Memory in the Real World

Memory in the Real World
Third Edition

**Edited by
Gillian Cohen and Martin Conway**

Psychology Press
Taylor & Francis Group

HOVE AND NEW YORK

First published 2008 by Psychology Press,
27 Church Road, Hove, East Sussex BN3 2FA

Simultaneously published in the USA and Canada
by Psychology Press
270 Madison Avenue, New York, NY 10016

*Psychology Press is an imprint of the Taylor & Francis Group, an Informa
Business*

Copyright © 2008 Psychology Press

Typeset in Sabon by Garfield Morgan, Swansea, West Glamorgan
Printed and bound in Great Britain by TJ International, Padstow, Cornwall
Paperback cover design by Lisa Dynan

British Library Cataloguing in Publication Data
A catalogue record for this book is available from the British Library

Library of Congress Cataloging-in-Publication Data
Cohen, Gillian.
    Memory in the real world / Gillian Cohen and Martin Conway. – 3rd ed.
        p. cm.
    Includes bibliographical references and indexes.
    ISBN 978-1-84169-640-9 (hardcover) – ISBN 978-1-84169-641-6 (pbk.)
    1. Memory. 2. Human behaviour. I. Conway, Martin A., 1952- II. Title.
    BF371.C59 2008
    153.1'2–dc22

                                                              2007019696

ISBN 978-1-84169-640-9 (hbk)
ISBN 978-1-84169-641-6 (pbk)

Contents

List of contributors

Gillian Cohen Formerly Department of Psychology, The Open University, UK

Martin A. Conway Institute of Psychological Sciences, University of Leeds, Leeds LS2 9JT, UK

Judi A. Ellis School of Psychology, University of Reading, Harry Pitt Building, Earley Gate, Whiteknights Road, Reading, Berkshire RG6 6AL, UK

Susan E. Gathercole Department of Psychology, University of York, York YO10 5DD, UK

J. Richard Hanley Department of Psychology, University of Essex, Colchester CO4 3SQ, UK

Caroline L. Horton Institute of Psychological Sciences, University of Leeds, Leeds LS2 9JT, UK

Elizabeth F. Loftus Department of Psychology and Social Behavior, 2393 Social Ecology 2, University of California – Irvine, Irvine, CA 92697-7085, USA

Chris J.A. Moulin Institute of Psychological Sciences, University of Leeds, Leeds LS2 9JT, UK

Akira R. O'Connor Institute of Psychological Sciences, University of Leeds, Leeds LS2 9JT, UK

Gabriel A. Radvansky Department of Psychology, University of Notre Dame, Notre Dame, IN 46556, USA

Alastair D. Smith Department of Experimental Psychology, University of Bristol, 12a Priory Road, Bristol BS8 1TU, UK

Céline Souchay Institute of Psychological Sciences, University of Leeds, Leeds LS2 9JT, UK

Rebecca G. Thompson Department of Experimental Psychology, University of Bristol, 12a Priory Road, Bristol BS8 1TU, UK

Helen L. Williams Institute of Psychological Sciences, University of Leeds, Leeds LS2 9JT, UK

Daniel B. Wright Department of Psychology, Pevensey Building, University of Sussex, Falmer BN1 9QH, UK

List of figures

List of tables

Preface to the third edition

This third edition of *Memory in the Real World* has been updated and now includes contributions from leading researchers in their specialist fields. The long-running controversy about the value of naturalistic research versus traditional laboratory research is reassessed and the two approaches are seen as complementary rather than opposed. This edition reflects the increasing links between cognitive psychology and neuropsychology, and the contribution of new methods such as imaging techniques are explored and evaluated. The scope of *Memory in the Real World* has been extended to include new chapters on consciousness and on memory impairment as well as on lifespan development in memory from childhood to old age. New studies of brain-damaged patients inform the understanding of memory in normal intact people. The focus is on how memory functions in everyday life and includes memory for plans and actions, routes and places, faces, names and voices, as well as thoughts and dreams, general knowledge and eyewitness testimony. The findings and observations of memory in real life are explained and interpreted by reference to current theories and models. In the explanation and interpretation of memory function, common-sense intuitions are frequently invoked. Everyday memory research is an area where common sense has a good deal to contribute. In particular, it is argued that where theory or data offend against common sense, it is a powerful indication that they should be carefully re-examined. The final chapter presents an overview with some speculations about the special characteristics that are needed if memory is to meet the demands of everyday life in the 21st century.

1 The study of everyday memory

Gillian Cohen

WHAT IS EVERYDAY MEMORY?

Function and context

Memory in the real world is often known as *everyday memory* and is concerned with the way memory is used as people go about their daily lives. Among the characteristic features of everyday memory research is its emphasis on the functional aspects of memory, that is, on what memory is for. Memory is viewed as part of a repertoire of behaviour designed to fulfil specific goals. For example, autobiographical memory functions to build and maintain personal identity and self-concept; prospective memory functions to enable an individual to carry out plans and intentions; spatial memory functions so that an individual can navigate in the environment, and so on. Bruce (1985) stated that ecological memory research must ask how memory operates in everyday life, identifying causes and processes; what functions it serves; and why it has evolved both ontogenetically and evolutionarily in this way.

Everyday memory is context-bound, not context-free. The kind of things people remember in everyday life include a great variety of different items such as, for example, remembering a shopping list or a recipe, remembering to telephone a relative or to fill up the car with petrol, recounting the arguments put forward at a meeting or the plot of a play seen on television, or remembering the amount of a bill that has to be paid. All these experiences are embedded in a rich context of ongoing events and scenes; they are influenced by a lifetime of past experiences, by history and culture, by current motives and emotions, by intelligence and personality traits, by future goals and plans. It is probably impossible to take all these factors into account, but everyday memory research does recognise the importance of the context in which an event occurs. Instead of discounting context, everyday memory researchers exploit the way that reinstating the context can facilitate retrieval. People remember details of an event they witnessed when they are reminded of aspects of the context such as the scene, or the preceding or succeeding events. Crime reconstructions rely on this effect when they use re-enactments to jog the memory of potential witnesses.

Everyday memory research also emphasises the fact that remembering usually occurs in a social context and that one of its main functions is to serve interpersonal communication. Memory is not just a private data bank; it is shared, exchanged, constructed, revised, and elaborated in all our social interactions. The importance of this aspect of memory emerges strongly from studies of collaborative remembering (see Chapter 9).

Its emphasis on function and on the social and situational context allows everyday memory research to bridge the gap between basic and applied research, and many practical applications have been developed. The findings can provide useful guidelines on how to structure a lecture or to frame instructions for using a gadget, to shape the advice a doctor gives to a patient, and how to maximise compliance of patients in keeping appointments, how to devise memory therapy and memory aids, and how to design road signs and physical environments.

Everyday memory is not confined to processing externally derived stimuli and generating external responses. Internally generated events are also considered to be an important aspect of everyday memory This emphasis is because in real life, as opposed to laboratory experiments, one of the main functions of memory (described in Chapter 10) is to support reflections, daydreams, plans, evaluations, and reasoning that take place mentally and may never issue in any overt physical response. Another important point to bear in mind is that naturally occurring memories are very often memories of memories rather than memories of the originally perceived objects and events. In everyday life, re-remembering is more common than first time or one-off acts of remembering.

This book reviews and assesses the research on all the main aspects of everyday life. It exemplifies theoretical, experimental, observational, and practical approaches and illustrates the way they are combined and integrated in current research.

THE EVERYDAY MEMORY CONTROVERSY

A bit of history

Over the last 25 years there has been a long-running controversy about the relative merits of traditional laboratory research in the psychology of memory versus the everyday memory approach. Initially, these two approaches were seen as polar opposites, but more recently researchers have treated them as complementary and mutually reinforcing. For almost 100 years, traditional laboratory research had dominated the study of memory, using formal experimental techniques to answer theoretical questions about the general principles that govern the mechanisms of memory. This type of experimental research began as a reaction against the kind of philosophical, introspective approach exemplified in William James' (1890) reflections on memory, sometimes called the "armchair" method. In an attempt to give psychology a status of genuine scientific respectability, the objective experimental methods employed by Ebbinghaus (1885/1964) were enthusiastically adopted and developed. The majority of these experiments were concerned with verbal learning. A typical experiment of this kind tests memory performance in situations where a few of the relevant factors are isolated and rigorously controlled and manipulated. Myriad other factors that may normally influence memory in everyday life are deliberately excluded. Using stimuli such as nonsense syllables, which are almost entirely devoid of meaning and of previously acquired associations, the experimenter controls the number, duration, and timing of the presentation of these stimuli. The participants are carefully selected and instructed; the environment is standardised; the delay before recall is fixed; and the mental events that occur during this retention interval are controlled as far as possible. Finally, the instructions for recall are presented and the experimenter can record the number and type of items that are recalled, and the order and timing of the responses.

Experiments like these reveal the limits of memory capacity and define the constraints that govern the system. Some general principles have emerged that have proved robust and reliable, and that generalise across a range of experimental situations. For example, the division of memory into a short-term store and a long-term store is widely accepted, and phenomena such as the bow-shaped curve of serial learning, the rate of decay, the role of rehearsal, and the effects of interference and of retention interval are well established. However, in the late 1970s the usefulness of this kind of research was challenged.

The winds of change

At the first conference on Practical Aspects of Memory in 1978, Ulric Neisser gave a talk entitled "Memory: What are the important questions?" in which he dismissed the work of the past 100 years as largely worthless. This talk was undoubtedly a milestone in the psychology of memory. Neisser believed that the important questions about memory are those that arise out of everyday experience. We ought, he claimed, to be finding out how memory works in the natural context of daily life at school, in the home, or at work. We should be finding out what people remember from their formal education; why some people have "better" memories than others; why we remember some things and not others; and how we remember such diverse things as poems and town layouts, people's names, and events from our childhood. The traditional laboratory experiments, according to Neisser, had failed to study all the most interesting and significant problems and had shed no light on them. He claimed that the experimental findings are trivial, pointless, or obvious and fail to generalise outside the laboratory. He advocated a new approach, concentrating on the detailed examination of naturally occurring memory phenomena in the real world, and paying special attention to individual differences. According to Neisser, psychologists should adopt an ethological approach, studying human memory in the same way that ethologists study animal behaviour in the field. Neisser proposed that memory research should have *ecological validity*. By this he meant that it should apply to naturally occurring behaviour in the natural context of the real world. Interestingly, by the end of this conference Neisser had become aware that many of the "important" and "ecologically valid" questions were already being explored. In fact, although he made some valid and important points, he had overstated his case.

Precursors of the change

It would be quite wrong to suppose that research into everyday memory only began abruptly as a result of Neisser's talk. Rather, he articulated a trend that had been slowly gathering strength over a long period. Long ago, both Galton (1883) and later Bartlett (1932) had addressed themselves to important questions about the rich and complex functioning of memory in natural contexts. Their ideas were allowed to lapse for many years but ecologically valid research began again both in Britain and in the United States during the Second World War. There was a new growth of applied psychology, when answers were urgently sought to practical questions about human performance in tasks like air traffic control (Broadbent, 1958), work on production lines (Welford, 1958), or Morse code operation (Keller, 1953). Research into topics like these broadened the scope of memory research and awakened interest in how memory functions in natural contexts outside the laboratory.

In addition, the school of *cognitive psychology* that evolved in the late 1960s adopted a much broader and more speculative approach to memory research than that of the traditional verbal learning experiments. Researchers confronted problems about memory strategies, and these led them to investigate many of the phenomena that characterise the use of memory in everyday life, such as, for example, the use of imagery and mnemonics (Paivio, 1969), the tip-of-the-tongue phenomenon (Brown & McNeill, 1966), and the advantages of categorical organisation (Mandler, 1967).

These examples illustrate the way that laboratory research using strict experimental methods had already begun to move away from the tradition of studying memory; memory for items of information stripped, as far as possible, of meaning, context, and personal significance. What Kihlstrom (1994) called the "cognitive revolution" brought about a new willingness to examine memory for richer and more meaningful material. By 1978 the winds of change were already beginning to blow, and the ideas that Neisser voiced had already begun to take shape.

Neisser's ideas had an enthusiastic reception and the wind of change has blown more and more strongly since 1978, bringing with it a rapidly accumulating, richly varied, and extremely interesting body of research into everyday memory. Indeed, this new wave of interest in the more practical aspects of cognition is not confined to the study of memory alone. Ecological validity has become something of a catchword and vigorous efforts are under way to relate many areas of cognitive psychology more closely to the mental activities of ordinary people going about their daily lives. Problems such as how doctors decide on a medical diagnosis or how gamblers decide to place their stakes; how juries assess the credibility of a witness; the skills involved in holding conversations, planning routes, recognizing disguised faces; and a very wide variety of naturally occurring memory phenomena ranging from memory for grocery lists and television news broadcasts to memory for school field trips and dietary intake have all been studied.

PROS AND CONS OF EVERYDAY MEMORY RESEARCH

The backlash: Limitations and problems

In 1989, Banaji and Crowder published a counterattack: "The bankruptcy of everyday memory". They argued that, in many studies of everyday memory, ecological validity is in inverse relation to generalisability. The study of memory in naturally occurring situations necessarily entails abandoning control over the encoding and storage stages. For example, in testing memory for classroom learning or memory for the details of a real traffic accident or a summer vacation, the researcher has no control over the original experience. There is no way of knowing how effectively the information was encoded and there is no control over the experience of the participants during the interval between encoding and retrieval. Banaji and Crowder argued that, in consequence, the results cannot be generalised from one situation to another.

The limitations and problems inherent in everyday memory research stem from weaknesses in the methodology. How can we draw conclusions about what causes people to forget something in everyday life when we have no control over potentially relevant factors? Consider, for example, memory for faces. In the real world, the researcher has no control over the initial learning phase: The degree of attention paid to the face when it was encountered; the number and duration of encounters; the importance and affective quality of the encounters; and the number and similarity of the faces encountered during the intervening period. How, then, can we infer what causes X to forget Y's face? The combination of lack of control and, in some cases, the absence of a strong theoretical framework means that everyday memory research is in danger of producing only a mass of interesting, but uninterpreted, observations and untested speculations. Because of these problems some researchers are inclined to dismiss everyday memory research as "soft" psychology, in contrast to the rigour and precision of the traditional experimental methods. Banaji and Crowder (1989) concluded that everyday memory research has failed to "deliver" any new theories, to add explanatory power, or to develop new methods that have the necessary rigour and precision. This scathing article provoked a spirited defence from everyday memory researchers.

The crux of the debate centres on the issues of control and generalisability. Without some form of control, either experimental or statistical, generalisability is weak and Banaji and Crowder believe it is better to sacrifice ecological validity and to maintain control and ensure generalisability. On the one hand, traditionalists claim that everyday memory research fails to generalise because uncontrolled factors are allowed to vary freely. On the other hand, everyday memory researchers believe that traditional research fails to generalise from the laboratory to real life. Defenders of everyday memory (e.g., Conway, 1993) have pointed out that the most rigorous methodology of the laboratory is no guarantee that the results will be of interest or will generalise beyond the experimental paradigm. It is possible to design experiments that conform to the highest standards of control and produce elegant quantitative data, but which only show how participants respond in that particular experimental paradigm and shed no light on how memory functions in any other situations.

The defence of everyday memory

There are some topics that can only be studied using the everyday memory approach in natural settings (Conway, 1991). One example is the retention of information over very long time spans. There is no way of finding out how well people remember what they learned in school or how well they remember the layout of cities they lived in long ago without emerging from the laboratory into the real world. Moreover, such studies, as will be seen in later chapters, have produced replicable and useful findings and show retention functions that are interestingly different from those obtained over shorter time spans in laboratory experiments.

It is one of the advantages of studying memory in the real world that it takes more account of individual differences. Differences of age, culture, sex, personality, and socioeconomic and educational background are important factors in everyday memory performance. Laboratory studies have often seemed to operate on the assumption that all human beings behave in the same way, basing generalisations on tests carried out on a fairly homogeneous sample of young college students. Once the researcher emerges into the real world, the great range and variety of human responses to the same situation has to be confronted.

Everyday memory research also differs from most traditional memory research in that the remembered information has often been learned incidentally rather than intentionally. This is an important difference that underlines the fact that everyday memory research is essentially about the norms and habits of memory function rather than being concerned with the limits of capacity. It is about what people choose to remember, or happen to remember, rather than what they are capable of remembering when pushed to the limits of their ability. The traditional laboratory experiment typically tests intentional memory and is concerned with establishing the limits of capacity. The primary aim of this type of research is to infer the nature of the mechanism, to deduce general principles, and to construct and test theoretical models. It is probably true to say that, in everyday life, naturally occurring memory tasks rarely tax capacity to its limits. Everyday memory differs in aims and scope as well as methods.

A TEMPEST IN A TEAPOT

In spite of the initial polarisation, many researchers began to recognise that their differences were not so fundamental and that the two approaches could be considered as complementary rather than opposed. Tulving (1991) described the dispute as a "tempest in a teapot" and Kvavilashvili and Ellis (1996) titled their article "Let's forget the everyday/laboratory controversy". In fact the dichotomy is breaking down, and many researchers use both approaches. Theories developed in the laboratory are applied and tested in real-world situations: Phenomena observed in the real world are analysed and tested in controlled laboratory conditions.

Some misconceptions about everyday memory

One common misconception is the view that everyday memory research has ecological validity and laboratory research does not. In a critical review of the controversy between real life and laboratory, Kvavilashvili and Ellis (2004) have analysed the concept of ecological validity, identifying its two main components as representativeness and generalisability. By representativeness they mean the extent to which the situation, task, and materials being studied correspond to a real, naturally occurring event in everyday life. By generalisability they refer to the degree to which the findings of a particular study will also apply to other similar real-life situations. Rather than being present or absent, both representativeness and generalisability can be viewed as a continuum and are present to varying degrees in both real-world and laboratory research. Using these criteria, Kvavilashvili and Ellis showed that some real-world research may fail the test of ecological validity because lack of controls limits its generalisability, while some experimental studies score more highly on both criteria. Ecological validity is not a property exclusive to everyday memory studies.

Another misconception is to suppose that everyday memory research relies on naturalistic observations, similar to the way that ethologists observe animals in field studies without attempting to control variables, to test hypotheses, or to derive a theoretical framework. Although there are some aspects of memory, such as early childhood memories, which are particularly difficult to study using formal controls, very little everyday memory research is purely naturalistic. Many issues are now being tackled by using a wide range of methods in a complementary fashion. Theories and findings derived from laboratory experiments direct the search for analogues in everyday life and the findings that originate from naturalistic studies are followed up in rigorous experiments, so that what might be called a hybrid method-ology has become commonplace. For example, Cohen and Faulkner (1986) used diary records of naturally occurring name blocks to confirm that elderly people report experiencing greater difficulty in remembering names; they then went on to design experimental analogues to explore this phenomenon with better control of the variables. Conway (1992) has analysed naturally occurring autobiographical mem-ories to develop a detailed theoretical model. Another good example of this kind of hybridisation comes from the studies of eyewitness testimony (see Chapter 3), where the effects of leading questions or misinformation identified in simulations of real-world events have been further explored in carefully controlled experiments designed to test hypotheses about the mechanism of memory distortion. Similarly, studies of face recognition move freely between the real world of identification lineups and analytic experiments testing the effects of specific variables such as inversion of the face.

These misconceptions are now widely recognised as such. Everyday memory research employs a wide range of methodologies, which are discussed in following sections

MOVING ON

The tempest in the teapot has largely blown itself out by now and the controversy between everyday memory and laboratory research has been replaced by other classifications. Most of these overlap with each other and may map loosely, but not exactly, onto the everyday memory dispute.

The storehouse versus correspondence metaphor

Koriat and Goldsmith (1996) encapsulated the characteristics of traditional labora-tory research in terms of what they call "the storehouse metaphor", as opposed to everyday memory research, which they think of in terms of the "correspondence metaphor". According to the storehouse metaphor, traditional laboratory research conceptualises memory as a storage space occupied by discrete units or items of information. The essence of this approach lies in counting these units: Memory is assessed in terms of quantity, of how many units are remembered, and by the factors that influence the amount of remembered information. By contrast, everyday memory research fits the correspondence metaphor, which stresses the degree of correspondence between the original input and what is remembered. Thus everyday memory research is concerned with memory quality; with how accurately, reliably, and completely memory preserves reality. According to this view, forgetting is not a matter of losing a number of items of information but of loss of correspondence, or deviation from reality. The correspondence metaphor carries with it the implication that memories should be considered holistically: Memory components are inter-related into complex wholes so that loss of accuracy in one part may affect the whole. This line of thinking makes a lot of sense when applied to memory for conversations, places, people, and complex events. Koriat and Goldsmith's emphasis on memory accuracy is reflected in a great deal of current everyday memory research. Their experiments have also shown that, whereas the quantity of responses (that is, the number of items retrieved) is usually not under conscious control, the accuracy of responses can be strategically controlled. Participants can opt to be absolutely correct or only approximately correct. The factors that govern strategic control of accuracy are of great importance in evaluating witness memory.

Quantitative versus qualitative research

Closely related to the storehouse/correspondence distinction, this classification is usually considered to be methodological. Quantitative research is associated with the use of experiments and statistics: Qualitative research is associated with exploring subjective experience. Capaldi and Proctor (2005) argue that this amounts to a difference in worldview, with the qualitative approach seeking to understand the meaning of a memory rather than how to predict or control it. However, many studies combine both qualitative and qualitative methods, being interested both in how much and in what kinds of things are remembered, and the distinction is also blurred in, for example, neuropsychological case studies and the use of imaging techniques.

Causal versus associative hypotheses

Wright (2006) has distinguished between causal and associative hypotheses. When a causal hypothesis is tested the causal variable is manipulated experimentally. For example, the length of time that a witness is allowed to view a lineup is varied to find whether this affects identification. An associative hypothesis seeks to estimate the probability that there is a relationship between events; for example, the probability that the experience of childhood abuse is correlated with subsequent criminal behaviour. Wright argues that, although both types of hypothesis are used in every-day memory research, they need to be carefully distinguished in terms of method-ology and especially in the interpretation of the findings. The generalisability of associative hypotheses depends on the population sampled and the size of the effect. The generalisability of causal hypotheses depends on the tightness of experimental control over relevant variables.

Basic versus applied research

Yet another dichotomy classifies research as basic or applied. Basic research, some-times called "blue skies" research, is undertaken in order to understand a phenom-enon, to construct and test a theory, to isolate causes and predict outcomes. Applied research has specific practical goals, such as designing flight deck instrumentation or improving traffic flow. However, once again the boundaries are not absolute. Blue skies research often yields applications and applied research may suggest theoretical developments.

METHODS OF EVERYDAY MEMORY RESEARCH

Everyday memory research employs a wide range of different methods, but these can be divided into three groups. The first draws its data from self-reports and relies on introspective evidence; the second involves the use of experimental methods that may be more, or less, naturalistic; the third group consists of methods used in cognitive neuropsychology and cognitive neuroscience that are applied to address issues in everyday memory.

Self-reports and introspection

Self-reports seem to provide a simple way of finding out how people's memories work in everyday life—by asking them. The researcher can record people's own observations about the way their memories function, collecting reports from individuals about the things they remember and the things they forget; the tricks and devices they use to prop up memory; the particular circumstances that are associated with success or failure. The use of self-reports may involve collecting oral histories and reminiscences, or it may involve the administration of formal questionnaires about memory. Participants may be asked to supply self-ratings of their own memory ability, or they may be asked to think aloud while they solve problems and produce a verbal protocol, or they may be asked to keep a diary recording the occurrence of memory phenomena such as absentminded lapses. All these procedures rely on introspection.

The recent use of introspective evidence by psychologists is another example of the way that the history of psychology exemplifies a kind of swings and roundabouts progression, with ideas being enthusiastically adopted, then discredited, and then reinstated. Early psychologists like Wundt and Freud based their theories on the introspections of their participants or patients, but during the Behaviourist period (roughly from the 1920s to the 1950s), only overt measurable behavioural responses were considered admissible as evidence. The importance, and even the existence, of mental events was discounted. However, the advent of cognitive psychology in the 1960s brought renewed interest in covert, unobservable mental processes such as imaging, reasoning, deciding, and planning. Introspective methods have been brought back into use and are now employed extensively in studying aspects of cognition like problem-solving and decision-making, as well as everyday memory.

This resurrection of introspective methods has not been without its critics (Nisbett & Wilson, 1977). They argued (p. 231) that "there may be little or no direct access to higher order cognitive processes". In particular, they claimed that causal reports, that is, reports about the causal influences on judgements and responses, are very inaccurate and are based more on people's preconceptions than on what actually influenced them. People may, for example, be unable to report accurately on what actually influenced their choice of a particular brand in a supermarket.

It is generally acknowledged that many of the very rapid mental processes that underlie activities like perceiving a complex scene, recognising a word, or speaking a grammatical sentence are simply not accessible to conscious awareness. Another mental process that takes place without conscious awareness is the so-called *pop-up* phenomenon. You may have the experience of finding that you cannot recall something, such as a person's name, although this may be a name that you know quite well. Such a retrieval block may persist, despite your best efforts, for hours or even days. Then, when you have given up and are thinking about something quite different, the forgotten name suddenly pops up into consciousness. In this situation, people are usually unable to report anything about the mental processes that produced the pop-up. Introspection fails to yield any information. In such cases, people are conscious of the end product of the mental operations, but not of the processes themselves. Nobody can introspect and make verbal reports about what is going on below the level of consciousness, and much of mental activity is unconscious.

Verbal protocols are a record of what people say when they are asked to think aloud as they perform a task. So, for example, practised participants can report the reasoning processes underlying the selection of a chess move. Their speech is recorded and later transcribed so that the mental processes that are reported can be analysed. The use of verbal protocols is a form of concurrent introspection. This has certain advantages over retrospective introspection in that there is less opportunity for editing and rationalising the report, and less chance of forgetting some of the mental processes. The protocol reveals the temporal sequence of mental operations, and the location and duration of the pauses in verbalisation convey information about the choice points. It is especially useful as a research tool for studying complex tasks of fairly long duration involving operations that are easy to verbalise. One disadvantage of using verbal protocols is that they are necessarily incomplete and they give no indication of what has been omitted. As already noted, some mental processes are not accessible to conscious introspection. Unconscious processes cannot be reported and unspoken thoughts remain mysterious. Another disadvantage is that individual participants may differ in the ease and spontaneity with which they can produce a running commentary on their thinking, and in the level of detail they report, so individual differences in the underlying thought processes may be obscured by individual differences in the spoken commentary. Verbal protocols may also be inaccurate if participants are trying to please the experimenter or to present themselves in a good light. They may not like to reveal the confused and muddled state of their mental processes and may tidy up the reported version so as to seem more impressive. Nisbett and Wilson (1977) have emphasised the shortcomings of verbal protocols, but Ericsson and Simon (1980) have defended the use of concurrent introspections and they have proved to be an informative way to study problem-solving and planning. Even so, some mental events may be difficult or impossible to express in words or, in some cases, the act of trying to verbalise what is going on in the head may interfere with or change the nature of the mental activity under scrutiny. Trying to introspect about how you read silently, for example, will almost certainly change the way you read, causing you to read more slowly and in a more word-by-word manner than you usually do when you are not thinking about it.

White (1988) argued that it is difficult to distinguish between mental *processes*, which are not accessible to consciousness, and mental *products*, which are accessible. It is clear that issues about the validity and reliability of introspective evidence will not go away. The relationship between conscious thought and subconscious or unconscious thought is one of the major issues confronting cognitive psychology at the present time.

The phenomenological approach

The admission that mental products are accessible to consciousness legitimises studies that use a phenomenological approach to study memory quality. The method typically involves asking participants to examine their own memories and to report the characteristics of these memories such as how vivid they are, and this may be combined with experimental manipulations. In studies of this kind Johnson (1988), Johnson, Foley, Suengas, and Raye (1988), and Suengas and Johnson (1988) asked participants to rate the sensory qualities, emotionality, amount of spatial and temporal detail, and amount of supporting context in designated memories, such as the memory of wrapping a parcel. The variables that were manipulated included whether the memory was of a real event that had actually occurred or of an event that had only been imagined; the recency of the events; and the amount and type of rehearsal. The experimenters then compared the ratings of memory qualities. The phenomenological reports of these qualities were validated by the fact that they varied systematically with whether the memory was real or imagined and with the recency of the event and the type of rehearsal.

Similar studies have used the phenomenological approach to compare the vividness of autobiographical memories from different decades of the lifespan (Cohen & Faulkner, 1988) and to examine the special qualities alleged to characterise the so-called flashbulb memories for dramatic public events (Cohen, Conway, & Maylor, 1994). Of course, phenomenological reports of this kind may sometimes be influenced by preconceptions. Participants may be aware that recent memories or highly emotional memories "ought" to be more vivid and their reports may reflect such beliefs rather than the phenomenological evidence. It is up to researchers to try to discriminate carefully between the effects of preconceptions and of genuine phenomenological qualities.

Surveys, questionnaires, and self-ratings

It is worth discussing the use of questionnaires at some length, as examples will be found in later chapters. Several different kinds of questionnaire can be distinguished. One type of memory questionnaire is a straightforward test of general factual knowledge and asks questions like "What is the date of the battle of Waterloo?" or "Who was the composer of Rigoletto?" This kind of memory test is used to plot the retention of knowledge over time, or to investigate differences in memory ability between different groups, or changes in memory ability that occur as a result of ageing, trauma, or dementia.

Another type of questionnaire is used in survey research to obtain information about people's activities, experiences, and opinions. For example, surveys may ask people how often they travel by bus or how many units of alcohol they consume each week, and are used primarily in developing public policies. However, Jobe, Tourangeau, and Smith (1993) underlined the fact that the design of survey research draws on current theories of memory and the results contribute to our understanding of everyday memory. A study of memory for dietary intake (Smith, Jobe, & Mingay, 1991) illustrated how far principles discovered in the laboratory—such as the effects of retention interval, the use of generic schemas to aid retrieval, and the organisation of items into related categories—were spontaneously implemented in a natural setting.

A different type of questionnaire has been called a metamemory questionnaire because it queries beliefs or judgements about memory. Metamemory questionnaires are not tests; their questions take a variety of different forms. Some are self-assessment questions that ask people to assess their own memory abilities by choosing the appropriate rating (e.g., *very good*, *good*, *fair*, *poor*, or *very poor*) in response to questions like "How good is your memory for the words of songs or poems?" or "How good is your memory for routes to places?" Alternatively, participants may be asked to assess the frequency of certain specified lapses of memory, as in "How often do you forget appointments?" or "How often do you want to tell a joke, but find you cannot remember it?" by rating the frequency of occurrence as *very often*, *often*, *occasionally*, *rarely*, or *never*. In other types of metamemory questionnaires, people are asked to predict their own performance in forthcoming tests. As well as asking for ratings of memory ability, metamemory questionnaires may ask participants what memory strategies, mnemonics, or reminders they employ; or whether they have detected any changes over time in their memory ability; or what beliefs and expectations they have about the way that memory works in general.

Self-assessments of memory ability are based on direct first-hand experience of success and failure in a wide range of everyday tasks over a long period. It seems reasonable, therefore, to assume that people should know about their own memory performance and be able to assess it accurately, but many researchers (e.g., Morris, 1984) have expressed serious doubts about the validity of self-ratings. These ratings have proved to have high *reliability* (i.e., if participants are asked to work through a questionnaire, and it is then administered again at a later date, there is a strong correlation between the original and the repeat ratings). However, *validity* appears to be low, because when the subjective ratings are correlated with scores on objective psychometric tests of memory ability, such as digit span (the number of digits that can be repeated back immediately after presentation of a list), or free recall of word lists, the correlations are low or nonexistent. For example, self-rated ability to remember telephone numbers correlates with digit span at only .4, and self-rated ability to remember faces correlates with tests of ability to recognise photographs of faces at .3 (Herrman, 1984). Several reasons for this low validity have been identified:

1   Self-assessment may reflect a person's self-image rather than his or her performance, and be distorted by modesty or pride. Self-assessment is also known to be influenced by anxiety, depression, and personality (Rabbitt, Maylor, McInnes, Bent, & Moore, 1995).

2   The Metamemory Paradox may operate, so that people who make the most errors are least likely to report them because they forget they have occurred.

3   Individual variation in the opportunity for error may also distort results. For example, some individuals may assess their memory for faces as excellent, but have few demands made on it because they seldom meet many new people. Differences in the opportunity for error may explain why elderly people paradoxically report fewer memory lapses overall than the young. Yet nobody supposes that their memory is better. Similarly, the fact that men report fewer lapses than women may be because some items in the questionnaires refer to shopping, and men tend to do less shopping (Rabbitt et al., 1995).

4   Using memory aids like diaries, address books, shopping lists, or knotted handkerchiefs may protect an individual from memory failures, so that few actually occur even though memory is poor.

5   Questions that ask "How often" or "How good" are ambiguous unless they specify a reference point. Providing an objective scale (e.g., instructing the participants that "often" should be taken to mean about once a week) or specifying comparisons (e.g., "How good are you as compared with an average person of your own age?") helps to increase precision.

6   Response biases may operate that inflate or reduce estimates of frequency. For example, the elderly may be anxious about the possibility of cognitive deterioration and be sensitised to errors. Zelinski, Gilewski, and Thompson (1980) found that whereas young people's self-assessments were quite unrelated to their test scores, elderly people's ratings had greater validity.

7   Low correlations between psychometric tests and self-assessments may be due simply to the fact that they are measuring different things. If so, it becomes necessary to ask which type of memory ability—the kind assessed by subjective reports or the kind measured by formal tests—is most important or relevant.

8   The knowledge that people are asked about in questionnaires may be implicit, so that they do not have explicit awareness of this knowledge. For example, in recognition tests that test implicit memory, people may do better than they thought they would.

The factors that govern the everyday performance on which self-assessments are based are different in so many ways from the factors that operate in formal laboratory tests that the lack of agreement is not surprising. The subjective memory beliefs expressed in self-assessment questionnaires should be validated against objective observations of everyday performance, rather than against laboratory tests. Some researchers (e.g., Broadbent, Cooper, Fitzgerald, & Parkes, 1982; Sunderland, Harris, & Baddeley, 1983) have tried to check the validity of self-assessments by having a partner or close relative provide a parallel set of ratings. If I rate my tendency to lose objects as very rare, this can then be checked against my partner's observations. In the case of normal intact participants these third-party ratings correlate only weakly with self-ratings, but for neurological patients the concordance is much higher. One reason for this discrepancy may be that in normal people the number of memory failures is relatively small. What are wanted, however, are more studies correlating self-assessments with ecologically valid tests that are close analogues of everyday situations, such as some of the tests in the Rivermead Behavioural Memory test battery (Wilson, Cockburn, & Baddeley, 1985) or Martin's (1986) study in which she validated participants' ratings of their own ability to keep appointments with objective records of how often they had missed appointments while serving on the participant panel.

Despite some doubts about their validity, self-assessment questionnaires have proved valuable in a number of ways. They have clearly indicated that people view their own memories as a set of specific abilities with specific strengths and weaknesses. Memory is not seen as being "good" or "bad" overall. Instead, people recognise that they may be good at remembering some things and poor at others. Self-assessment questionnaires provide a "profile" of memory ability that is considered more revealing than overall scores (Chaffin & Herrman, 1983).

As well as being used to differentiate individuals, questionnaires also provide an instrument for examining differences between groups like the young and the old (Cohen & Faulkner, 1984; Perlmutter, 1978) or studying changes over time following head injuries (Sunderland et al., 1983). In general, it is useful to know what people think about their memories because beliefs and expectations about memory performance (even if they are not accurate) affect many aspects of everyday behaviour, including people's preferences, the kind of tasks they are willing to tackle, and the way they respond to information dissemination. Despite some reservations and difficulties, if self-report data derived from protocols and questionnaires are used and interpreted with care and caution, they can be a valid and valuable source of information about memory in everyday life.

Naturalistic experiments

Many studies of everyday memory retain the experimental method, but attempt to devise experiments that are more naturalistic, more ecologically valid, or more representative of real life than the traditional laboratory experiment. Typically, such experiments involve testing people's memory for more natural material, such as stories, films, or maps, instead of the traditional lists of nonsense syllables, letters, or digits. In some cases, they may test memory for events that occurred naturally in the participant's daily life rather than for material selected and constructed by the experimenter. Thus, for example, researchers have devised tests of college teachers' ability to remember the names or faces of their former students (Bahrick, 1984).

The naturalistic experiment is essentially a compromise in which the researcher tries to ensure that the task and conditions are as close to those that obtain in real life as possible, while at the same time imposing enough control and standardisation of the procedure so that definite conclusions can be drawn from the findings. The aim is to ensure that memory in the more structured research context preserves the essential aspects of memory in the natural context. Of course, an experimental procedure can never be exactly the same as a real-life situation. A certain amount of ecological validity must be sacrificed to ensure that manageable and informative results are produced. The researcher must classify and compare; must exclude or ignore some variables and focus on others; must impose some form of measurement or testing; must interpret the findings and extract generalisations from them. In doing so, it is inevitable that the natural context of the memory act is changed to some extent. Using experimental methods also affects the participants' behaviour. In an experiment, participants know they are being tested. They may be anxious, bored, or eager to impress, and the material, or task, is liable to be more simplified and more orderly than real events.

Cognitive neuropsychology

Cognitive neuropsychology operates on the assumption that aspects of normal cognition such as memory can be studied by examining patterns of intact and impaired performance in brain-damaged patients. Their performance can shed light on everyday memory in several ways. The detailed investigation involved in diagnosis and rehabilitation breaks down the ability to perform everyday tasks into separable components that can be separately damaged or spared. This increases our understanding of how cognitive processes operate normally; how people can prop up and support failing abilities; and how far models or theories are correct in the assumptions they make about structures and processes and how they are inter-related.

Neuropsychological studies are typically carried out on single individuals rather than groups of patients because the individuals within a group tend to differ in important respects, such as: The site and extent of the damage; their pre-traumatic ability; the extent of recovery; age and gender. Many case studies report highly specific impairment of cognitive abilities following brain injuries. Single cases may demonstrate either associations or dissociations. Associations occur when damage to one function necessarily entails damage to another. Dissociations are shown when one function is impaired but another is intact. For example, recognition of living things such as vegetables or body parts can be damaged while recognition of non-living things such as musical instruments or precious stones is normal. The two kinds of recognition are dissociated. Hillis and Caramazza (1991) demonstrated a double dissociation with different individuals showing opposite patterns of impairment; intact recognition of nonliving things and damaged ability to recognise living things, or vice versa. Double dissociations of this kind provide a strong indication that the two functions are independent.

Specific deficits have also been reported for recognising faces and even a case of a farmer with impaired ability to recognise human faces but preserved ability to recognise the faces of sheep (McNeil & Warrington, 1993). Research on face recognition has also revealed dissociation between the ability to recognise facial expression, age, and gender and the impaired ability to recognise the identity of the person (e.g., Tranel, Damasio, & Damasio, 1988). These observations strongly suggest that there are functionally separate systems in the brain for recognising different kinds of things.

Cognitive neuropsychology has provided evidence for a number of theoretical models. Hierarchical models of object recognition are supported by evidence for specific deficits in ability to recognise an object visually, to name it, to understand its function, or to classify it (Forde & Humphreys, 1999). Models of face recognition and face naming also rest on neuropsychological evidence (Bruce & Young, 1986) (see Chapter 4), showing that these abilities can be independently damaged. Similarly the model of autobiographical memory proposed by Conway and Pleydell-Pearce (2000) gains support from detailed analysis of the disrupted memories of amnesic patients (Conway & Fthenaki, 2000) (see Chapter 13). The data from these patients, as well as supporting the theoretical model, gave striking evidence of the dependency of autobiographical memory on intact visual imagery. Tracing the patterns of dissociation and co-occurrence reveals the dependency relations and processing pathways involved in complex cognitive operations.

Cognitive neuroscience

The development of brain imaging techniques such as positron emission tomography (PET) scanning and magnetic resonance imaging (MRI) provide ways to observe the living, functioning brain at work. The PET scan measures the uptake of glucose by brain tissue during an activity such as speaking or reading. A participant is injected with radioactive elements that attach to glucose molecules. These emit positrons and show the rate at which cells consume the glucose during mental processes, so it is possible to observe which brain areas are most active. However, PET scanning has some drawbacks. It provides only a rather gross temporal resolution (within about 60 seconds) and limited spatial resolution (6–9 cubic millimetres). This means that observations of brain activity lag behind the actual event and do not pinpoint the activated brain area with absolute precision. MRI measures the energy given off by the billions of tiny magnets in brain tissue by placing them within a very strong magnetic field. Functional magnetic resonance imaging (fMRI) measures increased energy demands in activated areas of the neural network as local blood flow increases to deliver oxygen. If an fMRI is carried out while the participant is performing a task such as listening to music or solving mathematical problems, the image shows the parts of the brain that are activated. The fMRI technique has significant advantages over PET scanning. No injections are necessary and the spatial and temporal resolution is considerably finer. These techniques are now widely used to study both healthy and damaged brains.

Nevertheless there are problems in the interpretation of studies using imaging techniques because they measure blood flow rather than directly measuring neuronal activity. Blood flow changes are much slower, occurring over seconds, whereas the neuronal response occurs within a few hundred milliseconds. Another criticism is that MRI studies overstate the localisation of functions, overlooking complex inter-actions and dependencies between brain areas. In general, fMRI is not so useful for studying higher order processes, such as decision making and reasoning, which are less localized. It is also proving difficult to interpret the range of differences in the brain scans of different individuals doing the same task.

Imaging techniques can be used to locate the site of brain damage and to examine differences between the brains of individuals. fMRI studies have demonstrated that the exercise of particular skills can lead to a functional reorganisation of the brain. For example, it has been shown that London taxi drivers, renowned for their knowledge of the city layout and routes, have a larger than normal area of brain for representing spatial information (Maguire et al., 2001; see Chapter 6), and musicians and blind Braille readers have expanded regions representing the fingers of the skilled hand (Elbert, Panter, Wienbruch, Rockstroh, & Taub, 1995; Pascual-Leone & Torres, 1993). MRI has also been used to study differences between the brains of male and female (Haier, Jung, Head & Alkire, 2005), and normal and schizophrenic (Hulshoff et al., 2004) subjects.

CONCLUSIONS

As the two kinds of memory research, in the world of the laboratory and in the real world, continue to coexist and converge, it becomes increasingly clear that the relationship between memory in the laboratory and memory out in the real world is one of cross-fertilisation. The two approaches are not really antagonistic and it was mistaken to view them as such. Baddeley (1993) concluded that the hostilities that existed initially between researchers working in different traditions constitute a phoney war. The consensus view now is that laboratory research and everyday research are complementary. They exert a useful and mutually beneficial influence on each other. Laboratory research is enriched and extended; everyday research is disciplined and guided.

Everyday memory research provides a testing ground for the theories and findings that have resulted from 100 years of laboratory experiments. Studies of everyday memory test the range of situations to which the laboratory-based findings apply. Do they generalise to the real world? Can they be applied to naturally occurring phenomena? This relationship between the two approaches works to ensure that the laboratory experiments are not sterile. Laboratory research has a tendency, if left to itself, to become incestuous, endlessly exploring its own paradigms. Everyday research acts as a corrective to this tendency by opening up new lines of inquiry. The functional questions about what memory is for, which arise in the everyday context, provide a better basis for laboratory research than theory building for its own sake.

The benefits do not flow in one direction only. Everyday research also draws heavily on what has been learned in the laboratory. Although the results obtained in the laboratory are unlikely to be precisely replicated in the real world, some of the general principles, the organising concepts, and the distinctions and classifications derived from traditional studies can be carried over and used to give shape and structure to research on everyday memory. Throughout the chapters that follow, the studies of everyday memory that are described illustrate the debt that everyday memory research owes to the traditional approach. The findings are commonly interpreted in terms of these general principles even if the fit is, at times, rather loose. Distinctions like those between episodic and semantic memory, attentional and automatic processes, or constructive and copy theories are frequently employed. Models such as schema theory and production systems are applied and concepts such as levels of processing, metamemory, and scripts are used to make sense of the data and supply a guiding framework for further research. It would be unrealistic to suppose, however, that the data from everyday memory research are going to fit very neatly and precisely into the theoretical models. Because of the complex and wide-ranging nature of the topics studied, it is not to be expected that any one model should be able to account for all of the findings. The extent to which everyday memory research has borrowed and adopted the theories generated by traditional laboratory research underlines the fact that everyday memory research itself has so far been relatively unsuccessful in developing strong predictive theories of its own. In this respect, the critics appear to be vindicated.

In addition to the rapprochement between traditional memory research and everyday memory research, the naturalistic approach has helped to reduce the gulf between cognitive psychology and social psychology. Memory research that takes place in a real-world context cannot possibly ignore social factors. This is particularly obvious when social and cognitive psychologists come together in the study of collaborative remembering. Whatever criticisms have been made, the tradition of everyday memory research is now strongly established.

REFERENCES

Baddeley, A.D. (1993). *Human memory: Theory and practice*. Hove, UK: Lawrence Erlbaum Associates Ltd.

Bahrick, H.P. (1984). Memory for people. In J.E. Harris & P.E. Morris (Eds.), *Everyday memory actions and absentmindedness*. London: Academic Press.

Banaji, M.R., & Crowder, R.G. (1989). The bankruptcy of everyday memory. *American Psychologist, 44*, 1185–1193.

Bartlett, F.C. (1932). *Remembering*. Cambridge, UK: Cambridge University Press.

Broadbent, D.E. (1958). *Perception and communication*. London: Pergamon.

Broadbent, D.E., Cooper, P.F., Fitzgerald, P., & Parkes, K.R. (1982). The cognitive failures questionnaire (CFQ) and its correlates. *British Journal of Clinical Psychology, 21*, 1–18.

Brown, R., & McNeil, D. (1966). The "tip of the tongue" phenomenon. *Journal of Verbal Learning and Verbal Behaviour, 5*, 325–337.

Bruce, D. (1985). The how and why of ecological memory. *Journal of Experimental Psychology: General, 114*, 78–90.

Bruce, V., & Young, A. (1986). Understanding face recognition. *British Journal of Psychology, 77*, 305–327.

Capaldi, E.J., & Proctor, R.W. (2005). Is the world view of qualitative inquiry a proper guide for psychological research? *American Journal of Psychology, 118*, 251–269.

Chaffin, R., & Herrman, D.J. (1983). Self reports of memory abilities in young and old adults. *Human Learning, 2*, 17–28.

Cohen, G., Conway, M.A., & Maylor, E. (1994). Flashbulb memory in older adults. *Psychology and Aging, 9*, 454–463.

Cohen, G., & Faulkner, D. (1984). Memory in old age: "Good in parts". *New Scientist, 11 October*, 49–51.

Cohen, G., & Faulkner, D.M. (1986). Memory for proper names: Age differences in retrieval. *British Journal of Developmental Psychology, 4*, 187–197.

Cohen, G., & Faulkner, D.M. (1988). Life span changes in autobiographical memory. In M.M. Gruneberg, P.E. Morris, & R.N. Sykes (Eds.), *Practical aspects of memory: Current research and issues*. Vol. 1 (pp. 277–282). Chichester, UK: Wiley.

Conway, M.A. (1991). In defence of everyday memory. *American Psychologist, 46*, 19–26.

Conway, M.A. (1992). A structural model of autobiographical memory. In M.A. Conway, D.C. Rubin, H. Spinnler, & W.A. Wagenaar (Eds.), *Theoretical perspectives on autobiographical memory* (pp. 167–194). Dordrecht, The Netherlands: Kluwer Academic.

Conway, M.A. (1993). Method and meaning in memory research. In G.M. Davies & R.H. Logie (Eds.), *Memory in everyday life: Advances in psychology. Vol. 100*. Amsterdam: North-Holland/Elsevier.

Conway, M.A., & Fthenaki, A. (2000). Disruption and loss of autobiographical memory. In F. Boller & J. Graffman (Eds.), *Handbook of neuropsychology, Vol. 2* (2nd ed., pp. 281–312).

Conway, M.A., & Pleydell-Pearce, C.W. (2000). The construction of autobiographical memories in the self memory system. *Psychological Review, 107*, 261–288.

Ebbinghaus, H.E. (1964). *Memory: A contribution to experimental psychology*. New York: Dover. [Originally published 1885]

Elbert, T., Panter, C., Wienbruch, C., Rockstroh, B., & Taub, E. (1995). Increased cortical representation of the fingers of the left hand in string players. *Science, 270*, 305–307.

Ericsson, K.A., & Simon, H.A. (1980). Verbal reports as data. *Psychological Review, 87*, 215–225.

Forde, E.M.E., & Humphreys, G.W. (1999). A review of important case studies and influential theories. *Aphasiology, 13*, 169–193.

Galton, F. (1883). *Inquiries into human faculty and its development*. London: Macmillan.

Haier, R.J., Jung, R.E., Head, K., & Alkire, M.T. (2005). The neuroanatomy of general intelligence: Sex matters. *Neuroimage, 25*, 320–327.

Herrman, D.J. (1984). Questionnaires about memory. In J.E. Harris & P.E. Morris (Eds.), *Everyday memory, actions and absentmindedness*. London: Academic Press.

Hillis, A., & Caramazza, A. (1991). Category specific naming and comprehension impairment: A double dissociation. *Brain and Language, 114*, 2081–2094.

Hulshoff, P.H.E., Schnack, H.G., Mandl, R L.W., Cahn, W., Collins, D.L., Evans, A.C., &

Kahn, R.S. (2004). Focal white matter density changes in schizophrenia: Reduced inter-hemispheric connectivity. *Neuroimage, 21,* 27–35.

James, W. (1890). *The principles of psychology.* New York: Holt.

Jobe, J.B., Tourangeau, R., & Smith, A.F. (1993). Contributions of survey research to the understanding of memory. *Cognitive Psychology, 7,* 567–584.

Johnson, M.K. (1988). Reality monitoring: An experimental phenomenological approach. *Journal of Experimental Psychology: General, 117,* 390–394.

Johnson, M.K., Foley, M.A., Suengas, A.G., & Raye, C.L. (1988). Phenomenological characteristics of memories for perceived and imagined autobiographical events. *Journal of Experimental Psychology: General, 117,* 371–376.

Keller, F.S. (1953). Stimulus discrimination and Morse code learning. *New York Academy of Science, Series 2,* 195–203.

Kihlstrom, J.F. (1994). *Memory research: The convergence of theory and practice.* Paper presented at the Third Practical Aspects Conference, Washington, DC, July.

Koriat, A., & Goldsmith, M. (1996). Memory metaphors and the real life/laboratory controversy: Correspondence versus storehouse conceptions of memory. *Behavioral and Brain Sciences, 19,* 167–228.

Kvavilashvili, L., & Ellis, J. (1996). Let's forget the everyday/laboratory controversy. *Behavioral and Brain Sciences, 19,* 199–200.

Kvavilashvili, L., & Ellis, J. (2004). Ecological validity and the real life/laboratory controversy in memory research: A critical and historical review. *History and Philosophy of Psychology, 6,* 59–80.

Maguire, E.A., Gadian, D.G., Johnsrude, I.S., Good, C.D., Ashburner, J., Frackowiak, R.S.J., & Frith, C.D. (2001). Navigation-related structural change in the hippocampi of taxi drivers. *Proceedings of the National Academy of Sciences USA, 97,* 4398–4403.

Mandler, G. (1967). Organization and memory. In K.W. Spence & J.T. Spence (Eds.), *The psychology of learning and motivation: Advances in research and theory,* Vol. 1. London: Academic Press.

Martin, M. (1986). Ageing and patterns of change in everyday memory and cognition. *Human Learning, 5,* 63–74.

McNeil, J., & Warrington, E.K. (1993). Prosopagnosia: A face-specific disorder. *Quarterly Journal of Experimental Psychology, 46A,* 1–10.

Morris, P.E. (1984). The validity of subjective reports on memory. In J.E. Harris & P.E. Morris (Eds.), *Everyday memory, actions and absentmindedness.* London: Academic Press.

Neisser, U. (1978). Memory: What are the important questions? In M.M. Gruneberg, P.E. Morris, & R.N. Sykes (Eds.), *Practical aspects of memory.* London: Academic Press.

Nisbett, R.E., & Wilson, T.D. (1977). Telling more than we can know: Verbal reports on mental processes. *Psychological Review, 84,* 231–259.

Paivio, A. (1969). Mental imagery in associative learning and memory. *Psychological Review, 76,* 241–263.

Pascual-Leone, A., & Torres, F. (1993). Plasticity of the sensorimotor cortex representation of the reading finger in Braille readers. *Brain, 116,* 39–52.

Perlmutter, M. (1978). What is memory ageing the ageing of? *Developmental Psychology, 14,* 330–345.

Pollina, L.K., Greene, A.L., Tunick, R.H., & Puckett, J.M. (1992). Dimensions of everyday memory in young adulthood. *British Journal of Psychology, 83,* 305–321.

Rabbitt, P.M.A., Maylor, E.A., McInnes, L., Bent, N., & Moore, B. (1995). What goods can self-assessment questionnaires deliver for cognitive psychology? *Applied Cognitive Psychology, 9,* 127–152.

Richardson, J.T.E., & Chan, R.C.B. (1995). The constituent structure of self-assessment memory questionnaires: Evidence from multiple sclerosis. *Memory, 3,* 187–200.

Smith, A.F., Jobe, J.B., & Mingay, D.J. (1991). Retrieval from memory of dietary information. *Applied Cognitive Psychology, 5,* 269–296.

Suengas, A.G., & Johnson, M.K. (1988). Qualitative effects of rehearsal on memories for perceived and imagined events. *Journal of Experimental Psychology: General, 117,* 377–389.

Sunderland, A., Harris, J.E., & Baddeley, A.D. (1983). Do laboratory tests predict everyday memory? A neuropsychogical study. *Journal of Verbal Learning and Verbal Behaviour, 22,* 341–357.

Tranel, D., Damasio, A.R., & Damasio, H. (1988). Intact recognition of facial expression, gender and age in patients with impaired recognition of face identity. *Neurology, 38,* 690–696.

Tulving, E. (1991). Memory research is not a zero-sum game. *American Psychologist, 46,* 41–42.

Welford, A.T. (1958). *Ageing and human skill.* Oxford, UK: Oxford University Press.

White, P.A. (1988). Knowing more than you can tell: "Introspective access" and causal report accuracy 10 years later. *British Journal of Psychology, 79,* 13–45.

Wilson, B.A., Cockburn, J.E., & Baddeley, A.D. (1985). *The Rivermead Behavioural Memory Test.* Bury St. Edmunds, UK: Thames Valley Test Co.

Wright, D.B. (2006). Causal and associative hypotheses in psychology: Examples from eyewitness testimony. *Psychology, Public Policy and Law, 12,* 190–213.

Zelinski, E.M., Gilewski, M.J., & Thompson, L.W. (1980). Do laboratory tests relate to self-assessed memory ability in young and old? In L.W. Poon, J.L. Fozard, L.S. Cermak, D. Arenberg, & L.W. Thompson (Eds.), *New directions in memory and aging.* Hillsdale, NJ: Lawrence Erlbaum Associates, Inc.

2 Autobiographical memory

*Helen L. Williams, Martin A. Conway,
and Gillian Cohen*

What are autobiographical memories? Why do we need to remember events and experiences from our own lives? What makes us remember certain memories better than others? Are flashbulb memories really "special" types of memory? Questions such as these and the issue of how and why we remember the events and experiences that form our own personal history have interested psychologists for many years. Aspects of everyday memory such as memory for places and faces, objects and actions, which will be discussed in later chapters, are components within this broader framework of personal history. Memory for personal experiences comprises many different kinds of specific memories that together form the fabric of daily life and are recorded in autobiographical memory. This chapter will address the function of autobiographical memory, how autobiographical memories are organised and retrieved from memory, the impact of the self on memory, flashbulb memories and event characteristics of other memorable autobiographical events, and the fallibility of memory in the real world. However, before we begin to examine the nature of autobiographical memory in detail it is helpful to review a theoretical distinction that has guided research in this area over the past 30 years.

EPISODIC AND SEMANTIC MEMORY

Tulving (1972) distinguished between memory for personal experience and general world knowledge, and considered these as two separate and distinct memory systems. According to this distinction, *episodic memory* consists of personal experiences and the specific objects, people, and events that have been experienced at a particular time and place. *Semantic memory* consists of general knowledge and facts about the world. Table 2.1 shows the main features of the episodic–semantic distinction.

Tulving developed this distinction to clarify the difference between long-term semantic knowledge and the kind of knowledge acquired in verbal learning experiments, where learning a specific list of words constitutes an "episode". The distinction has since been extended to autobiographical memory, where memory for personal experiences is classed as a subsystem of episodic memory. However, further consideration has blurred the edges of the episodic–semantic distinction. For example, a person may know that last year they took a holiday to Italy (which would be termed "semantic" knowledge using Tulving's original conceptualisation), but the memory that this knowledge is referring to is both personal and universal

Table 2.1 The episodic–semantic distinction

	Episodic	Semantic
Type of information represented	Specific events, objects, people	General knowledge facts about the world
Type of organisation in memory	Chronological (by time) or spatial (by place)	In schemas or in categories
Source of information	Personal experience	Abstraction from repeated experience or generalisations learned from others
Focus	Subjective reality: the self	Objective reality: the world

("holiday" as a concept), and contains spatiotemporal knowledge of the individual holiday in question that is not semantic (see Conway & Holmes, 2005; Dritschel, Williams, Baddeley, & Nimmo-Smith, 1992). This highlights how episodic and semantic knowledge are not two separate, compartmentalised structures, but are in an interactive and interdependent relationship. Semantic knowledge is derived from personal experiences by a process of abstraction and generalisation. Episodic autobiographical memories are interpreted and classified in terms of general semantic knowledge in the form of schemas and scripts. In later developments of his theoretical distinctions, Tulving revised his concept of episodic memory to highlight that the distinguishing feature of episodic memory is that, when they are recalled, episodic memories come with *autonoetic consciousness* or *recollective experience*, i.e., a sense of oneself in the past and other associated episodic images, feelings or other memory details, which do not occur if other types of autobiographical knowledge are brought to mind (see Gardiner & Richardson-Klavehn, 2000, for a review; also Tulving, 1985).

WHAT ARE AUTOBIOGRAPHICAL MEMORIES?

Autobiographical memories are episodes recollected from an individual's life. The study of autobiographical memory has undergone a marked change in the last 35 years. Until then, the approach was almost exclusively psychoanalytic or clinical in orientation and diagnostic or therapeutic in aim. In the last 35 years researchers have adopted a cognitive approach and seek to interpret autobiographical memory within the theoretical framework of mainstream memory research. This undertaking has been fraught with difficulty because of the great quantity and variability of the data. It is a daunting task to try to discover the general principles that govern the encoding, storage, and retrieval of personal experiences accumulated over their lifetimes by different individuals with different personal histories. Nevertheless, some progress has been made, at least in defining the questions that are of most interest, and in exploring methods of gathering the data.

Personal experiences are usually stored without a conscious intention to memorise them and give rise to memories that can be of several different kinds. We can identify several dimensions of autobiographical memory:

1   Autobiographical memories may sometimes consist of biographical facts, for example, I may remember the fact that I was born in Liverpool without having any actual memory of having lived there. This kind of factual memory is what Tulving calls *noetic* and contrasts with the kind of *autonoetic* memory, which is experiential. For example, when I recall that I went to school in Wales I can relive the experience with associated sensory imagery and emotions.

2   Brewer (1986) argues that memories vary in the extent to which they are *copies* or *reconstructions* of the original event. Some personal memories seem like copies because they are vivid and contain a considerable amount of irrelevant detail. However, some personal memories are not accurate, and, rather than being raw experiences, they sometimes incorporate the interpretations that are made with hindsight, which suggests they are reconstructed. It seems plausible that the noetic type of memory is more likely to be reconstructed.

3   Autobiographical memories may be *specific* or *generic*, for example, I may remember eating lunch at a particular restaurant on a particular occasion, or I may have a generic memory of family dinners. Neisser (1986) has also noted that a personal memory may be one that is representative of a series of similar events and has termed this type of blended memory "repisodic".

4   Autobiographical memories may be represented from an *observer* perspective or from a *field* perspective. Nigro and Neisser (1983) found that when people examined their own memories some were remembered from the original viewpoint of the experiencer (the field perspective), but a larger number of memories seemed like viewing the event from the outside, from the point of view of an external observer. These "observer" memories cannot be copies of the original perception and must have been reconstructed. Nigro and Neisser reported that recent memories were more likely to be copy-type memories re-experienced from the original viewpoint, but older memories were more likely to be reconstructed ones seen from the observer's viewpoint. Robinson and Swanson (1993) replicated this finding and noted that field memories were more vivid. They asked students to recall personal memories from different periods of their lives, to report on the perspective of each memory, and to rate it for affect. In a later session they were asked to reinstate the memory in the original perspective or to recall it from the other perspective. Changing from a field to an observer perspective had the effect of diminishing affect. The findings showed clearly that it was possible to switch perspectives and most memories could be recalled in either the field or the observer mode, although it was harder to switch if the memory was old and not very vivid. The dynamic, unstable quality of autobiographical memory evidenced in this study is consistent with a reconstructive theory.

FUNCTIONS OF AUTOBIOGRAPHICAL MEMORY

Why do we have autobiographical memory? What function is served by the remembering, reflecting on, and retelling of memories of specific events from our past? Theoretical discussion on the functions of autobiographical memory has converged on three main theoretical positions—that autobiographical memory has directive, social, and self functions.

Directive

The directive function of autobiographical memory involves using memories of past events to guide and shape current and future behaviour, as an aid to problem-solving, and as a tool for predicting future behaviour (Baddeley, 1987). When we are confronted with a current problem, the general or schematic knowledge that has been abstracted from past experiences may not always be relevant and to solve the problem it may be more useful to search back through autobiographical memory to find a specific experience where a similar problem was encountered. Knowing how to behave in social and professional contexts or how to cope with practical problems such as changing a tyre or booking tickets for a concert can occur because we remember how it worked out last time a similar experience occurred. Pillemer (1998, 2003) emphasises the evolutionary significance and practical importance of this directive function of autobiographical memory and gives the example of how autobiographical memory directed behaviour on a large scale by discussing how the terrorist attack on the World Trade Center on September 11 2001 changed the behaviour of Americans. Pillemer (2003) notes how, in the weeks following this tragedy, Americans chose not to travel by air and avoided public places for fear of their personal safety. He highlights that although the "facts" of the tragedy would have contributed to this behaviour, the personal autobiographical memories of seeing the horrific images of the collapse of the Twin Towers on television would have directed behaviour by intensifying reactions, leading to the extreme protective behaviour carried out by individuals. On a more everyday level, when Goldsmith and Pillemer (1988) asked students to describe vivid memories of a parental statement, 46% of the memories indicated a directive function by describing advice or guidance.

Social

The social function of autobiographical memory is seen by some, such as Neisser (1988), as being the most fundamental function of memory. Sharing memories provides material for conversation and therefore facilitates social interaction, and people become friends by exchanging personal narratives. Self-disclosure of autobiographical memories with someone who was not there at the original event is a means of increasing intimacy, of pooling experiences, of giving and receiving understanding and sympathy, and of "placing ourselves" in a given culture and context. Reminiscing with someone who was present at the original event serves a social bonding function as well as heightening intimacy (Bluck, 2003; Fivush, Haden, & Reese, 1996). The importance of autobiographical memories in building and strengthening social bonds has been highlighted by research that has shown how social relationships can suffer when episodic remembering is impaired (Robinson & Swanson, 1990), and the social function of autobiographical memory has also been tied to potential evolutionary adaptivity (Neisser, 1988; Nelson, 2003). Sharing personal memories has been found to make a conversation seem more believable and persuasive (Pillemer, 1992a) and consequently it can help the speaker to educate and inform the listener, which may be particularly useful in parent–child interactions (Bluck, 2003; Fivush, Berlin, Sales, Mennuti-Washburn, & Cassidy, 2003).

Self

The defining characteristic of autobiographical memory is its relationship to the self: Events that are remembered are of personal significance and are the database from which the self is constructed (Conway, 2005). Memory for our own personal history is of great importance as it is an essential element of our personal identity, and many memory researchers view the interaction of the self and memory as the most important function of autobiographical memory. Autobiographical knowledge is proposed to constrain what the self is, has been, and can be in the future (Conway, 2005). To be in coherence with current aspects of the self, memories may be altered, distorted, and fabricated; memory and central aspects of the self are hypothesised as a coherent interdependent system where beliefs and knowledge about the self are confirmed and supported by specific autobiographical memories (Conway, 2005). Conway and Pleydell-Pearce (2000) proposed a model of autobiographical memory in which the working self and autobiographical memory are involved in a reciprocal relationship within a self-memory system (SMS). This model is discussed in the next section on the organisation and structure of auto-biographical memory.

Patients who have experienced loss of memory through trauma or disease illustrate the importance of memories to the concept of the self: Because these patients cannot recall their own personal history, in a very real sense they lose their sense of self. For older adults the practice of reminiscence therapy, where one reviews one's life history and reflects on memories, has been found to be useful in preserving a sense of identity as well as helping to gain a sense of perspective about life events—accepting successes and failures (Scogin, Welsh, Hanson, Stump, & Coates, 2005). For patients suffering from dementia, reminiscence therapy has also been found to improve cognition, mood, and general behavioural functioning (Woods, Spector, Jones, Orrell, & Davies, 2005).

There has been limited empirical research into the functions of autobiographical memory. In an early study, Hyman and Faries (1992) asked participants to describe memories that they frequently talked about and then to describe the situations in which they talked about them. Memories were coded as to how they were used in discussion and results showed that participants rarely described situations where memory had served a directive or problem-solving function; sharing of experiences with others, describing oneself to others, and sharing of information and advice were the more reported uses for autobiographical memories. In a second study, participants were asked to provide memories to cue words and here a distinction was seen between memories that were used for private self functions and memories that were used to inform others; no memories were described that could fall into the directive category. Although this work appears to show that the directive function of memory is not as important as other functions, the authors acknowledged that their methodology may have influenced this and that memories that guide current behaviour may be brought to mind more when in the process of tackling a problem than in casual conversation (Hyman & Faries, 1992; Pillemer, 2003).

More recently, Bluck, Alea, Habermas, and Rubin (2005) set out to test what function(s) people use their autobiographical memories for by creating the Thinking About Life Experiences questionnaire (TALE), which asked participants to what extent they thought about their life experiences in certain situations. Questions were developed that assess each of the three theoretical functions: directive, self, and social; examples of these questions can be seen in Table 2.2. Factor analysis on the TALE scores suggested to Bluck and colleagues that the three functions of directive, self, and social are not as clear-cut as was considered theoretically. They found that the directive function appears to be broader than originally thought, as it appears to include making sense of the past so to have a coherent view of the self with which to direct future behaviour. The self function was found to be narrower than previously conceptualised, as all the items reflected the idea of self-continuity across the lifespan, and the social function was deemed to reflect two different functions— developing relationships and nurturing relationships.

The findings of Bluck et al. (2005) provide a good starting point for further empirical research into the functions of autobiographical memory, but the authors themselves point out that there may be other functions of autobiographical memory that people are not aware of or able to reflect on, and important functions—such as the use of autobiographical memories to regulate emotions—that were not assessed by items on the TALE questionnaire. Pasupathi (2003) found that when people are retelling experiences they do so with the aim of regulating their emotional response, particularly when the initial experience was negative. However, regulation of emotion was found to be dependent on factors such as gender, goals for talking, and audience characteristics such as whether the listener agrees with the speaker's view of the event. With regard to how this function of autobiographical memory fits with the self, social, and directive functions, Pasupathi questions whether retelling of events for emotional regulation is just related to regulating the self, or whether it serves a social function by eliciting emotion from others. This interaction of functions, context, and individual differences is a rich area for future research.

Table 2.2 Example questions from the TALE questionnaire of Bluck et al. (2005)

Q. I think back over or talk about certain periods of my life . . .	Factor label
. . . when I feel that if I think about something bad that happened I can learn some lesson from it . . . when I am facing a challenge and want to give myself confidence	Directive
. . . when I am concerned about whether I am still the same type of person I was earlier . . . when I am concerned about whether my beliefs or values have changed over time	Self
. . . when I want to make someone else feel better by talking to them about my similar past experiences . . . when I want to strengthen a friendship by sharing old memories with friends	Nurturing relationships (social)
. . . when I want to develop a closer relationship with someone . . . when I hope to also learn more about that other person's life	Developing relationships (social)

ORGANISATION AND STRUCTURE OF AUTOBIOGRAPHICAL MEMORY

Autobiographical memories are not just a random collection but are grouped into related sets, organised and indexed so that they can be retrieved on demand, and a particular memory of a specific event has an internal structure of its own. In the 1970s, with the move towards a cognitive understanding of personal memories, theoretical ideas developed in the course of computer modelling provided a useful and illuminating starting point to our understanding of how people represent experiences in memory. Schank (1982a) and Schank and Abelson (1977) introduced the concept of a script, which is a particular kind of schema (see also Chapters 5 and 6) representing knowledge about events and experiences.

Scripts and schemas

A script is a general knowledge structure that represents the knowledge abstracted from a class of similar events, rather than knowledge of any one specific episode. Thus, people have scripts for familiar experiences like eating in restaurants, going shopping, visiting the dentist, and so on. Through everyday experience everyone acquires hundreds of such scripts. An example is shown in Figure 2.1.

A script consists of a sequence of actions that are temporally and causally ordered and are goal-directed. So you sit down *before* ordering; the waitress brings the food *because* you ordered it; you go to the cashier in *order* to pay; and the goal of the whole activity is to satisfy your hunger. The script also includes roles (e.g., the

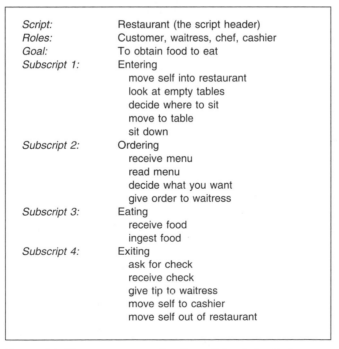

Script:	Restaurant (the script header)
Roles:	Customer, waitress, chef, cashier
Goal:	To obtain food to eat
Subscript 1:	Entering
	move self into restaurant
	look at empty tables
	decide where to sit
	move to table
	sit down
Subscript 2:	Ordering
	receive menu
	read menu
	decide what you want
	give order to waitress
Subscript 3:	Eating
	receive food
	ingest food
Subscript 4:	Exiting
	ask for check
	receive check
	give tip to waitress
	move self to cashier
	move self out of restaurant

Figure 2.1 The restaurant script (from Schank & Abelson, 1977). Reproduced with permission.

waitress) and props (e.g., the table, the menu), but notice that it does not contain details about the kind of food, the décor, the company, or the size of the bill. These details belong to specific episodes, or what Brewer and Tenpenny (personal communication to Cohen, 1996) call an instantiated script. When you remember a particular occasion, specific details can be inserted into the relevant slots in the general script. Scripts are broken up into subscripts, or scenes, which are hierarchically organised with a main action and subordinate actions.

Scripts allow us to supply missing elements and infer what is not explicitly stated. As well as guiding and enriching our understanding of events, scripts also provide an organising framework for remembering events. They explain the common observation that in remembering routine, familiar, often-repeated events we seem to have a generic memory in which individual occasions, or episodes, have fused into a composite.

The psychological reality of scripts has been demonstrated in a study by Bower, Black, and Turner (1979). They asked students to generate the component actions that comprise an event, and list them in order of occurrence. The events they asked about were attending a lecture, visiting a doctor, shopping at a grocery store, eating at a fancy restaurant, and getting up in the morning. There was very substantial agreement about the component actions and their sequence, as can be seen in Figure 2.2.

Subjects also agreed on how a given script was subdivided into scenes, and there was also evidence that they recognised that scripts were hierarchically structured with superordinate goals and subordinate goals.

Attending a lecture	**Visiting a doctor**
ENTER ROOM	*Enter office*
Look for friends	CHECK IN WITH RECEPTIONIST
FIND SEAT	SIT DOWN
SIT DOWN	Wait
Settle belongings	Look at other people
TAKE OUT NOTEBOOK	READ MAGAZINE
Look at other students	*Name called*
Talk	Follow nurse
Look at professor	*Enter examination room*
LISTEN TO PROFESSOR	Undress
TAKE NOTES	*Sit on table*
CHECK TIME	Talk to nurse
Ask questions	NURSE TESTS
Change position in seat	Wait
Daydream	Doctor enters
Look at other students	Doctor greets
Take more notes	Talk to doctor about problem
Close notebook	Doctor asks questions
Gather belongings	DOCTOR EXAMINES
Stand up	Get dressed
Talk	Get medicine
LEAVE	Make another appointment
	LEAVE OFFICE

Figure 2.2 Script actions listed by subjects for the events of attending a
      lecture and visiting a doctor (from Bower, Black, & Turner,
      1979). Copyright © Elsevier 1979. Used with permission.

Consistent and inconsistent events and schemas

In real life, events are not always routine repeated ones, and memories are not always generalised. Many events are unique, one-off experiences. Some events are first-time ones, never experienced before, or novel deviations from more familiar experiences. It is clearly nonsense to suppose that these events are not memorable, and common-sense observations suggest the contrary. The day you won the 100-metre sprint; the day little Johnny was sick in the doctor's waiting room; the time you hadn't enough money to pay the restaurant bill: These are the occasions that stand out in your memory. The unusual or atypical event seems to be more memorable than ordinary, run-of-the-mill occasions.

Experiments have confirmed these intuitions. Brewer and Treyens (1981, described also in Chapter 6) found that when memory was tested for objects in a room, schema-inconsistent objects were recalled better than schema-consistent objects. The same has been found to be true for schema-inconsistent actions (Bower et al., 1979). Nakamura, Graesser, Zimmerman, and Riha (1985) compared ability to remember script-relevant and script-irrelevant actions. Students attended a 15-minute lecture that was specially staged. During the lecture, the lecturer performed a number of actions that varied in relevancy to the lecture script. Examples are shown in Figure 2.3.

After the lecture, the students were given a recognition test in which they had to work through a list of actions, and identify those that had been performed by the lecturer. Irrelevant actions were recognised better than relevant actions, and the false alarm rate was three times higher for relevant actions than for irrelevant actions (i.e., subjects were much more likely to claim falsely that relevant actions had been performed when they had not).

These results have been interpreted in terms of the schema-plus-tag model. According to this model, the memory representation for a specific event consists of the instantiated script, which includes both script-relevant actions that actually occurred and script-relevant actions that were inferred, plus tags that correspond to the irrelevant, unexpected, or deviant aspects of the event. These distinctive tags are highly memorable, and serve as markers, or indices, for the retrieval of specific episodes. This modification of the original script model accounts for the way that

---

Relevant actions
Pointing to information on the blackboard
Opening and closing a book
Moving an eraser to the blackboard
Handing a student a piece of paper

Irrelevant actions
Scratching head
Wiping glasses
Bending a coffee stirrer
Picking up a pencil off the floor

Figure 2.3 Some of the relevant and irrelevant actions incorporated in a lecture (from Nakamura, Graesser, Zimmerman, & Riha, 1985). Used with permission.

novel or atypical occasions (like Johnny being sick on the doctor's carpet) seem to stick in memory.

Later research has suggested that the schema-plus-tag model is oversimplified. In a series of experiments by Brewer and Tenpenny (personal communication, 1996) subjects heard passages containing four types of item: script, instantiated script, irrelevant, and inconsistent. These items were either embedded in a familiar script or, for a group of control subjects, the same items occurred in a non-script context. Examples are shown in Figure 2.4.

After listening to the passages, subjects performed either a free recall test or a recognition test in which the sentences from the passage were mixed with foil sentences. The results showed that for script items, recall was good but recognition was poor, indicating that subjects rely on the pre-experimental generic script to generate recall responses, but this is not adequate to distinguish between target and foil sentences in recognition. Reliance on the pre-existing script in recall was also reflected in the high rate (over 50%) of intrusions. Instantiated script items were also well recalled, and recall of these items in the script condition was far superior to the control condition even though these cannot be derived from the pre-stored script. Brewer and Tenpenny argued that the script gave an advantage by guiding retrieval. Inconsistent items were well recalled and were also the most easily recognised and this is consistent with two schema-based mechanisms, attention and distinctiveness (see Chapter 6). Attention is directed toward items not consistent with the operative schema and these items also benefit from their distinctiveness in the context of the schema. As can be seen in Figure 2.5, there was no sign of an advantage for inconsistent items in the control non-script condition. Recall of irrelevant items was inferior to the other three item types, although the script condition was still better than the control condition, indicating that these items did stand out from the operative script. These results illustrate the extremely complex ways in which memory for elements of new experiences can be influenced by stored schemas and scripts.

The script condition

A restaurant

Gordon decided to go out for dinner. He went in the front door of the expensive restaurant. He was seated by the waiter. *He noticed that his shoe had come untied and tied it.* (Irrelevant) He ordered a drink. *He looked at the menu.* (Script) *He ordered lamb chops.* (Instantiated script) He looked around at the other patrons. He ate his salad. The waiter brought the main course. He ate slowly, enjoying every bite. *He walked through the forest.* (Inconsistent) He ordered dessert. He left a $5 tip. He went home quite pleased with his evening.

The non-script control version

Gordon went to the first football game of the season. He put a new record on his stereo. He cleaned the blackboard. *He noticed that his shoe had come untied and tied it.* He went to the library. *He looked at the menu. He ordered lamb chops.* He dribbled the basketball. He chose a window seat. He studied for his German quiz. He took his toaster in to be repaired. *He walked through the forest.* He swore to tell the truth. He got the lawnmower. He replaced a red bulb that had burned out.

Figure 2.4 Examples of a script and non-script passage from experiments by Brewer and Tenpenny (personal communication, 1996). Reproduced with the permission of the author.

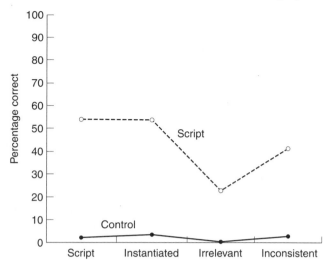

Figure 2.5 Recall scores for script and control conditions for each item type
(from Brewer and Tenpenny, personal communication). Reproduced
with the permission of the author.

The dynamic memory model

Developments and modifications of the original script model (Schank, 1982a, b)
have focused on this relationship between generalised event knowledge and memory
for specific episodes. Bower et al. (1979) noted in their experiment that people
tended to confuse elements from different scripts in memory. The existence of
confusions between actions occurring during the visit to the doctor and actions that
occurred during the visit to the dentist suggested that there exists some memory
structure that is common to both scripts. To account for this finding, Schank (1982a)
proposed that memories can be organised at many different levels of generality. He
also confronted another weakness of the original script model. He recognised the
fact that people can understand and remember an enormous range and variety of
different situations. The original model, in which each situation is interpreted by
means of pre-stored knowledge about a pre-set sequence of actions, is at once too
rigid and too cumbersome to cope with this fact. The number of scripts that would
be required would be highly uneconomical to store and pre-compiled scripts would
be too rigid to handle novel situations. Schank concluded that there must be higher
level of representations that are abstract and general enough to fit novel situations.
Another difficulty for Schank's original formulation is that life experiences do not
conform so neatly to categorised and compartmentalised units as script theory
implies. An experience of a picnic, for example, may involve eating and drinking,
games, quarrels, minor injuries, thunderstorms, and many other elements that
cannot be fitted into a single pre-compiled picnic script.

These observations led Schank to revise the original version of scripts and develop
a model that is more dynamic, more flexible, and more economical. The main
features of this version are:

1   Memory structures are constantly reorganised in the light of new experiences and repetitions of previous experiences, and links between structures reflect similarities between different experiences.

2   The new system is dynamic. Instead of using pre-stored, pre-compiled scripts to understand experiences and organise memories, memory structures are assembled as and when required. Different kinds of knowledge can be activated and linked up to create an appropriate representation for a particular occasion.

3   Instead of replicating elements that are common to many scripts (like entering a building, paying, taking a seat, etc., which belong to the cinema script, the restaurant script, the doctor script, and so on), these common elements are each represented separately at a higher, more general level, and can be called in and incorporated into the current script when required. So the generalised actions like entering and paying can be activated when a memory structure for a visit to a restaurant is being created, but the restaurant script itself now contains only the actions that are specific to restaurants, like calling a waitress, reading the menu, etc. This organisation, whereby generalised actions are common to different scripts, is more economical in storage and can account for the way people sometimes make confusions between related scripts.

4   The higher level generalised event representations have been called MOPs, short for memory organization packets. A MOP is a kind of high-level script that is linked to other related MOPs. In the picnic example, the memory of this particular picnic would involve weather MOPs, friendship MOPs, sports activities MOPs, and first-aid MOPs. The memory representation for this event would invoke general knowledge from all these MOPs as well as the standard picnic MOP.

5   As in the schema-plus-tag model, non-standard aspects of a particular occasion are stored as specific pointers, tags, or indices, which serve to retrieve the memory of a particular occasion. Standard occasions, or standard aspects of novel occasions, are absorbed into the relevant generalised event representations (the MOPs). The specific pointers provide the mechanism for the process Schank calls "reminding". You may be reminded of a particular episode by a friend who says, "Do you remember the time David fell in the river? You know, the day we got caught in a thunderstorm. You must remember, we played frisbee in a field of cows." The friend is *reminding* you of the event by activating successively the tags he thinks you are most likely to have used as indices.

6   Within this new dynamic memory system a particular episode, like going to a party, can therefore be stored at several different levels of generality, as:

> going to David's party last Saturday evening; *or*
> going to parties; *or*
> social interactions.

The system also allows for even more general, higher level representations, which Schank (1982a) has called TOPs or thematic organization points. Themes like "Getting what you want", "Achieving power", or "Failing to achieve a goal" are examples, and their existence is evident in conversational exchanges like the following:

"I just heard I didn't get the job."

"Bad luck. And I've failed my driving test again. Let's go and have a drink to cheer ourselves up."

The conversation illustrates how two disparate events can be organised under the high-level theme of failures. These high-level structures allow us to recognise similarities and analogies between superficially quite different events. In Schank's own example of the Steak and the Haircut, a friend's complaint that his wife would not cook his steak rare enough reminds the listener of occasions when a barber would not cut his hair short enough. The events are related to the common theme of failing to get a service performed in a sufficiently extreme form.

Schank's theories were originally developed in the process of writing programs for computer modelling of language-understanding, rather than being designed to account for human memory in everyday life, but they have been modified and adapted so as to explain experimental findings and observations. Some aspects, such as the emphasis on the need for economy of storage, may be more appropriate for the computer than for the human brain. However, the later versions of the model provide what is, on the whole, a convincing account of how people remember the events they experience in daily life.

Scripts and recollective experience

Recent work on scripts and schemas has explored their relationship to the phenomenological experiences of remembering. Schema-plus-tag and dynamic schema models both predict that schema-inconsistent information, which must be explicitly stored in episodic memory, should be remembered in a more vivid and detailed manner than schema-consistent information, which can be integrated into organisational knowledge structures that were used to process and store the original event. Lampinen, Faries, Neuschatz, and Toglia (2000) instructed participants to listen to a narrative of a character who carried out a number of script-based activities (e.g., washing his car). The participant's memory was then tested using the remember–know paradigm first introduced by Tulving (1985). In this paradigm, participants have to judge whether they *remember* an item being presented, or if they just *know* that it had been presented. *Remembering* involves conscious recollection of explicit details of the presentation experience, e.g., thoughts, perceptual details, emotional responses, whereas *knowing* involves feeling certain that the item had been presented before but with no recollection of any specific details of this presentation. Lampinen et al. (2000) found that more remember judgments were made for schema-inconsistent actions, indicating that participants' memories for these atypical actions were more experientially vivid than those for typical actions. Lampinen, Copeland, and Neuschatz (2001) replicated this finding using a room schemas paradigm similar to that of Brewer and Treyens (1981). In Lampinen and colleagues' experiment participants entered a room that was set up to resemble such an office. It contained 10 items that had been rated as typically appearing in a graduate students office and 10 items that were atypical to that setting. In a recognition test these atypical items were again more likely to be experienced in the remember sense than were the typical items. Both these studies demonstrate how schemas and expectations of what you should be seeing or hearing in a certain situation can influence the subjective experience of your memory for that situation.

Recent models of memory organisation

Scripts and schemas paved the way for more recent conceptualisations of how memory is organised. The consensus view emerging from a wide range of studies looking at the way in which people retrieve their memories is that there are two principles of organisation, temporal and thematic. Personal memories may be chronologically organised in a temporal sequence, like the memories of schoolteachers in Whitten and Leonard's study (1981), or in lifetime periods, sometimes called "extendures" (such as schooldays, college days, working in London, retirement, etc.). They may also be organised along themes such as illnesses, holidays, or parties.

The order in which people freely recall target events and the relative effectiveness of different instructions and different cues provide indications of the underlying organisation. Numerous studies have inferred the organisation of autobiographical memories by comparing the response times taken to retrieve personal memories to different cues. Subjects are supplied with a cue word and asked to respond as soon as a personal memory associated with the cue word comes to mind. Robinson (1976) compared the time taken to recall experiences involving an activity (e.g., throwing) or an object (e.g., car) with those involving an emotion (e.g., happy). He found that retrieval was slowest with emotion cues. This result suggests that people do not organise their memories in terms of the associated emotions. Robinson argued that this would be an inefficient form of organisation because many different experiences share the same emotions. This has been questioned recently by Schulkind and Woldorf (2005) who, instead of using emotion-word cues, asked participants to bring to mind memories in response to brief musical excerpts that had been rated in a pilot study for their affect (how positive or negative the music was) and their arousal (how intense the music was). Musical cues were chosen instead of emotion words as they suggested that emotion words may simply not elicit the same kind of emotional memories as something that induces a particular mood or the subjective experience of an emotion. Unlike other studies using musical cues, the participants were not told that the experiment had anything to do with emotion until after they had recalled all their memories; they were then asked to go back, date them, and rate them for valence (to what extent they were negative or positive) and arousal. Schulkind and Woldorf found that the valence of the music did indeed influence the valence of the memory elicited: The mean valence rating for memories that had been elicited by positive music was higher than that elicited by negative music. This finding suggests that emotion does have a role to play in the organisation of memory and Schulkind and Woldorf suggest that current models of the organisation of autobiographical memory need to consider the role of emotion more fully.

Reiser, Black, and Abelson (1985) investigated how script-like knowledge structures function in the organisation and retrieval of experiences. They compared the effectiveness of two different kinds of knowledge structure as a means of accessing personal memories. One kind of knowledge structure they called *activities*. These are script-like structures consisting of knowledge about sequences of actions undertaken to achieve a goal, for example, eating in restaurants, shopping in department stores, or going to libraries. The other kind of knowledge structure they termed *general actions*. These represent higher level knowledge about actions that can be components in many different specific activities. So paying, sitting down, buying tickets are examples of general actions that occur in many different scenarios.

Reiser et al. (1985) put forward the Activity Dominance Hypothesis, predicting that activities would be better retrieval cues than general actions because accessing specific activities, such as eating in restaurants, generates many inferences about food, décor, and service that can serve as further cues for retrieval of specific experiences. General actions are not "inference-rich" structures in this way; they do not constrain the area of search sufficiently and are too abstract to generate useful cues. To test their predictions, Reiser et al. asked subjects to recall specific personal experiences to fit an activity cue such as "went out drinking" or "had your hair cut" and a general action cue such as "paid at the cash register". They varied the order in which these two cues were presented. More experiences were successfully recalled and responses were faster when the activity cue was first. In everyday terms, you would find it easier to remember an occasion when you had your hair cut than an occasion when you bought a ticket. Reiser and his colleagues concluded that retrieval involves two stages: first, establishing a context, like haircuts, and second, finding an index or tag that identifies a particular experience within that context. Activities are knowledge structures at the optimal level of specificity. This is the level at which experiences are originally encoded, and is the level that provides the optimal context for search. This context-plus-index model is similar to the schema-plus-tag model.

Although the idea that there is an optimal level of specificity for search contexts is convincing, Reiser et al. (1985) only tested the efficacy of actions as retrieval cues, and did not compare actions with other cues such as locations or lifetime extendures, or the names of objects or emotions. Conway and Bekerian (1987) failed to replicate the findings of Reiser et al. and found that retrieval was facilitated when cued by lifetime period (e.g., schooldays, time at college), and suggested that people's memories of their own personal history are organised in terms of such periods. Moreover, Anderson and Conway (2007) have pointed out an important flaw in the design of Reiser et al.'s experiment. When they presented a general action before an activity cue the temporal order of events was reversed. For example, when "finding a seat" (the general action cue) preceded "going to the cinema" (the activity cue), the actual order in which these events occur was violated. Anderson and Conway repeated the experiment, selecting cues such as "parked the car" (general action) and "went to the cinema" (activity), which preserved the correct temporal order. They found no differences in the effectiveness of the two kinds of cue, but retrieval was faster when temporal order was preserved than when it was violated. They concluded that autobiographical memories are not indexed by activities or general actions but by themes and lifetime periods.

Barsalou (1988) has also questioned the Activity Dominance Hypothesis. Using the same paradigm as Reiser et al., he compared the effectiveness of activity cues (watching television), participant cues (your mother), location cues (in the cafeteria), and time cues (at noon). Retrieval time was not affected by cue type or by cue order, but participant cues elicited the most memories. He noted that goals, like passing an exam or learning to drive, were good cues for retrieving memories. Barsalou also conducted a free recall experiment in which students were asked to recall what they did last summer. The most frequently recalled events were extended events (taking a

trip to Europe), and repeated events (playing tennis). Only 21% of the recalled events were specific episodes. Organisational clusters could also be discerned in the recall protocols. From these data Barsalou concluded that, as shown in Figure 2.6, the highest level of organisation is chronological. Barsalou calls this level of the hierarchy "extended-event time lines", which are analogous to extendures or lifetime periods. Several different time lines may overlap concurrently. According to Barsalou, summarised events are represented at lower levels in the hierarchy.

Brown and Schopflocher (1998) performed a similar experiment where participants were first asked to recall a set of 14 autobiographical memories, either from important events from their life or from cue words. Participants then had to use each of these 14 memories to cue a second autobiographical memory. The data indicated that many different themes, not just activities, were used to cue the second memory from the first. In the important-event group, 50% of event pairs involved the same person, 43% occurred at the same location, 35% involved the same activity, and in 60% of pairs one event was identified as having caused the other. Organisational clusters were also studied by Lancaster and Barsalou (1997). Here participants were given sets of events to learn that again included a person, location, activity, and time. The first trial was always an incidental learning trial, i.e., participants were not explicitly told they would have to remember the events but

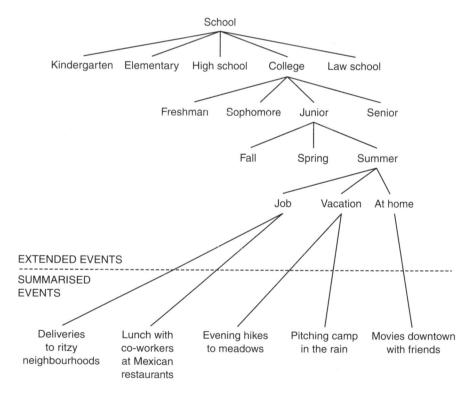

Figure 2.6 Hierarchical organisation of autobiographical memories. Summarised events at the lower levels are nested in extended time lines (from Barsalou, 1988). Reprinted by permission of Cambridge University Press.

instead had to rate each event as to how easy it was to image. Participants were then instructed to freely recall any full or partial events they could in any order that came to mind. This presentation and recall was then repeated in another trial, this time with the instruction to learn the events. The results showed that participants clustered events around each of the four elements but they tended to prefer clustering around the themes of person and activity. Participants were also able to pivot back and forth from activity to person clusters easily, i.e., when they had exhausted a cluster of events that had been performed by one person (e.g., Barbra Streisand), they were able to focus on a different element of the last event recalled (e.g., swimming), and then recall events that shared this theme. Lancaster and Barsalou concluded that people are able to organise events in memory dynamically, they can organise events in multiple ways, they can cross-classify events in different categories simultaneously, and they can also pivot from one organisation to another when retrieving memories.

Following the work of Barsalou (1988), a theoretical autobiographical memory framework was developed by Conway and Pleydell-Pearce (2000; and extended by Conway, 2005; Conway, Singer, & Tagini, 2004) called the self-memory system (SMS). The two main components of the SMS are the *working self* and the *autobiographical memory knowledge base*. The *self* or *working self* is thought of as a set of currently active goals or self-images that are organised through working memory into goal hierarchies that work together to constrain cognition, and therefore behaviour, so that the individual can operate on the world effectively. The working self controls access to the *autobiographical knowledge base, which* is made up of conceptual knowledge from two broad areas: lifetime periods and general events (Conway, 2005; Conway & Pleydell-Pearce, 2000). Knowledge is represented within this model in terms of its goal-relatedness. Within the SMS model the autobiographical knowledge base contains two types of information: autobiographical knowledge, which can range from highly abstract conceptual knowledge to conceptual knowledge that is event-specific and experience-near, and episodic memories. When these two systems are both involved in remembering, specific autobiographical memories can be formed. Within this conceptualisation of autobiographical memory the self is both the experiencer and the product of the experiences.

The autobiographical memory knowledge base

Figure 2.7 illustrates how Conway (2005) outlined how lifetime periods, general events, and episodic memories are organised within the autobiographical knowledge base and the distinctions between different types of conceptual autobiographical knowledge. The most abstract level is termed the "life story" and this is considered to be part of the conceptual self. An individual's life story contains their general factual and evaluative knowledge about themselves; it can also contain concepts or themes that refer to different selves, e.g., self as mother, self as colleague. These different self-images may have access to different knowledge, general events, and specific event memories in the autobiographical memory knowledge base. So, for example, the specific episode "meeting GC" is linked to the general event "last orders", to the theme of "activities" and the lifetime period of "working at pub X".

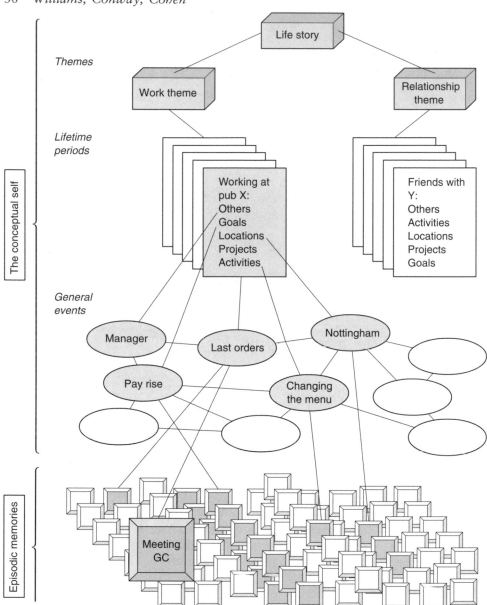

Figure 2.7 Knowledge structures in autobiographical memory. After Conway (2005). Reproduced by permission of Elsevier Inc.

Retrieval can occur in a top-down direction in response to queries like "What activities were you involved in when you worked at that pub?" or in a bottom-up direction in response to "How did you meet GC?"

Within this organisational hierarchy, relatively recent experiences, especially those occurring within the current lifetime period, are considered to be represented in terms of the goals of the working self that are currently active and dominating at the time. When goals change and new themes become the focus of the working self, an older version of the working self is stored in memory in the form of general events and their associated episodic memory clusters.

Episodic memory revisited

Within the SMS, conceptualisations of episodic memory have changed from Tulving's version (see Table 2.1) and from the original model put forward by Conway and Pleydell-Pearce (2000). In the current model, the term "episodic memory" has replaced the original term of "event-specific knowledge"; this was considered misleading as it simply referred to the content of episodic memories and did not encompass the sensory-perceptual-conceptual-affective processing which is summarised in episodic memories. The central characteristics of episodic memory are listed in Table 2.3.

One of the defining features of remembering, as conceptualised by the SMS, is represented by point eight in Table 2.3—recollective experience. Recollective experience or *autonoetic consciousness*, as originally discussed by Tulving, is the sense of "mental time travel" that is often experienced when recalling memories. Recollective experience entails a sense of the self in the past and a feeling of remembering that may be accompanied by imagery or other sensory-perceptual details of the original event. Recollective experience and the experience of remembering have become important areas of research and studies referring to them are discussed later.

As a recent model of memory organisation, the SMS provides a fluent model of how working memory, autobiographical knowledge, and the self interact to influence why we remember what we do from our everyday experiences. The SMS brings the self and memory closer together than any previous models of memory (e.g., Johnson & Chalfonte, 1994; Schank, 1982a, b). It is also consistent with responses to the TALE questionnaire of Bluck et al. (2005) discussed earlier, where the self was demonstrated not only to be related to the self function of autobiographical memory but also to the directive function, which was found to include making sense of the past in order to have a coherent self with which to direct future behaviour.

Table 2.3 Ten characteristics of episodic memory. After Conway (2005)

Ten characteristics of episodic memory
1 Retain summary records of sensory-perceptual-conceptual-affective processing derived from working memory
2 Retain patterns of activation/inhibition over long periods
3 Are mostly represented in the form of (visual) images
4 Represent short time slices, determined by changes in goal-processing
5 Represented roughly in their order of occurrence
6 Are only retained in a durable form if they become linked to conceptual autobiographical knowledge. Otherwise they are rapidly forgotten
7 Their main function is to provide a short-term record of progress in current goal-processing
8 They are recollectively experienced when accessed
9 When included as part of an autobiographical memory construction they provide specificity
10 Neuroanatomically they may be represented in brain regions separate from other (conceptual) autobiographical knowledge networks

Early diary studies of autobiographical memories

Diary studies also shed some light on how autobiographical memory is organised. Linton (1982) undertook a systematic 6-year study of her own memory for the events of her daily life. Each day she wrote on cards a brief description of at least two events that occurred on that day. Every month she reread two of these descriptions, which were selected at random from the accumulating pool, so that the retention period was varied. She then tried to remember the events described, to estimate the temporal order in which they occurred, and the date of each event. She also rated each memory for salience (importance) and for emotionality, both at the time of writing the description and again at the time of recall.

Linton noted two types of forgetting. One form of forgetting was associated with repeated events, such as regular trips to attend a committee meeting in another town. Over time, memories of particular trips became indistinguishable from each other, and she found she had only retained a generic composite memory. The specific memory of a particular occasion had been absorbed into a generalised event memory or, in other words, she had acquired a script for these events. This finding conforms to most people's own experience. Unique occasions are usually better remembered than repeated events, which blend into each other. A second type of forgetting also occurred. When she reread descriptions of some events she simply could not remember the event at all. Here it was not the case that similar events had been confused and amalgamated in memory, but that a single event had been forgotten. The number of events forgotten in this way increased steadily with each year of the study, and after 6 years had elapsed, 30% of the events recorded had been totally forgotten.

A surprising feature of Linton's study was her failure to find any strong relationship between rated importance and emotionality, and subsequent recall. Commonsense experience suggests that we remember important events, and those that roused strong passions better than those that were trivial or left us unmoved. However, Linton found that the emotionality and importance ratings she initially gave to an event did not correspond closely with those she gave later on using hindsight. It appears that the characteristics of an event at the time of encoding only affect memorability if the same qualities are still present at the time of recall.

To gain further insight into the way events are organised in memory, Linton also studied strategies of recall. She tried to recall all the events that occurred in a designated month. Introspective monitoring of her own attempts at recall showed that many events were organised chronologically and were recalled by a temporally ordered search. Some were organised in categories (themes) and were retrieved by working through named categories like parties or sporting activities. For events that were more than 2 years old, there was a shift away from chronological search toward a greater use of thematic search, reflecting a change in memory organisation. Linton's recall attempts also confirmed that events may be organised in terms of lifetime periods, which she called extendures, such as a job, a marriage, or living in a particular place. Within these extendures, specific events are embedded and can be accessed via the relevant extendure. The findings from Linton's diary study are therefore consistent with Barsalou's and Conway's views that memories are organised hierarchically, both chronologically and thematically. The results also emphasise the fragility of specific memories relative to higher level general event memories.

Wagenaar (1986) employed similar methods in recording 2400 events of his daily life over a period of 6 years. He specifically recorded each event in terms of *who*, *what*, *where*, and *when* plus some critical identifying detail. This format had two advantages. He was able to determine which of these facts about an event were best retained, and also which facts provided the best cues for retrieving the rest of the information. He also rated the *pleasantness*, *emotionality*, and *saliency* of each event. Saliency was defined as how often such an event might be expected to recur, so unique events were rated as highly salient, and routine events were rated low. Figure 2.8 shows the pro-forma for recording the events.

When memory was tested, each cue was presented in turn. For example, on trial 1, Leonardo da Vinci (the *who* cue) was supplied and Wagenaar had to try to recall *what* happened, *where*, and *when*. On trial 2, two cues were given; on trial 3, three cues; and on trial 4, all four cues were given and the question about the critical detail was posed. Cue order was varied systematically. The retention function showed that the percentage of questions answered correctly dropped over a 4-year period from 70% to 35%. Recall increased with the number of cues provided. Pleasant events were remembered better than unpleasant or neutral ones—a finding sometimes known as the *Pollyanna principle*—but retention was also related to the other rated dimensions of salience and emotionality. The order of efficacy of the retrieval cues when presented singly was *what, where, who, when*. *What* was by far the most powerful cue and *when* was almost useless. Chronological information was often missing from the memory of the event, and could not be used as a search criterion. Wagenaar concluded that only a few landmark events were precisely dated in memory, and events were, on the whole, not filed in memory by dates. In everyday terms, it is unlikely that you will remember if I ask you what happened on 17 July 4 years ago, but if I tell you that you went to watch a tennis match you would probably remember who played, where it took place, at roughly what period of the year, and what happened. The failure to remember when events occurred may seem to be at odds with the claim made in other studies that memories are chronologically organised, but that claim was based on evidence showing organisation into the large chunks of time that constitute lifetime periods, not precise days and dates. However, the power of the *what* cue does suggest that the predominant form of organisation is thematic, as discussed earlier.

Memory for dates

Although themes may be dominant, the ability to date memories is still crucial to the organisation of memory. The idea that memories are organised on a temporal dimension and retrieved by some form of chronological search raises questions about the accuracy of subjective dating, and much research has been undertaken into the issue of forward or backward bias in dating error.

Brown, Rips, and Shevell (1985) asked subjects to date the month of 50 news events from 1977 to mid-1982. They hypothesised that people seldom have a precise memory record of the dates of public events, so that dates are *estimated* rather than remembered. In this study they selected some events that subjects would know a lot about, and some events they would know little about, and predicted that dates of high-knowledge events (like "President Reagan shot") would be shifted toward the present, and dates of low-knowledge events (like "25 die in California mud slides")

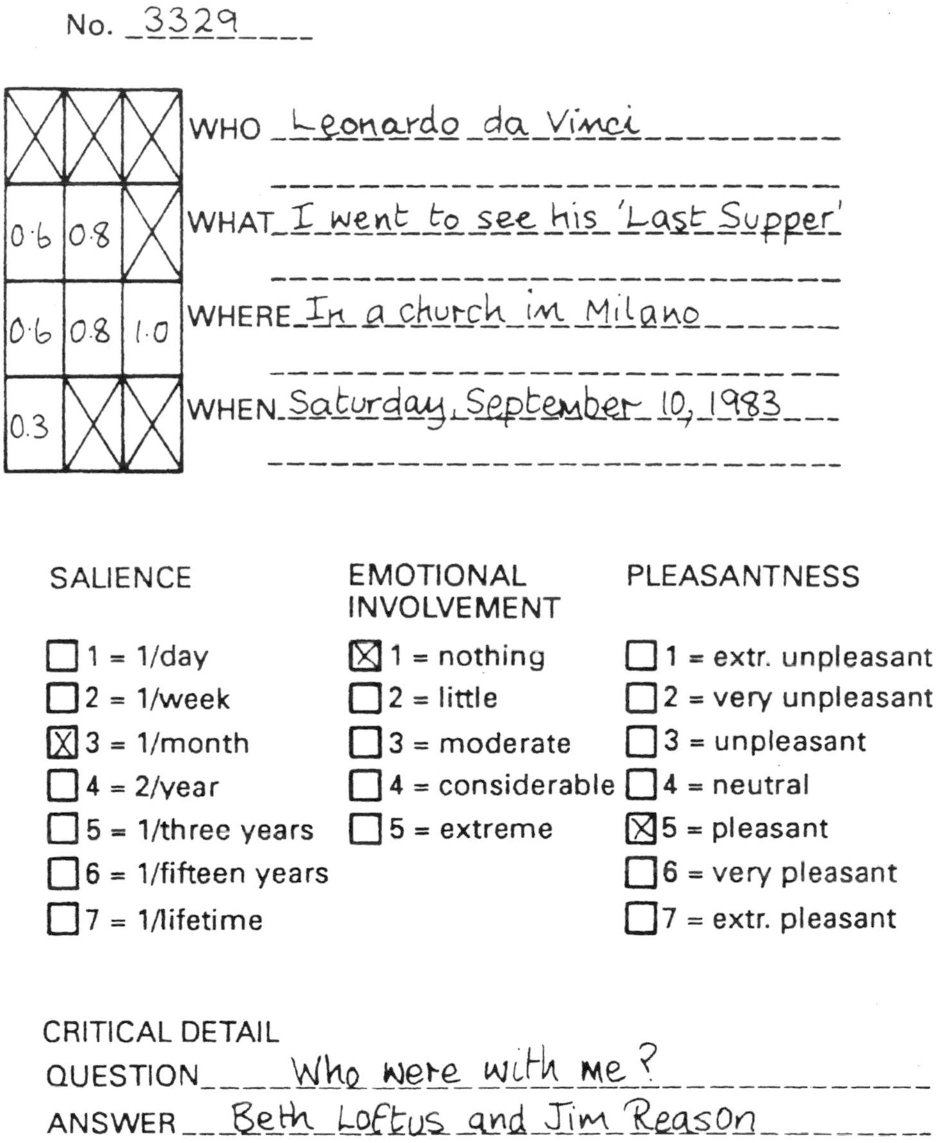

No. _3329____

WHO _Leonardo da Vinci_____

WHAT_I went to see his 'Last Supper'

WHERE_In a church in Milano_____

WHEN_Saturday, September 10, 1983____

SALIENCE	EMOTIONAL INVOLVEMENT	PLEASANTNESS
☐ 1 = 1/day	☒ 1 = nothing	☐ 1 = extr. unpleasant
☐ 2 = 1/week	☐ 2 = little	☐ 2 = very unpleasant
☒ 3 = 1/month	☐ 3 = moderate	☐ 3 = unpleasant
☐ 4 = 2/year	☐ 4 = considerable	☐ 4 = neutral
☐ 5 = 1/three years	☐ 5 = extreme	☒ 5 = pleasant
☐ 6 = 1/fifteen years		☐ 6 = very pleasant
☐ 7 = 1/lifetime		☐ 7 = extr. pleasant

CRITICAL DETAIL
QUESTION____Who were with me?_____
ANSWER __Beth Loftus and Jim Reason_____

Figure 2.8 An example of a recorded event from Wagenaar's diary study (1986).
Copyright © Elsevier 1986. Used with permission.

would be shifted toward the past. They suggested that estimation is based on the amount of information about the event that can be recalled. That is, people work on the assumption that information is progressively lost from memory over time, so the less that is remembered, the older the memory must be. The results conformed to the prediction. Dates of high-knowledge events were too recent by an average of 0.28 years, and dates of low-knowledge events were too remote by an average of 0.17 years. The number of propositions a subject could recall about an event was systematically related to the judged recency of the event.

People also estimate dates of public events using the strategy of relating the target event to autobiographical events or to some other, more easily dated public event; this is often called "anchoring" or association (Kemp, 1999). If a landmark event can be dated, and the temporal relationship of landmark to target is known, the target date can be estimated. For example, I can estimate the date of the Prince of Wales' wedding because I remember being on holiday in Switzerland at the time and seeing it on television in a hotel in the mountains, and I know the date of this holiday.

Loftus and Marburger (1983) confirmed that events are dated more accurately if a landmark is supplied as a temporal reference point. They noted that people usually overestimate the recency of events, especially ones that are very emotional and salient—a phenomenon known as *forward telescoping*—but this tendency was reduced by using landmarks. They compared responses to questions preceded by landmarks, e.g., *Since the eruption of Mount St. Helens did you . . .*, with responses to the same questions preceded by no landmark, e.g., *During the last six months . . .*, or the subject was instructed to supply a personal landmark to use as a reference point when answering the question. Forward telescoping was reduced by the use of all of these landmarks. Rubin and Baddeley (1989) also found forward telescoping in their study of people's memory for visits to the Applied Psychology Unit in Cambridge, with the size of the error increasing systematically with the time elapsed since the visit. They explained the phenomenon of forward telescoping in terms of two main factors. First, errors are larger for older events so more of these will be shifted into a different period, whereas the small errors that occur for recent events are not sufficient to shift them outside the correct period. Second, the recency effect preserves the dates of recent events so these are less likely to be shifted backward. The combination of these factors makes it more likely that dating errors will be forward shifts. Betz and Skowronski (1997) replicated this finding in a study where they asked participants to keep a diary. They found evidence of both *forward telescoping* for older events (near the start of the diary period) and evidence of *backward telescoping*, which they call *time-expansion*, the phenomenon of relatively young events (near the end of the diary period) being dated as older than they actually are.

Researchers have attempted to explain forward and backward telescoping through a number of different models. Huttenlocher, Hedges, and Prohaska (1988) and Rubin and Baddeley (1989) put forward the *boundaries effects model*, which is based on three assumptions: that without boundaries, dating of events is unbiased, that variability increases over time as memories decrease or decay, and that boundaries truncate the distribution as estimates beyond the boundaries are disallowed. In contrast to this model, the *associative approach* (Kemp, 1999) suggests that forwards telescoping occurs because of the anchors or landmarks used to date events. When an associate or anchor is found, the date of this event serves as a guide to the date of the event you are trying to date; however, this approach assumes that because the ability to retrieve relevant information decreases over time, the date of the anchor is typically going to be more recent than that of the target and this will therefore bias the dating of the target in a forward telescoping manner.

A recent study by Lee and Brown (2004) has found more support for the associative explanation for forward telescoping than for the boundaries effects model. In their study, four different groups dated 64 news events under different boundary conditions. In all conditions participants were provided with a date and told that this was the earliest possible date that the events could have occurred. The four different boundaries used were: January 1997 (the true boundary), January 1994, January 1991, and a no-boundary condition. The experiment was conducted at the end of 2001. Although the data from the first three conditions supported the boundaries effects model, evidence of forward and backward telescoping was also found in the condition where no date boundaries were imposed on responses, which cannot be explained by that model. To examine this further they looked at the date estimates for events that the participant had guessed (guesses were defined as events that had been rated by the participant, on a prior task, as an event that they did not know anything about). For these guessed estimates a backward telescoping effect was observed. Backward telescoping is the tendency to estimate unknown events near the midpoint of a range or earlier, i.e., backwards. When these biased guess responses were taken out of the analysis, Lee and Brown (2004) found that the different boundaries (1997, 1994, 1991 and no boundary) all showed the same level of forward telescoping and very little backward telescoping, indicating that it was not the different boundaries that had caused the effect. Lee and Brown (2004) therefore rejected the boundaries effects model and accepted the associative model to explain the forward telescoping effect in dating events.

Another bias that has been observed when people are recalling memories from their life is the *calendar effect*. Pillemer, Rhinehart, and White (1986) and Robinson (1986) found that when students have to freely recall events from the past year they recall more events from the beginnings and endings of school terms than from other times of the year. This finding suggests that people's recall is not only selective, but is also influenced by the over-riding structures of their lives. A number of explanations for this finding have been suggested. One possibility is that particularly important or salient events happen at the beginnings and endings of academic terms. This makes intuitive sense: You arrive at university for the first time and make friends with people you have never met before, or you return and see friends you have not seen at all over the summer. At the end of term you get stressed because of exams and then you say goodbye to friends and go home. Although the importance of events has been found to be related to the vividness of memories, Robinson (1986) found differing results regarding the effect of importance on the calendar effect with two groups of students. Another issue is that these studies could not verify the dates of events so participants could just have been showing a bias towards the boundaries of a term as these boundaries were used as anchors. In a series of experiments Kurbat, Shevell, and Rips (1998) tested these issues using four different paradigms. They tested students in schools with very different academic terms; asked participants to date events from the previous year that could be verified (e.g., the date of a concert on campus); compared memories for events elicited using holidays and special occasions (e.g., Valentine's day) as calendar markers as opposed to term boundaries; and asked participants to rate the importance of events. They found that schools with differing academic term cycles gave rise to calendar effects and that these related to their particular academic calendars. This effect did not appear to be due to the importance of events though, as participants were not found to rate the events from endpoints as more important than events that did not occur at endpoints. Accuracy of dating also did not play a significant role as the study, which asked participants to date events that could be verified, found that these estimates were not biased towards endpoint positions. In the experiment that compared holiday cueing to term-boundary cueing, endpoints were found to be retrieval aids: An explicit set of term dates maintained or enhanced the calendar effect whereas the alternative cues decreased the calendar effect. Kurbat et al. (1998) postulated that endpoints of periods such as academic terms are part of the web of generic information that each of us holds about school or university, and that these can be used to integrate personal memories into long-term memory. They also suggest that endpoints may be prominent because they appear to have control over activities, and particularly change in activities. When you are at university you encounter different people from when you are at home, you engage in different activities, and you have a different daily schedule. Endpoints can represent expectations about what can be done, and can also remind you of what you did (Kurbat et al., 1998).

An additional influence of boundaries was observed by Burt, Kemp, and Conway (2001), who retested people who had originally taken part in a diary study 10 years previously (Burt, 1992a, b). Instead of finding an effect of forward telescoping, as predicted, the authors observed a backward telescoping effect, with events being dated as having occurred longer ago than they actually did. Burt et al. (2001) suggested that this effect may have occurred because of the incidental establishment of an endpoint boundary when they were originally tested 10 years earlier. This landmark occasion of being tested on their diaries would have been more memorable and would have created a boundary before which all diary events must have occurred. A further explanation was suggested as being the association approach. Participants in the study had originally been tested on their memory for events that had taken place when they were aged between 10 and 16 years. Burt et al. (2001) posited that when participants were then retested, the contextual information available from similar or associated events was more likely to have come from the years before the age of 10 than the years after the age of 16, as their lives were more likely to involve more change after the age of 16. They may have left school, got a job, begun having romantic relationships, etc. Backward telescoping may have occurred because contextually similar events to those reported in the diaries came from an earlier period of childhood. This link between dating accuracy and life periods has introduced the idea of the self into the literature on memory for dates. Wilson and Ross (2003) found that negative events "feel older" than positive events and suggest that this is because negative events conflict with a person's current self-concept. When recalling a memory, the self-context associated with that memory or period of life may also be recalled. Comparing that self-concept with the current self-concept may lead to dating bias; if the self-concepts are very different the event in memory may be dated as older than if the self-concepts are judged as being similar (Skowronski, Walker, & Betz, 2003).

Thomsen and Berntsen (2005) also found that the self was very important to the organisation of memory by demonstrating that boundary effects also occur when you ask people to recall memories from a period of life that has definite boundaries, but these boundaries are specific to the individual and are not part of a collectively shared calendar. The period of life they chose to ask people about was their last romantic relationship. These findings were consistent with *personal narrative theory*, which suggests that more memories are typically recalled from the boundaries of periods because of the change in personal narrative script that has to occur at these points. Narrative structures are considered one form of organisation that gives an individual a coherent sense of self by linking past events into temporally, causally, and thematically organised arrays. This fits with the broader theory of the SMS (Conway, 2005; Conway & Pleydell-Pearce, 2000).

One important role for dating accuracy in the real world is when medical histories are elicited. The patient's ability to recall the dates and ordering of episodes and symptoms and their frequency and intensity is crucial for diagnosis. Means, Mingay, Nigam, and Zarrow (1988) have pointed out that in chronic health conditions, recurring events blended into a generic memory and were difficult to decompose. Their study showed that when people were trained to link events to personal landmarks, like birthdays or holidays, recall improved. Cohen and Java (1995), in their study of memory for medical history, found that 50% of health events that occurred in the previous 6 months were dated accurately to within 2 weeks and there was no difference between forward and backward shifts in dating errors. However, this was a relatively short time period and subjects spontaneously used personal landmarks. Loftus (1987) has noted that accuracy of dating improves when two time frames are interrogated instead of one. Asking whether X occurred (a) in the last 6 months and (b) in the last 2 months forces people to be more accurate and precise than simply asking whether X occurred in the last 6 months. People have also been found to be more accurate when asked to judge the age of an event in *absolute time format* as opposed to *relative time format* (Janssen, Chessa, & Murre, 2006). In absolute time format people are asked for the actual date on which an event occurred, whereas in relative time format they are asked how long ago, relative to the present, an event occurred. Janssen et al. (2006) also found that when dating personal events the absolute time format was preferred, whereas when dating news events participants preferred the relative time format. Another methodology used is the Judgment of Recency (JOR) technique, where participants are asked to judge which of two events occurred more recently. Skowronski et al. (2003) found that JOR accuracy is improved the greater the temporal distance between the two events and that JOR performance decreases as the youngest event of the pair becomes more distant in time. For example, if you are making a JOR for two events that took place 6 months apart, your accuracy will be better if the youngest event, i.e., the one that actually occurred more recently, occurred 10 months ago than if it occurred 20 months ago. This finding was linked to the relationships between past and present self-concepts as outlined earlier.

Brown, Shevell, and Rips (1986) collected verbal protocols from subjects during date estimation. In this study, both political events (Cyrus Vance resigns) and non-political events (Mount St. Helens erupts) were dated after lags of up to 5 years. Overall, 70% of the protocols contained temporal inferences of the kind "I know X happened just before Y and Y was about last autumn"; 61% of political events were related in this way to other political events and 31% to personal history. For non-political events, 25% were related to public events and 50% to personal history. It was easier to "place" non-political events within personally defined periods such as college terms, and to place political events within publicly defined periods such as the Reagan administration, but public and personal event histories were clearly interwoven and each provided a reference system for the other.

It follows from these findings that memories are dated more accurately if someone has a clearly defined time line. Skowronski and Thompson (1990) tested the hypothesis that women have a better developed temporal reference schema than men and are therefore better able to reconstruct the dates of past events. The idea behind this is that women are more concerned with keeping appointments, remembering the dates of birthdays and anniversaries, and more often keep personal diaries. In a meta-analysis of four dating studies they found that the dating accuracy of women was superior, although this difference is thought to be culturally induced rather than being a gender-specific difference.

Internal structure of specific memories

Anderson and Conway (1993) were interested in the internal structure of specific memories. Their subjects were asked to recall a memory and then to list details of that memory as fast as possible in one of four different ways: forward order of occurrence, reverse order from the most central detail to the least central, or free recall. Production rates were fastest for free recall and for forward-order recall; in the free recall condition it was evident that the order of production was influenced by the personal importance and distinctiveness of particular details. Figure 2.9 shows that in free recall the details of the remembered event "meeting Angela" deviated from the chronological forward order, with the important and distinctive detail "dancing with Angela" being reported earlier.

The general conclusion from this study again identified both temporal and thematic factors as organising principles.

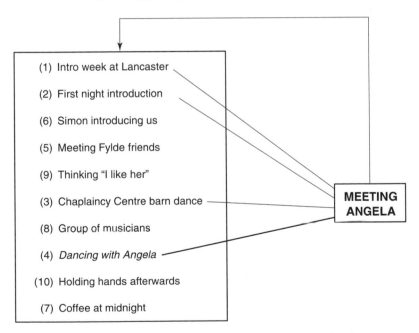

Figure 2.9 Organisation of knowledge of a specific autobiographical memory. Memory details are listed in forward chronological order from top to bottom and numbers in parentheses denote ordinal position in the free recall output (from Anderson & Conway, 1993). Reprinted by permission of the American Psychological Association and the authors.

Zacks, Tversky, and Iyer (2001) have examined the internal structure of memory in a different way. In a series of experiments they asked participants to watch videotapes of actors performing activities had been rated as familiar (e.g., doing the dishes), or unfamiliar (e.g., assembling a saxophone). Under various instruction conditions participants were asked to either describe the events as they watched them on the videotape, or to describe them from memory after the tape had finished. The element of interest here was how participants divided their descriptions up into discrete units or segments. Comparing the perceptual and memory descriptions, the authors found many similarities and concluded that the way an individual encodes an event in segments while they are initially experiencing it plays an important role in memory. One difference that they did observe, however, was that the verb semantics in the written descriptions from memory displayed a more schema-influenced account of the activity, which was less explicit about the physical actions performed by the actor but perhaps more related to the goals and plans of the actor. These findings suggest that even just a few moments after perceiving an event, our memory system is able to integrate what we have just witnessed with schemas that already exist in memory.

Availability of memories

An obvious question to ask is what kind of experiences people are most likely to remember from their past lives and, conversely, what kind of experiences they are most likely to forget. In ordinary everyday language we often speak of an experience as "unforgettable" and, in fact, we probably do have quite accurate intuitions about what kinds of events someone ought to be able to remember. If a person could not remember his or her own wedding, we would consider this abnormal; if he could not remember going to a party 10 years ago, we would not think this very unusual. However, remembering personal experiences is not always the result of effortful search and retrieval. Memories sometimes come to mind involuntarily and seem spontaneously elicited by some cue such as a thought, a phrase, a smell, a tune, or when we are reminded of them by a similar current experience.

Involuntary memories

Involuntary memories are conscious and unintentional recollections of personal experiences and have been described as being peculiarly vivid and emotional and having a strong feeling of immediacy. Involuntary memory retrieval appears to be quite a common experience in everyday life, with participants in a diary study reporting experiencing on average three to four involuntary memories per day (Berntsen, 1996). Recently Mace (2004) explored what types of cue are actually more likely to elicit involuntary memories. Cues were divided along two levels: Whether they were internal or external, and whether they were abstract, sensory/perceptual, or state. Internal cues were defined as having an internal source only, i.e., a bodily sensation, emotion, or thought. External cues were ones that came from the environment. Abstract cues were all thoughts or linguistic references to the original episode. Sensory/perceptual cues were those that provided sensory/perceptual referents to the original episode. State cues were physiological or emotional referents to the original episode. Participants were asked to keep a diary on them at all times for 2 weeks and record all instances when they experienced an involuntary memory. For each involuntary memory experienced they were asked to: record the date, time, cue; whether the cue was internal or external and abstract, sensory/perceptual or state; describe a thought experienced at retrieval; and describe the activity they were engaged in when the involuntary memory came to mind. Of the 811 involuntary memories recorded, 68% were found to have been elicited by abstract cues, whether internal (e.g., thoughts, 37%) or external (e.g., the words on a TV programme, 31%). It has been suggested by Haque and Conway (2001) that involuntary memories are examples of "direct retrieval"—where a cue directly activates information about an event. The findings of Mace (2004) demonstrate a similarity between involuntary and voluntary retrieval of memories. Voluntary memory retrieval often begins at the abstract level, involves elaboration and effort on the part of the remember, and terminates at the level of event-specific knowledge and recollective experience. In this study involuntary memories and their direct retrieval of recollective information were shown to be more likely to be elicited by abstract, more cognitively elaborate cues than any other form of cue, indicating that voluntary and involuntary memory retrieval processes are similar in this way. Work by Berntsen and colleagues has shown, however, that there are also many differences in involuntary and voluntary memory retrieval.

Berntsen (1998) directly compared retrieval of voluntary and involuntary memories by eliciting voluntary memories from participants using cues generated by the kinds of cues that had been found to elicit involuntary memories in a previous diary study. Berntsen found many differences between autobiographical memories that came to mind involuntarily in everyday life and memories retrieved voluntarily to word cues. Voluntary memories were found to refer to specific events less frequently than involuntary memories, and were also found to be more rehearsed, less recent, and less significantly emotionally positive than involuntary memories. In a later study, Berntsen and Hall (2004) extended these findings by demonstrating that involuntary memories also involved a greater physical reaction and impacted more on the mood of the individual experiencing the memory than did voluntary memory recall. Memories of specific episodes (which were more likely to be elicited in involuntary recall than in voluntary recall) were also found to be associated with more vivid recollection. Berntsen and Hall posit that this is related to the purpose of voluntary compared to involuntary recall. In daily life, autobiographical memories may be deliberately sought and retrieved in response to a query, or for comparison with a current experience. Voluntary memories may therefore be of a more generic style and involve less recollective experience than involuntary memories that are retrieved directly.

It is clear from our discussion so far that autobiographical memories can be accessed at a number of different levels and vary in availability; some are easy to retrieve and others are more elusive. Although organisation is one factor that influences accessibility of memories, several other factors are also important.

AUTOBIOGRAPHICAL MEMORY ACROSS THE LIFESPAN

It is well established that when people look back over their lives, memories from some parts of the lifespan are more readily available than from other parts. There is variability both in terms of quantity and quality, so that memories from some periods may be more numerous and more vivid than those from other periods.

Studies that focus on the retention of autobiographical memories over time and on the distribution of memories across the lifespan have used different methods, and addressed different issues. Rubin, Wetzler, and Nebes (1986) have collated the results of a number of studies (e.g., Crovitz & Schiffman, 1974; Rubin, 1982) that used word cueing and investigated the incidence of memories across the lifespan. With this method, subjects are presented with a list of cue words. For each cue word the subjects report the first autobiographical memory that comes to mind and, after completing the list, they supply the date of each reported memory. So, given the cue word "plum", a subject may respond "I remember making plum jam" and identify this memory as 10 years old. In these studies, the number of memories elicited from each period of the lifespan is then plotted. Rubin et al. reported that the data fitted a retention function with a linear relationship between the log of memory frequency and the log of recency of occurrence: That is, the mean number of memories elicited declined as a function of the age of the memories; there were many recent memories and fewer remote ones. Thus, the main trend reflects the normal course of forgetting. However, superimposed on this retention function, Rubin et al. noted a "reminiscence peak", seen in Figure 2.10, consisting of a disproportionate number of memories recalled from the period when the subjects were between 10 and 30 years old. Research into the types of memories typically recalled from the reminiscence peak, or bump, will be reviewed after the phenomenon of childhood amnesia is discussed in the next section. This third component of the distribution of memories

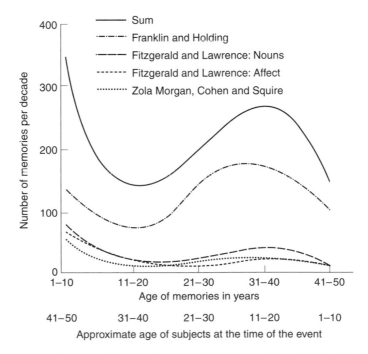

Figure 2.10 Distributions of memories across the lifespan (from Rubin, Wetzler, & Nebes, 1986). Reprinted by permission of Cambridge University Press.

across the lifespan, not apparent in Figure 2.10, is the small number of memories from the period when subjects were aged 0–5 years.

Further research has shown that the distribution of elicited memories across the lifespan is extremely sensitive to the method used. The recency effect observed by Rubin et al. (1986) was evident when subjects were asked to supply a memory for each of the word cues, and then go back through the memories they had produced and date them. Holding, Noonan, Pfau, and Holding (1986) asked their subjects to date each memory as it was produced, and found that this method produced a primacy effect, with memories being more numerous from the early part of the lifespan. They concluded that the dating process induced a chronological search. Cohen and Faulkner (1988) did not use word cueing, but simply asked subjects to produce and describe their most vivid memories. This technique also induced a forward-order chronological search through the lifespan and resulted in a preponderance of early memories. Thus, the incidence of memories from different parts of the lifespan varies according to the retrieval process being used. These methods do not test whether recent memories are better retained, or more easily elicited, than remote ones. They simply reflect the fact that when people retrieve memories by searching backwards through their past lives they produce more recent memories, and when they begin at the beginning and search forwards they produce more remote memories.

The accuracy and quality (as opposed to the incidence) of autobiographical memories is more consistently found to deteriorate with time elapsed. As in the studies by Linton (1982) and by Wagenaar (1986), and in Bahrick's (1984) data on teacher's memory for their students, information is lost over time, and Cohen and Faulkner (1988) also found that the self-rated vividness of autobiographical memories declined over time, with older memories being less vivid than recent ones. To summarise, it is clear that memory availability is influenced by age and time variables, including the length of time elapsed since the event, the age at which it was experienced, and the age of the person at the time of recall.

Childhood memory

There is a great deal of rather conflicting folklore on the subject of childhood memory. On the one hand, it is said that people remember very little of the experiences of their early years. On the other hand, some childhood memories appear to be retained with great vividness. For a recent review of the childhood memory literature, see Peterson (2002). Most people would agree that if they attempt to recall their personal history, they can retrieve a fairly continuous record for the years after the age of 6 or 7, but for the period before this age, memories are sparse and fragmentary, consisting of isolated vignettes of particular events. Freud (1916/1974) described this phenomenon as "childhood amnesia".

Childhood amnesia

The term "childhood amnesia" is used as a label for deficient recall, and does not necessarily imply that memory is completely lost. Initially, claims of childhood amnesia rested on clinical reports, anecdotes, and intuitions, but more recently there have been attempts to give a more precise definition and to provide an empirical demonstration. Wetzler and Sweeney (1986) pointed out that what needs to be demonstrated is deficient recall for the early childhood years that is independent of age at retrieval (current age) and of the length of the retention interval. That is, adults of all ages should exhibit a similar degree of childhood amnesia, and the loss of memory in the childhood years should be greater than would be predicted by the decay function, whereby forgetting increases with the passage of time. This approach concentrates on a quantitative criterion for childhood amnesia rather than on qualitative aspects of childhood memories.

One very interesting way to probe this "dark age" is to ask people to produce their earliest memory. Dudycha and Dudycha (1941) noted that the average age for earliest memories was around 42 months and Halliday (personal communication to Cohen) obtained a similar result with a mean of 39 months. Different studies therefore place the boundaries of childhood amnesia at different ages, ranging from 3 years (Sheingold & Tenney, 1982) to between 6 and 8 years (Freud, 1916/1974). Moreover, Usher and Neisser (1993) have shown that some events are remembered from earlier in childhood than others. They compared the earliest ages of recall for four different events: for birth of a sibling and for being hospitalised the earliest age was 2 years, and for death of a family member and for a family move the earliest age was 3 years. See the later section on cultural differences for a discussion of how the age of earliest autobiographical memory varies across cultures.

A range of explanations for the phenomenon of childhood amnesia are on offer (Pillemer & White, 1989, Wang, 2003; White & Pillemer, 1979). According to the Freudian explanation, early memories are present but, with the rejection of infant sexuality, memories are repressed and cannot be recalled to consciousness (Freud, 1905/1953). The deficit is thus a retrieval failure. Freud identified those early memories that can be recalled as "screen" memories, fabricated to block out emotionally painful realities. Although Freud's explanation is not now considered credible, a wealth of other theories have been developed to explain childhood amnesia. These attribute the dearth of early memories to inadequate encoding, neurological immaturity, or developmental changes in cognitive mechanisms.

It has been argued that very young children lack the linguistic ability to encode their experiences verbally, and lack the schemas within which they can represent and organise event memories (Schachtel, 1947). Recently Simcock and Hayne (2002) showed that the specific language skills that a child possesses at the time of an event influence what can later be recalled about the event verbally, i.e., at the age of 3 years a child is not able to describe an event experienced 1 year previously using anything but the language that was in his or her productive vocabulary at the time of the event. Children may also fail to use encoding strategies that elaborate and enrich the memory representation with semantic associations (Winograd & Killinger, 1983), or they may encode memories in ways that are inappropriate for the retrieval processes used at a later age. According to this explanation, developmental changes in coding and organisation produce a mismatch between the original coding and the subsequent retrieval cues. An example of this kind occurs when you try to remind a child of a particular event, such as a family trip to visit a relative. Your descriptions of the journey, the destination, and the relative, fail to evoke any memory in the child, but it turns out eventually that the child remembers the event in terms of the ice cream he or she was given at lunch. This type of example raises the possibility that we are underestimating the number of events that can be remembered from early childhood because we do not find the right triggers to elicit them. Other neurological explanations of childhood amnesia include theories based on neuro-logical maturation (e.g., Nelson, 1995), a shift in the nature of what children attend to (e.g., Fivush and Hamond, 1990), and changing knowledge structures or understanding of events (e.g., Usher and Neisser, 1993).

A more recent explanation of childhood amnesia has been offered by Perner (1992). He linked the ability to recall experiences to the development of "theory of mind". Children aged 3 and 4 years watched an object being put into a box or were told what was inside and were later asked what was in the box and how they knew. Both age groups could recall the object but only the 4-year-olds could explain how they knew. The older children had developed the ability to relate their knowledge to what they had experienced and, in Perner's view, this marks the beginning of autonoetic memory and the end of childhood amnesia. This suggestion has also been made in terms of the development of a concept of self by Harley and Reese (1999) and Howe and Courage (1993, 1997; Howe, 2000). In this framework children must develop a sense of self or personal frame of reference before personal memories can be encoded. Howe and Courage posit that the ability to visually recognize oneself marks the development of a sense of self, whereas Welch-Ross (1995) argues that more psychological complexity is needed. Welch-Ross also proposes that two meta-cognitive skills are required for the development of a sense of self: understanding the mental state of remembering, and understanding that knowing about an event is dependent on having had personal experience with that event.

Social interaction has also been proposed as playing a key role in the development of memory skills. For example, Fivush and colleagues have found that children of mothers who use an *elaborative style* of discussion recall more detailed event mem-ories than children whose mothers were low on elaboration (Fivush, 1994; Haden, Haine & Fivush, 1997). The likelihood is that there is no single explanation for childhood amnesia but that a multiplicity of factors are responsible. For example, Harley and Reese (1999) found that predictions from social-interaction and self-concept perspectives both independently contributed to the memory abilities of children.

Memories from early childhood

Failure to recall early childhood memories in later life does not mean that young children cannot remember their experiences. There is growing evidence of impressive memory ability in very young children. This revelation is a testament to the value of naturalistic field studies undertaken in the context of the child's daily life. Formal laboratory experiments seriously underestimate children's ability (Baker-Ward, 1993): There are several reasons why this is so. Children's memory is idiosyncratic. What is memorable to a child is not necessarily what would strike an adult as memorable. Children remember what makes sense to them and fail to remember what does not make sense. Children's memory is also socially determined in that they tend to remember what they want to communicate. Hudson (1990) has devel-oped a social interaction model of the development of autobiographical memory. Memories are jointly constructed, elaborated, and shaped in conversation between mother and child, as in the example shown in the box below, and children recall experiences better when their mothers have helped to provide a narrative format. Although laboratory experiments cannot create the social and motivational conditions that facilitate memory in everyday life, evidence has shown that children aged between 24 and 30 months will readily take part in conversations about past events with their mothers but also even with researchers who are relative strangers. Diary studies have also shown that children this young will initiate memory conversations with their mothers (see Peterson, 2002).

There is also evidence of implicit memory in preverbal infants as young as 9–21 months (McDonough & Mandler, 1994). Infants who have watched actions performed with a toy, such as listening to a toy telephone or feeding a teddy with a bottle, will imitate these actions at a later date, with the retention interval increasing with the child's age. Myers, Perris, and Speaker (1994) reported that two 5-year-old children even showed some verbal recall of a laboratory task involving nonverbal manipulation of toy animals, which they had taken part in when they were only 10–14 months old. Similarly, there are many parental anecdotes about young children who make straight for the cupboard where toys or biscuits are kept in a house they visited some time previously. These feats of implicit memory, although impressive, are obviously not equivalent to explicit recall.

---

21 months' Rachel (C) and her mother (M)
M: Did you see Aunt Gail and Uncle Tim last week?
C: Yes, yes, Uncle Tim.
M: What did we do with Aunt Gail and Uncle Tim?
C: Said bye-bye.
M: You said bye-bye to Aunt Gail and Uncle Tim?
C: Yes, go in car, in car.
M: Tim went in the car?
C: Aunt Gail with Uncle Tim.

Even at this early age, Rachel is contributing bits of information to this reconstruction of an episode that mother and child experienced together in the recent past. Six months later she could initiate and guide the recall:

27 months
C: Do you remember the waves, Mommy?
M: Do I remember the waves? What about the waves?
C: I go in the waves and I build a sand castle. And do you remember we swimmed? I swimmed in the waves and we did it again.

Joint construction of memories by a mother and child (from Hudson, 1990). Reprinted by permission of Cambridge University Press and the authors.

Once language has developed it becomes possible to study explicit recall, and one area that has been studied is the acquisition of scripts and the function of scripts in supporting memory. The box below shows examples of some of the scripts supplied by children of different ages in response to questions and prompts. Scripts for other events like getting dressed and going shopping were also elicited. These examples show that young children's event knowledge conforms to the defining features of scripts. Their scripts show temporal sequencing of actions and central goals, are consistent, and are expressed in a general form. Older children produced longer scripts with more detail and elaboration. Younger children's scripts were similar in form, but more skeletal. This finding supports Winograd and Killinger's conclusion that developmental differences in amount recalled stem from differences in the degree of elaboration at encoding. Nelson (1991) also stressed the importance of scripts and general event memories that allow the child to anticipate the future and act appropriately in the present.

Hudson and Nelson (1986) examined children's organisation of memory for events within the framework of schema-plus-tag, or context-plus-index models, whereby specific autobiographical events are organised in long-term memory in terms of their relationship to general event representations. Routine, repeated events, which conform to the same pattern, are absorbed into a general event representation and are not remembered as distinct occasions. However, novel, unique, or deviant occasions are retained as specific memories, although linked to the relevant general event representation. Autobiographical memories can therefore include a blend of specific knowledge about what happened on a particular occasion, and general knowledge that has been abstracted from past experience of similar occasions. Hudson and Nelson pointed out that this form of representation is essentially a developmental one, as the general event representations are progressively built up out of accumulating specific event representations. They sought evidence for qualitative changes in children's memory for events reflecting this development. The expectation was that age differences would exist in the relative proportions of general event knowledge and specific event knowledge.

In their first study, Hudson and Nelson examined 3- and 5-year-olds' memory for specific episodes of routine events that occurred the previous day (e.g., "What happened when you had dinner at home yesterday?"). They also studied their general knowledge about this class of event (e.g., "What happens when you have dinner at home?"). All the children produced more information in answer to the general dinner script question than in answer to the specific episode question. There were no age differences in the relative proportions of general event knowledge and specific event knowledge in their answers. They had relatively little recall for the last occurrence of a routine event, but when asked to recall a novel event, such as a trip to the zoo or the circus, their replies showed rich and detailed memory for these unique events.

Making cookies
Well, you bake them and eat them. (3;1)
My mommy puts chocolate chips inside the cookies. Then ya put 'em in the oven . . . Then we take them out, put them on the table and eat them. (4;5)

Add three cups of butter . . . add three lumps of butter . . . two cups of sugar, one cup of flour. Mix it up . . . knead it. Get it in a pan, put it in the oven. Bake it . . . set it up to 30. Take it out and it'll be cookies. (6;9)

First, you need a bowl, a bowl, and you need about two eggs and chocolate chips and an egg-beater! And then you gotta crack the egg open and put it in a bowl and ya gotta get the chips and mix it together. And put it in a stove for about 5 or 10 minutes, and then you have cookies. Then ya eat them! (8;8)

Birthday party
You cook a cake and eat it. (3;1)

Well, you get a cake and some ice cream and then some birthday (?) and then you get some clowns and then you get some paper hats, the animal hats and then and then you sing "Happy Birthday to you", and then then then they give you some presents and then you play with them and then that's the end and they go home and they do what they wants. (4;9)

First, uhm . . . you're getting ready for the kids to come, like puttin' balloons up and putting out party plates and making cake. And then all the people come you've asked. Give you presents and then you have lunch or whatever you have. Then . . . uhm . . . then you open your presents. Or you can open your presents anytime. Uhm . . . you could . . . after you open the presents, then it's probably time to go home. if you're like at Foote Park or something, then it's time to go home and you have to drive all the people home. Then you go home too. (6;7)

Well, first you open your mail box and get some mail. And then you see that there's an invitation for you. Read the invitation. Then you ask your parents if you can go. Then you . . . uhm . . . go to the birthday parry and after you get there you usually wait for everyone else to come. Then usually they always want to open one of the presents. Sometimes then they have three games, then they have the birthday cake then sometimes they open the other presents or they could open them up all at once. After that they like to play some more games and then maybe your parents come to pick you up. And then you go home. (8;10)

Examples of scripts for making cookies and for birthday parties from children aged 3–8 years (from Nelson & Gruendel, 1986). Reproduced with permission.

In a second experiment, Hudson and Nelson asked 5- and 7-year-olds about events that had been experienced a varying number of times. There was evidence that increasing familiarity with an experience produced increasing schematisation, with more general information and fewer particular details being reported. A further study examined children's memory for an untypical episode. New York children who made fairly frequent trips to museums were questioned about a particular trip to the Jewish Museum, which was unusual. One year later, memory for this specific occasion was well retained, but it had not been incorporated into the general museum script, and this general museum script had not been modified by the novel experience. Hudson and Fivush (1991) asked the children to recall the museum visit again 6 years later and found they were still able to recall some details.

Hudson also found that recall of specific memories of particular occasions depended on the cues that were used. Those children who could not remember the Jewish Museum visit after 1 year, when they were asked "What happened when you went to the Jewish Museum?", succeeded in recalling the occasion when asked about the archaeological activities that were shown in the museum. These children had filed the episode under an "archaeology" tag. This finding confirms the view that what seems like a loss of early memories may be due to a mismatch between how the event was encoded and the cues being used to try and retrieve it. As children's experience increases, and their knowledge of the world accumulates, the indices they use to tag specific episodes are likely to approximate more closely to probable retrieval cues, thus reducing the chance of mismatches.

Taken together, these studies showed that the relationship between general event representations and specific event memories that characterises adult memory is apparent as young as 3 years old. Structurally and functionally, autobiographical memory in young children is equivalent to autobiographical memory in adults. Routine events are absorbed into the general script; unique events are stored separately. There was no evidence of age-related changes in this basic structure between the ages of 3 and 7 years, but there was evidence that changes in autobiographical memory occurred as a function of increasing experience rather than age, and affected content rather than structure. Generalised event representations are clearly present and are used to guide encoding and retrieval, but they are simple and skeletal in content, and specific episodes may be indexed with inappropriate tags so that they cannot be retrieved later. Since the amount and nature of the input to the system appears to be a crucial factor in the development of memory organisation, it is tempting to speculate that there is some optimal mix of routine and novel experiences. If experience were too narrowly confined to an unvarying routine, scripts would be few and poorly elaborated; if experience were constantly changing, it would be difficult for the child to abstract general event knowledge and build general event representations.

In spite of this impressive evidence that children's memories are highly organised, many of the early memories that people report do not seem to fit this pattern. In Cohen and Faulkner's (1988) study, 21% of the events recalled from the first decade of the lifespan were categorised as trivia. Whereas the other memories from this period were clearly linked to general event representations for school, family, holidays, pets, etc., these trivial memories were apparently unrelated to any script or general event knowledge. They were memories of isolated scenes that seemed relatively pointless and devoid of context, and were rated as low in emotionality, importance, and frequency of rehearsal. Examples such as "sitting in the sandpit in the garden and looking at the sky through the leaves" or "walking along a road towards a beach" have the quality of scenes recalled from dreams. It is not clear why these memories should have been preserved or what significance, if any, they may once have had, since they seem to have become detached from any organising framework. One recent proposal is that these kinds of incomplete memories may mark the end of childhood amnesia and they have been termed *fragment memories* by Bruce et al. (2005). These authors asked participants to recall their earliest specific episodic memory of an event and their earliest memory fragment, which was described as being not a story with a beginning and an end but simply a disconnected piece of memory. For example, "I remember playing in the kitchen sink with a toy army man not really sure how I reached the sink, but I remember that there was music!" (Bruce et al., 2005, p. 572). The results demonstrated that participants were younger at the time of their earliest fragment memories (3.52 years) than at the time of their earliest event memories (4.36 years). Event memories were also rated as including more visual detail, sound, smell, touch, activity, details, and vividness than fragment memories. They also involved more activity, the location of the memory was clearer, and the events could be related to other events in memory as well as differing along a number of additional qualitative respects. These findings are consistent with the hypotheses that childhood amnesia ends with the formation of the cognitive self (Howe, 2000; Howe & Courage, 1993, 1997), or that childhood amnesia ends with the formation of a higher order cognitive system (Pillemer, 1998).

Research into the development of autobiographical memory in children has also focused on how long children retain memories for and how accuracy changes over this retention interval. Studies have tested these factors either by asking children about events that occurred to them in real life or by staging events, for which recall is then tested. Studies that have utilised parents as the providers of memory cues or even as the interviewers of their children have found that pre-school age children are able to recall events that occurred over a year earlier. Fivush and Hamond (1990) asked parents to talk with their children about events they thought they might remember, e.g., holidays, parties. After a 14-month interval, recall for these events was tested again and children were able to recall as much or even more information about the events they did remember (though some events were not remembered at all). Of the new information they provided after 14 months, 90% was judged to be accurate by their mothers. Using the staged play event of a "sick" teddy bear with 3- and 5-year-olds, Salmon and Pipe (1997) found differing results. After an interval of 1 year forgetting was found to be high, especially in the older group who initially had recalled more. Memories for real medical events have been the focus of a number of studies into children's long-term retention of autobiographical memories. Peterson and Whalen (2001) followed up children who had been admitted to the emergency room for injuries such as lacerations, bone fractures, second-degree burns, dog bites, and crushed fingers and tested their memory for what had happened during their visit to the hospital after 1 week, 6 months, 1 year, 2 years, and 5 years. Participants were aged between 2 and 13 at the time of the hospital visit and thus were aged between 7 and 18 at the 5-year follow-up. In each interview children were asked to freely recall the event first, before recall was prompted by use of wh- questions ("Where were you when it happened? Who was with you?"). After 5 years recall was generally very good, although older children recalled more, and were more accurate in this recall, than younger children. Details central to the event were also found to be better recalled than peripheral events (except for the youngest children who were aged 2 at the time of the event, they recalled central and peripheral events equally). Children were also better at recalling details of their injury than of their hospital treatment.

These studies show that there are differences in the recall levels elicited using different methodologies and that different paradigms yield varying age differences and childhood amnesia cut-off points. Better recall of events by older children could be down to a number of factors: Better understanding of the event at the time that it occurred, greater experience in describing events leading to rehearsal, or the memorability of the event in the first place—how exciting, shocking, unpleasant it was. Effects of memorability are discussed later. All these factors are yet to be integrated into a comprehensive account of the development of memory in childhood (Neisser, 2004).

The reminiscence bump

The reminiscence bump is the second component of the lifespan retrieval curve and represents an increase in retrieval for memories from between the ages of 10 and 30. It is usually found for all subjects over the age of about 35 years and has been replicated in various studies. Rubin, Rahhal, and Poon (1998) reviewed studies that had examined the reminiscence bump using a variety of techniques, and concluded that knowledge acquired during the period of reminiscence is highly accessible, more accessible than knowledge acquired outside this period, but not as accessible as knowledge of recent experiences. The reminiscence bump has been shown to exist for recall of films, music, and public events as well as for general autobiographical memories. Recent investigations have also found that it may be more prominent for positive experiences than for negative experiences (Rubin & Berntsen, 2003).

A number of different explanations have been suggested for the existence of the reminiscence bump. One suggestion was that memories from the reminiscence period were of first-time experiences and that was why they were more memorable, but actually this was true of only 20% of memories (Fitzgerald, 1988). They may not be first-time experiences but experiences during the reminiscence period may well be novel and distinctive and therefore may receive more elaborate cognitive processing and less interference from memories of previous events (Rubin et al., 1998). An event is more likely to be remembered as an episodic memory if it is a novel and distinctive event, as a script or schema will not yet exist for it. Novel events may also serve as reference points for later organisation. Conversely, theoretical accounts that focus on identity formation highlight adolescence and early adulthood as critical periods for the establishment of adult identity. In the SMS model of memory, Conway and Pleydell-Pearce (2000) view the reminiscence bump from this perspective and propose that preferential retention of events from this period is due to the fact that this time of life is primarily concerned with consolidation of the self. This ties in with Erikson's (1950, 1997) theory of psychosocial development, where the period of adolescence is associated with the formation of a mature personal identity. Evidence from Holmes and Conway (1999) supports this view of preferential encoding due to self-relevance of events experienced during the reminiscence period. In this study two slightly different reminiscence bumps were observed, an earlier peak from the period between the ages of 10 and 20, which was characterised by memory for public events, particularly events that reflected the cultural *zeitgeist* or spirit of the time; and a later bump, emerging between the ages of 20 and 30, which focused on personal memories relating to intimacy in relationships. These two peaks are taken to reflect development of social or generational identity and relationship identity respectively.

MEMORABLE EVENTS: SELF-DEFINING AND
FLASHBULB MEMORIES

What determines whether an event is going to stick in memory or be forgotten? As we saw from work using diary studies, forgetting is a very common occurrence (e.g., Linton, 1982), so what is remarkable about the events that are *not* forgotten in everyday life?

Event characteristics

Some of the factors that tend to make an event memorable are characteristics of the event itself, and operate at the time of encoding. Events that are personally import-ant, consequential, unique, emotional, or surprising are liable to be better remem-bered. These variables tend to co-occur so it is difficult to assess the relative contribution of each. Recall is also affected by variables that operate during reten-tion, such as how frequently the event is talked about or thought about. Rubin and Kozin (1984) asked a group of students to describe three of their clearest memories, and to rate them for national importance, personal importance, surprise, vividness, emotionality and how often they had discussed the event. The most commonly reported events concerned injuries or accidents, sports, and encounters with the opposite sex. Memories that were more vivid also received higher ratings for importance, surprise, and emotionality. A study by Sehulster (1989) confirmed the role of importance and rehearsal in making events particularly memorable. Sehulster tested his own ability to free recall details, dates, and casting of 284 opera performances seen over 25 years, and then checked his recall against the programmes. The importance of particular performances as rated by experts, and the amount of rehearsal opportunity as estimated from the availability of tapes, books, and TV showings, correlated with recall of the content and casting of the operas but did not influence recall of dates.

Cohen and Faulkner (1988) also reported that memory vividness correlated sig-nificantly with emotion, importance, and the amount of rehearsal. In their study, the relative power of these factors shifted with the age of the person who was remem-bering. For younger people, characteristics of the event itself, such as emotionality and importance, were the best predictors of memory vividness, but for elderly people the amount of rehearsal was the most powerful factor. The vividness of their remote memories was preserved because the events were often thought about and talked about. The events that were most often remembered were births, marriages, and deaths (22.2%), holidays (11.8%), trivia (8.2%), illness/injury (8%), education (8%), family (7.5%), war (6.1%), love affairs (5.1%), and recreations/sports (4.9%). Events in which the subjects were actors were remembered better than events in which they were only bystanders, and unique occasions and first times were remembered more often than generic events or last times.

A similar pattern was noted by Means and Loftus (1991) in a study of people's ability to recall health events such as visits to the doctor. Like Linton in her diary study, they found that similar, recurring events like repeated visits for chronic conditions were recalled less well than nonrecurring one-off visits. The recurring events blended into a generic "repisode" that was hard to decompose, but serious health events, which can be presumed to be more personally important, were remembered better than trivial ones. Cohen and Java (1995) also tested recall of health events, including illnesses, symptoms, injuries, and visits to health professionals, by subjects who had kept health diaries for 12 weeks. Three months later only 47% of these events were recalled. An unexpected finding was that people aged over 70 years had better recall than younger subjects and this was attributed to the greater importance they attached to their health problems.

Despite the wide variation in the methods used and in the type of memories that were probed, these studies have produced converging results. Events are better recalled if they are unique, important, and frequently rehearsed. These conclusions are therefore well supported, if not particularly surprising.

The relationship between event memorability and the self has also been explored recently. Conway and Holmes (2004) asked older adults to recall events from each decade of their lives. These memories were then coded according to which of Erikson's (1950, 1997) psychosocial stage of life they mapped on to. In Erikson's theory of development, over a lifetime an individual has to deal with different types of psychosocial problem during different lifetime periods. In childhood these problems centre around trust and mistrust. In adolescence, identity–identity confusion is the major hurdle. In adulthood the concern is intimacy versus isolation. Middle age is associated with generativity versus stagnation, and old age is marked by integrity versus despair. Conway and Holmes (2004) found that the themes elicited in older adults' memories were systematically related to the psychosocial stages of life proposed by Erikson. The events that were most memorable or most easily accessible from each decade of life were those that had an association with the psychosocial concern appropriate to that life period (see Table 2.4).

This is consistent with Conway and Pleydell-Pearce's model of autobiographical memory, which states that a factor that will increase the memorability of an event is how related it is to the self's current goals. The goals of the working self mediate encoding and therefore goal-relevant experiences are thought to be encoded in such a way that they are more easily accessible than non-goal-related experiences.

Self-defining memories

The affiliation between the self and memory is perhaps most apparent from the literature on *self-defining memories*. Researchers originally became interested in this

Table 2.4 From Conway and Holmes (2004). Number of memories produced by decade and stage (Experiment 1). Reproduced with permission of Blackwell Publishing.

Psychosocial stage	Decade						
	0 to 9	*10 to 19*	*20 to 29*	*30 to 39*	*40 to 49*	*50 to 59*	*60+*
Child	57	32	3	3	3	1	0
Identity	7	50	21	13	7	11	8
Intimacy	0	1	35	12	8	8	11
Generativity	2	3	19	32	40	26	18
Integrity	0	0	0	1	0	3	14
Unclassified	4	22	16	16	12	13	19
TOTALS	70	108	94	77	70	62	70

area due to the observation that people's autobiographies often contain descriptions of events that were "turning points" or self-defining moments. Singer and Salovey (1993) proposed that each of us holds a set of these self-defining memories, which contain significant knowledge on progress towards and attainment of personal goals. For example, memories associated with feelings of happiness and pride have been associated to attainment of goals and the smooth execution of personal plans. Pillemer, Picariello, Law, and Reichman (1996) found that both students and alumnae could recall very detailed vivid memories of interactions with professors and other teachers that significantly influenced their own academic careers. The following example comes from the preface of a book written by Endel Tulving:

> A number of years ago, a friend of mine, a respected and honoured psychologist, told me about a young colleague of his who was shortly going to be considered for tenure and promotion. My friend said that he was a very capable person, bright, hard-working, with many excellent ideas, and a demonstrated record of research accomplishment, but that, unfortunately, "he had not written his book yet". At the time of our conversation, I had been in the psychological research business for a long time, had published a number of papers in various journals, had been promoted to a full professor . . . But I, too, had not written my book yet. Trying to conceal my embarrassment, I changed the topic of conversation, but I never quite recovered from the emotional impact of the casual comment of my friend. From that day on I started thinking about writing "my book".
>
> p. vii *Preface* from *Elements of Episodic Memory* by Tulving, E. (1983)
> By permission of Oxford University Press and the author.

Self-defining memories such as this example (see also the discussion of this example by Pillemer, 1998, p. 67) are characterised by affective intensity, vividness, rehearsal, and links to other memories. In times of uncertainty self-defining memories have been proposed as being a landmark that can remind an individual of his/her identity (Blagov & Singer, 2004).

One area that has received particular attention from researchers is the development of the self in late adolescence. Thorne (1995) found that memories recalled by 20-year-olds corresponded to "developmental truths". Memories from childhood were typically about experiences to do with wanting help, approval and love, usually from parents, while memories from late adolescence and early adulthood described experiences relating to the themes of reciprocal love, assertiveness, and helping others. More recently, McLean and Thorne (2003) explored the differences between 19-year-olds' memories relating to parent–child relationships, and their memories relating to peer relationships. In this study memories of peer relationships were found to emphasise closeness whereas memories of parent relationships tended to be related to separation and conflict. The authors also examined how their participants had made meaning out of these experiences—how they had gained insight or learned lessons from these events, which were now self-defining memories. Experiences that had involved conflict were found to be most strongly associated with both gaining insight and learning lessons. These memories of conflict were also often accompanied by insight relating to issues such as beginning to understand one's own independence or a greater need for self-sufficiency. In a later study Thorne, McLean, and Lawrence (2004) have found that meaning was present in one-quarter of the memories provided by young adults (aged 18–23) and that meaning was more common in memories that contained references to tension. The relationship between the initial experiences, memories of those experiences, and the lessons and insights that they have brought about provides a link between the past and the present, giving the individual the ability to monitor the coherence of their psychological self-identity.

Self-defining memories have also been linked to personality styles. As part of a longitudinal study of students, Sutin and Robins (2005) found that the way in which students at the end of their third year of college described and evaluated a significant life experience from the preceding 3 years was correlated with their personality, well-being, and academic achievement during those 3 years. High positive affect in the memory description was related to higher levels of self-esteem and well-being, and levels of self-esteem, agreeableness, and conscientiousness showed a tendency to increase over the course of college for these students. High positive affect was also related to higher grades and improvements in grades across the college years. Achievement motivation was also found to be related to both higher grades and higher self-esteem and well-being. These findings support the idea the there is an important bidirectional relationship between personality and memory and that self-defining memories are some of the most prominent memories that link the auto-biographical knowledge base with the conceptual self. The development of self, which occurs at a heightened level during adolescence, involves both continuity and change and these two factors have been demonstrated in self-defining memory in a study by McAdams et al. (2006). After 3 years of college, the young adults in this study were found to have higher levels of emotional nuance and self-differentiation in their memories, and describe more emotionally positive memories and have a greater understanding of their own personal development, than they displayed in the first year of college. Continuity was shown in emotional tone, narrative complexity, agency, and growth.

As their name suggests, self-defining memories typically involve the self and relate to events that have been personally experienced. A different type of memory that can be equally detailed and vivid is memory for learning of a shocking or consequential public event.

Flashbulb memories

Flashbulb memory is a special case of witness memory. It is the term given to the unusually vivid and detailed recollection people often have of the occasion when they first heard about some very dramatic, surprising, important, and emotionally arousing event. Hearing the news that President John Kennedy had been shot, the bombing of Pearl Harbor, the first landing on the moon, the terrorist attacks on the World Trade Center in September 2001, or the death of Princess Diana, are among the examples that have been studied. Flashbulb memories typically encode what is called the "reception event" rather than the event itself. That is, they encode the circumstances in which the person first received the news and usually include the place, who was present at the time, what activities were going on, the affect occasioned by the event, and the source of the news. Once formed, flashbulb memories are apparently long-lasting and unchanged over time. Flashbulb memories are also distinguished by their phenomenological quality. They seem to have the peculiarly vivid character of an actual perception—what Brown and Kulik (1982) call "live quality"—and tend to include seemingly irrelevant and trivial details. However, there is considerable controversy about whether so-called flashbulb memories are different from other memories of events that are distinctive and personally significant. Are flashbulb memories special? There is also debate about how they originate and about the kind of information they incorporate.

Brown and Kulik (1982) suggested that there is a special neural mechanism triggered by high levels of emotion, surprise, and consequentiality. This mechanism, they claimed, causes the whole scene to be "printed" on the memory. Such a mechanism would have obvious evolutionary advantages, ensuring that the organism retains a vivid memory of the circumstances surrounding a potentially dangerous event. However, this account has been challenged by Neisser (1982) and McCloskey, Wible, and Cohen (1988). Neisser has argued in favour of a reconstructive theory, claiming that flashbulb memories are simply ordinary memories preserved by frequent rehearsal and retelling after the event, rather than special processes activated at the moment itself. They are not necessarily true or accurate because they are the product of successive reconstructions. According to this view, the perceived importance of the event is a crucial factor because it gives rise to frequent rehearsal, but surprise and emotion are not necessary for the memory formation. So, whereas Brown and Kulik stress the importance of factors such as emotion being present at the time of encoding, Neisser's reconstructive account places the emphasis on subsequent rehearsal.

Much of the debate has centred on whether flashbulb memories can be shown to be unusually accurate. If flashbulb memories can be shown to be inaccurate this tends to support Neisser's view. Neisser has cited cases where flashbulb memories recounted in great detail and good faith turned out to be inaccurate when independently checked. In his own recollection of hearing the news of Pearl Harbor in December 1941, he remembered that he was listening to a baseball game on the radio when the programme was interrupted by a newsflash. Neisser believed this memory must have been a fabrication because no baseball games are broadcast in December. However, Thompson and Cowan (1986) have discovered that a football game was actually broadcast at the relevant time, so Neisser's memory was inaccurate, but not completely wrong. McCloskey et al. (1988) also challenged the view that flashbulb memories have special qualities. Using a technique known as double assessment, they tested subjects' memory for the explosion of the space shuttle Challenger a few days after the event and again about 9 months later. They found inconsistencies between the two accounts and clear evidence of forgetting. In a similar double assessment study, Neisser and Harsch (1992) obtained similar results. On the basis of these findings they have argued that the strong claim that flashbulb memories are 100% accurate and immune to forgetting must be discarded. Against this view, others (e.g., Schmidt & Bohannon, 1988) have pointed out that no attempt was made to check on the emotional impact of the event on the subjects. It is possible, therefore, that those who showed forgetting may have had a lower level of emotional response and never encoded a true flashbulb memory. Brown and Kulik (1982) always maintained that flashbulb memories are only formed if the event is of high personal importance to the individual. In support of their view, they showed that the incidence of flashbulb memories varied systematically with personal involvement and perceived consequentiality. Black Americans had more flashbulb memories than white Americans for the deaths of Martin Luther King and Malcolm

X. In any case, in the McCloskey et al. study only 8% of the subjects showed forgetting and a remarkable 92% retained complete and accurate memories over the 9-month interval.

The weaker claim that flashbulb memories are significantly different from ordinary memories has also been challenged. As McCloskey et al. (1988) have pointed out, ordinary memories can also be accurate and long-lasting if they are highly distinctive, personally significant, and interesting. For these memories the observed level of recall can be explained by frequent rehearsal, and there is no need to postulate a special mechanism. So are flashbulb memories really different? Rubin and Kozin (1984) argued that so-called flashbulb memories are not essentially different in character from other vivid memories. They found that subjects rated some events of personal importance, such as graduating from high school, or an early romantic experience, as having flashbulb clarity, and the vividness of these memories was also related to rated values for surprise, emotionality, and consequentiality. Their findings failed to reveal any features that would clearly distinguish flashbulb memories from other vivid autobiographical memories.

Wright (1993) has also argued that flashbulb memories show evidence of schema-based reconstruction in the same way that ordinary memories do, so that there is no need to postulate a special mechanism. He studied memory for the Hillsborough disaster, a tragic event in 1989 when 95 people were crushed to death in a football stadium. He tested three different groups of people after 2 days, 1 month, and 5 months. Subjects tested after 5 months' delay were more likely to recall hearing the news with their families and on television and judged it to be more important both personally and socially. Wright concluded that their memory for the event had been reconstructed to fit a schema or stereotype, but it is difficult to be sure that between-group differences of this kind are really due to reconstructive processes introducing changes over time, rather than simply reflecting differences in the way the groups originally experienced the event.

A multinational study by Conway et al. (1994) sought evidence for flashbulb memories by investigating people's memory for learning the news of the resignation of the British Prime Minister Margaret Thatcher. Using a double assessment test–retest procedure they established that over 86% of British subjects had complete and accurate recall that met the criteria for flashbulb memory nearly 1 year later. By contrast, only 29% of non-British subjects had flashbulb memories. Analysis of ratings and questionnaire responses supplied by the subjects showed clearly that flashbulb memory formation was associated with high levels of emotional response, interest in politics, and the level of importance attached to the event. Most non-British subjects, who were not particularly interested or excited by the event, showed normal forgetting of the details. These results suggest that both memories for dramatic public events and vivid memories for highly significant personal experiences may receive special encoding that can only be triggered by emotion and consequentiality. In the absence of these causal factors memories do not have flashbulb quality.

Brown and Kulik (1982) based their claim that a special mechanism exists for flashbulb memories on the fact that they have a canonical structure. People remember *location* (where they were); *activity* (what they were doing); *source* (who told them); *affect* (what they felt); and *aftermath* (what happened next). However, according to Neisser (1982) there is no need to postulate a special mechanism to explain these uniformities because they are the product of "narrative conventions", the traditional schemas that govern the format for story-telling. If schema theory can explain the canonical form of flashbulb memories and frequency of rehearsal can explain why they are selectively well preserved, there is no need to invoke a special "print" mechanism. For Neisser, these special memories are primarily of social and cultural importance and function as "benchmarks" in the history of the individual.

Other researchers have studied developmental aspects of flashbulb memory in order to throw some light on the causal factors. Winograd and Killinger (1983) were interested in the development of flashbulb memories, and in whether dramatic events experienced by young children would be remembered in the same way as these events appear to be remembered by adults. They used subjects who were between the ages of 1 and 7 years at the time of John Kennedy's assassination and testing took place 16 or 17 years after this event. The subjects were asked questions about location, activity, the effect on those around them, the aftermath, how often it was discussed, and any additional details. They plotted recall as a function of age at the time of the event using two different criteria for recall. The lenient criterion was satisfied if the subject claimed to be able to recall the event and could supply information in answer to one of the questions. The stricter criterion was satisfied only when four questions could be answered. It is clear from Figure 2.11 that older children were more likely to remember the event and to recall more details about it.

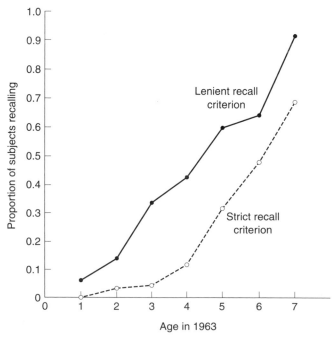

Figure 2.11 The proportion of subjects who could recall President Kennedy's assassination as a function of age at the time of the event (from Winograd & Killinger, 1983). Reproduced with permission of the authors.

The information most frequently recalled was location (90%), followed by activity (77%), source (70%), aftermath (43%), and other details (26%). The results did not support Neisser's (1982) view that the vividness of flashbulb memories is produced by frequent rehearsal because very little rehearsal was reported by any of the children. Moreover, if recall depends on reconstruction subsequent to the event, it is difficult to see why the age at encoding has such a strong effect on retention. The absence of flashbulb memories in the younger children seems more likely to be due to neurological immaturity or to their inability, due to lack of knowledge, to realise the importance of the event or to be surprised by it. Pillemer (1992b) studied children's memory for a dramatic event when a fire broke out at their preschool and police and fire engines arrived. Two weeks later two groups of children aged 3½ and 4½ years were asked questions about the event. Both groups recalled details of the event, but the older group were able to supply additional information about their location at the time, the emotion aroused by the event, and the cause of the fire. Retested 7 years later, only the older group had long-term memory for the event, showing flashbulb characteristics. This finding therefore supports Winograd and Killinger's (1983) conclusion that a process of maturation occurring about the age of 4 years is a prerequisite for flashbulb memory formation.

At the other end of the developmental spectrum, Yarmey and Bull (1978) investigated age differences in memory for the Kennedy assassination 12 years after the event and found that those aged 66 years and over had poorer recall of the event. A similar trend was noted by Cohen, Conway, and Maylor (1994), who examined age differences in the incidence of flashbulb memories for the Thatcher resignation. Although 90% of young subjects had flashbulb memories, only 42% of the elderly group met the criterion. A possible interpretation of this finding is that lowered levels of arousal associated with ageing are insufficient to trigger the special encoding mechanism necessary for flashbulb memory formation.

In 2003 a special issue of the journal *Applied Cognitive Psychology* focused on how research on flashbulb memories had advanced, or not, in recent years. In this special issue Kvavilashvili, Mirani, Schlagman, and Kornbrot (2003) compared flashbulb memories for the death of Princess Diana and the terrorist attacks of September 11 in British and Italian participants. For the British sample there were few differences between memories of the two events: Both were detailed, specific, and vivid even though the death of Diana had occurred 4 years prior to testing and the attacks on September 11 had only occurred 3 months earlier. Conversely, in the Italian sample, memories of September 11 were much more detailed than memories of learning about the death of Diana. This study also found that reports obtained 3 months after September 11 were somewhat less detailed than reports obtained 2–11 days after the attacks. Lee and Brown (2003) found similar results, with more contextual information being written in descriptions taken 1 day after September 11 compared to descriptions taken 10 days later, but in a retest 7 months later contextual information was low across all descriptions. This study also found that the consistency between the reports taken soon after the attack and 7 months later was low (66.5%). These results fit with those of McClosky et al. (1988) and Neisser and Harsch (1992), and add weight to their arguments that flashbulb memories are not especially accurate or immune to forgetting compared to other autobiographical memories.

In the special issue a study that again raises the issue of the effect of emotional response and personal involvement in formation and accuracy of flashbulb memories was carried out by Pezdek (2003). Participants in this study of memories of September 11 came from New York, California, and Hawaii and the prediction was that the New Yorkers would have the richest event memories, but that the other groups (California and Hawaii) would have more detailed autobiographical memories as they would have been less personally involved in the attacks. The New Yorkers were found to have more accurate memories for details of the event; for example, one question asked was "How much time passed between when the first tower was struck and when it collapsed?" (correct answer 108 minutes). Participants from Hawaii and California scored lower on event questions but higher on autobiographical memory details such as: Where were you when you heard the news? Who told you? What were you doing at the time? Pezdek suggests that these findings support the idea that people can "attach" their emotions to either of these types of memory and that this influences to what degree each one is rehearsed and remembered. Neisser (2003), in his commentary on the special issue, points out that New Yorkers may just have more detailed event memories for September 11 because of spending more time attending to media coverage of the event. This is also Neisser's criticism regarding the work of Smith, Bibi, and Sheard (2003), who reported that emotional arousal was correlated positively with event accuracy scores (.86) but that autobiographical memory was unaffected. Neisser's conclusions focus on the divide between studies that have not advanced the field much since the work of Brown and Kulik (1982) and those that have introduced new concepts to the area of flashbulb memory; for example, the work of Fivush, Edwards, and Mennuti-Washburn (2003b), who asked participants to write expressively about their experiences of September 11. The expressive writing paradigm has been used in health psychology and has been found to decrease feelings of depression and anxiety and improve general physical health (Pennebaker, 1997). In this paradigm participants are asked to write about their deepest thoughts and feelings continuously without regard for spelling or grammar; in this study this was repeated for 20 minutes per day for 5 days. Participants who had higher involvement in September 11, e.g., they had personally known someone who was killed or injured in the attacks, were found to utilise fewer cognitive processing words and positive emotion words in their writing. This supported previous findings, as cognitive processing is known to be affected by high levels of stress.

A recent study by Berntsen and Thomsen (2005) has also introduced a new methodology to the flashbulb memory literature. These authors compared memory accuracy for the reception of important news by comparing memory reports against objective records and a baseline obtained from participants who were too young to have experienced the original event. The events that were studied by Berntsen and Thomsen were the invasion (April 1940) and subsequent liberation (May 1945) of Denmark in the Second World War. For both days participants were asked to describe the weather and what day of the week the events took place. For the invasion they were asked the date that all inhabitants had to put up blackout blinds and for the liberation they were asked at what time the German capitulation was announced on the radio. They were also asked the standard flashbulb memory questions regarding where they were, what they were doing, who they were with, etc., at the time of both events. Two examples of memory descriptions are shown below.

Memory for the invasion, man, 79 years old (15 years old at the time of the event)
I was 15 years old and worked as the fourth farmhand at a farm called Thorupgaard. The 9th of April at 6 a.m., we went into the fields to plow and around 6:15 really many squadrons of planes came over us, and they were flying at such low altitude that the two horses I had to pull the plow were rearing and jumped over the ropes. I was really afraid and had great difficulties. The planes were flying over us for 15 to 20 minutes. I and the three other farmhands eventually got the horses calmed down and we talked a lot about what it all meant. All the planes had swastika on them, so we knew they were German planes . . .

Memory for the liberation, man, 81 years old (23 years old at the time of the event)
I was visiting my girlfriend at her parents' place. Five to ten minutes after [the announcement on the radio] everything was chaos, cheers, laughter, and happiness, flags out of all windows. German soldiers were dropping their weapons and handed out cigarettes to everyone—everything was joy and happiness. I went home an hour later. My brother and I had got our mother's permission to break a big ugly vase the day the war ended. My younger brother did so. He was 21 years old . . .

Both extracts from Berntsen and Thomsen (2005), reproduced with permission of the authors.

In this study, older adults' memories for details of learning the news of these momentous events (e.g., weather, time, day of the week) were found to be generally accurate, with 55% of answers being correctly answered (compared with 11% correct responses by the control group of younger adults). The authors concluded that this difference could not be put down to knowledge of history, inferences, or guessing and that personal memory must have served an important function in older adults' correct recall. This study was also able to examine the effects of social identity on personal memory, as participants were asked whether they had any ties to the Danish resistance movement, the German occupying power, or the Jewish community (few respondents indicated the last two ties). Participants who reported ties to the Danish resistance were found to have more accurate memories of the invasion and liberation and their descriptions had higher clarity than individuals who reported no ties. These findings fit with those of Conway et al. (1994) and suggest that social identity has a powerful role to play in long-lasting personal memories.

The flashbulb memory debate is still far from resolved. It is clear that some memories do exhibit remarkable persistence, clarity, and detail. Some of the factors associated with the formation and maintenance of these super-memories have been identified, but whether it is necessary to postulate a special mechanism, or whether they can be explained in terms of normal memory processes, is still disputed. Reconstructions may be inaccurate, particular details may be lost, and the unexpected may be disregarded. Conway (1995) maintained that the evidence for flashbulb memories is compelling and argued that they can be distinguished from other autobiographical memories. Autobiographical memories are actively constructed at retrieval and thus have a dynamic changeable quality; in contrast, flashbulb memories are considered to be fixed and highly durable. If flashbulb memories are accurate and long-lasting copies, rather than reconstructions, they are only encoded at the cost of some emotional distress. In general, the level of memory accuracy in particular situations is determined by a complex combination of motivational and affective factors and the operating characteristics of the mechanisms of encoding, storage, and retrieval. Flashbulb memories, in Conway's account, are more detailed and vivid, more holistic and integrated, than most autobiographical memories, and the formation of flashbulb memories is dependent on the preconditions of surprise, emotion, importance, and consequentiality. Conway's book reviews studies of flashbulb memory and the theoretical controversy surrounding it as well as providing a well-argued case for regarding flashbulb memories as "special". As highlighted by Neisser (2003), if future research into flashbulb memory is going to explore this argument, it needs to examine new avenues and methodologies.

CULTURAL DIFFERENCES IN AUTOBIOGRAPHICAL MEMORY

As was demonstrated in the Berntsen and Thomsen study above, an individual's social identity can influence the amount of detail in, and the accuracy of, their autobiographical memories. In addition to the suggestion that personal autobiographical memories serve the function of maintaining an individual's personal goals, beliefs, attitudes, and a coherent sense of self, other researchers have recently begun to focus on the function that remembering serves with regard to coherence of goals, beliefs, and self-identities at a cultural level.

Western cultures tend to be *independently oriented* and value individual autonomy, self-expression, and personal capability. An individual's perception of himself or herself will tend to be as an individual: distinct and unique, divorced from others and their social context. Contrastingly, Asian cultures are more *interdependently oriented* and value social rules, group harmony, interconnectedness, solidarity, and personal humility. Here people view themselves as part of a hierarchical social network of kinship. These cultural differences in conceptualisations of the self have led to research into the interactions between self, culture and autobiographical memory. Cross-cultural variations in autobiographical memory have been observed by a number of authors, e.g., Pillemer (1998), Röttger-Rössler (1993), Weintraub (1978) and Han, Leichtman, and Wang (1998). One of the first studies to directly test the relationship between culture, self-concepts, and earliest childhood memories was carried out by Wang (2001). American and Chinese college students in this study were asked to recall their first memory from childhood, rate this on a number of measures (e.g., rehearsal of this memory), and then complete 10 "I am . . ." statements. These statements were coded as either being *private self-descriptions* (e.g., "I am honest, happy, intelligent"); *collective self-descriptions* (e.g., "I am a student, a sister, a Lutheran"); or *public self-descriptions* (e.g., "I am deeply attached to my boyfriend"). They were also coded as positive, negative, or neutral. Memories were coded as being about the individual, the family, the neighbourhood, or school, as well as on a number of other dimensions such as emotionality and autonomous orientation. The results of this study showed that the average age of Americans' earliest childhood memories was 3.5 years whereas the earliest memories of the Chinese sample came from approximately 6 months later. In the analysis of memory descriptions Americans tended to write lengthy, emotionally elaborate, self-focused memories referring to specific one-off events whereas the Chinese participants' memories were more brief and more centred on collective activities, routines, and emotionally neutral events. When describing themselves in the *I am* statements, American participants were found to emphasise individual attributes whereas the Chinese participants described themselves to a greater extent in terms of social roles. Across both cultures participants who used more positive and self-focused terms were also found to provide more specific and self-focused memories. Together these results indicate a dynamic reciprocal relationship between individual and cultural influences on autobiographical memory construction and retrieval. These relationships between culture, self, and memory are depicted in Figure 2.12.

The finding that Americans tend to generate memories that are of unique one-time experiences that are more focused on their own roles and emotions whereas the Chinese are more inclined to focus on social interactions and collective activities was replicated in memories from across the lifespan in a study by Wang and Conway (2004). This work was part of a larger study by Conway, Wang, Hanyu, and Haque (2005), which recruited samples from China, Japan, England, Bangladesh, and America. Participants from each of these cultures were found to generate highly similar lifespan memory retrieval curves and these are shown in Figure 2.13. Periods of childhood amnesia and the reminiscence bump were found to be the same across cultures, although there were interesting cross-*country* differences with North

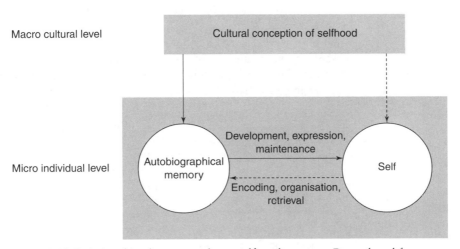

Figure 2.12 Relationships between culture, self, and memory. Reproduced from Wang and Conway (2004) with permission from Blackwell Publishing.

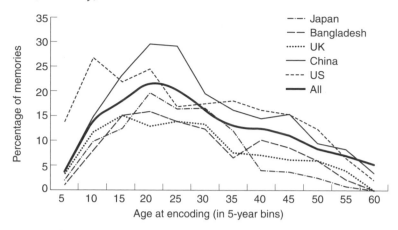

Figure 2.13 Lifespan retrieval curves from five countries. From Conway et al. (2005). Reproduced with permission of Sage Publications.

American participant showing the weakest childhood amnesia effect (i.e., they retrieved more memories from early childhood than the other groups).

The finding of highly similar lifespan retrieval curves across cultures in this study was unexpected, as in some Asian societies adulthood is not considered to start until the age of about 30, when a stable social network is formed. Conway et al. (2005) suggest that this finding could be due to the increased Westernisation of Asian cultures over the last 50 years, which may have brought about changes in the cultural norms regarding the timing of progression to adolescence and adulthood. It also could indicate universality in memory retrieval curves related to neurodevelopmental changes in the frontal lobes, which develop throughout childhood and into adolescence.

A different method of exploring the self–culture–memory relationship was recently used by Wang (2006). In this study participants' earliest childhood memories of self and others were cued using the specific words *self*, *mother*, *family*, *friend*, and *surroundings*. European Americans' earliest memories were again found to be from a younger age than were Taiwanese memories, and European Americans tended to recall more specific events and focus on individual roles and autonomy than did the memories from Taiwanese participants. With regard to the different memories recalled to the four cue words, across cultures memory for *mother* was found to come from the youngest age (American = 3.8 years, Taiwanese = 5.4 years), and the earliest memory for *self* came from 6–8 months later. Memory for *surroundings* came from about the same age as memory for mother, suggesting early development of knowledge about the physical environment. Memory for *friend* was the latest memory retrieved in both cultures (American = 5 years, Taiwanese = 6.33 years), which supports previous findings that the social self in relation to friendships develops in the late preschool years. Memories for events linked to the social self, and particularly the self in relation to mother, are therefore able to be formed before memories relating to the self as an individual. A child's conceptual self can only arise after he or she has formed interactional schemas and has been able to adopt the perspective of others present in his or her early years (Harter, 1998; Mead, 1982).

Mother–child interactions and how autobiographical memory styles are fostered during childhood and adolescence have been studied both within and between cultures. Leichtman, Wang, and Pillemer (2003) found that Western mothers talk about the past in more elaborate and emotional ways than mothers from Eastern cultures. In conversations with their children, Eastern mothers tend to place the child in a more collective setting, minimise emotions such as anger that may divide the child from the group, and instead highlight moral emotions and lessons. On the other hand, mothers from Western cultures focus on the child's own abilities and emotions. When discussing past events they will also provide rich and embellished information about the events being discussed and will elaborate and augment childrens' responses. Eastern mothers have been found to not use embellishment in conversations with their children, instead just repeating questions to try to elicit more information about the event being discussed (Wang & Brockmeier, 2002). These styles of reminiscing have been termed "high-elaborative" and "low-elaborative" respectively and have been shown to influence the amount of detail elicited in memory-sharing conversations and the elaborative style adopted by the child. This demonstrates how cultural styles of memory retrieval and memory content are directly passed down from mother to child through simple sharing of past experiences.

The language of encoding has also been found to be important for memory retrieval. As mentioned earlier, Simcock and Hayne (2002) showed that the specific language skills that a child possesses at the time of an event influence what can later be recalled about the event verbally. In a study of middle-aged immigrants who had fled from Poland to Denmark 30 years previously, Larsen, Schrauf, Fromholt, and Rubin (2002) found that when asked to recall memories to word cues (of which half were given in Danish and half in Polish), memories of events that had taken place in Poland were judged by the individual as being retrieved from memory in Polish whereas events that occurred after immigration were retrieved in Danish. Also, those who had immigrated at a younger age (24 years) now experienced more inner speech behaviours in Danish than late immigrators (average 34 years), i.e., they now thought in Danish. These results suggest that some element of autobiographical memory encoding takes language into account, or at least some linguistic elements feature in encoding specificity and subsequent retrieval. The acquisition of a second language in adulthood does appear to have identifiable effects on autobiographical memory.

The cultural practices that influence how autobiographical remembering is performed, as well as prevailing cultural ideas of selfhood, have been shown by these studies to determine the types of autobiographical memories recalled, both in experimental settings and in real-life scenarios. This burgeoning area of research is now being approached from a variety of different angles, and the huge array of beliefs, goals, and self-identities held in our ever-expanding multicultural world provide an excellent platform from which to launch further studies, including the influences of language and immigration on autobiographical memory and the passing-on of cultural identities from generation to generation.

FALSE OR TRUE? THE FALLIBILITY OF MEMORY

Research in autobiographical memory is complicated by the fact that most of the methods used are highly subjective, and rely on self-reports. There is often no way of

Original	Foil
_____ rode her bike through the park while I ran . . . I ran until I had to stop to get her out of the snow, walk her bike up a hill, etc. We were out an hour—it was beautiful out. Again it made me think how much I've enjoyed the city.	_____ rode her bike through the park while I ran . . . I ran until I had to stop to get her out of the snow, walk her bike up a hill, etc. We were out an hour—it was a mess out. Again it made me think how hard it is to adjust to the city.

Figure 2.14 An original memory and a foil where the evaluation has been changed (from Barclay & Wellman, 1986). Copyright © Elsevier 1986. Reproduced with permission.

checking whether the memories reported are veridical, but researchers have gone to considerable lengths to find ways of checking autobiographical memories. A person's recall of an event at one time can sometimes be checked against recall of the same event at a subsequent time, or against the recall of other people who may have experienced the same event. These methods have been used in the studies of flashbulb memory, discussed earlier, and eyewitness testimony reviewed in Chapter 3. For public memories there may be contemporary records, but for private memories tests of accuracy usually rely on the diary method, checking subsequent recall against the subject's own diary record.

Barclay and Wellman (1986) asked six adults to record three events every day for 4 months and then administered a recognition test after 3, 6, 9, 12, or 31 months. In the recognition test the original event descriptions were mixed with foil items that were of three different kinds. Some foils changed the description of the event, some changed the evaluation of the event, and some substituted a completely different event. Figure 2.14 shows one of the original memories and a foil that has changed the evaluation.

Hit rates for correct recognition ranged from 92% at the shortest interval to 79% at the longest, but false positive rates were high. Even for the completely different foils the false alarm rate was 22% and Barclay noted that false alarm rates were higher if the foil was semantically similar to the original event. He concluded that a process of schematisation takes place, with details being lost and memories becoming generic.

Conway, Collins, Gathercole, and Anderson (1996) reported a study in which two people kept diaries recording both true and false events and thoughts over a period of 5 months. Seven months later they tried to discriminate between the true and false records. Correct recognition for true memories was high and was associated with conscious recollection of the event, but false memories produced a high rate of false positive responses that were not associated with a distinct recollection. Events were recognised better than thoughts. In a later study Burt, Kemp, and Conway (2004) tested the memory of 11 participants who been involved in a longitudinal diary study and had originally recorded their daily events 13 years previously. Burt et al. constructed false events by transforming a true event given by the participant in one of seven ways: by changing the activity only, location only, participant only, activity and location, activity and participant, location and participant, and activity, location, and participant. Of all the false events, only 13% of memories were rated as remembered. Events where all details (activity, participant, and location) had been changed were found to be the least likely to be identified as false. Only 25% of these memories were rated as *never happened*; instead they were typically given ratings that related to memory failures (*the cues do not prompt any specific recollection*, or *it could be one of many similar events*), indicating that although the participant could recall the components of the event description, they could not identify the specific event memory from which they came. These studies illustrate the fallibility of autobiographical memory.

Reconstruction versus copy theories

The extent to which autobiographical memories are reconstructions or direct copies of the original event is related to the issue of accuracy. Historically, a number of different positions on this subject have been put forward. Barclay's (1993) ideas constitute a *strong reconstruction view* of autobiographical memory: He believes that new versions of the past are continually reconstructed. According to this view, people use their general knowledge and past experience to make plausible inferences about what might have happened. Reconstructed memories are therefore liable to conform to the general character of the original event but to be inaccurate in specific details.

Against this view, it is argued that memories often do contain specific details that are accurate. Brewer (1988) favours a more moderate *partial reconstructive view*. He gave his student participants a beeper set to go off at random intervals and asked them to record what they were doing, thinking, and feeling at that moment. Later, they were given recall and recognition tests and asked to rate the extent to which they could re-experience the event. He found that there was some degree of re-experiencing for the majority of events and considered this was evidence against the strong reconstructive position. The subjective feeling of re-experiencing is not a guarantee that a memory has not been reconstructed but Brewer found that accuracy, confidence, and degree of re-experiencing were highly intercorrelated. However, recollective experience, or the sensation of re-experiencing an event, has been found in a number of false memory studies. For example, Moulin, Conway, Thompson, James, and Jones (2005) found that patients who experience a persistent sense of *déjà vécu* (a sense of having lived through a particular experience or situation before) had recollective experience for items falsely recalled on memory tests. They also provided reasonable justifications for these memory errors at test, and the memory errors they made in everyday life. In an experiment with student participants, Heaps and Nash (2001) found that in discussion of a number of both true and false memories over a series of interviews, no differences were found between the recollective experience elements of image presence, image clarity, and whether the image associated with the memory was static or dynamic in the true and false memories. Current opinion holds that all memories are reconstructed, to some extent, each time they are brought to mind (Conway & Pleydell-Pearce, 2000).

False memories

It is well known that brain injuries can cause patients to confabulate, producing autobiographical memories that have no basis in fact (see Chapter 13 on memory dysfunction). The border between confabulation and reconstruction is not absolutely clear; it is well known that normal adults may confabulate details of real memories, and, as we have seen in the studies of eyewitness testimony (see Chapter 3), memories may be contaminated by misleading information. However, the question that currently preoccupies many researchers is whether normal adults may produce completely false confabulated memories of events that never occurred at all. Interest in false memories has been amplified recently by the spate of cases in which adults claim to have recovered repressed memories of sexual abuse that occurred in their childhood. Recovery of these memories usually takes place in the course of psychotherapy, and many researchers believe that the recovered events never took place, but have been implanted in disturbed and vulnerable people by the suggestions offered by the therapist. The phenomenon has been labelled *False Memory Syndrome (FMS)*, but it proves extremely difficult to find hard evidence to show that such memories are either true or false. To prove that the memory is true it would be necessary to have objective evidence that the abuse actually occurred, but this is usually lacking. Moreover, the existence of repressed memory, as distinct from normal forgetting, is itself controversial. Furthermore, a recent investigation by the British Psychological Society showed that in 134 out of 181 cases, memories of abuse were not suddenly recovered from total amnesia, but had been partially recalled previously over varying periods of time.

There has been a tendency, especially in the United States, for people to take up extreme positions, with some asserting that it is impossible to recover forgotten memories and attacking the concept of repression. The fact that some recovered memories, such as those involving being carried off by aliens in spaceships, are intrinsically unbelievable, is cited in support of this position. On the other hand, some people claim that a wide variety of psychological problems such as depression and eating disorders are indicative of sexual abuse in childhood, and that sufferers can be helped to recover forgotten memories of this abuse.

A more balanced view is that it may be possible to recover repressed memories later in life but that most recovered "memories" probably never happened. Lindsay and Read (1994) argued that memory recovery therapy can lead clients to create illusory memories. We know from studies of eyewitness testimony (Chapter 3) that gross inaccuracies are not uncommon and that memory is highly suggestible. It has certainly been clearly demonstrated that it is possible to implant false memories in a subject who comes to believe the false memory with a high degree of confidence. Studies by Bruck, Ceci, Francouer, and Barr (1995) have demonstrated that children's memory for what occurred during a medical examination can be influenced by post-event suggestions (e.g., "He looked into your ear, didn't he?"). This study also demonstrated that the longer the time that had elapsed since the event, and the more often the suggestions were repeated, the stronger the effects of the suggestions. In addition to misinformation distorting memories of actual events, Loftus and colleagues (Loftus, 1993; Loftus & Pickrell, 1995) have used a *memory implantation technique* to try to elicit entirely false autobiographical memories in participants. In this paradigm participants are asked to read descriptions of a number of true events that occurred to them as children and one false event, such as getting lost in a shopping mall or tipping over a bucket of punch at a wedding. With the assistance of the participant's parents the false event descriptions are typically endowed with numerous idiosyncratic details, such as the particular name of the shopping mall the child used to visit, or the child's favourite type of candy. Wade and Garry (2005) review the studies that have utilised this paradigm and state that, across studies, 37% of participants have remembered all or some details of the false event. Similar results have been found in children's memories. Ceci, Huffman, Smith, and Loftus (1994) interviewed young children, repeatedly asking them if they had ever experienced particular events, some of which had really occurred and some of which were fabricated (e.g., "Did you ever get your finger caught in a mouse-trap and have to go to hospital to get the trap off?"). More than half the children produced false narratives with compellingly vivid details. Thus, it is clear that false memories can be implanted in someone who then genuinely believes the memory to be true. Whether this is what is happening in some of the cases when memories of sexual abuse are "recovered" is not yet established, but it is clear that it could be happening. The possibility that some "recovered" memories are illusory is made more likely by the techniques employed, because some forms of memory recovery therapy encourage clients to believe strongly in memories that are sketchy or consist only of vague feelings. In a laboratory study that mimicked a psychotherapeutic situation, Loftus and Mazzoni (1998) asked participants to produce a dream report, which they then got "analysed" by an "expert clinician" who was really a confederate. The clinician informed the participant that their dream report suggested that they had been involved in a particular event in early childhood (either being in a dangerous situation or being lost). At 4-week follow-up, participants were found to be more confident that they had actually experienced the specified childhood event, although it is not known whether they had constructed an accompanying false memory to go with this increased confidence. In their review of the literature on FMS, Lindsay and Read (1994, p. 318) concluded that "the creation of illusory memories of childhood sexual abuse is not merely an abstract possibility but rather a tragic reality".

Recent reviews on the topic of False Memory Syndrome have highlighted that there is no empirical evidence that the syndrome exists and therefore suggest that the term should not be used; however, they do point out that the lack of supporting evidence is probably due to the fact that so little research has actually been done (Gleaves, Smith, Butler, & Spiegel, 2004). Within the FMS debate it has also been argued that it isn't important to decide whether FMS is in fact a syndrome or not; it is the accuracy of the memories that is critical. The counterargument against this is that mental health professionals are testifying in court cases relating to sexual abuse cases, describing FMS as being a scientific diagnosis and a psychopathology. Dallam (2001) concluded that, "in the absence of any substantive scientific support, 'False Memory Syndrome' is best described as a pseudoscientific syndrome that was developed to defend against claims of sexual abuse". Gleaves et al. conclude that experimental findings using techniques such as imagination inflation and memory implantation cast doubt on the accuracy and reality of false memories "recovered" in therapy. Nevertheless, most psychologists recognise that it is possible to retrieve forgotten memories of events that occurred long ago and that some recovered memories of sexual abuse may be true. More research is needed, as the situations in which false memories can or may be likely to occur are as yet unknown.

Factors that influence accuracy

It is arguable that forced-choice recognition experiments that use foils produce underestimates of the accuracy of autobiographical memory. The events that were tested in these studies were relatively mundane and trivial, and the foils were constructed so as to be confusing. In the ordinary circumstances of everyday life, when people try to recall autobiographical memories, they have the option of deciding they do not remember and so are less likely to make inaccurate responses. In experimental situations, when they are pushed into making yes/no responses to deliberately confusing items, it is not surprising that they make errors.

A number of factors have been identified that influence memory accuracy. It is commonly believed that highly stressful and emotional experiences leave indelible memories. Wagenaar and Groeneweg (1990) examined this idea in their study of the memories of concentration camp survivors. For 15 of the witnesses at the trial of Martinus De Rijke, a camp guard, their testimonies had been collected in 1943–1947 and were given again in 1984–1987. After 40 years, their experiences were generally well remembered but there was a marked loss of specific but essential details such as the names and appearance of torturers, and specific events such as seeing a murder and being brutally treated. The missing information appeared to be irretrievably lost and could not be recovered by cueing. Generic information about the daily routine was well remembered. The results of this study conform to the pattern found in more humdrum memories and do not support the view that very emotional experiences are never forgotten.

A study by Conway (1990) highlights the fact that memories may be altered to conform with current beliefs and attitudes, a sort of hindsight bias. Before they took an examination he asked students to report their expected grade; how much importance they attached to doing well; the number of hours they had spent in preparation; how well prepared they were; and how far they thought the grade they obtained would accurately reflect their knowledge and ability. Two weeks after the results of the examination were known they were asked to recall this information. Those who had grades worse than expected recalled working less hard; thought the grade less related to their true level of knowledge and ability; and thought the result less important than their original estimates. Those who did better than expected recalled the amount of work they had done correctly, but estimated the importance of the result more highly. Consistent with a reconstructive view, these findings suggest that personal memories are to some extent unstable and can be edited in the light of later experiences.

The strategies employed in verifying whether memories are false or true were examined recently by Wade and Garry (2005). In this study participants were asked to describe two scenarios. First they were asked to describe a real-life event where they had been unsure whether something they thought they remembered was actually a true memory. An example they were given was "You might have met up with an old friend and swapped those 'remember the time that we . . .' stories and started to remember something that you later realised did not occur." After describing this experience, participants were then given a passage to read that described the experimental paradigm of the "lost in the mall" scenario of Loftus and colleagues. Participants were asked to imagine that they had been a participant in the "lost in the mall" experiment and were asked to describe how they would have determined whether the "memory" they recalled about being lost in the mall was real or not. In both these tasks the most popular verification strategies chosen by participants were asking others such as family members, or using cognitive strategies such as concentrating, imagining, weighing up accounts of the event, and looking for inconsistencies. These results fit with the source monitoring framework, which posits that remembering involves reasoning and that people use the average differences in the qualitative characteristics of memories (e.g., perceptual, contextual, affective details) to distinguish between real and fantasy events (Johnson, Foley, Suengas, & Raye, 1988; Johnson, Hashtroudi, & Lindsay, 1993).

Relying on cognitive strategies, however, is not a good verification process. Imagining, which was listed by participants in Wade and Garry's (2005) study as a technique they would employ to verify a memory, has been shown to increase the belief that the event did occur (see Garry & Polaschek, 2000, for a review). The relationship between this belief in an event occurring and recalling an actual autobiographical memory of an event was recently investigated by Mazzoni and Memon (2003). In this study participants were asked to imagine one event occurring and were merely exposed to a description of another event. The two events differed along the lines of plausibility; the first event of having a milk tooth extracted by a dentist is highly plausible as occurring to children, whereas the second event used in this experiment, having a skin sample removed from your little finger, is not a procedure performed on children in the UK. Exposure and imagining were counterbalanced across these events. Results showed that after imagining an event occurring to them, participants not only had an increase in belief that the event had happened to them in childhood, but 40% of participants also reported having a memory for that event. The pattern of results was the same for the two events, although fewer memories were recalled in the less plausible skin sample condition. Overall, imagination alone was found to increase belief in a memory of an event and produce autobiographical memories of the event.

Plausibility and source monitoring errors have been suggested as being two of the three processes involved in the creation of false childhood memories (Hyman & Kleinknecht, 1999). The third process is memory construction. For a person to create a false memory, the event must first be considered plausible; for example, if you had never been to a mall before the age of 10 you would not consider it plausible that you had got lost in one at the age of 6. A memory of the event must then be constructed; this could be aided by tying the event to other events in memory or to self-knowledge, talking about the event, or, as we have seen above, imagining an event. When the event is considered plausible and an image is constructed the individual must then make a source monitoring error; they must falsely attribute that image as coming from memory rather than coming from their imagination (see Hyman and Loftus, 1998, for a review of these and other types of memory error). In experimental or eyewitness memory settings, factors such as desire to please the experimenter/interviewer and interrogative suggestibility will also be involved in the creation of false memories (Heaps & Nash, 2001).

It is common for information to be lost from autobiographical memory, for false details to be incorporated in true memories, and for completely false memories to be implanted by suggestion and imagination. Yet these findings are not representative of the normal functioning of autobiographical memory. In ordinary circumstances, when we are not deliberately misled or influenced by suggestion, memories may be inaccurate in detail but are usually accurate in general terms. Recently Brainerd and Reyna (2002, 2004) have put forward the *Fuzzy-Trace Theory* (*FTT*) of memory, which posits that the human brain holds both verbatim and gist traces of experience. Verbatim traces are conceptualised as integrated representations of a memory's form and associated item-specific information and are located in the memory targets (e.g., the font in which a word is printed). Conversely, gist traces are representations of semantic, relational and other elaborative information about the memory target and are therefore not part of the target itself, but are added to the target by the rememberer. There are five principal components of FTT:

1   That verbatim and gist traces are stored in parallel.
2   That verbatim and gist traces are retrieved separately.
3   That verbatim and gist traces are differentially accessible and therefore also preserved differentially.
4   That the retrieval of verbatim traces is accompanied by recollective experience whereas the retrieval of gist traces is accompanied only by familiarity.
5   That verbatim and gist memory develop at different ages during childhood.

Within this framework true memories can be represented by both verbatim and gist traces, whereas false memories can be represented by gist traces only. Thus, the predictions made by this model are that when memory is tested in a situation where verbatim traces are required for accurate recall, false memories should not occur; however, when memory is tested in a less optimal situation where both verbatim and gist traces may be called upon to aid recall, false memories or memory errors will occur. In autobiographical remembering there is a great deal that people can accurately remember, i.e., that certain events occurred, without needing to recall any further details—the gist is considered sufficient. This conceptual representation of events is considered to help the self-memory system avoid the potential information overload that would be associated with verbatim retrieval of episodic memories whenever memory was accessed, though as has been discussed in depth in the studies of false memory above, recalling some but not all the elements of an event may lead to the event being recalled falsely (e.g., Burt et al., 2004). Although most of the work on FTT has involved word-learning paradigms, extension of this area to the field of real-world false memory should be a fruitful area for future research.

CONCLUSIONS

Memory for personal experiences, as this chapter has illustrated, includes a wide-ranging variety of different types of memory. Researchers are forced to rely on relatively informal ways of gathering their data and cannot exclude or control the many factors that influence the encoding, retention, and retrieval of memories of personal experiences. In spite of these problems, theories and models developed in more formal cognitive studies are surprisingly successful at interpreting and making sense of the findings.

Although many aspects of autobiographical memory are still obscure, these studies have had considerable success, particularly in revealing the organisation and retrieval processes. The consensus of the findings indicates that organisation is both thematic and temporal, with types of events or actions being represented at different levels of generality/specificity. When people try to recall a particular episode from the past, retrieval processes access the level of categorisation or time period that provides the optimum context for search. This optimum level of representation is one that is rich and specific enough to generate useful cues and reminders. Particular episodes that are sufficiently distinctive, novel, deviant, or recent are not absorbed into generalised representations but are represented at the most specific level, where they can be identified by specific tags or stand out because they are distinctive or highly self-defining. Our self-image influences what personal experiences we recall and our memories of personal experiences are organised around self-concepts or themes that refer to different selves.

There is good evidence that memories lose specificity over time and become more generalised; that older memories tend to be less vivid and less accessible; and that accuracy declines with time and dating of memories is imprecise. False memories can be deliberately implanted and recognition tasks show a relatively high rate of false positive responses for false memories and false details of true memories. However, experimental paradigms tend to exaggerate the fallibility of autobiographical memory and underestimate the amazing quantity and quality of information that is retained over a lifetime.

REFERENCES

Anderson, S.J., & Conway, M.A. (1993). Investigating the structure of autobiographical memories. *Journal of Experimental Psychology: Learning, Memory and Cognition, 19,* 1178–1196.

Anderson, S.J., & Conway, M.A. (2007). *Why actions and contexts may not organise autobiographical memory: Further evidence against the activity dominance hypothesis.* Unpublished manuscript.

Baddeley, A.D. (1987). But what the hell is it for? In M.M. Gruneberg, P.E. Morris, & R.N. Sykes (Eds.), *Practical aspects of memory: Current research and issues* (pp. 3–18). Chichester, UK: Wiley.

Bahrick, H.P. (1984). Memory for people. In J.E. Harris & P.E. Morris (Eds.), *Everyday memory, actions and absentmindedness.* London: Academic Press.

Baker-Ward, L.A. (1993). A tale of two settings: Young children's memory performance in the laboratory and the field. In G.M. Davies & R.H. Logie (Eds.), *Memory in everyday life. Advances in psychology, 100* (pp. 13–41). Amsterdam: North-Holland.

Barclay, C.R. (1993). Remembering ourselves. In G.M. Davies & R.H. Logie (Eds.), *Memory in everyday life. Advances in psychology, 100* (pp. 285–309). Amsterdam: North-Holland.

Barclay, C.R., & Wellman, H.M. (1986). Accuracies and inaccuracies in autobiographical memories. *Journal of Memory and Language, 25,* 93–103.

Barsalou, L.W. (1988). The content and organisation of autobiographical memories. In U. Neisser & E. Winograd (Eds.), *Remembering reconsidered* (pp. 193–243). Cambridge, UK: Cambridge University Press.

Berntsen, D. (1996). Involuntary autobiographical memories. *Applied Cognitive Psychology, 10,* 435–454.

Berntsen, D. (1998). Voluntary and involuntary access to autobiographical memory. *Memory, 6,* 113–141.

Berntsen, D., & Hall, N.M. (2004). The episodic nature of involuntary autobiographical memories. *Memory & Cognition, 32,* 789–803.

Berntsen, D., & Thomsen, D.K. (2005). Personal memories for remote historical events: Accuracy and clarity of flashbulb memories related to World War II. *Journal of Experimental Psychology: General, 134,* 242–257.

Betz, A.L., & Skowronski, J.J. (1997). Self-events and other-events: Temporal dating and event memory. *Memory & Cognition, 25,* 701–714.

Blagov, P.S., & Singer, J.A. (2004). Four dimensions of self-defining memories (specificity, meaning, content, and affect) and their relationships to self-restraint, distress, and repressive defensiveness. *Journal of Personality, 72,* 481–511.

Bluck, S. (2003). Autobiographical memory: Exploring its functions in everyday life. *Memory, 11,* 113–123.

Bluck, S., Alea, N., Habermas, T., & Rubin, D.C. (2005). A tale of three functions: The self-reported uses of autobiographical memory. *Social Cognition, 23,* 91–117.

Bower, G.H., Black, J.B., & Turner, T.J. (1979). Scripts in text comprehension and memory. *Cognitive Psychology, 11,* 177–220.

Brainerd, C.J., & Reyna, V.F. (2002). Fuzzy-trace theory and false memory. *Current Directions in Psychological Science, 11,* 164–169.

Brainerd, C.J., & Reyna, V.F. (2004). Fuzzy-trace theory and memory development. *Developmental Review, 24,* 396–439.

Brewer, W.F. (1986). What is autobiographical memory? In D.C. Rubin (Ed.), *Autobiographical memory.* Cambridge, UK: Cambridge University Press.

Brewer, W.F. (1988). Memory for randomly sampled autobiographical events. In U. Neisser & E. Winograd (Eds.), *Remembering reconsidered* (pp. 21–90). Cambridge, UK: Cambridge University Press.

Brewer, W.F., & Tenpenny, P.L. (1996). *The role of schemata in the recall and recognition of episodic information.* Personal communication.

Brewer, W.F., & Treyens, J.C. (1981). Role of schemata in memory for places. *Cognitive Psychology, 13,* 207–230.

Brown, N.R., Rips, L.J., & Shevell, S.K. (1985). The subjective dates of natural events in very long-term memory. *Cognitive Psychology, 17,* 139–177.

Brown, N.R., & Schopflocher, D. (1998). Event clusters: An organization of personal events in autobiographical memory. *Psychological Science, 9,* 470–475.

Brown, N.R., Shevell, S.K., & Rips, L.J. (1986). Public memories and their personal context. In D.C. Rubin (Ed.), *Autobiographical memory.* Cambridge, UK: Cambridge University Press.

Brown, R., & Kulik, J. (1982). Flashbulb memory. In U. Neisser (Ed.), *Memory observed: Remembering in natural contexts.* San Francisco, CA: W.H. Freeman.

Bruce, D., Wilcox-O'Hearn, L.A., Robinson, J.A., Phillips-Grant, K., Francis, L., & Smith, M.C. (2005). Fragment memories mark the end of childhood amnesia, *Memory & Cognition, 33,* 567–576.

Bruck, M., Ceci, S., Francouer, E., & Barr, R. (1995). "I hardly cried when I got my shot!" Influencing children's reports about a visit to their pediatrician. *Child Development, 66,* 193–208.

Burt, C.D.B. (1992a). Reconstruction of the duration of autobiographical events. *Memory & Cognition, 20,* 124–132.

Burt, C.D.B. (1992b). Retrieval characteristics of autobiographical memories: Event and date information. *Applied Cognitive Psychology, 6,* 389–404.

Burt, C.D.B., Kemp, S., & Conway, M.A. (2001). What happens if you retest autobiographical memory 10 years on? *Memory and Cognition, 29,* 127–136.

Burt, C.D.B., Kemp, S., & Conway, M.A. (2004). Memory for true and false autobiographical event descriptions. *Memory, 12,* 545–552.

Ceci, S.J., Huffman, M.L.C., Smith, E., & Loftus, E.F. (1994). Repeatedly thinking about a non-event: Source misattributions among preschoolers. *Consciousness and Cognition*, *3*, 388–407.

Cohen, G., Conway, M.A., & Maylor, E. (1994). Flashbulb memory in older adults. *Psychology and Aging*, *9*, 454–463.

Cohen, G., & Faulkner, D. (1988). Life span change in autobiographical memory. In M.M. Gruneberg, P.E. Moms, & R.N. Sykes (Eds.), *Practical aspects of memory: Current research and issues*, *Vol. 1* (pp. 277–282). Chichester, UK: Wiley.

Cohen, G., & Java, R. (1995). Memory for medical history. *Applied Cognitive Psychology*, *9*, 273–288.

Conway, M.A. (1990). *Autobiographical memory: An introduction*. Milton Keynes, UK: Open University Press.

Conway, M.A. (1995). *Flashbulb memories*. Hove, UK: Lawrence Erlbaum Associates, Inc.

Conway, M.A. (2005). Memory and the self. *Journal of Memory and Language*, *53*, 594–628.

Conway, M.A., Anderson, S.J., Larsen, S.F., Donnelly, C.M., McDaniel, M.A., McClelland, A.G.R., Rawles, R.E., & Logie, R.H. (1994). The formation of flashbulb memories. *Memory & Cognition*, *22*, 326–343.

Conway, M.A., & Bekerian, D.A. (1987). Organization in autobiographical memory. *Memory & Cognition*, *15*, 119–132.

Conway, M.A., Collins, A.F., Gathercole, S.E., & Anderson, S.J. (1996). Recollections of true and false autobiographical memories, *Journal of Experimental Psychology: General*, *125*, 69–95.

Conway, M.A., & Holmes, A. (2004). Psychosocial stages and the accessibility of autobiographical memories across the life cycle. *Journal of Personality*, *72*, 461–480.

Conway, M.A., & Holmes, E.A. (2005). Autobiographical memory and the working self. In N. Braisby & A. Gellaty (Eds.), *Cognitive psychology*. Oxford, UK: Oxford University Press.

Conway, M.A., & Pleydell-Pearce, C.W. (2000). The construction of autobiographical memories in the self memory system. *Psychological Review*, *107*, 261–288.

Conway, M.A., Singer, J.A., & Tagini, A. (2004). The self and autobiographical memory: Correspondence and coherence. *Social Cognition*, *22*, 495–537.

Conway, M.A., Wang, Q., Hanyu, K., & Haque, S. (2005). A cross-cultural investigation of autobiographical memory—On the universality and cultural variation of the reminiscence bump. *Journal of Cross-cultural Psychology*, *36*, 739–749.

Crovitz, H.F., & Schiffman, H. (1974). Frequency of episodic memories as a function of their age. *Bulletin of the Psychonomic Society*, *4*, 517–518.

Dallam, S.J. (2001). Crisis or creation? A systematic examination of "false memory syndrome". *Journal of Child Sexual Abuse*, *9*, 9–36.

Dritschel, B., Williams, J.M.G., Baddeley, A.D., Nimmo-Smith, I. (1992). Autobiographical fluency: A method for the study of personal memory. *Memory & Cognition*, *20*, 133–140.

Dudycha, G.J., & Dudycha, M.M. (1941). Childhood memories: A review of the literature. *Psychological Bulletin*, *38*, 668–682.

Erikson, E.H. (1950). *Childhood and society*. New York: W.W. Norton & Company.

Erikson, E.H. (1997). *The life cycle completed*. New York: W.W. Norton & Company.

Fitzgerald, J.M. (1988). Vivid memories and the reminiscence phenomenon: The role of a self narrative. *Human Development*, *31*, 261–273.

Fivush, R. (1994). Young children's event recall: Are memories constructed through discourse? *Consciousness and Cognition*, *3*, 356–373.

Fivush, R., Berlin, L.J., Sales, J.M., Mennuti-Washburn, J., & Cassidy, J. (2003a). Functions of parent–child reminiscing about emotionally negative events. *Memory*, *11*, 179–192.

Fivush, R., Edwards, V.J., & Mennuti-Washburn, J. (2003b). Narratives of 9/11: Relations among personal involvement, narrative content and memory of the emotional impact over time. *Applied Cognitive Psychology*, *17*, 1099–1111.

Fivush, R., & Hamond, N.R. (1990). Autobiographical memory across the preschool years. In R. Fivush & J.A. Hudson (Eds.), *Knowing and remembering in young children* (pp. 223–248). New York: Cambridge University Press.

Fivush, R., Hayden, C., & Reese, E. (1996). Remembering, recounting, and reminiscing: The development of memory in a social context. In D. Rubin (Ed.), *Remembering our past: Studies in autobiographical memory* (pp. 341–359). Cambridge, UK: Cambridge University Press.

Freud, S. (1953). Childhood and concealing memories/infantile sexuality. In A.A. Brill (Ed.), *The basic writings of Sigmund Freud* (pp. 62–68/580–585). New York: The Modern Library. [Originally published 1905]

Freud, S. (1974). Introducing lectures on psychoanalysis. In J. Strachey (Ed.), *The standard edition of the complete works of Sigmund Freud*, Vol. 2. London: Pelican Books. [Originally published 1916]

Gardiner, J.M., & Richardson-Klavehn, A. (2000). Remembering and knowing. In E. Tulving & F.I.M. Craik (Eds.), *Handbook of memory* (pp. 229–244). Oxford, UK: Oxford University Press.

Garry, M., & Polaschek, D.L.L. (2000). Imagination and memory. *Current Directions in Psychological Science*, 9, 6–10.

Gleaves, D.H., Smith, S.M., Butler, L.D., & Spiegel, D. (2004). False and recovered memories in the laboratory and clinic: A review of experimental and clinical evidence. *Clinical Psychology—Science & Practice*, 11, 3–28.

Goldsmith, L.R., & Pillemer, D.B. (1988). Memories of statements spoken in everyday contexts. *Applied Cognitive Psychology*, 2, 272–286.

Haden, C.A., Haine, R.A., & Fivush, R. (1997). Developing narrative structure in parent–child reminiscing across the preschool years. *Developmental Psychology*, 33, 295–307.

Han, J.J., Leichtman, M.D., & Wang, Q. (1998). Autobiographical memory in Korean, Chinese, and American children. *Developmental Psychology*, 34, 701–713.

Haque, S., & Conway, M.A. (2001). Probing the process of autobiographical memory retrieval. *European Journal of Cognitive Psychology*, 13, 1–19.

Harley, K., & Reese, E. (1999). Origins of autobiographical memory. *Developmental Psychology*, 35, 1338–1348.

Harter, S. (1998). The development of self-representations. In W. Damon (Series Ed.) & N. Eisenberg (Vol. Ed.), *Handbook of child psychology: Vol. 3. Social, emotional, and personality development* (5th ed., pp. 553–617). New York: Wiley.

Heaps, C.M., & Nash, M. (2001). Comparing recollective experience in true and false autobiographical memories. *Journal of Experimental Psychology: Learning, Memory, and Cognition*, 27, 920–930.

Holding, D.H., Noonan, T.K., Pfau, H.D., & Holding, C. (1986). Date attribution, age and the distribution of lifetime memories. *Journal of Gerontology*, 41, 481–485.

Holmes, A., & Conway, M.A. (1999). Generation identity and the reminiscence bump: Memory for public and private events. *Journal of Adult Development*, 6, 21–34.

Howe, M.L. (2000). *The fate of early memories*. Washington, DC: American Psychological Association.

Howe, M.L., & Courage, M.L. (1993). On resolving the enigma of infantile amnesia. *Psychological Bulletin*, 113, 305–326.

Howe, M.L., & Courage, M.L. (1997). The emergence and early development of autobiographical memory. *Psychological Review*, 104, 499–523.

Hudson, J.A. (1990). The emergence of autobiographical memory in mother–child conversation. In R. Fivush & J.A. Hudson (Eds.), *Knowing and remembering in young children* (pp. 166–196). Cambridge, UK: Cambridge University Press.

Hudson, J.A., & Fivush, R. (1991). As time goes by—6th graders remember a kindergarten experience. *Applied Cognitive Psychology*, 5, 347–360.

Hudson, J.A., & Nelson, K. (1986). Repeated encounters of a similar kind—effects of familiarity on children's autobiographical memory. *Cognitive Development, 3,* 253–271.

Huttenlocher, J., Hedges, L.V., & Prohaska, V. (1988). Hierarchical organization in ordered domains: Estimating the dates of events. *Psychological Review, 95,* 471–484.

Hyman, I.E., & Faries, J.M. (1992). The functions of autobiographical memory. In M.A. Conway, D.C. Rubin, H. Spinnler, & W.A. Wagenaar (Eds.), *Theoretical perspectives on autobiographical memory* (pp. 207–221). Dordrecht, The Netherlands: Kluwer Academic.

Hyman, I.E. Jr, & Kleinknecht, E. (1999). False childhood memories: Research, theory, and applications. In L.M. Williams & V.L. Banyard (Eds.), *Trauma and memory*. Thousand Oakes, CA: Sage.

Hyman, I.E. Jr, & Loftus, E.F. (1998). Errors in autobiographical memory. *Clinical Psychology Review, 18,* 933–947.

Janssen, S.M.J., Chessa, A.G., & Murre, J.M.J. (2006). Memory for time: How people date events. *Memory and Cognition, 34,* 138–147.

Johnson, M.K., & Chalfonte, B.L. (1994). Binding complex memories: The role of reactivation and the hippocampus. In D.L. Schacter & E. Tulving (Eds.), *Memory systems* (pp. 311–350). Cambridge, MA: MIT Press.

Johnson, M.K., Foley, M.A., Suengas, A.G., & Raye, C.L. (1988). Phenomenal characteristics of memories for perceived and imagined autobiographical events. *Journal of Experimental Psychology: General, 117,* 371–376.

Johnson, M.K., Hashtroudi, S., & Lindsay, D.S. (1993). Source monitoring. *Psychological Bulletin, 114,* 3–28.

Kemp, S. (1999). An associative theory of estimating past dates and past prices. *Psychonomic Bulletin and Review, 6,* 41–56.

Kurbat, M.A., Shevell, S.K., & Rips, L.J. (1998). A year's memories: The calendar effect in autobiographical recall. *Memory & Cognition, 26,* 532–552.

Kvavilashvili, L., Mirani, J., Schlagman, S., & Kornbrot, D.E. (2003). Comparing flashbulb memories of September 11 and the death of Princess Diana: Effects of time delays and nationality. *Applied Cognitive Psychology, 17,* 1017–1031.

Lampinen, J.M., Copeland, S.M., & Neuschatz, J.S. (2001). Recollections of things schematic: Room schemas revisited. *Journal of Experimental Psychology: Learning, Memory and Cognition, 27,* 1211–1222.

Lampinen, J.M., Faries, J.M., Neuschatz, J.S., & Toglia, M.P. (2000). Recollections of things schematic: The influence of scripts on recollective experience. *Applied Cognitive Psychology, 14,* 543–554.

Lancaster, J.S., & Barsalou, L.W. (1997). Multiple organisations of events in memory. *Memory, 5,* 569–599.

Larsen, S.F., Schrauf, R.W., Fromholt, P., & Rubin, D.C. (2002). Inner speech and bilingual autobiographical memory: A Polish–Danish cross-cultural study. *Memory, 10,* 45–54.

Lee, P.J., & Brown, N.R. (2003). Delay related changes in personal memories for September 11, 2001. *Applied Cognitive Psychology, 17,* 1007–1015.

Lee, P.J., & Brown, N.R. (2004). The role of guessing and boundaries on estimation biases. *Psychonomic Bulletin and Review, 11,* 748–754.

Leichtman, M., Wang, Q., & Pillemer, D.P. (2003). In R. Fivush & C.A. Haden (Eds.), *Autobiographical memory and the construction of a narrative self: Developmental and cultural perspectives* (pp. 73–98). Mahwah, NJ: Lawrence Erlbaum Associates, Inc.

Lindsay, D.S., & Read, J.D. (1994). Psychotherapy and memories of childhood sexual abuse: A cognitive perspective. *Applied Cognitive Psychology, 8,* 281–338.

Linton, M. (1982). Transformations of memory in everyday life. In U. Neisser (Ed.), *Memory observed: Remembering in natural contexts*. San Francisco, CA: Freeman.

Loftus, E.F. (1987). *Remembering when*. Paper presented at the Second Practical Aspects of Memory Conference, Swansea, Wales.

Loftus, E.F. (1993). The reality of repressed memories. *American Psychologist, 48,* 518–537.

Loftus, E.F., & Marburger, W. (1983). Since the eruption of Mount St. Helens has anyone beaten you up? Improving the accuracy of retrospective reports with landmark events. *Memory and Cognition, 11,* 114–120.

Loftus, E.F., & Mazzoni, G.A.L. (1998). Using imagination and personalized suggestion to change people. *Behavior Therapy, 29,* 691–706.

Loftus, E.F., & Pickrell, J.E. (1995). The formation of false memories. *Psychiatric Annals, 25,* 720–725.

Mace, J.H. (2004). Involuntary autobiographical memories are highly dependent on abstract cuing: The Proustian view is incorrect. *Applied Cognitive Psychology, 18,* 893–899.

Mazzoni, G.A.L., & Memon, A. (2003). Imagination can create false autobiographical memories. *Psychological Science, 14,* 186–188.

McAdams, D.P., Bauer, J.J., Sakaeda, A.R., Anyidoho, N.A., Machado, M.A., Magrino-Failla, K., White, K.W., & Pals, J.L. (2006). Continuity and change in the life story: A longitudinal study of autobiographical memories in emerging adulthood. *Journal of Personality, 74,* 1371–1140.

McCloskey, M., Wible, C.G., & Cohen, N.J. (1988). Is there a special flashbulb mechanism? *Journal of Experimental Psychology: General, 117,* 171–181.

McDonough, L., & Mandler, J.M. (1994). Very long-term recall in infants: Infantile amnesia reconsidered. *Memory, 2,* 339–352.

McLean, K.C., & Thorne, A. (2003). Late adolescents' self-defining memories about relationships. *Developmental Psychology, 39,* 635–645.

Mead, G.H. (1982). *The individual and the social self.* Chicago: University of Chicago Press.

Means, B., & Loftus, E.F. (1991). When personal history repeats itself: Decomposing memories for events. *Applied Cognitive Psychology, 5,* 297–318.

Means, B., Mingay, D.J., Nigam, A., & Zarrow, M. (1988). A cognitive approach to enhancing health survey reports of medical visits. In M.M. Gruneberg, P.E. Morris, & R.N. Sykes (Eds.), *Practical aspects of memory: Current research and issues, Vol. 1.* Chichester, UK: Wiley.

Moulin, C.J.A., Conway, M.A., Thompson, R.G., James, N., & Jones, R.W. (2005). Disordered memory awareness: Recollective confabulation in two cases of persistent déjà vécu. *Neuropsychologia, 43,* 1362–1378.

Myers, N.A., Perris, E.E., & Speaker, C.J. (1994). Fifty months of memory: A longitudinal study in early childhood. *Memory, 2,* 383–415.

Nakamura, G.V., Graesser, A.C., Zimmerman, J.A., & Riha, J. (1985). Script processing in a natural situation. *Memory and Cognition, 13,* 104–114.

Neisser, U. (1982). Snapshots or benchmarks? In U. Neisser (Ed.), *Memory observed: Remembering in natural contexts.* San Francisco, CA: Freeman.

Neisser, U. (1986). Nested structure in autobiographical memory. In D.C. Rubin (Ed.), *Autobiographical memory.* Cambridge, UK: Cambridge University Press.

Neisser, U. (1988). Five kinds of self-knowledge. *Philosophical Psychology, 1,* 35–59.

Neisser, U. (2003). New directions for flashbulb memories: Comments on the ACP Special Issue. *Applied Cognitive Psychology, 17,* 1149–1155.

Neisser, U. (2004). Memory development: New questions and old. *Developmental Review, 24,* 154–158.

Neisser, U., & Harsch, N. (1992). Phantom flashbulbs: False recollections of hearing the news about Challenger. In E. Winograd & U. Neisser (Eds.), *Affect and accuracy in recall: Studies of "flashbulb" memories* (pp. 9–31). Cambridge, UK: Cambridge University Press.

Nelson, C.A. (1995). The ontogeny of human memory: A cognitive neuroscience perspective. *Developmental Psychology, 31,* 723–738.

Nelson, K. (1991). *Toward an explanation of the development of autobiographical memory.*

Keynote address presented at the International Conference on Memory, Lancaster, July 1991.

Nelson, K. (2003). Self and social functions: Individual autobiographical memory and collective narrative. *Memory, 11*, 125–136.

Nelson, K., & Gruendel, J. (1986). Children's scripts. In K. Nelson (Ed.), *Event knowledge: Structure and function in development*. Hillsdale, NJ: Lawrence Erlbaum Associates, Inc.

Nigro, G., & Neisser, U. (1983). Point of view in personal memories. *Cognitive Psychology, 15*, 465–482.

Pasupathi, M. (2003). Emotional regulation during social remembering: Differences between emotional elicited during an event and emotions elicited when talking about it. *Memory, 11*, 151–163.

Pennebaker, J.W. (1997). *Opening up*. New York: Guilford Press.

Perner, J. (1992). Grasping the concept of representation—its impact on 4-year-olds theory of mind and beyond. *Human Development, 35*, 146–155.

Peterson, C. (2002). Children's long-term memory for autobiographical events. *Developmental Review, 22*, 370–402.

Peterson, C., & Whalen, N. (2001). Five years later: Children's memory for medical emergencies. *Applied Cognitive Psychology, 15*, 7–24.

Pezdck, K. (2003). Event memory and autobiographical memory for the events of September 11, 2001. *Applied Cognitive Psychology, 17*, 1033–1045.

Pillemer, D.B. (1992a). Remembering personal circumstances: A functional analysis. In E. Winograd & U. Neisser (Eds.), *Affect and accuracy in recall: Studies of "flashbulb memories"* (4th ed., pp. 236–264). New York: Cambridge University Press.

Pillemer, D.B. (1992b). Preschool children's memories of personal circumstances: The fire alarm study. In E. Winograd & U. Neisser (Eds.), *Affect and accuracy in recall: Studies of "flashbulb memories"*. Cambridge, UK: Cambridge University Press.

Pillemer, D.B. (1998). *Momentous events, vivid memories*. Cambridge, MA: Harvard University Press.

Pillemer, D.B. (2003). Directive functions of autobiographical memory: The power of the specific episode. *Memory, 11*, 193–202.

Pillemer, D.B., Picariello, M.L., Law, A.B., & Reichman, J.S. (1996). Memories of college: The importance of specific educational episodes. In D.C. Rubin (Ed.), *Remembering our past: Studies in autobiographical memory* (pp. 318–337). New York: Cambridge University Press.

Pillemer, D.B., Rhinehart, E.D., & White, S.H. (1986). Memory of life transitions: The first year in college. *Human Learning, 5*, 109–123.

Pillemer, D.B., & White, S.H. (1989). Childhood events recalled by children and adults. *Advances in Child Development and Behavior, 21*, 297–340.

Reiser, B.J., Black, J.B., & Abelson, R.P. (1985). Knowledge structures in the organisation and retrieval of autobiographical memories. *Cognitive Psychology, 17*, 89–137.

Robinson, J.A. (1976). Sampling autobiographical memory. *Cognitive Psychology, 8*, 578–595.

Robinson, J.A. (1986). Temporal reference systems and autobiographical memory. In D.C. Rubin (Ed.), *Autobiographical memory* (pp. 159–188). Cambridge, UK: Cambridge University Press.

Robinson, J.A. (1992). First experience memories: Contexts and function in personal histories. In M.A. Conway, D.C. Rubin, H. Spinnler, & W. Wagenaar (Eds.), *Theoretical perspectives on autobiographical memory* (pp. 223–239). Dordrecht, The Netherlands: Kluwer Academic Publishers.

Robinson, J.A., & Swanson, K.L. (1990). Autobiographical memory: The next phase. *Applied Cognitive Psychology, 4*, 321–335.

Robinson, J.A., & Swanson, K.L. (1993). Field and observer modes of remembering. *Memory, 1*, 169–184.

Röttger-Rössler, B. (1993). Autobiography in question: On self presentation and life description in an Indonesian society. *Anthropos, 88*, 365–373.

Rubin, D.C. (1982). On the retention function for autobiographical memory. *Journal of Verbal Learning and Verbal Behavior, 21*, 21–38.

Rubin, D.C., & Baddeley, A.D. (1989). Telescoping is not time compression: A model of the dating of autobiographical events. *Memory and Cognition, 17*, 653–661.

Rubin, D.C., & Berntsen, D. (2003). Life scripts help to maintain autobiographical memories of highly positive, but not highly negative, events. *Memory & Cognition, 31*, 1–14.

Rubin, D.C., & Kozin, M. (1984). Vivid memories. *Cognition, 16*, 81–95.

Rubin, D.C., Rahhal, T.A., & Poon, L.W. (1998). Things learned in early adulthood are remembered best. *Memory & Cognition, 26*, 3–19.

Rubin, D.C., Wetzler, S.E., & Nebes, R.D. (1986). Autobiographical memory across the life span. In D.C. Rubin (Ed.), *Autobiographical memory*. Cambridge, UK: Cambridge University Press.

Salmon, K., & Pipe, M.-E. (1997). Props and children's event reports: The impact of a 1-year delay. *Journal of Experimental Child Psychology, 65*, 261–292.

Schachtel, E.G. (1947). On memory and childhood amnesia. *Psychiatry, 10*, 1–26.

Schank, R.C. (1982a) *Dynamic memory*. Cambridge, UK: Cambridge University Press.

Schank, R.C. (1982b). Reminding and memory organization. In W.G. Lehnen & M.H. Ringle (Eds.), *Strategies for natural language processing*. Hillsdale, NJ: Lawrence Erlbaum Associates, Inc.

Schank, R.C., & Abelson, R.P. (1977). *Scripts, plans, goals and understanding*. Hillsdale, NJ: Lawrence Erlbaum Associates, Inc.

Schmidt, S.R., & Bohannon, J.N. (1988). In defense of the flashbulb memory hypothesis: A comment on McCloskey, Wible, & Cohen (1988). *Journal of Experimental Psychology: General, 117*, 332–335.

Schulkind, M.D., & Woldorf, G.M. (2005). Emotional organization of autobiographical memory, *Memory & Cognition, 33*, 1025–1035.

Scogin, F., Welsh, D., Hanson, A., Stump, J., & Coates, A. (2005). Evidence-based psycho-therapies for depression in older adult. *Clinical Psychology—Science and Practice, 12*, 222–237.

Sehulster, J.R. (1988). Broader perspectives on everyday memory. In M.M. Gruneberg, P.E. Morris, & R.N. Sykes (Eds.), *Practical aspects of memory: Current research and issues, Vol. 1.* (pp. 323–328). Chichester, UK: Wiley.

Sehulster, J.R. (1989). Content and temporal structure of autobiographical memory: Remembering 25 seasons of the Metropolitan Opera. *Memory and Cognition, 17*, 590–606.

Sheingold, K., & Tenney, Y.J. (1982). Memory for a salient childhood event. In U. Neisser (Ed.), *Memory observed: Remembering in natural contexts*. San Francisco, CA: Freeman.

Simcock, G., & Hayne, H. (2002). Breaking the barrier? Children fail to translate their preverbal memories into language. *Psychological Science, 13*, 225–231.

Singer, J.A., & Salovey, A.P. (1993). *The remembered self*. New York: The Free Press.

Skowronski, J.J., & Thompson, C.P. (1990). Reconstructing the dates of personal events: Gender differences in accuracy. *Applied Cognitive Psychology, 4*, 371–381.

Skowronski, J.J., Walker, W.R., & Betz, A.L. (2003). Ordering our world: An examination of time in autobiographical memory. *Memory, 11*, 247–260.

Smith, M.C., Bibi, U., & Sheard, D.E. (2003). Evidence for the differential impact of time and emotion on personal and event memories for September 11, 2001. *Applied Cognitive Psychology, 17*, 1047–1055.

Sutin, A.R., & Robins, R.W. (2005). Continuity and correlates of emotions and motives in self-defining memories. *Journal of Personality, 73*, 793–824.

Thompson, C.P., & Cowan, T. (1986). Flashbulb memories: A nicer interpretation of Neisser. *Cognition, 22,* 199–200.

Thomsen, D.K., & Berntsen, D. (2005). The end point effect in autobiographical memory: More than a calendar is needed. *Memory, 13,* 846–861.

Thorne, A. (1995). Developmental truths in memories of childhood and adolescence. *Journal of Personality, 63,* 138–163.

Thorne, A., McLean, K.C., & Lawrence, A.M. (2004). When remembering is not enough: Reflecting on self-defining memories in late adolescence. *Journal of Personality, 72,* 513–542.

Tulving, E. (1972). Episodic and semantic memory. In E. Tulving & W. Donaldson (Eds.), *Organisation of memory.* New York: Academic Press.

Tulving E. (1983). *Elements of episodic memory.* Oxford, UK: Oxford University Press.

Tulving, E. (1985). Memory and consciousness. *Canadian Psychologist, 26,* 1–12.

Usher, J.A., & Neisser, U. (1993). Childhood amnesia and the beginnings of memory for four early life events. *Journal of Experimental Psychology: General, 122,* 155–165.

Wade, K.A., & Garry, M. (2005). Strategies for verifying false autobiographical memories. *American Journal of Psychology, 118,* 587–602.

Wagenaar, W.A. (1986). My memory: A study of autobiographical memory over six years. *Cognitive Psychology, 18,* 225–252.

Wagenaar, W.A., & Groeneweg, J. (1990). The memory of concentration camp survivors. *Applied Cognitive Psychology, 4,* 77–87.

Wang, Q. (2001). Cultural effects on adults' earliest childhood recollection and self-description: Implications for the relation between memory and the self. *Journal of Personality and Social Psychology, 81,* 220–233.

Wang, Q. (2003). Infantile amnesia reconsidered: A cross-cultural analysis. *Memory, 11,* 65–80.

Wang, Q. (2006). Earliest recollections of self and others in European American and Taiwanese young adults. *Psychological Science, 17,* 708–714.

Wang, Q., & Brockmeier, J. (2002). Autobiographical remembering as cultural practice: Understanding the interplay between memory, self and culture. *Culture & Psychology, 8,* 45–64.

Wang, Q., & Conway, M.A. (2004). The stories we keep: Autobiographical memory in American and Chinese middle-aged adults. *Journal of Personality, 72,* 911–938.

Weintraub, K.J. (1978). *The value of the individual: Self and circumstance in autobiography.* Chicago: University of Chicago Press.

Welch-Ross, M.K. (1995). An integrative model of the development of autobiographical memory. *Developmental Review, 15,* 338–365.

Wetzler, S.E., & Sweeney, J.A. (1986). Childhood amnesia: An empirical demonstration. In D.C. Rubin (Ed.), *Autobiographical memory.* Cambridge, UK: Cambridge University Press.

White, S.H., & Pillemer, D.B. (1979). Childhood amnesia and the development of a socially accessible memory system. In J.F. Kihlstrom & F.J. Evans (Eds.), *Functional disorders of memory.* Hillsdale NJ: Lawrence Erlbaum Associates, Inc.

Whitten, W.B., & Leonard, J.M. (1981). Directed search through autobiographical memory. *Memory & Cognition, 9,* 566–579.

Wilson, A.E., & Ross, M. (2003). The identity function of autobiographical memory: Time is on our side. *Memory, 11,* 137–149.

Winograd, E., & Killinger, W.A. (1983). Relating age at encoding in early childhood to adult recall: Development of flashbulb memories. *Journal of Experimental Psychology: General, 112,* 413–422.

Woods, B., Spector, A., Jones, C., Orrell, M., & Davies, S. (2005). Reminiscence therapy for dementia. *The Cochrane Database of Systematic Reviews,* Issue 2. Art. No.: CD001120.pub2. DOI: 10.1002/14651858.CD001120.pub2.

Wright, D.B. (1993). Recall of the Hillsborough disaster over time: Systematic biases of "flashbulb" memories. *Applied Cognitive Psychology, 7,* 129–138.

Yarmey, A.D., & Bull, M.P. (1978). Where were you when President Kennedy was assassinated? *Bulletin of the Psychonomic Society, 11,* 133–135.

Zacks, J., Tversky, B., & Iyer, G. (2001). Perceiving, remembering, and communicating structure in events. *Journal of Experimental Psychology: General, 130,* 29–58.

3 Eyewitness memory

Daniel B. Wright and Elizabeth F. Loftus

In the typical laboratory-based memory study, there are few consequences if the participants erroneously report what they have previously experienced. This is in sharp contrast to the consequences that memory errors can have in the real world. Eyewitness memory is not always accurate and errant identifications can lead investigations in wrong directions, can lead to guilty people remaining free, and can lead to innocent people being incarcerated—even on death row. In this chapter we describe how the dominant metaphor for memory used by people in general, and jurors in particular, namely that memory works like a videotape recorder, is wrong. Moreover people have other misconceptions about memory that they sometimes use to judge the eyewitness testimony that they hear in court cases. We review four areas of active research that highlight some errors of eyewitness memory.

THE FALLIBILITY OF EYEWITNESS MEMORY

Memory is an important aspect of human life. Memory of past events interacts with our present behaviours and thoughts to allow us to navigate through the present and plan for the future (Abelson, 1981). We rely on memory and take it for granted. We believe in our memories and we have to; otherwise we would have difficulty in everyday life. This leads us, as human beings, to assume that memories are always accurate. But research has shown that useful as memory sometimes is, it is far from perfect. We make many small errors all the time, and typically we do not notice them. Most errors are of no consequence, but sometimes errors occur in important situations, like a witness to a crime reporting erroneous information or identifying an innocent suspect. In these situations, even small errors can be crucial. That erroneous memory can have grave consequences has been revealed in recent years as DNA technology has shown that many individuals have been convicted of crimes they did not commit (Scheck, Neufeld, & Dwyer, 2003). Some of these people were on death row (e.g., Junkin, 2004).

The DNA cases are just a tip of the iceberg of miscarriages of justice for two reasons. First, only certain types of crime, like rape, tend to leave biological markers suitable for DNA analysis. Second, even when there is a biological marker, many defendants do not have access to DNA or the DNA has not been handled adequately. Scheck, Neufeld and Dwyer, and their colleagues involved with the *Innocence Project*, have made numerous recommendations for making DNA evidence more available (see http://www.innocenceproject.com/). As of April 13 2006, 175 people have been exonerated. These individuals, along with the amount of time each spent in prison, are shown in Figure 3.1. The innocence website provides further details of each of these tragic cases. Scheck and colleagues have argued that DNA exoneration could be a daily activity if access to DNA testing was routine, and they have been pushing for more access to DNA evidence. In the UK there are several "innocence" projects (see www.innocencenetwork.org) and many high-profile convictions which have been overturned on appeal (for example, see "Books" link on http://www.innocent.org.uk/). These high profile cases are just a small proportion of the all miscarriages of justice (Naughton, 2003).

To discover the cause of faulty convictions, Scheck and colleagues examined the evidence presented in these cases. In more than two-thirds of cases eyewitness evidence was involved and in most of the cases it was the primary evidence (Scheck et al., 2003, p. 365). Gross, Jacoby, Matheson, Montgomery, and Patil (2005) have examined exonerations from DNA evidence but also cases overturned by other

1–3	4–6	7–9	10–12	13–15	16–18	19–21	22–24	25–27
				Toney				
				Webb				
				Bauer				
				Mitchell				
			Dotson	Holdren				
			Linscott	Sarsfield				
			Kotler	Watkins				
			Daye	Youngblood				
			Honaker	Lavernia				
			Bullock	Robinson				
			Shepard	Smith				
			Cotton	Ochoa				
			Cruz	Washington	Green			
			Hernandez	Velasquez	Adams			
			Smith	Green	Rainge			
		Nelson	Jimerson	Bradford	Williams			
		Dabbs	Ortiz	Ollins	Johnson			
		Snyder	Byrd	Ollins	Abdal			
		Bloodsworth	Miller	Saunders	Charles	Gray		
	Vasquez	Scruggs	Mahan	Pierce	Butler	Brown		
	Woodall	Chalmers	Mahan	Pope	Washington	Townsend		
	Jones	O'DellHarris	Williamson	Thomas	Nesmith	Jean		
	Callace	Davis	Fritz	McSherry	Waters	Anderson		
	Brison	Davis	Jones	Webb	Fain	Mayes		
	Alejandro	Moto	Richardson	Godschalk	Johnson	Webster		
	Johnson	Webb	Atkins	McGee	Lloyd	Maher		
	Saecker	Mitchell	Miller	Bromgard	Sutherlin	Lowery		
	Durham	Reynolds	Criner	Echols	Bibbins	Willis		
	Hicks	Wardell	Danziger	Scott	Erby	Scott		
	Salazar	Gray	Krone	Avery	Avery	Charles	McMillan	
Green	Willis	Gregory	Dominguez	McCray	Laughman	Yarris	Gray	
DiazBravo	Cromedy	Dixon	Johnson	Richardson	Harrison	Hunt	Ruffin	
Piszczek	Reid	Gonzalez	Mercer	Salaam	Goodman	Good	Dedge	
Villasana	Cowans	Wyniemko	Holland	Santana	Moon	Brown	Whitfield	Evans
O'Donnell	Sutton	Jones	Powell	Wise	Booker	Woods	Williams	Terry
Alexander	Matthews	Rose	Rollins	Kordonowy	Rodriguez	Doswell	Waters	Diaz

Years in prison

Figure 3.1 The names of the first 163 people exonerated by DNA evidence and how many years each spent in prison for a crime they did not commit. Data from www.innocenceproject.com, October 25 2005.

means. They also found that erroneous eyewitness testimony, sometimes deliberate, is the most common evidence in these exonerations. This is particularly true for rape cases compared with murder cases, but they note that in murder cases there is often no eyewitness. Gross et al. describe how eyewitness identifications for rape victims should be more reliable than identifications for victims of more common crimes, like robbery, for which DNA evidence is seldom available. Therefore, the number of innocent people in prison is likely to be much larger than the number exonerated. In general, these analyses show that erroneous eyewitness testimony is the leading cause of wrongful conviction. Even prior to the DNA exoneration cases, it was clear to many that faulty eyewitness memory was "the greatest single cause of wrongful convictions" (Bailey & Aronson, 1971, p. 36). Bailey described how it is the mismatch between jurors' beliefs in the reliability of eyewitness memory and its true reliability that has caused the greatest problems.

How common is it for an eyewitness to be mistaken? The DNA cases, being the tip of an iceberg, cannot reveal this, but surveys of identifications in actual cases suggest it often occurs. There have been several surveys of identification parades in both the US and UK (Behrman & Davey, 2001; Slater, 1994; Tollestrup, Turtle, & Yuille, 1994; Valentine, Pickering, & Darling, 2003; Wright & McDaid, 1996). These surveys show a similar pattern. About 40% of the time no one is picked. About 20% of the time a filler (an innocent person chosen to stand with the suspect) is picked. About 40% of the time the suspect is picked. Different types of error can occur in these situations. When no one is picked this may mean that a guilty suspect is let go. When a filler is picked, this means that a guilty suspect may also be let go, but the filler is not charged.[1] However, the fact that a substantial proportion of eyewitnesses pick an innocent filler shows that many make mistaken identifications. An innocent suspect is arguably in a similar situation to an innocent filler, and therefore the 20% figure suggests that some innocent suspects are also identified. To calculate what proportion of chosen suspects are in fact innocent requires many assumptions, so the estimates should only be seen as approximate. Penrod (2003) estimates that when suspects are identified, about 15% of the time they are in fact innocent. If these estimates are all accurate, this suggests that about 40% of all identifications are errors. Penrod argues that if eyewitness testimony as a new kind of evidence, it would be difficult for prosecutors to argue that it was reliable enough to meet the stringent rules of evidence to be admissible.

One reason that memory errors are problematic is because people are unaware of memory problems when they judge the likely accuracy of a memory account to which they are listening. Several researchers have asked members of the public, students, law enforcement officers, therapists, etc. about their lay theories of human memory (for example, Benton, Ross, Bradshaw, Thomas, & Bradshaw, 2006). Many potential jurors believe a memory for every event is permanently stored in the mind, and remembering is simply finding where that accurate memory lies (Garry, Loftus, Brown, & DuBreuil, 1997). This folk theory of memory, which Neisser (1967) calls the *reappearance hypothesis*, is one that dominated much of the last century. It is one of many possible metaphors that people have for memory (Draaisma, 2000; Roediger, 1980), but for decades memory researchers have argued against this metaphor. For

---

1 There are exceptions. See http://www.psychology.iastate.edu/faculty/gwells/FillerCharged.htm accessed 28.01.2005.

example: "Some widely held views have to be completely discarded, and none more completely than that which treats recall as the reexcitement in some way of fixed and changeless 'traces'" (Bartlett, 1932, p. vi). Research, inspired in part by disputed cases involving eyewitness testimony, has shown that memories do not sit idly by waiting to reappear but are dynamic and malleable processes (Loftus, 1979). Because most people believe memories are indelible sources of information, jurors assign too much weight to them when making judgments about the guilt of defendants.

For example, Loftus (1974) gave participants a crime scenario where a man robbed a grocery shop and shot two people dead. There was some incriminating evidence, but not a large amount. When presented with this evidence, 18% of participants rendered a guilty verdict. For a second group of 50 participants, Loftus added the information that a store clerk saw the culprit and identified the suspect. Guilty verdicts were given by 72% of participants. Thus, there were four times more guilty verdicts when eyewitness testimony was present. Further, the participants seemed uncritical about how reliable the eyewitness was. Another group of 50 participants were told that the eyewitness had very poor vision. Even with the vision difficulty, 68% of participants rendered a guilty verdict. Research shows that potential jurors are impressed with eyewitness testimony and often have difficulty evaluating its reliability. This is one of the main reasons for allowing expert testimony on the topic. An alternative to expert testimony is having the judge explain the reliability of memory to the jury. However, Wise and Safer (2004) tested judges in the US and found that the judge's knowledge about how memory works was inaccurate in several areas. In the next section we discuss four areas of active research about eyewitness memory. Eyewitness memory research is one of the largest areas of applied cognitive research and therefore our review is selective. For more detailed coverage see papers in Toglia, Read, Ross, & Lindsay (2006).

SITUATIONS AFFECTING THE RELIABILITY OF EYEWITNESS TESTIMONY

Post-event information

The malleability of memory can be demonstrated by showing participants a video or slide show and then presenting them with misleading post-event information. For 30 years researchers have used this method to show that memories can be distorted, created, and even made less accessible by information presented after a person sees an event (Loftus, 2005). One early demonstration involved participants who watched films of traffic accidents (Loftus & Palmer, 1974, Exp. 2). Some of the participants were asked to estimate the speed of the automobiles when they "hit" and others were asked to estimate the speed when they "smashed". The participants given the verb "smashed" provided higher speed estimates than the "hit" participants. Further, when asked if there was shattered glass at the scene of the crash, only 14% of those in the "hit" condition errantly remembered shattered glass compared with 32% of those in the "smashed" condition who remembered nonexistent glass.

Biasing questions like the hit/smashed example show one way in which post-event information can subtly become part of a person's memory. Other examples include: asking if an eyewitness saw *the* gun a person was carrying, because it suggests there was a gun; verbal utterances after the eyewitness answers, like: "are you sure?" and "thank you"; and many nonverbal responses like smiling or nodding when the eyewitness answers in a way that confirms the questioner's beliefs. There is much work on how nonverbal communication can influence how both humans and other animals answer questions. Consider the following example: Around the turn of the 19th century, Clever Hans, a horse, was able to answer a variety of questions correctly by tapping with his hoof (see papers in Sebeok & Rosenthal, 1981). Clever Hans was able to pick up subtle cues—movements of 1 millimetre—from the person asking the questions, which indicated whether the number of hoof taps were correct. Hans could only give correct answers when someone present knew the answer. Orne (1981) and Rosenthal (1981) compared the Clever Hans effect with the demand characteristics and expectancy effects shown in psychology experiments with human participants, where humans both consciously and unconsciously provide others with the responses that they want or expect. Given Clever Hans' achievements, it is easy to understand how humans can pick up on the beliefs and desires of a police investigator, and therefore provide biased responses. The explanation for the remarkable behaviour of Clever Hans was only found through double-blind experiments. This is why recent guidelines in the US advocate that the police investigators in charge of identification parades do not know which person is the suspect (Technical Working Group for Eyewitness Evidence, 1999). In the UK the person conducting the identification parade usually knows who the suspect is (see Kebbell, 2000, for how the UK matches up with the US guidelines).

One of the most common ways for witnesses to encounter misinformation is when talking with other eyewitnesses (Paterson & Kemp, 2006). For example, in the Oklahoma bombing, Timothy McVeigh rented the truck that he used in the tragedy. CCTV and the taxi driver who dropped him off indicated that he was alone. Three people from the truck rental shop saw him. Two of them initially did not recall other individuals accompanying McVeigh. The third person gave a good description of McVeigh, but also recalled him with another person. After discussion with his co-workers, his recollection spread into their memories. The other two people soon recalled an accomplice and one of the biggest manhunts in US history began. The FBI now believe McVeigh was alone when he rented the truck (Memon & Wright, 1999; Schacter, 2001; Wright, Self, & Justice, 2000).

The Oklahoma bombing case and numerous other incidents prove that misleading post-event information can distort other people's memories. From a forensic perspective, three important questions are: How can the justice system limit eyewitnesses exposure to misleading post-event information? Are there situations in which eyewitnesses may be particularly prone to accepting this information? How should the legal system treat a memory that has been exposed to post-event information?

For the first question, it is important to avoid biasing questions and not to lead the witness. The cognitive interview (Fisher & Geiselman, 1992) is a technique developed for police interviews and is widely used in both the UK and the US. It involves many different facets, including the avoidance of direct and biasing questions. Overall it increases the amount of accurate information, but it also sometimes increases the amount of inaccurate information (Koehnken, Milne, Memon, & Bull, 1999). While there are disagreements about the value of some of the individual facets of the cognitive interview, all concerned agree it is best to avoid biasing questions. However, this is not simple. While some interviews are clearly bad, even when interviewers do a very good job trying to avoid biasing questions, it can be difficult to avoid having some biased questions over the course of a long interview. Sometimes a biasing question may not be for a particularly important issue, but sometimes it may be. It is often necessary to look back at interviews and the language used for specific questions. Therefore, it is important to video interviews. Subtle cues, as in the case of Clever Hans, will be more difficult to identify. After all, numerous people watched Hans perform mathematics and were not able to detect the subtle cues from the questioners. The ideal solution would be that interviewers should not have knowledge about the case. While this can and should be done with identification parades, it may be difficult to implement for many interviews.

The second question is: Which situations increase the likelihood that the post-event information will distort people's memories? There are studies of individual differences; for example, very young and very old people tend to be more suggestible (Ceci & Bruck, 1993; Cohen & Faulkner, 1989), as do people who score high on measures of dissociation (see papers in Read & Winograd, 1998). There is currently much valuable research trying to identify what moderates how suggestible people are to misleading post-event information, often called the misinformation effect.

Finally, if it is known that a witness has encountered post-event information or has heard another eyewitness account, it is important for the justice system to realise that the report is no longer independent. Over a quarter of the first 74 DNA exonerations involved multiple eyewitnesses identifying an innocent suspect. It is not clear how many of these eyewitnesses spoke with each other prior to the identification (or received input about other identifications), but if Paterson and Kemp's (2006) findings generalise to these cases, it is likely that many of them did, and therefore one person's faulty memory could have affected others. It is important to look at the questioning of eyewitnesses and to ask if they could have received information about the case from other sources. When witnesses talk with each other the evidence they produce should not be treated as independent (Gabbert, Memon, & Wright, 2006).

The fate of the original memory

When people are misled by false post-event information, what has happened to the original memory? Numerous researchers have asked this question and proposed different possibilities. It is clear in certain circumstances that each of these explanations accounts for some of the data. The main explanations are:

1   *The vacant slot* explanation states that when the original information is not encoded, which is bound to happen in many cases, the misinformation will be accepted because there is no information that contradicts it.
2   *The coexistence* explanation states that separate memory representations exist for both the original and the post-event information. Participants will sometimes choose the post-event information because: (a) they believe that they are supposed to (*demand characteristics*); (b) their memory for the post-event information is more accessible so they believe that version must be correct (*memory strength*); and (c) they incorrectly believe that the post-event information was shown in the original presentation (*source misattribution*).

3 *The blend* explanation states that the resulting memory is a combination of the two. In an extreme version the post-event information could overwrite the original information (*substitution*).

4 *The response bias* explanation points out that many of the methods used to study the effects of post-event information bias the participant towards reporting the misinformation. This explanation was originally put forward in McCloskey and Zaragoza (1985), and while subsequent research has shown that response bias cannot account for all responding, it is important that researchers consider their methods carefully.

Researchers are no longer looking for any single account of the misinformation effect, but for the situations in which each of these explanations is most likely to occur.

Duration estimation

A young woman was alone in the bedroom of her Newcastle flat. Unaware that she was home, a male intruder burst into her room, saw her, and fled. The police investigator asked the woman how long the intruder was in the room. This is important because the longer the intruder was present, the longer the eyewitness has to see him, and this relates to how reliable the memory is. She said it was about 10 seconds. Does this seem reasonable? Are people generally good about saying how long something takes? Would the 10-second estimate have seemed more reasonable if we had said: "A male intruder walked into her room, looked around and saw her, and then went out of the room"? These are the kind of questions that are important in an eyewitness context. In this particular case, the woman identified a suspect. The case was brought to trial but the charges were dropped, partially because of a report on the reliability of eyewitness memory when only a brief glance at the culprit could be made. Thus, the 10-second estimate was critical.

Ten seconds is a long time. If an intruder went into a room, saw another person and left as quickly as possible, this would take only a few seconds. When questioning an eyewitness, a barrister could ask: "So, you say you saw the culprit for about [*PAUSE* for 10 seconds] this long?" A 10-second silence will seem long and the eyewitness will often say that it was not for that long, and that "10 seconds" just meant a short time. This illustrates several different aspects of duration estimation that we will discuss.[2]

First and foremost, duration estimations are often inaccurate (e.g., Loftus, Schooler, Boone, & Kline, 1987; Memon, Hope, & Bull, 2003). To see how systematic the distortions can be, consider a study that asked students to estimate the duration of an unexpected event. When one of us was lecturing, a student ran in and yelled: "I'm sick and tired of psychology, it's boring, you're boring, it's all boring." The lecturer asked him to calm down and then the student grabbed the lecturer's

---

2 We are just discussing retrospective duration estimation. There is a large field of social and organisational psychology concerned with prospective duration estimation, estimating how long it will take to complete a task.

briefcase and ran out the door with the lecturer chasing him. From the time the student entered the lecture hall to when the lecturer left the hall, 19.8 seconds elapsed. Students were asked to estimate how long the person was in the room. The mean estimate was over 30 seconds and more than 10% of students said that the incident lasted more than 1 minute (Pedersen & Wright, 2002). People often overestimate the duration of brief events.

To understand why people often given unreliable temporal estimates it is necessary to look at how people perceive elapsed time and how they estimate magnitudes generally. Time can be described in many different ways (Fraser, 1987). Calendar and clock time are society's creations and, while they map onto some regularities that we experience, for example the diurnal cycle and our heart rates, they do not map perfectly onto how we experience time. The amount of information that we are experiencing and physiological changes can both affect how we estimate time. If we experience more information, like more notes in a musical piece, we remember the duration as being longer (Ornstein, 1969).[3] People often use the number of events that they remember as a crude measure for the amount of time elapsed. Physiological changes include giving drugs to affect people's internal clocks and this has the predicted effect on temporal judgments.

The way that people remember events is also important for how duration estimates are constructed. At the beginning of this section we described an intruder entering a room.

> *A male intruder burst into her room, saw her, and fled*

The words used here suggest rapid movement. While factually equivalent, if we had said:

> *A male intruder walked into her room, looked around and saw her, and then went out of the room*

the wording suggests a slower tempo, and therefore this suggests that the intruder was in the room for a longer time. Burt (1992, 1993; Burt & Popple, 1996) has done a series of studies that show how describing an event using words that imply rapid speed is related to duration estimates: the faster the implied speed, the shorter the duration. Burt relates these findings to the post-event information effect and, in a same way as the advice given for post-event information more generally, it is important to avoid biasing questions for temporal estimates.

In summary, estimating how long something took to happen is a difficult task. Mapping psychological time onto clock and calendar time is a very recent requirement in our evolution and we are poor at these tasks. Therefore, it is necessary to be cautious accepting temporal estimates as necessarily accurate. It is worth asking eyewitnesses how they made their estimates.

---

3 This is different from concurrent duration estimation: How long something seems to take while it is being experienced. Periods without much information, like a 10-second pause in a barrister's question, seem longer than periods with much information.

Own-race bias

In 33 of the first 74 DNA exonerations where mistaken identity was an issue, a white eyewitness wrongly identified a black suspect (Scheck et al., 2003, p. 366; for details on one of the cases see http://www.pbs.org/wgbh/pages/frontline/shows/dna/ accessed April 13 2006). Research has found that in general people have more difficulty recognising faces of strangers from other races than faces of people from their own race (Meissner & Brigham, 2001). This is called the *own-race bias* (ORB), sometimes referred to as the phenomenon of cross-racial identification. Despite this being a robust phenomenon that has been observed for decades, there is still disagreement about why it occurs. The different possibilities include: people have more contact with others of their own race and therefore have become "experts" recognising these races; race is a particular feature or dimension used in representing faces and the salience of this dimension is different for other race faces; people pay more attention to own-race faces, etc. Most of the explanations are not exclusive, and all should be viewed within the societal context where racism and segregation still exist.

The basic finding, that people are better at recognising faces of their own race, is well documented. Ninety per cent of eyewitness testimony experts questioned by Kassin, Tubb, Hosch, and Memon (2001) thought it was sufficiently reliable for expert testimony. From a legal standpoint, an important question is how much better people are at recognising faces of their own race. The *Daubert* criteria, which are the criteria judges in the US have for deciding whether an expert is allowed to testify on a particular topic, suggest that knowing the error rate is important for admitting expert testimony. It is important to look at the different rescarch procedures used in order to gauge the size of the effect.

The most common procedure used to study ORB involves showing participants a sct of face photographs of people from different races and then showing them a much larger set and asking participants whether they were previously shown each of these faces. These studies are useful for understanding the effect, but lack ecological validity because these situations are atypical of those encountered by eyewitnesses. In particular, participants are aware that they are in a study and that they should attend to all the faces that they are shown. Researchers have also looked at actual cases. As these are real cases, this procedure has more ecological validity, but it is more difficult to make causal attributions because it is not possible to know whether eyewitnesses are in similar situations when viewing a culprit from another race as when viewing a culprit from the same race. A compromise between these approaches is conducting field experiments where a confederate interacts with people of different races, and then a researcher tells the people that they are in a study and asks them to make an identification. Because of ethical concerns, only fairly benign interactions between the participant and the to-be-identified person have been used, and thus one could question whether the same results would occur with more violent or upsetting interactions. Nonetheless, the body of work in this area shows that ORB is a robust phenomenon, occurring with a wide variety of procedures.

Meissner and Brigham (2001) have done a meta-analysis of the laboratory studies. They observed that the odds of correctly identifying a photograph as being previously shown were 1.4 times higher if the photograph subject was of the same race as the participant than if the photograph subject was of a different race. This means that for every correct identification of somebody from another race, you would expect 1.4 correct own-race identifications, a fairly large difference. Similarly, the odds of falsely identifying a photograph of someone from another race were 1.6 times higher than for own-race identifications.

Valentine et al. (2003, Table 12) compared own- and cross-race identifications using actual parades in London. One difficulty in making conclusions from real identifications is not knowing whether the suspect is, in fact, the culprit. The police often treat suspect identifications as "correct". From Penrod's (2003) analysis, approximately 85% of the time when a suspect is identified, the suspect is the culprit, so one could infer that most of these are correct. The odds for suspect identifications was 1.4 times higher for own-race identifications than for cross-race identifications. Cross-race parades were more likely to produce filler identifications and no identifications.

Finally, Wright, Boyd, and Tredoux (2001) conducted a field experiment where either a black or a white confederate approached either a black or a white participant in shopping centres in England and South Africa. The confederate asked a couple of questions such as where the cinema was. Two minutes later a research assistant approached the participant, explained the purpose of the study, and asked them to make an identification. They found the odds of a correct identification were about 3 times more likely for own-race identifications than for cross-race identifications. They also found that the odds of filler identification were about 1.7 times higher for cross-race identifications. These are higher estimates than Meissner and Brigham found. There are several possible explanations: One is that the laboratory studies underestimate the size of the effect because they do not take into account that people may pay more attention to others during own-race interactions than during cross-race interactions. This deserves further research.

The own-race bias is well established, but it appears that it might not be the only own-group bias. Both own-age and own-gender memory recognition biases have been observed. For example, Wright and Stroud (2002) showed both young (18–33-year-olds) and middle-aged (35–55-year-olds) people videos of simulated crimes where the culprit was in one of these two age bands. They found that people were more accurate at picking the culprit from a parade if they were in the same age group as the culprit. Similarly, there appears to be an own-gender bias, where people have better memory for those of their own gender. This may seem counterintuitive in our predominantly heterosexual society, but from an evolutionary standpoint it may be better to have good memory for the large number of sexual competitors than the smaller number of sexual mates (Wright & Sladden, 2003).

The justice system can take into account own-race bias in two ways. First, police investigators, judges, and jurors could be warned that cross-race identifications tend to be less reliable than own-race identifications. However, they should be warned about the size of the effects so that they do not assume that all cross-race identifications are wrong and that all own-race identifications are accurate. The odds of an accurate identification is about two times higher for own-race than for other-race identifications. Second, when constructing identification parades, police could put extra safeguards in for cross-race identifications (see Wells & Olson, 2001, for details). This might include using extra fillers with cross-race parades and being particularly careful about the selection of fillers when the suspect is from a different race from the people constructing the parade (which was one of the original reasons for establishing identification suites in the UK, see Wright & McDaid, 1996). More research is necessary to see if these recommendations should also apply to other own-group biases.

Changes in identification parades

The traditional identification parade (called a lineup in the US) involves the eyewitness looking at several people, including the suspect, at the same time. The guidelines in the UK for how to conduct these parades are part of the Police and Criminal Evidence Act, or PACE, have been in place for several decades, and continue to evolve as a function of advances in memory research, changes in law, and advances in technology. Current guidelines are available on http://police.homeoffice. gov.uk/operational-policing/powers-pace-codes/pace-codes.html (accessed February 16 2006). Similarly, guidelines have been produced in the US for conducting parades there (available from http://www.ncjrs.org/pdffiles1/nij/178240.pdf, accessed February 16 2006).

Research about identification parades can be divided into examining how structural changes to the procedure affect performance and if there are any ways to differentiate accurate from inaccurate identifications. These are often called system and estimator variables, respectively (Wells, 1978). The police guidelines tend to focus on the structural changes and that will be the focus here. The main findings with respect to estimator variables are that people tend to be more accurate if they make a rapid identification and there is a moderate positive relationship between identification accuracy and how well the person thinks they have performed (Wells & Olson, 2003; Wright & Skagerberg, 2007). There have been two main changes in the UK in the past few decades with respect to system variables. The first was a move from conducting parades in different police stations to conducting them in specialised identification suites (Wright & McDaid, 1996). Not only did this ensure greater uniformity in how the parades were conducted, but it greatly eased the administrative burden because they were more efficient. For example, they kept lists of people and their descriptions so they could arrange parades with more ease than police stations, and many of the buildings were physically designed for parades so that it was possible to keep separate suspects, eyewitnesses, and fillers, and to film the procedures.

The second major change in the way UK parades are conducted is that video parades are now used (Valentine et al., 2003). Rather than having to arrange to get fillers for every parade, video images of people can be downloaded from a system containing tens of thousands of images. The images show the people looking towards the camera, turning left, and turning right. The police at the suites put together a video parade, which can then be shown to eyewitnesses whenever they can make it to the suite. The practical advantages to this system are immense for police operations. Initial research comparing live parades and video parades (Valentine & Heaton, 1999) suggested that video parades produced fairer parades, and this led the government to urge suites to use videos. Given the practical advantages, there are virtually no live parades in the UK any more.

The change to video parades brings with it a major structural change. With a live parade, eyewitnesses view all the people in the parade simultaneously. Lindsay and Wells (1985) have argued that this can make the task like a forced-choice problem, where the eyewitness may try to choose the person who looks most like how they remember the culprit. This may be all right if the suspect is the culprit, because they should look most like themselves, but it is not if the suspect is innocent and happens to look more like the culprit than any of the other people. Because of that Lindsay and Wells have argued that sequential parades should be used, where the eyewitness views each person individually and either says that person is or is not the culprit. If the eyewitness says the person is not the culprit the next person is shown, but if the eyewitness identifies the person the parade ends. According to Lindsay and Wells, sequential lineups require the eyewitness to make absolute judgements about each person rather than relative judgements. Sequential lineup procedures are being adopted in many US jurisdictions, but the procedure remains controversial (McQuiston-Surrett, Malpass, & Tredoux, 2006). The UK video parades have one element of the sequential lineup, that the people are viewed individually, but in the UK the eyewitness has to look at all the people in the parade at least twice, so it is not a pure sequential lineup.

The combination of specialist suites and the technology of video parades have meant that UK identification parades have changed greatly over the past 20 years and continue to improve as more basic and evaluative research is conducted.

CONCLUSIONS

The primary cause of false convictions is faulty eyewitness memory. We examined four ways in which memory can be erroneous. First, while memory may seem to be about a single past event, how that memory is constructed is based both on how it is reconstructed in the present and also on experiences of similar events between encoding and retrieval. Second, duration estimates are often poor. People use different strategies to estimate time, so it is important to ask how they constructed their estimates and, if possible, provide them with strategies to help accurate construction. Third, own-race bias is a problem in many eyewitness cases: People are better at recognising individuals of their own race, and this appears true for other groups also (e.g., age, gender). Finally, there have been important procedural changes in UK identification parades, and strides continue to be made to lessen the chance of false identifications and increase the chance of culprit identifications.

For certain types of case, DNA evidence is making the justice system more reliable. However, because all culprits do not leave biological markers and in many cases the identity is not an issue, DNA is not a panacea for miscarriages of justice. Certain types of police investigation and certain types of case rely on human memory, even with all its imperfections. It is vital that psychologists helped to inform police investigators, jurors, and judges about the malleability of memory, and advice on how to make memories more reliable.

REFERENCES

Abelson, R.P. (1981). Psychological status of the script concept. *American Psychologist, 36,* 715–729.
Bailey, F.L., & Aronson, H. (1971). *The defense never rests.* New York: Stein & Day.
Bartlett, F.C. (1932). *Remembering: A study in experimental and social psychology.* Cambridge, UK: Cambridge University Press.

Behrman, B.W., & Davey, S.L. (2001). Eyewitness identification in actual criminal cases: An archival analysis. *Law and Human Behavior, 25,* 475–491.

Benton, T.R., Ross, D.F., Bradshaw, E., Thomas, W.N., & Bradshaw, G.S. (2006). Eyewitness memory is still not common sense: Comparing jurors, judges and law enforcement to eyewitness experts. *Applied Cognitive Psychology, 20,* 115–129.

Burt, C.D.B. (1992). Reconstruction of the duration of autobiographical events. *Memory & Cognition, 20,* 124–132.

Burt, C.D.B. (1993). The effect of actual event duration and event memory on the reconstruction of duration information. *Applied Cognitive Psychology, 7,* 63–73.

Burt, C.D.B., & Popple, J.S. (1996). Effects of implied action speed on estimation of event duration. *Applied Cognitive Psychology, 10,* 53–63.

Ceci, S.J., & Bruck, M. (1993). The suggestibility of children's recollections: An historical review and synthesis. *Psychological Bulletin, 113,* 403–439.

Cohen, G., & Faulkner, D. (1989). Age differences in source forgetting: Effects on reality monitoring and on eyewitness testimony. *Psychology & Aging, 4,* 10–17.

Draaisma, D. (2000). *Metaphors of memory.* Cambridge, UK: Cambridge University Press.

Fisher, R.P., & Geiselman, R.E. (1992). *Memory enhancing techniques for investigative interviewing: The Cognitive Interview.* Springfield, IL: C.C. Thomas.

Fraser, J.T. (1987). *Time, the familiar stranger.* Amherst, MA: University of Massachusetts Press.

Gabbert, F., Memon, A., & Wright, D.B. (2006). Memory conformity: Disentangling the steps towards influence during a discussion. *Psychonomic Bulletin & Review, 13,* 480–485.

Garry, M., Loftus, E.F., Brown, S.W., & DuBreuil, S.C. (1997). Womb with a view: Memory beliefs and memory-work experiences. In D.G. Payne & F.G. Conrad (Eds.), *Intersections in basic and applied memory research* (pp. 233–255). Mahwah, NJ: Lawrence Erlbaum Associates, Inc.

Gross, S.R., Jacoby, K., Matheson, D.J., Montgomery, N., & Patil, S. (2005). Exonerations in the United States, 1989 through 2003. *Journal of Criminal Law and Criminology, 95,* 523–560.

Junkin, T. (2004). *Bloodsworth: The true story of the first death row inmate exonerated by DNA.* Chapel Hill, NC: Algonquin Books.

Kassin, S.M., Tubb, V.A., Hosch, H.M., & Memon, A. (2001). On the general acceptance of eyewitness testimony research: A new survey of the experts. *American Psychologist, 56,* 405–416.

Kebbell, M.R. (2000). The law concerning the conduct of lineups in England and Wales: How well does it satisfy the recommendations of the American Psychology-Law Society? *Law and Human Behavior, 24,* 309–315.

Koehnken, G., Milne, R. Memon, A., & Bull, R. (1999). A meta-analysis on the effects of the cognitive interview. *Psychology, Crime & Law, 5,* 3–27.

Lindsay, R.C.L., & Wells, G.L. (1985). Improving eyewitness identification from lineups: Simultaneous versus sequential lineup presentations. *Journal of Applied Psychology, 70,* 556–564.

Loftus, E.F. (1974). Reconstructing memory: The incredible eyewitness. *Psychology Today, 8,* 116–119.

Loftus, E.F. (1979). *Eyewitness testimony.* Cambridge, MA: Harvard University Press.

Loftus, E.F. (2005). Planting misinformation in the human mind: A 30-year investigation into the malleability of memory. *Learning & Memory, 12,* 361–366.

Loftus, E.F., & Palmer, J.C. (1974). Reconstruction of automobile destruction: An example between language and memory. *Journal of Verbal Learning and Verbal Behavior, 13,* 3–13.

Loftus, E.F., Schooler, J.W., Boone, S.M., & Kline, D. (1987). Time went by so slowly: Overestimation of event duration by males and females. *Applied Cognitive Psychology, 1,* 3–13.

McCloskey, M., & Zaragoza, M. (1985). Misleading post-event information and memory for events: Arguments and evidence against memory impairment hypotheses. *Journal of Experimental Psychology: General, 114,* 1–16.

McQuiston-Surrett, D.E., Malpass, R.S., & Tredoux, C.G. (2006). Sequential vs. simultaneous lineups: A review of methods, data, and theory. *Psychology, Public Policy and Law, 12,* 137–169.

Meissner, C.A., & Brigham, J.C. (2001). Thirty years of investigating the own-race bias in memory for faces: A meta-analytic review. *Psychology, Public Policy, & Law, 7,* 3–35.

Memon, A., Hope, L., & Bull, R. (2003). Exposure duration: Effects on eyewitness accuracy and confidence. *British Journal of Psychology, 94,* 339–354.

Memon, A., & Wright, D.B. (1999). The search for John Doe 2: Eyewitness testimony and the Oklahoma bombing. *The Psychologist, 12,* 292–295.

Naughton, M. (2003). How big is the "iceberg"? A semiological approach to quantifying miscarriages of justice. *Radical Statistics, 81,* 5–17.

Neisser, U. (1967). *Cognitive psychology.* New York: Appleton-Century-Crofts.

Orne, M.T. (1981). The significance of unwitting cues for experimental outcomes: Towards a pragmatic approach. In T.A. Sebeok & R. Rosenthal (Eds.), *The Clever Hans phenomenon: Communication with horses, whales, apes, and people* (pp. 152–159). New York: The New York Academy of Sciences.

Ornstein, R.E. (1969). *On the experience of time.* Harmsondsworth, UK: Penguin Books.

Paterson, H.M., & Kemp, R.I. (2006). Co-witnesses talk: A survey of eyewitness discussion. *Psychology, Crime, & Law, 12,* 181–191.

Pedersen, A.I.C., & Wright, D.B. (2002). Do differences in event descriptions cause differences in duration estimates? *Applied Cognitive Psychology, 16,* 769–783.

Penrod, S. (2003). Eyewitness identification evidence: How well are witnesses and police performing? *Criminal Justice Magazine, 54* (Spring), 36–47.

Read, J.D., & Winograd, E. (1998). Individual differences and memory distortion: Introduction. *Applied Cognitive Psychology, 12,* S1–S4.

Roediger, H.L. (1980). Memory metaphors in cognitive psychology. *Memory & Cognition, 8,* 231–246.

Rosenthal, R. (1981). Pavlov's mice, Pfungst's horse, and Pygmalion's PONS: Some models for the study of interpersonal expectancy effects. In T.A. Sebeok & R. Rosenthal (Eds.), *The Clever Hans phenomenon: Communication with horses, whales, apes, and people* (pp. 182–198). New York: The New York Academy of Sciences.

Schacter, D.L. (2001). *The seven sins of memory: How the mind forgets and remembers.* Boston: Houghton-Mifflin Company.

Scheck, B., Neufeld, P., & Dwyer, J. (2003). *Actual innocence: When justice goes wrong and how to make it right.* New York: New American Library.

Sebeok, T.A., & Rosenthal, R. (Eds.) (1981). *The Clever Hans phenomenon: Communication with horses, whales, apes, and people.* New York: The New York Academy of Sciences.

Slater, A. (1994). *Identification parades: A scientific evaluation.* Police Research Award Scheme. London: Police Research Group, Home Office.

Technical Working Group for Eyewitness Evidence. (1999). *Eyewitness evidence: A guide for law enforcement* (NCJ No. 178240). Washington, DC: US Department of Justice, Office of Justice Programs.

Toglia, M., Read, J.D., Ross, M., & Lindsay, R.C.L. (Eds.) (2006). *Adult eyewitness testimony: A handbook.* Hillsdale, NJ: Lawrence Erlbaum Associates, Inc.

Tollestrup, P.A., Turtle, J.W., & Yuille, J.C. (1994). Actual victim and witnesses to robbery and fraud: An archival analysis. In D.F. Ross, J.D. Read, & M.P. Toglia (Eds.), *Adult eyewitness testimony: Current trends and developments* (pp. 144–160). Cambridge, UK: Cambridge University Press.

Valentine, T., & Heaton, P. (1999). An evaluation of the fairness of police line-ups and video identifications. *Applied Cognitive Psychology, 13,* S59–S72.

Valentine, T., Pickering, A., & Darling, S. (2003). Characteristics of eyewitness identification that predict the outcome of real lineups. *Applied Cognitive Psychology, 17,* 969–993.

Wells, G.L. (1978). Applied eyewitness testimony research: System variables versus estimator variables. *Journal of Personality and Social Psychology, 36,* 1546–1557.

Wells, G.L., & Olson, E.A. (2001). The other-race effect in eyewitness identification. What do we do about it? *Psychology, Public Policy, and Law, 7,* 230–246.

Wells, G.L., & Olson, E. (2003). Eyewitness identification. *Annual Review of Psychology, 54,* 277–295.

Wise, R.A., & Safer, M.A. (2004). What US judges know and believe about eyewitness testimony. *Applied Cognitive Psychology, 18,* 427–443.

Wright, D.B., Boyd, C.E., & Tredoux, C.G. (2001). A field study of own-race bias in South Africa and England. *Psychology, Public Policy, and Law, 7,* 119–133.

Wright, D.B., & McDaid, A.T. (1996). Comparing system and estimator variables using data from real lineups. *Applied Cognitive Psychology, 10,* 75–84.

Wright, D.B., Self, G., & Justice, C. (2000). Memory conformity: Exploring misinformation effects when presented by another person. *British Journal of Psychology, 91,* 189–202.

Wright, D.B., & Skagerberg, E.M. (2007). Post-identification feedback affects real eye-witnesses. *Psychological Science, 18,* 172–178.

Wright, D.B., & Sladden, B. (2003). An own-gender bias and the importance of hair in face recognition. *Acta Psychologica, 114,* 101–114.

Wright, D.B., & Stroud, J.N. (2002). Age differences in lineup identification accuracy: People are better with their own age. *Law and Human Behavior, 26,* 641–654.

4 Memory for people: Faces, names, and voices

J. Richard Hanley and Gillian Cohen

Remembering people is a crucial element of everyday life, both in social interaction and in work and family life. Memory for people differs from memory for objects in a number of ways. One of the most important differences is that person recognition demands identification at the level of the individual, whereas for object recognition it is often sufficient to identify the category. We commonly recognise someone as John Smith or as our next-door neighbour, but we recognise an apple as an apple, not as a particular apple. Recognising people as individuals allows us to behave consistently to the same person and differently to different people, but it is usually unnecessary to tune our behaviour so finely for individual apples. Although memory for faces, names, and voices form separate sections in this chapter, remembering people in everyday life frequently involves all of these as well as information about other aspects of their physical appearance, the context in which we encounter them, and their biographical details. It makes sense to think of memory for people as a single system in which all this information is integrated.

It is also important to note that investigations of memory for people quite clearly demonstrate the importance of everyday memory research. Strong theoretical advances have been based on the convergence of studies of face processing in the laboratory, everyday performance in natural situations, patterns of neurological impairment, and computational modelling. Each line of research has informed and illuminated the others.

RECOGNISING FACES

Remembering faces is a skill that is in daily use, but in real life we are not often called on to recognise people by their faces alone. Faces are rarely seen in isolation, even in photographs. Information about a person's identity is also supplied by body build, clothes, gait, voice, and the context in which the person is encountered. We know very little about the relative contribution of these different aspects of personal identity to the recognition process, but mistakes and difficulties of identification suggest that they are important cues. Clothes and context are both liable to change, and therefore ought to be less reliable as cues, but experience suggests that we do rely on them to a considerable extent. It would probably be hard to recognise your bank manager in a bar or your dentist in evening dress. Young and Bruce (1991) called this the Little Red Riding Hood effect—even wolves can seem like grandmothers if they are in the right cottage and wearing the right clothes. A striking demonstration of this phenomenon is Sinha and Poggio's (1996) illusion, in which context dramatically influences our recognition of former US President Bill Clinton and his deputy Al Gore (see Figure 4.1).

Matching different views of faces

As Figure 4.1 suggests, when taken out of context, and stripped of all the additional information that normally accompanies them, our ability to recognise faces can be extremely poor. Indeed, we sometimes have problems even in matching two views of an unfamiliar face. Take a look at the faces that are presented in Figure 4.2a and b. In each case, is the face of the person at the top present in the lineup below? If so, which one is he? These examples are taken from a study by Bruce et al. (1999), in which the target face was present in the array on 50% of occasions. Even though the pictures were taken on the same day, Bruce et al. showed that on approximately 30% of trials participants either claimed the face was present in the lineup when it was absent or matched the face to that of a different person when the target was present. Given that we are fallible at matching unfamiliar faces when the different views of the face are available for detailed scrutiny at the time of testing, it is not surprising that eyewitnesses make errors when they attempt to match one of a series of faces in a lineup with a mental representation of a previously unfamiliar face that is stored in memory. Similar errors of eyewitness recognition of suspects in police lineups were described in Chapter 3. The target appears at position 3 in (a) and is absent in (b).

Kemp, Towell, and Pike (1997) reported a similarly low level of performance in an unfamiliar face-matching task when they examined the ability of cashiers in a supermarket to match a recent colour photograph of a face on a credit card with the face of a person who was using the card to pay for goods. The cashiers found it particularly difficult to reject fraudulent cards where an attempt had been made to

Figure 4.1 Take a close look at this photograph of Bill Clinton and Al Gore. Although the figure at the back appears to be Al Gore, both faces are in fact identical photographs of Bill Clinton. It is Al Gore's hairstyle, suit, and location in the background that appear to make us believe it is him. From Sinha and Poggio (1996). I think I know that face . . . *Nature*, *384*, 404. Copyright © 1996 Nature Publishing Group. Reproduced with permission.

(a)   (b)

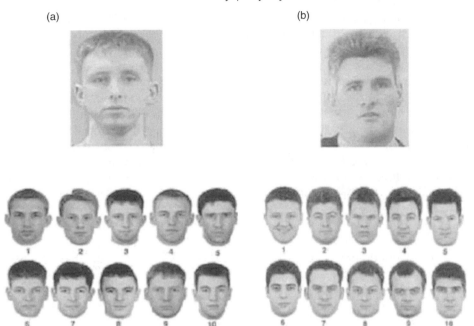

Figure 4.2 It is difficult to match different views of unfamiliar faces. Is the face
of the person at the top present in the line-up below? The answers
are in the text. Reproduced with permission from Bruce et al. (1999).
Copyright © 1999 American Psychological Association.

match the features of the face on the card with the face of the person making the
purchase. Kemp and his colleagues concluded that it is unlikely that the introduction
of cards containing photographs of their owners would lead to a significant
reduction in credit card fraud. Matching different views of well-known faces, as
opposed to unfamiliar ones, is a much easier task. For example, Bruck, Cavanagh,
and Ceci (1991) showed, even after a gap of 25 years, that classmates could match
faces from a college yearbook with current photos of the same people much more
successfully than participants who had never seen the faces before.

Variables that influence memory for faces in experimental studies

Experimental studies have indicated a number of factors that influence how well we
can remember unfamiliar faces in laboratory experiments in which participants view
a series of faces and are subsequently asked to distinguish between target faces and
distractors (faces not presented earlier).

The view of the face that is presented at test

Given the errors that occur with unfamiliar face matching, it might seem strange that
recognition memory for unfamiliar faces is often quite good in laboratory studies.
For example, in one of Backmann's (1991) experiments, his young participants

(age 19–27 years) correctly recognised 84% of pictures of 30 unfamiliar faces that they had been shown 20 minutes earlier, and falsely identified only 4% of distractors. However, as in many experimental studies, the view of the face that Backmann presented at test was the same as that shown at encoding. When different views of a face are presented at encoding and test, recognition is very much lower and slower (e.g., Bruce, 1982; Logie, Baddeley, & Woodhead, 1987; Newell, Chiroro, & Valentine, 1999). If the same view of a face is presented at encoding and at test, there is a danger that recognition becomes a test of pictorial memory for visual features of the photograph presented rather than a memory test for the face itself. It is crucial that a different view of the target face is presented at recognition if the test is to reflect the processes involved in face rather than picture recognition (see Bruce, 1982).

Distinctiveness

The everyday intuition that highly distinctive faces are easier to remember than faces that are ordinary and typical has also been confirmed experimentally (Valentine & Bruce, 1986; Valentine & Moore, 1995). In the Valentine and Bruce study, participants were shown photos of famous and unfamiliar people and were asked to rate each face for how well it would stand out in a crowd. On the basis of these ratings, the faces were classified as distinctive or typical. Different participants were then shown the faces in a mixed sequence and asked to respond as quickly as possible whether each face was familiar or not. Average response time was significantly faster for the distinctive faces. It is now established that typical faces are less likely to be recognised correctly than distinctive faces, but are more likely than distinctive faces to be recognised incorrectly (e.g., Shepherd, Gibling, & Ellis, 1991). The effects of distinctiveness occur with unfamiliar as well as with familiar faces. These findings are consistent with the results of studies investigating the effects of caricature. Rhodes, Brennan, and Carey (1987) used a computer program to exaggerate the distinctive features of line drawings of faces and found that the resulting caricatures were easier to recognise than the originals. Because caricature enhances distinctiveness, this result confirms the conclusion that distinctive faces are easier to recognise than typical ones.

Valentine (1991) has suggested a form of representation that explains why distinctive faces are easier to recognise than typical ones. He postulates a model in which a particular face is represented by its location in multidimensional face space. The dimensions of this space include features such as colour of hair and size of nose, and more holistic characteristics like overall face shape. Typical faces that share many of the same values on these dimensions (e.g., blue eyes and brown hair) will be clustered together; distinctive faces that have unusual values on dimensions (e.g., auburn hair and green eyes) will occupy an area where few other faces are located. According to this model, identifying a face involves locating it in the multidimensional space and, obviously, it is easier to pick out a distinctive face in a relatively empty area than a typical one in a crowded area.

Valentine, Chiroro, and Dixon (1995) argue that this model can also provide an explanation of the other-race bias in face processing. This is the finding that people are better at recognising faces of their own race than faces of a different race. For example, Chiroro and Valentine (1995) found that black participants from

Zimbabwe recognised black faces better than white faces whereas white participants from the UK remembered white faces better than black faces. Valentine and his colleagues argue that other-race faces will tend to be clustered together in multi-dimensional space because the dimensions that are optimal for representing own-race faces do not produce equally distinct representations of faces from other races.

Familiarity

Valentine, Pickering, and Darling, (2003) found that suspects were much more likely to be identified in a police lineup if they were already known to the witness before the crime took place. Similar results have been obtained in the laboratory. Bruce (1982) showed that familiar faces were more accurately recognised in a memory test than unfamiliar faces and found that familiar faces were recognised more quickly than unfamiliar faces both when different and when same views of the faces were presented at recognition. Klatzky and Forrest (1984) found superior recognition for famous than unfamiliar faces and showed that the effect persisted even when participants could not remember the names of the famous faces. Bruce suggested that a number of different codes are potentially available to remember a face (e.g., pictorial qualities of the photographic image, the structural features of the person's face, semantic knowledge about the person, and the name of the person) and that more of these codes are available for familiar than unfamiliar faces.

Recognition of familiar faces and the influence of configural processing

So far, we have seen that it is much easier to match two views of a familiar face than two views of an unfamiliar face, and that it is much easier to recognise familiar people in police lineups and laboratory studies of face memory than it is to recognise previously unfamiliar people. There are many other findings in the literature that also indicate that there is a crucial difference between the processing of familiar and unfamiliar faces. For example, Bruce (1982) showed that, unlike unfamiliar faces, accuracy of recognition memory for familiar faces is unaffected by a change of view between encoding and test. Megreya and Burton (2006) have shown that although people who are good at recognising unfamiliar faces also tend to be good at a variety of other visual processing tasks, there is no correlation between unfamiliar and familiar face recognition ability (see also Bahrick, 1984).

One explanation of these differences is that the type of visual information crucial for recognition of familiar faces is used less often with unfamiliar faces. Ellis, Shepherd, and Davies (1979) found that features in the inner part of the face (eyes, nose, and mouth) are more important than features in the outer part (hair and face shape) in recognition of familiar faces. However, for unfamiliar faces there was no difference between the use of inner and outer features. These findings suggest that the mental representation of a face undergoes some change as the face becomes more familiar, with the more expressive inner features becoming increasingly important as we get to know a person better (Ellis & Shepherd, 1992). It is now widely accepted that these inner features form a pattern or "configuration" that is crucial for the recognition of familiar faces. Farah (1991) argued that the configural or holistic processing that is required for face identification involves "the ability to identify by getting an overview of an item as a whole in a single glance". She claimed that written words and objects are identified by first identifying their component parts (letters and visual features, respectively). However, this is not what happens with faces. It is true, she argues, that faces do have nameable parts (nose, eyes, mouth, etc.), but what distinguishes one face from another is the spatial organisation of these components relative to each other, not the shape or size of an individual feature. In other words, the visual information that we use to identify a familiar face is higher level second-order relationships rather than the shape of a particular visual feature. Once we have learnt the configural information that distinguishes one face from another, recognition of that face becomes easy; we are genuine experts at recognising familiar faces. Before we have learnt a face, however, we depend more on unreliable visual features such as face shape and hairstyle.

Striking evidence for the importance of configural information in identifying familiar faces was provided by Young, Hellawell, and Hay (1987). They produced a set of composites by attaching the top half of a photograph of one celebrity's face (e.g., Margaret Thatcher) onto the bottom half of the face of a different celebrity (e.g., Princess Diana). A new facial configuration emerged when the two different face halves were put together, and participants took much longer to name the two people who were shown in the top or bottom of the composite than when the two halves were presented separately. When the faces were inverted (presented upside down), however, it actually became easier to identify the famous people in the two halves of the composite.

Although configural information is most likely to be used in recognition of familiar faces, it can also play a role in unfamiliar face recognition. Tanaka and Farah (1993) asked participants to learn names for faces. The faces were sometimes normal, and sometimes scrambled (see Figure 4.3). For example, participants learned that a face constructed (using Mac-a-Mug computer software) with a particular combination of features was called Larry. At test, they were asked to: (1) identify a single feature such as Larry's nose when seen as one of a pair of isolated noses; (2) identify Larry's face when seen as one of a pair of normal faces differing only in the nose; and (3) identify Larry's face when seen as one of a pair of scrambled faces, again differing only in the nose. Tanaka and Farah argued that if facial features are represented separately, then memory for a particular feature should be as good when it is seen in isolation as when it is seen in the context of the whole face. If faces are represented configurally, then it should be more difficult to recognise isolated features. The results showed that features learned in the context of a whole normal face were better recognised when seen in a whole normal face. This advantage did not hold for scrambled faces or when the faces were inverted.

It has been known for many years that recognition of faces is disproportionately difficult when they are inverted (Yin, 1969), and the results of Young et al. (1987) and Tanaka and Farah (1993) suggest that inversion exerts a particularly large disruptive effect on configural processing. According to Farah, processing of inverted faces must therefore be carried out by the feature-based object recognition system, which is not so badly affected by inversion because it processes individual features. Moscovitch, Winocur, and Behrmann (1997) and Moscovitch and Moscovitch (2000) have provided a fascinating study of a neuropsychological patient (CK) that is directly relevant to these differences between face and object processing. CK's ability to recognise and name familiar faces was preserved despite severe problems in

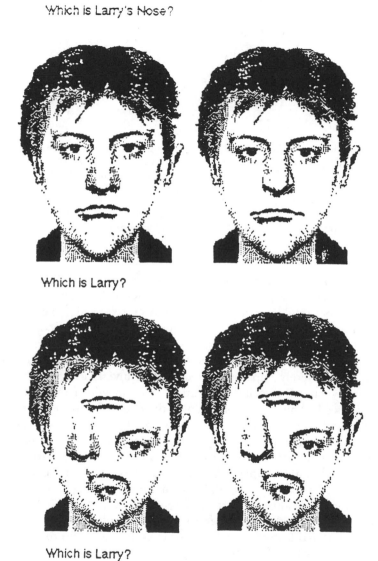

Figure 4.3 Examples of test pairs with isolated noses (top), noses set in normal face contexts (middle) and in scrambled faces (bottom). From Tanaka & Farah (1993) *Quarterly Journal of Experimental Psychology A, 46A,* 225–246. www.informaworld.com. Reproduced with permission.

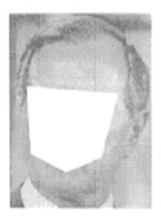 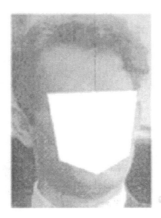 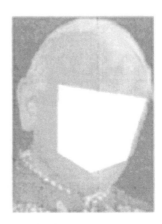

Figure 4.4 Patient CK was impaired at recognising faces such as these in which the internal features have been removed. The identities of these faces can be found in the text. Reproduced with permission. Originally published in Moscovitch and Moscovitch (2000). Super face inversion effects for isolated internal or external features, and for fractured faces. *Cognitive Neuropsychology*, *17*, (1–3), 201–219. Copyright © Psychology Press (http://www.psypress.co.uk/journals.asp).

recognising objects. He could recognise familiar faces when they were presented as cartoons, when they were presented as caricatures, when they were presented in disguise, and when a single internal feature had been removed. He could also recognise famous faces when all of the external features had been removed, and when they were vertically misaligned. On these tasks (where the configural information appears to be preserved in the visual stimulus) he outperformed normal controls. Crucially, however, CK was severely impaired at recognising inverted famous faces. He also performed poorly on other facial recognition tasks in which the configural information was reduced or absent (recognition of the external features of famous faces, see Figure 4.4, and recognition of horizontally misaligned famous faces). Although normal controls were inconvenienced by these manipulations, they all performed very much better than CK. Presumably this is because their object recognition system (unlike that of CK) is able to perform some degree of compensatory feature-based processing on a face when the configural information is missing. On the basis of CK's preserved and impaired pattern of performance with faces, Moscovitch et al. (1997, p. 592) concluded that the ability to identify faces depends crucially on the "spatial relations of the internal features of a face (the eyes, the nose and the mouth) to each other" and is quite separate from the ability to recognise objects. The faces in Figure 4.4 are George Bush (Senior), Tom Hanks, and Pope John Paul II.

The use of inverted faces has also shed some important light on two areas of research, namely the own-race bias effect that was described earlier in this chapter, and the verbal overshadowing effect. One possible explanation for the own-race bias effect is that it comes about because configural information is more difficult to process in other-race than in own-race faces. If so, then the own-race face effect should be much less marked when faces are inverted. This is precisely what has been observed (Rhodes et al., 1987). The same also seems to be true of the verbal

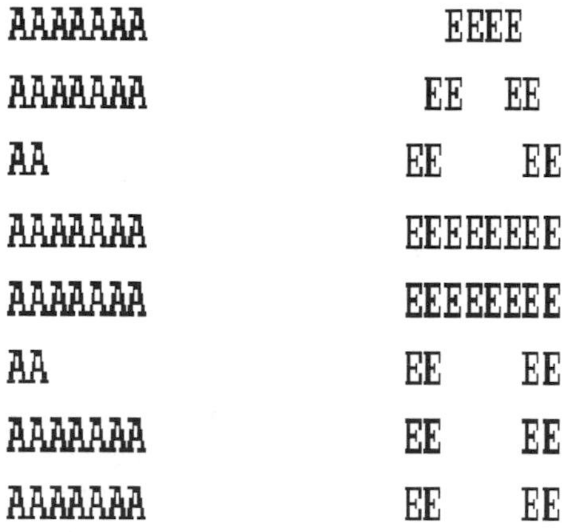

```
AAAAAAA                    EEEE
AAAAAAA                  EE    EE
AA                       EE      EE
AAAAAAA                  EEEEEEEE
AAAAAAA                  EEEEEEEE
AA                       EE      EE
AAAAAAA                  EE      EE
AAAAAAA                  EE      EE
```

Figure 4.5 An example of Navon figures.

overshadowing effect. Witnesses who were asked to describe a suspect verbally before seeing a lineup were less successful at identification. Describing a face verbally may predispose a witness to focus on individual features of the face and ignore the configural information when the lineup takes place (presumably because a configuration is very difficult to verbalise). Consistent with this suggestion, the effect of verbal overshadowing was no longer significant when the recognition test comprised inverted faces (Fallshore & Schooler, 1995).

This account of verbal overshadowing raises the possibility that performance might improve if a witness is encouraged to focus on configural information at the time of test. Macrae and Lewis (2002) investigated this issue by asking witnesses to a simulated robbery to perform a letter processing task that encouraged either configural ("global") processing or featural ("local") processing (see Navon, 1977) just before they took part in a lineup test. Both groups were shown large letters that were made up of different smaller letters (for an example, see Figure 4.5). Participants in the global condition were asked to name the large letters, and participants in the local condition were asked to name the small letters. The results revealed significantly better face recognition performance by those who had named the large letters than by controls who had performed an unrelated task. Those who had named the small letters performed significantly worse at recognition than the controls. As with the results of Tanaka and Farah (1993), these findings suggest that configural information can be used to recognise unfamiliar faces, and that performance will improve to the extent that witnesses are able to employ this form of processing at test. Macrae and Lewis' finding also raises the question of whether other forms of face processing might also benefit if participants have recently performed a global processing task. This is an issue that is likely to receive a lot of attention from researchers in the next few years.

Everyday errors in recognising familiar people

Although we are very much better at recognising familiar faces than faces that we have seen in a single episode, recognition of familiar people is not infallible. In the same way that Reason and Mycielska (1982) collected slips of action (see Chapter 5) and attempted to infer the underlying mechanism, Young, Hay, and Ellis (1985) studied naturally occurring errors in recognising familiar people and developed a model of person recognition based on an analysis of the types of error that were reported. They persuaded 22 participants (mostly undergraduates at Lancaster University) to keep a written record of any errors that they made in recognising other people over an 8-week period. A total of 922 incidents were recorded, and while one of the diarists contributed no fewer than 97 of them, even the lowest scoring subject reported 13 incidents.

One of the most interesting aspects of the study was the finding that over 850 of these incidents could be categorised as falling into one of *four* basic categories. First, there were many occasions when a diarist mistook one person for another. This type of error frequently occurred when viewing conditions were poor, and was generally ended when the observer caught a better view of the person in question. This was certainly not the case in the remaining three categories, however, and these are worth examining in some detail.

Failure to recognise a familiar face

One hundred and fourteen incidents involved diarists completely failing to recognise a familiar person. Here are three examples.

> I was walking past Blackpool College, where I used to be a student. I thought "why is that man staring at me?" About 10 minutes later, when he was gone, I realized that it was my old art tutor.

> I bought a record in a shop in town and I thought the assistant behaved in a strange, over-familiar sort of way . . . A few days later I was told that our neighbour's son had got a Christmas job on the record counter in that shop. Despite having lived next door to him for 3 years, and having talked to him many times before, I hadn't recognized him.

> A friend called Jayne decided to come and stay with me for a few days in Lancaster. When I opened the door to her, I didn't recognize her at first, as she had had her hair cut.

It is clear that failures such as these did not come about simply because of inadequate viewing conditions or because the diarists did not know these faces well enough or only paid cursory attention to them. In the first example, the failure seems to have occurred because the face had not been seen for some time prior to the incident. In the second, the face was seen in an unexpected context, and in the third the physical features of the face were slightly different from normal. The similarity between the three incidents is that they are all failures of face recognition per se. This is not true of the next type of incident, however.

Failure to "place" a person

Two hundred and thirty three incidents occurred when a face felt familiar to the diarist but they were unable to recall any information as to who the person might be. Here are some examples:

A woman at another table looked very familiar at first, but I couldn't pin it down to anyone. In the end I decided that I didn't know her at all.

I was at the theatre when I saw someone in the audience that I thought I knew. I didn't know who she was till I saw her with her sisters and parents, who I know better.

I went to a meeting at the Trades Hall. I don't usually go there. I was sure I knew someone who was there but after 2 hours, I still can't think why or from where.

The first example suggests that faces can "ring a bell" even when they ultimately turn out not to be familiar at all, and the final example reminds us how tantalising the situation can be when further information about the person remains elusive. However, well over 50% (135/233) of incidents of this kind were successfully resolved when the person in question was brought to mind. The second and third examples again demonstrate the effect of context in face recognition. They suggest that faces often feel "familiar-only" when they are seen in a context in which they are not typically encountered, and that resolution occurs when the person is subsequently seen in their normal context, as in the second example. Overall, it appears that this type of error is generally not a failure of the face recognition system, since the face itself has been correctly classified as familiar. The failure has occurred at a subsequent processing stage, where *person* recognition starts to take over from *face* recognition.

Failure to recall full details about a person

The final type of failure almost always occurred under circumstances where a person had been recognised but their name was temporarily inaccessible. One hundred and ninety incidents of this type were recorded in which the subject knew exactly who the person was. Almost always, the subject could remember what the person did for a living (99%), and where they were typically encountered (92%), but simply couldn't remember the person's name. Here are two examples:

> I was reading the *Radio Times*. I saw a photograph of an actor I knew, but couldn't remember the name. I thought it was Paul something. I knew the name well [Paul Schofield], and just had to wait until it popped into my mind; I expected it to come in a few seconds.
>
> In a store I spoke to a woman at the checkout. I knew her face, knew her child came to playgroup, but couldn't remember her name . . . I only remembered her name when retelling the story to a workmate.

Failures of this kind occurred despite the fact that the people concerned were often highly familiar, and were not necessarily seen in an unusual context. The missing information was subsequently retrieved in over 50% of cases, and often emerged within 10 seconds of the incident starting. As in the two examples above, appropriate "semantic" information about the person often came to mind even though the name was inaccessible. In addition, in certain circumstances, the diarist could accurately recall information about the name itself, such as the number of syllables it contained and the identity of the initial letter. In such situations, where a word is temporarily inaccessible but its recall is felt to be imminent, an individual is said to be in a "tip-of-the-tongue" (TOT) state.

Difficulties such as these, which are specific to retrieval of the name itself, were strikingly similar to some previously reported by Yarmey (1973). Yarmey performed an experimental study of name retrieval that was based on Brown and McNeill's (1966) classic investigation of TOTs. Brown and McNeill had given participants definitions of obscure English words (e.g., *sampan, sextant*) and had attempted to discover the nature of the information about the word that was available when they were in a TOT state. Yarmey gave his participants photographs of famous people and asked them to record any information about the celebrity that they could retrieve when they felt that they knew their name but couldn't access it in memory. Yarmey reported that when a participant had been in a genuine TOT state, they were able to provide accurate information about the number of syllables there were in the name (73% correct for first names, and 79% correct for last names), and the identity of the first letter (68% correct for first name, and 59% correct for last names). For more discussion of the TOT state see Chapter 12 on Memory and Consciousness.

The errors that were never reported

What about the errors that were *not* reported by any of the diarists in Young et al.'s (1985) paper? This was perhaps the most striking aspect of the entire study, and it provided important evidence about the nature of the relationship between remembering a person and remembering their name. Out of the 190 records in which there was a failure to recall full details about a person, there was not a single incident in which the person's name was recalled without the participant first being able to retrieve some information about their occupation or where they were typically encountered. That is, the diarists never seemed to report situations such as "I remembered that she was called Sally Sharp, but I couldn't recall what she did or where I knew her from". In principle, there seems to be no reason why this sort of failure could not occur, and the absence of such errors is almost certainly a vital clue about the nature of the system involved in identifying familiar faces. It suggests that retrieval of a name is critically dependent upon recall of *semantic* information about the person in question. As we will see, this is by no means the only piece of evidence indicating that there are no direct associations between faces and names.

Bruce and Young's (1986) model of face processing

Young et al. (1985) used the diary study data to put forward the sequential stage model of person recognition that is shown in Figure 4.6. They concluded that person recognition is a graded process, with levels of recognition varying from "seeming familiar" to full identification. Everyday errors in which a familiar face is classified as unfamiliar (or vice versa) reflect a problem at the first stage of the model, which requires the activation in memory of the appropriate face recognition unit (FRU) for the person one is attempting to recognise. FRUs contain representations of the physical appearance of known faces, with every familiar face having its own recognition unit. They allow recognition of a face regardless of the view of the face that is seen. At this stage, a face that activates one of the stored representations is judged to be familiar. The context in which a face is seen will also influence the probability that an FRU will reach threshold and signal that the face is familiar. If an FRU

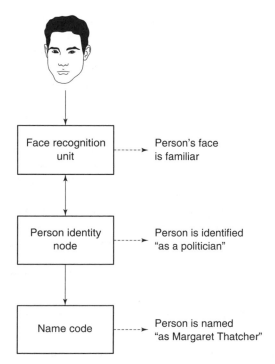

Figure 4.6 Levels of person recognition (adapted from Young, Hay, & Ellis, 1985).

reaches threshold, then access to the next stage becomes possible, at which a person identity node (PIN) must be activated. The PIN contains biographical information, such as the person's occupation and nationality. Failures to place a person are caused by problems in accessing the PIN from the FRU. Finally, activation of the PIN allows access to the third stage, where there is a further lexical store that contains the person's name. TOT states are caused by a failure to access the name store despite access to biographical information about the person stored at the PIN. The sequential organisation of the stages also explains why failures of recognition in which the name of a person is recalled without any biographical information do not occur. This is because the name code cannot be accessed unless the PIN containing the biographical information has already been activated.

Although the results of diary studies contain interesting data, one must be careful not to invest them with too much significance. The experimenter cannot investigate the errors as they occur, and must rely on the accuracy of the diarists' own recollection of the incidents. Hanley and Cowell (1988) and Hay, Young, and Ellis (1991) therefore investigated, under laboratory conditions, the errors that participants made whilst attempting to identify photographs of celebrities. These experiments supported the diary study and the sequential stage model in suggesting that identification can break down at three distinct stages: at the level of the face, at the level of the person, and at the level of the name. They also demonstrated once again that only those participants who could supply the person's occupation could also recall their name.

Hanley and Cowell (1988) further tested the sequential model by giving participants cues to help them recall a name when they were experiencing different types of identification problem. A second view of a face helped participants to name a known face when they had originally found the face unfamiliar. Information about the celebrity's occupation helped participants to name a face when they had originally been unable to place a person. The celebrity's initials helped name recall when participants were in a TOT state. Overall, the effectiveness of a particular retrieval cue appeared to be directly related to its ability to assist the recognition system at the precise stage in the sequence at which it had become stalled.

In 1986, Bruce and Young put forward an elaborated version of the stage model, retaining the same basic components but integrating them within a broader framework of other functions of facial information and different ways of recognising people by their names or voices. This model is shown in Figure 4.7. The initial stage of structural encoding converts the input face to a description that is independent of the particular viewpoint and expression. In addition to the person identification route of FRU, PIN, and name generation, which is retained from the earlier model, there are three independent modules operating in parallel. Expression analysis yields information about the person's mood and feelings; facial speech analysis carries out lip-reading; and directed visual processing selectively processes information, such as age, sex or race, that does not require identification of the person as familiar.

The effects of brain injury on the ability to recognise familiar people

Although everyday errors in recognising people can be a source of temporary embarrassment and frustration for us, they are of relatively little consequence when put beside the devastating effects that brain injury can have on the lives of those unfortunate individuals whose ability to identify other people has become

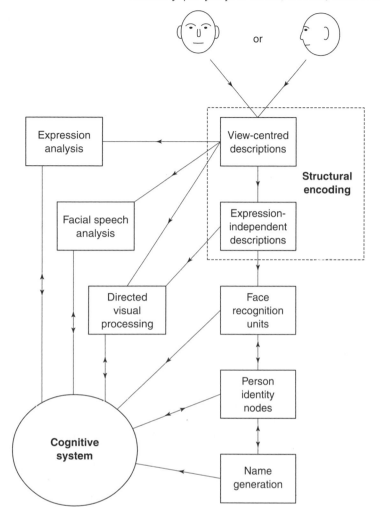

Figure 4.7 A model of face recognition (adapted from Bruce & Young, 1986). Reprinted by permission of The British Psychological Society and the author.

permanently impaired. The impairment that is experienced by a particular patient can often be remarkably specific, totally disrupting certain aspects of face processing while leaving others unaffected. Furthermore, the precise nature of the deficit often varies in quite striking ways from one patient to another. One of the advantages of Bruce and Young's (1986) model was that it provided an extremely useful framework for investigating the diverse problems that these individuals can experience.

A complete inability to recognise faces that were once familiar can be seen in prosopagnosia, a disability that encompasses the faces of friends and relatives as well as celebrities, and seems to prevent the patient from learning new faces in addition to preventing the recognition of faces that were familiar before the illness started. As an illustration of the severity of the impairment, LH (Levine, Warrach & Farah, 1985) does not recognise his wife at a party unless it has been arranged beforehand that she will wear something distinctive in her hair such as a ribbon. Another patient, Larry (Bauer, 1984), apparently bumped into his own reflection in a mirror and apologised, quite unaware of the fact that the face in front of him was his own. Although PH (Young & De Haan, 1988) was good at distinguishing between famous and un-familiar names, he performed at chance when asked to decide which of two faces was that of a famous person. De Renzi, Faglioni, Grossi, and Nichelli (1991) showed that many patients with prosopagnosic problems (whom they refer to as having "apper-ceptive" prosopagnosia) have widespread general visual processing problems. Other individuals with prosopagnosia (whom they refer to as "associative" prosopagnosics) seem to be accurate at identifying objects and at determining the age of a face.

Patients also exist who are unable to learn new faces but have no difficulty in recognising faces that they knew before their illness started. For example, ELD (Hanley, Young, & Pearson, 1989) performed very badly on a recognition test for unfamiliar faces and was unable to recognise faces of people who had become famous since the time of her illness. However, she was able to recognise faces of celebrities who had become famous several years earlier, and performed well on recognition memory tests for familiar faces of this kind. ELD could learn new verbal material (for example she could identify virtually all celebrities from their names) but had problems remembering other types of recent visual information, such as the layout of places that she had never visited before. Tippett, Miller, and Farah (2000) report an even more specific case (CT) who performed well on standardised tests of recent visual memory, including memory for new visual patterns, despite an inability to recognise faces of people he had met since his illness started. Tippett et al. refer to this condition as "prosopamnesia".

Prosopagnosic and prosopamnesic individuals still know who people are despite their inability to recognise their faces. Other patients with person recognition impairments, however, have difficulties in remembering people from their faces, names, and voices (e.g., De Haan, Young, & Newcombe, 1991; Ellis, Young, & Critchley, 1989; Hanley, Pearson, & Young, 1990). The impairment observed in De Haan et al.'s case (ME) was reminiscent of the everyday error of failing to place a familiar person; ME experienced preserved familiarity but was unable to recall further information about many people whose faces and names she clearly still recognised. BD (Hanley et al., 1989) and KS (Ellis et al., 1989) also had problems in recognising faces, names, and voices of people he once knew well. It appeared that these people had become completely unfamiliar to them.

Finally, the counterpart of failure to retrieve full details about a person is observed in a word-finding deficit known as "anomia". Patients with anomia can often recall lots of details about familiar people, such as their occupations. However, they are unable to retrieve people's names. Some patients with anomia have general word-finding difficulties that encompass the names of both objects and people (e.g., Flude, Ellis, & Kay, 1989; Hanley, 1995). Others, including PC (Semenza & Zettin, 1988), have problems that are confined to the retrieval of proper names. PC gave the correct name for pictures of fruit, vegetables, body parts, colours, letters, transport, furni-ture, and types of pasta but could name nobody other than his son. He also had problems in recalling other types of proper name such as the names of rivers, mountains, and cities.

Many of these impairments can be readily explained in terms of Bruce and Young's (1986) sequential processing framework. Apperceptive prosopagnosic patients would appear to have problems at the level of structural encoding, whereas associative prosopagnosics seem to have problems at the level of the face recognition units. Prosopamnesic patients appear to be unable to form new face recognition units but can still access old ones. ME would appear to be able to activate FRUs but has problems in accessing the PINs for people she finds familiar. Anomic patients can access PINs, which contain biographical information about people, but are unable to access the name store.

Beyond Bruce and Young (1986)

In 1990, Burton, Bruce, and Johnston put forward the Interactive Activation and Competition (IAC) model (see also Burton, Bruce, & Hancock, 1999). This is a computational model of familiar face processing that reformulates the central identification route of the Bruce and Young model in a parallel connectionist format. However, it differed in a few crucial respects from Bruce and Young (1986). The stages are replaced by three separate pools of units, with units in different pools being linked by bidirectional excitatory connections. In the IAC model, FRUs do not themselves signal familiarity. Their role is to pass on activation to a modality-free person identity node (PIN), which represents the point at which the face and voice recognition systems converge. There is one PIN for each known person and, in effect, the person is represented at the PIN. The PIN receives activation not only from the FRU, but also from other systems that process the written or spoken name (NRUs) and the voice (VRUs are not shown in Figure 4.8). It is the level of activation at the PIN that determines whether or not a person is found familiar. In Bruce and Young (1986), PINs contained semantic information, but in the IAC model they act as a multimodal gateway to a separate semantic information pool that contains biographical facts about familiar people. As can be seen in Figure 4.8, a particular semantic unit such as "royal" might be linked to several different PINs.

The new conceptualisation of PINs means that the IAC model can provide a parsimonious account of the impairments experienced by BD and KS (Ellis et al., 1989; Hanley et al., 1989) by assuming that they have a problem at the level of the PINs. The new role of PINs leads to a specific prediction concerning patient ME's (De Haan et al., 1991) ability to recognise the faces and names of people that she finds familiar but for whom she cannot supply any semantic information. In such situations, the PIN must have reached threshold and this means that activation has reached the point in the model at which face and name recognition have converged. If so, ME should be able to match the faces and names of people despite being unable to recall any information about them. This prediction was upheld.

Another advantage of Burton et al.'s model is that it provides a plausible explanation of the striking finding that some associative prosopagnosic patients show evidence of covert recognition of faces that they do not find familiar. For example, PH showed covert recognition on a variety of behavioural tasks including priming from faces that he did not find familiar. Covert recognition was shown by the finding that, although he did not consciously recognise the face of Prince Charles, it acted as a prime so that PH was significantly quicker at recognising the name of Princess Diana if he had been shown a picture of Prince Charles' face a few milliseconds earlier (Young, Hellawell, & De Haan, 1988b). Burton, Young, Bruce, Johnston, and Ellis (1991) demonstrated that the IAC model can account for this finding by

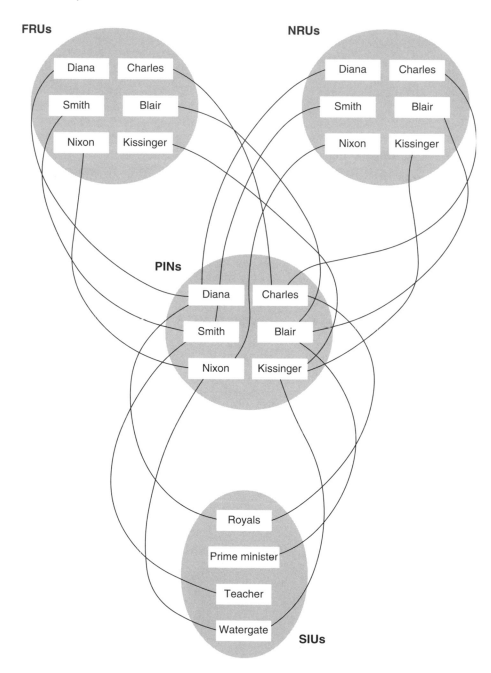

Figure 4.8 Basic components of Burton et al.'s (1990) interactive activation and competition model (IAC) model of face recognition. Reproduced with permission. Originally published in Young, A.W. and Burton, M. (1999). Simulating face recognition: Implications for modelling cognition. *Cognitive Neuropsychology*, *16*, (1), 1–48. Copyright © Psychology Press (http://www.psypress.co.uk/journals.asp).

assuming that face recognition units still work normally in associative prosopagnosia but that the connections from the FRUs to the PINs have been severely weakened. These weak connections mean that, for prosopagnosics, known faces feel unfamiliar but weak connections still allow some activation of the PIN to take place when a known face is seen. Such activation of the PIN provides the basis for an explanation of priming in prosopagnosia. Associative connections between the PINs of people who are often seen together (which exist because such people share information in the semantic pool) mean that the PIN of Princess Diana will start to become activated whenever Prince Charles' FRU is activated. So, Diana's name is classified as familiar more quickly when preceded by Prince Charles' face even though his face is not overtly recognised.

A different type of covert recognition in prosopagnosia was reported by Bauer (1984). Normal participants show larger skin conductance responses (SCRs) when looking at known faces than at unknown faces. Bauer demonstrated that this also turns out to be the case in prosopagnosia. For example, Larry (Bauer, 1984) had an elevated skin conductance response when he heard the name of a face that he was looking at despite the fact that he did not find the face familiar. Breen, Caine, and Coltheart (2000) argued that an area of the brain known as the amygdala, which is part of the limbic system, produces elevated SCRs to familiar faces. It is already established that the amygdala is involved in attaching emotional responses to memories and is active during face perception (Hirstein & Ramchandran, 1997). Breen et al. argue that connections between the FRUs and the amygdala mean that the amygdala will receive stronger signals from familiar than unfamiliar faces. They argue that the connections between the FRUs and the amygdala are intact in prosopagnosia despite the weakened connections between the FRUs and the PINs. As a consequence, prosopagnosic patients produce normal SCRs from known faces despite the absence of overt recognition.

Breen et al. (2000) also suggest that this account can provide an explanation of a very different pattern of performance that is observed in psychiatric patients with Capgras delusion, who believe that a loved one has been replaced by an imposter. Individuals with Capgras delusion show *reduced* SCRs to familiar faces but are not necessarily impaired at overt face recognition (Ellis, Young, Quayle, & De Pauw, 1997; Hirstein & Ramchandran, 1997). Breen et al. argue that the connections between the FRUs and the PINs are intact in Capgras delusion but the links between the FRUs and the amygdala are severely weakened. The consequence is weak SCRs to familiar faces despite unimpaired overt recognition.

Bruce and Young (1986) suggested that person-specific semantic knowledge is represented in some sense separately from the rest of the semantic system. Recent theorising is consistent with this suggestion. Following Caramazza and Shelton (1998), who argued that knowledge is fractionated into distinct semantic memory systems for animals, plants, and artefacts, several authors (e.g., Gentileschi, Sperber, & Spinnler, 2001; Kay & Hanley, 1999; Miceli et al., 2000) have suggested that knowledge about familiar people may also be stored in its own distinct area of semantic memory. After all, an expertise in rapid retrieval of information about familiar people has obvious evolutionary salience in terms of everyday interaction and communication, and has clear adaptive value in distinguishing "friend" from "foe". It would therefore make sense for a specialised semantic memory system for people to exist. One important line of evidence for this claim is the observation that patients such as KS (Ellis et al., 1989) who are unable to recall biographical information about familiar people, are unimpaired at retrieving other types of information from semantic memory such as knowledge about the properties of objects and animals. Crucially, evidence of a double dissociation has recently emerged between KS and patients who have severe problems in retrieving information about objects from semantic memory but who seem to have entirely preserved knowledge of familiar people (Kay & Hanley, 2002; Thompson et al., 2004).

One possible explanation of why knowledge about familiar people and objects might be stored separately comes from the work of Barry, Johnston, and Scanlan (1998). It is widely believed that representations of objects and animals in semantic memory might be associated by the features that they share and the superordinate category to which they belong. In contrast, Barry et al. claim that knowledge about people might be structured by social relationships (e.g., people who work together, people who live together) rather than by superordinate categories (e.g., film stars) or semantic features (e.g., friendly people). Alternatively, Valentine, Brennen, and Brédart (1996) argue that the key difference may be that, unlike semantic representations of objects and animals, knowledge about a familiar individual is bound together by an abstract person identity node (PIN). They argue that PINs prevent unwanted general information about politicians from becoming available whenever we see a picture of Tony Blair. Although it may be useful to automatically activate general information about fruit whenever we see an apple, more *precise* semantic information is required when we encounter a person that we know. The suggestion that was made earlier in this section, that patient KS (Ellis et al., 1989) may have an impairment at the level of the PINs, is certainly consistent with Valentine et al.'s ideas.

An issue that has only recently started to attract some interest concerns our ability to access specific personal memories about familiar people (e.g., the memory of seeing a particular actor perform in a film at the cinema). Damjanovic and Hanley (in press) found that participants were able to recall episodic memories of this kind for just over half (55%) of famous faces that they found familiar. Nevertheless, participants were less successful at recalling episodic information about familiar people than at recalling semantic information (which was available on over 90% of occasions that a famous face was found familiar). One possible explanation is that whereas semantic information is relatively consistent across time, each episode in which a familiar person is encountered is different, making it difficult to bring any one of them to mind. Westmacott and Moscovitch (2003) found that certain famous names were much more likely than others to be associated with retrieval of personal memories. Furthermore, these personally salient names were read and recognised more quickly than less salient names, even when the two sets were equally familiar to the participants. These findings suggest that episodic memory might be more important in person recognition than has hitherto been suspected.

MEMORY FOR NAMES

Are names stored separately from other information about people?

One of the most interesting and controversial claims made by Bruce and Young (1986) was that names are stored in a separate store from other types of information that we know about people, and that recall of names is contingent on recall of semantic information. A number of subsequent studies performed by Andy Young and his colleagues tested this claim by comparing the time it takes to retrieve names and occupations when we see a face. For example, Young, Ellis, and Flude (1988a) collected a set of photographs of famous people of whom half were politicians and half were entertainers. Moreover, half of them were called Michael (e.g., Michael Caine, the film star) and half were called David (e.g., David Owen, the former Liberal Democrat leader). On half of the experimental trials, the participants made decisions as quickly as they could about a face's first name and on half the trials they made decisions about a face's occupation. The results showed that it took approximately 50 milliseconds longer to press a button signifying that the name of a face was David than that it was the face of a politician. More recent research by Carson, Burton, and Bruce (2000) has shown that even after participants had received extensive practice at naming each of a series of famous faces, they were still significantly slower at recalling their names than at recalling their occupations.

Consistent findings were obtained from studies that compared the learning of names and occupations of previously unfamiliar people. Cohen and Faulkner (1986) tested recall of information from fictional minibiographies. For example, participants heard: "James Gibson is a policeman who lives in Glasgow and wins prizes for ballroom dancing", and later attempted to fill in blanks in a written version of this biography. Recall of first names and surnames was much poorer than recall of place names, occupations, and hobbies.

McWeeny, Young, Hay, and Ellis (1987) were concerned with testing different possible explanations for the difficulty of retrieving names:

1   *Arbitrariness:* Occupations of faces might be easier to recall than their names because context and visual appearance can give clues to a person's occupation, but not to his or her name (apart from the gender of their first name). This is because names are arbitrarily related to their referents in the sense that the person I know as Ann (or John) might equally well have been called by another name.
2   *Frequency:* Names of people may be words that are encountered less frequently than names of occupations.
3   *Imageability:* Names of people are often not so easy to image as names of occupations.

All these factors, which might favour recall of occupations, were systematically eliminated in their experiment. Participants viewed 16 photos of unfamiliar middle-aged men's faces one at a time and were told each man's name and occupation (both names and occupations were arbitrarily assigned to faces). The faces were presented without visible background or clothing to eliminate any contextual cues; frequency of names and occupations was matched and, in some examples, the same word (e.g., Baker or Potter) was interchanged so that it sometimes functioned as a surname and sometimes as an occupation. Consequently, the imageability, frequency, and meaningfulness of the words used as names and occupations were equated. Even when these factors were controlled there remained a vast difference between memory for names and memory for occupations. The percentage of trials on which participants

recalled the correct occupation but not name (75%) far exceeded the trials on which they recalled the correct names but not the correct occupation (5%).

These findings were replicated by Craigie and Hanley (1997), who tested a further prediction of the sequential stage model. Because the model states that recalling an occupation is part of the process of naming a face, it follows that a newly learned name should be much easier to recall from a description of a person's occupation than from seeing their face. This prediction was confirmed. In another study Brennen, Baguley, Bright, and Bruce (1990) studied the TOT experience when a name is on the tip of the tongue but is proving difficult to access. They asked participants to answer trivia questions about familiar people, such as:

> *Who played Basil Fawlty's Spanish waiter Manuel?*
> *Which actor is better known as Captain James T Kirk?*

The key issue was whether a photo of a face would help an individual to recall the name of a familiar person during a TOT experience. The sequential stage model would predict that a photograph would be of no value in resolving a TOT state because it provides no information that could help the system at the point at which it is failing (i.e., the link between stored semantic information and the name store). If, contrary to Bruce and Young (1986), there is a direct link between a face and its name in memory, then providing a face should prove highly beneficial. The results strongly supported the sequential stage model. A photo led to the resolution of only 14.5% of TOT states. This figure was not significantly higher than the number of TOTs that were resolved by simply repeating the question (10.7%).

Despite these successes, the sequential stage model has not gone unchallenged. In line with their parallel activation IAC model shown in Figure 4.8, Burton and Bruce (1992) suggested that names and occupations are represented together in the same semantic store, but that it is particularly difficult to retrieve names from this store. The difficulty with names comes about because a name is typically unique to an individual whereas occupations tend to be shared by many people. For example, most of us know many film stars but only one person whose name is *Heath Ledger*. Hence a unique name can only accrue activation from a single source. Burton and Bruce were able to demonstrate that their IAC model took much longer to recall unique facts about people than shared facts, and claimed as a consequence that they had solved the problem of why names are so difficult to recall. The key factor was their *uniqueness*.

Unfortunately, this explanation very soon ran into problems because it had difficulty in explaining the performance of two anomic patients reported by Hanley (1995) and Harris and Kay (1995). According to Burton and Bruce, these patients should encounter just as many problems in recalling unique semantic facts about people as in recalling their names. This prediction did not hold. For example, BK (Harris & Kay, 1995) could even recall a famous person's catchphrase (e.g., Magnus Magnusson's "I've started so I'll finish") despite being unable to retrieve his name.

What is different about names that results in their storage in a separate memory store from occupations? In a learning study, Cohen (1990) found that if occupations or possessions were rendered meaningless by using nonsense words, then recall of these was as poor as recall of names. She argued that names are difficult to recall because they are *meaningless*. For example, learning the surname of a new acquaintance does not allow us to deduce any further information about that person: It does not follow that because a person's name is *Butcher* they will share anything in common with other people with that surname or with people who work as butchers. However, learning that the person is employed as a school teacher provides important information about them (e.g., that they work with young people and earn a salary). Hanley (1995) argued that what are stored in the semantic system are conceptual representations (e.g., film star) that are separate from the symbols that we use in written or spoken language. This can be seen from the fact it is possible to refer to concepts by different synonymous verbal labels (e.g., movie star or film star). A name, however, is nothing more than a lexical symbol and therefore representations of names belong in the speech production system rather than in the semantic system.

Valentine, Brédart, Lawson, and Ward (1991) provide a different alternative from the sequential stage model. In their view, names and occupations are represented in different stores, but both stores have direct connections with a person's PIN. Like Burton and Bruce (1992), they argue that names are more difficult to recall than occupations because they are unique. However, the existence of separate stores for names and occupations means that they can accommodate the finding (which proved fatal to Burton and Bruce) that anomic patients can recall unique semantic facts about people even though they cannot name them (Hanley, 1995; Harris & Kay, 1995). However, Valentine and his colleagues themselves acknowledge that if there are direct associations between PINs and names, then it is puzzling that we do not occasionally name people without recalling additional information about them. In an attempt to bolster their case, they point to a report of an Alzheimer's patient (Mme DT) who was described by Brennen, David, Fluchaire, and Pellat (1996). Mme DT did name three out of a large set of faces without recalling specific biographical information about the three people concerned. However, these three individuals were people who may have been quite difficult for a patient with dementia to categorise because they were all iconic figures who were famous for a variety of different reasons. It was also clear that Mme DT did know that they were famous. It would therefore be imprudent to claim that the case of Mme DT has serious implications for models of face naming.

Are proper names more difficult to recall than common names?

We have seen that semantic facts about people, such as occupations, are easier to recall than names. Some theorists have made an additional claim that common names are generally easier to recall than proper names. Such a prediction cannot be derived directly from Bruce and Young (1986), because their sequential stage model makes no claims about the processes that are involved in naming objects. However, the prediction does follow from a model of face and object naming put forward by Burke, Mackay, Worthley, and Wade (1991), which is called the "node structure theory". Figure 4.9 illustrates the representation of the occupation "baker" (common name) and "Baker" (proper name) according to this theory. As can be seen in the upper panel, a number of propositional (semantic) nodes representing information about bakers converge on the lexical node for the common name "baker". If the connections between any one of the four semantic nodes and the lexical node is weak, there are three other nodes available to activate the lexical node and prevent a failure

(a) Semantic system

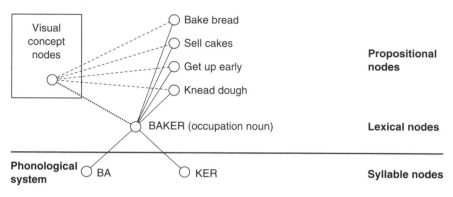

(b) Semantic system

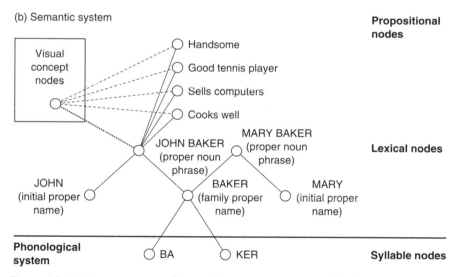

Figure 4.9 Basic components of the node structure (NST) model of proper name retrieval (from Mackay & Burke, 1990. In T. Hess (Ed.) *Aging and cognition: Knowledge organization and utilization.* pp. 1–51. North-Holland). Reprinted by permission of the publishers and author. Copyright © Elsevier 1990.

to access the name. In contrast, a proper noun phrase intervenes between the semantic features and the lexical node for the proper name "Baker". This means that the lexical node is connected only indirectly to the semantic attributes of the named individual. If the connections between the proper noun phrase and the lexical node are weak, then there are no additional connections that could compensate in order to allow name retrieval to take place. In summary, proper name retrieval in this model is made vulnerable by the fact that, unlike common name retrieval, the lexical node for proper names receives direct activation from only a single source.

How strong is the evidence for the claim that proper names are disproportionately hard to recall? At one time the existence of proper name anomic patients such as PC (Semenza & Zettin, 1988), who are unable to recall proper names but are unimpaired at recalling common names, might have been seen as evidence for this claim. However, Lyons, Hanley, and Kay (2002) reported a case of a patient with "common name anomia" who seemed to have the opposite problems to PC. When asked to name a set of 62 famous *faces* ranging from very easy (e.g., *Charlie Chaplin*) to very difficult (e.g., *William Holden*), FH named 43/62 correctly. The average score by unimpaired age-matched controls was 42.2/60. When asked to name a set of objects, however, his performance placed him within the lowest performing 1% of the population. For example, when asked to name a set of 62 objects ranging from very easy (e.g., *mushroom*) to very difficult (e.g., *tantalus*), FH named only 15/62 correctly whereas the average score by age-matched controls was 41.2/60. FH was therefore much better at naming people than objects (e.g., he named *Bob Geldof* but not a camel). The existence of common name anomia makes it difficult to argue that proper name anomia comes about because proper names are generally harder to recall than common names. The most parsimonious explanation of this double dissociation is that common name anomia is the result of an impairment to the connections from the object semantic system to the lexical system, and proper name anomia is caused by an impairment to the connections from the person semantic system to the lexicon.

Reason and Lucas (1984) carried out a diary study designed to investigate naturally occurring occasions when memory for a word is blocked and people experience a TOT state. The corpus of data collected by Reason and Lucas included blocking of both common names and proper names, and confirms that blocks are particularly likely to be reported for proper names (77%). In a similar study, Cohen and Faulkner (1986) asked participants to record details of any name blocks they experienced during a 2-week period. The majority (68%) of blocks were for names of friends and acquaintances. Burke et al. (1991) themselves carried out a diary study in which retrieval failures and TOTs states were reported more frequently for proper names than for object names and abstract words. However, these results from diary studies do not indicate that proper names are more difficult to recall than common names. If many more attempts are made to recall proper names, then it would follow that there should be more retrieval failures for them. An experimental study is therefore required in which a set of faces and objects matched for familiarity is presented for naming. If the number of *don't know* responses for the two sets is matched, then the key issue is whether there will be more TOTs for names of faces. An experiment that comes close to achieving this was reported by Rendell, Castel, and Craik (2005), and they found no evidence that young participants encounter more difficulties in recalling proper names than common names.

The diary studies also show that old people report more TOTs for proper names than do young people. This finding has been confirmed by the results of laboratory experiments. For example, Cross and Burke (2004) showed that older adults were less likely than younger adults to recall names of famous people and more likely to report TOT states despite the fact that the number of *don't know* (DK) responses was equivalent for the younger and older participants. Rendell et al. (2005) also reported that older participants had more retrieval failures for proper names than young participants, but reported no age-related differences of this kind for common names. In terms of the node structure model (see Figure 4.9), these results suggest that access to the semantic nodes is preserved in old age, but that the connections to the lexical or phonological nodes for proper names are weakened in old age.

When elderly people suffered name blocks they tended to report that they experienced a complete mental blank, with no names at all coming to mind. However, when younger participants attempted to retrieve a blocked name, they often found that other names came to mind instead of the target. These nontarget candidates were nearly always recognised as being incorrect, but were persistent and difficult to set aside. They were often phonologically similar to the target name (e.g., *Sylvia* instead *of Cynthia*, or *Ken* instead of *Kevin*). Sometimes the nontarget candidates were contextually related to the target name (*Carter* instead of *Reagan*). Reason and Lucas (1984) also recorded that candidate names were elicited on 59% of blocks. They describe these nontarget items as "mockers" that impede access to the target, but Cohen and Faulkner's (1986) participants reported that in the process of rejecting nontarget candidates they sometimes retrieved additional information about the target name. When several nontarget candidates were elicited, these could be graded as more or less similar to the target. In one example, the target name was *Kepler*. The first letter and first vowel sound were retrieved. Candidates, in order of occurrence, were *Keller, Klemperer, Kellet,* and *Kendler*. All of these were rejected, but *Keller* was recognised as being closest to the target, and the additional information that the target name was foreign came to light during evaluation of the candidates. Nontarget candidates may sometimes be stepping stones toward recall, rather than mockers.

Exactly the opposite pattern of performance from that seen in the elderly can be observed in bilingual adults. Roberts, Garcia, Desrochers, and Hernandez (2002) reported that bilinguals experienced more TOT states and recalled fewer names of pictured objects than monolinguals. Gollan, Bonanni, and Montoya (2005) argued that bilinguals who speak both languages relatively often will experience more retrieval failures because they have less practice in recalling the name of an object in any one language. If so, then these differences should disappear for the recall of proper names because, as Gollan et al. point out, *Bill Clinton* has the same name in other languages as in English. These predictions were supported; Gollan et al.'s Spanish–English bilinguals produced more TOTs than monolingual English speakers when naming objects in English, but not when naming familiar people.

What makes some names easier to remember than others?

The results of Burke et al.'s (1991) diary study suggested that the probability of a retrieval failure was linked to the frequency and recency of use of the name. Names that had not been used frequently, or not for a long time, were more likely to be blocked. An experimental study by Hanley and Chapman (in press) showed that famous names that had previously been rated as being of lower familiarity were associated with more retrieval failures than more familiar names. However, Cohen and Faulkner's (1986) diary study showed that the attempt to retrieve very well-known names can sometimes lead to retrieval failures. This fluctuating availability of well-known names suggests that retrieval failure often results from dynamic variations in the retrieval process, rather than defective encoding or storage.

Hanley and Chapman (in press) also compared recall of names that contains three words (e.g., Sarah Michelle Gellar) with those that require two (Gwyneth Paltrow). They found that there were more retrieval failures for the surnames of people whose name contains three elements. There was no difference in the number of *don't know* responses, so access to semantic information about people with three names appeared good. The problem seemed to be at the lexical retrieval or phonological retrieval stage. Famous names are stage names chosen by the individuals themselves, so it seems odd that celebrities would choose to be known by three-name stage names if it makes their names more prone to TOTs. One possible explanation is that although having three words in a name appears to hinder recall, it may improve recognition of a person's name as familiar because it makes the name more distinctive. Consistent with this suggestion, Valentine and Moore (1995) showed that participants were worse at recalling a newly learned name when the name was unusual (less than one occurrence per 50,000 entries in a telephone directory) than when it was common (more than one occurrence per 500 entries in the directory). However, Valentine et al. (1991) showed that when participants are asked whether a surname was that of a famous person, it took less time to recognise an unusual surname than a common surname.

Stevenage and Lewis (2005) examined how readily participants can recall the real name of actors and actresses who are associated with a very well-known character name (e.g., Calista Flockhart/Ally McBeal). Stevenage and Lewis reported that participants produced fewer correct recalls and many more retrieval failures (trials where the name was reported to be known but could not be recalled) for actors with two names than for equally familiar actors who were associated with only a single name (e.g., Meg Ryan). In order to explain these findings, Stevenage and Lewis provided an explanation based on the "fan" effect, which states that an association with multiple units within a pool in a network increases competition in that pool. It follows that the more facts that a participant knows about a person (in this case their real name and the name of the character they play), the more difficult it is likely to be to recall any one of these facts. The fan effect can also explain why three-word names are difficult to recall.

MEMORY FOR VOICES

In everyday life situations, voices sometimes play a part in recognising people, as when we detect a familiar voice across a crowded room or pick up the phone and recognise the voice of a friend. Although a voice may be totally unexpected and there are no contextual cues to aid identification, we are often able to identify the speaker immediately. Nevertheless, we are nothing like as skilled at voice recognition as at familiar face recognition, and on many occasions we are unable to put a name or occupation to a voice even though we are confident that it is a familiar voice and not the voice of a stranger.

Voices that we know extremely well, such as those of close work colleagues, can often be recognised almost without error (Bricker & Pruzansky, 1966). However, Clarke and Becker (1969) found that only around 60% of familiar voices were recognised correctly, and that performance did not improve very much even after weeks of training. This finding suggests that familiar voice recognition is much more difficult than familiar face recognition. This was confirmed in an experiment by Hanley, Smith, and Hadfield (1998), who presented half their participants with famous faces and the other half with famous voices. Fewer famous voices than faces were found familiar (70% versus 95%), and more voices than faces of non-famous people were considered to be familiar. However, Hanley et al. did not merely demonstrate that familiar voices are harder to recognise than faces. As we saw from the section on familiar face recognition, when we see a face that feels familiar we are almost always able to retrieve information about the person concerned, such as their occupation or where they are typically encountered. Hanley et al. found a quite different pattern when they presented voices of famous people instead of their faces. Overall, the occupations of only 50–60% of voices found familiar could be retrieved. There were therefore many more failures to place familiar voices than faces (situations in which the person feels familiar but no information about them can be retrieved). Damjanovic and Hanley (in press) matched the level of recognition performance in the faces and voices conditions by blurring the faces. Their results showed that semantic memories and episodic memories were significantly more likely to be recalled from blurred faces than from voices.

Such findings are consistent with research on episodic memory for previously unfamiliar faces and voices, which shows that a recently seen face is much more likely to be correctly recognised than a recently heard voice. For example, Yarmey, Yarmey, and Yarmey (1994) performed an experiment in which participants were approached by a young woman in a public place and engaged in conversation for about 15 seconds. On a recognition test 5 minutes later, they were twice as likely to correctly identify this woman from a photograph of her face (57%) than from a tape recording of her voice (28%). With longer delays, earwitness performance is even worse. Clifford (1983) tested the ability of shopkeepers and bank clerks to recognise the voice of a male stooge who entered the bank or shop, introduced himself, explained that he had lost his chequebook and card, and asked what steps he should take. The researcher later asked the shop assistant or bank clerk to participate in a voice-identification test. In this situation, when testing was not anticipated, identification was at chance level after 4 hours' delay.

Voice recognition improves if a person's face is visible when the voice is presented at recognition (Armstrong & McKelvie, 1996). However, there is evidence that the presence of the face at encoding actually reduces the ability to subsequently recognise the person's voice. If the voice is presented alone at learning and at test, then voice recognition is markedly improved (Cook & Wilding, 1997; McAllister, Dale, Bregman, McCabe & Cotton, 1993). Cook and Wilding refer to this as the "face overshadowing effect". By comparison, the detrimental effects on face recognition of hearing a voice are relatively small. These findings suggest that faces are such a powerful stimulus that they divert attention away from the voice when a person is encountered. Consistent with this conclusion, Armstrong and McKelvie showed that voice recognition was improved if participants' attention was directed to the voice at encoding by informing them that their ability to recognise voices would subsequently be tested.

One implication of the face overshadowing effect is that blind people might be superior at recognising voices than sighted people. As Yarmey (1995) points out in his review of earwitness studies, however, there is very limited support for this claim. Winograd, Kerr, and Spence (1984) found no evidence of superior voice recognition in congenitally blind adults relative to controls. Although Bull, Rathborn, and Clifford (1983) found that blind listeners performed better on a short-term memory test for voices, voice recognition was not influenced by the severity of the visual impairment experienced by the "blind" participants in this study. It is important to note that these studies investigated memory for once-heard voices rather than the ability to recognise voices of familiar people.

Several studies indicate that the ability to recognise once-familiar voices can be severely disrupted by brain injury (e.g., Neuner & Schweinberger, 2000; Van Lancker, Kreiman, & Cummings, 1989). Neuner and Schweinberger described three patients who performed at chance levels when attempting to recognise voices, despite being able to recognise other kinds of sound just as well as controls. These three individuals were also as good as controls at recognising famous people from their name and from their face. These findings therefore support the view that different input systems are responsible for familiar voices (voice recognition units) from those involved in familiar face and name recognition.

Van Lancker, Cummings, Kreiman, and Dobkin (1988) reported a double dissociation between the ability in brain-injured patients to recognise familiar voices and the ability to discriminate between two unfamiliar voices. Cook and Wilding (1997) found a nonsignificant correlation between the ability to recognise famous voices and the ability to recognise a voice that had been presented earlier for the first time. These findings suggest that, as we saw with faces, the ability to remember familiar voices may rely to some extent on different components of the voice-processing system from those involved in recognising once-heard voices.

Voices, as we already noted, have been integrated within the Bruce and Young (1986) and the Burton and Bruce (1992) models of face recognition, with a separate input route accessing the PINS so that the model does represent the role of the voice in making judgements about identity. However, as well as conveying information about a person's identity, voices carry information about age, sex, and national, regional, and social origins, and we also tend to make judgements about character on the basis of voice. Yarmey (1993), in his study of stereotypes for faces and voices, found that there were significant correlations between rated voice characteristics and rated personality traits. For example, high voices were associated with weak personalities and soft voices with submissive personalities. Voices may express mood, affect, and emotions even more clearly than faces. These considerations suggest that further routes for voice expression analysis (mirroring the route for facial expression analysis) and for directed voice processing of semantic information need to be incorporated in the model.

CONCLUSIONS

Although the topic of memory for voices is still under-researched, great progress has been made in understanding the processes of face recognition and name recall. In both these areas, researchers using a wide range of different methodologies, including formal experiments, naturalistic observations, neuropsychological case studies, and computer simulations, have pooled their findings and sought to construct theoretical frameworks that take account of them all. Although it is clear that we are experts at recognising familiar faces, the same cannot be said for our ability to remember faces that we have seen only once. Our ability even to match different views of unfamiliar faces is far from perfect. It appears that configural information (the spatial relationship between the internal features of a face) is critical for remembering a person's face, and our ability to store this information appears to require that we have considerable exposure to a face before the configural information becomes stored in memory. Exactly how unfamiliar faces become familiar is likely to be a major topic of research in the next few years.

It is apparent that memory for faces and memory for proper names constitute special systems in that they can be independently impaired. Both the identification of faces and the retrieval of proper names incur the added difficulty attaching to individuation. As opposed to tasks that only require classification, individuation requires an extra level of discrimination and precision so that, although it is easy to say that something is a face, it is a great deal harder to decide whose face it is. Interestingly, both face recognition and name recall elicit a wide range of individual differences in ability Many people are not at all good at recognising faces or at remembering names, and the line between normal and pathological performance is blurred.

REFERENCES

Armstrong, H.A., & McKelvie, S.J. (1996). Effect of face context on recognition memory for voices. *Journal of General Psychology, 123*, 259–270.

Backmann, T. (1991). Memory for unfamiliar faces. *Memory and Cognition, 19*, 63–71.

Bahrick, H.P. (1984). Memory for people. In J.E. Harris & P.E. Morris (Eds.), *Everyday memory, actions and absentmindedness*. London: Academic Press.

Barry, C., Johnston, R.A., & Scanlan, L.C. (1998). Are faces special objects? Associative and semantic priming of face and object recognition and naming. *Quarterly Journal of Experimental Psychology, 51A*, 853–882.

Bauer, R. (1984). Autonomic recognition of faces and names in prosopagnosia. *Neuropsychologia, 22*, 457–469.

Breen, N., Caine, D., & Coltheart, M. (2000). Models of face processing and delusional misidentification: A critical review. *Cognitive Neuropsychology, 17*, 55–71.

Brennen, T., Baguley, T., Bright, J., & Bruce, V. (1990). Resolving semantically induced tip-of-the-tongue states for proper nouns. *Memory and Cognition, 18*, 339–347.

Brennen, T., David, D., Fluchaire, I., & Pellat, J. (1996). Naming faces and objects without comprehension. *Cognitive Neuropsychology, 13*, 93–110.

Bricker, P.D., & Pruzansky, S. (1966). Effects of stimulus content and duration on talker identification. *Journal of the Acoustical Society of America, 40*, 1441–1449.

Brown, R., & McNeill, D. (1966). The "tip of the tongue" phenomenon. *Journal of Verbal Learning and Verbal Behavior, 5*, 325–327.

Bruce, V. (1982). Changing faces: Visual and non-visual coding processes in face recognition. *British Journal of Psychology, 73*, 105–116.

Bruce, V., Henderson, Z., Greenwood, K., Hancock, P., Burton, A.M., & Miller, P. (1999). Verification of face identities from images captured on video. *Journal of Experimental Psychology: Applied, 5*, 339–360.

Bruce, V., & Young, A. (1986). Understanding face recognition. *British Journal of Psychology, 77*, 305–327.

Bruck, M., Cavanagh, P., & Ceci, S. (1991). Fortysomething: Recognising faces at one's 25th reunion. *Memory & Cognition, 19*, 221–228.

Bull, R., Rathborn, H., & Clifford, B.R. (1983). The voice recognition accuracy of blind listeners. *Perception, 12*, 223–226.

Burke, D.M., Mackay, D.G., Worthley, J.S., & Wade, E. (1991). On the tip of the tongue:

What causes word finding failures in young and older adults. *Journal of Memory and Language, 30,* 542–579.

Burton, M., & Bruce, V. (1992). I recognise your face but I can't remember your name: A simple explanation. *British Journal of Psychology, 83,* 457–480.

Burton, A.M., Bruce, V., & Hancock, P.J.B. (1999). From pixels to people: A model of familiar face recognition. *Cognitive Science, 23,* 1–31.

Burton, M., Bruce, V., & Johnston, R. (1990). Understanding face recognition with an interactive activation model. *British Journal of Psychology, 81,* 361–380.

Burton, M., Young, A.W., Bruce, V., Johnston, R., & Ellis, A. (1991). Understanding covert recognition. *Cognition, 39,* 129–166.

Caramazza, A., & Shelton, J. (1998). Domain-specific knowledge systems in the brain: The animate–inanimate distinction. *Journal of Cognitive Neuroscience, 10,* 1–34.

Carson, D.R., Burton, M., & Bruce, V. (2000). Putting names to faces. A review and test of the models. *Pragmatics and Cognition, 8,* 9–62.

Chiroro, P., & Valentine, T. (1995). An investigation of the contact hypothesis of the own-race bias in face recognition. *Quarterly Journal of Experimental Psychology, 48A,* 879–894.

Clarke, F.R., & Becker, R.W. (1969). Comparison of techniques for discriminating among talkers. *Journal of Speech and Hearing Research, 12,* 747–761.

Clifford, B.R. (1983). Memory for voices: The feasibility and quality of earwitness evidence. In S.M.A. Lloyd-Bostock & B.R. Clifford (Eds.), *Evaluating witness evidence.* Chichester, UK: Wiley.

Cohen, G. (1990). Why is it difficult to put names to faces? *British Journal of Psychology, 81,* 287–297.

Cohen, G., & Faulkner, D. (1986). Memory for proper names: Age differences in retrieval. *British Journal of Developmental Psychology, 4,* 187–197.

Cook, S., & Wilding, J. (1997). Earwitness testimony: Never mind the variety, hear the length. *Applied Cognitive Psychology, 11,* 95–111.

Craigie, M., & Hanley, J.R. (1997). Putting faces to names. *British Journal of Psychology, 88,* 157–171.

Cross, E., & Burke, D.M. (2004). Do alternative names block young and older adult's retrieval of proper names? *Brain & Language, 89,* 174–181.

Damjanovic, L., & Hanley, J.R. (in press). Recalling episodic and semantic information about famous faces and voices. *Memory & Cognition, 45.*

De Haan, E.H.F., Young, A.W., & Newcombe, F. (1991). A dissociation between the sense of familiarity and access to semantic information concerning familiar people. *European Journal of Cognitive Psychology, 3,* 51–67.

De Renzi, E., Faglioni, P., Grossi, D., & Nichelli, P. (1991). Apperceptive and associative forms of prosopagnosia. *Cortex, 27,* 213–221.

Ellis, A., Young, A.W., & Critchley, E.M.R. (1989). Loss of memory for people following temporal lobe damage. *Brain, 112,* 1469–1483.

Ellis, H.D., & Shepherd, J.W. (1992). Face memory—theory and practice. In M.M. Gruneberg, P.E. Morris, & R.N. Sykes (Eds.), *Practical aspects of memory: Current research and issues,* Vol. 1. Chichester, UK: Wiley.

Ellis, H.D., Shepherd, J.W., & Davies, G.M. (1979). Identification of familiar and unfamiliar faces from internal and external features: Some implications for theories of face recognition. *Perception, 8,* 431–439.

Ellis, H.D., Young, A.W., Quayle, A.H., & De Pauw, K.W. (1997). Reduced autonomic responses to faces in Capgras delusion. *Proceedings of the Royal Society London B, 264,* 1085–1092.

Fallshore, M., & Schooler, J.W. (1995). The verbal vulnerability of perceptual expertise. *Journal of Experimental Psychology: Learning, Memory, & Cognition, 21,* 1608–1623.

Farah, M. (1991). Patterns of co-occurrence among the associative agnosias. *Cognitive Neuropsychology, 8,* 1–19.

Flude, B.M., Ellis, A.W., & Kay, J. (1989). Face processing and retrieval in an anomic aphasia: Names are stored separately from semantic information about people. *Brain and Cognition, 11,* 60–72.

Gentileschi, V., Sperber, S., & Spinnler, H. (2001). Crossmodal agnosia for familiar people as a consequence of right infero-polar temporal atrophy. *Cognitive Neuropsychology, 18,* 439–463.

Gollan, T.H., Bonanni, M.P., & Montoya, R.I. (2005). Proper names get stuck on bilingual and monolingual speakers' tip of the tongue equally often. *Neuropsychology, 19,* 278–287.

Hanley, J.R. (1995). Are names difficult to recall because they are unique ? A case study of a patient with anomia. *The Quarterly Journal of Experimental Psychology, 48A,* 487–506.

Hanley, J.R., & Chapman, E. (in press). Partial knowledge in a tip-of-the-tongue state about two and three word proper names. *Psychonomic Bulletin & Review.*

Hanley, J.R., & Cowell, E. (1988). The effects of different types of retrieval cues on the recall of names of famous faces. *Memory & Cognition, 16,* 545–555.

Hanley, J.R., Pearson, N.A., & Young, A.W. (1990). Impaired memory for new visual forms. *Brain, 113,* 1131–1148.

Hanley, J.R., Smith, T., & Hadfield, J. (1998). I recognise you but I can't place you: An investigation of familiar-only experiences during tests of voice and face recognition. *The Quarterly Journal of Experimental Psychology, 51A,* 179–195.

Hanley, J.R., Young, A.W., & Pearson, N.A. (1989). Defective recognition of familiar people. *Cognitive Neuropsychology, 6,* 179–210.

Harris, D., & Kay, J. (1995). I know your face, but I can't remember your name. Is it because names are unique? *British Journal of Psychology, 86,* 345–358.

Hay, D.C., Young, A.W., & Ellis, A.W. (1991). Routes through the face recognition system. *Quarterly Journal of Experimental Psychology, 43A,* 761–791.

Hirstein, W., & Ramchandran, V. (1997). Capgras syndrome: A novel probe for under-standing the neural representation of the identity and familiarity of persons. *Proceedings of the Royal Society London B, 264,* 437–444.

Kay, J., & Hanley, J.R. (1999). Person-specific knowledge and knowledge of biological categories. *Cognitive Neuropsychology, 16,* 171–180.

Kay, J., & Hanley, J.R. (2002). Preservation of memory for people in semantic memory: Further category-specific semantic dissociation. *Cognitive Neuropsychology, 19,* 113–133.

Kemp, R., Towell, N., & Pike, G. (1997). When seeing should not be believing photographs, credit cards and fraud. *Applied Cognitive Psychology, 11,* 211–222.

Klatzky, R.L., & Forrest, F.H. (1984). Recognising familiar and unfamiliar faces. *Memory & Cognition, 12,* 60–70.

Levine, D.N., Warrach, J., & Farah, M. (1985). Two visual systems in mental imagery: Dissociation of "what" and "where" in imagery disorders due to bilateral posterior cerebral lesions. *Neurology, 35,* 1010–1018.

Logie, R.H., Baddeley, A.D., & Woodhead, M.M. (1987). Face recognition, pose, and ecological validity. *Applied Cognitive Psychology, 1,* 53–69.

Lyons, F., Hanley, J.R., & Kay, J. (2002). Anomia for common names with preserved retrieval of names of people. *Cortex, 38,* 23–35.

Macrae, C.N., & Lewis, H.L. (2002). Do I know you? Processing orientation and face recognition. *Psychological Science, 134,* 194–196.

McAllister, H.A., Dale, R.H.I., Bregman, N.J., McCabe, A., & Cotton, C.R. (1993). When eyewitnesses are earwitnesses: Effects on visual and voice identifications. *Basic and Applied Social Psychology, 14,* 161–170.

McWeeny, K.H., Young, A., Hay, D.C., & Ellis, A.W. (1987). Putting names to faces. *British Journal of Psychology, 78,* 143–149.

Megreya, A.M., & Burton, A.M. (2006). Unfamiliar faces aren't faces: Evidence from a matching task. *Memory & Cognition, 34*, 865–876.

Miceli, G., Capasso, R., Daniele, A., Esposito, T., Magarelli, M., & Tomaiuolo, F. (2000). Selective deficit for people's names following left temporal damage: An impairment of domain-specific conceptual knowledge. *Cognitive Neuropsychology, 17*, 489–516.

Moscovitch, M., & Moscovitch, D. (2000). Super face inversion effects for isolated internal or external features, and for fractured faces. *Cognitive Neuropsychology, 17*, 201–219.

Moscovitch, M., Winocur, G., & Behrmann, M. (1997). What is special about face recognition? *Journal of Cognitive Neuroscience, 9*, 555–604.

Navon, D. (1977). Forest before the trees: The precedence of global features in visual perception. *Cognitive Psychology, 9*, 353–383.

Neuner, F., & Schweinberger, S.R. (2000). Neuropsychological impairments in the recognition of faces, voices and personal names. *Brain & Cognition, 44*, 342–366.

Newell, F.N., Chiroro, P., & Valentine, T. (1999). Recognising unfamiliar faces: The effects of distinctiveness and view. *Quarterly Journal of Experimental Psychology, 52A*, 509–534.

Reason, J.T., & Lucas, D. (1984). Using cognitive diaries to investigate naturally occurring memory blocks. In J.E. Harris & P.E. Morris (Eds.), *Everyday memory, actions and absentmindedness*. London: Academic Press.

Reason, J.T., & Mycielska, K. (1982). *Absentminded? The psychology of mental lapses and everyday errors*. Englewood Cliffs, NJ: Prentice-Hall.

Rendell, P.G., Castel, A.D., & Craik, F.I.M. (2005). Memory for proper names in old age: A disproportionate impairment. *Quarterly Journal of Experimental Psychology, 58A*, 54–71.

Rhodes, G., Brennan, S.E., & Carey, S. (1987). Identification and ratings of caricatures: Implications for mental representations of faces. *Cognitive Psychology, 19*, 473–497.

Roberts, P.M., Garcia, L.J., Desrochers, A., & Hernandez, D. (2002). English performance of proficient bilingual adults on the Boston Naming Test. *Aphasiology, 16*, 635–645.

Semenza, C., & Zettin, M. (1988). Generating proper names: A case of selective inability. *Cognitive Neuropsychology, 5*, 711–721.

Shepherd, J.W., Gibling, F., & Ellis, H.D. (1991). The effects of distinctiveness, presentation time and delay in face recognition. *European Journal of Cognitive Psychology, 3*, 137–145.

Sinha, P., & Poggio, T. (1996). I think I know that face . . . *Nature, 384*, 404.

Stevenage, S.V., & Lewis, H.G. (2005). By which name should I call thee? The consequences of having multiple names. *Quarterly Journal of Experimental Psychology, 58A*, 1447–1461.

Tanaka, J.W., & Farah, M. (1993). Parts and wholes in face recognition. *Quarterly Journal of Experimental Psychology, 46A*, 225–246.

Thompson, S.A., Graham, K.S., Williams, G., Patterson, K., Kapur, N., & Hodges, J.R. (2004). Dissociating person-specific from general semantic knowledge: Roles of the left and right temporal lobes. *Neuropsychologia, 42*, 359–370.

Tippett, L.J., Miller, L.J., & Farah, M.J. (2000). Prosopamnesia: A selective impairment in face learning. *Cognitive Neuropsychology, 17*, 241–255.

Valentine, T. (1991). A unified account of the effects of distinctiveness, inversion and race in face recognition. *Quarterly Journal of Experimental Psychology, 43A*, 161–204.

Valentine, T., Brédart, S., Lawson, R., & Ward, G. (1991). What's in a name? Access to information from peoples' names. *European Journal of Cognitive Psychology, 3*, 147–176.

Valentine, T., Brennen, T., & Brédart, S. (1996). *The cognitive psychology of proper names*. London: Routledge.

Valentine, T., & Bruce, V. (1986). The effects of distinctiveness in recognizing and classifying faces. *Perception, 15*, 525–536.

Valentine, T., Chiroro, P., & Dixon, R. (1995). An account of the own-race bias and the contact hypothesis in terms of a face space model of face recognition. In T. Valentine (Ed.),

Cognitive and computational aspects of face recognition: Explorations in face space. London: Routledge.

Valentine, T., & Moore, V. (1995). Naming faces: The effects of facial distinctiveness and surname frequency. *Quarterly Journal of Experimental Psychology, 48A,* 849–878.

Valentine, T., Pickering, A., & Darling, S. (2003). Characteristics of eyewitness identification that predict the outcome of real lineups. *Applied Cognitive Psychology, 17,* 969–993.

Van Lancker, D.R., Cummings, J.L., Kreiman, J., & Dobkin, B.H. (1988). Phonagnosia: A dissociation between familiar and unfamiliar voices. *Cortex, 24,* 195–209.

Van Lancker, D.R., Kreiman, J., & Cummings, J. (1989). Voice perception deficits: Neuro-anatomical correlates of phonagnosia. *Journal of Clinical and Experimental Neuropsychology, 11,* 665–674.

Westmacott, R., & Moscovitch, M. (2003). The contribution of autobiographical significance to semantic memory. *Memory & Cognition, 31,* 761–774.

Winograd, E., Kerr, N.H., & Spence, M.J. (1984). Voice recognition: Effects of orienting task, and a test of blind versus sighted listeners. *American Journal of Psychology, 97,* 57–70.

Yarmey, A.D. (1973). I recognise your face but I can't remember your name: Further evidence on the tip-of-the-tongue phenomenon. *Memory and Cognition, 3,* 287–290.

Yarmey, A.D. (1993). Stereotypes and recognition: Memory for faces and voices of good guys and bad guys. *Applied Cognitive Psychology, 7,* 419–431.

Yarmey, A.D. (1995). Earwitness speaker identification. *Psychology, Public Policy and Law, 1,* 792–816.

Yarmey, A.D., Yarmey, A.L., & Yarmey, M.J. (1994). Face and voice identifications in showups and lineups. *Applied Cognitive Psychology, 8,* 453–464.

Yin, R.K. (1969). Looking at upside down faces. *Journal of Experimental Psychology, 81,* 141–145.

Young, A.W., & Bruce, V. (1991). Perceptual categories and the computation of "grandmother". *European Journal of Cognitive Psychology, 3,* 5–49.

Young, A.W., & De Haan, E.H.F. (1988). Boundaries of covert recognition in prosopagnosia. *Cognitive Neuropsychology, 5,* 317–336.

Young, A.W., Ellis, A.W., & Flude, B. (1988a). Accessing stored information about familiar people. *Psychological Research, 50,* 111–115.

Young, A.W., Hay, D.C., & Ellis, A.W. (1985). The faces that launched a thousand slips: Everyday difficulties and errors in recognising people. *British Journal of Psychology, 76,* 4956–523.

Young, A.W., Hellawell, D., & De Haan, E.H.F. (1988b). Cross-domain semantic priming in normal subjects and in a prosopagnosic patient. *Quarterly Journal of Experimental Psychology, 40,* 561–580.

Young, A.W., Hellawell, D., & Hay, D. (1987). Configural information in face perception, *Perception, 16,* 747–759.

5 Memory for intentions, actions, and plans

Judi A. Ellis and Gillian Cohen

PROSPECTIVE MEMORY

What is prospective memory?

Everyday memory does not only consist of a record of past events. As well as remembering what has happened in the past, we also use memory to encode our future or delayed intentions and plans. Most importantly, we need to remember to actually perform the intended actions, while memory is also involved in keeping track of ongoing actions and of the actions we intend to carry out in the future. This type of memory is known as prospective memory. Everyday memory research places a particular emphasis on memory functions and remembering to carry out daily tasks is one of the most basic of these functions. If this kind of memory is impaired, people can be severely compromised in their ability to live an independent life.

Prospective memory is used to describe both the tasks that we want to carry out and the processes that support the performance of these tasks. It includes forming an intention, which includes the decision to act in a particular way in the future (the intent), what we want to do (an action) and when we want to do it (a retrieval cue), together with plans concerned with how we perform that action at the appropriate moment, e.g., passing on a message when you see your friend Jane. Thus we have to remember both what we want to do and when we want to do it. In everyday life prospective memory is almost continuously active. We go through the day employing prospective memory to remember to pay the gas bill, phone a relative, buy more cat food, raise a point at a meeting, look up a reference in the library, and so on. In some cases, failures of prospective remembering may have serious, or even catastrophic, consequences. The safety of many people may depend on the prospective memory of pilots, doctors, and those in charge of machinery. On a more everyday level, our health may depend on our ability not only to remember to take medicine but also to remember whether or not we have taken it at the prescribed time, so that we don't take either too much or too little—something that may be especially important in old age when we may have to take multiple medications.

The term prospective memory was designed to draw a distinction between memory for future actions (prospective memory) and retrospective memory, which is concerned with the recall of events that occurred in the past. A major point of interest, therefore, is the relationship between prospective and retrospective memory. Baddeley and Wilkins (1984) have pointed out that, in practice, the distinction between the two kinds of memory is not absolutely clear-cut because prospective memory necessarily includes some elements of retrospective memory. In remembering my plan to phone my mother, I also remember, retrospectively, her number and how to use the phone, and not to call while she is watching her favourite television programme. However, despite this overlap between the two kinds of memory, there are numerous distinguishing features. Prospective memory differs from retrospective memory at the encoding stage, as prospective plans are often self-generated and do not necessarily involve initial learning, but the difference between the two is perhaps more marked at the retrieval stage. In most retrospective memory tasks the amount of information that has to be recalled is often fairly substantial, e.g., when you last went to the doctor and what she told you to do. In prospective memory, by contrast, the amount of information that has to be remembered is usually small, in that we need only remember that we want to post a letter, call the plumber, or whatever. However, although we may have relatively little to remember, this task is not a trivial one—the most common cause of a prospective memory error is failure to recall that intended action at the appropriate moment, e.g., when passing a postbox on our way to work.

The findings from some studies suggest that there may be a dissociation between prospective memory ability and retrospective memory ability. Kvavilashvili (1987), for example, found no significant correlation between retrospective and prospective memory. In her study those participants who were good at the prospective task of remembering to give a message to the experimenter were not necessarily good at recalling the content of the message, and vice versa. Wilkins and Baddeley (1978) actually found a negative correlation. They designed a prospective memory study to simulate remembering to take pills at a specific time. Subjects had to press a button on a small box at 8.30 a.m., 1.00 p.m., 5.30 p.m. and 10 p.m. each day for 7 days. The apparatus in the box recorded the time of each button press. Lateness of response increased across the 7 days, and across each day, with early responses being more accurate than later ones, perhaps because later in the day there were more competing activities, providing a greater source of distraction. The same participants were also given a retrospective memory test of free recall of lists of unrelated words. It emerged that those who had good retrospective verbal memory did poorly on the prospective task, a phenomenon that Wilkins and Baddeley described as the "absentminded professor effect".

Although there are logical and functional differences between prospective and retrospective memory, it is by no means clear that prospective memory is a distinct and separate type of memory. It is not too surprising that prospective memory for taking medicine does not correlate strongly with the kind of retrospective memory involved in recall of word lists from long-term memory because these are very different tasks. When the tasks are more similar a different result emerges. Hitch and Ferguson (1991) compared prospective and retrospective memory in a study that tested the ability of members of a film society to recall, retrospectively, the names of films they had seen in the past and to recall, prospectively, the names of films they intended to see in the future. The two kinds of memory showed interesting correspondences. Retrospective memory for past films showed the usual recency effect, with better recall of more recent films. As shown in Figure 5.1, prospective memory for future films showed an analogous proximity effect; films one planned to see earlier were better remembered.

For both past and future films, memory was inversely related to the total number of films and there was a small but significant correlation between an individual's

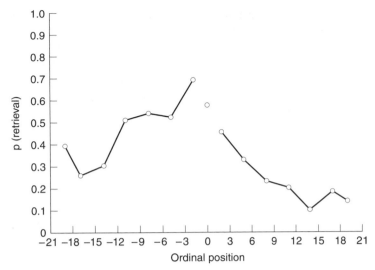

Figure 5.1 Proportion of films retrieved as a function of ordinal position in subjects' film diaries (zero = current film; negative numbers = past films; positive numbers = future films). From Hitch, G.J. and Ferguson, J. (1991). Prospective memory for future intentions: Some comparisons with memory for past events. *European Journal of Cognitive Psychology*, 3, 285–295. Copyright © Psychology Press (http://www.psypress.co.uk/journals.asp).

retrospective and prospective memory. More recently, researchers have taken a different approach to understanding the relationship between retrospective and prospective memory by examining whether particular variables have the same or a different effect on each type of memory task (Einstein & McDaniel, 1990). Different effects would suggest that prospective memory is a distinct form of remembering while similar ones would suggest commonalities between the two types of task; cf. Hitch and Ferguson's examination of recency effects. Another source of information is the data that comes from the use of neuroimaging techniques such as fMRI (functional magnetic imaging) or PET (positron emission tomography) to identify the brain areas that are activated when a prospective memory task is being encoded, retained, and performed, and to contrast this with those areas activated during a comparable retrospective memory task (see, for example, Burgess, Quayle, & Frith, 2001). Although it is still not clear how far prospective memory should be regarded as a distinct and separate type of memory, as will become apparent in this chapter this may be because the performance of a prospective memory task appears to rely on cognitive processes other than memory.

Types of prospective memory

Prospective memory is probably much too broad a category to be useful. Each of the components of an intention can encompass a number of variations. If we consider the nature of the decision to act, one distinction that can be drawn concerns the origin of the intention: Whether it is self-generated or imposed by someone else. It is also the case that some intentions are of vital importance and have high priority while others are much less important and have low priority. It is not necessarily the case that a prospective plan is implemented if it is retrieved at the appropriate moment; different intentions may compete with each other for our time. Some will be postponed, some will be truncated, and others will be discarded altogether. Other distinctions relate to the action that we want to perform. Some prospective tasks, for example, involve remembering to perform routine actions such as posting a letter whereas others involve novel actions or novel modifications of familiar actions, such as performing a familiar action at different times or in a novel context. Similarly, a prospective memory task may describe a single isolated action or a set of related or unrelated actions, and these actions may be either specific and detailed (e.g., going to a particular shop and buying a particular brand of cat food) or more vague or general (e.g., do the shopping); for further discussion see Kvavilashvili and Ellis (1996).

The point about specificity applies to the cue as well as the action content of the intention, i.e., the criteria for when the action should be recalled and performed. Ellis (1988), for example, distinguished between "pulses" and "steps". A pulse intention specifies an exact time at which it must be implemented (e.g., 3.15 on Tuesday afternoon). A step intention describes a larger time window (e.g., before the library closes; next time I see him; after I've finished everything else I have to do today). Ellis found that pulses are better recalled than steps, are judged to be more important, and people are more likely to use an external memory aid such as a diary to remind them of pulses. Einstein and McDaniel (1990) have distinguished two kinds of prospective memory on the basis of the cues that trigger retrieval. Time-based prospective memory requires performance either at a specific time or after some period of time has elapsed, cf. pulses and steps. In event-based prospective memory, by contrast, the cue is an object, person, or event (e.g., seeing your friend Jane should remind you to pass on the message to her). Time-based prospective memories are generally harder to remember because the passage of time has to be monitored and remembering is self-initiated, whereas in event-based prospective memory the reminder is physically present in the environment. Einstein and McDaniel (1991) showed that elderly people had no deficit in event-based memory but were poorer at time-based tasks. These differences between various types of prospective memory are potentially significant because they are likely to influence its efficiency. Both theoretical and common-sense considerations suggest that novel, high-priority event-based plans that are part of a network of related plans are more likely to be remembered (Ellis, 1996).

Methods of studying prospective memory

Devising methods for studying prospective memory presents a challenge, particularly when one considers the huge variety of intentions that we form, as well as the need to schedule and prioritise between several intentions that should be performed in a given time period. The methods that have been adopted include questionnaires and diary studies, field experiments and laboratory experiments, as well as the adaptation of the latter for use in neuroimaging (e.g., fMRI, PET) and electrophysiological (e.g., ERP, EEG) studies. Questionnaires and diary studies are employed to investigate naturally occurring intentions; field experiments are ones in which the experimenter prescribes the task but the participants carry it out in their everyday life, e.g., Wilkins & Baddeley's (1978) pill-taking task; and laboratory experiments are experimenter-generated and conducted in a relatively novel environment.

Questions about prospective memory have been incorporated in a number of questionnaires, for example, "How often do you forget to keep an appointment?" or "How often do you forget to take things with you when you go out?" or "How often do you forget to say something you intended to say?" Problems about the validity of self-assessments of this kind were discussed at greater length in Chapter 1. One difficulty is that people may not always be aware of their prospective memory failures. Of course, failure to implement some plans will be noticed because they have serious consequences or earn bitter reproaches, but other failures may well pass unnoticed. In their pill-taking study, run as a field experiment, Wilkins and Baddeley (1978) noted that although people remembered when they had performed their intended actions, they tended to be unaware of omissions. This finding suggests that self-assessment of prospective memory ability is likely to be inaccurate. Moreover, the generic nature of the questions that are typically posed does not take account of the specific characteristics of particular intentions; as noted earlier, these can influence the likelihood that they will be performed, e.g., the importance of the appointment that has been made.

Several questionnaire studies indicate that older adults report better prospective memory than do young people (Harris & Sunderland, 1987). Logically, this could arise if older people are more likely to fail to notice their errors or, having noticed them at the time, forget about them later. However, Martin (1986) argues that older adults are essentially accurate in their self-assessment. She found not only that older adults rated their memory as better than a young group for keeping appointments, paying bills, and taking medicine, but also that objective records of their attendance at appointments confirmed their superiority. However, questionnaire responses do not reveal how far successful prospective remembering was due to the use of external reminders and how far the respondents relied on their own memory. The apparent superiority of elderly people could also arise if their lifestyle is more relaxed, so that the demands on prospective memory are less severe for them than for the young. All these factors make it unlikely that questionnaire responses can provide an accurate reflection of prospective memory ability. Ellis's (1988) study, which identified step and pulse intentions, is an example of a diary study, used to investigate some of the variables that influence performance on naturally occurring intentions.

A method that potentially provides a more objective evidence of success or failure is the field experiment. Here, researchers set people a specific task, such as remembering to post a postcard or make a phone call to the experimenter at a designated time. This method allows the experimenter to vary factors such as the retention interval, the number and spacing of the to-be-remembered actions, and the incentives that are offered for successful performance. Sometimes, these prospective memory tasks are incorporated into an interview (West, 1984). In West's study, remembering to keep the interview appointment was one test of prospective memory. Participants were also told at the start of the interview that they should remember to locate a folder and hand it to the interviewer at the end of the session. A number of problems can arise with field experiments like these. Although the experimenter can manipulate some of the relevant variables, there is no way of controlling other, potentially relevant variables operating during the retention interval, such as the amount of rehearsal and the number of competing tasks. Maylor (1990) used a telephone call task and later debriefed her older adult participants about the strategies they had used. She classified these as conjunction cues (mentally linking making the phone call to another routine event), external cues (using notes, diaries, alarm clocks), and internal cues (relying on memory, rehearsing the task, mentally reviewing a schedule). The old-old participants did less well than the young-old, but only when they were relying on internal cues. Thus, the results of the experiment were misleading unless underlying strategies were disclosed and taken into account.

Field experiments appear to have high ecological validity; they incorporate actions that retain some resemblance to naturally occurring ones and the task takes place during one's everyday activity. However, by taking part in everyday life they sacrifice experimental control and the findings are therefore difficult to interpret. Moreover, the actions are a little contrived—sending a blank postcard to an experimenter is a less than meaningful task. Thus one not only loses experimental control but also fails to gain important information on naturally occurring intentions. Another problem is that the number of observations (e.g., the number of telephone calls made or postcards posted) per subject is low, making the data difficult to interpret.

Laboratory studies of prospective memory can suffer from different problems (see Kvavilashvili, 1992, for a review). West (1986) designed an experiment varying the load on prospective memory. She asked her participants to carry out a sequence of up to 14 actions (such as put the comb on the table, put the toothbrush in the bag) and recorded omission errors and order errors for young and older subjects. There was a clear age deficit in ability to carry out the longer action sequences. However, the task is a very artificial one. In everyday life people seldom need to memorise 14 unrelated actions—they would write them down—and there is likely to be a coherent reason why these tasks need to be performed in a specific order, thereby providing some cues for retrieval.

A number of recent studies have built prospective memory tasks into a text-processing paradigm in which people are asked to remember to underline certain target words in the text, put a tick at the end of a page, and get up and switch off the room lights at the end of a passage (e.g., Evans, Wilson, & Baddeley, 1994). Other experimenters have embedded a prospective task into a short-term memory task (e.g., Einstein & McDaniel, 1990). Here, the primary task is to study a list of words for subsequent recall and the prospective task is to press a key when a target word occurs. Again, these could be considered to be artificial tasks. However, even when a laboratory study of prospective memory involves a naturalistic task, the unfamiliar environment of the laboratory may affect the results. Ceci, Baker, and Bronfenbrenner (1988) studied the behaviour of children who had to remember to take cakes out of the oven after 30 minutes. As shown in Figure 5.2, the frequency and pattern of clock checking was significantly different when the task was performed at home and when it was performed in the laboratory. At home, the children checked the clock often in the first 10 minutes but then only infrequently until the last few minutes. Ceci et al. suggested that the children used the frequent initial checks to calibrate their subjective psychological clock with the objective external clock and then were able to rely on internal monitoring. This interpretation was confirmed by the fact that the same calibration strategy was evident even if the clock was made to run faster or slower than normal. In the laboratory, by contrast, clock checking was 30% more frequent and showed a different pattern, increasing in frequency across the 30-minute period.

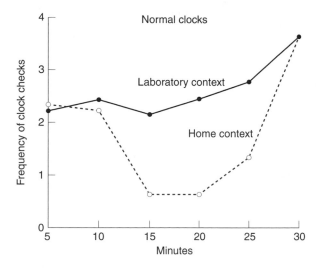

Figure 5.2 Children's frequency of monitoring a clock during cooking in a
laboratory and home context. From Ceci, S.J., Baker, J., and
Bronfenbrenner, U. (1988). Prospective memory: Temporal
calibration and context. In M.M. Gruneberg, P.E. Morris, and R.N.
Sykes (Eds.), *Practical aspects of memory: Current research and
issues* (pp. 360–365). Copyright © 1988 John Wiley & Sons Ltd.
Reproduced with permission.

Ceci et al.'s (1988) study is important because it demonstrates that an interesting
strategy for time-based prospective remembering was only revealed in naturalistic
conditions. Clearly, performance on a particular task may be sensitive to the context
in which it is performed. However, this particular task—remembering to take a cake
out of the oven—is a more unusual one when performed in the laboratory than when
performed at home. One conclusion that can be drawn from this finding, therefore,
is that when an everyday task is placed in a laboratory context it may lose its
ecological validity; it may be more important to ensure that the task—whatever it
is—is one that it is sensible and reasonable to ask someone to do in that context.
Thus, asking someone to press a specific key whenever a particular word appears
(prospective memory task) while they carry out a series of short-term memory tests
in the laboratory may be a more realistic and meaningful prospective memory task
than asking them to bake a cake in the laboratory!

Prospective memory efficiency

Research on prospective memory is primarily concerned with identifying the factors
that promote successful remembering or induce failure. Typically researchers have
investigated factors that affect performance at the following phases of prospective
memory, described by Ellis (1996; see also Brandimonte, 1991):

- formation and encoding of the intention (action, cue, intent);
- retention interval (period prior to opportunity to perform action);

- performance interval (period during which cue is expected to occur);
- initiation and execution of action;
- evaluation of outcome.

Motivation and emotional factors

The nature of the prospective task is a factor that can affect performance in any of the above phases. Another important factor in prospective memory is motivation, which can affect both compliance and memory. For a prospective act to be performed, the actor must not only remember to perform it but also must be willing to perform it. A patient may remember a hospital appointment, but not feel like going, or may remember to take prescribed medication, but decide not to take it. These are examples where poor motivation, rather than a failure of prospective memory, has caused a failure of compliance. But the level of motivation may also affect whether the prospective act is recalled at an appropriate moment when the cue occurs. It is a truism that very important appointments are rarely missed. When a job interview is make-or-break, you get there on time. A high level of motivation may ensure that an elaborate reminder system is set up and the sequence of events is carefully planned and frequently rehearsed.

These common-sense observations have been confirmed experimentally. Meacham and Singer (1977) gave participants eight postcards to post back one a week for 8 weeks. One group was offered a cash incentive for posting on time, which produced a small improvement in performance. Poon and Schaffer (1982) asked participants to phone in 25 times over a 3-week period, at specific times. Although a cash incentive had no effect on the proportion of calls remembered, payment did improve the accuracy of timing for older but not for young participants. The effect of incentives may not be very striking, but it seems probable that self-generated motivation in naturally occurring prospective memory tasks is a more powerful factor. Thus the few studies that have been conducted on perceived importance of an intention do tend to show a positive relationship between importance and prospective remembering (e.g., Ellis, 1988; Kliegel, Martin, McDaniel, & Einstein 2001; Kvavilashvili, 1987). Recent research indicates that intention importance has its main impact during the performance interval by improving performance when the characteristics of the intention make it more likely that people will use strategic (attentionally demanding) processes (Kliegel, Martin, McDaniel, & Einstein, 2004b). Thus, importance improves performance on a time-based but not on an event-based task (Kliegel et al., 2001). However, importance can impact on the performance of some event-based tasks. Kliegel et al. (2004), for example, found an effect of importance when there was a mismatch between the processing focus of an ongoing task (rating the pleasantness and other characteristics of words) and the focus needed to recognise prospective memory cue words that appeared in the ongoing task (detecting words that included either a "p" or a "q").

Other factors that are potentially relevant have so far received little attention. These include emotion and personality traits and states such as levels of anxiety and stress, and the effects of fatigue and illness. Cockburn and Smith (1994), in one of the few studies that have addressed these problems, found a complex relationship between level of anxiety and performance on a prospective memory task. Their findings suggested that both low and high levels of anxiety can be beneficial, but intermediate levels produce more failures, perhaps because at this level there is sufficient anxiety to produce errors but not enough to induce the extra effort needed to overcome them. Mood can also affect performance; depressed participants have been shown to complete fewer time-based intentions (Rude, Hertel, Jarrold, Covich, & Hedlund, 1999). Interestingly, there was a positive relationship between the frequency with which people checked the time (by pressing a computer key to display a clock on the monitor) and prospective memory performance. However, the nondepressed participants monitored the passage of time more frequently. Similar findings, using mood induction with a nonclinical population, have been reported by Kleigel et al. (2005). Personality differences also may be important; for example, people with Type A personalities, who are highly conscientious, tense, competitive worriers, were better at prospective memory tasks that they perceived as being important either to themselves or to someone else (Searleman & Gaydusek, 1989).

Using strategies and reminders

Other important influences on performance come from variations in how the task is encoded and the kind of strategies and reminders we use to ensure that we retain the content of the intention during a delay period and to prompt its retrieval at the appropriate moment. Meacham and Leiman (1975) gave people postcards to post back at varying intervals up to 32 days later. Half the participants were given coloured tags to hang on their key chains as a reminder, and there was some evidence that this improved performance. Einstein and McDaniel (1990) confirmed this finding on the benefits of an external memory aid in a laboratory study. The nature of the retrieval cue that should prompt intention recall and performance during a performance interval is also relevant. McDaniel and Einstein (1993) have demonstrated that cues that are highly distinctive, unfamiliar, and specific are particularly effective (see also Brandimonte & Passolunghi, 1994). A real-life example of this is the loud beeping signal that reminds me to turn off the car lights when I park. Of course, recognition of a retrieval cue is not sufficient for successful performance; we also need to recall the action encoded with that cue. Findings reported by McDaniel, Guynn, Einstein, and Breneiser (2004) indicate better prospective remembering when there was a close association between a cue and response (e.g., see the cue word spaghetti, write sauce) than when they were nonassociated (e.g., thread–pencil).

Many people spontaneously devise their own reminders (cf. Maylor's 1990 analysis of the strategies older people used for her telephone task). Moscovitch (1982) has suggested that the superior performance of older people in some prospective memory tasks may be due to increasing use of and reliance on external reminders. Older people are known to make more use of written reminders in diaries and notes (Moscovitch, 1982), and Harris (1980) reported that middle-aged women also made extensive use of reminders such as calendars and wall charts to remember family birthdays and social commitments. Other people make knots in handkerchiefs, leave objects where the eye will fall on them, or write in biro on their hands. Differences in the extent to which people devise internal and external reminders, and use them efficiently, as well as differences in the effectiveness of a memory aid for a particular intention, may underlie observed differences in prospective task performance between individuals, age groups, or sexes. Tying a knot in your hankie is a very nonspecific reminder, telling you only that you have something to do but not what it is, nor when you should do it!

Time factors

Time factors such as the length of the retention interval, the time of day, and the regularity with which a time cue appears have been studied experimentally. By analogy with retrospective memory, and in line with the proximity effect in Hitch and Ferguson's (1991) study of memory for films, it would be expected that prospective memory would decline as the retention interval increased. However, Wilkins (1976) varied the retention interval in a postcard task from 2 to 36 days, but found no effect of increasing delay. This finding has been replicated in several laboratory experiments using shorter time intervals, such as 15–30 minutes (Einstein, Holland, McDaniel, & Guynn, 1992; Guynn, McDaniel, & Einstein, 1998; Loftus, 1971) and indicates that prospective memory does not operate like retrospective memory, in this respect at least. One important characteristic of these experiments is that the contrast was always between different delay periods (e.g., an opportunity to perform an intention after 2 minutes or after 20 minutes) and not between no-delay (immediate performance) and a delay. When Brandimonte and Passolunghi (1994) examined performance in immediate and delayed conditions, they found forgetting after a 3-minute interval that was filled with an attentionally demanding task, suggesting that prospective memory forgetting may occur during the first minute or two after forming an intention (see also Einstein, McDaniel, Williford, Pagan, & Dismukes, 2003). Therefore prospective and retrospective memory appear similar with respect to the effects of immediate versus delayed performance, but may differ in the effects of increasing delays.

Harris and Wilkins (1982) have studied the effect of response spacing by asking their participants to hold up a card at 3- or 9-minute intervals while watching a film. They found no effect of response spacing and no effect of the stage of the film on prospective remembering. The interesting finding in this study was that people sometimes forgot to make the response even though they had checked the time within the previous 10 seconds. This finding supports Brandimonte and Passolunghi's (1994) suggestion that forgetting in prospective memory can occur in the first few seconds or minutes after the intention is formed. In everyday life we often have to carry out concurrent tasks; many of our intentions have to be recalled and carried out while we are engaged on other, often more routine, tasks such as remembering to take medication during, before, or after a meal. We are often distracted from our prospective intentions as, absorbed in one activity, we forget to interrupt it and do something else. The amount and type of concurrent activity are likely to be important factors in naturally occurring prospective memory. Ellis and Nimmo-Smith (1993), for example, noted that their subjects reported that their naturally occurring intentions were more likely to be recollected (during a retention interval) when their concurrent task required little attention. It has also been suggested that we might use natural breaks in our everyday tasks to recollect and evaluate upcoming intentions Laboratory studies have provided some support for this conjecture. Hicks, Marsh, and Russell (2000) found that providing breaks in activity led to improved prospective memory performance, with both long and shorter retention intervals (2.5, 5, and 15 minutes), and that longer intervals with breaks led to higher performance overall, presumably because they give more opportunities for a review of one's intentions.

Theoretical perspectives on prospective memory

Explanations of prospective memory draw on the theoretical principles and models derived from research on retrospective memory. One theoretical issue concerns the nature of the memory representation for future intentions. In a key set of experiments on this question, Goschke and Kuhl (1993) reported an "intention-superiority effect" in which the content of an intention appears to be held in a higher state of activation than other types of information in memory. In what they describe as the postponed intention paradigm, their participants learned a number of short activity scripts, each consisting of five short noun-verb phrases (e.g., light the candles) that described a particular activity (e.g., setting a dinner table). Some of these actions had to be executed later and some had to be recalled. They found that words from the to-be-executed scripts were recognised faster than words from the to-be-recalled scripts, and this effect was attributed to a heightened level of persisting activation for to-be-performed intentions. This phenomenon has been replicated and extended by Marsh and colleagues, who found that this effect persists when the intention is interrupted but disappears if the intention is either cancelled or performed (Marsh, Hicks, & Bink, 1998; Marsh, Hicks, & Bryan, 1999).

Koriat, Ben-Zur, and Nussbaum (1990) argued that if an intention is encoded verbally then memory should be better if it is tested by verbal recall than when tested by actual performance of the intention. If the representation is encoded in a motoric form, by acting it out during learning, then memory should be better when tested by performance. The results of their experiments showed that when participants had to remember a series of noun–verb phrases (e.g., pick up the book), performance was better when these phrases were performed at test. This superiority for phrases that people expected to recall through performance at test occurred even when recall was—unexpectedly—tested verbally. Koriat et al. (1990, p. 577) concluded that "the encoding of future tasks entails an internal symbolic enactment of the tasks which enhances memory", but did not rule out the possibility that the representation may include a mixture of verbal, imaginal, and motoric elements. Interestingly, Brandimonte and Passolunghi's (1994) findings support this suggestion. They found that forgetting after a short 3-minute delay occurred not only when the delay period was filled by an attentionally demanding activity, as reported earlier, but also when it was filled by an undemanding motor task ("drawing" circles in the air); importantly, however, forgetting did not occur when the delay period was filled by an undemanding verbal task (counting from 1 to 10).

Another theoretical issue concerns the mechanism of prospective memory. The idea that the central executive component of working memory schedules, controls, and monitors actions can be applied to prospective memory. This account is also consistent with the concept of a Supervisory Activating System (SAS), proposed by Norman and Shallice (1986), which acts to maintain goals and resist distractions, and is also capable of interrupting and changing ongoing behaviour in response to current environmental conditions. (Baddeley, 1993), adopted Norman and Shallice's SAS as a model of central executive function.) Norman and Shallice have identified the frontal lobes of the brain with the operation of the SAS. The frontal lobes are responsible for planning, organising, and controlling actions, and patients who have sustained damage to the frontal lobes show a *frontal lobe syndrome* that includes increased distractibility and inability to allocate attention effectively. In Norman and Shallice's model these patients are said to be reliant on the operation of a contention scheduling system that is responsible for the routine selection of action. Although they perform normally on many cognitive tests, these patients are distinguished by a disabling inability to organise their daily lives. Shallice and Burgess (1991) tested three patients with severe frontal lobe damage on a range of tasks including analogues of real-life planning. The Six Element Task required them to schedule and carry out two sets of three different tasks (dictating a route, solving 35 arithmetic problems, and writing the names of 100 pictured objects) within 15 minutes. Relative to control subjects, the patients were unable to allocate their time between the tasks. The Multiple Errands Task required them to carry out eight different errands (buying a loaf, buying throat pastilles, writing down the name of a shop, etc.) in a shopping precinct. Again the patients performed very poorly, breaking the rules and failing to complete the tasks, and although they were able to memorise the instructions, they seemed unable to organise their performance. Shallice and Burgess (1991) identified deficits in formulating, modifying, and evaluating an overall plan, and for creating triggering markers for the individual tasks within the plan. Goldstein, Bernard, Fenwick, Burgess, and McNeil (1993) reported very similar patterns in the performance of another patient with unilateral frontal lobectomy. The relationship demonstrated in these studies between frontal lobe damage and impaired prospective memory is consistent with the theoretical model in which these functions are controlled by the Supervisory Attentional System, or the central executive component of working memory.

Attentional or executive processes are important also for theoretical models of prospective memory retrieval processes. Successful retrieval, during a performance interval, relies on processing a retrieval cue in the ongoing task, recognising that it is a cue for an intended action, and retrieving and performing that action. Einstein and McDaniel (1996) summarised two opposing views on the attentional requirements of intention retrieval: the automatic activation model, in which retrieval is achieved with few demands on attentional resources, and a notice+search model that makes greater demands on attentional resources. At that time the findings from laboratory experiments could be accommodated by both of these models. Subsequent research has revealed a number of conflicting findings that have led to the proposal of a multiprocess model of retrieval (McDaniel & Einstein, 2000; see also Ellis, Milne, & McGann, 1997). According to this model, the attentional or strategic demands of future intention retrieval vary as a function of the characteristics of each of the different components of a prospective memory task (including the retention/delay interval and the ongoing task), and of the individual undertaking that task (e.g., age, personality). Recent research has employed a number of different methods to study the conditions under which retrieval requires attentional resources. These include investigation of the performance of younger and older adults (older adults are thought to have reduced attentional resources), children at different ages (attentional resources increase with age in children), and young adults under full or divided attention (using divided attention tasks that make varying demands on executive resources). More recently, Smith (2003; Smith & Bayen, 2004) has introduced a new method that examines the "costs" of prospective memory retrieval on the performance of the ongoing task in which the retrieval cue is embedded (ongoing task latency and/or accuracy). Current findings support the notion that the attentional demands of prospective memory task retrieval vary with the characteristics of that task (see, for example, Marsh, Hicks, & Cook, 2005; McGann, Ellis, & Milne, 2002).

Output monitoring

One relatively neglected aspect of prospective remembering is being able to recall the outcome of one's intention: Did you or did you not carry out the action as intended? The term "output monitoring" was employed by Koriat, Ben-Zur, and Sheffer (1988) to describe this. Two errors are possible here: omissions, due to the incorrect belief that you have performed the action when in fact you haven't, and repetitions, which arise from an incorrect belief that you didn't perform an action when in fact you did. Marsh, Hicks, Hancock and Munsayac (2002) have developed a laboratory paradigm that can distinguish between these errors. Their participants are asked to make one response when they see a retrieval cue for the first time (press / key) and a different response when it appears for a second occasion (press = key) *and* they recall having responded to it when it first occurred. This allows us to look at performance when the cue appears for a second time after both a correct (pressed /) and incorrect (no action) response on its first appearance. Marsh et al. found that younger adults' omissions occurred because they (wrongly) thought they had carried out an action, whereas some repetition errors were due not to failure to see a cue word, but to the wrong belief that they had not made a prior response. It is of interest to note that both young and older adults can become confused about whether or not they have completed their intentions (Einstein, McDaniel, Smith, & Shaw, 1998). Further research on this aspect of prospective remembering should clarify whether the underlying causes of these errors differ in these two age groups.

ABSENTMINDED SLIPS OF ACTION

Errors of prospective memory involve failing to carry out a plan or to comply with an instruction to do something. These can be distinguished from absentminded slips of action. As defined by Norman (1981), a slip is an error that occurs when a person does an action that is not intended. Errors of this kind arise during the performance of an action sequence. So, absentminded slips of action usually take the form of doing the wrong thing, whereas errors of prospective memory take the form of forgetting to do it at all.

Slips of action are a common experience in daily life and occur both in speech and in nonverbal behaviour. In this chapter we will be concerned with errors in nonverbal actions. We all find ourselves, from time to time, doing things like pouring coffee into the sugar bowl or throwing cheques into the waste-paper basket. By analysing the nature and incidence of these kinds of slips, researchers have been able to infer some of the characteristics of the mechanisms that control the performance of action sequences.

Classifying slips of action

Reason (1979) asked 35 volunteers to keep a diary record of their slips of action. In two weeks the diaries yielded 400 of these slips, and Reason was able to identify several different categories of error:

1   *Repetition errors:* Forgetting that an action has already been performed and repeating it, e.g., "I started to pour a second kettle of boiling water into the teapot, forgetting I had just filled it". Reason called these "storage failures" and 40% of his corpus consisted of repetition errors of this kind.
2   *Goal switches:* Forgetting the goal of a sequence of actions and switching to a different goal, e.g., "I intended to drive to a friend's house but found myself driving to work instead" or "I went upstairs to fetch the dirty washing and came down without the washing, having tidied the bathroom instead". These slips (which Reason called "test failures") formed 20% of his corpus.
3   *Omissions and reversals:* Omitting or wrongly ordering the component actions of a sequence, e.g., filling the kettle but failing to switch it on, or putting the lid on a container before putting something in it. In Reason's study 18% of the errors were of this kind.
4   *Confusions/blends:* Confusing objects involved in one action sequence with those involved in another sequence, e.g., taking a tin-opener instead of scissors into the garden to cut flowers. Or confusing the actions from one sequence with actions from another sequence, as in the case of a woman who reported throwing her earrings to the dog and trying to clip dog biscuits on to her ears. In these cases, there has been cross-talk between two programmes and different action sequences have been confused with each other. About 16% of errors in Reason's study were confusions.

Although the diary records produced good descriptive evidence for the occurrence of these different types of error, the reported incidence of each kind may not be a very accurate record of actual incidence. A particular kind of slip may be reported as more frequent because it is more disruptive and therefore more noticeable. Slips that involve confusions are likely to be particularly memorable because they tend to produce rather ludicrous results, but other slips of action may go unnoticed.

Automatic and attentional processes

Some characteristic features have been identified from the classification of slips. The most important finding is that slips of action occur predominantly with highly practised, overlearned, routine activities. Making cups of tea and coffee, for example, are activities that give rise to many of the reported slips of action. This is partly because actions that occur very frequently provide more opportunities for slips to occur. However, the predominance of errors in making tea and coffee is not just evidence of a national obsession, but also arises because these are routine, repeated actions. To understand the underlying mechanism, researchers have applied the distinction between *automatic* and *attentional processes* formulated by Shiffrin and Schneider (1977). Highly practised actions become automatic and can then be carried out according to pre-set instructions, with little or no conscious monitoring or need for attentional resources. Reason and Mycielska (1982) called this mode of action control an "open loop" system.

Automatic, or open loop, processes differ from attentional, or closed loop processes. Attentional processes are under moment-to-moment control by a central processor, which monitors and guides the action sequence, modifying performance according to feedback about changes in external circumstances and internal needs and intentions. A good example of this distinction between automatic and attentional processes occurs when you are driving a car. Emerging from a road junction is (or ought to be) an attentional process. The traffic must be scanned, and distances and speeds assessed, and the driver is consciously thinking about the actions that need to be implemented. In contrast, for the practised driver, changing gears is an automatic process. The actions involved do not need to be consciously monitored and can usually be carried out successfully while the driver is attending to something quite different, like chatting to a passenger or calculating petrol consumption. Automatic action sequences have the advantage that they can be carried out while the conscious mind is free to engage in other parallel activities. However, automatisation can lead to slips of action. Even automatic actions may need intermittent attention to keep them on the right track, and slips of action occur if attention is not shifted to the ongoing action at a critical point in the sequence.

Predisposing conditions

An action sequence (or programme) that is in frequent use is "stronger" than one that is used less often. There is a tendency for a stronger programme to take over from a weaker programme, particularly if some component stages are common to both, and this type of slip is sometimes known as a "strong habit intrusion" or a "capture error". Slips of action often occur at junctions where two programmes share a particular component and there is an involuntary switchover to the stronger programme. William James (1890) describes these switchovers as "strong habit intrusions". In his example, a person went into the bedroom to change his clothes, took off one garment, and then got undressed completely and went to bed. The stronger "going to bed" programme took over from the "changing clothes" programme because both shared the common components of entering the bedroom and removing the jacket. The types of slip classed as goal switches and confusions may both occur because of strong habit intrusions.

Another predisposing condition, besides automaticity and competition from stronger habits, has been identified by Reason (1984). Any need for change in a well-established routine is liable to produce errors. In one of his examples, someone who had decided to give up sugar on cornflakes sprinkled it on as before. In the same way, the ex-smoker's hand goes to his pocket to take out the cigarettes that are no longer there.

In addition to these predisposing circumstances, there are predisposing internal states. Some individuals are much more prone to make these kinds of error than other people, but many people find that slips of action increase with tiredness, illness, or stress. Broadbent, Cooper, Fitzgerald, and Parkes (1982) developed the Cognitive Failures Questionnaire (CFQ) to serve as an index of an individual's susceptibility to slips of action, as well as other failures of memory and perception. Respondents were asked to assess the frequency with which they experienced specific examples of cognitive failure, for example "Do you forget whether you've turned off the light or fire, or locked the door?" on a five-point scale ranging from *never* to *very often*. They found that CFQ scores were not related to either performance on tests of immediate and delayed memory or perception as measured by performance on a word identification task. Martin and Jones (1984) found that CFQ scores correlated significantly with ability to perform two tasks at the same time, indicating that poor ability to deploy attention and allocate processing resources effectively is associated with frequent slips of actions as well as other forms of cognitive failure. CFQ scores were also related to forward digit span, which tests ability to maintain a set of items in the correct serial order. This ability is also involved in carrying out action sequences, and the kind of slips classified as omissions and reversals arise as a result of breakdown in the maintenance of the correct serial order for components in an action sequence. In addition, Martin and Jones also reported an association between frequent cognitive failures and high anxiety.

Theoretical perspectives

Both Reason (1984) and Norman (1981) have developed explanatory models of action control to account for absentminded slips of action. Common to both models is the concept of an *action schema*. An action schema is a knowledge structure representing the sensorimotor knowledge that constitutes an action sequence. Schemas are linked together in related sets, and several action schemas may be operative simultaneously. Schema theory is described in more detail in Chapter 6, and the theoretical models of slips and errors are reviewed by Berry (1993).

Reason's model

In Reason's model there are three levels of control. At the schema level, control is by automatic pre-programmed instructions built into the schemas; the activation of a particular schema initiates the action sequence. Schemas can be activated by sensory information or by another, already active, schema. At this level, activation is influenced by recency and frequency of use. Schemas that have been implemented more recently or more frequently (the "strong habit" schemas) have lower thresholds and are more easily activated. The second level of control in Reason's model is the intention system, which generates goals, and can also activate the schemas that are appropriate for achieving these goals. The intention system assembles plans, monitors ongoing activity, and corrects errors. It has a limited capacity, so that only one plan is maximally active at any one time. At the third level, the attentional control system acts to increase or suppress the activation of particular schemas, deploying attentional resources in accordance with the goals of the intention system. Reason conceptualises the complete set of schemas as a "cognitive board" on which attentional resources in the form of an "attentional blob" are moved around and may be concentrated on one particular schema or diffused over several, as shown in Figure 5.3.

In this model, some action sequences require little or no attentional resources. These are the automatic, open loop, schema-driven ones. Other, higher level, closed loop action sequences involving complex decision-making require much more attention. Slips of action occur because of the faulty deployment of attention. For example, the allocation of attention may be too fixed and narrowly concentrated on

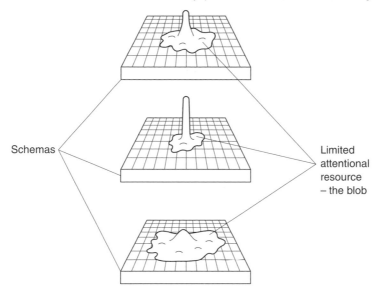

Figure 5.3 The cognitive board with attentional resources more or less concentrated (from Reason, 1984). Copyright © Elsevier 1984. Reproduced with permission.

a very limited number of schemas. This model is mainly a descriptive one and does not generate novel predictions.

In a later model, Reason (1990) has outlined the Generic Error Modelling System (GEMS). This system distinguishes between *skill-based slips*, in which actions are not executed as planned, *rule-based mistakes*, and *knowledge-based mistakes*. Whereas skill-based slips are failures of monitoring, rule-based mistakes and knowledge-based mistakes are problem-solving failures that do not involve attentional failures. Rule-based mistakes arise because the wrong rule is selected from the stored repertoire, but knowledge-based mistakes arise when the individual has no rule-based solution adequate to deal with the problem. Rule-based mistakes may take the form of applying a good rule in the wrong situation, or using a poor rule. Knowledge-based mistakes may reflect a lack of relevant knowledge or an inaccurate mental model of the problem. This analysis has been able to provide an account of a wide range of errors from pouring the tea into the sugar bowl to nuclear power plant disasters like Chernobyl.

Norman's model

Norman's (1981) model emphasised the hierarchical organisation of schemas, which work together in organised groups, as in Figure 5.4. He called the highest level "parent schemas". These correspond to global intentions or goals (e.g., "having a cup of tea"). Subordinate level "child schemas", or subschemas, correspond to component actions necessary to achieve the overall goal ("getting out the teapot" or "boiling water"). The activation level of each schema is determined by internal events (plans, needs, intentions) and by external events (the current situation). Each schema also has a set of triggering conditions that must be fulfilled for it to be

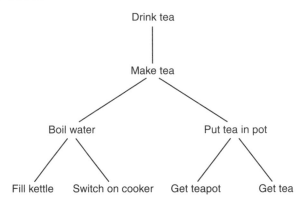

Figure 5.4 A hierarchy of action schemas for making tea.

implemented. These consist of external events and circumstances. A given schema operates when the activation level is above threshold, and the current situation matches the triggering conditions. So, in the tea-drinking example, the intention to have a cup of tea activates the whole set of schemas related to this goal, and the state of the boiling water might constitute the triggering conditions for initiating the teapot-filling subschema.

Slips of action, according to Norman's model, result from faulty specification of the overall intention, faulty activation of the schemas, or faulty triggering. Particular examples of slips can be classified in terms of these causes. The specification of the intention to go to work may be inadequate if it fails to specify the intended form of transport, and could result in getting into the car when you meant to take the bus. Strong habit intrusions or goal switches, like driving to the wrong destination, can be explained as faulty activation. So, for example, the frequently used "going to work" schemas are more highly activated and may take over from the less frequent, less activated "visiting a friend" schemas. In Norman's terminology, this is a capture error. Tidying up the bathroom instead of fetching the washing is also a case of faulty activation. The mess in the bathroom matches the triggering conditions for the bathroom-tidying schema and causes it to be activated. Norman called this kind of slip a data-driven error because the switch originates from externally cued activation. Reversals and repetitions occur when the triggering of an action sequence is faulty, and blends or confusions result if two different schemas are triggered simultaneously. Slips are not always due to competing schemas, but may result if activation is inadequate or fizzles out. In this case, you may be found standing in a room and wondering why you went to it and what you intended to do there. The original intention is no longer activated. Alternatively, you may simply omit to perform the intended action—forgetting to collect your coat from the cleaners, or failing to turn off the electric fire. The activation is insufficient to sustain the performance of the actions. The key feature of Norman's model was the idea that action sequences can be represented at different levels, from a global, general representation of the overall goal at the highest level to specific subordinate actions at the lowest level.

Norman's model and the original version of Reason's model obviously have a good deal in common. In Norman's model, the postulated mechanism for action control is able to account for the different types of error that are observed. Although

Reason's model does not offer such a fine-grained explanation, his claim that slips of action can be ascribed to faulty deployment of attention is supported by Martin and Jones' (1984) finding that ability to divide attention efficiently is related to the incidence of slips. Norman's model was expanded and extended in the Norman and Shallice (1986) model, described earlier, to account for errors made by people who have sustained damage to their frontal lobes (see also Cooper & Shallice, 2000).

Heckhausen and Beckman (1990) have stressed the need to integrate slips of action into a general theory of intentional behaviour. In their view, actions are guided by mentally represented intentions of two kinds: goal intentions and instrumental intentions. The latter are further subdivided into initiation, implementation, and termination intents. They also distinguish between two control modes. Processing with a wide goal span encompasses a range of overlapping or unrelated activities and is automatic and unconscious; in processing with a narrow goal span all attentional capacity is absorbed by the current ongoing activity. Narrow goal span is associated with unfamiliar and difficult actions. They found that most slips of action occurred with wide goal control and these could be categorised in terms of the initiation, implementation, or termination phase of action. Their model is similar to Reason's but lays more emphasis on the role of intents and includes problems in terminating actions.

Although many of the examples of slips of action are of trivial everyday actions, similar slips that may have catastrophic consequences occur in driving, flying planes, operating machinery, medicating patients, and so on. Important lessons about training procedures, the design of equipment, the avoidance of fatigue, and the development of effective cues can be derived from theoretical analyses of slips of action and mistakes such as GEMS (Reason, 1990). Applied psychology and theoretical cognitive psychology are interdependent in this area.

PLANNING

What is planning?

Prospective memory involves remembering what to do and when to do it. Most research on planning and mental rehearsal has been concerned with how to do it. As defined by Hayes-Roth and Hayes-Roth (1979), a plan is the "predetermination of a course of action aimed at achieving some goal". According to Battman (1987, p. 4), a plan is "an ordered set of control statements to support the efficiency of actions and the preparation of alternative actions for the case of failure". In everyday life, people spend a lot of time planning how to do things. This is particularly true when a prospective task is a novel or complex one involving a sequence of actions, and when decisions have to be taken about which actions will produce the best results. People plan journeys and holidays; what to buy for dinner and what to plant in the garden; how to play a hand of bridge or behave at a job interview. Actions that don't typically require planning are those that are very simple or very routine, automatic, or purely impulsive. For most people several daily activities involve some degree of planning.

Mental practice is a form of planning that consists of mentally simulating an action sequence. This has been found effective in assisting acquisition and enhancing performance in a wide variety of skills and sports such as golf, skating, and diving (Annett, 1991). Planning is also a type of problem-solving by mental simulation, envisaging the circumstances and running through possible actions, evaluating the consequences, and selecting the optimal actions and the optimal order for executing them. Planning depends on memory. Knowledge derived from past experience and stored in long-term memory must be retrieved and used in formulating possible plans, and in constructing representations of hypothetical events. A working memory buffer store is needed to hold tentative or incomplete plans while these are being evaluated or revised. Recently, Philips and her colleagues have questioned the benefits of such preplanning activities, due in part to the demands that these make on working memory, and have provided findings that support a more important role for online planning (Phillips, Wynn, Gilhooly, Della Sala, & Logie, 1999; Phillips, Wynn, McPherson, & Gilhooly, 2001). Online or "opportunistic" planning (Hayes-Roth & Hayes-Roth, 1979), discussed below, is thought to place a smaller load on memory than full preplanning and to be more consistent with naturalistic planning.

Individual differences in planning

Everyday observations suggest that people differ in the amount of planning they habitually do. We all know people who rush into things without stopping to think at all and others who obsessively think through every detail before embarking on a course of action. There has been little formal investigation of these differences so far. Giambra (1979) analysed the content of daydreams (defined as thoughts unrelated to the current task) and found that for all age groups the majority of daydreams were of the type he called "problem-solving" and involved planning future activities. Young males were the exception to this generalisation: They had more daydreams of love and sex than of problem-solving. Females of all ages had more problem-solving daydreams than males. This finding has also emerged from a questionnaire used in a pilot study by Cohen and Faulkner (unpublished). Females reported spending more time on mental planning; they planned in more detail, and formulated more alternative plans in case of difficulties. Elderly people also reported more planning than young people. The reasons underlying these differences are not clear, but probably include personality, level of anxiety, work load, and the importance of efficient performance. Another influence may be one's level of impulsivity or the degree to which one values speed over accuracy (Owen, 1997). As Phillips et al. (2001, p. 596) suggest, "choosing to spend a long time preplanning may reflect personality characteristics rather than the efficiency of planning".

The travelling salesman task

Battman (1987) studied the planning involved in the "travelling salesman problem". He was interested primarily in the function of planning and also in individual differences in planning. Battman argued that planning entails an investment of time and effort. It is therefore only cost-effective if it improves efficiency and/or reduces anxiety in the execution phase. But planning is not always helpful. If the plan is inadequate, or if circumstances change, it may be a positive disadvantage.

Battman compared the performance of two groups of participants in a version of the travelling salesman task in which his participants had to act as chain store supervisors, visiting 10 stores in one day. Three of the visits had to be made at pre-arranged times, plus or minus 10 minutes, and people had to make decisions about marketing or finance at each store. They were provided with access to a map and information about average between-store travel times and the average time needed to handle a problem within a store. In addition, they could change any of the appointment times, provided this was done at least 25 minutes beforehand. Arriving early for an appointment meant wasting time; arriving late entailed making a second visit. One group of participants was instructed to plan before beginning the task. They could fix intermediate goals and write out a schedule of visits. The other group was not instructed to plan ahead.

The participants instructed to plan performed more efficiently. They kept more appointments punctually, completed more visits, spent less time driving between stores, and made more use of the ability to change appointments. As well as these indices of efficiency, level of stress was monitored during performance. The findings differed according to the intelligence of the subjects. High-IQ participants who planned were more stressed on the first trial, but benefited on later trials. Planning was cost-effective for them because it improved efficiency and reduced anxiety. For low-IQ participants planning brought no reduction in anxiety; although it increased their efficiency, keeping to the plan was effortful and a high level of stress was maintained. Battman concluded that generating and executing a plan can, in some circumstances, be more demanding than simply responding in an ad hoc way or "making it up as you go along" cf. opportunistic or online planning. Most of us can probably think of people we know who are meticulous planners, but who appear to suffer a good deal of agitation in trying to execute these plans.

Planning errands

A detailed study of planning by Hayes-Roth and Hayes-Roth (1979) used verbal protocols to study the way people plan a day's errands. Their participants' task was to produce a plan for completing as many as possible of the errands listed below, moving around the hypothetical town shown in the map (Figure 5.5).

You have just finished working out at the health club. It is 11.00 and you can plan the rest of your day as you like. However, you must pick up your car from the Maple Street parking garage by 5.30 and then head home. You'd also like to see a movie today, if possible. Show times at both movie theatres are 1.00, 3.00, and 5.00. Both movies are on your "must see" list, but go to whichever one fits most conveniently into your plan. Your other errands are as follows:

- pick up medicine for your dog at the vet
- buy a fan belt for your refrigerator at the appliance store
- check out two of the three luxury apartments
- meet a friend for lunch at one of the restaurants
- buy a toy for your dog at the pet store

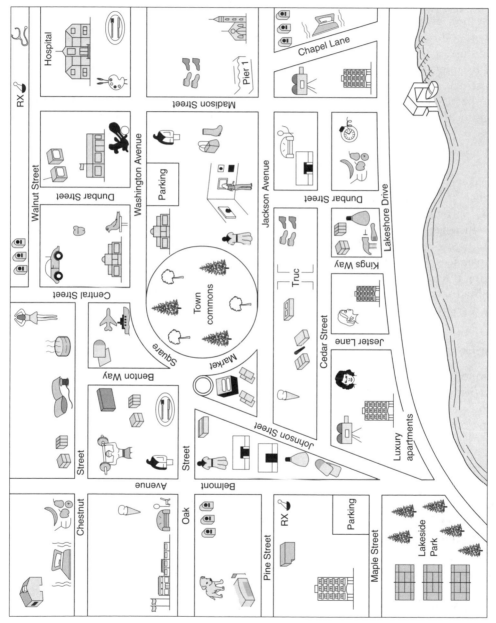

Figure 5.5 The town map for the errand planning task. From Hayes-Roth & Hayes-Roth (1979) *Cognitive Science, 3,* 275–310. www.informaworld.com. Reproduced with permission.

- pick up your watch at the watch repair shop
- special order a book at the bookstore
- buy fresh vegetables at the grocery store
- buy a gardening magazine at the newsstand
- go to the florist to send flowers to a friend in hospital.

1   Let's go back down the errand list. Pick up medicine for the dog at veterinary supplies. That's definitely a primary, anything taking care of health. Fan belt for refrigerator. Definitely a primary because you need to keep the refrigerator. Checking out two of three luxury apartments. It's got to be a secondary, another browser. Meet the friend at one of the restaurants for lunch. All right. Now, that's going to be able to be varied I hope. That's a primary, though, because it is an appointment, something you have to do. Buy a toy for the dog at pet store. If you pass it, sure. If not, the dog can play with something else. Movie in one of the movie theatres. Better write that down, those movie times, 1, 3, or 5. Write that down on my sheet just to remember. And that's a primary because it's something I have to do. Pick up the watch at the watch repair. That's one of those borderline ones. Do you need your watch or not? Give it a primary. Special order a book at the bookstore.

2   We're having an awful lot of primaries in this one. It's going to be a busy day.

3   Fresh vegetables at the grocery. That's another primary. You need the food. Gardening magazine at the newsstand. Definitely secondary. All the many obligations of life.

4   Geez, can you believe all these primaries?

5   All right. We are now at the health club.

6   What is going to be the closest one?

7   The appliance store is a few blocks away. The medicine for the dog at the vet's office isn't too far away. Movie theatres—let's hold off on that for a little while. Pick up the watch. That's all the way across town. Special order a book at the bookstore.

8   Probably it would be best if we headed in a southeasterly direction. Start heading this way. I can see later on there are a million things I want to do in that part of town.

9   No we're not. We could end up with a movie just before we get the car. I had thought at first that I might head in a southeasterly direction because there's a grocery store, a watch repair, a movie theatre all in that general area. Also, a luxury apartment. However, near my parking

lot also is a movie, which would make it convenient to get out of the movie and go to the car. But I think we can still end up that way.

10   All right. Apparently the closest one to the health club is going to the vet's shop. So I might as well get that out of the way. It's a primary and is the closest. We'll start . . .

[The experimenter mentions that he has overlooked the nearby restaurant and flower shop.]

11   Oh, how foolish of me. You're right. I can still do that and still head in the general direction.

12   But, then again, that puts a whole new light on things. We do have a bookstore. We do have. OK. Break up town into sections. We'll call them northwest and southeast. See how many primaries are in that section. Down there in the southeast section, we have the grocery store, the watch repair and the movie theatre. In the northwest section we have the grocery store, the bookstore, the flower shop, the vet's shop, and the restaurant.

13   And since we are leaving at 11.00, we might be able to get these chores done so that some time when I'm in the area, hit that restaurant. Let's try for that. Get as many of those out of the way as possible. We really could have a nice day here.

14   OK. First choose number one. At 11.00 we leave the health club. Easily, no doubt about it, we can be right across the street in 5 minutes to the flower shop. Here we go. Flower shop at 11.05. Let's give ourselves 10 minutes to browse through some bouquets and different floral arrangements.

Thinking aloud protocol; from the errand-planning task. From Hayes-Roth & Hayes-Roth (1979) *Cognitive Science*, *3*, 275–310. www.informaworld.com. Reproduced with permission.

The tinted box above reproduces one of the verbal protocols. This typical participant started by defining the goal and tasks and classifying errands as high-priority or low-priority. He began by sequencing the errands from the start point, forming clusters of errands based on priority and on adjacency. There are frequent revisions of the plan, and at a later stage, some sequencing backward in time from the final errand (picking up the car at 5.30). The mental simulation of one stage of the plan guides the later stages, and consists of mentally timing the actions and inferring the consequences. Planning occurs at different levels of abstraction, sometimes involving specific items and sometimes higher order clusters.

Hayes-Roth and Hayes-Roth noted that planning was opportunistic. As this participant's protocol illustrates, people did not formulate an overall global plan and then proceed to fill in the stages by successive refinements, but jumped about between levels with many shifts and changes. Instead of being controlled in a top-down direction by higher order principles and pre-set goals, the plan was under multi-directional control, many decisions being influenced on a moment-to-moment basis by new facts that came to light as planning proceeded. Planning was incremental, with tentative decisions becoming gradually firmer, and alternative plans were considered in parallel.

The cognitive model they formulated to represent these aspects of the planning process included a working memory buffer, which they call the *blackboard*, where different forms of knowledge interact. The different kinds of knowledge include:

1   Knowledge of the overall task (the metaplan).
2   A set of possible actions, procedures for implementing them, and outcomes (plans).
3   A list of desirable attributes (such as quick, adjacent) for these plans (plan-abstractions).
4   A knowledge base of specific data about errand routes and locations. The model also has an executive for taking decisions and for allocation of resources. A computer simulation of this model produced a protocol broadly similar to that produced by a human participant, but the computer's plan was more feasible. It sacrificed more of the low-priority errands and, unlike the human participant's plan, it could have been completed in the available time.

In the errand-planning task the problem lies in selecting and ordering actions. The constraints are mainly of time and distance and the task involves a number of goals that are interdependent, a knowledge base that is equivalent to long-term memory, and the blackboard for carrying out evaluations and decision processes that is equivalent to working memory.

Theoretical perspectives

Planning, like prospective memory and carrying out action sequences, depends on the operation of working memory and the allocation of attention and also on the way plans are represented in memory.

Types of representation

The types of representational system that are current in cognitive psychology today fall into three basic types. These are propositional, analogical, and procedural (Rumelhart & Norman, 1985). In propositional systems knowledge is represented as a set of symbols arranged to constitute statements of facts or rules. Much of the factual knowledge used in planning is represented as propositions. For example, the knowledge that you can get a bookstore to order books for you or that restaurants serve lunch between 12.30 and 2 p.m. can be represented propositionally.

Procedural representations encode knowledge about how to perform actions like making appointments or ordering books, and this knowledge is stored in the form of a set of procedures. Procedural knowledge must necessarily be involved at the stage when planned actions are executed.

Analogue representational systems are ones in which the objects and events being represented map directly on to the representation. An analogue representation is more like a copy of the real thing. Some kinds of information involved in planning might be better represented analogically. An analogical representation of the spatial layout of the town allows relations like next to and nearest to to be read off directly, and hypothetical moves can be evaluated in terms of locations and distances. The same information could be represented propositionally, but the analogical form has certain advantages. Analogical representations are dynamic: They are readily transformed, rotated, and dismantled. They can be constructed from different viewpoints, they can represent change and movement, and they are specific and determinate. Whereas propositions are truth functional (i.e., they are either true or false), analogical models can be hypothetical. These characteristics of analogical representations are well suited to mental planning tasks, but they also have some shortcomings. It is not easy to see how some kinds of information can be represented in an analogue form. Temporal and causal factors, quantifiers like "all", "some", "several", and relations like negation are easier to represent propositionally.

It is important to note that these different forms of representation are not mutually exclusive. Different aspects of the real world may be represented in different ways, and a particular object or event may be represented in different ways at different times. It is a reasonable assumption that the memory representations used in planning are of more than one kind. This type of difficulty might be resolved by adopting a hybrid model that combines both kinds of representation.

Hybrid models

Kosslyn, Chabris, Marsolek, and Koenig (1992) incorporates both propositions and analogue imagery in his model. He postulates a "deep representation", which stores propositional knowledge in long-term memory. Also in long-term memory there is what Kosslyn calls a "literal representation", consisting of sets of coordinate points. From the deep and literal representations, a "surface representation" in the form of an analogue spatial image can be generated as a temporary visual display, and there are processes that can scan the image, and can expand, contract, or rotate it. This kind of multiple representation model is well suited to the demands of planning, particularly plans that involve spatial judgements.

An alternative model of multiple representation has been proposed by Johnson-Laird (1983), who suggests that "What we remember consists of images, models, propositions and procedures for carrying out actions" (p. 447). The central component in this set of representations is the *mental model*. Mental models "play a central and unifying role in representing objects, states of affairs, sequences of events, the way the world is, and the social and psychological actions of daily life. They enable individuals to make inferences and predictions, to understand phenomena, to decide what action to take and to control its execution, and, above all, to experience events by proxy" (p. 397).

According to Johnson-Laird, mental models are representations that constitute a working model of the real world, although they may be incomplete or simplified. They are derived from perception and from verbal information. Mental models may be physical or conceptual. Physical mental models are analogue in form and can represent relations, space and time, change, and movement. Conceptual mental models can represent more abstract features such as negation. Mental models are specific, but can be used to represent hypothetical states of affairs. They are intermediate between propositions and images because they represent a mapping, or interpretation, of propositional representations and can be used to generate images. Mental models, as described by Johnson-Laird, are not fixed structures, but dynamic models that can be constructed as and when they are required, and this makes them particularly well suited to planning because they are able to simulate dynamic actions and events. In this, they appear to have the advantage over the images in Kosslyn's model, which only represent static scenes and objects and are limited in the kind of transformations they can undergo. Cognitive processes like planning appear to require a hybrid form of representation that is dynamic and that can represent hypothetical states of affairs. Mental models fulfil these criteria better than other systems of representation.

Planning and prospective memory

As noted earlier, research on planning tends to be concerned primarily with planning how to perform different actions, processes that are clearly relevant for the performance of a prospective memory task or future intention. Prospective remembering, however, is concerned also with the circumstances when we should recall and carry out our intentions, therefore when-planning, as well as planning-how, may be important. The importance of extrinsic or when-planning has been acknowledged in a series of studies reported by Patalano and Seifert (1997), building on the concept of opportunistic planning illustrated by Hayes-Roth and Hayes-Roth. They extended this model by examining the "problem of recognizing the relevance of a pending goal in memory given circumstances in the current environment" (p. 4). In other words, the need to recognise that a situation (retrieval cue) is an appropriate one for performing an intention—prospective remembering. Patalano and Seifert's (1997) findings suggest that these intentions are stored as goals in long-term memory that are associated, at encoding, with potential features of the environment representing "opportunities". In prospective memory terms this is akin to encoding not only what we want to (the action) but also the association between this and its retrieval cue(s)—the when aspects of the intention representation. A comparable model, described by Ellis (1996), is based on studies of naturally occurring intentions and takes account of the structure and organisation of everyday activities.

Planning-when processes may be particularly important in everyday situations when, unlike many of the laboratory studies described earlier, we have several intentions to perform and have to prioritise and schedule these. Relatively few studies, real-world or laboratory-based, have been conducted on this important aspect of prospective remembering and those that have taken place have been based on the six-element and multiple errand task, described earlier, that Shallice and Burgess (1991) designed to provide simulations of everyday planning or multitasking. In a follow-up study, the Six Element Task was modified to provide measures of pre-planning, plan following, and intention performance (Burgess, Veitch, de Lacy Costello, & Shallice, 2000). Examination of the behaviour of brain-damaged patients and matched healthy control participants revealed three components of multitasking: retrospective memory, prospective memory, and planning. Moreover, prospective memory appeared to be supported by processes in left frontal regions whereas right dorsolateral regions were implicated in planning. The importance of executive processes, assumed to be based at least in part on neuronal processes in the prefrontal cortex, has been supported by further studies conducted by Kleigel, Eschen, and

Thöne-Otto (2004a), using a new analogue of the Six Element Task. Interestingly, in their study healthy older adults showed a similar pattern of performance to the (younger) patients, in that they were worse on the intention formation and performance phases of their task.

CONCLUSIONS

In this chapter we have considered several aspects of memory for plans and actions, including the ability to execute plans, and the slips that occur when actions are not executed according to plan; the ability to remember to implement prospective plans; as well as how and why people make plans. All these topics relate to naturally occurring behaviour in everyday life, but each has been illuminated and interpreted by the application of formal theories of memory, attentional mechanisms, and action representation and coordination developed in the context of traditional laboratory experiments. They have also led to the development of experimental paradigms that seek to simulate some important aspects of these real-world tasks. Although there is still considerable scope for improvement here, particularly the simulation of multiple intention designs and the provision of richer contexts in which planning and multitasking of these intentions takes place, current findings have served to provide theoretical frameworks that can be tested in both the laboratory and the real world. It is also worth noting that the involvement of attentional and other executive processes in future intention and action completion has led to increased interest in this area from cognitive neuroscientists and neuropsychologists. The application of neuroimaging and other neuroscience techniques, together with patient studies, has improved and will continue to improve theory development and tests, leading to improved advice and assistance for everyday activities, particularly for vulnerable groups in society (e.g., older adults, young children, and people with frontal lobe damage).

REFERENCES

Annett, J. (1991). Skill acquisition. In J.E. Morrison (Ed.), *Training for performance: Principles of applied human learning* (pp. 13–51). Chichester, UK: Wiley.

Baddeley, A.D. (1993). *Human memory: Theory and practice.* Hove, UK: Lawrence Erlbaum Associates Ltd.

Baddeley, A.D., & Wilkins, A.J. (1984). Taking memory out of the laboratory. In J.E. Harris & P.E. Morris (Eds.), *Everyday memory, actions and absentmindedness.* London: Academic Press.

Battman, W. (1987). Planning as a method of stress prevention: Will it pay off? In I.G. Sarason & C.D. Spielberger (Eds.), *Stress and anxiety, Vol. 10.* New York: Hemisphere.

Berry, D.C. (1993). Slips and errors in learning complex tasks. In G.M. Davies & R.H. Logie (Eds.), *Memory in everyday life: Advances in psychology, Vol. 100* (pp. 137–171). Amsterdam: North-Holland.

Brandimonte, M. (1991). Ricordare il futuro. *Giornale Italiano di Psicologia, 3,* 351–374.

Brandimonte, M., & Passolunghi, M.C. (1994). The effect of cue familiarity, cue distinctiveness and retention interval on prospective remembering. *The Quarterly Journal of Experimental Journal of Experimental Psychology, 47A,* 565–587.

Broadbent, D.E., Cooper, P.F., Fitzgerald, P., & Parkes, K.R. (1982). The cognitive failures questionnaire (CFQ) and its correlates. *British Journal of Clinical Psychology, 21,* 139–177.

Burgess, P.W., Quayle, A., & Frith, C.D. (2001). Brain regions involved in prospective memory as determined by positron emission tomography. *Neuropsychologia, 39,* 545–555.

Burgess, P.W., Veitch, E., de Lacy Costello, A., & Shallice, T. (2000). The cognitive and neuroanatomical correlates of multitasking. *Neuropsychologia, 33,* 261–268.

Ceci, S.J., Baker, J., & Bronfenbrenner, U. (1988). Prospective memory: Temporal calibration and context. In M.M. Gruneberg, P.E. Morris, & R.N. Sykes (Eds.), *Practical aspects of memory: Current research and issues* (pp. 360–365). Chichester, UK: Wiley.

Cockburn, J., & Smith, P.T. (1994). Anxiety and errors of prospective memory. *British Journal of Psychology, 85,* 273–282.

Cooper, R., & Shallice, T. (2000). Contention scheduling and the control of routine activities. *Cognitive Neuropsychology, 17,* 297–338.

Einstein, G.O., Holland, L.J., McDaniel, M.A., & Guynn, M.J. (1992). Age-related deficits in prospective memory: The influence of task complexity. *Psychology and Aging, 7,* 471–478.

Einstein, G.O., & McDaniel, M.A. (1990). Normal aging and prospective memory. *Journal of Experimental Psychology: Learning, Memory and Cognition, 16,* 717–726.

Einstein, G.O., & McDaniel, M.A. (1991). *Aging and time versus event-based prospective memory.* Paper presented at the 32nd meeting of the Psychonomic Society, San Francisco, CA.

Einstein, G.O., & McDaniel, M.A. (1996). Retrieval processes in prospective memory: Theoretical approaches and some new empirical findings. In M. Brandimonte, G.O. Einstein, & M.A. McDaniel (Eds.), *Prospective memory: Theory and applications* (pp. 115–141). Mahwah, NJ: Lawrence Erlbaum Associates, Inc.

Einstein, G.O., McDaniel, M.A., Smith, R.E., & Shaw, P. (1998). Habitual prospective remembering and aging: Remembering intentions and forgetting actions. *Psychological Science, 9,* 284–288.

Einstein, G.O., McDaniel, M.A., Williford, C.L., Pagan, J.L., & Dismukes, R.K. (2003). Forgetting of intentions in demanding situations is rapid. *Journal of Experimental Psychology: Applied, 9,* 147–162.

Ellis, J.A. (1988). Memory for future intentions: Investigating pulses and steps. In M.M. Gruneberg, P.E. Morris, & R.N. Sykes (Eds.), *Practical aspects of memory: Current research and issues, Vol. 1.* Chichester, UK: Wiley.

Ellis, J.A. (1996). Prospective memory or the realization of delayed intentions: A conceptual framework for research. In M. Brandimonte, G.O. Einstein, & M.A. McDaniel (Eds.), *Prospective memory: Theory and applications* (pp. 1–22). Mahwah, NJ: Lawrence Erlbaum Associates, Inc.

Ellis, J.A., Milne, A., & McGann, D. (1997). *Conceptual and perceptual processing in prospective remembering.* Paper presented at the International Workshop on Prospective Memory, Leuven.

Ellis, J.A., & Nimmo-Smith, I. (1993). Recollecting naturally occurring intentions: A study of cognitive and affective factors. *Memory, 1,* 107–126.

Evans, J.J., Wilson, B.A., & Baddeley, A.D. (1994). *An instrument for the clinical assessment of prospective memory.* Poster presented at the Third Practical Aspects of Memory Conference, Washington, DC.

Giambra, L.M. (1979). Sex differences in daydreaming and related mental activity from the late teens to the early nineties. *International Journal of Aging and Human Development, 10,* 1–34.

Goldstein, L.H., Bernard, S., Fenwick, P.B.C., Burgess, P.W., & McNeil, J. (1993). Unilateral frontal lobectomy can produce strategy application disorder. *Journal of Neurology, Neurosurgery and Psychiatry, 56,* 274–276.

Goschke, T., & Kuhl, J. (1993). Representation of intentions: Persisting activation in memory. *Journal of Experimental Psychology: Learning, Memory and Cognition, 19,* 1211–1226.

Guynn, M.J., McDaniel, M.A., & Einstein, G.O. (1998). Prospective memory: When reminders fail. *Memory and Cognition, 26,* 287–298.

Harris, J.E. (1980). Memory aids people use: Two interview studies. *Memory and Cognition, 8,* 31–38.

Harris, J.E. (1984). Remembering to do things: A forgotten topic. In J.E. Harris & P.E. Morris (Eds.), *Everyday memory, actions and absentmindedness.* London: Academic Press.

Harris, J.E., & Sunderland, A. (1987). Effects of age and instruction on an everyday memory questionnaire. *Canadian Journal of Psychology, 41,* 175–192.

Harris, J.E., & Wilkins, A.J. (1982). Remembering to do things: A theoretical framework and an illustrative experiment. *Human Learning, 1,* 123–136.

Hayes-Roth, B., & Hayes-Roth, F. (1979). A cognitive model of planning. *Cognitive Science, 3,* 275–310.

Heckhausen, H., & Beckman, J. (1990). Intentional action and action slips. *Psychological Review, 97,* 36–48.

Hicks, J.L., Marsh, R.L., & Russell, E.J. (2000). The properties of retention intervals and their effect on retaining prospective memories. *Journal of Experimental Psychology: Learning, Memory and Cognition, 26,* 1160–1169.

Hitch, G.J., & Ferguson, J. (1991). Prospective memory for future intentions: Some comparisons with memory for past events. *European Journal of Cognitive Psychology, 3,* 285–295.

James, W. (1890). *The principles of psychology.* New York: Holt.

Johnson-Laird, P.N. (1983). *Mental models.* Cambridge, UK: Cambridge University Press.

Kleigel, M., Eschen, A., & Thöne-Otto, A.I.T. (2004a). Planning and the realization of complex intentions in traumatic brain injury and normal aging. *Brain and Cognition, 56,* 43–54.

Kliegel, M., Jäger, T., Phillips, L.H., Federspiel, E., Imfield, A., Keller, M., & Zimprich, D. (2005). Effects of sad mood on time-based prospective memory. *Cognition and Emotion, 19,* 1199–1213.

Kliegel, M., Martin, M., McDaniel, M.A., & Einstein, G.O. (2001). Varying the importance of a prospective memory task: Differential effects across time- and event-based prospective memory. *Memory, 9,* 1–11.

Kliegel, M., Martin, M., McDaniel, M.A., & Einstein, G.O. (2004b). Importance effects on performance in event-based prospective memory tasks. *Memory, 12,* 553–561.

Koriat, A., Ben-Zur, H., & Nussbaum, A. (1990). Encoding information for future action: Memory for to be-performed tasks versus memory for to-be-recalled tasks. *Memory and Cognition, 18,* 568–578.

Koriat, A., Ben-Zur, H., & Sheffer, D. (1988). Telling the same story twice: Output monitoring and age. *Journal of Memory and Language, 27,* 23–39.

Kosslyn, S.M., Chabris, C.F., Marsolek, C.J., & Koenig, O. (1992). Categorical versus coordinate spatial representations: Computational analysis and computer simulations. *Journal of Experimental Psychology: Human Perception and Performance, 187,* 562–577.

Kvavilashvili, L. (1987). Remembering intentions as a distinct form of memory. *British Journal of Psychology, 78,* 507–518.

Kvavilashvili, L. (1992). Remembering intentions: A critical review of existing experimental paradigms. *Applied Cognitive Psychology, 6,* 507–524.

Kvavilashvili, L., & Ellis, J.A. (1996). Varieties of intention: Some distinctions and classifications. In M. Brandimonte, G.O. Einstein, & M.A. McDaniel (Eds.), *Prospective memory: Theory and applications* (pp. 23–51). Mahwah, NJ: Lawrence Erlbaum Associates, Inc.

Loftus, E. (1971). Memory for intentions: The effect of presence of a cue and interpolated activity. *Psychonomic Science, 23,* 315–316.

Marsh, R.L., Hicks, J.L., & Bink, M.L. (1998). The activation of completed, uncompleted and partially completed intentions. *Journal of Experimental Psychology: Learning, Memory and Cognition, 24*, 350–361.

Marsh, R.L., Hicks, J.L., & Bryan, E. (1999). The activation of unrelated and cancelled intentions. *Memory and Cognition, 27*, 320–327.

Marsh, R.L., Hicks, J.L., & Cook, G.I. (2005). On the relationship between effort toward an ongoing task and cue detection in event-based prospective memory. *Journal of Experimental Psychology: Learning, Memory and Cognition, 31*, 68–75.

Marsh, R.L., Hicks, J.L., Hancock, T.W., & Munsayac, K. (2002). Investigating the output monitoring component of event-based memory performance. *Memory and Cognition, 30*, 302–311.

Martin, M. (1986). Aging and patterns of change in everyday memory and cognition. *Human Learning, 5*, 63–74.

Martin, M., & Jones, G.V. (1984). Cognitive failures in everyday life. In J.E. Harris & P.E. Morris (Eds.), *Everyday memory, actions and absentmindedness*. London: Academic Press.

Maylor, E.A. (1990). Age and prospective memory. *Quarterly Journal of Experimental Psychology, 42A*, 471–493.

McDaniel, M.A., & Einstein, G.O. (1993). The importance of cue familiarity and distinctiveness in prospective memory. *Memory, 1*, 23–41.

McDaniel, M.A., & Einstein, G.O. (2000). Strategic and automatic processes in prospective memory retrieval: A multiprocess framework. *Applied Cognitive Psychology, 14*, S127–S144.

McDaniel, M.A., Guynn, M.J., Einstein, G.O., & Breneiser, J. (2004). Cue-focused and reflexive-associative processes in prospective memory retrieval. *Journal of Experimental Psychology: Learning, Memory and Cognition, 30*, 605–614.

McGann, D., Ellis, J.A., & Milne, A. (2002). Conceptual and perceptual processes in prospective remembering: Differential influences of attentional resources. *Memory and Cognition, 30*, 1021–1032.

Meacham, J.A., & Leiman, B. (1975). *Remembering to perform future actions*. Paper presented at the American Psychological Association meeting, Chicago.

Meacham, J.A., & Singer, J. (1977). Incentive in prospective remembering. *Journal of Psychology, 97*, 191–197.

Moscovitch, M. (1982). A neuropsychological approach to memory and perception in normal and pathological aging. In F.I.M. Craik & S. Trehub (Eds.), *Aging and cognitive processes*. New York: Plenum Press.

Norman, D.A. (1981). Categorisation of action slips. *Psychological Review, 88*, 1–15.

Norman, D.A., & Shallice, T. (1986). Attention to action: Willed and automatic control of behavior. In R.J. Davidson, G.E. Schwartz, & D. Shapiro (Eds.), *Consciousness and self-regulation: Advances in research and theory, Vol. 4* (pp. 1–18). New York: Plenum Press.

Owen, A.M. (1997). Cognitive planning humans: Neuropsychological, neuroanatomical and neuropharmacological perspectives. *Progress in Neurobiology, 53*, 431–450.

Patalano, A.L., & Seifert, C.M. (1997). Opportunistic planning: Being reminded of pending goals. *Cognitive Psychology, 34*, 1–36.

Phillips, L.H., Wynn, V., Gilhooly, K.J., Della Sala, S., & Logie, R.H. (1999). The role of memory in the Tower of London task. *Memory, 7*, 209–231.

Phillips, L.H., Wynn, V.E., McPherson, S., & Gilhooly, K.J. (2001). Mental planning and the Tower of London task. *The Quarterly Journal of Experimental Psychology, 54A*, 579–597.

Poon, L.W., & Schaffer, G. (1982). *Prospective remembering in young and elderly adults*. Paper presented at the American Psychological Association meeting, Washington, DC.

Reason, J.T. (1979). Actions not as planned: The price of automatisation. In G. Underwood & R. Stevens (Eds.), *Aspects of consciousness, Vol.1*. London: Academic Press.

Reason, J.T. (1984). Absentmindedness and cognitive control. In J.E. Harris & P.E. Morris (Eds.), *Everyday memory, actions and absentmindedness*. London: Academic Press.

Reason, J. (1990). *Human error*. New York: Cambridge University Press.

Reason, J.T., & Mycielska, K. (1982). *Absentminded? The psychology of mental lapses and everyday errors*. Englewood Cliffs, NJ: Prentice-Hall.

Rude, S.S., Hertel, P.T., Jarrold, W., Covich, J., & Hedlund, S. (1999). Depression-related impairments in prospective memory. *Cognition and Emotion, 13*, 267–276.

Rumelhart, D.E., & Norman, D.A. (1985). Representation of knowledge. In A. Aitkenhead & J.M. Slack (Eds.), *Issues in cognitive modelling*. Hove, UK: Lawrence Erlbaum Associates Ltd.

Searleman, A.E., & Gaydusek, K.A. (1989). *Relationship between prospective memory ability and selective personality variables*. Paper presented at the Annual Meeting of the Psychonomic Society, Atlanta, GA.

Shallice, T., & Burgess, P.W. (1991). Deficits in strategy application following frontal lobe damage in man. *Brain, 114*, 727–741.

Shiffrin, R.M., & Schneider, W. (1977). Controlled and automatic processing: Perceptual learning, automatic attending and a general theory. *Psychological Review, 84*, 127–190.

Smith, R.E. (2003). The cost of remembering to remember in event-based prospective memory: Investigating the capacity demands of delayed intention performance. *Journal of Experimental Psychology: Learning, Memory and Cognition, 29*, 347–361.

Smith, R.E., & Bayen, U.J. (2004). A multinomial model of event-based prospective memory. *Journal of Experimental Psychology: Learning, Memory and Cognition, 30*, 756–777.

West, R.L. (1984). *An analysis of prospective everyday memory*. Paper presented at a meeting of the American Psychological Association, Toronto.

West, R.L. (1986). Everyday memory and aging. *Developmental Neuropsychology, 2*, 324–344.

Wilkins, A.J. (1976). *A failure to demonstrate the effects of retention interval*. Unpublished manuscript, cited in J.E. Harris (1984).

Wilkins, A.J., & Baddeley, A.D. (1978). Remembering to recall in everyday life: An approach to absentmindedness. In M.M. Gruneberg, P.E. Morris, & R.N. Sykes, (Eds.), *Practical aspects of memory*. London: Academic Press.

6 Memory for places: Routes, maps, and object locations

Alastair D. Smith and Gillian Cohen

FUNCTIONS AND CHARACTERISTICS OF SPATIAL MEMORY

Spatial memory encodes information about location, orientation, distance, and direction. It enables us to remember scenes and to navigate our environment. We can recognise places as familiar and recall routes from one location to another. We can devise novel routes or shortcuts for reaching a goal. Spatial memory is also used for locating objects, and for remembering how they might be found. This may range from coding landmarks along routes, such as a service station on the motorway, to everyday objects lying around the house, such as a set of keys. Memory for scenes and for the layout of objects within scenes mediates our interaction with the immediate environment. All these functions involve representation of the spatial layout of the environment.

Spatial representations in memory also allow us to process internally generated information. We are able to revisit known places mentally; work out and evaluate routes without actually travelling; search for objects and scan possible locations without leaving the sofa. Whilst space is not inherently hierarchical, Neisser (1988) suggested that we tend to represent it mentally as nested hierarchical structures, with local representations nested inside global ones. This structure enables us to locate, for example, a particular restaurant in a particular street, but also within a district, city, and country: Cognitive space is relational. Bryant (1992) has argued that we have a separate spatial representation system that is independent of other memory systems. Neisser (1988) also speculated that spatial memory could be a specific memory module and there is ample neuropsychological evidence (e.g., Marshall & Halligan, 1995) for dissociations of spatial memory from verbal memory so that, following strokes or traumas, patients may perform normally in tests of verbal memory but be impaired in tests of spatial memory, or vice versa. It is apparent, however, that the kind of spatial ability that is measured in psychometric tests in the laboratory, or by the clinician, is not very similar to the kind of spatial ability required in everyday life. Kirasic (1991) devised a series of tests to examine spatial memory for the layout in both a familiar and an unfamiliar supermarket. The tests were scene recognition (identifying photographs taken in the supermarket); distance ranking (for the distances of specified items from a specified start point); route execution (walking the shortest route to pick up seven different items); and map placement (placing pictures of items in the correct locations on a floor plan of the supermarket). Participants also performed a battery of psychometric tests of spatial ability such as the Form Board, Cube Comparison, and Building Memory tests. Correlations between the supermarket tests and the formal psychometric tests were very weak. Why should there be this disparity? Perhaps it is because spatial cognition in everyday life is operating in a far richer environment. Another important characteristic of spatial cognition as it is exercised in real-world tasks is that the spatial environment is related to the self. The self is present as the traveller of routes, the observer of scenes, the searcher for objects, so that spatial knowledge in natural settings is almost invariably self-referential. In recent years, however, research in this area has benefited from a greater variety of methodological approaches. As will be apparent in this chapter, functional imaging, animal models, and controlled large-scale navigational tasks have supplemented traditional cognitive experiments. The result is a more comprehensive set of accounts for the representation of spatial knowledge, and how that information is used for us to efficiently interact with the spatial world around us.

MEMORY FOR ROUTES

Navigating in the environment

In everyday life people have to find their way around within buildings, within cities, or across country. They may be pedestrians or they may be using various forms of transport. The environment may be simple or complex, and there may be many or few landmarks. Most importantly, spaces will vary in their familiarity: Navigation may require a map or directions, or we may rely on memories of previous experience. Familiarity has a large impact on the type of information that is used to negotiate our environment, and successful navigation, as we will see later, is primarily based upon the manner in which the information is represented. For example, Hartley, Maguire, Spiers, and Burgess (2003) demonstrated that a familiar route is coded in an action-based manner, whereas following a novel route utilises a form of "cognitive map" (O'Keefe & Nadel, 1978; Tolman, 1948).

This highlights a key distinction that has been drawn between route-based information and "map-like" information. In a familiar environment, navigation is a matter of following routes that lead from a starting point through to a given destination, via a series of known points. This is dependent upon the ability to recognise a landmark and to couple it to a given instruction (e.g., turn left at the police station). It has been suggested that this is akin to learning stimulus–response pairs (Thorndyke, 1981). This kind of representation is formed using an egocentric frame of reference: Knowledge is related to your particular view of world and the position of your body within in. This form of coding means that you can specify the side of your body on which you will encounter a part of your route (e.g., pass the pub on your left, and turn right at the following junction). Whilst route knowledge can become highly automated, requiring little conscious control (Hartley et al., 2003), it is also very inflexible. Problems can arise if you emerge from a building or a shopping centre by an unfamiliar exit and have difficulty reorienting yourself with respect to the known routes. Or, if you have learned a route in one direction only, it will be unfamiliar if you need to traverse it in the opposite direction. In this case, landmarks must be recognised from different viewpoints and changes of direction transposed. In less familiar environments, or ones that you do not have preferred routes within, navigation is more likely to rely on map-like representations. In comparison to route knowledge, this information is coded in allocentric space, which means that landmarks are coded by their absolute Euclidian relationship between each other, independent of your position within that space. A map does not specify how you will move from one location to another. Rather, it forms a flexible representation that enables you to navigate from any point in the environment. In some circumstances you may need to find a shortcut or a new route. To work out a quick way to the station, or to reorient yourself after your known route is blocked by a newly imposed restriction, you have to be able to orient yourself in respect to your destination, remember the spatial relationships that hold between alternative routes, and to infer that a given sequence of turns will bring you approximately to its location. Janzen, Schade, Katz, and Herrmann (2001) demonstrated that detour-finding strategies differ depending on the way in which you initially learn about the environment. In their study, participants who had learned a bird's eye map-like (allocentric) view of space preferred to take right-angled routes around an obstacle, whereas participants who had learned an observer's (egocentric) view of space preferred to take obliquely oriented detours. The most frequently used detours were the ones that brought individuals back to the original path that they were following.

Navigating in a completely novel environment may involve following route instructions or a map. This will involve matching the actual environment to the described representation (linguistic or pictorial). Therefore you will have to abstract and simplify in order to extract the essential skeleton of the road layout from the cluttered scene in front of you. It will also be necessary to match the landmarks you encounter against your mental representation of their form. Of course, if the pre-scribed route you are following is in memory, you may get lost because your memory is inaccurate. Equally, if the map or directions are available in front of you, you may make navigation errors if you cannot match them to the area you are travelling through, as, for example, when minor roads are omitted.

Individual differences in memory for routes

Most people would agree that individuals vary very considerably in navigational ability. Some have a poor sense of direction, such that if placed in a maze or an unfamiliar town, they have little idea which direction they have come from, or which direction they should be heading for. Some are notoriously poor map readers and seem to be unable to transform the pictorial information into something that tallies with the environment around them. Other people have a good sense of direction and a good track record as successful navigators. There are a variety of possible bases for these individual differences, at many different levels, and we here consider a small range.

Kozlowski and Bryant (1977) examined the relationship between self-assessed "sense of direction" and a variety of performance measures. In one experiment they walked participants through a maze of underground service tunnels beneath a university campus, from a start point to an endpoint and back again. Individuals were divided on the basis of their self-assessed sense of direction into good and poor groups. On return to the start, they had to point to the location of the endpoint. In this unfamiliar environment, there was no difference between good and poor groups on the first trial, but on later trials those with a good sense of direction improved more than the poor group. Kozlowski and Bryant concluded that this kind of directional orientation is not automatic but requires effort, attention, and repeated exposures. Those with a "good sense of direction" are those who are able to benefit from experience and acquire an accurate cognitive map. It is not clear, however, whether a sense of direction can be regarded as a unitary ability that mediates performance in a variety of spatial tasks, or a constellation of different abilities (such as visuospatial memory, ability to estimate angular relations and distances, ability to visualise, and spatial reasoning) that reinforce each other.

Maguire et al. (2001) studied a group with a more externally validated sense of direction. A group of London taxi drivers, who had all acquired a large amount of navigational experience and undergone extensive training (referred to as "The Knowledge"), underwent a structural MRI examination. Using voxel-based morphometry (VBM), their grey matter density was compared to that of control participants without such extensive navigational experience. The authors discovered that the posterior hippocampal formation was significantly larger in the taxi driver group. Furthermore, the volume of this formation was correlated with the amount of time spent as a taxi driver: Individuals with more experience had more grey matter. This supports the claim that the posterior hippocampus stores spatial representations of the environment. Furthermore, it shows that the area is plastic, and undergoes structural change depending on the amount of navigational experience that we have.

A more fundamental distinction between individuals is that of sex, and there is some evidence that males and females perform differently on large-scale spatial tasks. Male rodents tend to demonstrate better memory than female rodents when negotiating a radial arm maze, and this has been related to the organisational effects of male gonadal hormones (e.g., Williams & Meck, 1991). This difference also seems to extend to humans, with men performing better than women in a virtual water maze task (Astur, Ortiz, & Sutherland, 1998) and in a virtual maze of halls and doorways (Moffat, Hampson, & Hatzipantelis, 1998). However, it seems that this might be due to particular task demands, and that men and women, in fact, tend to use different strategies. Dabbs, Chang, Strong, and Milun (1998) compared men and women on a variety of spatial tasks (e.g., map reading, giving directions) and found that men tended to conceive space in metric Euclidian terms, with specification of distance and direction. In comparison, women were much more likely to think in terms of landmarks and categorical relations (i.e., left and right). Some researchers have failed to find a sex difference in virtual radial arm mazes, and this might be because extra-maze landmarks are utilised particularly well by female participants, removing the usual male superiority for navigation without landmarks (Levy, Astur, & Frick, 2005). An additional factor that may affect the presence or absence of sex differences is the observation that female spatial abilities fluctuate during the menstrual cycle (Hampson, 1990), with better performance in the menstrual stage and poorer performance in the preovulatory stage.

MEMORY FOR MAPS

A study by Thorndyke and Stasz (1980) focused on individual differences in ability to acquire knowledge of an environment by studying maps. In this task, participants studied a map and had to memorise the absolute and relative positions of the named objects and places shown, so that they could draw the map from memory in a recall test. After six study-test trials, they were also asked to solve some route-finding problems from memory. The two maps used, a town map and a country map, are shown in Figures 6.1 and 6.2, respectively.

Three of the participants were experienced in the use of maps. DW was a retired army officer who had taught recruits to use field maps. FK was a retired air force pilot experienced with military maps, and NN was a scientist who worked with geographical data and cartography. Five other participants were inexperienced with maps. Both expert and novice participants were asked to verbalise the strategies they used while studying the maps and their verbal protocols were recorded and analysed. An extract from one of the protocols is shown in the box below.

The task revealed large individual differences. On trial 5, the best participant (DW) scored 100% and the poorest scored 19%. Surprisingly, the expert participants did not necessarily outperform the novices. Although DW was outstandingly good, FK was 6th out of the eight participants and NN was the poorest of all. The verbal protocols revealed that different acquisition strategies were associated with good map learning. Good and poor learners differed in three ways.

---

1   Um. First I notice that there's a railroad that goes up through the middle of the map.

2   And then, the next thing I notice is there's a river on the top left corner, and let's see.

3   There's a main street and . . . I guess I'd try and get the main streets first.

4   That would be Market and Johnson and Main. Try to get the relationship of those.

5   On these two streets, they both start with an M.

6   Then I'd just try to get down the other main streets, that, uh,

7   Victory Avenue comes below the golf course, and

8   then goes straight down and

9   becomes parallel with Johnson, and . . .

10   I guess I'd try to learn the streets that are parallel first, parallel to each other.

11   Just try to remember which, in which order they come.

12   I guess with this one I could, since there's a sort of like a forest, I could remember that this is Aspen, and um,

13   let's see, and Victory, I guess I could relate it to the golf [course], winning the golf [match].

A verbal protocol from a subject studying the town map (from Thorndyke & Stasz, 1980). Copyright © Elsevier (1980). Reproduced with permission.

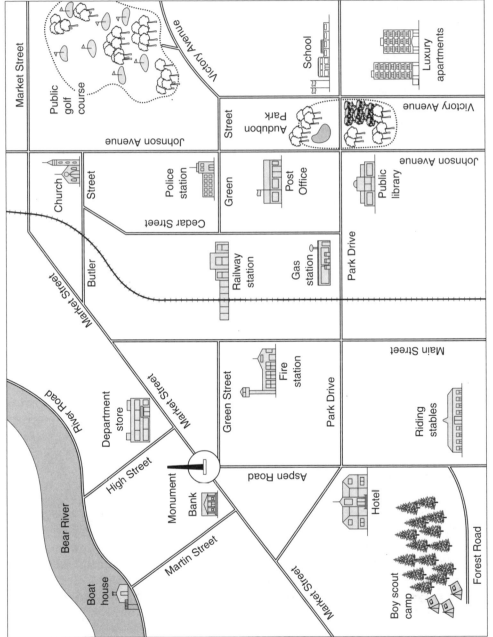

Figure 6.1 The town map (from Thorndyke & Statz, 1980). Copyright © Elsevier (1980). Reproduced with permission.

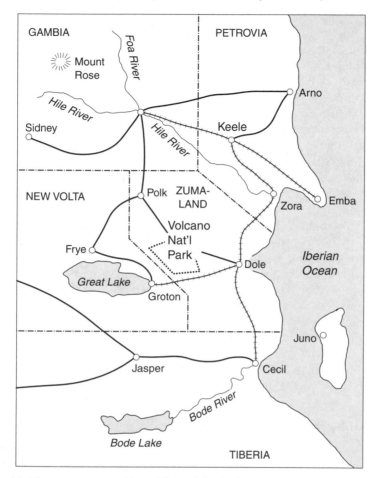

Figure 6.2 The country map (from Thorndyke & Stasz, 1980). Copyright ©
Elsevier (1980). Reproduced with permission.

1 *Allocation of attention*: Good learners partitioned the map into areas and
   focused attention on one area at a time before shifting to a fresh one. The
   protocol in the box above exemplifies this homing-in strategy. Poor learners
   adopted a more diffuse global approach, trying to learn the whole map at once.
2 *Encoding strategies*: Good learners reported using visuospatial imagery to
   encode patterns and spatial relations. Poor learners used no imagery, and relied
   on verbal rehearsal of named elements or verbal mnemonics.
3 *Evaluation*: Good learners tested their own memory to find out how they were
   doing and then focused on areas they had not learned. Poor learners did not do
   this efficiently.

Learning from maps

In a second experiment, Thorndyke and Stasz tested the effects of instructing
participants to use the more effective techniques. Those participants who had high
scores on tests of visual memory benefited from the training, but those with poor

visual memory failed to improve. Neither the greater experience of the expert participants nor training in optimal strategies was sufficient to guarantee efficient map learning. A good visual memory appeared to be a prerequisite. However, Gilhooly, Wood, Kinnear, and Green (1988) suspected that the failure of the experts to show superior skill might be due to the fact that the maps used in these tests were simplified planimetric maps without contours, which gave little scope for the exercise of expertise.

When they compared the ability of groups of experts and novices to remember contour maps they found that the experts were better at remembering contour features, although there was no difference between the groups when memory for noncontour features like place names, roads, and buildings was tested. Trained map readers do have superior memory for the more specialist aspects of maps.

Rossano and Hodgson (1994) tested the hypothesis that people learn maps in a global-to-local fashion and they also compared the effectiveness of different learning strategies. Participants learned the "five countries" map shown in Figure 6.3 in one of four different learning conditions.

In the ad lib condition participants studied the map in their own way; in the imagery condition they were told to form a mental picture so that they would be able to draw the map; in the story condition they read a story about a plague spreading across the countries; and in the verbal condition they were asked to make up phrases to describe the location of the elements in the map. Map recall scores showed that, as predicted, countries were remembered better than provinces, which in turn were better remembered than cities, confirming that map learning was global-to-local. The imagery instructions were most effective in improving recall.

Map knowledge and route knowledge

It is fortunate, perhaps, for those who are no good at it, that studying a map is not the only way to acquire knowledge of the environment. It can also be learned directly from the experience of moving around. Thorndyke and Hayes-Roth (1982) set out to compare the kind of spatial knowledge that results from these two modes of learning. They tested two groups of participants for their knowledge of a large complex building. The map knowledge group learned from floor plans. The navigational or route knowledge group was composed of people who worked in the building. Each group included people at two different levels of experience. A series of tests were administered.

1   *Distance:* (a) Estimate the straight-line distance between two named locations, and (b) estimate the route distance (walking from one location to the other).
2   *Orientation:* (a) Point to the location of one place when standing at another location, and (b) point to the location of one place while imagining yourself standing at some other location.
3   *Location:* Mark designated locations on an incomplete plan.

Route knowledge participants were better at estimating route distances and at orientation. Map knowledge participants were better at estimating straight-line distances and marking locations. Thorndyke and Hayes-Roth concluded that map knowledge (sometimes called survey knowledge) is good for representing global

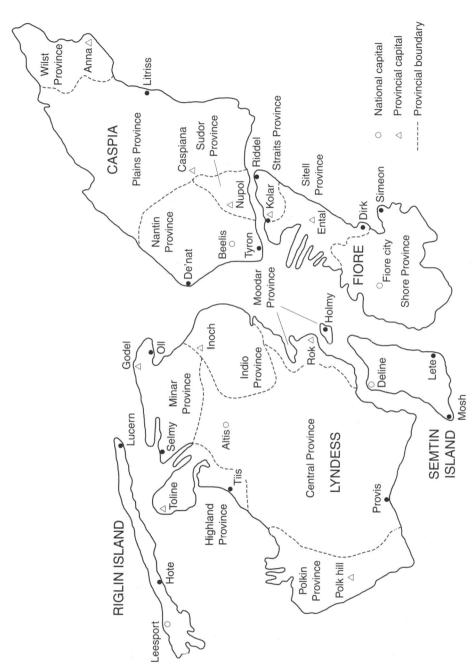

Figure 6.3 The five countries map. From Rossano, M.J. and Hodgson, S.L. (1994). The process of learning from small-scale maps. *Applied Cognitive Psychology*, 8, 565–582. Copyright © 1994 John Wiley & Sons Ltd. Reproduced with permission.

relationships and gives direct access to distance and location information. It provides a *bird's-eye view*, but this is difficult to transform into a different view. Navigational knowledge is based on sequentially organised procedural knowledge acquired by traversing the routes, and results in a *ground-based view*. However, the results suggested that route knowledge can be used to generate map knowledge. Mental simulation of navigation (i.e., imagining yourself walking around) yields information about routes, distances, and locations, and information about orientation and straight-line distance can be computed from route knowledge. Comparison of participants with high and low experience suggested that with increasing experience, navigationally acquired route knowledge undergoes qualitative changes, becoming more flexible. Thorndyke and Hayes-Roth (1982) claimed that this ground-based view becomes effectively translucent, so relationships between points can be "seen" despite intervening obstructions. The best all-round performance in this experiment was achieved by the highly experienced navigators.

The distinction between route knowledge and map knowledge is not hard and fast. If Thorndyke and Hayes-Roth are correct in claiming that route knowledge is transformed into map knowledge with experience, there must be transitional stages in between, and experience confirms that one kind of spatial knowledge can be converted into the other. You can derive a route from studying a map, and you can construct a map from knowledge of routes. However, we can still distinguish between the two kinds of knowledge. Route knowledge is typically small-scale knowledge of local areas, acquired episodically from personal navigational experiences. It is represented from a ground-based, egocentric point of view in terms of sequentially organised procedures for getting from one point to another. Map knowledge is larger-scale, and represents global spatial relations topologically from a bird's-eye point of view.

Using a different paradigm, Tversky (1991) also differentiated between route knowledge and map or survey knowledge. In her experiments the two kinds of knowledge are exemplified in different forms of verbal description. Route descriptions take the reader on a mental tour presenting information sequentially and relating it to the traveller's own body position (left, right, in front, behind). Survey descriptions take a perspective from above and describe the locations of landmarks in terms of canonical directions (north, south, east, west), as in the following extracts from examples of descriptions of a resort area shown in Figure 6.4.

Route description
. . . to reach the Pigeon Lake area drive south along Bay Road until you reach, on your left, the point where the Forest Highway dead-ends into Bay Road. From this intersection, you can see in the distance that Bay Road continues to Matilda Bay . . . You turn left on to Forest Highway and travel about 40 miles until on your right you reach Horseshoe Drive. Horseshoe Drive is the only road you can take to get into the Pigeon Lake region. Turning right onto Horseshoe Drive you see on your left, Pigeon Lake . . .

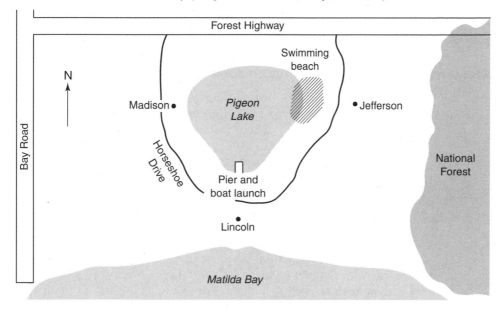

Figure 6.4 Map of resort area (from Taylor & Tversky, 1992). Reprinted by permission of Academic Press, Inc. and the author. Copyright © Elsevier 1992. Reproduced with permission.

Survey description
. . . The resort area is bordered by four major landmarks: the National Forest, Matilda Bay, Bay Road, and the Forest Highway. The eastern border is made up of the National Forest . . . the southern border is made up of Matilda Bay. Two major roads, Bay Road and the Forest Highway form the other two borders of the region. Bay Road runs north–south along the western border of this region . . .

(Tversky, 1991, p. 111).

Tversky was interested in whether these two kinds of description produced different mental representations or whether both produced a common perspective-free representation. Participants in her experiments read detailed descriptions (either route or survey) of fictitious environments and afterwards made true/false judgements about statements. True statements were either verbatim statements about the location of landmarks extracted from the text, or they were inference statements containing information that could be inferred from the text. The results showed no difference in speed or accuracy between route and survey descriptions, so Tversky and colleagues concluded that, irrespective of the perspective of the description, the reader constructs a spatial mental model of the environment that is perspective-free. Her findings contrast with those of Thorndyke and Hayes-Roth (1982), and, as we will see in the next section, this viewpoint is not supported by behavioural navigational tasks (e.g., Wang & Spelke, 2000).

Mental representation of spatial information

As mentioned earlier, another way of distinguishing route and survey knowledge is in relation to one's own bodily perspective. Egocentric representations are those constructed from observer experience, where features are coded in relation to your position in space. In comparison, allocentric knowledge is more "map-like" in conception, and refers to an enduring, orientation-free representation of space. More recent studies consider spatial representation within these terms, and have sought to ascertain which of these representations forms the primary basis for human navigation, and how the different types of information interact.

Wang and Spelke (2000) highlight an important factor relating to these two forms of representation: egocentric information is constantly updated as the individual moves and can provide a basis for action, whereas allocentric information is enduring, providing the basis for long-term storage of spatial coordinates. This distinction has been found with animals, as well as humans. For example, insects use a system of path integration to navigate, whereby the vector between a foraging animal and its nest is constantly updated with each movement (Gallistel, 1990). In comparison, rodents are also able to navigate along novel routes, and also from novel starting points, suggesting that they have formed a more stable representation of the environment as a whole, or a "cognitive map" (O'Keefe & Nadel, 1978; Tolman, 1948). Wang and Spelke (2000) conducted a series of experiments to test whether human navigation depends primarily on one representation or the other. The general task was for participants to point to non-visible targets within a room, first with their eyes open, and then blindfolded following a small rotation, and blindfolded following extended self-rotation that led to a state of disorientation. The findings suggest that navigation (within moderately sized environments, at least) depends on active transformation and updating of information relative to the body. With or without vision, participants were able to accurately estimate target locations as long as they were able to remain oriented and update their representation of the environment with their movement. In conditions where they became disoriented, participants could no longer accurately locate target positions. If a landmark was visible (Exp. 5: a light visible through an opaque blindfold) then disorientated participants could reorient themselves to the remembered geometry of the room, but were unable to accurately locate the configuration of targets within the space. The authors argue that egocentric updating is the primary basis for navigation, and that a "cognitive map" is constructed by adding environmental details to the same system (rather than it being an entirely separate system).

Researchers have also employed functional neuroimaging techniques to distinguish different forms of spatial representation. Maguire et al. (1998a) used positron emission tomography (PET) to measure cortical activity whilst participants navigated through a virtual reality town. They found the right hippocampus to be more active when navigating, compared to following a trail of arrows through the town (requiring no navigational skills). Furthermore, when heading direction to a target location was more accurate, there was increased activation in this area. There was also consistent activation in the right inferior parietal cortex, and this was not modulated by navigation or trail-following conditions. The authors argue that this demonstrates a cooperative network between hippocampal and inferior parietal cortices that enables effective navigation. The hippocampus is seen as providing an allocentric representation of the environment, allowing a perspective-free computation of routes from any starting point and to any destination. In turn, the inferior parietal lobe transforms these coordinates into body-centred (egocentric) terms to enable active movement through the environment. As such, the parietal areas were active during both navigation and trail-following, as both conditions involved the computation of turning and heading information, along with the position of environmental elements relative to the body. Hartley et al. (2003) support this distinction between map-based and action-based representations. Their study compared the following of a novel path with a familiar well-worn route, and they found that the hippocampus was specifically involved in computing a novel route. For familiar routes, however, an entirely different network of motor and somatosensory areas was activated. The absence of hippocampal involvement suggests that repeated rehearsal of a route leads to action-based egocentric representations of space, which render active perceptual spatial processing less necessary and might be seen as a form of autopilot.

Damage to specific brain areas can also indicate the manner in which spatial information is represented, especially when a very discrete aspect of navigation is disrupted. In the last century or so, a number of neuropsychological cases have been reported where patients seem to present a deficit in way-finding, often termed "topographical disorientation". Aguirre and D'Esposito (1999) reviewed these cases and suggested a taxonomical system to differentiate the functional bases of navigational difficulty:

1 *Egocentric disorientation.* This deficit is associated with damage to posterior parietal areas, and is often associated with spatial deficits other than navigation (i.e., mental rotation, spatial span). Patients are particularly impaired at representing the locations of objects relative to the body. Whilst their object and landmark recognition appears to be intact, these patients are unable to combine that information with an egocentric frame of reference. As such, they have difficulties learning and describing routes, being unable to associate bodily position with a given landmark.

2 *Heading disorientation.* These patients appear to have a specific inability to derive directional information from landmarks, in the face of intact recognition and egocentric processing. There are few cases that fit this category, but those that do have damage to the posterior cingulate region, an area that has been identified as representing heading direction in rodents.

3 *Landmark agnosia.* The key component of this deficit is an inability to recognise salient features of the environment for the purposes of navigation. Whilst patients can recognise objects, and some distinguish different classes of building, there seems to be a particular deficit in representing these objects as having landmark value. This tends to result from damage to the lingual gyrus, and suggests that this brain area represents classes of object with specific reference to topography, separate to the visual identification of objects.

4 *Anterograde disorientation.* Cases that fit this category have difficulties primarily with novel environments. Following damage to the parahippocampal area, patients have been reported to demonstrate difficulties in learning new routes,

but have preserved topographical knowledge acquired before their lesion. Patients do not tend to present any general memory impairments, highlighting the role of the parahippocampus in the acquisition of novel topographical knowledge.

The types of case described above indicate that effective navigational behaviour is based on various forms of representation, from egocentric appreciation of landmarks to the formation of allocentric cognitive maps for novel spaces. These forms of knowledge are based within a functional sphere that we might refer to as perception and action. However, there is some evidence that spatial behaviour is also partially dependent on linguistic factors. Hermer and Spelke (1994, 1996) studied reorientation behaviour in adults and young children (18–24 months). In animal studies, rats and non-human primates have been shown to use the geometric shape of an area to reorient, and do not make use of local landmarks (such as a visual feature or an olfactory cue). Hermer and Spelke's experiments took place within a small rectangular room with a box in each corner. Participants observed an object being hidden in one of the corners and then underwent a disorientation process. Afterwards they were asked to locate the object that had been hidden. In one condition the room was entirely devoid of all landmarks, and participants could only use the shape of the room to guide their search behaviour. In this condition, both adults and children split their search equally between two geometrically appropriate corners (as do rats and non-human primates). In another condition, one of the smaller walls was of a different colour to the rest of the room, thus providing a landmark. Here, adults were able to utilise the wall to search accurately in the correct location, showing a flexible ability to conjoin geometric and landmark information. In comparison, children continued to divide their search between the geometrically appropriate corners, despite the fact that some of them drew reference to the existence of the coloured wall. This suggests that, like rodents, young children are unable to use landmark information for reorientation. In further experiments with older children (3–7 years), they found that successful search behaviour coincided with the emergence of spatial language, especially "left" and "right" (around 6 years).

As a result of these findings, Hermer and Spelke (1994, 1996) argue that flexible spatial memory relies on language, which forms a basis for the combination of different types of spatial information. To support this thesis, Hermer-Vasquez, Spelke, and Katnelson (1999) present experiments with adult reorientation during verbal shadowing. Again, participants searched for the hidden object, but were required continuously to shadow (immediately repeat aloud) verbal speech information during the entirety of the procedure. In this case, their performance became like that of children and rats, in that they did not use the landmark to guide their search behaviour. However, when participants were required to shadow nonverbal rhythmic streams, they were able to use the coloured wall to locate the hidden object accurately. It was argued that this further demonstrates the necessity of language as a platform with which to combine spatial information. When participants were unable to use linguistic processes (due to continuous verbal shadowing) they lost the flexibility and performed as children without those linguistic representations of space. Other groups have questioned these findings, owing to differences found in attempts to replicate the reorientation procedure. For example, Learmonth, Nadel, and Newcombe (2002) found that young children could not use landmarks to reorient in a small space (like that of Hermer & Spelke) but could effectively combine landmark and geometric information in a larger room. This suggests that there may be additional factors that affect this kind of spatial behaviour, and that the nature of the environment may be as important as the linguistic terms available to represent it.

Verbal descriptions do not, as a rule, specify space as completely and precisely as maps, models, or actual experience. Descriptions may be indeterminate in that they fail to specify the distances between objects or they use indeterminate expressions like "A is beside B", which leaves their relative positions unspecified. This type of indeterminate information can be represented mentally as a set of propositions but not as an image or mental model, where information has to take a determinate form. Tversky (1991) argued that people encode multiple different kinds of representations of spatial information and this view is widely accepted. It is likely that several factors determine which type of representation dominates. One factor is the form of the input, whether it is a map, a verbal description, or a visual or navigational experience. Another factor is the function of the representation; for example, whether it is used for computing distance or relative locations, for finding short cuts or retracing known routes, for moving the furniture around or finding a parking space.

Spatial information processing: Inferences and estimates

Spatial information processes include both the construction of the representation and processes of consultation that occur when information is extracted from the memory representation. When information is explicitly represented, it may be read off directly, but when information is not explicit in the representation, processes of spatial inference and spatial transformation are needed to extract it. The relative positions of some objects, their relative distances, and orientations may be unspecified or indeterminate but this information can often be inferred.

In propositional representations, spatial locations may be hierarchically arranged, so, for example, the proposition "Scotland is north of England" is superordinate to "Edinburgh is in Scotland" or "Newcastle is in England". The information that Edinburgh is in Scotland is, in our example, already stored as a proposition and can be accessed directly. The information that Edinburgh is north of Newcastle is not stored directly, but is implicit and can be inferred by logical deduction from this set of propositions.

Spatial inferences are not always accurate, however. Stevens and Coupe (1978) asked participants to judge the relative positions of one city to another (e.g., Reno to San Diego). The errors that were made showed that participants derived their answers by inferences from superordinate propositions that express the spatial relationship between Nevada and California. Because Nevada lies east of California, they assume (wrongly) that Reno lies east of San Diego. Similarly, in the United Kingdom, if people are asked whether Bristol lies east or west of Edinburgh, they tend to infer (again wrongly) that Bristol must be west because it lies on the west coast and Edinburgh lies on the east coast.

Information about distance and orientation can also be inferred when it is not stored directly. Byrne (1979) asked participants to estimate walking distances between pairs of locations in and around the town of St Andrews, Scotland. These included short routes and longer routes; routes in the town centre and routes in the suburbs; straight routes and routes with changes of direction. People tended to overestimate the short routes, those with more changes of direction, and the town centre routes where there were more landmarks. Byrne concluded that distance estimation was based on the number of identifiable segments in the route. The larger the number of segments, the greater the estimated distance.

Byrne also tested participants' ability to draw from memory the angles between the roads at familiar junctions. The results showed that all types of angles were normalised towards the right angle. Inaccurate estimates of angles would necessarily distort inferences about direction and orientation, so this tendency would explain why it is that short cuts do not always take you to your intended destination. Memory for places, and being able to find your way around, depend on the accuracy and completeness of the mental representation of spatial knowledge, and also on the processes employed to read out or compute the required information.

MEMORY FOR OBJECTS AND OBJECT LOCATIONS

In everyday life, memory for objects has two main functions. The first involves object identification. We rely on memory representations to identify and classify objects, to recognise what they are and what category of objects they belong to. The second function involves memory for the location of objects. Because we are constantly moving around in our environment and changing the locations of the objects with which we interact, we need to remember where objects are, and we also need to be able to recognise them when we have found them. This latter point may seem obvious and trivial but research has shown that memory for the visual appearance of common objects is sometimes very imprecise and poorly specified. This may explain why people looking for a mislaid object can fail to "see" it when it is in plain view.

Landau and Jackendoff (1993) drew on their analysis of language to gain insight into spatial cognition and, in particular, into the nature of representation of objects and places. They concluded that there may be distinct separate spatial cognitions systems for representing *what* and *where*. The descriptions used to refer to objects when concerned with their identity (the *what* system is engaged) use rich and complex terminology to describe their shape and surface. When the same objects are in the role of landmarks or reference points (the *where* system is engaged), descriptions are restricted to very schematised features. Rather similarly, Tversky (1995) has developed a theory of memory for the visuospatial world that distinguishes between memory for figures, objects, or elements of a scene, and memory for the spatial relations between them. There is also some neurological evidence of double dissociations between object recognition ability and ability to localise objects in space and in relation to each other (Farah, Hammond, Levine, & Calvanio, 1988), which supports the view that these are separate systems. Nevertheless, in everyday life the business of finding mislaid objects seems to involve both kinds of spatial cognition.

Memory for object location

Losing objects

Forgetting where you put something, misplacing, or losing objects is a common and frustrating experience in everyday life. The lapse of memory may be only temporary.

The moment when you realise you cannot remember where you parked the car is usually short-lived and the memory is recovered quite soon. In other cases, forgetting is complete, the memory is never recovered, and the missing object may never be located. The questions of interest are why we sometimes forget an object's location, and how we set about trying to find missing objects. Several different causes of error in object location can be distinguished:

1 *Absentmindedness:* The object has been put in an unusual, unintended place by mistake, and the participant does not remember putting it there.
2 *Updating errors:* The object has been put in one of several familiar places. The participant has memories of putting it in all of these places on different occasions, but cannot remember which memory is the most recent one.
3 *Detection failures:* The object has been put in its proper place. The participant looks there, but fails to detect it.
4 *Context effects:* Tversky (1995) has pointed out that memory for locations is relative to other contextual elements in the scene and to a higher order frame of reference (such as the walls of the room, or a map of the world), and these may introduce distortions. For example, Gestalt principles of grouping and common fate may mean items are remembered as being closer together than they really were.

In trying to locate missing objects there are also several different kinds of search strategy that can be employed:

1 *Action replay strategy:* The participant tries to reconstruct mentally the sequence of actions, and so retrieve the memory of placing the object.
2 *Mental walk strategy:* The participant can generate visual images of locations in which the object might be placed and mentally inspect these locations to see if the object is present.
3 *Reality-monitoring strategy:* The participant can generate images of putting the object in various possible locations, and employ the reality-monitoring criteria described in Chapter 10 to judge whether any of these correspond to reality.
4 *Physical search:* Instead of mental searching for the object, the participant can physically search possible locations.

Tenney (1984) administered a "lost and found" questionnaire to young and elderly participants. She expected to find that elderly people misplaced objects more often than the young, and she generated two preliminary hypotheses about why we lose things. The first hypothesis attributed such incidents to memory problems. Tenney suggested that elderly people might be more absentminded than the young, and lack of attention to ongoing activities would cause them to put objects down inadvertently in unintended places. Tenney's second hypothesis attributed object loss to detection failures. She suggested that elderly people might have more difficulty in finding objects because of perceptual difficulties caused by sensory handicaps, or poor search strategies. Participants were asked to report any incidents of losing objects occurring within a 2-week period. Approximately 30% of the participants experienced such an incident, but young and elderly participants did not differ in the number of incidents reported.

The absentminded hypothesis

Participants were also asked to supply self-ratings on an absentmindedness scale. Although there was again no age difference, object losers (unsurprisingly) rated themselves as more absentminded than those who had not lost any objects. The absentminded hypothesis received further support from the fact that in 62% of the incidents the objects were left in unintended places and in 58% of these cases the participant had no recollection of ever having put the object there. Tenney divided the misplaced objects into common objects (misplaced by more than one participant) and unique objects (misplaced by only one participant). Common objects included pen, pencil, chequebook, keys, money, glasses, watch, and jewellery. Although it is not clear from her data exactly how many incidents involved common objects, it does seem as if a substantial number of incidents occurred in the course of routine activities handling routine objects. In these circumstances, failures of memory for object location can be interpreted in the same way as slips of action (see Chapter 5). They occur during routine activities that are under automatic control. Because of the lack of conscious attentional monitoring, the action of misplacing the object is not adequately encoded in memory, and the object's location cannot be recollected later. This kind of explanation fits those cases when the participant has no memory of putting the object in the place where it is eventually found.

The perceptual hypothesis

Tenney (1984) found that some of the object-losing incidents fitted the perceptual hypothesis. Elderly people reported a higher incidence of cases where object-misplacing involved defective search or failure of detection, but even young people reported some occasions when they found the object in plain sight (6.8%), in a place where it was usually kept (21.5%), or in a place where they had already looked (23.75%). Although it seems odd that people should fail to find an object when it is in its usual place, this is obviously quite a common experience. Sometimes, of course, the object may be partly concealed or obscured by other objects, but when an object is in plain sight it may be undetected if memory for the object's appearance is incomplete, inaccurate, or based on an inappropriate orientation. Failures of object detection may therefore be linked to the process of mental rotation. When searching for an object, the searcher generates a visual image of the missing object in the expected location and looks for a match. If the target object is at an unusual orientation (fallen over, lying askew) it will not match the visual image unless either image or stimulus is mentally rotated into alignment. Failure to carry out the appropriate mental rotations could account for cases when objects in plain view are not found. Tversky (1995) has pointed out that many objects have a "canonical" view. Teapots and horses are easiest to recognise when seen sideways on, but for clocks and telephones the frontal view is canonical.

The memory-updating hypothesis

Another explanation, not suggested by Tenney (1984), also rests on the fact that many misplaced objects are those that are handled very frequently. This hypothesis suggests that when you try to recall an object's location, the problem is one of correctly dating the memory that is retrieved. You may remember putting the car keys on the hall table, or the chequebook in the desk drawer, but is this the memory from the last, most recent time you used the keys or chequebook, or is it derived from some previous occasion? Bjork (1978) reminded us of the importance of updating in every sphere of everyday life. You need to remember where you parked the car today, not last week. You need to know your current car's registration number, not the number of the car you had before. You need to know what are trumps in the hand of bridge you are playing now. Bjork also pointed out that very many jobs, from short-order cook to air traffic controller, require continual memory updating. Effective management of any enterprise requires accurate updating of information about supplies, orders, personnel, etc. There is a very general need to forget, erase, or override information that is no longer current, and replace it with the most recent version. When we make mistakes about object locations, it is often because this updating process has failed and we retrieve an outdated memory.

Bjork distinguished two mechanisms of updating: *destructive updating*, whereby earlier versions are completely destroyed, and *structural updating*, whereby earlier versions are preserved but order and recency information is built into the series by some structural principle. In his experiment, the task tested memory for paired associates. The stimulus word remained the same, but was paired with a different response word on each trial (e.g., frog–rope; frog–plum, etc.). As well as testing total recall of all the response words, the task tested updating by asking participants to recall the most recent response word. Participants were given different instructions. In the *destructive updating condition*, they were told to imagine writing the words on a blackboard, erasing the previous response word, and filling in the new one on each trial. In the *ordered rehearsal condition*, they were told to rote rehearse the items in order of presentation. In the *structural updating condition*, they were given a story line to connect the items, and in the *imagery condition*, they had to form a mental picture relating the items (e.g., a frog with a rope), then undo the picture and replace the old item with the new one on each trial (e.g., replace the rope with a plum). Participants reported that they were unable to carry out the destructive instructions. The structural condition produced the best updated recall of the most recent item, but total recall was poor in this condition, indicating that some destruction of earlier items may have occurred.

Where did I park?

Remembering where you parked the car is usually a problem of updating. You can probably recall parking it in several places and can image the car in each of these. But which is today's memory? As Bjork's (1978) participants reported, although it is often useless in everyday life to remember outdated information, we do not seem to be able to erase it at will. Various strategies can be employed to cope with the car-parking problem. I tend to use an action replay strategy. When I cannot remember where I parked the car today, I trace back through a sequence of activities (Which direction did I come from as I approached the building I work in? Did I arrive early, when the nearest parking slots would have been vacant?) In effect, I supply a story line in order to identify the most recent of my parking memories. By elaborating the memory in this way I can place it in the right temporal context.

Da Costa Pinto and Baddeley (1991) studied memory for car parking in Cambridge in a series of experiments. Their findings showed a clear recency effect and suggested that both decay over time and interference from repeated parking events affected recall. Both factors affect the discriminability of the target memory from other parking events. This study is consistent with the interpretation of the recency effect offered by Baddeley and Hitch (1993). They suggested that the advantage for recent events derives from two factors; an implicit priming factor causes gradually declining activation and so makes the most recently presented items easiest to reactivate (they call this the "light bulb analogy"), and an output factor such that there is an explicit strategy of retrieving the last items first. The parking study is an elegant demonstration of the way in which naturalistic research can be used to test the scope and generalisability of theoretical concepts.

Lutz, Means, and Long (1994) also carried out a naturalistic study of memory for car parking in which 32 university staff were asked to indicate on a map the exact space in which they had parked that day and the 3 preceding days. Accuracy of recall was good for the same day but declined for the previous days. For the same day, 88% of the staff were accurate within three spaces, but for the most remote day only 58% maintained this level of accuracy. Some individuals made wild errors, even forgetting which parking lot they had used. People used a variety of strategies to help them remember where they had parked. The most popular strategy was to eliminate the problem by sticking to a favourite parking spot. Other commonly used strategies were relating the car to a visual landmark or mentally retracing the action. Both these strategies seemed to include a strong imagery component and few participants reported encoding the information verbally. The decline in memory for parking on previous days suggests that these outdated memories may fade fairly rapidly and so lose their power to interfere with the most recent memory.

Objects and the self

In an earlier section we saw that navigation involves updating spatial information with movement, so that the environment is represented egocentrically, with reference to the body. Evidence suggests that this is the same for our memory of object locations. Simons and Wang (1998) demonstrated this by presenting participants with an array of objects on a circular table, and then lowering a curtain over the table. Participants were either led around the table to a new point, or the table was rotated by an equivalent amount. When asked to detect whether one of the objects had changed position after the curtain was raised, participants were more accurate following self-rotation, rather than rotation of the table. In another study (Wang & Simons, 1999), participants rotated the table themselves, and therefore had full view and control of the rotational movement. Despite this, their performance was still more accurate when they had walked around the table to an equivalent viewpoint. These findings suggest that self-motion leads to an updating of object location information that is more accurate than object-based transformations.

Some forms of memory for object location are likely to rely on mental image manipulation. For example, when individuals view an object array that has been rotated, they may mentally rotate the display so that the image matches their previous view of the array. They can then compare between the two representations and ascertain whether a change has occurred. Support for this comes from Diwadkar and McNamara (1997), who examined the recognition of spatial layouts from a variety of different views (i.e., rotations of the object array). They found that the time taken to respond was chronometrically proportionate to the angular rotation of the array from its original position. This suggests that participants were mentally rotating the display in an analogue manner, similar to that described by Shepard and Metzler (1971). Mental rotation can be conceived differently depending on the strategy that an individual takes: One can imagine the object rotating, while one's viewpoint is fixed, or one can imaging moving around a fixed object to view it from another position (Kosslyn, Thompson, Wraga, & Alpert, 2001). In an interesting parallel to the findings of Simons and Wang (1998), Wraga, Creem, and Proffitt (2000) found that participants demonstrated more accurate memory for an object array when they imagined moving around the display than when they imagined the display rotating. Not only does this support arguments for egocentric representation of object locations, but it also suggests that spatial updating does not rely on proprioceptive or vestibular stimulation.

Memory for a common object

Memory representations of objects need to be sufficiently precise and fine-grained to support the kinds of discriminations that are usually made. We need to be able to discriminate between an apple and a pear, and possibly between a William pear and a Conference pear, but we may not need to discriminate between one banana and another. There is a case for arguing that memory representations of common objects are only as precise and accurate as they need to be. It has been noted that people are often unable to report the layout of numbers on a telephone dial or pad and that even typists cannot reconstruct the keyboard. Nickerson and Adams (1982) confirmed experimentally that people have surprisingly poor memory for the visual appearance of common objects. They asked 20 participants to draw each side of a US one-cent piece. Out of a total of eight features (four on each side), the mean number of features correctly reproduced was only three, and nearly half of these were mislocated. Nickerson and Adams considered the possibility that performance was poor because, although people often need to recognise coins, recall is rarely required. However, on a recognition test, where participants had to select the correct version from 15 drawings of different versions, only half the participants were correct. More recently, Richardson (1992) tested people's ability to recall the orientation of the monarch's head on British coins and found there was a bias to recall the profile incorrectly as facing left. He suggested that people develop a left-facing schema from their experience with the orientation of the head on stamps and erroneously apply this to coins.

Foos (1989) found that elderly people were particularly poor at recognising coins and telephone dials. Thirty per cent of young adults identified the correct drawing of a coin and 40% identified the correct layout of the telephone dial. None of the elderly participants identified the coin and only 7% identified the dial. However, in spite of their poor performance, the elderly were more confident in their responses. It seems that people only remember enough of the visual properties of objects to be able to make the quite gross discriminations required in everyday life. In the case of coins, knowing the size, shape, and colour of metal is sufficient and it is unnecessary to know anything about the inscriptions and symbols on the coin faces. If memory for the visual appearance of other common objects is similarly vague, it is not so surprising that people sometimes fail to find an object that is in its proper place.

Objects and navigation

As we explore the world, objects can serve as landmarks to facilitate our navigation. A useful landmark may range from a tower block to a fire hydrant—it is not necessarily the size of the object that is useful, but rather its navigational significance. If an object appears at a location at which a decision needs to be made (e.g., turn left or right), then it is more likely to be remembered than another object at a non-decision point (see Blades & Medlicott, 1992). In a study by Janzen and Van Turennout (2004), participants observed a film sequence that displayed a route through a virtual museum. Their stated task was to remember the route that was followed and the objects along the way, as if they were training to be a guide. On the route there were objects placed at decision points (i.e., intersections) and non-decision points (i.e., simple turns). Half of the objects were toys and half were non-toys; participants were asked to pay particular attention to the toys in order to guide a children's tour through the museum. This particular manipulation allowed the authors to control for attention, as there were an equal number of attended and non-attended objects at decision and non-decision points. Following the observation phase, participants were scanned using event-related fMRI while they performed a simple object recognition task. They were shown a selection of objects that were present in the museum (toys and non-toys, at decision and non-decision points) interleaved with a selection of novel toys and non-toys. Their task was to indicate whether they had seen it in the previous film. Elements from this procedure are illustrated in Figure 6.5.

Behavioural results showed no differences in the accuracy of recognition memory for attended vs unattended objects, or decision-point vs non-decision-point objects, although participants responded significantly faster to attended objects (i.e., toys). However, imaging data demonstrated that brain activity was modulated by the navigational relevance of objects. Parahippocampal activity was greater for objects that had been placed at a decision point than those that appeared at a non-decision point. This demonstrates the importance of the parahippocampal gyrus for object-location memory, and suggests that the brain automatically distinguishes between navigationally relevant and irrelevant objects when we explore our environment. Crucially, the decision-point related activity was shown to be unrelated to explicit attention during the study phase (i.e., toys vs non-toys), which rules out the possibility that participants simply paid more attention to objects at decision points. Furthermore, the increase observed in parahippocampal activity for decision-point objects was present even for forgotten objects, which is evidence for an implicit retrieval of navigational information. It seems that navigational information is automatically and often unconsciously acquired as we learn routes, and that objects and landmarks relevant to our navigation can be stored for later use in the absence of spatial information (even if not explicitly remembered). The involvement of parahippocampal areas for the encoding of salient object locations is also supported by the findings of Maguire, Burgess, Donnett, O'Keefe, and Frith (1998b), who

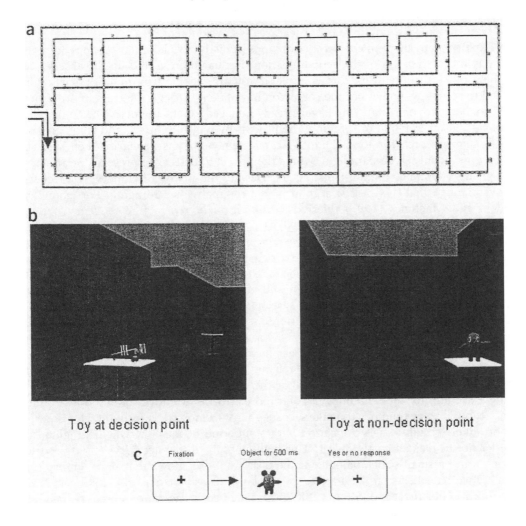

Figure 6.5 Virtual museum and recognition task from Janzen and Van
   Turennout (2004). (a) The aerial perspective of the virtual museum.
   Participants started the tour in the direction of the arrow. The
   squares indicate tables on which the objects were placed. (b)
   Examples of scenes that participants viewed during the study phase.
   Shown here are two attended objects (toys) placed at a decision point
   and a non-decision point from the viewpoint of the participants. (c)
   During a recognition task, participants were presented with objects
   from the virtual museum that were randomly intermixed with new
   objects, and then they indicated by button press whether or not they
   had seen the object in the prior film sequence. Reprinted by
   permission from Macmillan Publishers Ltd: Nature Neuroscience,
   Janzen and Van Turennout, *Selective neural representation of objects
   relevant for navigation,* copyright © 2004.

found increased activity in this region when navigating a virtual environment with relevant landmarks, compared to a featureless environment.

Exploring an environment without obvious or distinctive landmarks can require us to pay more attention to the actual location that has been visited, in the absence of salient objects to orient us. For example, if you are picking fruit in an orchard, you need to somehow remember the route you have taken through the trees in order not to go back to one that you have already relieved of its bounty. This might be considered an example of foraging, the process by which animals, and some groups of humans, search for food. Human search behaviour has primarily been studied using the visual search paradigm, where the task is to detect the presence or absence of a target stimulus amongst distracters. Despite the many differences, researchers have claimed that this task is a good model for real-world foraging. For example, Klein and MacInnes (1999) referred to *inhibition of return* (the tendency not to return an item that has just been fixated) as a "foraging facilitator". Gilchrist, North, and Hood (2001) investigated the extent to which visual search does resemble foraging in a paradigm that required participants to walk around an array of search locations (film canisters) in a room. The task was to detect the presence or absence of a target (a marble) by bending down and checking each location (by shaking the canister). As with standard visual search findings, search times increased proportionally with the number of locations in the room, and the ratio between the target-present and target-absent slopes was 1:2. However, there were far fewer revisits to locations that had already been inspected than one would expect in a visual search task, where individuals often refixate elements a number of times during a trial. Gilchrist et al. (2001) argued that the difference in effort required to search might account for these findings. It is far more effortful to moves one's body around the search display than it is to make saccades across a monitor screen; therefore one is more likely to tag a visited location with some kind of memory when foraging, in order not to make a costly revisit. This highlights the difference between large-scale search and a small-scale analogue of the task, and also shows that our memory for where we have been can be affected by the kind of task we are undertaking.

Smith, Gilchrist, and Hood (2005) investigated large-scale search behaviour further by manipulating the effort required to search. Child participants (aged between 5–8 years) performed searches in an automated version of the foraging paradigm. This took the form of an isolated square room without obvious landmarks. Embedded in the floor was a grid of search locations, each consisting of two lights and a switch (see Figure 6.6). A randomised display of search locations (green lights) was presented, and children were required to search for the target (a red light) by pressing the switch at each location until they had located the one that illuminated the adjacent red light. In one condition children performed the search with their preferred hand, and in another they used their non-preferred hand. The authors found that when children searched with their non-preferred hand, they made more erroneous revisits to previously checked locations than when they were using their preferred hand. It therefore seems that when the motor response was more effortful (i.e., using the non-preferred hand) children demonstrated poorer memory for where they had previously been. Note that this is in an opposing direction to that predicted by Gilchrist et al. (2001): Whereas they suggested that increased effort may be associated with better memory for where one has been, Smith et al. (2005) found that increased effort is associated with poorer memory. Individual differences were also

Figure 6.6 Children's search behaviour in large-scale space: Developmental components of exploration. Reproduced from Smith, Gilchrist, and Hood (2005). Reprinted with permission from Pion Press.

measured in this experiment, and the authors found that those children with a longer visuospatial short-term memory span (as measured by the Corsi Block Tapping task) tended to perform their searches in a faster time and with fewer overall visits than children with a shorter span. However, search efficiency was unrelated to their general fluid intelligence. This demonstrates the importance of spatial memory in navigation, especially when organising an efficient search and remembering one's route through a uniform environment. The findings also show that efficiency can be affected by the physical nature of the search: For children, the more demanding their interaction with the space, the less capacity they seem to have for remembering their path. This is something that changes with development; as our memory and physical capabilities improve, so do our foraging abilities. This tallies with anthropological reports of the development of foraging participation in hunter–gatherer societies (Jones, Hawkes, & Draper, 1994).

MEMORY FOR SCENES

In real life it is not always necessary to remember the location of a single object, or of an array discretely arranged in one sector of space. It is more likely that we will need to interact with objects that are distributed all around us. Brewer and Treyens (1981) tested people's ability to remember objects in a room. The rationale and interpretation of this experiment was based on schema theory, so it is necessary to outline the main principles of schema theory first.

Schema theory

Schema theory is able to provide a theoretical explanation of considerable generality for many phenomena in everyday memory. It can account for the fact that many of our experiences are forgotten, or are reconstructed in a way that is incomplete, inaccurate, generalised, or distorted. Schema theory emphasises the role of prior knowledge and past experience, claiming that what we remember is influenced by what we already know. According to this theory, the knowledge we have stored in memory is organised as a set of schemas, or knowledge structures, which represent generic knowledge about objects, situations, events, or actions that has been acquired from past experience.

Bartlett (1932) introduced the idea of schemas to explain why, when people remember stories, they typically omit some details, introduce rationalisations and distortions, and reconstruct the story so as to make more sense in terms of their own knowledge and experience. According to Bartlett, the story is "assimilated" to pre-stored schemas based on prior knowledge. Although for many years Bartlett's ideas were neglected, in recent years schemas have been given a central role in memory.

Schemas represent all kinds of generic knowledge from simple knowledge, such as the shape of the letter "A", for example, to more complex knowledge such as knowledge about political ideologies or astrophysics. Like the action schemas described in Chapter 5, knowledge schemas may be linked together into related sets, with superordinate and subordinate schemas. So, for example, the schema for "table" would be linked to schemas for "furniture", "rooms", and "houses". A schema has slots that may be filled with fixed compulsory values, or with variable optional values. A schema for a boat would have "floats" as a fixed value, but has "oars" and "engine" as variable values. Schemas also supply default values. These are the most probable or typical values. If you are thinking about some particular boat, and you cannot remember the colour of the sails, the boat schema might supply the default value "white" as being the most probable value to fill the colour slot. "Schema" is used as a general term to cover all kinds of general knowledge. More closely specified versions of schemas are called *scripts*, which consist of general knowledge about particular kinds of events, or *frames*, which consist of knowledge about the properties of particular objects or locations. Scripts are discussed in more detail in Chapter 2.

Pre-existing schemas operate in a top-down direction influencing the way we encode, interpret, and store the new information coming in. According to schema theory, new experiences are not just passively "copied" or recorded in memory. A memory representation is actively constructed, integrating the old generic information in the schema with new information from the current input using processes that are strongly influenced by schemas in a variety of ways, as outlined by Alba and Hasher (1983):

1 *Selection:* The schema directs attention and guides the selection of what is encoded and stored in memory. Information that is relevant to whichever schema is currently activated is more likely to be remembered than information that is irrelevant.
2 *Storage:* A schema provides a framework within which current information relevant to that schema can be stored.
3 *Abstraction:* Information may undergo transformation from the specific form in which it was perceived to a more general form. Specific details of a particular

experience tend to drop out, whereas those aspects that are common to other similar experiences are incorporated into a general schema and retained.

4   *Normalisation:* Memories also tend to be distorted so as to fit in with prior expectations and to be consistent with the schema. They are sometimes transformed toward the most probable or most typical item of that kind. People may remember what they expected to see rather than what they actually saw. An example of the way schemas may influence memory for common objects by normalisation comes from a study by French and Richards (1993), who found that when participants were asked to draw a clock with Roman numerals from memory after examining it for 1 minute, 10 of the 14 participants represented the 4 as IV. In fact, all clocks and watches with Roman numerals represent the 4 as IIII. In this striking example, schema-based memory of the normal form of representation overrode the perceptual experience.

5   *Integration:* According to schema theory, an integrated memory representation is formed that includes information derived from the current experience, prior knowledge relating to it, and default values supplied by the schema.

6   *Retrieval:* Schemas may also aid retrieval by providing cues. People may search through the schema in order to retrieve a particular memory. When the information that is sought is not represented directly, it can be retrieved by schema-based inferences. (If you know that John has measles, you can infer, from your measles schema, that he won't come to the party.)

Brewer and Tenpenny (personal communication, 1996), in a similar analysis of schema mechanisms, list directing attention, providing a framework, integrating old and new information, and guiding retrieval, but add two further mechanisms, distinctiveness and verification. A schema provides a background against which new information not consistent with the schema becomes distinctive. This mechanism renders a pig in the living-room more distinctive and more memorable than the same pig in the farmyard. The schema also supplies a criterion for verifying new episodic information. If it is inconsistent with the schema it needs to be double-checked (is it really a pig in the living-room?).

The most important prediction from schema theory is that what is normal, typical, relevant, or consistent with pre-existing knowledge will be remembered better than what is unexpected, bizarre, or irrelevant. However, intuitively, this prediction is not entirely convincing and the results of experimental testing have not always supported it. Critics of schema theory have pointed out that it often seems to be what is odd or unusual that tends to remain in memory. To account for this finding, schema theory has been modified in a somewhat ad hoc fashion to create a schema-plus-tag model in which the memory representation is composed of generic information derived from the schema plus the novel, deviant, or unexpected information that is appended in the form of a tag. Alternatively, Brewer and Tenpenny's distinctiveness mechanism provides a more convincing account of the tendency to remember what is bizarre.

Memory for objects in a room

Brewer and Treyens (1981) set up an experiment that tested the predictions from schema theory. Participants were called one at a time to serve in an experiment.

When they arrived they were asked to wait in a room and left there alone for 35 seconds. They were then called into another room and given the unexpected task of recalling everything they had seen in the first room. This first room was arranged to look like a graduate student's office, and contained 61 objects. Some of the objects were schema-relevant, that is, they were objects people would expect to find in such a room, such as a table, typewriter, coffee pot, calendar, posters, etc. Other objects were schema-irrelevant (e.g., a skull, a toy top, a piece of bark). A different set of participants were asked to rate all the objects on two scales, a schema-expectancy scale and a saliency scale. For the schema-expectancy scale, they rated "how likely the object would be to appear in a room of this kind". For the saliency scale, they rated how noticeable the object was. The mean number of items correctly recalled was 13.5 per participant. Responses included some items, such as books and telephone, that had not actually been present, but were probable in the context. These had been inferred from the schema. Recall correlated with both schema expectancy ratings and with saliency ratings. That is, the most probable items and the most noticeable items were most often remembered. Items that formed part of the room itself, like walls and doors, were also frequently recalled. Brewer and Treyens refer to these as *frame objects*. Table 6.1 lists the items that were most frequently recalled.

It is clear that, contrary to the predictions of schema theory, bizarre objects with low schema expectancy, like the toy top and the skull, were also recalled quite frequently. The results also demonstrated the normalising influence of schemas on memory for location. When participants were asked to recall the exact location of objects in the room, they tended to shift the objects toward a canonical location. For example, a note pad was remembered as being on the desk when it was really lying on the seat of a chair.

Brewer and Treyens' experiment showed that people remember objects that are typical, normal, and consistent with the currently active schema better than objects that do not fit the schema. Schema-consistent objects are more likely to be encoded; they are better retained because they are stored in a permanent framework, and they are more likely to be retrieved by schema-guided search processes. The experiment also provided evidence of schema-induced errors. People remembered the expected objects whether they actually saw them or not, and they remembered things in their expected places when they were elsewhere.

However, the experiment also shows that schemas are not the only factor at work. Saliency, as well as schema-expectancy, affected what was remembered. Very noticeable objects were more likely to be recalled. Brewer and Treyens (1981) did not distinguish between perceptual saliency and the kind of distinctiveness conferred by incongruity, but the results suggested that some objects, such as the skull, were remembered because they were bizarre and incongruent in that setting. These objects benefit from what Brewer and Tenpenny (personal communication, 1996) subsequently called the distinctiveness mechanism. Other studies (e.g., Lampinen, Copeland, & Neuschatz, 2001; Mäntylä & Backman, 1992) have found that memory for schema-inconsistent information in a visual scene may actually be superior to memory for schema-consistent information. In everyday life, if you ask someone to recall the contents of a kitchen or a garage that they have just seen, you might also find that they remember any very distinctive, surprising, or peculiar objects better than the highly probable, schema-consistent objects. Note, however,

Table 6.1 Items recalled in an experiment testing memory for objects in a room (from Brewer & Treyens, 1981), copyright © Elsevier 1981. Reproduced with permission.

Object	No. participants[a]	Object	No. participants
Chair (next to desk)	29	Frisbee	3
Desk	29	Jar of coffee	3
Wall[b]	29	Poster (in addition to	
Chair (in front of desk)	24	those in room)[c]	3
Poster (of chimp)	23	Screwdriver	3
Door[b]	22	Snoopy picture	3
Table (worktable)	22	Rotary switches	3
Shelves	21	Cactus	2
Ceiling[b]	16	Cardboard boxes	2
Table (with coffee)	15	Coffee cup[c]	2
Skinner box	14	Computer cards	2
Child's chair	12	Papers on bulletin board	2
Door[b]	12	Pens[c]	2
Light switch[b]	12	Pot (for cactus)	2
Toy top	12	Solder	2
Brain	11	Vacuum tube	2
Parts, gadgets (on worktable)	11	Window[c]	2
Swivel chair	11	Wires	2
Poster on ceiling	10	Ball[c]	1
Books[c]	9	Brain (in addition to that in room)[c]	1
Ceiling lights[b]	9		
Poster (of food)	9	Brick	1
Typewriter	9	Computer surveys	
Bulletin board	8	(on floor)	1
Clown light switch	8	Curtains[c]	1
Coffee pot	8	Decals on walls[c]	1
Skull	8	Desk (in addition to those in room)[c]	1
Mobile	7		
Road sign	7	Doorknob[b]	1
Calendar	6	Eraser	1
Wine bottle	6	Fan	1
Football-player doll	5	Glass plate (covering desk)[c]	1
Jar of creamer	5	Globe	1
Pipe (cord)	5	Hole in wall (for pipe)	1
Postcards	5	Homecoming button	1
Tennis racquet	5	Lamp[c]	1
Blower fan	4	Magazines	1
Coloured patterns on		Nails[c]	1
ceiling lights	4	Packets of sugar	1
Piece of bark	4	Paper (on desk chair)	1
Papers on shelf	1	Scissors	1
Pencil holder[c]	1	Screws[c]	1
Pencils	1	Teaspoon	1
Filing cabinet[c]	3	Picnic basket	1
Pliers[c]	1	Umbrella	1
Saucer	1	Wrench	1
Telephone[c]	1		

[a] Maximum number of participants = 30.
[b] Frame object.
[c] Inferred object, i.e., an object not in the office.

that even if people tend to remember whatever is not consistent with the schema, this still implies the existence of a schema. The results of this experiment conform to Brewer's (1994) view that the primary way that schemas facilitate recall is by guiding the retrieval process to locate new episodic information for recall, and the primary reason why schemas induce errors is because the new episodic information is integrated with the old generic information and the two cannot always be distinguished.

Brewer and Treyens' finding, that memory for the *position* of items in a room was influenced by stored knowledge about where things ought to be, has also been noted by Mandler and Parker (1976). They showed people pictures of organised scenes and unorganised scenes as shown in Figure 6.7, and asked them to reconstruct these scenes from memory, either immediately afterwards or 1 week later.

The organised scene was reconstructed much more accurately, but when testing was delayed for a week, there was an interesting difference in the accuracy of placement on the vertical and the horizontal dimensions. Vertical positions were remembered better. Mandler and Parker (1976) suggested that vertical placement is predictable from stored knowledge of spatial relations. We know that pictures are on walls, and are higher than chairs, which are on the floor, but horizontal placement is not predictable and there is no way of guessing whether the flowerpot should be on the left or right of the television set.

CONCLUSIONS

Spatial memory can be considered a separate system, but it does not operate independently of other kinds of memory. Instead, it interacts with a variety of informational sources, including knowledge about the nature and function of objects, people and their activities, and awareness of our bodies in space. Studies of memory for maps, routes, and layouts have suggested that spatial memory is not tied to one form of representation. People can construct multiple different forms of representation and can translate one form into another to meet the demands of the current task. Some of the studies reported in this chapter might seem to emphasise the fallibility and weaknesses of spatial memory for places and object locations. This is partly a reflection of research techniques rather than an objective evaluation. Researchers deliberately contrive tasks with a level of difficulty that ensures a substantial proportion of errors simply because the nature of the errors and the pattern of incidence yield more information about the underlying mechanism than successful performance can reveal. However, some of the more recent experiments included here give a better idea of how well memory functions in the real world. Memory efficiency in everyday life ultimately needs to be judged in the street, not in the laboratory, but researchers are beginning to employ techniques to improve the validity of their lab-based studies. These range from virtual reality displays (e.g., Maguire et al., 1998a, b) to large-scale search environments (e.g., Smith et al., 2005). Such studies benefit from being able to provide elements that are key to empirical enquiry, such as controllability and parametric measurement. However, we also look forward to developing techniques that will allow us to measure human spatial cognition accurately in our natural environments.

Figure 6.7 Examples of an organised scene (top) and an unorganised scene (bottom) (from Mandler & Parker, 1976). Reproduced with permission of the American Psychological Association and the authors.

REFERENCES

Aguirre, G.K., & D'Esposito, M. (1999). Topographical disorientation: A synthesis and taxonomy. *Brain, 122,* 1613–1628

Alba, J.W., & Hasher, L. (1983). Is memory schematic? *Psychological Bulletin, 93,* 203–231.

Astur, R.S., Ortiz, M.L., & Sutherland, R.J. (1998). A characterization of performance by men and women in a virtual Morris water task: A large and reliable sex difference. *Behavioural Brain Research, 93,* 185–190.

Baddeley, A.D., & Hitch, G. (1993). Recency re-examined. In S. Dornic (Ed.), *Attention and performance, Vol. VI* (pp. 647–667). Hillsdale, NJ: Lawrence Erlbaum Associates, Inc.

Bartlett, F.C. (1932). *Remembering.* Cambridge, UK: Cambridge University Press.

Bjork, R.A. (1978). The updating of human memory. In G.H. Bower (Ed.), *The psychology of learning and motivation: Advances in research and theory, Vol. 12.* New York: Academic Press.

Blades, M., & Medlicott, L. (1992). Developmental differences in the abilities to give route directions from a map. *Journal of Environmental Psychology, 12,* 175–185.

Brewer, W.F. (1994). *The paradoxical role of schemata in memory accuracy.* Paper presented at the Third Practical Aspects of Memory Conference, Washington, DC, July.

Brewer, W.F., & Tenpenny, P.L. (1996). *The role of schemata in the recall and recognition of episodic information.* Personal communication.

Brewer, W.F., & Treyens, J.C. (1981). Role of schemata in memory for places. *Cognitive Psychology, 13,* 207–230.

Bryant, D.J. (1992). A spatial representation system in humans. *Psycholoquy,* May 24 1992.

Byrne, R.W. (1979). Memory for urban geography. *Quarterly Journal of Experimental Psychology, 31,* 147–154.

Dabbs, J.M., Chang, E.L., Strong, R.A., & Milun, R. (1998). Spatial ability, navigation strategy, and geographic knowledge among men and women. *Evolution and Human Behavior, 19,* 89–98.

Da Costa Pinto, A., & Baddeley, A.D. (1991). Where did you park your car? Analysis of a naturalistic long-term recency effect. *European Journal of Cognitive Psychology, 3,* 297–313.

Diwadkar, V.A., & McNamara, T.P. (1997). Viewpoint dependence in scene recognition. *Psychological Science, 8,* 302–307.

Farah, M.J., Hammond, K., Levine, D., & Calvanio, R. (1988). Visual and spatial mental imagery: Dissociable systems of representation. *Cognitive Psychology, 20,* 439–462.

Foos, P.W. (1989). Age differences in memory for two common objects. *Journal of Gerontology: Psychological Sciences, 44,* 178–180.

French, C.C., & Richards, A. (1993). Clock this! An everyday example of a schema-driven error in memory. *British Journal of Psychology, 84,* 249–253.

Gallistel, C.R. (1990). *The organization of learning.* Cambridge, MA: MIT Press.

Gilchrist, I.D., North, A., & Hood, B. (2001). Is visual search really like foraging? *Perception, 30,* 1459–1464.

Gilhooly, K.J., Wood, M., Kinnear, P.R., & Green, C. (1988). Skill in map reading and memory for maps. *Quarterly Journal of Experimental Psychology, 40,* 87–107.

Hampson, E. (1990). Estrogen-related variations in human spatial and articulatory-motor skills. *Psychoneuroendocrinology, 15,* 97–111.

Hartley, T., Maguire, E.A., Spiers, H.J., & Burgess, N. (2003). The well-worn route and the path less traveled: Distinct neural bases of route following and wayfinding in humans. *Neuron, 37,* 877–888.

Hermer, L., & Spelke, E.S. (1994). A geometric process for spatial reorientation in young children. *Nature, 370,* 57–59.

Hermer, L., & Spelke, E.S. (1996). Modularity and development: The case of spatial reorientation. *Cognition, 61,* 195–232.

Hermer-Vasquez, L., Spelke, E.S., & Katnelson, A.S. (1999). Sources of flexibility in human cognition: Dual-task studies of space and language. *Cognitive Psychology, 39,* 3–36.

Janzen, G., Schade, M., Katz, S., & Herrmann, T. (2001). Strategies for detour finding in a virtual maze: The role of the visual perspective. *Journal of Environmental Psychology, 21,* 149–163.

Janzen, G., & Van Turennout, M. (2004). Selective neural representation of objects relevant for navigation. *Nature Neuroscience, 7,* 673–677.

Jones, N.B., Hawkes, K., & Draper, P. (1994). Foraging returns of Kung adults and children— why didn't Kung children forage? *Journal of Anthropological Research, 50,* 217–248.

Kirasic, K.C. (1991). Spatial cognition and behaviour in young and elderly adults: Implications for learning new environments. *Psychology and Aging, 6,* 10–18.

Klein, R.M., & MacInnes, W.J. (1999). Inhibition of return is a foraging facilitator in visual search. *Psychological Science, 10,* 346–352.

Kosslyn, S.M., Thompson, W.L., Wraga, M.J., & Alpert, N.M. (2001). Imagining rotation by endogenous versus exogenous forces: distinct neural mechanisms. *NeuroReport*, *12*, 2519–2525.

Kozlowski, L.T., & Bryant, K.J. (1977). Sense of direction, spatial orientation and cognitive maps. *Journal of Experimental Psychology: Human Perception and Performance*, *3*, 590–598.

Lampinen, J.M., Copeland, S.M., & Neuschatz, J.S. (2001). Recollections of things schematic: Room schemas revisited. *Journal of Experimental Psychology: Learning, Memory, and Cognition*, *27*, 1211–1222.

Landau, B., & Jackendorff, R. (1993). "What" and Where" in spatial language and spatial cognition. *Behavioral and Brain Sciences*, *2*, 217–238.

Learmonth, A.E., Nadel, L., & Newcombe, N.S. (2002). Children's use of landmarks: Implications for modularity theory. *Psychological Science*, *13*, 337–341.

Levy, L.J., Astur, R.S., & Frick, K.M. (2005). Men and women differ in object memory but not performance of a virtual radial maze. *Behavioral Neuroscience*, *119*, 853–862.

Lutz, J., Means, L.W., & Long, T.E. (1994). Where did I park? *Applied Cognitive Psychology*, *8*, 437–530.

Maguire, E.A., Burgess, N., Donnett, J.G., Frackowiak, R.S.J., Frith, C.D., & O'Keefe, J. (1998a). Knowing where and getting there: A human navigation network. *Science*, *280*, 921–924.

Maguire, E.A., Burgess, N., Donnett, J.G., O'Keefe, J., & Frith, C.D. (1998b). Knowing where things are: Parahippocampal involvement in encoding object locations in virtual large-scale space. *Journal of Cognitive Neuroscience*, *10*, 61–76.

Maguire, E.A., Gadian, D.G., Johnsrude, I.S., Good, C.D., Ashburner, J., Frackowiak, R.S.J., & Frith, C.D. (2001). Navigation-related structural change in the hippocampi of taxi drivers. *Proceedings of the National Academy of Sciences USA*, *97*, 4398–4403.

Mandler, J.M., & Parker, R.C. (1976). Memory for descriptive and spatial information in complex pictures. *Journal of Experimental Psychology: Human Learning and Memory*, *2*, 38–48.

Mäntylä, T., & Backman, L. (1992). Aging and memory for expected and unexpected objects in real world settings. *Journal of Experimental Psychology: Learning, Memory and Cognition*, *18*, 1298–1309.

Marshall, J.C., & Halligan, P.W. (1995). Seeing the forest or only half the trees? *Nature*, *373*, 521–523.

Moffat, S.D., Hampson, E., & Hatzipantelis, M. (1998). Navigation in a "virtual" maze: Sex differences and correlation with psychometric measures of spatial ability in humans. *Evolution and Human Behavior*, *19*, 73–87.

Neisser, U. (1988). What is ordinary memory the memory of? In U. Neisser & E. Winograd (Eds.), *Remembering reconsidered* (pp. 356–373). Cambridge, UK: Cambridge University Press.

Nickerson, R., & Adams, M.J. (1982). Long-term memory for a common object. In U. Neisser (Ed.), *Memory observed: Remembering in natural contexts*. San Francisco, CA: Freeman.

O'Keefe, J., & Nadel, L. (1978). *The hippocampus as a cognitive map*. Oxford, UK: Oxford University Press.

Richardson, J.T.E. (1992). Remembering the appearance of familiar objects: A study of monarchic memory. *Bulletin of the Psychonomic Society*, *30*, 389–392.

Rossano, M.J., & Hodgson, S.L. (1994). The process of learning from small-scale maps. *Applied Cognitive Psychology*, *8*, 565–582.

Shepard, R.N., & Metzler, J. (1971). Mental rotation of three-dimensional objects. *Science*, *171*, 701–703.

Simons, D.J., & Wang, R.F. (1998). Perceiving real-world viewpoint changes. *Psychological Science*, *9*, 315–320.

Smith, A.D., Gilchrist, I.D., & Hood, B.M. (2005). Children's search behaviour in large-scale space: Developmental components of exploration. *Perception, 34*, 1221–1229.

Stevens, A., & Coupe, P. (1978). Distortions in judged spatial relations. *Cognitive Psychology, 10*, 422–437.

Taylor, H.A., & Tversky, B. (1992). Spatial mental models derived from survey and route descriptions. *Journal of Memory and Language, 31*, 261–292.

Tenney, Y.J. (1984). Aging and the misplacing of objects. *British Journal of Development Psychology, 2*, 43–50.

Thorndyke, P.W. (1981). Spatial cognition and reasoning. In J. Harvey (Ed.), *Cognition, social behaviour, and the environment*. Hillsdale, NJ: Lawrence Erlbaum Associates, Inc.

Thorndyke, P.W., & Hayes-Roth, B. (1982). Differences in spatial knowledge acquired from maps and navigation. *Cognitive Psychology, 14*, 450–489.

Thorndyke, P.W., & Stasz, C. (1980). Individual differences in procedures for knowledge acquisition from maps. *Cognitive Psychology, 12*, 137–175.

Tolman, E.C. (1948). Cognitive maps in rats and men. *The Psychological Review, 55*, 189–208.

Tversky, B. (1991). Spatial mental models. In G.H. Bower (Ed.), *The psychology of learning and motivation: Advances in research and theory*, Vol. 27 (pp. 109–145). San Diego, CA: Academic Press.

Tversky, B. (1995). Memory for pictures, environments, maps and graphs. In D. Payne & F. Conrad (Eds.), *Practical aspects of memory*. Hillsdale, NJ: Lawrence Erlbaum Associates, Inc.

Wang, R.F., & Simons, D.J. (1999). Active and passive scene recognition across views. *Cognition, 70*, 191–210.

Wang, R.F., & Spelke, E.S. (2000). Updating egocentric representations in human navigation. *Cognition, 77*, 215–250.

Williams, C.L., & Meck, W.H. (1991). The organizational effects of gonadal hormones on sexually dimorphic spatial ability. *Psychoneuroendocrinology, 16*, 155–176.

Wraga, M., Creem, S.H., & Proffitt, D.R. (2000). Updating displays after imagined object and viewer rotations. *Journal of Experimental Psychology: Learning, Memory and Cognition, 26*, 151–168.

7 Memory for knowledge: General knowledge and expert knowledge

Gillian Cohen

There is more to everyday memory than mundane matters like remembering to pay the bills or feed the cat. Everyday memory involves retrieving and using stored knowledge of many different kinds in the appropriate contexts. These different kinds of knowledge include knowledge acquired formally from education or training, as well as knowledge that is picked up incidentally. In the course of daily life, a person may need to use practical, theoretical, and expert knowledge in domains such as mathematics, music, electrical wiring, chess, cookery, stock markets, and many more specialised topics. Everyday memory is not just concerned with the trivial and the commonplace.

The distinction between two kinds of long-term memory, episodic memory and semantic memory, was first put forward by Tulving (1972). Previous chapters have been mainly concerned with episodic memories that are acquired by personal experience and that represent specific objects, people, places, and events in a specific spatiotemporal context. This chapter examines semantic memory for general factual knowledge about the world, as well as the kind of knowledge that underlies specialised expertise. The distinction between episodic and semantic memory is not absolute because semantic knowledge can built up by abstraction from personal experiences. However, the important difference between the two kinds of knowledge is that semantic knowledge consists of objective general facts and episodic knowledge consists of subjective specific facts.

REPRESENTATION OF KNOWLEDGE

The knowledge stored in human memory forms a very large database (Nickerson, 1977) but nobody knows, as yet, how large it is. In any case, the most interesting questions concern what information is stored in memory, and how it is organised and retrieved, rather than how much information is in store. Current models of semantic memory have tended to focus on either conceptual knowledge or relational knowledge.

Conceptual knowledge

Conceptual hierarchies

These models assume that concepts are the basic units of knowledge and that these represent objects and events and are organised into categories. In an early version proposed by Collins and Quillian (1969), conceptual categories are organised hierarchically with the most general superordinate concepts at the highest level and the most specific concepts at lower levels. So, for example, in Figure 7.1 a hierarchy with living things at the superordinate level would have plants and animals at a lower level, with the animal branch dividing further into birds, mammals, fish, etc., and with specific individuals like Rover the dog at the lowest level of all. The model achieves great economy in storage because the properties common to all exemplars of a category (such as *grows, breathes, can fly*) need only be represented once at the higher levels and are inherited by all the exemplars at lower levels. The information that a robin lays eggs can be retrieved by the inference that a robin is a bird and that birds lay eggs. In any information system, whether it is a computer or a human memory, information may be pre-stored and represented explicitly, or it may be computable by the application of inferential procedures to other information that is in store. There is a trade-off between pre-storage and computation. Pre-storage is very expensive in terms of storage space and, if large amounts of information are pre-stored, very efficient search and retrieval processes are required to locate and access particular items. For knowledge that is not very likely to be in frequent use it may be uneconomical to have it pre-stored. Having knowledge that is implicit, but not pre-stored, like the fact that birds grow, saves space; but implicit information takes more time to compute and errors occur if incorrect inferences are made.

There has been considerable behavioural evidence in support of this model. Reaction times to verify statements such as *"a canary is a bird"* mirror the theoretical "distance" of the conceptual nodes in the model. The patterns of semantic deficit observed in patients with semantic dementia also fit the model, with specific knowledge being lost first and memory for general features of objects being more robust (Hodges, Graham, & Patterson, 1995; Warrington, 1975).

Modality-specific systems

More recently there have been doubts and criticisms of this type of model. Storing properties with superordinates may be economical in storage but not optimal for

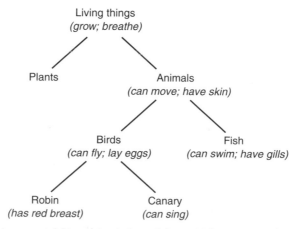

Figure 7.1 A conceptual hierarchy (adapted from Collins & Quillian, 1969). Reproduced with permission of the American Psychological Association and the authors.

access. The model also has trouble in accommodating variants and exceptions, like canaries that fail to sing or cats without fur, and individual people would probably have incomplete or idiosyncratic hierarchies reflecting individual variation in education and experience. Theories of conceptual representation, such as hierarchical networks, generally assume that concepts are represented as abstract and amodal propositions. That is, they are separate from the modality-specific system of perception so that the concept of a bird, for example, is represented as a set of propositions rather than as a visual image. An alternative view has been put forward by Barsalou, Simmons, Barbey, and Wilson (2003) and Goldstone and Barsalou (1998).

Instead of sensory information being transduced into an amodal representation, as shown in Figure 7.2a, it is stored in association areas and can be reactivated, as in 7.2b. This re-enactment of the sensory information underlies the mental imagery that occurs in remembering, in language comprehension, and in planning actions. The re-enacted representation can be multimodal, capturing sounds, smells, and tactile qualities. Barsalou et al. (2003) have found considerable experimental evidence in support of modality-specific conceptual processing. For example, they compared the performance of participants instructed to use imagery with a group given no such instruction in yes/no decision tasks such as deciding *Does a pony have a mane?* They found no difference between the groups. The amodal view predicts a difference, since the uninstructed group would base their response on an amodal representation, while the imagery group would use a visual image of a pony to decide. The results conformed to the prediction of the modality-specific theory; that both groups would spontaneously use re-enacted imagery so there would be no difference. Striking evidence also comes from neuroimaging studies (Martin, 2000), which showed that conceptualising the colour, shape, or motion of objects activated the corresponding modality-specific areas of the brain. As shown in Figure 7.3, the model can represent multiple instances of a given concept and can also produce both types and tokens. A simulation or re-enactment can represent a particular instance, or *token*, of a category (such as Rover the dog, or my car) but the system can also integrate information across instances and produce a generalised *type*.

The differences between theories that assume abstract amodal representation of concepts and theories that assume modality-specific systems is not unbridgeable. Rogers et al. (2004) implemented a parallel distributed processing model based on neuropsychological studies of patients with selective deficits in naming and categorising tasks. The model combines an amodal abstract semantic system with multiple connections to modality-specific perceptual systems that provide input to, and output from, the semantic system. The representation of conceptual knowledge is currently very much a live issue and is engaging researchers from cognitive science, neuropsychology and cognitive psychology.

Relational knowledge

Much of human knowledge is incomplete, inconsistent, vague, and uncertain. Nickerson distinguished between fuzzy relational knowledge and absolute knowledge such as quantitative facts. Relational knowledge includes facts such as *Potatoes are bigger than peas; France is north of Spain; Alexander the Great lived before*

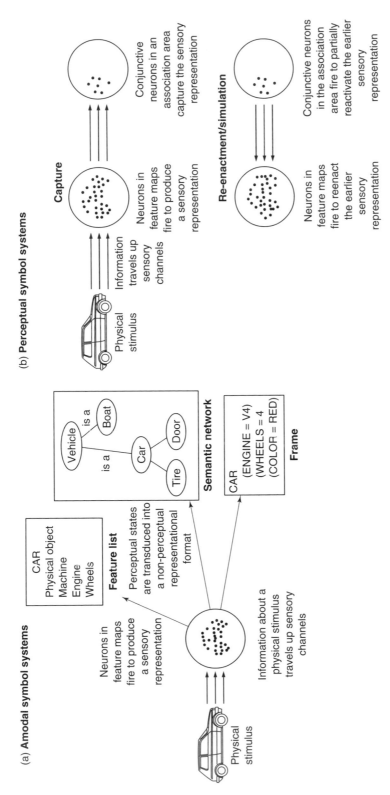

Figure 7.2 Reprinted from *Trends in Cognitive Sciences*, 7, Barsalou, Simmons, Barbey, and Wilson, *Grounding conceptual knowledge in modality-specific systems*, pp. 84–91, copyright © 2003, with permission from Elsevier. (a) In amodal symbol systems, neural representations are established initially to represent objects in vision. Subsequently, however, these neural representations are transduced into another representation language that is amodal, such as a feature list, semantic network, or frame. Once established, these amodal descriptions provide the knowledge used in cognitive processes, such as memory, language, and thought. (b) In perceptual symbol systems, neural representations similarly represent objects in vision. Rather than being transduced into amodal descriptions, however, visual representations are partially captured by conjunctive neurons in nearby association areas. Later, in the absence of sensory input, activating these conjunctive neurons partially re-enacts the earlier visual states. These re-enactments contribute to the knowledge that supports memory, language, and thought. This figure illustrates knowledge acquired through vision, but analogous accounts exist for acquiring knowledge in the other modalities (e.g., audition, action, emotion).

(a) **Capture of multiple instances in a simulator**

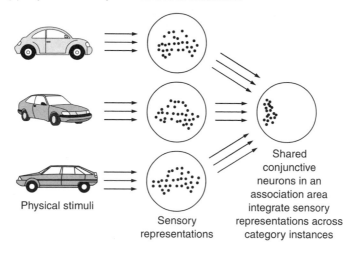

Physical stimuli

Sensory representations

Shared conjunctive neurons in an association area integrate sensory representations across category instances

(b) **Production of different simulations by a stimulator**

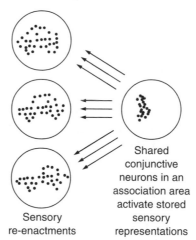

Sensory re-enactments

Shared conjunctive neurons in an association area activate stored sensory representations

Figure 7.3 Reprinted from *Trends in Cognitive Sciences*, 7, Barsalou, Simmons, Barbey, and Wilson, *Grounding conceptual knowledge in modality-specific systems*, pp. 84–91, copyright © 2003, with permission from Elsevier. (a) As multiple instances of a category are encountered, neural representations of them arise in vision. Because conjunctive neurons in visual association areas are tuned to particular conjunctions of visual features, a common set of conjunctive neurons captures the visual representations of the category's instances, which tend to share visual features. Sets of conjunctive neurons in other association areas (not shown) similarly capture a category's instances on other modalities (e.g., audition, action, emotion). In higher-order association areas (also not shown), common conjunctive neurons integrate modality-specific information for a category across modalities. (b) Once a simulator develops for a category, it later produces specific simulations of the category. On a given occasion, a subset of conjunctive neurons in the simulator produces one particular simulation in the visual system. This simulation could represent a given instance, an average of several instances, or a variety of other possibilities, depending on which subsets of stored information become active. Re-enactments typically occur on multiple modalities simultaneously, producing a multimodal simulation of the category, not just on vision (as shown).

Napoleon, which represent relative differences in magnitude, location, and temporal order. He pointed out that people are more likely to know these kind of relationships than to know actual sizes, dates, weights, speeds, ages, monetary values, or whatever. This observation lends support to Nickerson's contention that much of our knowledge is approximate rather than exact. The model of the world that we have in our heads is vague and inexact. And, as he convincingly points out, this kind of approximate knowledge is all that is needed for most decisions and actions in everyday life. For most purposes, we do not need to know precise numerical values. We need to be able to make rough estimates and fairly crude relational judgements. Much of our knowledge is also imprecise because it is probabilistic. Predictions about what the weather will be like tomorrow, when the plums will be ripe, the state of the bank balance next month, and the chances of catching a train, are couched in terms of probabilities.

Analogical reasoning

According to Spellman, Holyoak, and Morrison (2001), models of conceptual knowledge have tended to neglect the importance of semantic relations. Hummel and Holyoak (2005) argued that the ability to acquire and manipulate relationally defined concepts is a fundamental aspect of human thinking. The ability to interpret and respond to a current experience depends crucially on being able to recognise that it is analogous to a previous experience. It is rare for an experience to be an exact replica of one that has occurred before, so this recognition involves being able to perceive relational parallels. Analogical reasoning is a complex skill but, in everyday life, it underlies many of our decisions. People make choices about what make of car to buy or what kind of food may make them ill on the basis of past experiences that are relationally similar. In more formal situations, analogies are consciously sought and more rigorously evaluated. The political analyst considers analogies between the wars in Iraq and Vietnam; the chess player considers the move that was successful in a previous game. Kroger, Holyoak, and Hummel (2004) emphasise that *sameness* is the fundamental element in analogical reasoning, which involves the ability to recognise that objects or situations are essentially the same in spite of differences. In their example, the analogy between *West Side Story* and *Romeo and Juliet* exists at a high level of abstraction and can be recognised when the differences are seen to be irrelevant. Cohen (2000) has pointed out that analogies are more transparent when concepts are represented at a high level of generality.

Hummel, Holyoak, and colleagues have developed a model of cognitive architecture called LISA (Learning and Inference with Schemas and Analogies), which represents objects and their relational roles as patterns of distributed activation and is based on the neural structure of the brain. Propositions such as "*John loves Sally*" are stored in long-term memory as part of a hierarchy of units representing features (*human, male*) and relational roles (*John + lover*). Analogical reasoning requires working memory so the model correspondingly has a capacity-limited working memory. It has the ability to retrieve semantic information and to inhibit competing, but irrelevant, information in order to make inferences and detect analogies by a process of guided pattern recognition. This model is supported by both experimental and neuropsychological evidence. Spellman et al. (2001), using lexical decision and naming tasks, found participants showed relational priming in these tasks. When asked to make a lexical decision or name words in a target pair such as *bear–cave* they were faster if the preceding pair, such as *bird–nest*, had the same semantic relationship (*lives in*) than if the preceding pair, such as *window–glass*, had a different relationship. The relational priming effect was found only if the participants were instructed to attend to the relationship, which suggests that analogical mapping is not always automatic, but that it occurs when required. This finding makes sense in terms of everyday functioning. We look for analogies when we need to figure out how to do something or what is likely to happen next, but could easily be overwhelmed if analogies came to mind automatically and unsought.

The breakdown of analogical reasoning has been studied by Morrison et al. (2004). They investigated the role of the prefrontal cortex and the anterior temporal cortex in patients with frontotemporal lobar degeneration, using a picture analogy and a verbal analogy task. For example, in Figure 7.4 the two pictures could be matched because they share the same visual feature (a man) or because they depict the same relation (a dog breaking its lead to get away from a man to chase a cat and a dog breaking away from a rope tied to a tree to chase a cat). These patients performed significantly worse than controls in selecting a relational match rather than a feature-based match. The pattern of errors showed that frontal lobe patients made errors due to impaired working memory and failure to inhibit irrelevant information, but temporal lobe patients made errors showing loss of knowledge from semantic memory. Their performance was simulated using the LISA model, which was able to account for the nature of the deficits.

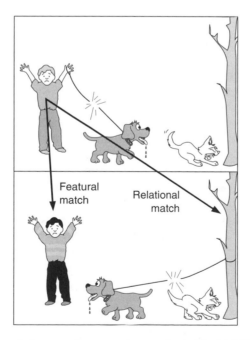

Figure 7.4 An example from a picture analogy task used by Tohill and Holyoak (2000). Reprinted from the *Journal of Cognitive Neuroscience*, 16, Morrison et al., A neurocomputational model of analogical reasoning and its breakdown in frontotemporal lobe degeneration, pp. 260–271, copyright © 2004, with permission from Elsevier.

Inferential knowledge

The amount of knowledge that can be retrieved far exceeds the knowledge that is actually stored in memory. This is because memory is not just a repository of facts, but a set of processes that allow further information to be inferred, calculated, estimated, or guessed. Whereas some facts have been learned explicitly, such as, for example, *the sum of 2 and 4 is 6*; *whales are mammals*; *the Aswan dam is in Egypt*, much knowledge is implicit or tacit and consists of facts that are unlikely to have been learned explicitly, but which can be inferred from other knowledge.

Camp, Lachman, and Lachman (1980) demonstrated the psychological reality of this distinction between pre-stored and computable knowledge. They selected a set of questions likely to be retrieved by direct access. These were questions like *"What was the name of the flying horse in mythology?"* Subjects either know or do not know that the answer is *Pegasus*. Many of the direct access questions involved proper names because these are not computable—they cannot be inferred. Another set of questions were inferential questions such as *"What direction does the Statue of Liberty face?"* or *"Which US President was the first to see an airplane?"* Subjects were unlikely to know the answers to these questions, but they could figure out the answer by inferential processes. Camp et al. found that reaction times to respond "true" when told the answers to direct access questions averaged 1.97 seconds, whereas reaction times to respond "true" to the answers to the inferential questions averaged 2.85 seconds. The additional retrieval time for inference questions reflects the reasoning processes necessary to retrieve the answer. Explicit knowledge can be accessed directly; implicit or tacit knowledge has to be retrieved by means of inferential processes or computation.

Much of our everyday knowledge about the world is implicit and different kinds of inferences are used to access it. We make temporal, spatial, and mathematical inferences constantly in everyday life, figuring out, for example, that John is older than Bill because John was born in 1960 and Bill in 1969; or that Paris is further away from London than Calais because you reach Calais first. Spatial inferences about distance, location, and orientation were discussed in Chapter 6, and temporal inferences are used to date the autobiographical events described in Chapter 2. All these examples show that human knowledge, although limited, is extremely elastic. What we don't know we can infer, guess, estimate, or predict. We can produce a plausible—if uncertain—answer. It is relatively rare that we are completely at a loss. In human memory, reliance on fuzzy knowledge and implicit knowledge, and on inferential processes in addition to direct access to explicitly pre-stored information, has the effect of making a limited amount of knowledge go a long way.

LONG-TERM MAINTENANCE OF KNOWLEDGE

The previous section focused on issues about the nature of knowledge, but inter-esting questions can also be asked about the maintenance of knowledge. How permanent is knowledge once acquired? In his 1978 talk at the Practical Aspects of Memory conference (see Chapter 1), Neisser suggested that one of the important questions that memory research should address concerns what people retain of the knowledge they acquired during the years of their formal schooling. Educators have studied children's memory for what they learn at school over relatively short retention intervals of months, rather than years, but when we come to assess the value of education in the longer term we want to know how much people remember in the years after they have left school. What, if any, of the information we acquire with so much effort in our schooldays constitutes permanent knowledge? Because these issues have to be studied over long time spans, they are outside the scope of traditional laboratory methods, and have been neglected until recently, when the more adventurous approach of everyday memory research has encouraged some psychologists to tackle them.

Studies of long-term retention of knowledge

Spanish and mathematics

Bahrick (1984) has conducted a series of studies of long-term retention of Spanish learned at school. Surmounting formidable methodological problems, his landmark study spanned retention intervals of up to 50 years and attempted to identify the conditions of original learning that determine the longevity of the knowledge acquired. The subjects were 773 individuals who had learned Spanish in high school. The time that had elapsed between studying the language and being tested varied from 0 to 50 years. A control group of 40 subjects, who had never received any instruction in Spanish, was also included in the study to establish a baseline for performance that could be achieved by guessing, or by incidentally acquired knowledge. The subjects who had learned Spanish supplied information about the level of their original training (how many courses they had taken), the grades they had attained, and how much they had used the language during the retention interval. The tests included reading comprehension, and recall and recognition tests for vocabulary, grammar, and idioms. The results showed that retention was predictable from the level of original training. People who had learned more remembered more, so that retention depended on the amount of the original learning. When the recall test scores were expressed as a percentage of the original grades, up to 40% of the original performance was maintained after 50 years, and on recognition tests up to 60% was maintained.

Interim use of the language was negligible, so that no effects of rehearsal were evident. The most interesting finding can be seen in Figure 7.5. Three components can be discerned in the retention function. Knowledge declined exponentially for about 3–6 years, but after this retention stabilised, and there was little further loss for a period of up to 30 years before a final slight decline. This final period corresponds to a time when the subjects were 60–70 years old and may represent the effects of ageing rather than of the retention period. It is clear, however, that much of the original knowledge remains accessible even after 50 years.

According to Bahrick (1984), this knowledge has entered the *permastore*. On the basis of the discontinuous character of the retention function, he argued that there had been a discrete transition of knowledge into the permastore and that a minimum level of original training was necessary for this transition to take place. When the original training was insufficient, the knowledge would not be entered into the permastore and would only be retained for a shorter period.

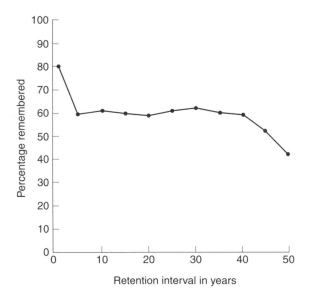

Figure 7.5 Idealised retention curve for the very long-term retention of Spanish (adapted from Bahrick, 1984). Reproduced with permission of the author.

Commenting on these results, Neisser (1984) suggested that there was no need to assume the existence of a knowledge permastore. Whereas Bahrick's explanation assumes that language learning involves acquiring responses that are *reproduced* when retrieval takes place, Neisser argued that knowledge is *reconstructed*, rather than being reproduced. In his view, the enduring component of language knowledge does not consist of specific responses, but of generalised schemas, a structured system of knowledge of the Spanish language that enables people to reconstruct correct responses. Acquisition of knowledge schemas depends on the level of original training, as Bahrick's data confirmed. According to this interpretation, the information that is lost in the early years of the retention interval consists of isolated bits and pieces not closely related to the general schema. Neisser claims that retention of systematic schematised knowledge is enduring because it is protected from interference by its unique and specialised nature. Schema-based knowledge is not forgotten because other knowledge is not sufficiently similar to cause interference. On this interpretation, the discontinuity in Bahrick's retention curves does not reflect two different stores—a vulnerable store with a 5-year span and a permastore—but two different kinds of knowledge—isolated items and integrated schemas.

Bahrick and Hall (1991) extended this research to the domain of mathematics and investigated long-term retention of mathematics by 1600 former students at retention intervals up to 50 years. They compared the performance of two groups, one who had studied up to the level of calculus and another group who had not reached this level. The two groups produced very different retention functions. Those who had studied to an advanced level showed very little forgetting; those who had not showed a steady decline. This study therefore confirms that the level of the original knowledge is a powerful determinant of subsequent retention.

Philosophy, psychology, and anthropology

Further studies have examined different knowledge domains. Naveh-Benjamin (1988) has studied retention of knowledge acquired in university courses of philosophy, psychology, and anthropology, comparing a zero retention interval with retention intervals of 1 and 2 years. He was particularly interested in how the knowledge structures changed over time. In order to examine this, he first asked the university teachers who had taught the courses to arrange different elements of knowledge into conceptual hierarchies, with general concepts at the highest level and specific concepts at the lowest level. When the subjects were tested, they were shown a conceptual hierarchy with some empty nodes and had to select items from a set of alternatives and place the correct item at the correct node. This test revealed a loss of information from 70% at the zero retention interval to 46% after 2 years. The loss of information was greatest at the lowest level of the conceptual hierarchy, whereas the higher level concepts were better retained. The test also showed that the relationships between higher order concepts and low-level specific examples were especially vulnerable to the effects of the passage of time. Knowledge became fragmented as people tended to forget the links between concepts.

Cognitive psychology and classic novels

Conway, Cohen, and Stanhope (1991) studied retention of knowledge of cognitive psychology. This knowledge had originally been acquired as part of participants' university degree courses and a range of tests probed memory for names and concepts, general principles and specific facts, and experimental design and statistics. Conway et al. used testing retention intervals of up to 12 years. The findings showed that, as in Bahrick's studies, there was a rapid loss of information over the first 3 years, after which knowledge remained stable (see Figure 7.6). The results were also not altogether consistent with Neisser's schema-based account of knowledge retention. As in Naveh-Benjamin's study, general principles were retained better than specific facts, but a great deal of specific information was remembered. A test of memory for conceptual relations showed very poor retention, although this type of knowledge might be supposed to be inherent in a schema. On Neisser's account, concepts, which can be reconstructed from a schema, should be retained better than proper names, which cannot. The comparison of retention of names and concepts showed that memory for names initially declined more, but both types of knowledge subsequently stabilised at the same level. Interestingly, there was very little forgetting for the principles of experimental design and statistical analysis. Conway et al. (1991) reflected that this might be procedural knowledge because it was acquired and implemented in practical work, and suggested that procedural knowledge is more robust than declarative knowledge. Unlike Bahrick's subjects, all the former students in this study had received the same level of training, but, nevertheless, those who had achieved higher grades for coursework showed better long-term retention. Similar results were also obtained by Stanhope, Cohen, and Conway (1993), who examined long-term retention of classic novels studied as part of a university course. An initial decline was followed by stable retention. Memory for higher level superordinate information was better than memory for very specific details, but a

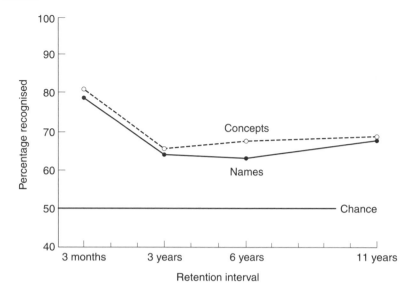

Figure 7.6 Percentages of correct responses to names and concepts in the
    recognition test (based on data from Conway, Cohen, & Stanhope,
    1991).

great deal of specific information was nevertheless retained and it is difficult to see how this could have been reconstructed from a schema.

Taken together, these studies show that in a variety of knowledge domains a substantial amount of knowledge is retained over long periods of time even when it is not rehearsed or used. Factors that influence this long-term retention include the amount and spacing of original training; the level of expertise originally achieved; whether the knowledge is declarative or procedural, high-level general knowledge or low-level specific knowledge; and the extent to which it can be reconstructed from schemas. Conway, Cohen, and Stanhope (1992, p. 480) speculated that it may be important to track the retention of knowledge and the retention of understanding separately: "The knowledge structures which support understanding may consist of integrative concepts or mental models that serve to cross-reference and organize the knowledge domain—our suggestion is that when a knowledge domain remains unused then the first type of knowledge to be lost is that of structures supporting understanding."

Knowledge updating

Whether or not some of our knowledge is immutably lodged in a permastore, knowledge sometimes has to be revised. Some of the facts we thought to be true turn out to be false, or to need modification. New knowledge supersedes old knowledge that is outdated, or irrelevant, or contradicted. As in any information storage system, the information that is stored in memory needs to be corrected and updated.

Some researchers who have studied the process of knowledge updating have noted a *knew-it-all-along effect* (Wood, 1978). When people have been given new facts that contradict their previous knowledge they appear to be unable to remember what they originally believed, and claim to have known it (i.e., the new fact) all along. Apparently, the new knowledge is immediately assimilated with the previous knowledge, and any inconsistencies are eliminated so as to produce an updated version. An update-and-erase mechanism of this kind may be an efficient kind of information storage, but it represents a limitation of metamemory. The knew-it-all-along effect appears to indicate that, although people may know what they know, they are not very accurate at knowing what they used to know.

Hasher, Attig, and Alba (1981) examined the fate of discredited information in a complex experiment that involved asking subjects to rate a set of plausible statements about current affairs, the arts, sports, etc. on a seven-point *true–false* scale. Subsequently, they were given feedback about the truth or falsity of the statements, followed by further information either confirming or discrediting the feedback. Finally, when they were asked to reproduce their original ratings, it was apparent that these had shifted in line with the feedback. Even when the feedback had been discredited, subjects were still influenced by it. However, in a second experiment, Hasher et al. did succeed in inducing subjects to ignore disconfirmed information. It was more effectively discredited when they were told it had been deliberately misleading, not just a mistake. This time the re-ratings did not differ from the original ratings, showing that the subjects had returned to their original knowledge state. This finding suggests that old knowledge is not necessarily completely erased when it is contradicted, but can be recovered. The results also showed that it was easier to shift a belief from false to true than from true to false. People are more reluctant to change their views in response to falsifying evidence. A similar bias has been noted in studies of problem-solving (e.g., Wason, 1960) in which subjects generate a hypothesis in an attempt to solve a problem, and resist evidence that the hypothesis is false.

In everyday life, knowledge-updating is likely to be even more complex than in Hasher et al.'s experiment. There are three different processes that make knowledge-updating necessary. One of these is contradiction, as in the experiment. You may believe that the highest mountain in the United Kingdom is Snowdon until someone tells you this is not true. If the new information is sufficiently authoritative, you will probably discard the original belief. Another process that necessitates knowledge-updating is change. Little Willy changes from a small boy into a young man, or the neighbours trade in their Metro for a Volvo, or the new bypass is now the quickest route to the city. In these cases, the old knowledge is not so much wrong as obsolete. Another process that enforces knowledge revision is the accumulation of counter-examples. A belief that cream and butter are good for you may need revising in the face of growing evidence that high-cholesterol foods are damaging to health. In some of these examples, knowledge-updating is a gradual process, with old knowledge being eroded over time, and gradually giving way to a new belief. While this process is going on a person may dither between two contradictory beliefs, or may be in a state of suspended disbelief, or may simply be confused. When knowledge-updating occurs as a result of change, the old knowledge is not necessarily forgotten or discarded, but may be maintained alongside the new knowledge. Naturally occurring knowledge-updating is much more complicated and variable than the kind of knowledge-updating that has so far been studied in laboratory experiments.

EXPERT MEMORY

The nature of expertise

General world knowledge is the kind of information that is shared by many educated adults in the same culture. It includes miscellaneous and relatively superficial information about history, geography, science, literature, current events, and so on. Expert knowledge, on the other hand, consists of a body of tightly integrated, domain-specific knowledge about some particular defined area such as nuclear physics, 18th-century chamber music, computer programming, or chess. The difference between the two kinds of knowledge is mainly one of depth and interrelatedness. Although the distinction is not a sharp one, expert knowledge is more detailed, more cohesive and integrated, and less likely to be common to the majority of the population. The deployment of expertise involves skills as well as knowledge, but the balance of skill and knowledge varies with the nature of the domain of expertise. The role of skill is probably more important for expert typists and expert dancers; the role of knowledge is more important for expert historians or literary critics. However, in some domains much of an expert's knowledge is implicit and even the experts themselves find it difficult to specify and describe it.

How does an expert differ from a novice? According to Bradley, Paul, and Seeman (2006), an expert is "someone who is characterized by superior performance within a specific domain of activity". Ericsson and Pennington (1993) reviewed three different views about the nature of expertise: the *talent view*, the *knowledge view*, and the *acquired mechanisms view*. According to the talent view, people who become experts start off with special inborn capacities that allow them to develop superior performance. Ericsson and Pennington discount the role of talent in expert performance on two grounds. First, research has generally found that the superior level of ability in experts is confined to the domain of their expertise. Experts in chess are not necessarily experts at Scrabble. Second, a high level of expertise is almost invariably associated with a high level of practice. Nevertheless, it is arguable that some kinds of expertise do require innate characteristics whereas others do not. It is possible that anyone can become an expert cook or an expert bridge-player with sufficient motivation and practice, but physical skills in sport or dance may require specific physical characteristics that cannot be acquired. In other domains of expertise, such as music or art, the respective contributions of innate talent and training are more controversial.

The role of knowledge in expertise is undisputed. Nobody becomes an expert chess player or physician without acquiring a great deal of specialist knowledge and tests of knowledge are predictive of performance. When someone ceases to be a novice and becomes an expert in some particular knowledge domain, changes that are both qualitative and quantitative have taken place in the knowledge structures stored in memory. This is broadly true whether we are talking about formal knowledge domains like chess or computer programming, or less formal ones like birdwatching or cookery. Despite the fact that knowledge structures and reasoning strategies vary from one domain to another, some of the qualities that characterise an "expert", and some of the changes that are associated with expertise, are similar in different domains. It is, of course, almost tautologous to state that experts know more than novices about their area of expertise. They are also able to acquire and retain new information better than novices, and to utilise stored knowledge more effectively. It might be supposed that, as the amount of knowledge in store increases, search processes would be more complex and it would become more difficult to locate and retrieve particular items of information to order. However, this is not what happens. So, how does an expert manage to handle a greatly expanded amount of knowledge without being overwhelmed by it?

The answer lies in the *acquired mechanisms view* of expertise. Experts acquire cognitive mechanisms and cognitive strategies that allow them to handle the enlarged knowledge base effectively:

1 Organisation and chunking. One of the most powerful of these mechanisms is chunking. Experts recode information into large, information-rich chunks and link the chunks with powerful associations (Chase & Simon, 1973; Gobet & Waters, 2003).
2 Selective encoding. Experts home in on the most important information and filter out irrelevant or unimportant details. Experts also encode anticipatory scenarios, which allow them to respond faster and more accurately to dynamic situations as they unfold (Didierjean & Marmeche, 2005; Ferrari, Didierjean, & Marmeche, 2006).
3 Using strategies to extend basic capacity limitations so that, for example, the capacity of working memory is enhanced (Ericsson & Kintsch, 1995).

The most important issues concern the representation and structure of expert knowledge in memory and how far the acquisition of expert knowledge depends on innate natural talent, general cognitive ability, or intensive training and practice. The domains of expertise that have received most attention include music, chess, and field sports.

Expert memory for music

The effects of expertise on memory are clearly evident in the domain of music. Memory for music has a number of special features that distinguish it from other forms of memory discussed in previous chapters. One of these is the enormous range of individual differences. Most people can remember simple melodies, but training and experience produce expert musicians with the ability to remember musical pieces that are many times greater in number, length, and complexity. In this respect, remembering music is quite unlike remembering language. Most people can remember some poetry and a few quotations, but individuals are not trained to be able to reproduce whole novels from memory (although a few mnemonists with exceptional memories may set out to learn telephone directories). Despite some parallels, there are striking differences between memory for music and for language. One of the most obvious is that for many untrained individuals music is a purely receptive ability. They may be able to remember and recognise familiar music, but are unable to reproduce it and are even more unlikely to be able to create new musical sequences. This pattern of ability is not regarded as in any way abnormal. By contrast, the ability to reproduce language and to generate well-formed novel outputs is universal and inability is abnormal. Memory for music is primarily receptive and there are huge variations in ability between trained and untrained individuals. There are some striking analogies between music and mathematics, both being concerned with creating order and elegance out of abstract patterns. Exceptional ability in music, like exceptional ability in mathematics, is highly specific and sometimes develops in early childhood. However, music is unlike mathematics in the way it arouses and engages the emotions, and the emotional and dramatic aspects of music are an important factor in its memorability.

The talent versus training debate

One way in which individuals differ in their ability to remember music is in the possession of absolute pitch. If absolute pitch is a crucial component of expertise, it is important to know whether it is an inborn gift or whether it is the result of training. Absolute or perfect pitch is the ability to produce, name, or remember pitches on an absolute basis and is popularly believed to be an innate endowment. However, Sloboda (1985) claims that almost all musicians who begin training before the age of 6 years have absolute pitch and almost none of those who begin training after the age of 11 have it, suggesting that it is not innate but that there is a critical period for its development.

Studies of musical prodigies, from Mozart onwards, have been invoked in support of the view that musical talent is inborn. Typically, such prodigies have extraordinary memory for music although, because they are so young, the amount of training they have received is limited. Ruthsatz and Detterman (2003) studied Derek, a 6-year-old prodigy, in order to test their theory that a high level of general intelligence is linked to musical ability. Derek played several instruments to professional standards but had received little formal training and did not practise intensively. They concluded that his high general intelligence, exceptional short-term memory, and high scores on tests of musical ability compensated for the lack of training and practice.

However, the idea that general intelligence is an essential component is inconsistent with the evidence from individuals who have exceptional musical skill combined with mental retardation. The proportion of musical savants among autistic children has been estimated at 10% but in mentally retarded children at 0.06%. They are predominantly male, suggesting that the ability is sex-linked, and all of them have absolute pitch. However, as Miller (1989) points out, their talent does not emerge fully formed. Most of them have received some training and encouragement. Their exceptional musical skill is commonly linked with severe visual defects, language impairment, and generally low IQ. This interesting pattern of impairment and spared ability tells us something about the characteristics required for musical skill. Miller carried out careful tests on Eddie, a 5-year-old boy, and found that he and other savants did exceptionally well in tasks requiring retention of harmonic information, but were no better than other musicians in remembering material without any tonal element. He suggested that their superior memory for chords and melodies is due to having absolute pitch, which enables them to carry out rapid and accurate encoding, but he emphasised that musical savants are not like tape-recorders. The fact that they are better at remembering structured, meaningful musical patterns, and show sensitivity to musical constraints, suggests a more abstract, organised representation. Sloboda, Hermelin, and O'Connor (1985) investigated a musical savant, NP, who had exceptional memory for music but poor short-term memory and general IQ. In contrast, Young and Nettlebeck (1995) tested a 13-year-old autistic savant, TR, who had remarkable musical memory but also had a normal short-term memory span. Taken together, these studies suggest that exceptional memory for music depends on having innate or early-acquired ability and absolute pitch, together with some combination of training, practice, and a high level of general intelligence and short-term memory, but not all of these components are necessary.

Mental representations of experts and novices

Experts have hierarchical mental schemas capable of representing abstract higher order groupings, whereas novices represent small-scale patterns of adjacent notes. A concert pianist may be required to produce over 1000 notes a minute for periods of up to 30 minutes (Chaffin & Imreh, 1994). How can this prodigious feat of memory be sustained? Performers establish multiple independent memory codes including motor, conceptual, auditory, and visual codes. The ability of expert performers to memorise a piece involves general knowledge of the principles of construction and the ability to encode the specific piece in terms of groupings and structural markers (Williamson & Egner, 2004), and to relate it to familiar styles and patterns. Experts are able to grasp the global structure and overall architecture of a composition. Bigand (1993) has identified two kinds of abstract musical knowledge structure. The first is a system of relations among musical categories such as pitch, duration, loudness, and timbre. The second is a lexicon of abstract patterns that occur frequently. People who have substantial listening experience have knowledge of stylistic conventions and can extract abstract patterns such as recurrent melodies, the metrical construction, and harmonic framework, which helps them to reconstruct a piece. These differences in the way music is represented in memory underpin the huge gulf between the ability of expert musicians to remember music and the ability of the untrained novice. Novices and non-musicians lack these higher order abstract knowledge structures or have only a limited amount of knowledge that is implicit rather than explicit. Similar differences, described in the next section, have been found between expert and novice chess players, but the advantage conveyed by expertise is perhaps even more striking in the case of music. One example is the often-cited instance of the young Mozart being able to transcribe accurately the score of Allegri's *Miserere* after hearing it twice. It has been suggested that this feat reflects a kind of "eidetic" auditory memory, but Sloboda argued that it could be explained in terms of Mozart's general musical knowledge and the relatively simple structure of the piece.

Expert memory for chess

Chase and Simon (1973) carried out a classic study of the differences between expert and novice chess players. Three subjects with different levels of expertise—a beginner, a class A player, and a Master—were allowed 5 seconds to study a chess board with a game in progress, and were then asked to reconstruct the board positions from memory. If the reconstruction was not complete and accurate the original board was presented and viewed again, and the procedure was repeated until a perfect reconstruction was achieved. The Master needed fewer attempts to achieve a perfect reconstruction than the class A player or the novice. On average, the Master placed 16 pieces correctly at the first attempt to reconstruct a middle game. The class A player placed 8 pieces correctly and the beginner only 4. However, when the subjects were asked to reconstruct chess boards in which the pieces were placed at random, there were no differences between them. This result showed that the Master did not just have superior memory ability. Expertise does not improve memory in general; experts only have better memories for meaningful, properly structured information in their particular knowledge domain.

Chase and Simon believed that chess experts perceive board positions in terms of relations between groups of pieces so, whereas novices have to memorise the position of each individual piece, the expert only has to remember the group. They tested this "perceptual chunking hypothesis" in a further study. Subjects again had to reconstruct board positions, but this time, instead of relying on memory, they were allowed to look back at the original board as often as they needed to. Monitoring the number of "looks" revealed the size and composition of the perceptual chunks. The expert player memorised larger chunks with each glance at the board, and each chunk represented a meaningful cluster of related pieces. The expert organised information into chunks in accordance with the relational patterns resulting from the attacking and defensive moves that occur in the game. The main effects of expertise and meaningfulness on recall performance constitute the most robust and important finding and extend to a variety of domains including field sports and electronics.

However, the chunking theory of Chase and Simon has since been challenged and modified. Template Theory (TT) (Gobet & Waters, 2003; Simon & Gobet, 2000) retains the idea of chunks but includes additional knowledge structures called templates, which contain information about more pieces, and also have slots that can represent locations as well as tactical plans and strategies. An alternative theory, known as the Constraint Attunement Hypothesis (CAH), has been proposed by Vicente and Wang (1998) and emphasises goal-related constraints in the stimulus environment rather than the cognitive processes. According to this theory, experts represent the domain as a hierarchy with five levels of increasing abstraction from board pieces at the lowest level, to strategies and purpose at the highest levels. Levels are connected by means–ends relationships. These two theories, TT and CAH, are difficult to differentiate experimentally as they make similar predictions, but Gobet and Waters claim that results from a study manipulating the degree of randomisation favoured the Template Theory.

Didierjean and Marmeche (2005) and Ferrari et al. (2006) demonstrated that experts' memory includes mental representations of anticipated situations as well as current perceptions. In the domain of basketball they showed that expert players, but not novices, took longer to make same–different judgements for pairs of configurations representing game positions if the different member of the pair was the "next-most-likely" position. The experts had encoded this development of the game in anticipation and so had difficulty in rejecting it. In a similar study, expert chess players participated in an old–new recognition test for board positions. Experts made more false recognition responses than novices when new items were probable developments from the old items viewed in the study phase. These studies provide clear evidence that expert memory is dynamic and anticipatory.

In chess, as in music, expertise is linked to a high degree of practice. However, Horgan and Morgan (1990) studied young players and showed that, although chess performance was highly correlated with the amount of experience, there was also a significant correlation between chess skill and scores on tests of spatial reasoning ability. This finding suggests that exceptional cognitive ability underpins the acquisition of chess expertise. It seems evident that all three components of expertise—talent, knowledge, and acquired mechanisms—are involved to varying degrees in the different domains of expertise considered here. Interest, motivation, and long hours of persevering application and practice are also essential ingredients. Beyond these fairly obvious conclusions it is difficult to generalise across different areas of expertise. The most striking common feature is the enormous advantage in memory that is conferred by expertise in any domain.

CONCLUSIONS

This chapter has emphasised that large amounts of knowledge are stored in semantic memory and that the amount of knowledge available can be greatly expanded by inferential processes. Stored knowledge tends to be inexact, relative, or probabilistic, but this kind of knowledge is "good enough" for most everyday purposes. Although much of the knowledge acquired from formal education and not subsequently used or refreshed is lost from memory, a surprisingly substantial residue is retained almost indefinitely. There is also evidence that knowledge is not simply forgotten over time but may also be deliberately discarded or modified. These considerations emphasise the fact that knowledge structures are dynamic, not fixed. Knowledge structures change as expertise develops and fragment or become inaccessible as information is lost. Some types of knowledge are more durable and are retained over long periods of time; other kinds of knowledge are lost more rapidly. Processes of revision, updating, and reorganisation are occurring continuously throughout our lives, and this is especially true of everyday knowledge. Whereas expert knowledge in domains such as chess or computer programming is encapsulated, everyday knowledge tends to be interactive. Knowledge about transport is interwoven with knowledge about the environment, pollution, politics, and personal plans and activities, and changes in one domain force changes in the other domains. Expert knowledge is organised in accordance with functions, rules, or frequently occurring patterns, and these structures make it more robust.

REFERENCES

Bahrick, H.P. (1984). Semantic memory content in permastore: Fifty years of memory for Spanish learned in school. *Journal of Experimental Psychology: General, 113*, 1–35.

Bahrick, H.P., & Hall, L.K. (1991). Lifetime maintenance of high school mathematics content. *Journal of Experimental Psychology: General, 120*, 20–33.

Barsalou, L.W., Simmons, W.K., Barbey, A.K., & Wilson, C.D. (2003). Grounding conceptual knowledge in modality-specific systems. *Trends in Cognitive Sciences, 7*, 84–91.

Bigand, E. (1993). Contributions of music to research on human auditory cognition. In E. Bigand & S. McAdams (Eds.), *Thinking in sound: The cognitive psychology of human audition* (pp. 231–277) Oxford, UK: Clarendon Press.

Bradley, J.H., Paul, R., & Seeman, E. (2006) Analysing the structure of expert knowledge. *Information and Management, 43*, 77–91.

Camp, C.J., Lachman, J.L., & Lachman, R. (1980). Evidence for direct access and inferential retrieval in question answering. *Journal of Verbal Learning and Verbal behavior, 19*, 583–596.

Chaffin, R., & Imreh, G. (1994). *Memorizing for piano performance.* Paper presented at the Third Practical Aspects of Memory Conference, Washington, DC, July.

Chase, W.G., & Simon, H.A. (1973). Perception in chess. *Cognitive Psychology, 4,* 55–81.

Cohen, G. (2000). Hierarchical models on cognition: Do they have psychological reality? *European Journal of Cognitive Psychology, 12,* 1–36.

Collins, A.M., & Quillian, M.R. (1969). A spreading activation theory of semantic processing. *Psychological Review, 82,* 407–428.

Conway, M.A., Cohen, G., & Stanhope, N. (1991). On the very long-term retention of knowledge acquired from formal education: Twelve years of cognitive psychology. *Journal of Experimental Psychology: General, 120,* 395–409.

Conway, M.A., Cohen, G., & Stanhope, N. (1992). Very long-term memory for knowledge acquired at school and university. *Applied Cognitive Psychology, 6,* 467–482.

Didierjean, A., & Marmeche, E. (2005). Anticipatory representation of visual basketball scenes by expert and novice players. *Visual Cognition, 12,* 265–283.

Ericsson, K.A., & Kintsch, W. (1995). Long-term working memory. *Psychological Review, 102,* 211–245.

Ericsson, K.A., & Pennington, N. (1993). The structure of memory performance in experts: Implications for memory in everyday life. In G.M. Davies & R.H. Logie (Eds.), *Memory in everyday life: Advances in psychology, Vol. 100* (pp. 241–277). Amsterdam: North-Holland/Elsevier.

Ferrari, V., Didierjean, A., & Marmeche, E. (2006). Dynamic perception in chess. *Quarterly Journal of Experimental Psychology, 59,* 397–410.

Gobet, F., & Waters, A.J. (2003). The role of constraints in expert memory. *Journal of Experimental Psychology: Learning, Memory and Cognition, 29,* 1082–1094.

Goldstone, R.L., & Barsalou, L.W. (1998). Reuniting cognition and perception: The perceptual basis of rules and similarity. *Cognition, 65,* 231–262.

Hasher, L., Attig, M.S., & Alba, J.W. (1981). I knew it all along: Or did I? *Journal of Verbal Learning and Verbal Behavior, 20,* 86–96.

Hodges, J.R., Graham, N., & Patterson, K. (1995). Charting the progression in semantic dementia: Implications for the organization of semantic memory. *Memory, 3,* 463–495.

Horgan, D.D., & Morgan, D. (1990). Chess expertise in children. *Applied Cognitive Psychology, 4,* 109–128.

Hummel, J.E., & Holyoak, K.J. (2005). Relational reasoning in a neurally plausible cognitive architecture. *Current Directions in Psychological Science, 14,* 153–157.

Kroger, J.K., Holyoak, K.J., & Hummel, J.E. (2004). Varieties of sameness: The impact of relational complexity on perceptual comparisons. *Cognitive Science, 28,* 358.

Martin, A. (2000). Category-specificity and the brain: The sensory-motor model of semantic representation of objects. In M.S. Gazzaniga (Ed.), *The new cognitive neurosciences* (2nd ed., pp. 1023–1036). Cambridge, MA: MIT Press.

Miller, L.K. (1989). *Musical savants: Exceptional skill in the mentally retarded.* Hillsdale, NJ: Lawrence Erlbaum Associates, Inc.

Morrison, R.G., Krawczyk, D.C., Holyoak, K.J., Hummel, J.E., Chow, T.W., Miller, B.L., & Johnson, B.J. (2004). A neurocomputational model of analogical reasoning and its breakdown in frontotemporal lobar degeneration. *Journal of Cognitive Neuroscience, 16,* 260–271.

Naveh-Benjamin, M. (1988). Retention of cognitive structures learned in university courses. In M.M. Gruneberg, P.E. Morris, & R.N. Sykes (Eds.), *Practical aspects of memory: Current research and issues, Vol. 2* (pp. 383–388). Chichester, UK: Wiley.

Neisser, U. (1978). Memory: What are the important questions? In M.M. Gruneberg, P.E. Morris, & R.N. Sykes (Eds.), *Practical aspects of memory.* London: Academic Press.

Neisser, U. (1984). Interpreting Harry Bahrick's discovery: What confers immunity against forgetting? *Journal of Experimental Psychology: General, 113*, 32–35.

Nickerson, R.S. (1977). Some comments on human memory as a very large data base. *Proceedings of the Third International Conference on Very Large Data Bases*, Tokyo, October, 1991.

Rogers, T.T., Lambon Ralph, M.A., Garrard, P., Bozeat, S., McClelland, J.L., Hodges, J.R., & Patterson, K. (2004). Structure and deterioration of semantic memory: A neuropsychological and computational investigation. *Psychological Review, 111*, 205–235.

Ruthsatz, J., & Detterman, D.K. (2003). An extraordinary memory: The case study of a musical prodigy. *Intelligence, 31*, 509–518.

Simon, H.A., & Gobet, F. (2000). Expertise effects in memory recall: Comment on Vicente and Wang. *Psychological Review, 107*, 593–600.

Sloboda, J.A. (1985). *The musical mind: The cognitive psychology of music*. Oxford, UK: Clarendon Press.

Sloboda, J.A., Hermelin, B., & O'Connor, N.O. (1985). An exceptional musical memory. *Music Perception, 3*, 155–170.

Spellman, B.A., Holyoak, K.J., & Morrison, R.G. (2001). Analogical priming via semantic relations. *Memory and Cognition, 29*, 383–393.

Stanhope, N., Cohen, G., & Conway, M.A. (1993). Very long-term retention of a novel. *Applied Cognitive Psychology, 7*, 239–256.

Tohill, J.M., & Holyoak, K.J. (2000). The impact of anxiety on analogical reasoning. *Thinking & Reasoning, 6*, 27–40. (http://www.psypress.co.uk/journals.asp).

Tulving, E. (1972). Episodic and semantic memory In E. Tulving & W. Donaldson (Eds.), *Organization of memory*. New York: Academic Press.

Vicente, J.J., & Wang, J.H. (1998). An ecological theory of expertise effects in memory recall. *Psychological Review, 105*, 33–57.

Warrington, E.K. (1975). Selective impairment of semantic memory. *Quarterly Journal of Experimental Psychology, 27*, 635–657.

Wason, P.C. (1960). On the failure to eliminate hypotheses in a conceptual task. *Quarterly Journal of Experimental Psychology, 12*, 129–140.

Williamson, A., & Egner, T. (2004). Memory structures for encoding and retrieving a piece of music: An ERP investigation. *Cognitive Brain Research, 22*, 36–44.

Wood, G. (1978). The knew-it-all-along effect. *Journal of Experimental Psychology: Human Perception and Performance, 4*, 345–353.

Young, R.L., & Nettlebeck, T. (1995). The abilities of a musical savant and his family. *Journal of Autism and Developmental Disorders, 25*, 231–248.

8 Situation models in memory: Texts and stories

Gabriel A. Radvansky

Part of everyday memory is the ability to remember the situations that are described in conversation, texts we read, films we see, and so on. This memory requires a mental representation that will capture the important aspects of a described event. This representation, in some sense, serves as mental analogue for the situation in the world. By remembering a mental analogue of the situation, we are remembering the described event. These mental representations of described situations are called *situation models* (Van Dijk & Kintsch, 1983; Zwaan & Radvansky, 1998). This chapter will look at a number of ways that memory for events is influenced by the use of these situation models. A general description of memory for situations is first provided. After this, the chapter will look at the long-term memory for events, how the dynamic characteristics of events can change memory as we update our understanding of the event, and how event memory is affected by the natural ageing process.

LEVELS OF COMPREHENSION AND MEMORY

When you read a story in a newspaper or hear a story on the news, it is important what words were used to convey the message. However, as time passes, the precise wording used becomes less and less important, and our memory for that information becomes progressively worse. Over long periods of time what we remember is not the exact wording used, but the situation that was described. Research on memory for language and text has delineated between three levels of mental representation (Van Dijk & Kintsch, 1983): the surface form, the propositional textbase, and the situation model. The *surface form* is essentially a person's memory for the exact words and syntax used. While precise wording may be important, verbatim memory is generally very poor. Memory for the surface form is very fragile and may be forgotten within a few minutes or even seconds (Sachs, 1967), unless there is extensive practice (Noice & Noice, 2002) or wording is critical, as with jokes (Kintsch & Bates, 1977).

In comparison to the surface form, the *propositional textbase* is a more abstract representation. The textbase is a mental representation of the ideas conveyed by the text, independent of the precise wording used. For example, the sentences "The girl hit the boy" and "The boy was hit by the girl" differ in their wording, but essentially mean the same thing. This common underlying idea would be the textbase. While the textbase is remembered longer than the surface form, people still tend to forget this information at a fairly rapid rate. As will be seen, textbase information begins to be lost after a few minutes of reading a text.

The referential memory for a described situation is the *situation model* (Johnson-Laird, 1983; Van Dijk & Kintsch, 1983; Zwaan & Radvansky, 1998). This is a memory representation for the situation described by a text apart from memories of the text itself. A situation model is a mental simulation of the event being described. While these mental representations isomorphically capture the important components of a situation, they are not complete and do not capture every aspect of an event. There are a number of components that can be identified in a situation model (Wyer & Radvansky, 1999). First, a situation is embedded in a *spatial–temporal framework*. This is a location in space that the situation unfolds in, and the span of time in which the situation operates. The spatial–temporal framework provides the context that defines a static situation (e.g., Bower & Morrow, 1990; Radvansky & Zacks, 1991; Radvansky, Zwaan, Federico, & Franklin, 1998).

Within the spatial–temporal framework are a number of *tokens* that stand for the entities, such as people, animals, objects, abstract concepts, etc. Associated with these tokens are various relevant *properties*, including external (e.g., physical) and internal (e.g., mental or emotional) properties. Finally, there are *structural relations* among the tokens, including spatial, social, and ownership relations. The probability that these components are included in the situation model is a function of the degree to which they involve an actual or likely interaction among those elements (Radvansky & Copeland, 2000; Radvansky, Spieler, & Zacks, 1993; Radvansky, Wyer, Curiel, & Lutz, 1997).

In addition to moments in time, a situation model can capture dynamic aspects of an event. This is done by joining a series of spatial–temporal frameworks by *linking relations* including temporal and causal relations. These relations are presumably grounded in the tokens of the situation model that stand for the entities that are undergoing transition in the situation. During the reading of a text, reading times increase when there are breaks in causal coherence (Zwaan, Magliano, & Graesser, 1995) and temporal contiguity (Zwaan, 1996; Zwaan et al., 1995). Furthermore, the degree of causal connectivity of story constituents is a primary predictor of recall and summarisation (see Van den Broek, 1994).

Unlike the surface form and textbase, memory for the situation model is much more durable, lasting for long periods of time. For example, when you think about a newspaper article you may have read, you are unlikely to remember the wording of the article, but are likely to remember the events in the world that the article was describing. This is the superior memory of the situation model relative to the surface form and textbase.

This differential memory of the surface form, textbase, and situation models levels over time has been illustrated most clearly in a study by Kintsch, Welsch, Schmalhofer, and Zimny (1990; see also Radvansky, Zwaan, Curiel, & Copeland, 2001). In this study, people were given texts to read. They were then tested for their memory of the text immediately after reading, 40 minutes later, 2 days later, or 4 days later. The results of this study are shown in Figure 8.1. What was observed was that although memory at all three levels of representation were relatively high immediately after reading, as time passed there were marked differences in the rate of forgetting.

An important aspect of this study is that it used a method developed by Schmalhofer and Glavanov (1986) to separate out memory for the three levels of

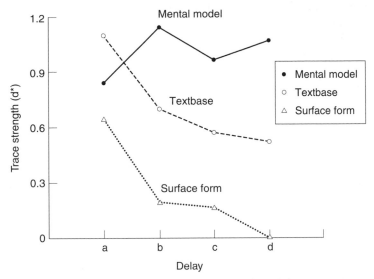

Figure 8.1 Results of the Kintsch, Welsch, Schmalhofer, and Zimny (1990) study showing the forgetting of information at the surface form and textbase levels, but relatively well-preserved memory at the situation model level. Redrawn from data reported by Kintsch, Welsch, Schmalhofer, and Zimny (1990), *Journal of Memory and Language*, 29, 133–159.

representation. This analysis uses the rate at which people say they remember verbatim, paraphrase, inference, and incorrect statements as having been read before. A signal detection analysis is applied to these data by strategically comparing these different types of item. For the surface form, memory performance declined very rapidly after the first 40 minutes, and within a few days, people were essentially at chance in their ability to discriminate between sentences that had actually been read, and those that captured the same meaning, but differed in their wording.

For the textbase, the rate of forgetting was less pronounced. Although there was some evidence of forgetting even after 40 minutes, it was not as extreme as with the surface form representation. Over the next few days, performance did decline over time, although people were still above chance in their ability to discriminate ideas that were in the text versus those that could be inferred, but were not explicitly mentioned. In comparison, memory at the situation model level showed no appreciable forgetting across the various retention intervals. In some ways, this result is not too surprising. After all, when we read something, we are often not overly concerned with the words themselves, but with the situation that is being described. We care about the events, not the words, and so our memory is oriented around remembering the described circumstances rather than the language used.

LONG-TERM MEMORY FOR SITUATIONS

This portion of the chapter will look at long-term memory for described situations and how the structure of situations influences how well different pieces of information are retained and retrieved in memory. Given that situation models are efficiently retained longer than other sorts of memory traces, and that these memories capture the described events, it is expected that this will have a meaningful influence on long-term memory performance. Specifically, memory should be more situation-based rather than language-based. That is, people should make memory judgements based on whether the information matches the described situation, not based on linguistic correspondences.

Sentence memory

A classic illustration of this sort of situation-based memory comes from work on sentence memory. Specifically, it has been shown that people are more likely to misidentify a sentence that is different from one heard earlier if it describes the same situation. The classic example of this is a study by Bransford, Barclay, and Franks (1972; see also Garnham, 1981; Jahn, 2004). In this study people heard sentences such as "Three turtles rested on a log and a fish swam beneath them". Later, these people were likely to mistakenly identify the sentence "Three turtles rested on a log and a fish swam beneath it" as having been heard before. This error occurs because both of these sentences describe the same situation. This is in comparison to a condition in which people heard sentences such as "Three turtles rested beside a log and a fish swam beneath them". In this case, people are much less likely to mistakenly say that they heard the sentence "Three turtles rested beside a log and a fish swam beneath it" because this more clearly describes a different situation, even though the change in wording between these two versions of the sentence is the same as the change in wording in the first pair.

Overall, what these sorts of studies show is that people's memory even for simple sentences is guided by a memory for the described situation, not a memory for the language itself. People depend on their situation models to make memory decisions. They do not have very good memories for the language used to make those descriptions.

The use of situation models during memory retrieval, even for simple sentences, can be clearly seen in work on the fan effect. A *fan effect* is an increase in retrieval time or error rates on a recognition test that accompanies an increase in the number of newly learned associations with a concept (Anderson, 1974). In other words, the more new things a person learns about something, the harder it is to retrieve any one of them. For example, suppose people first memorised a set of sentences that included "The bulletin board is in the school" "The bulletin board is in the city hall" and "The bulletin board is in the car dealership". Then, during a recognition test, because there are three places that the bulletin board is in, people will take longer to verify any one of these sentences compared to a condition in which only one thing was learned about the bulletin board. This memory retrieval slow-down is the fan effect.

According to a situation model view, the reason this interference effect occurs is because people are creating a separate situation model for each location the bulletin board is in. This is because each of those three sentences is likely to be interpreted as referring to a different situation in the world. As such, what we have are three separate situation models about the bulletin board stored in long-term memory. During retrieval, when the person is presented with a fact to verify, such as "The

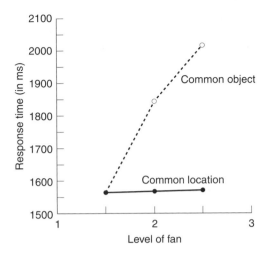

Figure 8.2 Different interference effect for multiple location (one object in multiple location) and single location (multiple objects in one location) conditions. Level of fan refers to the number of associations with either an object or location. Drawn from data reported by Radvansky, Spieler, and Zacks (1993) *Journal of Experimental Psychology: Learning, Memory, and Cognition, 19,* 95–114.

bulletin board is in the car dealership", not only is the car dealership model activated, but so are the school and city hall models, because they also contain a bulletin board. As such, these related and irrelevant models interfere with the retrieval of the appropriate one, producing interference and slowing retrieval down, producing a fan effect.

In comparison, suppose as part of the set of sentences, people learned the sentences "The potted palm is in the hotel" "The pay phone is in the hotel" and "The ceiling fan is in the hotel". Under these circumstances, although there are three different sentences about the hotel, it is easy for people to imagine a single situation that is consistent with these three facts. As such, people can integrate this information into a common situation model, and store that one model in memory. Then at retrieval, when a person needs to recognise any one of those facts, because there is only a single situation model about the hotel, there are no related and irrelevant models that would be activated and produce interference. As such, no fan effect is observed (Radvansky, 1999; Radvansky et al., 1993; Radvansky & Zacks, 1991). This differential interference effect for multiple location and single location conditions can be seen in Figure 8.2.

This differential interference effect is not specific to spatial locations, but applies to situation models more generally, and how people conceive of the way that situations are structured in the world. For example, if people memorise sentences about people in small locations that typically contain only a single person (such as a dressing room at a store) then the information is organised into situation models oriented around the person (who can travel from place to place as a sequence of events) rather than the location (Radvansky et al., 1993). Also, situation models are organised around people for statements of ownership rather than objects (Radvansky et al., 1997), or around common time periods (Radvansky et al., 1998). Thus, people are using their understanding of events in the world to create situation models, and then using these situation models during retrieval, which can then influence memory performance.

This sort of interference effect is not only observed when people memorise sets of individual sentences, but also when people have extensive prior knowledge and are reading longer texts. In a study by Bower and Rinck (2001), people first memorised a map of a building. An example of one of these maps is shown in Figure 8.3. This building had many rooms, with several objects in each room. Moreover, different instances of some of the objects could occur in multiple rooms. For example, two or three rooms could have a desk. After memorising the map, people read narratives that described events that occurred within that building. On critical trials, sentences mentioned objects that were either grouped together in a single room, or that occurred in multiple rooms. What was observed was that people showed evidence of interference when there were several instances spread across multiple locations, but not when there were several objects in one location. Thus, the principles of memory and the use of situation models to structure information and influence retrieval were observed both with simple sentences and with more complex event descriptions.

Overall, there is clear evidence that when people remember information they have heard or read, there is a tendency to rely on situation models of the described situations rather than a memory for the text itself. This tendency becomes more pronounced as time passes, and the memories become older and older. Moreover, how information is structured and organised into situation models can have a profound impact on how the information is retrieved later. For example, information that has been integrated into a common situation model can be remembered with more facility than information that refers to common situational elements, but is stored across multiple situation models.

Narrative memory

While the research on sentence memory is instructive, people are often called upon to remember complex sets of information, such as that presented in the context of a narrative. As mentioned earlier, the Schmalhofer and Glavanov (1986) analysis of people's memory for text shows that they retain their situation model representations for a longer period of time than their more text-oriented representations. However, different aspects of a situation model are differentially remembered depending on the role they play in the situation. In this section, we look at some factors that can influence performance, such as functional relations, causality, and stereotypes.

People create situation models of the narratives they hear and read. These situation models are made up of a number of components that correspond to different elements of the situation, including information about the spatial–temporal framework, entities, their properties, structural relations such as spatial and ownership relations and linking relations, such as temporal and causal relations (Wyer & Radvansky, 1999; Zwaan & Radvansky, 1998). The relative importance of each of these components varies with the role it plays in the situation.

One distinction that can be made is between different types of structural relations. Take the example of spatial relations that convey how different entities in a situation

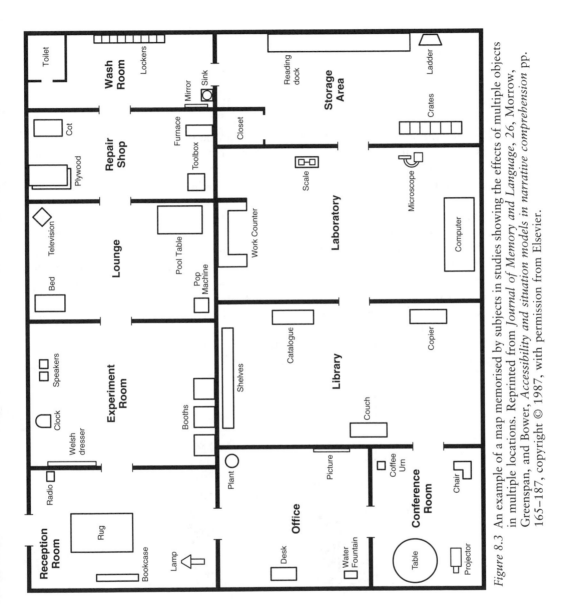

Figure 8.3 An example of a map memorised by subjects in studies showing the effects of multiple objects in multiple locations. Reprinted from *Journal of Memory and Language, 26*, Morrow, Greenspan, and Bower, *Accessibility and situation models in narrative comprehension* pp. 165–187, copyright © 1987, with permission from Elsevier.

are oriented with respect to one another. When people read about the arrangement of objects with respect to a story protagonist, if they are sufficiently motivated, they will create situation models to capture this framework. Thus, objects that are directly ahead of the protagonist will be directly ahead in the situation model. Objects that are to the right will be to the right in the model. This has implications for the availability of information within a situation model. Specifically, the availability of information retrieved from a situation model varies as a function of characteristics of the real world, and how the story protagonist would interact with those objects if that were a real environment. In a study by Franklin and Tversky (1990), people read stories that described the relative position of objects with respect to the story protagonist. Then people were probed for information about those objects.

What Franklin and Tversky (1990) found, as can be seen in Figure 8.4, was that the availability of information about objects in working memory was greatest for items along the above–below axis, intermediate for objects along the front–back axis, and least available for objects along the left–right axis. The thinking is that objects along the above–below axis are most available because this dimension of space is clearly defined by presence of gravity and the asymmetry of a person's body along this axis. Information along the front–back axis is moderately available because, while the environment does not clearly define this axis, the asymmetry of a person's front versus back does. Finally, the left–right axis is the most difficult to use because it is neither clearly defined by the environment nor a person's body, because we are symmetrical (more or less) along the left–right axis. Thus, the availability of information in working memory is influenced by the structure of a person's situation model and how this model is being used.

Not all spatial relations between entities are important to understanding the situation. For example, suppose it is raining. If a person were to stand next to the

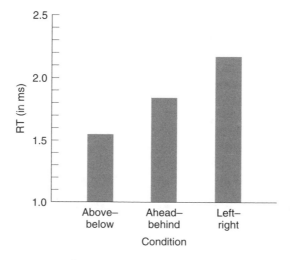

Figure 8.4 Availability of object information in working memory as a function of the spatial orientation relative to a story protagonist. Drawn from data reported by Franklin and Tversky (1990) *Journal of Experimental Psychology: General, 119,* 63–76.

bridge there is no functional relation here, and it would not be important for people to remember this spatial relation. However, if a person were to stand below the bridge, this would serve the function of keeping the person out of the rain and not getting wet. Because the spatial relation between the two entities (the person and the bridge) serves some function, there is now some reason to remember it. This distinction between functional and nonfunctional relations has important consequences for event memory. Specifically, people are more likely to remember functional relations than nonfunctional ones (Radvansky & Copeland, 2001). This is because the functional relations are the more important ones in the content of the event.

This influence of functional relations even extends to sentence memory. As a reminder, Bransford et al. (1972) were able to show that people mistakenly remembered sentences that described the same situation as an original one. More recent work by Jahn (2004) has found that this can be affected by the presence or absence of causal relations. Specifically, if people read sentences about animals in spatial relation to one another, they were more likely to make memory errors when the sentences were consistent with a causal predator–prey relation than when that relation was absent. This predator–prey relation is a functional one that is critical to a person understanding the described event. This further supports the idea that people are creating situation models of events and using them to make memory decisions, even when the information is conveyed by something as small as a single sentence. Moreover, how these situation models are structured is based on how entities interact in the world.

The influence of causal information on memory for situation is very clearly observed in studies of narrative comprehension that have looked at how causal structure influences memory for a narrative. In general, a given piece of narrative information is more likely to be remembered if it is causally more important. Causal importance is quantified at the beginning of a study by having an experimenter indicate, for each text unit (such as a sentence), whether it is causally connected to other events that have occurred in the story, and if so which ones (Trabasso & Sperry, 1985; Trabasso & Van den Broek, 1985). Through this type of analysis, a causal network of the story can be readily derived. What this network will indicate is the degree to which a given text element is causally connected to the other portions of the text. This is important because it has been found that sentences that have a greater number of causal connections are remembered better than sentences that have a lesser number. Thus, people are using the causal structure of described situations to create situation models, and this causal structure has a direct influence on memory performance. This importance of causal connectedness on memory for situations not only applies to those situations that are read about, but also those that are experienced and are represented in autobiographical memory (Radvansky, Copeland, & Zwaan, 2005a).

The importance of causal relations in memory for situations can also be observed in the ability of people to use causal inferences they derive from texts as they read them. For example, in one study by Singer, Halldorson, Lear, and Andrusiak (1992), people read brief stories that either did or did not imply a causal relation among situational elements. For example, if a person first read the sentence "Mark poured the bucket of water on the bonfire" followed by the sentence "The bonfire went out," then they were later able to verify more quickly the statement "Does water extinguish fire?" than if the first sentence that was read was "Mark placed the bucket of water by the fire." This suggests that when situation models are created, the memory for an inferred causal relation can influence later performance. People have situation models in memory that include not only information about what was read, but also about what was implied.

This memory for causal relations can be exploited during retrieval. In a series of studies (Duffy, Shinjo, & Myers, 1990; Keenan, Baillet, & Brown, 1984; Myers, Shinjo, & Duffy, 1987), people were presented with sentence pairs. Later they were given the first sentence and asked to recall the second. Recall was more successful when the sentences were casually related than when they were not. This further supports the idea that causal relations are stored in our memory for situations and can be used to retrieve information at a later point.

The aspects of narrative memory that have been considered so far are somewhat neutral, in that they involve physical or natural causal relations among entities. However, people actively evaluate social aspects of the situations they are confronted with. Among the social implications of stories are the social stereotypes that may become involved and prejudices that the reader may have. These may be used to evaluate the story characters that can become incorporated into the situation models that are created and stored in memory. We all have stereotypes of people that we carry around with us in our heads, even if we don't agree with or believe in the stereotypes. That is, we know what the stereotypes are, even if we don't accept their application. These stereotypes can sometimes provide information that would be incorporated into a person's situation model, and then this situation model is used to make decisions. If these decisions are based on stereotypical information, then a person may act in a prejudicial manner even if they want to be egalitarian.

When a person reads a text, inferences need to be made because not all of the information needed to understand it is explicitly stated. People rely on their general knowledge to make these inferences, and most of the time this occurs in a rapid and unconscious manner. One of the potential sources of information in long-term memory that could be used to make inferences is our stereotypes. What can happen is that people unconsciously make inferences using their stereotypes to fill in the gaps of the text. Later, when people need to remember information they read earlier, they will have a hard time distinguishing between what was read and what was inferred. As such, people are more likely to think mistakenly that the stereotypical information that they inferred had actually been read (Radvansky, Copeland, & Von Hippel, 2006). A person may therefore think and act in a prejudicial manner towards the person they had read about earlier.

MEMORY AND UPDATING SITUATIONS

While some situations are static states-of-affairs, others are more dynamic courses-of-events, in which the situation changes and develops over time (Barwise & Perry, 1983). Memory must take into account this dynamic aspect of situations in two general ways. First, as a person is actively processing information about an ongoing situation in a text they are reading, they need to be able to update the contents of their working memory so that they continue to think about information that is relevant to the current situation, but so that newly irrelevant information is removed from the current situation model and is not actively maintained in working memory.

The other thing that memory must do is keep track of the sequence of events as they occur for the time when this information needs to be later reconstructed.

There are a number of ways that the situations we read about can change. One type of change that can occur is a change in spatial location; people we read about can move from one location to another. Often, this sort of change is viewed as a significant change in the ongoing situation, and readers need to update their situation models. When they do this, relevant information needs to remain in the highly active foreground in working memory, whereas information that was relevant in the prior location, but less relevant in the current situation, should be removed from a high state of availability in working memory.

In one study of spatial updating, Glenberg, Meyer, and Lindem (1987; see also Radvansky & Copeland, 2001; Radvansky, Copeland, Berish, & Dijkstra, 2003a) had people read brief texts in which a critical object was either associated with or dissociated from the story protagonist. Then the protagonist moved to a new location. An example of this is the story below:

> John was preparing for a marathon in August. After doing a few exercises, he put on/took off his sweatshirt and went jogging. He jogged halfway around the lake without much difficulty. Further along his route, however, John's muscles began to ache.

According to situation model theory, things that were associated with the protagonist should stay in the foreground of the situation model because they move to the new location with the protagonist. However, objects that were dissociated from the protagonist should not be carried along to the new location, and so would not be relevant to that situation, and should fall away from the foreground of the situation model. This was tested in Glenberg et al.'s study by asking people questions or presenting memory probes that referred to the critical object in the story (in this case the sweatshirt) that was either associated with or dissociated from the story protagonist.

What Glenberg et al. (1987) observed was that information about the critical object was less available when it was dissociated than when it was associated. People were faster to respond to questions or probes that referred to a critical object that was associated with the story protagonist, and thus maintained when the spatial shift occurred, relative to dissociated objects that remained in the prior location. Thus, spatial updating of a situation model as a person strives to understand the described situation affects the working memory availability of information about objects in that situation.

The monitoring of situational information across spatial shifts takes into account not only information about the current state of the situation, but general world knowledge about the larger context. This is most clearly seen in a series of studies by Bower and colleagues (e.g., Morrow, Greenspan, & Bower, 1987; Rinck & Bower, 1995). In these studies, people first memorise a map of a building with multiple rooms and multiple objects in each room, like the one shown in Figure 8.8. Then, after the map is memorised, people read narratives about characters moving about in those buildings. During reading, people were probed for information about objects in those buildings. In essence, what was found was that as the distance from the story protagonists' current location in the building to the objects increased, there was an increase in processing time. This spatial gradient suggests that people are updating their situation models when there are spatial shifts, and that people take into account the broader context in which that situation is embedded.

While people can monitor spatial shifts in long-term memory, this does not mean that they always do so. For example, people do not show the spatial gradient of availability when they are not focused on the protagonist (Wilson, Rinck, McNamara, Bower, & Morrow, 1993) or do not have extensive prior knowledge about the larger spatial layout (Zwaan, Radvansky, Hilliard, & Curiel, 1998). The structure of the situation model is more likely to affect memory retrieval when cognitive processing is oriented towards understanding the unfolding events, but not otherwise. Thus, situation models do not necessarily have an overpowering influence on cognitive processes but are likely to have an influence in everyday memory use, since most of what we think about are the events and situations in our world. When situation model processing is engaged, the structure of a situation model can over-come other mental structures and organisations. For example, if people memorise a map in a way that emphasises a temporal ordering (e.g., Clayton & Habibi, 1991; Curiel & Radvansky, 1998), during simple memory retrieval, a temporal organiza-tion of the information is observed. However, if people need to use that information to process events, such as reading the stories that were used by Bower and colleagues, they exhibit the spatial gradient of availability (Curiel & Radvansky, 2002). Essentially, the use of situation models in working memory causes the knowledge to be mentally restructured to capture the organisation of an event as it would occur in the world, and not reflect the prior structure of the information in long-term memory.

Another way that a situation can change is that there could be a shift in time (e.g., Radvansky et al., 2003a; Zwaan, 1996). Shifts in time vary in their importance in monitoring knowledge in working memory depending on the size of the time shift. For relatively short shifts, based on a reader's knowledge of how long events typically last, the situation model in working memory may require little or no modification, whereas for larger time shifts beyond the normal duration of an event of a particular type, people will need to update their situation models in some way (Anderson, Garrod, & Sanford, 1983). For example, if a reader is told that a person has started watching a movie, an hour later the person is still likely to be watching the movie, but 5 hours later the situation may well have changed. These larger time shifts are cues to readers to update their situation models by creating a new spatial–temporal context. Again, some of the information from the previous event will be relevant in the new situation, and other information will become irrelevant.

A study by Zwaan (1996) looked at temporal updating in a way that is somewhat similar to the Glenberg et al. (1987) study described earlier. In that study, people read texts that described a person engaged in an activity. Then there was a statement that indicated either a short or a long temporal shift. Here is an example of one of the stories used:

> Today was the grand opening of Maurice's new art gallery. He had invited everybody in town who was important in the arts. Everyone who had been invited had said that they would come. It seemed like the opening would be a big success. At seven o'clock, the first guests arrived.
> Maurice was in an excellent mood. He was shaking hands and beaming. A *moment/day later*, he turned very pale. He had completely forgotten to invite the

local art critic. And sure enough, the opening was very negatively reviewed in the weekend edition of the local newspaper. Maurice decided to take some Advil and stay in bed the whole day.

Again, the idea was that information that was relevant to the first situation, but temporally limited, should still be available. However, after a longer time shift, information about the protagonists' activities should be removed from working memory. In this case, a reader could be probed with the word "beaming" after the temporal shift sentence, with the task of verifying whether it had occurred before. When the temporal shift was a short one, people should be faster to verify the probe than after a long shift. After a long temporal shift, information that was relevant to the previous event, but not to the current situation, should have been removed from the foreground of the situation model in working memory.

What was found in Zwaan's (1996) study was that people were, in fact, slower to verify these probes when there had been a long temporal shift than when there had been only a short shift. These results further support the idea that people are creating mental simulations of the world when they read about events that happen in the world, and that these situation models are updated to take into account the current state of affairs. Working memory contents are being managed to keep relevant information available, whereas less relevant information is removed when it no longer pertains to the current situation.

Events can change in more subtle ways than by shifts in time and space. Another set of elements of a situation that can change are the goals and desires of the people involved. When people read a text, they need to keep track of what the story characters want and are trying to achieve. This provides an understanding of what motivates people to do different things, and helps explain why they take various actions. In other words, what happens in a narrative situation is often driven by the intentions of the characters. When a person's goals change, the situation changes as well. Goals can change in a situation in a number of ways, including becoming a goal for a person, becoming more or less important, or being completed and no longer relevant. Our focus here will be on cases in which a person's goal has been completed. This type of goal change nicely parallels the work on spatial and temporal shifts we have covered up to this point.

Essentially, when a person completes a goal, information about the need for that person to achieve that goal has to be removed from working memory. This is because it no longer motivates a person's actions. For example, if Jimmy wants a bike, and then gets one, then there is no reason to think that any of his future actions involve him trying to get a bike. This process of updating goal information was assessed in a study by Suh and Trabasso (1993; see also Lutz & Radvansky, 1997; Radvansky & Curiel, 1998). In that study, people read a series of stories in which the characters had explicitly stated goals. At a later point during the story, the protagonist was able either to complete that goal successfully or not. What was found was that information about the goal became much less available when the goal was completed, but remained highly available in working memory if it was not. Thus, when people are reading, the situation model they create is actively monitoring events in the world by regulating the active contents of working memory. This applies to many aspects of a situation, including non-perceptual changes such as a shift in goal relevance.

This work on understanding how people remember events that they read from a text is important in other domains, not just memory for text. For example, take the finding by Glenberg et al. (1987) that, when people read about a spatial shift, they retain information about objects that were associated with the story protagonist, but remove information about dissociated objects from the foreground of their situation model. A study by Radvansky and Copeland (2006) extended this finding to interaction with events in virtual reality. In their study, people navigated a virtual environment, picking up and setting down objects along the way. They also probed people for the names of objects they were either carrying or had just set down. What they found was that the Glenberg et al. (1987) result recurred in these virtual reality environments. Specifically, memory for objects was worse for objects that had been set down as compared to objects that were currently being carried. Moreover, if a person walked through a doorway, a marked spatial shift, memory for the objects was even worse, particularly for those that the person was carrying. Essentially, walking through doorways causes forgetting.

AGEING

Now that we've covered a number of issues relating to memory for situations in normal, college-aged people, let's look at how these principles of memory and comprehension can be extended to older adults. Old age brings with it a number of psychological changes (see Chapter 11). For example, relative to younger adults, older adults process information more slowly (Salthouse, 1996), are more likely to make errors on memory tests (Johnson, 2003), are less able to maintain information in working memory (Craik & Byrd, 1982), and are less able to suppress irrelevant information from entering the current stream of processing (Hasher & Zacks, 1988). Because of the importance for creating, maintaining, and retrieving information from situation models to everyday comprehension and memory, it is also of interest to see how the natural ageing process affects this.

As mentioned earlier, after people read a text, memory for that information can be analysed at three levels: the surface form, textbase, and situation model (e.g., Kintsch et al., 1990). Using the sort of analysis that was described earlier to tease apart memory at these three levels, we can then assess how younger and older adults differ or are the same. This was done in a study by Radvansky et al. (2001), who found that older adults had poorer memory than younger adults at the surface form and textbase levels. This is consistent with a great deal of work on ageing and memory (see Johnson, 2003). However, what is interesting is that at the situation model level, the older adults did as well as, if not better than, the younger adults. Thus, while there are declines at lower levels, memory at the situation model level was relatively well preserved. Older adults are as able as younger adults to construct situation models of a described event, and then remember them later.

As a reminder, when people construct situation models they are taking information from a text that they are reading and combining it with inferences they draw from their prior knowledge about the world, and how the described situation is likely to be operating. While this process seems to work well for older adults in general, there are some ways in which their age-related deficits can hinder their performance. An example of this would be cases where people make and retain inferences about things that they read although they feel these are inappropriate. For example, in one study by Hamm and Hasher (1992), people read texts that initially misled them about what sort of situation the protagonist was in. Then, part-way through the story, it was made clear that another situation was operating. An example of one of those stories is presented below:

> Carol was not feeling well and decided to find out what was wrong. She called her friend who was a nurse to ask her for some advice. The friend told Carol what to do. Carol went into town and apprehensively entered the large building hoping to find an answer. She walked through the doors and took an elevator to the third floor. She found a book that seemed relevant to her problem. Carol then went to the main desk and checked out the book for two weeks so that she could read it at home. When she left the building she saw that it had started snowing hard and she hailed a taxi to take her home.

In this story, it initially implies that the building Carol is going into is a hospital. However, this is misleading, and the passage then makes clear that the building is a library. One of the problems that older adults have is in suppressing inappropriate information (Hasher & Zacks, 1988). Consistent with this, older adults not only made inferences about the correct interpretation of the situation (that Carol went to a library), but they continued to hold on to the inappropriate interpretation (that the building was a hospital) after it was made clear that another was operating. That is, they were maintaining two different situation models of the same description.

In another study by Radvansky et al. (2006), people read texts about stereotyped members of the community, such as African–Americans and Jews. It was found that older adults were more likely to draw and maintain inferences about the story characters consistent with the stereotypes. That is, older people were more likely to draw inferences based on their stereotypes and to integrate them into their situation model. These situation models with a greater amount of stereotype-consistent information were then used to make memory decisions later. This occurred even in face of the fact that older adults were more motivated to be egalitarian than the younger adults. These older adults' memories led them to be prejudicial against their will.

Evidence for the idea that older adults are using situation models in memory in a manner similar to younger adults can also be seen in a study by Radvansky, Gerard, Zacks, and Hasher (1990), in which people were presented with confusable and non-confusable sentences, similarly to the study by Bransford et al. (1972). In this study, younger and older adults were confusing sentences that had been heard before with ones that were different, but plausibly described the same situation. Both groups made fewer confusions for sentences that were unlikely to be interpreted as describing the same situation. Thus, older adults, like younger adults, use their situation model memories to make decisions about what has and has not been presented before.

The influence of situation models on memory retrieval is similar across younger and older adults. Specifically, younger and older adults both show fan effect interference during memory retrieval for information that is shared across multiple models in memory, although the older adults show larger interference effects. However, both younger and older adults are able to avoid this interference if they can integrate this information into a single situation model (Radvansky, Zacks, & Hasher, 1996, 2005b). Thus, the use of situation models in memory not only affects how information is encoded, but also how it is retrieved, showing that this use of situation models in retrieval is similar across age groups.

This age-invariant influence of situation models can also been seen in the selective processing of causal information. A study by Radvansky, Copeland, and Zwaan (2003b) involved having people read stories conveying functional or non-functional spatial relations. What was observed was that the older adults showed a memory benefit for functional information, like the younger adults. Moreover, this benefit was greater for older adults such that the normal memory deficit that is observed with ageing was completely absent. Thus, when older adults are creating situation models as they read, they are more likely to select out and encode that information that is more central or important to understanding the situation, and are less likely to encode more peripheral details of an event they are reading about.

Finally, work on situation models in memory and ageing also shows that older adults process situation model information in working memory in a manner similar to younger adults. This is evident when they are presented with a situation in which people need to update their situation models. Situation model updating involves an increase in the processing load on working memory resources because a person needs to maintain aspects of the situation that continue to be relevant, remove elements that are no longer relevant, and incorporate new elements that are important in the new situation. This all needs to be done relatively quickly and with a minimum of error in order for successful understanding to be achieved. Despite the general processing difficulties older adults have with working memory and other aspects of cognition, it does not appear that older adults have any greater difficulty with this updating process per se. Research has found that older adults are as effective as younger adults in updating their situation models when there has been a shift in space or time (Radvansky et al., 2003a) or after the successful completion of a character's goal (Radvansky & Curiel, 1998). Thus, older adults are also effective in processing situation models in working memory as well as having preserved abilities in long-term memory.

Not only does long-term memory for situations appear to be well preserved in older adults, but the way that they manage information about a described situation also appears to be similar to that of younger adults. Studies looking at the updating of situation models in working memory with ageing show that, across situational shifts, older adults continue to maintain information that is relevant, and success-fully remove information that has become irrelevant. Thus, there is a preserved ability to handle information in memory when that information is integrated into a person's interpretation of a set of circumstances.

CONCLUSIONS

This chapter has looked at what situation models are and how they influence and are influenced by various memory processes. These situation models are referential representations that capture the circumstances that a text describes; they are not representations of a text itself. Thus, in the real world, these are the memory rep-resentations that people are most likely to use in their day-to-day activities. This is supported by the finding that many memory decisions involve the use of information that is stored in a situation model, and that these sorts of representations are the most enduring. We care about the events that we read about. It is much rarer that we are interested in the language used to describe those events.

Situation models in memory help us integrate not only a text that we may read but also the inferences we draw. By putting all of this information together in a more complete understanding of the world we can improve our memory for those events. Even the active comprehension of events and situations in working memory reflects some of the advantages that can occur when we possess an awareness of the structure of the situation and how it unfolds. This ability is relatively robust. The ability to create and use situation models when comprehending text appears to reflect a more primitive ability to understand situations, and this is used in remembering events that are experienced through film or even in an interactive environment. Furthermore, although there are a number of cognitive declines that accompany age-related changes in the nervous system, we retain the ability to remember the events that we have encountered, even when we only read about those events.

REFERENCES

Anderson, A., Garrod, S.C., & Sanford, A.J. (1983). The accessibility of pronominal antecedents as a function of episode shifts in narrative texts. *Quarterly Journal of Experimental Psychology: Human Experimental Psychology, 35(A),* 427–440.

Anderson, J.R. (1974). Retrieval of propositional information from long-term memory. *Cognitive Psychology, 6,* 451–474.

Barwise, J., & Perry, J. (1983). *Situations and attitudes.* Cambridge, MA: MIT Press.

Bower, G.H., & Morrow, D.G. (1990). Mental models in narrative comprehension. *Science, 247,* 44–48.

Bower, G.H., & Rinck, M. (2001). Selecting one among many referents in spatial mental models. *Journal of Experimental Psychology: Learning, Memory, and Cognition, 27,* 81–98.

Bransford, J.D., Barclay, J.R., & Franks, J.J. (1972). Sentence memory: A constructive versus interpretive approach. *Cognitive Psychology, 3,* 193–209.

Clayton, K., & Habibi, A. (1991). Contribution of temporal contiguity to the spatial priming effect. *Journal of Experimental Psychology: Learning, Memory, and Cognition, 17,* 263–271.

Craik, F.I.M., & Byrd, M. (1982). Aging and cognitive deficits: The role of attentional resources. In F.I.M. Craik & S. Trehaub (Eds.), *Aging and cognitive processes* (pp. 191–211). New York: Plenum Press.

Curiel, J.M., & Radvansky, G.A. (1998). Mental organization of maps. *Journal of Experimental Psychology: Learning, Memory, and Cognition, 24,* 202–214.

Curiel, J.M., & Radvansky, G.A. (2002). Mental maps in memory retrieval and comprehension. *Memory, 10,* 113–126.

Duffy, S.A., Shinjo, M., Myers, J.L. (1990). The effect of encoding task on memory for sentence pairs varying in causal relatedness. *Journal of Memory and Language, 29,* 27–42.

Franklin, N., & Tversky, B. (1990). Searching imagined environments. *Journal of Experimental Psychology: General, 119,* 63–76.

Garnham, A. (1981). Mental models as representations of text. *Memory & Cognition, 9,* 560–565.

Glenberg, A.M., Meyer, M., & Lindem, K. (1987). Situation models contribute to fore-grounding during text comprehension. *Journal of Memory and Language*, 26, 69–83.

Hamm, V.P., & Hasher, L. (1992). Age and the availability of inferences. *Psychology and Aging*, 7, 56–64.

Hasher, L., & Zacks, R.T. (1988). Working memory, comprehension, and aging: A review and a new view. G. Bower (Ed.), *The psychology of learning and motivation: Advances in research and theory*, Vol. 22 (pp. 193–225). San Diego, CA: Academic Press.

Jahn, G. (2004). Three turtles in danger: Spontaneous construction of causally relevant spatial situation models. *Journal of Experimental Psychology: Learning, Memory, and Cognition*, 30, 969–987.

Johnson, R.E. (2003). Aging and the remembering of text. *Developmental Review*, 23, 261–346.

Johnson-Laird, P.N. (1983). *Mental models: Towards a cognitive science of language, inference, and consciousness*. Cambridge, MA: Harvard University Press.

Keenan, J.M., Baillet, S.D., & Brown, P. (1984). The effects of causal cohesion on comprehension and memory. *Journal of Verbal Learning and Verbal Behavior*, 23, 115–126.

Kintsch, W., & Bates, E. (1977). Recognition memory for statements from a classroom lecture. *Journal of Experimental Psychology: Human Learning and Memory*, 3, 150–159.

Kintsch, W., Welsch, D., Schmalhofer, F., & Zimny, S. (1990). Sentence memory: A theoretical analysis. *Journal of Memory and Language*, 29, 133–159.

Lutz, M.F., & Radvansky, G.A. (1997). The fate of completed goal information in narrative comprehension. *Journal of Memory and Language*, 36, 293–310.

Morrow, D.G., Greenspan, S.L., & Bower, G.H. (1987). Accessibility and situation models in narrative comprehension. *Journal of Memory and Language*, 26, 165–187.

Myers, J.L., Shinjo, M., & Duffy, S.A. (1987). Degree of causal relatedness and memory. *Journal of Memory and Language*, 26, 453–465.

Noice, T., & Noice, H. (2002). Very long-term recall and recognition of well-learned material. *Applied Cognitive Psychology*, 16, 259–272.

Radvansky, G.A. (1999). The fan effect: A tale of two theories. *Journal of Experimental Psychology: General*, 128, 198–206.

Radvansky, G.A., & Copeland, D.E. (2000). Functionality and spatial relations in situation models. *Memory & Cognition*, 28, 987–992.

Radvansky, G.A., & Copeland, D.E. (2001). Working memory and situation model updating. *Memory & Cognition*, 29, 1073–1080.

Radvansky, G.A., & Copeland, D.E. (2006). Walking through doorways causes forgetting. *Memory & Cognition*, 34, 1150–1156.

Radvansky, G.A., Copeland, D.E., Berish, D.E., & Dijkstra, K. (2003a). Aging and situation model updating. *Aging, Neuropsychology and Cognition*, 10, 158–166.

Radvansky, G.A., Copeland, D.E., & Von Hippel, W. (2006). *Stereotype activation, prejudice and aging*. Manuscript submitted for publication.

Radvansky, G.A., Copeland, D.E., & Zwaan, R.A. (2003b). Aging and functional spatial relations in comprehension and memory. *Psychology and Aging*, 18, 161–165.

Radvansky, G.A., Copeland, D.E., & Zwaan, R.A. (2005a). A novel study: The mental organization of events. *Memory*, 13, 796–814.

Radvansky, G.A., & Curiel, J.M. (1998). Narrative comprehension and aging: The fate of completed goal information. *Psychology and Aging*, 13, 69–79.

Radvansky, G.A., Gerard, L.D., Zacks, R.T., & Hasher, L. (1990). Younger and older adults' use of mental models as representations for text materials. *Psychology and Aging*, 5, 209–214.

Radvansky, G.A., Spieler, D.H., & Zacks, R.T. (1993). Mental model organization. *Journal of Experimental Psychology: Learning, Memory, and Cognition*, 19, 95–114.

Radvansky, G.A., Wyer, R.S., Curiel, J.C., & Lutz, M.F. (1997). Situation models and abstract ownership relations. *Journal of Experimental Psychology: Learning, Memory, and Cognition, 23*, 1233–1246.

Radvansky, G.A., & Zacks, R.T. (1991). Mental models and the fan effect. *Journal of Experimental Psychology: Learning, Memory, and Cognition, 17*, 940–953.

Radvansky, G.A., Zacks, R.T., & Hasher, L. (1996). Fact retrieval in younger and older adults: The role of mental models. *Psychology and Aging, 11*, 258–271.

Radvansky, G.A., Zacks, R.T., & Hasher, L. (2005b). Age and inhibition: The retrieval of situation models. *Journal of Gerontology: Psychological Sciences, 60B*, 276–278.

Radvansky, G.A., Zwaan, R.A., Curiel, J.M., & Copeland, D.E. (2001). Situation models and aging. *Psychology and Aging, 16*, 145–160.

Radvansky, G.A., Zwaan, R.A., Federico, T., & Franklin, N. (1998). Retrieval from temporally organized situation models. *Journal of Experimental Psychology: Learning, Memory, and Cognition, 24*, 1224–1237.

Rinck, M., & Bower, G.H. (1995). Anaphor resolution and the focus of attention in situation models. *Journal of Memory and Language, 34*, 110–131.

Sachs, J.S. (1967). Recognition memory for syntactic and semantic aspects of connected discourse. *Perception & Psychophysics, 2*, 437–442.

Salthouse, T.A. (1996). The processing-speed theory of adult age differences in cognition. *Psychological Review, 103*, 403–428.

Schmalhofer, F., & Glavanov, D. (1986). Three components of understanding a programmer's manual: Verbatim, propositional, and situational representations. *Journal of Memory and Language, 25*, 279–294.

Singer, M., Halldorson, M., Lear, J.C., & Andrusiak, P. (1992). Validation of causal bridging inferences in discourse understanding. *Journal of Memory and Language, 31*, 507–524.

Suh, S.Y., & Trabasso, T. (1993). Inferences during reading: Converging evidence from discourse analysis, talk-aloud protocols, and recognition priming. *Journal of Memory and Language, 32*, 279–300.

Trabasso, T., & Sperry, L.L. (1985). Causal relatedness and importance of story events. *Journal of Memory and Language, 24*, 595–611.

Trabasso, T., & Van den Broek, P.W. (1985). Causal thinking and the representation of narrative events. *Journal of Memory and Language, 24*, 612–630.

Van den Broek, P. (1994). Comprehension and memory of narrative texts: Inferences and coherence. In M.A. Gernsbacher (Ed.), *Handbook of psycholinguistics* (pp. 539–588). San Diego, CA: Academic Press.

Van Dijk, T.A., & Kintsch, W. (1983). *Strategies in discourse comprehension.* New York: Academic Press.

Wilson, S.G., Rinck, M., McNamara, T.P., Bower, G.H., & Morrow, D.G. (1993). Mental models and narrative comprehension: Some qualifications. *Journal of Memory and Language, 32*, 141–154.

Wyer, R.S., & Radvansky, G.A. (1999). The comprehension and validation of social information. *Psychological Review, 106*, 89–118.

Zwaan, R.A. (1996). Processing narrative time shifts. *Journal of Experimental Psychology: Learning, Memory and Cognition, 22*, 1196–1207.

Zwaan, R.A., Magliano, J.P., & Graesser, A.C. (1995). Dimensions of situation model construction in narrative comprehension. *Journal of Experimental Psychology: Learning, Memory, and Cognition, 21*, 386–397.

Zwaan, R.A., & Radvansky, G.A. (1998). Situation models in language comprehension and memory. *Psychological Bulletin, 123*, 162–185.

Zwaan, R.A., Radvansky, G.A., Hilliard, A.E., & Curiel, J.M. (1998). Constructing multidimensional situation models during reading. *Scientific Studies of Reading, 2*, 199–220.

9 Collaborative and social remembering

Rebecca G. Thompson

If asked to think for a moment about everyday situations that involve the use of memory, many of the situations that come to mind will contain an interpersonal, collaborative component. Humans are social creatures, which means that a large proportion of their cognitive processes take place within social settings. So what are the effects of social interactions on cognitive processes? The common adages "two heads are better than one" and "too many cooks spoil the broth" highlight interesting patterns of human behaviour. They suggest that in some situations the presence of other people facilitates performance, while in others it hinders. The field of social psychology has long been interested in this phenomenon. The classic conformity studies of Asch (1956) and obedience studies of Milgram (1963) draw attention to the detrimental effects that social interactions can have on an individual's performance. However it is only fairly recently that cognitive psychologists (in particular memory researchers) have embraced the idea that the mere presence of others may have an impact on an individual's performance. Memory research has traditionally tested individual participants in isolation. This is because memory processes have generally been regarded as an "intrapersonal phenomenon". While this approach has generated valuable models of human memory processes, it has disregarded any influences that social interactions may have on such memory processes. This is the focus of collaborative memory research.

COLLABORATION ON PHYSICAL TASKS: EXAMPLES FROM SOCIAL PSYCHOLOGY

Before the discussion turns to the impact of collaboration on memory performance, let us consider examples of the effects of collaboration on physical tasks, as these have provided the foundation for collaboration memory research. Ringleman, a psychologist working in Germany in the early part of the 20th century (unpublished work, cited in Moede, 1927), investigated the "social effects" of working with others on a physical rope-pulling task. Ringleman observed that individual participants pulled the rope at a pressure of 63kg. Surprisingly, groups of three pulled the rope at 160kg, only two-and-a-half times greater than the performance of an individual. Groups of eight participants pulled the rope at a pressure of 248kg, less than four times the individual pulling rate. Ringleman's results provide an intriguing contradiction to the intuitive perception that group work will be highly productive. Instead, the results revealed that increasing the number of individuals pulling on the rope was not correlated with an increased level of pressure being exerted on the rope. Latane, Williams, and Harkins (1979) replicated this result using different physical tasks including hand clapping and shouting, and concluded that the sum of the individual performances was greater than group performance, which was later termed *social loafing*.

COLLABORATIVE MEMORY RESEARCH

In its simplest form, the field of collaborative memory research (CMR) explores memory performance in the presence of other people. It attempts to identify the effect that social interactions has on an individual's memory performance. The hypothesis common throughout the research is "does social interaction have a positive (facilitatory) effect, a negative (inhibitory) effect (as in physical tasks), or no effect on performance when compared to either an individual performance or to a predicted level of performance?" In other words, can the product of a collaborative group remembering be greater than the sum of the individual participants' recall? In addition to the overall product of collaborative memory process (how much is recalled), CMR explores features of memory processes that are unique to social settings, features that cannot be observed when individuals work alone on a task. These include; process gain (new information produced as a result of the collaborative setting) and process loss (previous individually recalled information is lost on a subsequent collaborative recall). For the purpose of this chapter the use of the term "group" will be defined as *two or more individuals who actively interact with each other*.

Pooling versus collaboration

If asked to predict the performance of a collaborating group compared to an individual performance, predictions would most probably coincide with the logical intuition that "two heads (or more) are better than one", thus predicting a larger performance for the group. Taken in absolute terms, examples from the literature provide evidence for this, with group performance exceeding individual performance (Stephenson, Clark, & Wade, 1986; Vollrath, Sheppard, Hinsz, & Davis, 1989). However, the observation that a group performance exceeds an individual performance is not conclusive proof that collaboration facilitates performance. This is because collaborating groups have the potential to outperform individuals in the absence of any collaborative processes, simply by the pooling of outputs (e.g., 1+1 = 2; Lorge & Soloman, 1955). For example, if two participants independently learn and recall a 10-item word list, Person A may recall five items, a,b,c,d,e while Person B recalls six items d,e,f,g,h,j. The joint performance, with all things being equal, of Persons A+B in the *absence* of any interaction between Person A and B would be nine items (a,b,c,d,e,f,g,h,j). To account for this CMR draws a clear distinction between "group effects", which result in a larger performance due to pooling of abilities, and "genuine collaborative effects", which are only produced through collaborative processes (Clark, Hori, Putnam, & Martin, 2000).

Collaborating groups versus nominal groups

The distinction between group effects and collaborative effects is achieved experimentally by comparing the performance of collaborating or interacting groups to the performance of nominal or non-interacting groups. Nominal groups are groups in name only and consist of two (or more) individuals who work alone during all phases of an experiment. The performances of the nominal participants are combined during the data analysis stage of the research; two or more nominal participants' data are treated as if they had worked together collaboratively. For example, if nominal participant A recalled items a,b,c,d,e while nominal participant B recalled items d,e,f,g,h,j then the combined performance of participants A and B would be a,b,c,d,e,f,g,h,j. The scores from the nominal group act as a predictor for the performance of a collaborating group. This approach provides a much more informative experimental methodology and has been used in recent collaborative memory studies (e.g., Weldon, Blair, & Huebsch, 2000).

The comparison of nominal and collaborating group performance produces three predictions. (1) If collaboration has *no* effect on performance, collaborative performance will be *equal* to nominal performance. (2) If collaboration *benefits* or *facilitates* performance, then collaborating performance will be *greater than* nominal performance. (3) If collaboration *negatively* affects performance, collaborative performance will be *less than* the nominal group performance.

EXPERIMENTAL METHODOLOGIES IN COLLABORATIVE MEMORY RESEARCH

A variety of experimental methodologies are utilised in CMR. Each has its unique advantages and limitations.

Independent versus repeated measures designs

As in other fields of psychology research, there are two types of experimental design used in CMR. Repeated measures designs require the same participants to complete two (or more) separate testing sessions (Meudell, Hitch, & Boyle, 1995; Meudell, Hitch, & Kirby, 1992; Weldon & Bellinger, 1997), whereas in independent sample designs participants form different groups (i.e., nominal versus collaborative) and are tested only once. Participants in repeated measures methodologies are initially tested individually on the task (first testing session). This allows an individual participant's performance to be established. Additionally this performance forms a baseline level for comparison to subsequent testing sessions (either collaborative or individual). In the second testing session, participants are divided into different groups (collaborative or nominal) to perform the task again. Repeated measures designs are advantageous in terms of allowing the identification of new emergent memories (process gain) and levels of information loss (process loss) to be analysed across trials. Independent designs, on the other hand, utilise a single test session. Participants form two or more groups (nominal, collaborative) and perform the task only once.

Product versus process analysis

The dependent variable of interest also drives the experimental design employed in CMR. Both the overall product produced during collaboration and the processes involved in obtaining the collaborative output are of interest. Determining the product of the group permits the quantitative comparison of the outputs from collaborating versus nominal groups, while the qualitative analysis helps elucidate all of the processes, stages, and steps involved in achieving the collaborative output. This type of analysis allows identification of "process loss" and "process gain". Process loss is defined as items recalled in an initial test session that are not recalled at a subsequent testing session, while process gain incorporates items that were not recalled initially but are recalled during a subsequent session. Steiner (1972) summarises the collaborative output as: *Actual productivity = potential productivity – losses due to faulty processes.*

Collaboration on cognitive tasks

The findings reported from collaboration on physical tasks lead naturally to the question: "Does collaboration affect cognitive performance?" Does the presence of a collaborator negatively affect cognitive performance in the same way as is observed on the physical tasks? Early indications suggesting that this may be the case included studies by Taylor, Berry, and Block (1958) and Dunnette, Campbell, and Jaastad (1963). Both studies compared the performance of brainstorming groups to the performance of nominal groups. Remarkably, the results from both studies concurred with the physical tasks results, i.e., collaborating groups produced fewer novel ideas compared to the pooled performance of individuals working alone during a brainstorming session. Bouchard and Hare (1970) later replicated these findings using a range of group sizes and concluded that group brainstorming "inhibits rather than facilitates creative thinking, and pooled individual effort is a far more productive procedure than group effort" (p. 51).

Collaboration on memory tasks—product analysis

Surprisingly, the counterintuitive findings reported on physical tasks and brainstorming tasks have been reported on memory tasks. The lower performance of a collaborating group when compared to the performance of a nominal group has been robustly reported on a variety of tasks including story recall (Andersson & Rönnberg, 1996) and word list retrieval (Basden, Basden, Bryner, & Thomas, 1997). Weldon and Bellinger (1997) reported that when the performance of collaborating groups is compared to individual performance, collaborating performance exceeds individual performance. However, when collaborating group performance is compared to a nominal group performance on the same task, collaborating performance is lower than that of the nominal group. Weldon and Bellinger replicated this effect on a number of tasks, including semantic picture recall, word recall, and episodic story recall tasks. These findings suggest that although group performance on a memory task is generally greater than individual performance, the social interaction among collaborating group members fails to facilitate performance beyond that predicted by the performance of a nominal groups.

Collaboration on memory tasks—process analysis

In addition to comparing the overall product of collaboration, CMR explores the processes involved in reaching the collaborative output. This involves identifying whether the collaborative process has an effect on the quality of the responses given by participants. Meudell and colleagues state that collaboration can only be considered advantageous if there is a greater amount of new or emergent information produced in collaborating group conditions compared to the individual (and nominal) conditions (in repeated measures designs) (Meudell et al., 1992, 1995). They propose that cross-cueing processes have the potential to play a major role in producing new items during the collaborative process. Meudell and colleagues based their reasoning on the work of Tulving and Pearlstone (1966), who reported that when participants were provided with a category cue at recall (if they were unable to recall an item from a list) they subsequently were able to recall more items than participants who were not provided with category retrieval cues. Tulving suggested that there is a quantifiable difference between the "accessibility" and "availability" of items in memory. To investigate new item production in collaboration, Meudell and colleagues (1992, 1995) employed a repeated measures procedure on a categorised word list retrieval task. Participants first recalled a word list individually (R1), followed by a subsequent recall (R2), which was performed either collaboratively or individually again. Meudell et al. (1995) reported that collaborating groups did not produce more new items from the word list than the individual participants, despite being provided with the opportunity to cross-cue each other with word list categories as a natural part of the collaborative process. Other manipulations revealed that the failure of collaborating participants to cross-cue each other was not related to task complexity or the familiarity of the stimulus. Meudell et al. (1995) concluded that the collaborating participants appeared to reminisce their individual performance jointly rather than generating "cues" to cross-cue the collaborator in an attempt to access previously unavailable materials. Further evidence for the lack of cross-cueing between collaborating individuals is provided by Basden, Basden, and Henry (2000). Similarly Clark et al. (2000) argued that effective cross-cueing between individuals that can result in new memory production is a very rare phenomenon. The reason for this is that for Person A's retrieval cues to trigger new memories in Person B, the retrieval cues have to be more effective for Person B than they are for Person A. This reasoning is in line with the work of Mantyla and Nilsson (1983), among others, who state that one's own retrieval cues are the most effective at cueing production of information from memory.

ACCURACY OF COLLABORATIVE MEMORY RECALL

The accuracy of collaborative output has been detrimentally affected in certain situations and improved in others. Using a simulation of a police interrogation, Stephenson et al. (1986) reported an overall higher accuracy of the collaborating groups' performance compared to individual performance. However, the collaborating groups were overconfident in the accuracy of the inaccurate responses they gave. This effect was more prevalent in an immediate recall condition compared to a delayed recall condition. Similarly Basden, Basden, Thomas, and Souphasith (1998) reported that collaborating groups of participants made more false intrusions in their memory output than did the nominal groups. These findings suggest that working collaboratively may decrease the threshold for accepting an erroneous response into a memory recall. Additionally, group members may become more responsive to normative influences, resulting in a tendency for the group members to go along with others' responses even if these contradict an individual's own beliefs.

Numerous other examples are cited in the collaborative memory literature of the reduced accuracy of collaborative group output. Schneider and Watkins (1996) reported "response conformity" in a recognition memory test. Participants working in pairs had to give a positive or negative response to a list of words (a positive response was given to words presented previously and a negative response to new words). The results revealed that participants produced responses that "conformed" to the previous participant's response regardless of whether this response was correct or incorrect. In order to control the number of positive and negative responses given, Schneider and Watkins replaced one of the participants with a confederate. Despite this, an identical pattern of results was found. Wright, Self, and Justice (2000) demonstrated that erroneous post-event information presented by another participant lowered the accuracy of an individual's memory report. Furthermore, Roediger, Meade, and Bergman (2001) investigated the effects of misinformation on collaborating participant pairs (one participant and one confederate). Participants were shown a common household scene, containing a variety of common objects. The scene was presented for either a short duration (15 seconds) or a long duration (60 seconds). During a collaborative recall test participants had to recall six items from the scene. The confederate occasionally presented false information (objects that were not presented in the scene). After a brief delay all participants free recalled the items from the scene. Participants who had worked with a collaborator made a larger number of intrusion errors than the control participants. Additionally, more errors were produced in the short study duration than in the longer study duration, suggesting that a participant's confidence in their responses (more confidence associated with longer exposure durations) had an effect on the extent to which erroneous information was accepted into their subsequent report.

Contrary to the above, Clark et al. (2000) reported that the accuracy of responses on a recognition memory task was facilitated through collaboration. They reported that collaborating groups correctly identified more target items than did the nominal groups. However, this collaborative facilitation did not extend to the rejection of distractor items. These results, on a recognition memory task, are in contrast to collaborative performance on free recall memory tasks. Clark hypothesises that free recall tasks are too restrictive in nature and therefore not conducive to collaboration. For Person A to be able to influence Person B's memory, Person A has to recall an item or produce a retrieval cue that Person B failed to recall for the process of collaboration to be beneficial (in terms of generating new materials). However, for recognition performance to be considered beneficial, Person A has only to argue successfully that they remember seeing a presented item previously for it to be accepted by Person B. Therefore there are fewer cognitive demands placed on the collaborating individuals during a collaborative task.

Additionally, Ross, Spencer, Linardatos, Lam, and Perunovic (2004) reported that when older adults collaborated on naturalistic shopping list recall tasks (with their spouse) fewer errors were produced compared to the nominal groups (although nominal performance was greater than collaborative). Ross et al. suggest that the process of collaboration leads to participants attaching a higher level of certainty to information given, thereby increasing the accuracy of responses. Therefore the accuracy of the collaborative output is dependent upon both participant and task variables.

COLLABORATIVE INHIBITION: A COUNTERINTUITIVE PARADIGM

The collaborative memory studies detailed above show that despite the output of a collaborating group being larger than an individual performance, the collaborating group performance does not exceed the predicted performance of a nominal group. This is in terms of the overall product of collaboration and in the quality of the information recalled or produced. This intriguing counterintuitive effect has been termed "collaborative inhibition" (CI) as shown in Figure 9.1.

Social explanations of collaborative inhibition (CI)

Explanations of CI fall into two categories: social and cognitive. Social explanations propose that CI results from low levels of motivation between group participants to work together and poor coordination between them to achieve the aims and goals of the task (see Steiner's theory of process loss—Steiner, 1972). Latane et al.'s (1979) social loafing theory offers a related example of CI, stating that an individual in a group situation may work less efficiently compared to when working alone. This reduction in productivity is assumed to be due to a decrease in the perception of accountability held by an individual for the group output.

Paulus and Dzindolet (1993) claim that the lower performance of brainstorming groups (compared to nominal groups) is directly influenced by social factors arising

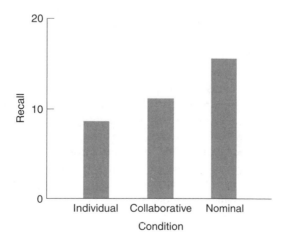

Figure 9.1 An example of collaborative inhibition where collaborative performance exceeds individual performance but is less than the performance of the nominal group. From Thompson 2002, unpublished dissertation.

from the interaction between group members during the collaborative process. Paulus et al. presented collaborating participants with information concerning the performance of other "external" collaborating groups. Knowledge that the external collaborating groups were performing to a lower level reduced the performance of the collaborating group, suggesting that the inhibited productivity of collaborating groups may result from members of the group attempting to match their performance to other group members or even to external groups (if this is known).

Cognitive explanations of collaborative inhibition

Cognitive explanations attempt to unravel the factors influencing CI because social explanations such as low levels of motivation do not comprehensively account for the full range of reported findings. For example, Weldon (2000) manipulated levels of motivation in collaborating individuals in three ways: (1) offering monetary rewards ($60) to the group who recalled the most information during a task; (2) setting a minimum level of retrieval required from a group before participants were allowed to leave an experiment; (3) increasing group cohesion before the collaborative task was undertaken. Despite high levels of motivation between group members to complete the task, collaborating groups of participants still failed to outperform the nominal groups (although in some cases increases in motivation did increase overall recall).

Furthermore, Finlay, Hitch, and Meudell (2000) provided additional evidence that CI results from more than poor levels of motivation and coordination of goal objectives. In a three-stage successive free recall experiment, they reported that material recalled individually in test 1 was lost (not recalled) when participants worked collaboratively in test 2. Importantly, the lost material was later recovered when working again alone in phase three of the experiment. This suggests a transient disruption in retrieval of previously available materials as a direct result of the collaborative process. However, the most convincing evidence available to date that CI is likely to be the result of cognitive processes is provided by Wright and Klumpp (2004). In this study participants either worked individually or in pairs (where a strict turn-taking procedure was employed). Participants recalled (by writing down) a list of previously studied words. Participant pairs were either shown or not shown what their collaborator had written down. CI was observed in participants' recall when shown the recalled items, while performance in the not-shown participants equalled the nominal group performance. This finding suggests that it is exposure to the product of a collaborator's recall that is disruptive rather than the being in the presence of a collaborator.

Each of the cognitive explanations centres on the notion that each individual in a collaborative situation is equipped with a unique set of strategies and techniques to retrieve information from their memory. However, these strategies are extremely vulnerable to disruption, which includes the presence of a collaborator and their retrieval cues.

Retrieval strategy disruption

Retrieval strategy disruption, or interference with one's ability to reconstruct knowledge from memory, has been proposed as an explanation. Central to this explanation is the concept of retrieval cue ineffectiveness (Mantyla & Nilsson, 1983). Mantyla stated that an individual's own retrieval cues are the most effective at cueing memory retrieval. In contrast, retrieval cues generated externally by other individuals (including a collaborator) are less effective at cueing recall from memory. Therefore a collaborator's retrieval cues are redundant and their presence is disruptive.

Evaluation apprehension and production blocking

An alternative explanation is "evaluation apprehension" proposed by Diehl and Stroebe (1991). In a series of four experiments Diehl et al. concluded that collaborating participants often experience evaluation apprehension. This means that collaborating participants set a high criterion for selecting which items are to be recalled and produced publicly. As a result they hold back and inhibit potential contributions in an attempt to avoid the embarrassment of producing an erroneous response in front of group members or peers. This in turn reduces the overall productivity of the group. Earlier work by Diehl and Strobe (1987) suggested that while members of a group wait to respond with their contributions (as a natural part of a group process), disruption occurs to their thought processes. This disruption directly reduces the group output and is termed "production blocking".

Part set cueing

Comparisons are frequently cited in the collaborative memory research between the negative effects of collaboration and the disruption caused to memory retrieval during the part set cueing phenomenon (Basden & Basden, 1995; Meudell et al., 1995). Reduced levels of recall (inhibition) are robustly reported in part set cueing experiments. A typical part set cueing task has two phases. In the first, participants study a set of to-be-remembered stimuli. In a second phase, individual participants recall the information in one of two conditions: (1) free recall the information, or (2) are provided with part of the to-be-remembered list as a cue to recall. However, rather than aiding memory, the presentation of part of the list actually inhibits recall, i.e. participants recall fewer of the remaining non-cued items. It is reasoned that additional exposure to part of the list strengthens the representation of these items within the memory system. Therefore stronger traces are formed for the cued items, which in return inhibits the retrieval of the non-cued items (Rundus, 1973).

Basden et al. (1997) explored the hypothesis that the responses of collaborating individuals act as part set cues for their collaborators. They reported that CI was greater for categorised lists of words with a few categories and lots of examples per category, rather than a larger number of categories with fewer items per category. Basden et al. claimed that the larger lists experienced more CI as retrieval strategies are vitally important in such a list. Additionally, CI was reduced when participants were forced to organise their output by category, thus minimising retrieval disruption.

Cognitive overload

An alternative cognitive explanation of CI is that the collaborative process places heavy demands on the working memory system. Collaborating individuals are required to coordinate their personal thought processes with those of their collaborator. Thus the price of the increase in demands placed on the processing resources of the working memory system is an inhibited output.

Reduction of collaborative inhibition

Can anything be done to reduce CI and promote productive collaborative interactions? A number of studies have focused on situational variables (tasks demands) and individual variables (age and gender of the collaborating participant) that may achieve this, and these will now be addressed in turn.

Friends vs non-friends

Andersson and Rönnberg (1995, 1996, 1997) report differential effects of collaboration on different group constellations. On a free recall task, collaborating groups of friends displayed less CI than groups of unacquainted individuals (strangers). However, as in previous studies, neither collaborating group (friend or strangers) outperformed the nominal group performance (Andersson & Rönnberg, 1995). Andersson and Rönnberg propose that over time friends develop a unique, implicit and highly specific way of communicating and sharing ideas with each other and this reduces the levels of CI experienced during a collaborative recall. The lack of this knowledge places collaborating groups of strangers at a disadvantage. This reasoning is similar to the concept of a transactive memory system (Wegner, Raymond, & Erber, 1991), which forms a unique distributed memory system held between friends or couples. The joint memory system is greater and more powerful than the individual member's memory. Group members can act as external memory aids or systems for each other.

In addition to acting as an external memory aid, friends develop familiar body language and methods of communicating with each other that can optimise exchange of information and may facilitate memory retrieval. Interestingly, Andersson (2001) reported no gender differences in the negative effects of CI, which suggests that men and women are affected negatively to the same extent during the collaborative process. To summarise, although studies suggest that working with a friend reduces CI, it does not reverse the effect to allow collaborating performance to exceed that of the nominal group.

Task demands: Semantic vs episodic and explicit vs implicit tasks

The extent to which CI is observed is shown to be related to the type of materials used in the collaborative task. If we briefly consider everyday collaborative memory situations, a pattern of situations emerge that draw or rely upon a shared knowledge base such as a jointly shared experience or historical event. These events are considered to be semantic in nature. Therefore the nature of everyday collaborative tasks is in contrast to the tasks that have been used in the collaborative memory literature, most of which are based on episodic memory tasks, e.g., encoding and subsequent recall of unrelated word lists or story recall tasks. It is therefore of theoretical interest to explore the effects of collaboration on a range of memory tasks, including those that have a rich, interconnected, meaningful, and shared semantic structure.

Collaboration on semantic memory tasks

Semantic memories and information includes general knowledge that has been acquired over a long period of time. Unlike episodic information, semantic knowledge is not explicitly linked to a temporal context (Tulving, 1972). Additionally, it forms the basis of shared personal information. Due to the rich, interconnected, shared nature of semantic materials it is logical to reason that it may be possible to produce efficient retrieval cues during a collaborative process that may cue the production of new emergent memories. This is something that appears to be unachievable when using episodic materials. Because semantic information has rich interconnections with other information stored in the memory system, it is also reasonable to assume that when retrieval cues are produced for the materials, they have the potential to be expanded upon by the other members of the collaborating group. This expansion in return has the potential to trigger memory production in other members of the group. This is in contrast to the cues generated for episodic information, which are considered to be ineffective at cueing retrieval of information from a collaborator's memory. Andersson and Rönnberg (1996) reported that a semantic task (a 20-item semantic memory test for historical information) was less affected by CI than an episodic task (a historical story learning and recall task). With collaborating group performance on the semantic task equalling the nominal group performance, there was an absence of CI. However, on the episodic story recall task, collaborative memory performance was lower than the nominal performance, demonstrating the presence of CI. Similarly, Weldon (2000) reported results from a pilot study that revealed a positive effect (facilitation) was observed on a collaborative general knowledge task where collaborating groups (of three participants) performed better on the task than the nominal groups.

Why is there a difference between episodic and semantic tasks?

The differential patterns of performance on episodic and semantic collaborative tasks can be linked back to the retrieval cue effectiveness hypothesis. The retrieval of semantic information can be achieved with relatively unspecific retrieval cues. This is because semantic knowledge draws on a rich interconnected knowledge database, so there are many potential routes to access the information. However, episodic information represents knowledge relating to a specific episode, and access to this information requires very specific retrieval cues. The information is thought to be less organised and more weakly represented within the memory system, thereby increasing the need for retrieval cues that are specific enough to access the information. This is difficult enough for oneself and becomes even more difficult when trying to produce an effective retrieval cue for a collaborator.

Cued vs free recall tasks

As well as a difference in the type of materials used in collaborative memory (episodic vs semantic), there are also differences in the task demands used, the main one being the type of retrieval strategies required to complete the task (e.g., free recall versus cued recall). Weldon (2000) speculated that an effective way to reduce levels of CI is to use cued recall tasks. Cued recall tasks provide a cue and retrieval context for recall process. An example of a cued recall task is a word-stem completion task. In this task participants are provided with the first couple of letters or an incomplete letter string (the stem) of the to-be-remembered word as a cue to retrieval (e.g., TR_ _ _ for TRAIN). Providing a retrieval cue at test reduces reliance on individual retrieval strategies as the cued recall test *"provides distinctive, direct, target specific information to facilitate retrieval"* (Weldon, 2000, p. 104), therefore bypassing disruption to an individual's retrieval strategies. Free recall tasks, on the other hand, allow an individual to recall previously learnt items in any order. This permits an individual to search their memory randomly for items, a technique unique and specific to each individual. Therefore when such collaborative memory tasks are used it is unlikely that there will be consistency between the recall strategies of the members of the collaborating group.

Collaborative relationships and task demands

Andersson and Rönnberg (1996) reported an interaction between the task demands (episodic vs semantic) and the relationship between the collaborators (friends, spouses, and strangers). No difference was reported between the performance of collaborating friends and strangers on a semantic memory task. However, the friends outperformed the strangers on the episodic task. It is reasoned that this is due to the semantic information being drawn from a shared knowledge base, which makes it easier to generate retrieval cues that are effective for a collaborator (even when they are a stranger). Therefore the effect of friendship is not universal across all collaborative memory tasks.

Encoding specificity

A further attempt to minimise CI has been to ensure that the learning and retrieval contexts of materials are congruent. Tulving and Thomson (1973) proposed the encoding specificity hypothesis, which states that a rich encoding context (or learning environment) that is congruent with the retrieval context promotes efficient memory retrieval. Therefore CI might be the result of a mismatch between the initial encoding context of the information (typically experienced individually) and the retrieval context, which occurs in the presence of one or more collaborators. In support of this, Andersson and Rönnberg (1995) identified that when collaborating, individuals encoded to-be-remembered items together (in an episodic task) and they actually outperformed the nominal groups. Similarly, Finlay et al. (2000) reported reduced levels of CI when collaborating participants encoded the test materials together in a similar order, compared to when the test materials were encoded individually but recalled collaboratively. These results suggests that individuals who encode the test materials together (reducing the mismatch between encoding and retrieval contexts) are able to produce similar representations of the information, which subsequently enables them to produce more efficient retrieval cues for their collaborator.

Group size

The number of individuals in a collaborating group has been identified as being influential in determining the presence or absence of CI. Groups of two participants (dyads) generate a performance level that is usually equal to the nominal performance. Therefore, by definition, dyads do not exhibit CI (see Andersson & Rönnberg, 1995; Meudell et al., 1992, 1995). However, when group size is increased to three individuals or larger (triads plus), the negative effects of collaboration become evident; collaborating group performance < nominal performance (see Basden et al., 1997, 2000; Weldon & Bellinger, 1997). The reduction of group performance as a function of group size can be linked to Steiner's (1972) process loss hypothesis: As group size increases, the efficiency and cohesion of communication between group members lessens, making it harder to communicate groups goals. Additionally, members of large collaborating groups will have less opportunity to make individual contributions. As the formality of responding during group situations increases, group productivity suffers. Steiner proposed that process loss will be reduced as long as individuals have a clear understanding of their unique role and contribution to group process.

AGE DIFFERENCES IN COLLABORATIVE AND SOCIAL REMEMBERING

All of the research detailed above (with the exception of Ross et al., 2004) has been conducted on young adults, typically undergraduate students. Therefore the effect that collaboration has on different age populations is of interest. However, in comparison to the studies discussed above this topic has received relatively little attention. It could be hypothesised that the presence of CI and the failure to generate new information through cross-cueing is a direct result of the restrictive use of young adults as participants. Therefore a number of interesting questions are raised, including: Do collaborating young adults compete with collaborators rather than engaging fully in the task? Do young adults feel inhibited in the presence of strangers? Are the younger adults performing to an optimum level of performance in the initial testing session of a repeated measures design, leaving little scope for gain in a subsequent test session? It is impossible to answer any of these questions simply by considering the research discussed above. Thus the discussion now turns to a review of collaborative memory studies in young (<16 years) and older (>65 years) individuals.

Collaborative memory in children

Unfortunately, there appear to be only two studies on the effects of collaboration on the memory performance of children. This lack of research is a shame, as collaboration and any potential effects hold significant implications for the education process. In the first study, Andersson (2001) reported that collaboration negatively affected performance on a spatial recognition memory task in collaborating dyads of 7-year-olds and 15-year-olds. However, the negative effects of collaboration were reduced when participants worked with a friend. Less negative effects (i.e., CI) were reported in the collaborating 15-year-olds compared to the 7-year-olds.

In the second study, Leman and Oldham (2005) reported an opposite pattern of results, with younger children being less affected by the collaborative process than older children. Leman and Oldham investigated the collaborative memory performance of 7- and 9-year-olds on an episodic word list recall task. In this task the participants were read aloud a list of words, followed by a 2-minute silence. Participants were then asked to recall the words aloud either collaboratively or individually. There were three collaborative groups: two 7-year-olds, two 9-year-olds, or one 7-year-old and one 9-year-old; participants in these groups performed this task together, while participants in the nominal groups performed the task alone. Unlike the results observed in young adult participants, no CI was observed in the 7-year-olds; their collaborative performance equalled that of the nominal groups. CI was observed, however, in collaborating groups of 9-year-olds and in the mixed-age groups (a 7-year-old and a 9-year-old). The study suggests that CI does not affect younger children to the same extent as older children.

Collaborative memory and the older adult

There is emerging evidence that suggests that when older adults collaborate and actively interact with others whilst performing a cognitive task (especially a memory task) their performance does not display the same patterns of cognitive inhibition as observed in younger adults. In some older adults' studies performance is facilitated (Ross et al., 2004; Thompson, 2002), while in others, under certain conditions performance of the collaborating participants equals the nominal groups (see Johansson, Andersson, & Rönnberg, 2005). Research also suggests that older adults approach the collaborative task differently to young adults, which results in them utilising the collaborative situation positively in order to compensate for the everyday cognitive difficulties associated with the healthy ageing process (Dixon, 1999).

The cognitive ageing literature provides evidence for a number of deficits in a variety of cognitive domains, including decreases in episodic memory, working memory capacity, and processing speed. It is generally accepted that older adults perform at a lower level than younger adults on many laboratory-based memory tasks. However, in contrast to the laboratory-observed deficits in cognitive performance, older adults maintain high levels of functioning outside the laboratory, i.e., in the real world. Therefore it is of theoretical interest to identify the processes underlying these contradictory patterns of behaviour, and collaboration may perhaps play a role.

Collaboration as a compensation strategy

Dixon (1999) proposed that the process of collaboration and the presence of a collaborator (equipped with their retrieval cues) may act as a compensatory mechanism/buffer for age-related cognitive decline. Compensatory mechanisms operate by replacing a redundant or ineffective mechanism or strategy with one that is effective, which helps promote a higher level of cognitive performance. Compensatory mechanisms take numerous forms, including: structural mechanisms, where alternative areas of the older adult's brain are recruited when performing a cognitive task (e.g., Cabeza et al., 1997); internal strategies, including mnemonics (e.g., method of loci); and external compensatory mechanisms, including memory prompts (diaries, calendars). Research has identified that older adults benefit and rely more on the use of external memory aids, compared to younger adults who generally use internal memory strategies (Maylor, 1990). Craik, Anderson, Kerr, and Li (1995) claim that older adults are "less able to 'self initiate' effective encoding and retrieval operations, but if such operations are guided and supported by the external environment, they can perform quite well" (p. 218). Additionally, Backman (1996) reported that older adults' memory performance maintains "a reserve of abilities" and this potential can be accessed through the use of various training strategies (including organisation and mnemonic strategies).

Dixon (1999) proposed that collaboration offers an ecologically valid example of an external memory aid/compensatory mechanism, with the presence of another individual or a collaborator providing a source of "online" metacognition, constantly monitoring and providing feedback on responses and strategies produced to maximise performance.

Collaborative expertise hypothesis

Dixon (1999) additionally suggested that older adults possess a level of "collaborative expertise". This is the result of a lifetime of experience in collaborative situations. It is suggested that this collaborative expertise may promote the production of more efficient retrieval cues by the older adult during a collaborative situations. To investigate this, Dixon and Backman (1993) compared the collaborative story recall performance of older adult married couples who had been married for 40 years plus, to that of young adult married couples and older adult unacquainted dyads. Of particular interest was whether the collaborative expertise of the older adults could lead to an increase in accuracy and efficiency. It was reported that married older couples performed as well as married young couples in the overall gist recall of a story. However, older adult unacquainted pairings performed less well than did the young adults. This suggests that the married older adults were able to draw from their shared "resource bank" in order to complete the task and overcome the age-related deficits in performance.

Collaborative memory in older adults: Empirical evidence

Gould and Dixon (1993) reported qualitative differences in the performance of collaborating older adult married couples and collaborating young adult married couples on a story-retelling task concerning the last vacation the participants had taken together. The main difference was the number of words used to express events in the story: Older adults used more words and non-recall statements to describe an event than the younger adults. This result should be considered with reference to the everyday word-finding problems experienced by many older adults. However, the additional verbiage may be advantageous in some situations in terms of providing elaborations and extra details that may prompt memory recall in collaborating participants.

Dixon and Gould (1998) reported evidence that both young and older adults benefited from the presence of an unacquainted collaborator when retelling a complex narrative compared to the same-aged nominal participants, suggesting that older adults may benefit from performing episodic memory tasks in the presence of others in real-life everyday situations. Comparison of young and older adult married couples on the same task revealed similar levels of performance for the two age conditions, further supporting the notion that age-related cognitive decline could be compensated for when older adults are able to collaborate on cognitive tasks.

Dixon, Fox, Trevithick, and Brudin (1997) investigated collaborative problem solving in young and older adults on a fixed and unrestricted problem-solving task. In the fixed task participants had to identify a single object from a 42-object display. Participants were allowed to ask 20 questions (with yes/no answers) in order to identify the object in the fixed task and solve the unrestricted task. It was reported that older adults produced a larger number of inefficient hypothesis scanning questions than did the young adults in an attempt to reach the solution. However, both the young and older adults produced similar levels of efficient questions. This suggests that collaborative problem-solving is beneficial for older adults.

Using a naturalistic design (as opposed to the laboratory tasks described above), Johansson, Andersson, and Rönnberg (2000) investigated collaborative memory performance on a retrospective memory task that required older adult participants to recall episodic information learnt during a visit to a university campus. During the same visit participants completed a prospective memory task, which involved performing a number of actions during their visit (i.e., reminding the experimenter to fetch a book from the library). The performance of three dyad groups of older adult participants was compared (married couples, unacquainted dyads and nominal dyads). It was reported that the collaborating groups suffered from collaboration compared to the nominal participants on both the prospective and retrospective memory tasks. Interestingly, the performance of the married couple dyads did not display a reduction in CI as has previously been shown in younger adults, although a subpopulation of the married couples that reported a strong reliance on transactive memory performed at the same level as the nominal group. Similarly, Ross et al. (2004) reported increased accuracy in the performance of collaborating older adults on a shopping list recall task, despite the collaborating group performance being less than that of the nominal performance overall. The results of Johansson et al. and Ross et al. suggest that an active and supportive spouse or collaborator may indeed help to boost memory performance on tasks of everyday remembering for healthy older adults.

CONCLUSIONS

The study of collaborative memory provides an excellent insight into how the presence of others impacts on what and how information is retrieved from memory. Taken at face value, two heads are certainly better than one; when people recall together, the amount recalled is more than by a solitary individual. However, this observation arises from nothing more than the simple pooling of individual performances (group processes) rather than as a result of any true collaborative processes. This is revealed when the performance of a collaborating group is compared to the predicted performance of a nominal group. On a variety of tasks the performance of collaborating groups is shown to be equal to or less than that of the nominal group, and this affect is intensified as group size is increased. Therefore it appears that too many cooks really do spoil the broth. This counterintuitive observation has been termed "collaborative inhibition".

However, it cannot be concluded that the negative affect of collaboration is a universal phenomenon; rather the effects are dependent upon the age of participants (children, young adults, and older adults) and the task demands (episodic versus semantic and cued versus free recall). Young adults experience collaborative inhibition to a greater extent than older adults, who appear to benefit from the collaborative process under certain situations (e.g., increased accuracy of responses). Similarly, semantic memory tasks and cued recall tasks are more suited to a collaborative recall situation than are episodic memory tasks and free recall tasks.

REFERENCES

Andersson, J. (2001). Net effect of memory collaboration: How is collaboration affected by factors such as friendship, gender and age? *Scandinavian Journal of Psychology, 42*, 367–375.

Andersson, J., & Rönnberg, J. (1995). Recall suffers from collaboration: Joint recall effects of friendship and task complexity. *Applied Cognitive Psychology, 9*, 199–211.

Andersson, J., & Rönnberg, J. (1996). Collaboration and memory: Effects of dyadic retrieval on different memory tasks. *Applied Cognitive Psychology, 10*, 171–181.

Andersson, J., & Rönnberg, J. (1997). Cued memory collaboration: Effects of friendship and type of retrieval cue. *European Journal of Cognitive Psychology, 9*, 273–287.

Asch, S.E. (1956). Studies of the independence and submission to group pressure: 1: A minority of one against a unanimous majority. *Psychological Monographs, 70*, Whole No. 416.

Backman, L. (1996). Utilizing compensatory task conditions for episodic memory in Alzheimer's disease. *Acta Neurologica Scandinavia Supplement, 165*, 109–113.

Basden, D.R., & Basden, B.H. (1995). Some tests of the strategy disruption interpretation of part-list cuing inhibition. *Journal of Experimental Psychology: Learning, Memory and Cognition, 21*, 1656–1669.

Basden, B.H., Basden, D.R., Bryner, S., & Thomas, R.L. (1997). A comparison of group and individual remembering: Does collaboration disrupt retrieval strategies? *Journal of Experimental Psychology: Learning, Memory, and Cognition, 23*, 1176–1189.

Basden, B.H., Basden, D.R., & Henry, S. (2000). Costs and benefits of collaborative remembering. *Applied Cognitive Psychology, 14*, 497–507.

Basden, B.H., Basden, D.R., Thomas, R.L., & Souphasith, S. (1998). Memory distortion in group recall. *Current Psychology: Developmental, Learning, Personality, 16*, 225–246.

Bouchard, T.J., & Hare, M. (1970). Size, performance, and potential in brainstorming groups. *Journal of Applied Psychology, 54*, 51–55.

Cabeza, R., Grady, C.L., Nyberg, L., McIntosh, A.R., Tulving, E., Kapur, S., Jennings, J.M., Houle, S., & Craik, F.I.M. (1997). Age-related differences in neural activity during memory encoding and retrieval: A Positron Emission Tomography study. *The Journal of Neuroscience, 17*, 391–400.

Clark, S.E., Hori, A., Putnam, A., & Martin, T.P. (2000). Group collaboration in recognition memory. *Journal of Experimental Psychology: Learning, Memory and Cognition, 26*, 1578–1588.

Craik, F.I.M., Anderson, N.D., Kerr, S.A., & Li, K.Z.H. (1995). Memory changes in normal aging. In A.D. Baddeley, B.A. Wilson, & F.N. Watts, (Eds.), *Handbook of memory disorders* (pp. 211–241). Chichester, UK: Wiley.

Diehl, M., & Stroebe, W. (1987). Productivity loss in brainstorming groups: Toward the solution of a riddle. *Journal of Personality and Social Psychology, 53,* 497–509.

Diehl, M., & Stroebe, W. (1991). Productivity loss in idea-generating groups: Tracking down the blocking effect. *Journal of Personality and Social Psychology, 61,* 392–403.

Dixon, R.A. (1999). Exploring cognition in interactive situations; the aging of N+1 minds. In T.M. Hess & F. Blanchard-Fields (Eds.), *Social cognition and aging* (pp. 267–289). San Diego, CA: Academic Press.

Dixon, R.A., & Backman, L. (1993). The concept of compensation in cognitive aging: The case of prose processing in adulthood. *International Journal of Aging and Human Development, 36,* 199–217.

Dixon, R.A., Fox, D.P., Trevithick, L., & Brudin, R. (1997). Exploring collaborative problem solving in adulthood. *Journal of Adult Development, 4,* 195–208.

Dixon, R.A., & Gould, O.N. (1998) Younger and older adults collaborating on retelling everyday stories. *Applied Developmental Science, 2,* 160–171.

Dunnette, M.D., Campbell, J., & Jaastad, K. (1963). The effects of group participation on brainstorming effectiveness for two industrial samples. *Journal of Applied Psychology, 47,* 30–37.

Finlay, F., Hitch, G.J., & Meudell, P.R. (2000). Mutual inhibition in collaborative recall: Evidence for a retrieval-based account. *Journal of Experimental Psychology: Learning, Memory and Cognition, 26,* 1556–1567.

Gould, O.N., & Dixon, R.A. (1993). How we spent our vacation: Collaborative storytelling by young and old adults. *Psychology and Aging, 8,* 10–17.

Johansson, A., Andersson, J., & Rönnberg, J. (2000). Do elderly couples have a better prospective memory than other elderly people when they collaborate? *Applied Cognitive Psychology, 14,* 121–133.

Johansson, A., Andersson, J., & Rönnberg, J. (2005). Compensating strategies in collaborative remembering in very old couples. *Scandinavian Journal of Psychology, 46,* 349–359.

Latane, B., Williams, K., & Harkins, S. (1979). Many hands make light work: The causes and consequences of social loafing. *Journal of Personality and Social Psychology, 37,* 822–832.

Leman, P.J., & Oldham, Z. (2005). Do children need to learn to collaborate? The effect of age and age differences on collaborative recall. *Cognitive Development, 20,* 33–48.

Lorge, I., & Soloman, H. (1955). Two models of group behaviour in the solution of Eureka-type problems. *Psychometrika, 20,* 139–148.

Mantyla, T., & Nilsson, L.G. (1983). Are my cues better than your cues? *Scandinavian Journal of Psychology, 24,* 303–312.

Maylor, E.A. (1990). Age and prospective memory. *Quarterly Journal of Experimental Psychology, 42A,* 471–493.

Meudell, P.R., Hitch, G.J., & Boyle, M.M. (1995). Collaboration in recall: Do pairs of people cross-cue each other to produce new memories? *The Quarterly Journal of Experimental Psychology, 48A,* 141–152.

Meudell, P.R., Hitch, G.J., & Kirby, P. (1992). Are two heads better than one? Experimental investigations of the social facilitation of memory. *Applied Cognitive Psychology, 6,* 525–543.

Milgram, S. (1963). Behavioural study of obedience. *Journal of Abnormal and Social Psychology, 67,* 391–398.

Moede, W. (1927). Die Richtlinien der Leistungs-psychologie. *Industrielle Psychotechnik, 4,* 193–207.

Paulus, P.B., & Dzindolet, M.T. (1993) Social-influence processes in group brainstorming. *Journal of Personality and Social Psychology, 64,* 575–586

Roediger, H.L., Meade, M.L., & Bergman, E.T. (2001). Social contagion of memory. *Psychonomic Bulletin & Review, 8,* 365–371.

Ross, M., Spencer, S.J., Linardatos, L., Lam, K.C.H., & Perunovic, M. (2004). Going shopping and identifying landmarks: Does collaboration improve older people's memory? *Applied Cognitive Psychology, 18*, 683–696.

Rundus, D. (1973). Negative effects of using list items as recall cues. *Journal of Verbal Learning and Behavior, 12*, 43–50.

Schneider, D.M., & Watkins, M.J. (1996). Response conformity in recognition testing. *Psychonomic Bulletin & Review, 3*, 481–485.

Steiner, I.D. (1972). *Group process and productivity.* New York: Academic Press.

Stephenson, G.M., Clark, N.K., & Wade, G.S. (1986). Meetings make evidence? An experimental study of collaborative and individual recall of a stimulated police interrogation. *Journal of Personality and Social Psychology, 50*, 1113–1122.

Taylor, D.W., Berry, P.C., & Block, C.H. (1958). Does brainstorming facilitate or inhibit creative thinking? *Administrative Science Quarterly, 3*, 23–47.

Thompson, R.G. (2002). *Collaborative memory in young and older adults.* Unpublished doctoral dissertation, Bristol University.

Tulving, E. (1972). Episodic and semantic memory. In E. Tulving & W. Donaldson (Eds.), *Organization of memory* (pp. 382–404). New York: Academic Press.

Tulving, E., & Pearlstone, Z. (1966). Availability versus accessibility of information in memory for words. *Journal of Verbal Learning and Verbal Behavior, 5*, 381–391.

Tulving, E., & Thomson, D.M. (1973). Encoding specificity and retrieval processes in episodic memory. *Psychological Review, 80*, 352–373.

Vollrath, D.A., Sheppard, B.H., Hinsz, V.B., & Davis, J.H. (1989). Memory performance by decision-making groups and individuals. *Organizational Behaviour and Human Decision Processes, 43*, 289–300.

Wegner, D.M., Raymond, P., & Erber, R. (1991). Transactive memory in close relationships. *Journal of Personality and Social Psychology, 61*, 923–929.

Weldon, M.S. (2000). Remembering as a social process. *The Psychology of Learning and Motivation, 40*, 67–120.

Weldon, M.S., & Bellinger, K.D. (1997). Collective memory: Collaborative and individual processes in remembering. *Journal of Experimental Psychology: Learning, Memory and Cognition, 23*, 1160–1175.

Weldon, M.S., Blair, C., & Huebsch, P.D. (2000). Group remembering: Does social loafing underlie collaborative inhibition? *Journal of Experimental Psychology: Learning Memory and Cognition, 26*, 1568–1577.

Wright, D.B., Self, G., & Justice, C. (2000). Memory conformity: Exploring misinformation effects when presented by another person. *British Journal of Psychology, 91*, 189–202.

Wright, D.B., & Klumpp, A. (2004). Collaborative inhibition is due to the product, not the process, of recalling in groups. *Psychonomic Bulletin & Review, 11*, 1180–1083.

10 Memory for thoughts and dreams

Caroline L. Horton, Martin A. Conway, and Gillian Cohen

There is a wealth of research investigating how we remember events or experiences that have physically occurred. There is also evidence to suggest that the different ways in which a person views or thinks about an experience alters their memory of it, such as whether it was an important, typical, or emotional experience. Yet relatively little is known about how we remember such views or thoughts, largely because it is very difficult to study. We know that it is very important to remember thoughts as well as external events and experiences; it is necessary to have knowledge of what has happened and whether it was real or imagined. So, the research in this area has tended to focus on "reality monitoring"; the checking of whether something that happened was internal, such as a thought, or external. This theory was devised by Marcia Johnson and her colleagues, and is the focus of this chapter. Source monitoring is an extension of the reality-monitoring framework and refers to the process of identifying the source of a memory.

In addition, in our everyday lives there are other types of experiences that we may remember but which did not actually happen to us. Recalling a film or television programme is a different kind of experience to remembering having gone shopping yesterday, but you were there watching the film with your own eyes. Dreaming, on the other hand, is a unique experience whereby you can see and feel things that you aren't actually experiencing externally. As a result, memory for these kinds of experiences is also unique. Whereas little is understood about how we remember thoughts, it is generally agreed that our remembering of dreams is very poor. Why is this? How does remembering thoughts and dreams differ from our usual everyday autobiographical remembering? Why are these memories important? And how can we study them?

REALITY MONITORING

What is reality monitoring?

Imagine you are in a lecture listening to a presentation. You may start thinking about some of the issues that are being discussed and you may have a theory that helps you understand certain concepts. You might think that your theory is a particularly good idea, and wish to remember it at a later stage. When recalling that idea at a later stage, it may well be necessary to distinguish your theory from your lecturer's presentation; that is, the internal thoughts from the external actions. In order to do this you may engage in source monitoring; the strategy by which you pinpoint the origin of that memory. Reality monitoring is an aspect of this strategy, which refers to the process by which you identify whether the source of a memory was internal or external. Source monitoring differs in that it requires a discrimination to be made between the sources of external memories. Both the reality monitoring and the source monitoring frameworks are similar.

There are several aspects of this process of deciphering the source of a memory. Indeed, many studies have adopted methods that investigate such differences. For instance, experiments requiring participants to identify whether an event was perceived or imagined (Johnson, Foley, Suengas, & Raye, 1988; Suengas & Johnson, 1988) investigated the processes at work when monitoring an event's reality (perceived) as opposed to its internal source (imagined). Here participants compared memories of a social occasion with memories of a dream, fantasy, or unfulfilled intention. Other methods adopted include comparing actions—both with and without objects (Sussman, 2001)—versus imaginings; watching films or thinking about films; talking about something or thinking about something; listening to words, thinking about words, or writing words; intended actions versus past actions; events which have happened to you or to someone else. There are cases whereby fantasy and reality are confused. There is even an experiment whereby participants distinguished between dreams that they had told to someone versus dreams that someone had told them (Johnson, Kahan, & Raye, 1984).

Johnson et al. (1988) suggested that reality monitoring is a two-stage process in which the qualitative differences between actual and imagined events are used as a guide. First, then, the characteristics of the event in question are assessed, to note whether they resemble a typical internally or externally generated experience. The characteristics can be perceptual (e.g., colours), contextual (e.g., order of events), semantic (meaningful information, generally about what happened), cognitive/emotional (e.g., how one felt at the time), and the cognitive operations employed at the time of the event being experienced, either as a thought or as an event being encoded as a memory (Sluzenski, Newcombe, & Ottinger, 2004). There is more contextual detail in the external memories, for example. Second, the amount of active cognitive operations offers clues as to the origin of the event. More cognitive operations are present in memories of internally generated events. As a result of these different cognitive processes the characteristics of internal memories, such as thoughts, differ qualitatively from the characteristics of external events that have been experienced. So, these two stages of the reality-monitoring decision process complement one another. It is the differences between these types of characteristic that guide a person's judgements about whether something that has happened was internal or external.

Deciding whether an event, experience, or thought was internally or externally derived—that is, reality monitoring—is only one decision process in a source monitoring task. The source of a memory could refer to a number of different attributes: who said it (e.g., yourself or someone else), where it occurred (e.g., at home or at school), or when it occurred (e.g., in childhood or recently), to name but a few. Deciding upon these sources may be very important and, like reality monitoring, a source monitoring decision process may be either automatic or conscious and controlled. It relies upon the same criteria: comparing the characteristics of different kinds of memories and comparing the cognitive operations involved. Johnson, Hashtroudi, and Lindsay (1993) describe the source monitoring framework in great detail. Whereas it is largely similar to that of the reality-monitoring framework, some of its implications are more far-reaching than the simple decision between and externally and internally derived experience. That is, experiments examining source monitoring could involve identifying the source of two internally generated memories (such as thoughts) or two externally occurring memories (actual events). So, the characteristics of different kinds of thoughts or imagined events are especially important when making a source monitoring decision. As these are more similar to one another than when comparing the characteristics of, for example, perceived versus imagined events, more strategic processes may be required than when reality monitoring.

Failures of reality monitoring

Everyday examples

In everyday life, imperfect reality monitoring is quite common in normal intelligent adults. Children are more likely to confuse fantasy and reality, which Flavell, Flavell, and Green (1983) have found results from the borderline between what is real and imaginary being unclear (see the later section on the development of reality monitoring).

Upon repeating a story of a personal event, memory for the original event can often become confused with the memory for the story or version of the event. This is a reality-monitoring error, and occurs when someone is unable to discriminate between the original event (an external event) and a different version of the event, perhaps some more script-like account (an internal creation).

Some confusion occurs when the memory of a planned or intended action is confused with the memory of an actual performed action. When leaving your house to walk to the shop, you may wonder whether you locked the door or not, and so return home to check on this. Upon arriving home you find your door safely locked. This everyday action can become problematic as it is difficult to discern between the memory for the actual event (having locked the door) and the memory script—like a schema of this typical action that is repeated at least daily (see Chapter 2 on autobiographical memory).

Sometimes these confusions are not necessarily between a plan and action but, more strictly speaking, between a recent and previous performance of a particular action. Similarly, you may have intended to buy a particular item when shopping, but not be able to recall whether you did this or simply thought of doing so. Other confusions between planned actions and actual actions concern the misplacing of objects, whereby you thought you put your tea down on the coffee table, but in fact you only planned the action and the tea is still in the kettle! All of these kinds of experience are common in everyday life, and remind us that although there are usually many clues as to whether an event was real or imagined, mistakes can be made. On the whole, the more realistic the experience, the more confusing it can be.

Serious failures—clinical examples

Failures of reality monitoring can sometimes extend beyond everyday occurrences and become more problematic. They can be characteristic of schizophrenia, dementia, delirium, and intoxication, as well as other states of mental abnormality that involve hallucinations or obsessions. In these disorders there is usually an inability to distinguish between the real and the imaginary in current experience as well as in past experience. So, this is a problem of present consciousness as well as a memory issue.

There are two types of error that can result from a failure of reality monitoring. The type of error depends upon the direction of the confusion. When a plan or imagined act is mistaken for the memory of a real act, the consequence is an omission error. If, on the other hand, the memory of a performed action is mistaken for the memory of a plan, the result is a repetition error. A second dose of medicine is taken, or two sugars are put in your coffee.

An obvious example whereby reality and fantasy are confused occurs in individuals suffering from delusions; strong beliefs that something has happened or exists, when in reality it does not. Also, when people hallucinate they are seeing or hearing (in the case of auditory hallucinations, i.e., hearing voices) things that are not actually there. Source monitoring is particularly interesting here, as there appear to be clues that an internal experience is occurring externally. So, reality monitoring breaks down. According to Garrett and Silva (2003) in an experiment comparing "voices" of auditory hallucinations and real speakers, similarities between the characteristics of these types of voice may partly account for why patients believe their voices are real. Of course, this account does not consider the cause of those hallucinations, and therefore reality-monitoring frameworks are probably unable to completely explain these confusions, which are symptomatic of the complex disorder, schizophrenia.

Another example may be seen as more of an extension of everyday failures of reality monitoring: Recall the scenario whereby you cannot be sure whether or not you locked the door on leaving your house. Such confusions between memories for everyday actions and scripts of those actions often result in some kind of checking behaviour. This is a behaviour that most of us can be familiar with. However, repeated checking behaviours resulting from more severe and frequent memory failures can be characteristic of sufferers of obsessive-compulsive disorder (OCD) (for a review see Ecker, 2001). Such behaviours are examples of repetition errors. The tasks that individuals are concerned about having performed or not are often ones that may be a potential threat to safety, such as turning the gas hob off. Sufferers can become increasingly concerned about these issues, feeling increasingly threatened by them, and the problem escalates.

Koriat, Ben-Zur, and Sheffer (1988) attributed repetition errors—when people repeat an action because they are unaware that they have already performed it—to defective output monitoring. They distinguished between two models of output monitoring, online cancellation and retrospective judgements. Online cancellation processes may operate to erase or tag a plan once it has been executed, just as I might strike out or tick the items on a shopping list when I have bought them. Alternatively, executed plans may simply lose activation so that they are unlikely to be reactivated. In the absence of cancellation processes, retrospective checks may establish whether an act has been performed. These checks may be internal or external. We can check the external consequences by trying the door handle to see if it has been locked, or looking in the cupboard to see if we have already bought the ingredient for our recipe. Alternatively, we can carry out an internal check, examining the memory trace of the act and making a reality-monitoring judgement about it. Of course, this option seems more practical in everyday life. Radomsky, Gilchrist, and Dussault (2006) have provided an alternative explanation of this relationship between checking (reality monitoring) and memory; they argue that rather than failures of memory inducing checking behaviours, repeated checking can make us doubt our memory.

Another type of reality-monitoring error affects judgements of frequency. The judged frequency of occurrence of a particular event may be inflated if that event is frequently imagined, just as the frequency of actually performing an action increases the difficulty of reality monitoring. The internally generated memories are added to the externally derived ones. Johnson (1985) suggests that people's subjective estimates of how often they have been ill or unhappy could be influenced by the frequency with which episodes of illness or unhappiness have been thought about; thus depression can reinforce itself.

Applications of reality monitoring

Some recent research has been conducted using the reality-monitoring framework in more applied situations. Three examples are shown here, two relating to remembering criminal events: eyewitness testimony and the cognitive interview (see Chapter 3 on eyewitness memory for an explanation of the cognitive interview). Finally the issues of false, "recovered" memories of abuse are considered.

Hekkanen and McEvoy (2005) asked students to make source monitoring judgements for a variety of stimuli that had been either seen on slides, read, or neither of these. This paradigm could be applied to situations involving eyewitness testimony, as their definition of source misattribution errors were consistent with the literature on eyewitness testimony. They found that "the proportion of source misattribution errors was greater for schema-typical than for schema-atypical items, and the proportion of errors on suggested items was greater than that on control items" (p. 759). This reinforces the difficulty with reality monitoring when labelling realistic, everyday behaviours. It is well documented in memory research that the more distinctive an encoded event, experience, or stimulus, the more easily retrievable it is. This may be because more information is encoded, thus allowing for more "retrieval paths", or it may be that it simply differs so much from other memories that it stands out, possibly in terms of the semantic organisation, thus making it more accessible as it is not easily confused with other, semantically similar, memories. Johnson, Raye, Foley, and Foley (1981) provide some evidence for this phenomenon. In one experiment participants found it more difficult to identify the origin of highly typical instances of a category than to identify more unusual instances. So, participants were required to generate instances (e.g., apple) in response to category cues (e.g., fruit). An individual who had generated the typical "apple" would be more likely to mistake its origin than the one who generated "pomegranate". In addition, the proportion of errors increased under the long delay, reflecting the sensitivity of both the memory systems at work and of the reality-monitoring processes themselves.

Larsson and Granhag (2005) conducted an experiment whereby participants had their memories for both observed and imagined events scrutinised with the cognitive interview. They found that observed events produced more visual, affective, spatial, and temporal information in the cognitive interview statements, compared to the imagined events. This alternative methodology provides more support for the reality-monitoring model; that there are characteristic differences between internally and externally produced memories.

The accuracy of reality monitoring is crucial in the context of recovered memories. When people "recover" memories of abuse that they suffered in childhood, they make a reality-monitoring judgement that these events actually occurred. In some cases it appears that these are false memories that have been constructed by the patient on the basis of suggestions from a therapist, and the claim that they are real recovered memories represents a failure of reality monitoring. Despite this being a controversial issue, there are individuals who believe that in some cases the events did not actually occur. Rather, they have been suggested to the individual in a therapeutic context. So, how might it be possible that an individual believes something actually did happen when they have only thought about it? We know that memories for events that occurred early on in our lives are poor (see section on childhood amnesia in Chapter 2). So, in this case the characteristics of an event itself are not really discernible from the typically less-detailed thoughts, in this case, of abuse. Also, some individuals might recognise "typical" signs of an abusive past in themselves. Here, these clues are implying that the abuse might have happened, in the same way as information about conceivable events may indicate that a memory is fantasy as opposed to reality.

The reality-monitoring model

Evaluation of qualitative attributes

The characteristics of external versus internal memory traces are said to be qualitatively distinct, as shown in Table 10.1. For example, higher levels of perceptual and contextual information as well as supporting memories characterise perceived events as compared to imagined events (Johnson et al., 1988). In line with Sluzenski et al. (2004), Johnson and Raye (1981) claimed that "memories originating from perception should have more perceptual information . . . more contextual information . . . and more meaningful detail, whereas memories originating from thought should have more information about the cognitive operations (e.g., sensory, perceptual or reflective processes) that generated them" (p. 67). These characteristics can vary across a number of dimensions, and are said to reflect differences in perception and imagination as originally experienced.

Table 10.1 Qualitative differences between external and internal memories. (A plus sign indicates that an attribute is more likely to be present.)

Attributes	Memories	
	External	*Internal*
Contextual attributes: space and time	+	−
Sensory attributes visual: auditory, haptic	+	−
Detail and complexity	+	−
Coherence	+	−
Schematic quality	−	+
Cognitive operations: imaging, reasoning, decision processes	−	+

So far, the reality-monitoring model seems to clearly distinguish between internally and externally generated memories. So, how does this model account for the failures of reality monitoring? There are two ways in which the reality-monitoring process can break down. A target memory may be uncharacteristic of its class (e.g., an especially vivid imagination), or the person may fail to engage in reasoning on the basis of prior knowledge or may engage in faulty reasoning. The former claim appears to make sense; schematic or typical memories exemplify experiences that may contain less detail than a more novel event would contain, and thus be more characteristic of an imagined event. However, the "faulty reasoning" may require further elaboration and investigation.

Anderson (1984) elaborated upon Johnson and Raye's model (1981), which claimed that errors in reality monitoring are caused by confusability of the memory traces. We know that self-generated memories differ characteristically from externally generated memories. But different kinds of self-generated memories, such as memories of performed actions and memories for imagined actions, are more similar to one another than internal–external memories. Anderson added the idea that this occurs when information is coded directly onto the memory trace in the form of a tag and errors occur when the tag is lost. The confusability explanation predicts that errors should reflect a gradient of similarity. That is, the greater the degree of similarity between origins, the greater the probability of confusing them. The origin tag explanation, on the other hand, predicts that all types of confusion would be equally likely because, once a tag is lost, origin identification must be pure guesswork. Luckily the gradient of similarity provides a testable hypothesis. Anderson's experiments used simple line drawings as stimuli. Participants had to trace the drawings (the Perform condition), imagine tracing them (Imagine), or watch someone else trace them (Look). It was found that participants were most likely to confuse the self-generated memories (Perform and Imagine) than confuse the self-generated memories with other-generated (Look) memories. Anderson concluded that these findings were consistent with Johnson and Raye's model, as participants had judged the origin of memories by evaluating qualities of the trace rather than by inspecting the origin tags.

Coherence and plausibility

So, the typical characteristics of thoughts or actual experiences are not quite sufficient to produce totally accurate reality monitoring. For memories that fall into the region of uncertainty, Johnson and Raye (1981) suggested that different methods of evaluation could be employed. One method is to invoke criteria of coherence and plausibility. External memories ought to make sense in terms of our knowledge of the world. Internal memories, like fantasies and dreams, can sometimes be recognised because they violate natural laws or conflict with other knowledge. A dream in which you fly or are invisible is unlikely to be true. We have already considered these issues when we thought about individuals who suffer with delusions—here reality checking is impaired and things that are unreal seem to be true. People can sometimes check on the reality of a memory by trying to recall supporting context. If you can remember that when you locked the back door the key was stiff, and the cat was on the wrong side, the memory is probably of a performed action and not an imagined one. This mirrors the idea of distinctiveness proposed before—the more unique the memory, the more memorable it is. Another criterion is based on confidence. People appear to operate a strategy that has been called the "It had to be you" effect (Johnson & Raye, 1981). This strategy is used to determine whether a memory is of an action performed by oneself or by someone else. If a memory is of an experience that seems typical of their own kinds of memories or experiences, someone would be likely to be quite confident about its origin. The absence of such confidence may result in attributing the origin to another person. This strategy of assessing confidence that an event is one's own is employed in source monitoring in addition to simply determining whether something was internally or externally produced.

In short, in order for reality monitoring to take place, there should be some kind of supporting evidence or knowledge that the memory is in line with other normal activity (i.e., coherent with it) and for something to have actually occurred as an action it should be plausible and should obey natural laws—for instance, flying violates the law of gravity so it cannot have actually taken place externally.

Experimental evidence

Johnson and her colleagues have conducted numerous experiments in order to investigate reality monitoring further. The two major aspects of the reality-monitoring model will be discussed; effects resulting from characteristic similarities and differences between internally and externally generated memories, and the role of cognitive operations in making a reality-monitoring judgement.

The effect of qualitative similarity

As mentioned previously, knowledge about the characteristics of internally and externally generated memories aids the reality-monitoring process and so, if those characteristics are similar, or atypical of a particular memory type (e.g., an especially vivid and detailed thought or plan), reality-monitoring judgements can be inaccurate. Individual differences in reality monitoring have been employed to test the effect of qualitative similarity. In other words, some people are better at reality monitoring than others. Johnson, Raye, Wang, and Taylor (1979) tested the prediction that people who are unusually good at forming vivid and detailed visual images should be especially poor at reality monitoring, as their vivid internal memories would be confusingly similar to externally derived memories. Conversely, people who are poor at imaging should be better able to distinguish their vaguer images from real memories. Prior to the experiment, participants were divided into good and poor imagers on the basis of their abilities at recalling details of a picture that they had been presented with. Although this was more of a memory task than a task differentiating between good and poor imagers, it can be argued that visual memory abilities are important in reality monitoring. During the actual experiment participants were required to look at pictures of common objects. For some of the trials just the name of the object was given and participants had to imagine it. So, the variable here was whether the object had actually been seen (an externally occurring memory) or imagined (an internally generated memory). Later, participants had to unexpectedly judge the number of times each picture had been seen, ignoring the times it had been imagined. So, the participants had to engage in reality monitoring.

Results were in line with the hypothesis—that is, those participants in the good imaging group claimed that they had seen the pictures more often, and poor imagers were less affected. So, the judged frequency was inflated by the number of times they had imagined the item. Other individual differences paradigms may be useful in future research, especially those exploring relationships with different kinds of specific memory ability.

Johnson and her colleagues have found further support for her model of reality monitoring by studying phenomenological judgements about memories with different origins (Johnson, 1988; Johnson et al., 1988; Suengas & Johnson, 1988). They asked subjects to remember real or imaginary autobiographical events and then rate these memories for factors such as sensory qualities, emotions, supporting events, and spatial and temporal details. In another study they asked subjects to perform an action (having coffee, wrapping a parcel) or to listen to a description of these events and imagine doing them. Ratings of the memories for the real and the imagined actions were then compared. These ratings revealed clear differences. Real memories received higher ratings for sensory qualities and had more details of the setting. Differences were also apparent in the rate of forgetting and the effects of rehearsal. The clarity of imagined memories declined faster than the clarity of real memories and the difference between real and imagined memories increased over time, but rehearsal of the emotional quality of the memories blurred the difference. Heaps and Nash (2001) also found significant differences between true and false autobiographical memories, with true memories being richer along a host of dimensions, including recollective experience being more emotionally intense and having clearer imagery. These studies demonstrate how phenomenological evidence can be strengthened by manipulating factors, such as retention interval and rehearsal, and noting whether the phenomenological ratings conform to the theoretical predictions.

Some of the effects reported by Johnson and her colleagues are not vast, and in some cases there is no independent evidence that the attempt to manipulate the nature of the mental representation and covert processes was successful. Nevertheless, a substantial body of confirmation for her model has accumulated.

The role of cognitive operations

The second major aspect of the reality-monitoring theory focuses upon the role of cognitive operations. That is, the more difficult an item is to generate in thought, the greater the amount of cognitive operations that will be present in the memory trace, so the more easily it will be recognised as self- (i.e. internally) generated. This second part of the reality-monitoring process (with the first relating to characteristics of the two types of memory) is slightly more difficult to investigate experimentally. Johnson et al. (1981) asked participants to identify which words they had generated themselves and which had been generated by the experimenter. The words were instances (e.g., dog) generated in response to category cues (e.g., animal). In order to manipulate the variable of cognitive operations involved, a first letter cue was sometimes added when participants had to recall the words. In the cases of the cue being present (e.g., animal, d) the identification of origin was less accurate. The authors explained these findings by arguing that the added cue elicited the response automatically and so reduced the need for cognitive operations in generating the response, and the reduced cognitive component made the memory harder to identify as self-generated. This interpretation relied on the idea that automatic processes occur without involving cognitive operations such as search and selection.

In another experiment, participants were required to identify whether they had themselves related a dream to their partner, or vice versa (Johnson et al., 1984). Pairs of subjects woke and gave each other reports of real dreams and made-up pseudo-dreams. Later, the subjects could distinguish between the pseudo-dreams they had made up when awake and real dream reports because the latter lacked traces of constructive processes. Although they are distinguishable, in Johnson's view, dreams, imaginings, and real memories are all products of the same cognitive system but vary in the contribution of different subsystems. Dreams are generated primarily by the reflective subsystem. It is assumed that when individuals have to make reality-monitoring decisions between internally self-generated items and externally other-generated items, the role of cognitive operations is a more reliable source than comparisons of their characteristics. The effortful process involved in thinking may be encoded along with the memory for the thought itself, reflecting how episodic memory and reality monitoring are related.

Johnson (1985) applied her reality-monitoring model to the recall of memories under hypnosis, to explain how this recall is not only poor, it is so inaccurate that more false memories can be yielded when hypnotised (e.g., Dywan & Bowers, 1983). Johnson suggested that, when under hypnosis, memories generated are produced without the exercise of cognitive operations. In addition, they may be particularly vivid and therefore resemble externally generated memories more than internal ones. So, the vital clues used in the reality-monitoring process are atypical. Such memories are similar to memories for dreams, which are also perceptually detailed although produced without such cognitive operations being present. However, in this case reality monitoring is not known to be poor—people can usually distinguish between dreams and actual events (Johnson et al., 1984). This may be due to the slightly different, more fantasy-like content of dreams, such as being able to fly.

The development of reality monitoring

Certain studies have been interested in how reality monitoring develops and changes over time, so different age groups have been compared. Young children and older adults have especially been the focus of attention.

Foley, Johnson, and Raye (1983) tested 6-, 9-, and 17-year-olds in a task that required them to discriminate between words that had been said and those that had been heard (say vs listen), or between those that had been said and those that had been thought (say vs think). The young children had no difficulty in the say–listen condition in discriminating between what they had said themselves and what someone else had said. They were also able to discriminate between words spoken by two different speakers (i.e., two external sources), but 6-year-olds were more likely to confuse the two self-generated sources, saying and thinking. Foley and Johnson (1985) also noted a similar developmental pattern in memory for the origin of actions. The younger children distinguished doing and watching, but not doing and imagining. It has been suggested that instead of being unable to discriminate between internal sources, young children have problems when two sources were very similar.

To test this, Roberts and Blades (1995) devised a task in which the perform condition required children to hide counters under objects and the imagine condition required them to pretend to do so. This requirement was intended to ensure that the imagining did actually occur. Both conditions involve internal sources and both actions were very similar. In a surprise memory test the children were told the names of the objects and asked whether each was in a real or a pretend hiding place. The results showed no difference between children and adults in the proportion of confusions, so, clearly, children are not necessarily unable to distinguish between reality and fantasy and the preconditions for age effects in reality-monitoring judgements remain to be established.

More recently Sussman (2001) compared participants aged 4, 8, and 12 years and adults in their ability to distinguish between performed, imagined, or new actions. In line with previous research, the 4-year-olds struggled most with the task, and reality-monitoring ability seemed to increase developmentally. Sluzenski et al. (2004) note how a number of studies have found similar patterns of reality monitoring over time, with the ability to discriminate between internally and externally derived experiences kicking in at around the age of 4 years, when participants tend to perform at above chance level in such tasks. However, younger children tend not to be used in these experiments, presumably due to the complexity of the tasks. By the age of 6 the abilities have developed somewhat, although they are not mature. Actions generated by other people, for instance, are particularly troublesome to monitor at this age. Errors in reality monitoring are also evident in participants aged 10, although it seems that there is little development, on the whole, after this time (Sussman, 2001).

So, why the difficulty with reality monitoring? Johnson's model accounts for errors in reality monitoring in adults, but it may be that children struggle with the task for different reasons. The relationship between episodic memory abilities and reality monitoring has been investigated, to see whether poor episodic memory prevents a memory trace from subsequently being monitored accurately. Sluzenski et al. (2004) hypothesised that, although in previous studies memory for source has been uncorrelated with memory for the events themselves, this has been a result of "memory for the events" having been defined inappropriately. Specifically, event memory has been explored using recognition style tasks. Sluzenski et al. were more interested in memory for details composing those events, which they deem is a more valid measure of "memory for events". Results indicated that developmental effects were replicated, as outlined above, with 4-year-olds performing especially poorly on the reality-monitoring tasks. As these younger participants also performed relatively poorly on the memory for event details tasks, the authors conclude that reality monitoring is linked to episodic memory abilities. Interestingly, the tasks were repeated after a 1-week delay, and the younger participants still performed badly even though they had remembered more about the real than imagined events. The reality monitoring-model implies that the characteristic differences between real and imagined events should provide clues for accurate reality monitoring, so the difficulty may lie in recognising that those characteristics are typical of a particular type of experience. The authors offer an alternative explanation; that the younger participants struggle with the episodic component of such memories, as well as the strategic difficulties of reality monitoring itself. Support for this came from correlation analyses that linked episodic memory abilities to reality monitoring at the different developmental stages. Although these correlations exist, the extent to which these memories can be considered episodic is questionable. The details recalled may not be embedded in experience-based information, as indicated by the difficulties that 4-year-olds have with reality monitoring of non-self-performed actions. Thus, a general issue of how autobiographical the memories are may be more crucial here, and requires further investigation. Sluzenski et al. were able to suggest that the prefrontal cortex is a brain structure largely involved in reality monitoring, as well as other areas such as the hippocampus that are known to be involved in memory generally.

As mentioned earlier, Flavell et al. (1983) have noted how in early childhood there is some degree of confusion over real and imagined experiences. This may be functional, for instance the creation of imaginary friends may provide company for growing infants or may serve to promote the development of a theory of mind. This idea may be supported by the finding in Sussman's (2001) experiment that the 4- and 8-year-old groups seemed more likely to confuse imagined actions with performed actions, and the youngest participants especially seemed to find it difficult distinguishing the imagined actions from the others.

At the other end of the developmental spectrum, Cohen and Faulkner (1988, 1989) found that elderly people made more false positive errors in a reality-monitoring task. They were more likely to misidentify actions they had only imagined, or actions that had not occurred at all, as ones they had performed themselves. There was evidence that elderly people have a lower criterion for deciding that a memory is a "real" externally derived one, but age-related deficits in the very young and very old may also be partly due to failure to encode distinctive features on the memory trace.

None of these experiments, however, is very closely analogous to reality monitoring in everyday life, and Cohen and Faulkner noted that the self-rated incidence of reality-monitoring errors in daily life correlated only weakly with errors in their experimental task. In the laboratory tasks, when words are used as stimuli, they are isolated words occurring without context and do not form part of a meaningful message. When actions are the stimuli, they are not goal-directed and do not form part of an overall plan schema. Most of the experimental tasks are not sufficiently like naturally occurring instances of reality monitoring for us to be able to draw conclusions about how people normally distinguish internal and external memories in everyday life.

Conclusions

It is evident that although there is a bulk of supporting evidence for the reality-monitoring model, only one model has been proposed to account for the process by which internally and externally generated memories are differentiated. Whilst the work of Johnson and her colleagues is well conducted and convincing, using sophisticated designs that produce consistent findings, effect sizes (the distance between means when comparing different groups or conditions) are not always large. It is also worth remembering that complicated experiments may not necessarily be ecologically valid, especially when considering that the topic being investigated is impossible to measure directly and thus to validate.

However, the reality-monitoring model currently offers a comprehensive account for the ways in which individuals make judgements about the source of particular kinds of memories—in this case, between internally and externally generated ones. To recap, it is proposed that people make these important decisions by using characteristics information from the memory in question. If it is particularly detailed and supported by contextual information, it is likely that the memory is of an actual event. If, on the other hand, the memory is characteristically less detailed and involves more cognitive operations, it may well have been self-generated. It is worth remembering that these processes are likely to work together and, indeed, complement one another. Kensinger and Schacter (2005) exemplify this in their study manipulating the emotionality of memories. It was found that emotional memories, as opposed to emotionally neutral memories, can be less prone to reality-monitoring errors. This may reinforce the effect of distinctiveness, whereby the less typical a memory is, the more identifiable its source. So, the emotionality of an event may provide more contextual information at the time of encoding, and thus provide a particular kind of characteristic information, enabling a more accurate reality-monitoring judgment to be made. The emotionality may also act upon cognitive operations in specific ways, allowing for an accurate judgement to be made. Research such as this supports the reality-monitoring model, although it does not explain exactly how these effects occur. Kensinger and Schacter also used fMRI techniques to locate the brain regions involved in these processes. The continued study of reality-monitoring processes, probably focusing more upon brain activity, may well elucidate exactly which cognitive functions are at work when internal–external source judgements are made.

MEMORY FOR DREAMS

Introduction

So far in this chapter we have considered how and why individuals discriminate between memories that have been internally generated compared to events or actions that have actually happened. Dreams are exceptional experiences that can produce feelings and memories as if they have actually been experienced, even though they have been "generated" to some degree internally. As a result, memories of dreams are fascinating research material.

Dreams are a common element of everyday life, but are seldom mentioned in the literature on everyday memory. Yet most people are interested in the content of their dreams, puzzled by the elusive quality of memory for dreams, and fascinated by the strange relationship between the events they experience in real life and the echoes of these events in their dreams. Also, for the cognitive psychologist, interesting questions arise about how far memory for dreams conforms to the same theoretical principles as waking memory or whether it is fundamentally different. An account of memory in everyday life cannot be complete unless it includes memory for dreams because a substantial proportion of our everyday lives is spent in sleeping and dreaming. Moreover, a few cognitive psychologists are beginning to realise, somewhat belatedly, that the relationship between memory and dreaming poses many interesting and important questions that a comprehensive model of cognition should be able to answer. Memory is involved at three different stages of dreaming. First, memories of previously experienced real events are incorporated and represented within dreams, so memories form the content of dreams. Here, questions arise about what determines the particular memories that are selected and reproduced in dreams and the extent to which they are distorted. Second, memory processes are at work within the dream, organising, sequencing, and monitoring the dream narrative. At this stage, the issues centre on how far these processes in dreams are similar to the same processes in waking cognition. The third role of memory comes at the stage of dream recall. On waking, we remember only a very small proportion of our dreams, so the most important questions are why dreams are so difficult to recall, and why some individuals remember dreams more often and in more detail.

In order to try and investigate some of these themes and questions, we first need to consider what dreams are, how and if they differ from the characteristics of normal autobiographical memories, and if this information might help elucidate this issue.

Remembering one's dreams is part of autobiographical memory, as dreams are unique experiences that have only happened in their precise form to one individual. However, as will be demonstrated, remembering dreams differs greatly from normal autobiographical remembering for waking experiences and events. First and foremost, memory for dreams is relatively poor (e.g., Reed, 1974), so models and theories tend to focus upon its inadequacy. In addition, it is especially difficult to measure dreaming behaviours due to their characteristics. Specifically, although certain dream characteristics are measurable, dream details rely upon subjective reports, and there are no validity measures for these. There are two main methods that are adopted in order to try and measure memory for dreams. A quantitative method frequently adopted simply counts up how many dreams were recalled in a specific time period, regardless of what kind of dreams they are. This is referred to as dream recall frequency (DRF). The alternative approach assesses the dream in more detail by requesting information about the characteristics of dreams, such as emotionality or bizarreness, and these are usually plotted on some sort of rating scale. It has been well documented that certain features of events make them more memorable in waking life, such as bizarreness (Bartlett, 1932, cited in Cipolli, Bolzani, Cornoldi, De Beni, & Fagioli, 1993), emotionality, and novelty. These trends have certainly also been acknowledged in the dream literature, e.g., bizarreness (Cipolli et al., 1993) and emotionality (Schredl & Doll, 1998). Bizarre situations appear in dreams that would not happen in waking life (e.g., Cipolli et al., 1993), and the proportion of such events to non-bizarre events is about 2:1. After a delayed recall, bizarre events were more memorable, suggesting a clear advantage for such memories. Such strange memories also provide clues in reality monitoring situations; a memory of flying through the air is much more likely to be a dream than an actual event.

Kemp, Burt, and Sheen (2003) followed up on Johnson et al.'s (1984) experiment on the reality monitoring of dreams. Some interesting comparisons were observed between remembering dreamt and actual experiences, with more detail being provided overall for actual experiences. This subsequently allowed more accurate reality-monitoring judgements to be made. The findings suggest that the more recent the dream, the more contextual details are included in the memory, the more accurate the reality-monitoring decision. There also seems to be a recency effect in some form. Dreams were significantly less memorable than normal memories, which may be either the result of the two types of memories being stored in different ways, or encoded differently due to different information accompanying the memories.

Whilst aspects of remembering dreams are comparable to remembering waking experiences, substantial differences between memory for dreams and events exist. A variety of research has tried to classify the characteristics of dreams. This may account for the memory differences. Foulkes (1979) reviews the literature assessing the differences between home-recalled dreams, which usually utilise spontaneous morning reports, and laboratory-controlled dreams, in which participants are often awakened at particular times throughout their sleep cycle. Dreams recalled in home environments are more likely to have occurred longer ago than the laboratory dreams, which may account for the characteristic and content differences between these two types of dream report. Specifically, Hall and Van de Castle (1966), who developed a famous dream coding system, found that dreams spontaneously recalled in the laboratory were significantly longer than "spontaneous" home dreams, suggesting that greater selectivity takes place when at home—possibly due to individuals not focusing upon their dreams when in their everyday routines. In addition, home dreams are more likely to be generally dramatic and emotional than laboratory dreams. While this could be accounted for by a lack of environmental input affecting dream content when in a laboratory-controlled environment, it may well be that specific features of dreams (such as bizarreness or emotionality) make them more memorable, as with waking events. As dreams reported from a home setting are likely to be slightly older than the laboratory dreams (as it often takes longer for a participant to report their dreams at home than in the laboratory), the home dreams may have to be slightly more memorable in order to be recalled at all.

As the characteristics of dreams differ from normal autobiographical memories for waking experiences, with dreams being less detailed along a whole host of measures (Horton & Conway, 2006a; Johnson et al., 1984; Kemp, Burt, & Sheen, 2003), we should consider what happens when we dream.

What happens when we dream?

When we go to sleep at night we enter different stages of sleep. Healthy individuals, indeed all mammals, will progress through these stages in a systematic cycle that occurs every 90 minutes or so. In humans, on average about 2 hours of a normal night are spent in REM sleep, in periods lasting from 5 to 40 minutes and becoming longer later in the night. Each stage is characterised by specific patterns of EEC and EEG activity, and can be broadly divided into periods of rapid eye movement (REM) and non-rapid eye movement (NREM). Different regions of the brain are also active compared to waking. So, the study of dreaming has been taken over by neuro-scientists, on the whole, as opposed to cognitive psychologists.

Aserinsky and Kleitman (1953) published groundbreaking findings about the association between dreaming and REM sleep. Dreaming is generally thought to occur in REM stages of sleep, due to the brain activity being relatively heightened at this time compared to the NREM stages. It is sometimes called paradoxical sleep, as although you are asleep, the brain is receiving sensory input as if awake. Countless studies have found that if people are woken up when in REM sleep, they are more likely to report a dream, compared to when they are woken from NREM sleep. However, the physiology of REM sleep has not provided a complete explanation of dreaming as some REM sleep occurs without dreaming, and some dreaming occurs without REM sleep. On about 80% of occasions when people are woken from REM sleep they are able to report an ongoing dream. It seems likely, therefore, that some REM sleep occurs without concomitant dreaming, and this conclusion is reinforced by the fact that REM sleep is found in neonates and decorticates, where dreaming is thought to be improbable (Goodenough, 1978). Dreaming has also been found to occur in NREM sleep (Herman, Ellman, & Roffwarg, 1978), although the amount is substantially less. However, experimenters have recently found that by framing the question differently (e.g., "What was going through your mind just before I called you?"—see Battaglia, Cavallero, & Cicogna, 1987—as opposed to "What were you dreaming?"), dream reports can be gained from periods of NREM sleep. The type of dreams differ, though; REM dreams are generally typical of what we think dreams are like, whereas NREM dreams are more vague and less themed like a story (Battaglia et al., 1987).

What the discovery of the strong correlation between dreaming and REM sleep has achieved is to provide a methodology for dream research. Previously, researchers had to rely on diaries in which people recorded their dreams at home, but the accumulation of data by this method is slow because people typically report only two or three dreams each week. By contrast, when subjects are brought into the laboratory to sleep and are awakened during REM sleep, several dream reports can be collected each night. The laboratory method also has other advantages. Although home-dream reports tend to be of vivid, emotional, and bizarre dreams, these turn out to be misleadingly unrepresentative. REM-sleep wakings produce more mundane, realistic, coherent, and well-formed dreams, which are nothing like the weird and strange dreams in the home-dream reports (Cavallero & Foulkes, 1993). In the laboratory, the conditions of recall can be controlled and manipulated so that the effect of distractions and delay intervals can be systematically assessed and pre-sleep stimulation can be presented so as to study its effect on dream content. It has become possible, therefore, to apply the methods of cognitive psychology to dream research and to search for commonalities between memory processes in waking life and memory processes in dreams. However, dream research is still entirely dependent on self-reports, and there is no way in which dreams can be judged as accurate or not accurate. Studies are usually restricted to very small numbers of subjects (perhaps because sleeping in a lab and being woken up several times a night is not an attractive prospect), and results have tended to vary from one laboratory to another. For whatever reason, cognitive psychologists have so far shown rather little interest in dream research.

Origins of dream events

A major distinction between REM and NREM dreams lies in the actual content and make-up of those dreams themselves. Whilst REM dreams may be considered to be bizarre, these ratings are only in comparison to waking memories (cf. Cipolli et al., 1993). Whereas REM dreams may involve some bizarre situations and experiences (such as flying), on the whole they comprise normal and mundane activities—events and memories from waking life. Clearly, then, there is an interesting and complex relationship between dreaming and memory. Specifically, episodic memory (see Chapter 2) for particular experiences must be important in dreaming, as they reappear in some form in REM dreams, leading researchers such as Rauchs and colleagues (2004) to conclude that REM sleep is important in episodic memory consolidation. They found that "remember" but not "know" responses in a recollective experience paradigm task were reduced in participants deprived of REM as opposed to slow-wave sleep (see section on recollective experience in Chapter 12 for an explanation of the recollective experience paradigm and examples of memories that are recalled with *remembering* or are just *known*). Some of the same researchers (Rauches, Desgrange, Foret, & Eustache, 2005), however, review literature showing that NREM sleep improves episodic memory abilities more than REM sleep. This discrepancy is difficult to resolve; however, the validity of the recollective experience paradigm distinguishes between strictly episodic memories featuring autonoetic consciousness and memories of waking experiences. This study was the first to use such a design. Nielsen and Stenstrom (2005) note that dreams tend to lack such autonoetic consciousness, which may account for the more consistent finding from numerous studies that NREM dreams contain more episodic references than REM dreams.

There is a whole host of evidence that, during dreaming, material seen or encountered during the day is somehow re-experienced, reaffirming the continuity hypothesis. Freud (1900/1953) referred to this as the "day residue" hypothesis. It has been demonstrated via, for example: blind individuals dreaming without visual images (e.g., Hurovitz, Dunn, Domhoff, & Fiss, 1999); speakers of a second language dreaming in that language if they have been speaking it during the day; even rapid eye movements following the same course as waking eye movements from the day. Thus it would seem to follow that dream material, specifically, would include episodic memories from the previous day. This certainly seems to be the case to a certain extent, although it is apparent that the sensation of dreaming does not obey similar constraints to waking thoughts.

A comparison between REM and NREM dreams by Foulkes, Bradley, Cavallero, and Hollifield (1989) also suggested that the different physiological states give rise to different types of dream—not just characteristically, but in terms of their make-up. They compared two REM dreams and two NREM dreams reported by each of 16 young men. They concluded that REM dreams are more elaborated and include a broader range of mnemonic origins, including episodic memories, general knowledge, and self-knowledge. This may be due to their increased recallability. In their study, judges scored the degree of correspondence between the dream report and the real-life source identified by the dreamer. They found that REM and NREM dreams did not differ in the number of identified sources but that NREM dreams showed closer correspondence to the original sources.

Fosse, Fosse, Hobson, and Stickgold (2003) investigated this relationship further by examining the replay of episodic memories in dreams. The premise for this is that memory consolidation occurs during sleep (see Cipolli, 1995, for a review). Although sleep following some period of learning seems to improve memory, it is generally assumed that this is due to memory consolidation during sleep as opposed to there being less interference or decay than when awake. That is, there is a whole host of evidence that learning and memory performance is improved after a period of sleep. Certain studies have investigated this in terms of specific sleep stages (e.g., Cavallero, Foulkes, Hollifield, & Terry, 1990). Fosse et al.'s (2003) premise was that episodic memories may also be consolidated during the night, and they chose to see whether such memories were incorporated into dreams or not. Twenty-nine participants kept a record of their waking events in detail over a period of 14 days. They also recorded their dreams and scored them for any signs of incorporation of the episodic memories. The researchers found that only 1.4% of the 299 dreams that had been scored contained any replay of episodic events from the participants' recent waking lives. As a result it was concluded that "sleep has no role in episodic memory consolidation" (p. 1). However, such a conclusion should only be drawn tentatively, for the following reasons.

It has already been mentioned that REM dreams are more coherent and memorable than NREM dreams. Also, these REM dreams are less likely than NREM dreams to contain episodic memories. So, it may well have been that Fosse et al.'s participants were scoring the incorporation of episodic memories into REM dreams, in which case it was unsurprising that such a low rate of events has been incorporated. Future studies should try to differentiate between REM and NREM dreams. Also, the incorporation of specific types of memories into dreams may not reflect the consolidation of such kinds of memories. Instead, it could be that memory consolidation is not related to dreaming at all. However, there could be some interesting relationship between events that are important to the self and whether they are incorporated into dreams or not. Finally, Fosse and colleagues operationalised memory consolidation as occurring only when episodic memories that had been reported from participants' waking lives had been totally replayed in exactly the same way as they had initially been experienced. So, some episodic memories that had not been reported may have been incorporated into the dreams. Also, the incorporation may not have taken the form of total replay. In fact, 65% of the dream reports seemed to reflect some aspects of waking life experiences. This proportion may have been higher if the judgements had been less strict. All in all, the relationship between episodic memory and dreaming is not a simplistic one, although it may be unwise to claim that there is no relationship there at all on the basis of this study.

Freud postulated a theory of dreaming (1900/1953) that relates to the ideas of Fosse and colleagues, without being so strict about the definitions of events involved, or about dreaming generally. Here the dream event may be a reflection of a real event that is anticipated rather than reflecting something that has actually occurred. Freud acknowledged that many dream events are echoes of experiences in recent days, including unsolved problems and preoccupations. Some have their origin in ongoing sensory or somatic events, like a rattling window or a bout of indigestion, but in his view, almost all dreams contain an element of wish fulfilment. Freud also emphasised that many dreams are related to childhood experiences and he cited cases where childhood memories that were completely inaccessible in waking life surfaced in dreams. The main idea was that dreams are composed of experiences from the preceding day with there being some consolidatory role or purpose, although that, too, was not specified. This "day residue" idea provides a functional account of dreaming in terms of memory if events from each day need to be consolidated.

The "dream-lag" effect (Nielsen, Kuiken, Stenstrom, & Powell, 2004) continues Freud's focus on the temporal order of the dream–memory relationship. This effect illustrates how dream recall alters quite systematically over a week. Effects lasting in such a timeframe are referred to as "circaseptan"; that is, about seven days. Nielsen et al. demonstrate how events that have occurred in the past 1–2 days are likely to appear in dreams, although events from days 3–5 are not. Then, events that occurred about 5–7 days prior to the dream are again likely to be incorporated into dreams. This mimics a free recall curve in which primacy and recency effects are shown. However in this case, the timeframe is circaseptan. Nielsen et al. (2004) found both of these effects, although ANOVAs indicated that this was only the case for the females, in their predominantly female sample.

It does seem that the continuity between dreaming and waking extends beyond the re-experiencing of episodic experiences and memories, as highlighted by trends of individual differences. The continuity hypothesis (Schredl & Hofmann, 2003) claims that there are similarities between dreaming and waking memory, specifically, episodic memory for particular experiences and episodes. Schredl and Hofmann wanted to test the continuity hypothesis in terms of which waking-life activities, i.e., exactly which memories, are re-experienced by being incorporated into dreams. They studied individual differences in the relationship between dream content and waking experiences. They commented that a significant positive correlation between dreams and waking life content would provide support for any form of the continuity hypothesis, and such results have been found. However, this simplistic idea has been reinforced and elaborated upon in numerous other studies, which have extended the time period and pinpointed the specific processes involved. Schredl and Hoffman emphasise the need for the continuity hypothesis to be defined and modelled more clearly.

Of course, it is often impossible to identify any origin in waking life for the content of a dream. Antrobus (1978) pointed out that dream events may be, as Freud maintained, a symbolic or metaphorical representation of real events or, alternatively, the dream may be a distorted representation of the waking event. Freud's theory of dreaming claimed that "dream thoughts" were completely transformed by "dream work". In this case, there is scope to try to determine whether the distortion or transformation arises randomly or is due to systematic cognitive operations. Antrobus believes that the dream and the corresponding real event share common organisation and relational features, and has supported this view with evidence from a study in which subjects were trained, when awake, to associate a tone with a particular vignette. The tone was then presented when the subject was asleep and the sleeper was subsequently wakened and asked to provide a dream report. In one example, the subject learned to associate the tone with a vignette of a man cutting the bark of a tree with a cane knife. When the tone was presented during sleep the subject dreamed of himself cutting a pie with a kitchen knife, so here there was a high degree of correspondence between the pre-sleep event and the dream event. Cipolli, Battaglia, Cavallero, Cicogna, and Bosinelli (1992) also studied the incorporation of pre-sleep stimuli into dreams, although they used a design relying much less on interpretation of content. They gave subjects lists of phrases to study before sleeping and found a high proportion were reproduced in subsequent dreams, although in a considerably distorted form. In one example, the phrase "the sword is pulled from the stone" gave rise to the dream report "I was trying to pull the cork from the bottle", thus preserving the relationship but changing the components. Antrobus has suggested that the distortion of reality that occurs in dreams can be accounted for if there is a disruption of the link between visual features and semantic features. Dreams often seem to contain bizarre and contradictory elements, and this hypothesised disruption might explain the kind of contradiction cited by Antrobus, in which a dream character is identified by the dreamer as his brother but as having the appearance of a little girl. It is clear from these examples that methods exist for studying the mechanisms underlying the correspondence, or lack of correspondence, between dream and reality. Given the attention that cognitive psychologists are currently devoting to issues about accuracy and distortion in waking memory, it is of particular interest to speculate whether the same mechanisms operate in dreaming.

Cognitions during dreams

This section has so far been concerned with the content of dreams and whether episodic memories of some kind can be identified within them. Indeed, when talking to people about dreaming they are usually interested in the content to some degree. However there is more to dreaming than just the content. It has been briefly mentioned how brain activity is different to that of waking life during the different stages of sleep. Researchers may use individuals' abilities during dreaming to investigate the more subjective accounts of such activity. So, cognitive abilities during dreaming should reflect what is going on in the brain. Specifically, assessing memory functions and comparing them to normal autobiographical remembering may offer some insight into our understanding of dreaming.

De Witt (1988) has argued against what he calls the "hallucinatory movie" view that characterises dreaming as a passive sensory experience so that dreaming is like watching a movie. This idea is consistent with introspective reports that dreams seem to be revealed or discovered rather than self-generated. Like a movie, dreams often have characters, places, and actions in meaningful scenarios, and there is often a narrative plot that has continuity and development. However, in opposition to the hallucinatory movie view, De Witt has put forward the "impaired consciousness model". According to this model, the dream is actively constructed and is at least partly under the dreamer's control, but normal processes of reality construction and reality monitoring are impaired or inoperative. De Witt's conclusions were based on students' responses to a questionnaire about characteristics of their dreams. Ten attributes of dreams are listed, and the percentage of respondents whose dreams exhibited these attributes are shown in parentheses:

1 Visual images are vague and unstable (46%).
2 Factual information is "just known" without any evidence (56%).
3 Bizarre occurrences are accepted as normal (67%).
4 Events are grossly misinterpreted (e.g., a group of people in a swimming pool was accepted as a maths class) (46%).
5 There are abrupt shifts of continuity and scene changes (70%).
6 The dreamer assumes different identities (59%).
7 The dreamer has multiple points of view, often inconsistent with each other (62%).
8 Prior events within the dream are invented (e.g., the dream began in a drugstore but later the dreamer "remembered" its beginning in a sick friend's house) (46%).
9 Earlier parts of the dream are distorted (36%).
10 Events that are anticipated or feared turn into actual happenings within the dream (e.g., the dreamer saw a cliff-edge, was afraid of falling, then did fall) (60%).

Solms (1997) adopts a very different approach to dreaming, both theoretically and methodologically. Solms has investigated dreaming from a clinicoanatomical perspective, asking his patients about their dreams and thus collecting a large number of dream reports from a number of patients suffering from various different kinds of brain impairments. Whilst investigating which brain regions are implicated in dreaming, Solms reports that damage to the part of the brain involved in motivation, the ventromedial quadrant of the frontal lobe, leads to a cessation of dreaming. In line with continuity theories, patients are also less motivated in waking life. As a result, Solms convincingly argues that Freudian theory is neuropsychologically plausible. In contrast, activation-synthesis accounts such as those proposed by Hobson, Pace-Schott, and Stickgold (2000) state that a certain level of cortical activation such as that experienced in REM sleep is required in order to dream. Such activation is claimed to involve random firings of neurons in active brain regions. The dream is the result of an individual trying to piece together the random thoughts and images that emerge from this activation. These theories can account for the clearly non-random themes and images in dreams. Solms and Hobson are often portrayed as having opposite views on this matter.

These attributes are not consistent with dreams being passively experienced, but rather suggest construction and control processes that differ from those in waking life. In particular, the most striking feature is the absence of any attempt to maintain consistency, either within the dream or between dream events and general knowledge. Within the dream, the characters, scenes, and events shift and change unpredictably and there are gross discrepancies between dream events and the dreamer's knowledge of the real world. Moreover, such discrepancies appear to be either unrecognised or unheeded by the dreamer. Some researchers (e.g., Cavallero & Foulkes, 1993) emphasise the continuity between cognitive processes in waking and cognitive processes in dreaming, but De Witt's data underline some striking and important differences. It is paradoxical that, in the area of dream research, some studies are concerned with showing the bizarre nature of dreams, whereas others (e.g., Montangero, 1991) stress that dreams are essentially coherent and orderly. It seems possible to support both views by judicious choice of examples.

Montangero (1991) has developed methods of analysis designed to discover the principles of sequential organisation in dreams. Dreams almost always have a sequence of actions and scenes so that questions arise as to the nature of the mechanism that regulates the progression from one scene to another, and whether dream sequences are organised in the same way as waking narratives. Montangero's participants were wakened after about 10 minutes of REM sleep and asked to report their dream and then to reconstitute the precise order of events within the dream. The taped report was played back next day and they were asked if they recalled anything more. Dream events were then partitioned by two judges into semantic units at three hierarchical levels corresponding to the main situation, steps within the situation, and subdivisions of these steps. Once the component units had been established, the type of connecting link between them was identified. Five main types of link were identified:

1   Plausible continuation (e.g., "I go out—I meet a friend").
2   Narrative links consisting of a triggering event, a desired outcome, and intermediate steps toward the outcome.

3   Scripts in which events conform to a stereotypical sequence. These include dreams of visiting a restaurant or going on a plane.
4   Teleonomic links in which successive events involve goals or intentions, means, and results. In Montangero's example, "I had to find a way to open up a secret passage. I pressed a tile and the passage opened before me."
5   Causal links (e.g., "The rubber dinghy hit a stone, sprang a leak, and we fell into the water").

Connecting links may exist between semantic units and also between sequences of units, but there may also be breaks between unconnected sequences. This method of analysis yields a dream description in terms of the number of semantic units and breaks, the length of the sequences, and the type of connections. However, the types of connections just listed are clearly not mutually exclusive and particular examples may be difficult to classify. The summary of a dream report shown in the box below consists of five sequences.

---

1   Dreamer drives up a mountain road with her father, hears an alarming noise while her father says that there is a strange noise; they stop and see that they have a flat tyre. The father says that this is always happening to him. He decides to change the tyre.
2   Dreamer and her father decide to go to a mountain resort restaurant. Father says they must look for plates; dreamer gets porcelain plates; father says they are not suitable, paper plates will do.
3   Dreamer and members of her family sit down at a table in a mountain resort restaurant. A woman (her godmother) at another table gets up, goes towards them and kisses them. She says she has two boys. First boy comes up to their table, greets them and leaves. Dreamer thinks he is too young. Second boy comes and greets them, then leaves. His head is not visible, as in a badly framed movie picture.
4   Dreamer outside the restaurant.
5   Dreamer is sitting with a friend, in a room, looking at photographs. Dreamer pins the pictures on the wall. Friend makes a comment about a picture of herself. Suddenly the dreamer sees the real scene, as if she was standing beside the photographer who took the picture. Then dreamer and friend look at a picture of a horse. Again, dreamer sees the real scene and she notices that the photographer had not intended to photograph the horse, but a boy who was standing beside it. Dreamer laughs at the photographer's error.

A dream narrative. From Montangero, J. (1991). How can we define the sequential organization of dreams. *Perceptual and Motor Skills*, 73, 1059–1073. Copyright © Perceptual and Motor Skills, 1991.

As Montangero (1991) points out, this dream shows good continuity with only one major break, and includes plausible, script-based, causal, and teleonomic connecting links. The comparison of sequential organisation in dreams and in waking narratives is clearly a rich field of research, but the conclusions seem to be too dependent on the particular dream selected for analysis and the subjective judgements of the researchers. Dream experiences, as compared with normal waking experiences or stories generated when awake, are characterised by spatial and temporal discontinuity, by lack of plausibility, by frequent shifts of point of view and of scenario, by changes of mood and goals, by the actor's relative lack of control, by the vagueness and indeterminacy of the experience, and by the dreamer's acceptance of the inexplicable.

It is interesting to note, however, that there is evidence of a continuum of coherence when comparisons are made between waking fantasies, NREM dreams, and REM dreams. Reinsel, Antrobus, and Wollman (1992) compared dream reports when sleepers were wakened and waking fantasies that were generated by subjects relaxed in a quiet dim room. Judges then rated the resulting reports for bizarreness on the basis of discontinuities and improbabilities. Surprisingly, this measure of bizarreness was highest for the waking fantasies, next highest in REM dreams, and lowest in NREM dreams, decreasing with the level of cortical activation. The authors suggested a cognitive interpretation of these findings. When external stimulation is minimised and cortical arousal is low, then spreading activation is too sluggish to activate top-down processing and so impose the constraints of general knowledge. This explanation is in line with De Witt's view that normal operations of construction and monitoring are impaired during dreaming. The idea that memory in dreams and waking memory share the same cognitive mechanisms operating at different levels of efficiency is further supported by Kerr's (1993) observation that lesions in brain-damaged patients can cause parallel impairment of visual imagery in both waking life and in dreams.

According to Cicogna and Bosinelli (2001), "all the operations involved in dream generation are obviously unconscious" (p. 35). The dreamer is rarely aware of dreaming, the major exception being lucid dreaming (see Schredl & Erlacher, 2004), wherein a dreamer is aware that he or she is dreaming at the time. This occurs in about 3% of dreams (Cicogna & Bosinelli, 2001). Thus, in the majority of cases, the processes involved in dreaming differ greatly from the conscious awareness characteristic of waking thought, which may reflect profound differences between remembering dreams and remembering normal autobiographical experiences, if the self is less central in dreams. Both lucid dreaming and self-reflection in dreams was increased experimentally by Purcell and colleagues (Purcell, Mullington, Moffitt, Hoffmann, & Pigeau, 1986), who manipulated the learning of remembering dreams. The group engaging in the most self-reflective and lucid dreaming over the course of the experiment had learned attention patterning schemas in waking, and thus had utilised mnemonics as a memory aid. Other memory aids, such as attention control, also significantly increased self-reflection and lucid dreaming, but to a lesser extent. Here the link between memory, dreams, and the centrality of the self in dreams are clearly linked, although in a more complex way than the close relationship between autobiographical memory and the self (see Conway, 2005).

So, although the characteristics of dreams may differ quite substantially from autobiographical memories, it seems that cognitive activity whilst dreaming is not as distinct from waking cognition as originally thought. Especially bizarre or emotional dreams may be encoded in the same way as normal autobiographical memories that are especially bizarre or emotional; thus there may not be too much difference at the stage of encoding between the actual dreams and events at the time of them being experienced. Let us focus on the remembering of the experience of dreams.

Dream recall

Why are dreams so difficult to recall in normal circumstances? It is clear from the huge discrepancy between the frequency of home-dream reports and the frequency of laboratory reports from REM sleep that we recall very few of our dreams and are usually unaware of having dreamed. Dream recall is extremely fragile and elusive. The slightest distraction on waking, or a brief delay before the recall attempt, is enough to disrupt the memory. Even if we do recall a dream on waking, it tends to vanish from memory later in the day and cannot be re-recalled. Goodenough (1978, 1992) reviewed two types of explanation for dream-recall failure. The first type of explanation centres on the content of dreams and the second on the nature of sleep and its effects on memory processes.

Content-centred theories of dream-recall failure

In support of this theory, Goodenough describes an experiment in which subjects were classified as habitual dream reporters—participants who frequently and consistently reported dreams—and as non-reporters—participants who were consistently unable to report dreams upon waking. Subjects were wakened at home by phone calls until they had each provided five dream reports. These reports were then presented to other subjects, who were tested for recall of the dreams and found the dreams of the non-reporters harder to remember. This result suggests that the content of non-reporters' dreams influenced retrievability, but Goodenough points out that their initial dream reports may have been vaguer or less vivid, so that it was the nature of the report rather than of the dream itself that was affecting recall. There is evidence that dramatic, emotional, and salient dreams are more likely to be recalled and that non-reporters do appear to have less salient dreams. Repression theories also centre on the content of dreams but, whereas the salience hypothesis predicts better recall of highly emotional dreams, repression theory predicts that intensely emotional dreams will be forgotten. There seems, however, to be no clear link between indices of repressive personality and dream-recall failure, and no link between repressive personality and the nature of dream content. Another content-centred explanation suggests that dreams are forgotten because, like scrambled texts, their content is disorganised. However, Goodenough noted that no relationship between ratings of disorganisation for initial dream reports and ability to re-recall the content had been found. It has also been suggested that the problem is motivational, and dreams are not remembered because we consider them to be unimportant and irrational. It is true that dream reporters tend to be more interested in their dreams than non-reporters, but this is more likely to be an effect than a cause of their superior dream recall.

A very different kind of theory explaining why we forget so many aspects of dreams was postulated by Freud (1900/1953). As part of the psychodynamic framework, dreams are made up of hidden fears and wishes that are so undesirable, individuals try not to allow them to become conscious. As a result, the defence mechanism of repression operates to disallow dream material from entering conscious memory upon waking. Although the specific cognitive operations are not outlined in Freud's early work, his theory (and indeed other psychodynamic ideas on dreaming by Jung and Adler, for example) is definitely worth a read.

Memory process explanations for dream-recall failure

Memory for dreams is relatively poor (e.g., Reed, 1974) and the memory traces seem to decay rapidly. However, research currently being conducted in our lab (e.g., Horton & Conway, 2006a, b) implies that if the memory trace is retained it remains in the memory store indefinitely, just like normal long-term memories. Processes such as displacement, whereby new material is encoded in favour of dreams, and rehearsal, whereby focusing upon a dream memory improves how well remembered it is, require further investigation. These processes are active in waking autobiographical memory. In addition, storage and retrieval may be similar in memory for dreams as well as normal semantic and autobiographical memory.

Dreams tend to be especially emotional and bizarre, so they are not easily comparable to other autobiographical memories. But why are they so difficult to recall? Isn't it typical for these kind of experiences to be especially memorable? As dreams are so different to other kinds of autobiographical memories, there may be a problem at encoding, with less detail being encoded to form an accessible memory trace. This could be explored by comparing levels of processing or state-dependent memory accounts of recalling dreams compared with waking autobiographical memories. Alternatively, the difference could lie at the level of retrieval. Typical psychodynamic conceptions of the unconscious may be able to shed light on why dreams are more inaccessible than normal memories, although this theory cannot be investigated easily in the laboratory.

According to Goodenough's theory, the ability to recall any dream, irrespective of its content, is impaired by the effects of sleep on memory processes. Memory process explanations point to the fact that dream recall exhibits several similarities with waking recall. For example, dream recall shows a recency effect, with dreams from later in the night being remembered better than those from earlier in the night, and a list-length effect, with a decline in re-recall when a larger number of dreams have been reported. On the assumption, then, that general memory processes are operating, it has been suggested that dream-recall failure may be explained in terms of state-dependency, with a mismatch of the sleep state and the waking state contributing to poor recall. Alternatively, it has been suggested that consolidation of memory traces is impaired by sleep. On this view, transfer to long-term memory does not take place, so recall is better if the dream is still in short-term memory when the sleeper wakes. However, against the consolidation hypothesis, there is evidence that the problem lies at the retrieval stage. Botman and Crovitz (1989) examined the effects of different types of cue on facilitating dream recall. They asked subjects to free recall their dreams first, and then presented them with cues that were either:

1 Cues relating to childhood events such as animal, car, fear, mother, house.
2 Cues relating to the subject's experiences of the previous day.
3 Colour words.

The childhood-event cues were ones that had been found effective in cueing real autobiographical memories. Both the childhood cues and the cues from the previous day facilitated additional dream recall. This finding fits with the everyday experience of being reminded of forgotten dreams by naturally occurring cues that bear some relation to the dream content. Botman and Crovitz put forward the interesting idea that the difficulty of retrieving dreams should be seen in terms of the context-plus-index model of memory (Reiser, Black, & Abelson, 1985; see Chapter 2) in which retrieval consists of accessing first the context and then the specific indices. Because dreams do not have contexts, this kind of retrieval process would be unable to access them. Cohen (1974), in a suggestion that is easily testable, discusses the interference hypothesis: New stimuli encountered upon awakening interfere with the memory trace for a dream.

As can be seen, there are too many explanations of dream-recall failure rather than too few. It is clear, however, that a satisfactory explanation must account for the fact that dreams can usually be recalled if the dreamer is wakened from REM sleep, but only seldom if waking occurs naturally. An explanation in terms of dream content cannot account for this. It seems more likely that characteristics of the physiological state that intervenes between REM sleep and natural waking are responsible for the fragility of memory for dreams.

A number of different measures of memory ability have been proposed in accounting for variance in dream recall. However, different types of memory do not seem to be related to dream recall in a simplistic, illustrative way. As dreaming involves the visual system so heavily, the visual cortex is highly active when dreaming, and visual memory has therefore been hypothesised to relate to dream recall frequency (DRF).

Cory, Ormiston, Simmel, and Dainoff (1975) assessed visual memory ability as an explanation of dream recall. A significant positive correlation was found. Consistent links between visual memory and DRF have also been reported for elderly persons (e.g., Waterman, 1991) and patients with dementia (Brunner et al., 1972; Kramer, Roth, & Trinder, 1975; both cited in Schredl, Wittman, Ciric, & Götz, 2003b).

Correlates of dream recall: Individual differences

Individual differences in dream recall are marked—perhaps even more so than individual differences in waking memory ability. Those designated as home-dream non-reporters only recall their dreams infrequently and also report dreams less frequently when wakened from REM sleep in the laboratory. It is not clear, therefore, whether they have poorer memory for dreams or whether they dream less often than those who are classed as home-dream reporters. Butler and Watson (1985) reasoned that dream quality determines the probability of recall. As we have seen, highly salient dreams that are vivid, emotional, bizarre, and active are more likely to be recalled, so that the ability to recall dreams may be linked to the ability to generate salient dreams. Butler and Watson predicted that this ability would be linked to specific cognitive skills. To test this hypothesis, they woke subjects during every REM period and recorded the incidence of dream reports, rated the salience of the reported dreams, and correlated these measures with the subjects' scores on tests of cognitive ability. The results showed that subjects with low scores on the Wechsler Block Design test produced dream reports on 48.5% of wakings; subjects with high scores produced 83.5% dream recall. Significant correlations were also obtained between dream recall and subtests of the Wechsler Memory Scale and tests of visualisation ability. Kerr (1993) has also noted that scores derived from the Betts Questionnaire for rated vividness of visual imagery and ability to control and manipulate images correlated with frequent dream recall. These findings serve to emphasise the continuity between cognitive processes in waking life and those involved in dreaming. It is worth noting that both Butler and Watson's visual ability measures, and those of Kerr, were not based specifically upon visual memory ability. Instead, visualisation ability may relate to traits such as fantasy proneness, which has been found to correlate with dream recall (e.g., Schredl et al., 2003b), whilst the likelihood of rating images as vivid may reflect a tendency to see images or thoughts clearly.

Other factors besides differences in cognitive skills also contribute to individual differences in dreaming. Reinsel et al. (1992) found that light sleepers reported 71% dreams in NREM sleep, whereas heavy sleepers reported only 21%. Heavy sleepers are thought to have insufficient cortical arousal to generate dreaming. Age and gender differences in dream reporting have also been observed. Kahn, Fisher, and Lieberman (1969) found that women recalled more dreams than men, and a group of elderly people aged 66–87 only recalled dreams on 55% of REM wakenings as compared to 87% for young adults. However, Waterman (1991), who studied the dream reports of 80 men and women aged between 45 and 75, found no age differences in dream frequency or in the length of the dream narrative. He measured general intelligence, visuospatial IQ and, as a test of visual memory, recall from a silent clip of Bergman's film *Wild Strawberries*. All these scores, especially memory for the film, correlated significantly with the length of the dream reports but not with dream frequency. This pattern of results makes sense if the length of the report depends on the same memory processes as waking memory tasks, but the incidence of dreaming is controlled by other factors, such as physiological ones. An age-related decline in the emotionality of dreams is also likely to have a physiological explanation. One possibility that has not received much consideration is that home-dream non-reporters are more susceptible to distraction and interference so that their recall is more likely to be disrupted. On this assumption, dream reporting would be linked to measures of attentional capacity and distractibility.

Several personality traits have been found to relate to DRF. Individuals who are "thin boundaried", that is, "unusually empathic, unusually open in psychological interviews, quickly and intensely involved in relationships, and have a fluidity of thoughts and feelings" are more likely to remember their dreams than "thick boundaried individuals" (Hartmann. 1991, p. 311). This trait is a psychodynamic notion of being "closer" to subconscious experience if thin boundaried. Boundary thinness has been found to correlate significantly with remembering longer, more detailed dreams, and the dreams being more emotional and vivid (Hicks, Bautista, & Hicks, 1999). Thin boundaried persons also appear to regard their dreams more highly; i.e., they attribute importance to dreams (Schredl, Kleinferchner, & Gell, 1996a). According to Hartmann, Rosen, and Rand (1998), "the trait continuum ranging from thick to thin boundaries is similar to the state continuum running from focused waking thought to dreaming, and (that) both continua refer to the same aspects of cortical activity" (p. 31), which provides a potential neurological explanation for this effect, although it fails to explain why some individuals are more likely to lie at a particular point on the continuum. It must also be emphasised that this relationship is merely correlational, not causal; that is, the cortical activity may be a result, as opposed to a precipitant, of this behavioural trait. Thus, the notion of thin boundaries being conceived as a psychodynamic trait of individual differences may be inaccurate. Rather, it is a level of cortical activation.

Another individual difference effect relating to remembering dreams is the essence of being "open to experience", which is one of the Big Five personality traits. Participants highly open to experience have been found to describe the most unknown characters in their dreams (characters who they do not know in their waking life), whereas "agreeable" individuals have been found to dream of a greater number of characters generally—including both known and unknown characters (Bernstein & Roberts, 1995).

Previous research has also been confirmed by Schredl, Ciric, Götz, and Wittmann (2003a), showing that, despite openness-to-experience and thin boundaries demonstrating reliable and significant relationships with rate of dream recall, attitudes towards dreaming, when included, increase the correlation coefficients considerably. Thus dream recall and attitudes or dreaming behaviours should be distinguished. This has particular implications for Schonbar's (1965) lifestyle hypothesis, which claims that a likelihood of remembering dreams forms part of a broader way of living; and is influenced by more than simple personality traits or cognitive functioning. Schredl, Nurnberg, and Weiler (1996b) further investigated these relationships, and the findings partly confirmed Schonbar's lifestyle hypothesis of dream recall. In addition, gender was also influential: Being female was a strong indicator of remembering dreams. This is a common finding.

However, this relationship between personality and dream recall frequency is not always clear-cut. Schredl (2002) failed to replicate the often-cited correlation between openness to experiences and dream recall frequency in a simple questionnaire case study. None of the six subsections of the openness to experiences personality trait (fantasy, aesthetics, feelings, actions, ideas, and values) was associated with recalling dreams, although the highest (yet still insignificant) relationship was with the "feelings" subsection, demonstrating the possible role that emotion plays when investigating these traits. Schredl notes that the usual findings about individual differences may result from certain individuals training themselves to recall dreams. This may especially be the case in individuals who hold a positive attitude towards dreams.

Also, Beaulieu-Prevost and Zadra (2005) challenged the idea of a simplistic relationship between attitudes towards dreams and dream recall frequency, in a study that has interesting methodological implications. Attitude towards dreams and diary DRF were independently related to estimated DRF, the measure usually adopted in studies claiming that a positive correlation exists between DRF and attitude towards dreams. According to this study, this only seems to be the case in questionnaire studies. Diary studies certainly differ in their operationalisation of DRF. Also, estimations of DRF were found to be inaccurate, with attitude towards dreams mediating this effect. Thus ". . . the choice of DRF measures has a direct and significant impact on the pattern of the relation between people's DRF and their attitude towards dreams" (p. 919).

Overall there are a number of factors that have been implicated as accounting for individual differences effects in dream recall. The effect of gender is a profound, well-documented one, with males being less likely to recall their dreams than females (e.g., Schredl et al., 1996b). Despite this being such a robust finding, few proposals have been put forward in an attempt to account for these differences.

Models of dreaming

Schredl et al. (2003b) tried to model the widespread variance in dream recall by using a statistical procedure known as structural equation modelling, in order to try and identify the factors involved in home dream recall. Only 8.4% of the variance was accounted for by the four factors that were significantly correlated with incidence of dream recall: personality, creativity, nocturnal awakenings, and attitude towards dreams. This extremely low value for accounted variance may imply there are other, as yet unexplained or immeasurable, variables influencing dream recall frequencies.

Schredl's model reflects two important aspects of this kind of research: First, there are a multiplicity of influences upon recalling dreams, including social (e.g., attitudes), cognitive (e.g., visual memory), biological (e.g., sleep) and psychological (e.g., stress) factors. Second, there is such a large amount of variance that has still not been accounted for. This may be because dream recall is a complicated product of a number of cognitive processes.

Antrobus (1991) and Fookson and Antrobus (1992) have explored the potential of connectionist modelling to provide a theoretical account of dreaming. There are two key assumptions that underlie their model: first, that the cerebral cortex is activated, and second, that sensory input is absent or inhibited. In REM sleep the cortex is apparently as active as it is in a waking state, yet there is little or no response to external stimulation. Both sensory and motor response subsystems are inhibited. Thus, during sleep, the pattern of distributed activation and inhibition is different from the waking state and, deprived of constraints from bottom-up sensory input, the system is dependent on its own self-generated reverberating activation. In the absence of external stimulation, rather than the conceptual modules controlling the production of visual images, image production by visual modules drives the interpretation by conceptual modules. When parallel distributed processing (PDP) networks are operating normally, bizarre combinations and bizarre sequences are not created because incompatible units are inhibited, but during sleep normal constraints based on the conditional probabilities of co-occurrence are not operating. Fookson and Antrobus have simulated the production of imagery and of sequences including bizarre and improbable combinations in their DREAMIT (Distributed Recurrent Activation Model of Imagery and Thought) models. DREAMIT-S is a single-layered network composed of 90 units representing features, objects, persons, and places, as well as abstract concepts such as values and roles. The network can create an integrated set of schemata integrating, for example, the "I-as-student" role with units for physics, college, and books, but cannot model sequence production. To achieve this, DREAMIT-BP, a multilayered model with back propagation, was constructed. To mimic the conditions prevailing during sleep, the output of the forward-propagation phase is folded back to the input layer. This model proved capable of generating sequences and also produced dream-like discontinuities and improbable combinations of features, as well as the repetitive loops that are sometimes experienced in dreams. This line of research, bringing together neural and cognitive analyses of dreaming, offers a valuable testbed for further predictions.

Functions of dreams

Ideally, models of dreaming should be linked to its function, but there is currently no agreement about the function of dreaming. Ellman and Weinstein (1991) distinguish four different accounts:

1   According to Crick and Mitchison (1986), REM sleep is a sort of reverse learning whereby the neural networks are cleared.
2   According to the opposite view, REM sleep is necessary for memory consolidation.
3   REM dreams are considered to provide endogenous stimulation necessary to maintain cortical function.
4   REM dreams are thought to fire a self-stimulation system that is positively rewarding. This would explain why REM sleep deprivation produces a rebound increase in dreaming.

In addition, Revonsuo (2000) posits an evolutionary function of dreaming. It is argued that dreams provide a situation in which threats can be simulated, so that the appropriate way to deal with the behaviour has been practised in case it is ever necessary in waking life. This theory has sparked a lengthy debate regarding the functionality of dreaming.

The memory consolidation function of dreaming, especially of REM sleep, has also been extensively studied. A number of mechanisms have been proposed in accounting for the relationship between physiology and improved memory after sleeping through different stages. Nielsen and Stenstrom (2005) briefly review these, outlining the proposed mechanisms by which reduced information flow (Stickgold, Hobson, Fosse, & Fosse, 2001), theta activity (Johnson, 2005), increased cortisol (Payne & Nadel, 2004), and connections between dispersed cortical networks and hippocampal-neocortical connections (Paller & Voss, 2004) can account for the consolidation of different kinds of memories (both declarative and episodic) whilst asleep.

Freud also considered the function of dreaming. He believed that dreams serve as a safety valve for desires that are censored during conscious waking life. The DREAMIT model does not offer a functional account of dreaming. However, although it is difficult to reconcile with either the first or second of these views, it could be consistent with the third or fourth.

CONCLUSIONS

Research on thoughts and dreams provides an excellent illustration of the strengths and weaknesses of everyday memory research. On the plus side of the equation, cognitive psychologists have risen to the challenge of investigating particularly inaccessible aspects of memory and have had considerable success in devising useful methodologies. Although ultimately dependent on the quality of people's self-reports, these methods incorporate experimental manipulations and the effectiveness of the manipulations in influencing the responses provides some validation for the self-reports. On the negative side, the theoretical accounts are weak: Models of reality monitoring are more descriptive than explanatory, but the development of connectionist models of dreaming holds promise for more powerful theorising. However, theoretical concepts derived from studies of memory for external stimuli and events have proved useful for interpreting internal memories. Interpretation of reality monitoring has employed concepts of visual imagery, automatic and attentional cognitive operations, and self-reference. Interpretation of dreaming has invoked concepts of interference, retention interval, salience, and narrative construction. This kind of theoretical overlap suggests that externally derived memories and internally derived memories can be accounted for within a unitary cognitive system.

REFERENCES

Anderson, R.E. (1984). Did I do it or did I only imagine doing it? *Journal of Experimental Psychology: General, 113*, 594–613.

Antrobus, J.S. (1978). Dreaming for cognition. In A.M. Arkin, J. Antrobus, & S. Ellman (Eds.), *The mind in sleep* (pp. 569–581). Hillsdale, NJ: Lawrence Erlbaum Associates, Inc.

Antrobus, J.S. (1991). Dreaming: Cognitive processes during cortical activation and high afferent thresholds. *Psychological Review, 98*, 96–121.

Aserinsky, E., & Kleitman, N. (1953). Regularly occurring periods of eye motility and concominant phenomena during sleep. *Science, 118*, 273–274.

Bartlett, F.C. (1932). *Remembering*. Cambridge, UK: Cambridge University Press.

Battaglia, D., Cavallero, C., & Cicogna, P. (1987). Temporal reference of the mnemonic sources of dreams. *Perceptual and Motor Skills, 64*, 979–983.

Beaulieu-Prevost, D., & Zadra, A. (2005). Dream recall frequency and attitude towards dreams: A reinterpretation of the relation. *Personality and Individual Differences, 38*, 919–927.

Bernstein, D.M., & Roberts, B. (1995). Assessing dreams through self-report questionnaires— relations with past research and personality, *Dreaming, 5*, 13–27.

Botman, H.I., & Crovitz, H.F. (1989). Dream reports and autobiographical memory. *Imagination, Cognition and Personality, 9*, 213–224.

Brunner, R., Kramer, M., Clark, J., Day, N., Trinder, J., & Roth, T. (1972). Dream recall in chronic brain syndrome patients. *Psychophysiology, 9*, 139–140.

Butler, S.F., & Watson, R. (1985). Individual differences in memory for dreams: The role of cognitive skills. *Perceptual and Motor Skills, 61*, 823–828.

Cavallero, C., & Foulkes, D. (1993). *Dreaming as cognition*. Hemel Hempstead, UK: Harvester-Wheatsheaf.

Cavallero, C., Foulkes, D., Hollifield, M., & Terry, R. (1990). Memory sources of REM and NREM dreams. *Sleep, 13*, 449–455.

Cicogna, P., & Bosinelli, M. (2001). Consciousness during dreams. *Consciousness and Cognition, 10*, 26–41.

Cipolli, C. (1995). Symposium: Cognitive processes and sleep disturbances: Sleep, dreams and memory: An overview. *Journal of Sleep Research, 4*, 2–9.

Cipolli, C., Battaglia, D., Cavallero, C., Cicogna, P., & Bosinelli, M. (1992). Associative mechanisms in dream production. In J. Antrobus & M. Bertini (Eds.), *The neuropsychology of sleep and dreaming*. Hillsdale, NJ: Lawrence Erlbaum Associates, Inc.

Cipolli, C., Bolzani, R., Cornoldi, C., De Beni, R., & Fagioli, I. (1993). Bizarreness effect in dream recall. *Sleep, 16*, 163–170.

Cohen, D.B. (1974). Toward a theory of dream recall. *Psychological Bulletin, 81*, 138–154.

Cohen, G., & Faulkner, D. (1988). The effects of aging on perceived and generated memories.

In L.W. Poon, D.C. Rubin, & B. Wilson (Eds.), *Cognition in adulthood and later life*. Cambridge, UK: Cambridge University Press.

Cohen, G., & Faulkner, D. (1989). Age differences in source forgetting: Effects on reality monitoring and eyewitness testimony. *Psychology and Aging, 4*, 10–17.

Conway, M.A. (2005). Memory and the self. *Journal of Memory and Language, 53*, 594–628.

Cory, T.L., Ormiston, E., Simmel, E., & Dainoff, M. (1975). Predicting the frequency of dream recall. *Journal of Abnormal Psychology, 84*, 261–266.

Crick, F., & Mitchison, G. (1986). REM sleep and neural nets. *Journal of Mind and Behaviour, 7*, 229–250.

De Witt, T. (1988). Impairment of reality constructing processes in dream experience. *Journal of Mental Imagery, 12*, 65–78.

Dywan, J., & Bowers, K. (1983). The use of hypnosis to enhance recall. *Science, 222*, 184–185.

Ecker, W. (2001). The relevance of memory processes for the understanding of compulsive checking. *Zeitschrift für klinische Psychologie und Psychotherapie, 30*, 45–54.

Ellman, S.J., & Weinstein, L.N. (1991). REM sleep and dream formation: A theoretical investigation. In S.J. Ellman & J.S. Antrobus (Eds.), *The mind in sleep: Psychology and psychophysiology* (2nd ed.). New York: Wiley.

Flavell, J.H., Flavell, E.R., & Green, F.L. (1983). Development of the appearance-reality distinction. *Cognitive Psychology, 15*, 95–120.

Foley, M.A., & Johnson, M.K. (1985). Confusions between memories for performed and imagined actions: A developmental comparison. *Child Development, 56*, 1145–1155.

Foley, M.A., Johnson, M.K., & Raye, C.L. (1983). Age-related changes in confusion between memories for thoughts and memories for speech. *Child Development, 54*, 51–60.

Fookson, J., & Antrobus, J. (1992). A connectionist model of bizarre thought and imagery. In J. Antrobus & M. Bertini (Eds.), *The neuropsychology of sleep and dreaming* (pp. 197–214). Hillsdale, NJ: Lawrence Erlbaum Associates, Inc.

Fosse, M.J., Fosse, R., Hobson, J.A., & Stickgold, R.J. (2003). Dreaming and episodic memory: A functional dissociation? *Journal of Cognitive Neuroscience, 15*, 1–9.

Foulkes, D. (1979). Home and laboratory dreams: Four empirical studies and a conceptual reevaluation. *Sleep, 2*, 233–251.

Foulkes, D., Bradley, L., Cavallero, C., & Hollifield, M. (1989). Processing of memories and knowledge in REM and NREM dreams. *Perceptual and Motor Skills, 68*, 365–366.

Freud, S. (1953). The interpretation of dreams. In J. Strachey (Ed.), *The standard edition of the complete psychological works of Sigmund Freud (Vols 4 and 5)*. London: Hogarth. [Originally published 1900]

Garrett, M., & Silva, R. (2003). Auditory hallucinations, source monitoring, and the belief that "voices" are real. *Schizophrenia Bulletin, 29*, 445–457.

Goodenough, D.R. (1978). Dream recall: History and current status of the field. In A.M. Arkin, J.S. Antrobus, & S.J. Ellman (Eds.), *The mind in sleep: Psychology and psychophysiology* (1st ed., pp. 113–140). Hillsdale, NJ: Lawrence Erlbaum Associates, Inc.

Goodenough, D.R. (1992). Dream recall: History and current status of the field. In A.M. Arkin, J.S. Antrobus, & S.J. Ellman (Eds.), *The mind in sleep: Psychology and psychophysiology* (2nd ed., pp. 143–171). Hillsdale, NJ: Lawrence Erlbaum Associates, Inc.

Hall, C.S., & Van de Castle, R.L. (1966). *The content analysis of dreams*. New York: Appleton-Century-Crofts.

Hartmann, E. (1991). *Boundaries in the mind*. New York: Basic Books.

Hartmann, E., Rosen, R., & Rand, W. (1998). Personality and dreaming: Boundary structure and dream content. *Dreaming, 8*, 31–39.

Heaps, C.M., & Nash, M. (2001) Comparing recollective experience in true and false autobiographical memories. *Journal of Experimental Psychology: Learning, Memory and Cognition, 27*, 920–930.

Hekkanen, S.T., & McEvoy, C. (2005). Source monitoring in eyewitness testimony: Implicit associations, suggestions, and episodic traces. *Memory and Cognition, 33*, 759–769.

Herman, J.H., Ellman, S.J., & Roffwarg, H.P. (1978). The problem of NREM dream recall re-examined. In A.M. Arkin, J.S. Antrobus, & S.J. Ellman (Eds.), *The mind in sleep: Psychology and psychophysiology* (1st ed.). Hillsdale, NJ: Lawrence Erlbaum Associates, Inc.

Hicks, R.A., Bautista, J., & Hicks, GJ. (1999). Boundaries and level of experience with six types of dreams. *Perception and Motor Skills, 89*, 760–762.

Hobson, J.A., Pace-Schott, E.F., & Stickgold, R. (2000). Dreaming and the brain: Toward a cognitive neuroscience of conscious states. *Behavioural and Brain Sciences, 23*, 793–1121.

Horton, C.L, & Conway, M.A. (2006a). *Comparing the characteristics of autobiographical memories and memories for dreams.* Paper presented at the Toward a Science of Consciousness conference, Center for Consciousness Studies, Tucson, Arizona, April.

Horton, C.L., & Conway, M.A. (2006b). *Comparing the retrieval of dreams and autobiographical memories: A recall versus recognition diary study.* Paper presented at the International Conference on Memory (ICOM-4), Sydney, Australia, July.

Hurovitz, C.S., Dunn, S., Domhoff, G.W., & Fiss, H. (1999). The dreams of blind men and women: A replication and extension of previous findings, *Dreaming, 9*, 183–193.

Johnson, J.D. (2005). REM sleep and the development of context memory. *Medical Hypotheses, 64*, 499–504.

Johnson, M.K. (1985). The origin of memories. In P.C. Kendall (Ed.), *Advances in cognitive behavioral research and therapy, Vol. 4.* London and New York: Academic Press.

Johnson, M.K. (1988). Reality monitoring: An experimental phenomenological approach. *Journal of Experimental Psychology: General, 117*, 390–394.

Johnson, M.K., Foley, M.A., Suengas, A.G., & Raye, C.L. (1988). Phenomenological characteristics of memories for perceived and imagined autobiographical events. *Journal of Experimental Psychology: General, 117*, 371–376.

Johnson, M.K., Hashtroudi, S., & Lindsay, S. (1993). Source monitoring. *Psychological Bulletin, 114*, 3–28.

Johnson, M.K., Kahan, T.L., & Raye, C.L. (1984). Dreams and reality monitoring. *Journal of Experimental Psychology: General, 113*, 329–344.

Johnson, M.K., & Raye, C.L. (1981). Reality monitoring. *Psychological Review, 88*, 67–85.

Johnson, M.K., Raye, C.L., Foley, H.J., & Foley, M.A. (1981). Cognitive operations and decision bias in reality monitoring. *American Journal of Psychology, 94*, 37–64.

Johnson, M.K., Raye, C.L., Wang, A., & Taylor, T. (1979). Facts and fantasy: The role of accuracy and variability in confusing imaginations with perceptual experiences. *Journal of Experimental Psychology: Human Learning and Memory, 5*, 229–246.

Kahn, E., Fisher, C., & Lieberman, L. (1969). Dream recall in the normal aged. *Journal of the American Geriatric Society, 17*, 1121–1126.

Kemp, S., Burt, C.D.B., & Sheen, M. (2003). Remembering dreamt and actual experiences. *Applied Cognitive Psychology, 17*, 577–591.

Kensinger, E.A., & Schacter, D.L. (2005). Emotional content and reality-monitoring ability: fMRI evidence for the influences of encoding processes. *Neuropsychologia, 43*, 1429–1443.

Kerr, N. (1993). Mental imagery, dreams and perception. In C. Cavallero & D. Foulkes (Eds.), *Dreaming as cognition* (pp. 18–37). Hemel Hempstead, UK: Harvester Wheatsheaf.

Koriat, A., Ben-Zur, H., & Sheffer, D. (1988). Telling the same story twice: Output monitoring and age. *Journal of Memory and Language, 27*, 23–39.

Kramer, M., Roth, T., & Trinder, J. (1975). Dreams and dementia: A laboratory exploration of dream recall and dream content in chronic brain syndrome patients. *International Journal of Aging and Human Development, 6*, 169–178.

Larsson, A.S., & Granhag, P.A. (2005). Interviewing children with the cognitive interview:

Assessing the reliability of statements based on observed and imagined events. *Scandinavian Journal of Psychology, 46,* 49–57.

Montangero, J. (1991). How can we define the sequential organization of dreams. *Perceptual and Motor Skills, 73,* 1059–1073.

Nielsen, T.A., Kuiken, D., Alain, G., Stenstrom, P., & Powell, R.A. (2004). Immediate and delayed incorporations of events into dreams: Further replication and implications for dream function. *Journal of Sleep Research, 13,* 327–336.

Nielsen, T.A., & Stenstrom, P. (2005). What are the memory sources of dreaming? *Nature, 437,* 1286–1289.

Paller, K.A., & Voss, J.L. (2004). Memory reactivation and reconsolidation during sleep. *Learning and Memory, 11,* 664–670.

Payne, J.D., & Nadel, L. (2004). Sleep, dreams, and memory consolidation: The role of the stress hormone cortisol. *Learning and Memory, 11,* 671–678.

Purcell, S., Mullington, J., Moffitt, A., Hoffmann, R., & Pigeau, R. (1986). Dream self-reflectiveness as a learned cognitive skill. *Sleep, 9,* 423–437.

Radomsky, A.S., Gilchrist, P.T., & Dussault, D. (2006). Repeated checking really does cause memory distrust. *Behaviour Research and Therapy, 44,* 305–316.

Rauchs, G., Bertran, F., Guillery-Girard, B., Desgranges, B., Kerrouche, N., Denise, P., Foret, J., & Eustache, F. (2004). Consolidation of strictly episodic memories mainly requires rapid eye movement sleep. *Sleep, 27,* 395–401.

Rauchs, G., Desgranges, B., Foret, J., & Eustache, F. (2005). The relationship between memory systems and sleep stages. *Journal of Sleep Research, 14,* 123–140.

Reed, H. (1974). The art of remembering dreams. *Quadrant, 9,* 48–60.

Reinsel, R., Antrobus, J., & Wollman, M. (1992). Bizarreness in dreams and waking fantasy. In J. Antrobus & M. Bertini (Eds.), *The neuropsychology of sleep and dreaming.* Hillsdale, NJ: Lawrence Erlbaum Associates, Inc.

Reiser, B.J., Black, J.B., & Abelson, R.P. (1985). Knowledge structures in the organisation and retrieval of autobiographical memories. *Cognitive Psychology, 17,* 89–137.

Revonsuo, A. (2000). A reinterpretation of dreams: An evolutionary hypothesis on the function of dreaming. *Behavioral and Brain Sciences, 23,* 877–901.

Roberts, K.P., & Blades, M. (1995). Children's discrimination of memories for actual and pretend actions in a hiding task. *British Journal of Developmental Psychology, 13,* 321–333.

Schonbar, R.A. (1965). Differential dream recall frequency as a component of "life style". *Journal of Consulting Psychology, 29,* 468–474.

Schredl, M. (2002). Questionnaires and diaries as research instruments in dream research: Methodological issues. *Dreaming, 12,* 17–26.

Schredl, M., Ciric, P., Götz, S., & Wittmann, L. (2003a). Dream recall frequency, attitude towards dreams and openness to experience. *Dreaming, 13,* 145–153.

Schredl, M., & Doll, E. (1998). Emotions in diary dreams. *Consciousness and Cognition, 7,* 634–646.

Schredl, M., & Erlacher, D. (2004). Lucid dreaming frequency and personality. *Personality and Individual Differences, 37,* 1463–1473.

Schredl, M., & Hofmann, F. (2003). Continuity between waking activities and dream activities, *Consciousness and Cognition, 12,* 298–308.

Schredl, M., Kleinferchner, P., & Gell, T. (1996a). Dreaming and personality: Thick vs. thin boundaries. *Dreaming, 6,* 219–223.

Schredl, M., Nurnberg, C., & Weiler, S. (1996b). Dream recall, attitude toward dreams, and personality. *Personality and Individual Differences, 20,* 613–618.

Schredl, M., Wittmann, L., Ciric, P., & Götz, S. (2003b). Factors of home dream recall: A structural equation model. *Journal of Sleep Research, 12,* 133–141.

Sluzenski, J., Newcombe, N., & Ottinger, W. (2004). Changes in reality monitoring and episodic memory in early childhood. *Developmental Science, 7,* 225–245.

Solms, M. (1997). *The neuropsychology of dreams: A clinico-anatomical study.* Hillsdale, NJ: Lawrence Erlbaum Associates, Inc.

Stickgold, R., Hobson, J.A., Fosse, R., & Fosse, M. (2001). Sleep, learning, and dreams: Offline memory reprocessing. *Science, 294,* 1052–1057.

Suengas, A.G., & Johnson, M.K. (1988). Qualitative effects of rehearsal on memories for perceived and imagined complex events. *Journal of Experimental Psychology: General, 117,* 377–389.

Sussman, A.L. (2001). Reality monitoring of performed and imagined interactive events: Developmental and contextual effects. *Journal of Experimental Child Psychology, 79,* 115–138.

Waterman, D. (1991). Aging and memory for dreams. *Perceptual and Motor Skills, 73,* 45–75.

11 Memory changes across the lifespan

Chris J.A. Moulin and Susan E. Gathercole

INTRODUCTION

Across the lifespan, people experience changes in their abilities, skills, and goals. Cognitive psychologists interested in development investigate the ways in which these change, and what that can tell us about cognitive processes. In the real world, implicit assumptions about these changes are part of the fabric of society, which places age limits on various activities as a control for competency and responsibility. The majority of societies, for example, do not permit an individual to drive until an age between late adolescence and early adulthood as a means of ensuring that drivers have sufficient levels of cognitive development and responsibility to handle a car safely. Education systems similarly enshrine assumptions about changing cognitive competence with age, with changes in the delivery of teaching, classroom organisation, curriculum content, and expectations of the independence of learner as a function of age. Further on in the lifespan, older adults in many societies are expected to retire at a particular age; retirement ages are often lower for employments that involve robust challenges to physical strength and decision-making, such as piloting. Elderly drivers may also need to demonstrate their capability to drive safely.

Many cognitive psychologists interested in both applied and theoretical work have studied these changes in the context of memory. Consider the lifespan retrieval curve shown in Chapter 2. As our goals change and our memory abilities develop, the accessibility of memories for our own life events also change. Before the age of 3 years, very few memories are available (e.g., Rubin, Wetzler, & Nebes, 1986). This developmental pattern is particularly interesting as it appears children have memories at the time, although they cannot access them later in life (Conway, 2005). Understanding childhood amnesia will illuminate the processes involved in autobiographical memory, and some key features of childhood cognition, too.

The lifespan retrieval curve is quite unique as a phenomenon, since it covers the whole of life: from infancy to old age. In fact, unless you test people who are old enough, the standard pattern of childhood amnesia, the reminiscence bump, a period of forgetting, and a recent period of superior memory do not appear. Typically, memory researchers focus either on childhood development (the acquisition of knowledge and skills) or cognitive ageing (the loss of knowledge and skills). In fact, developmental psychology has come to refer almost uniquely to childhood development, and psychologists also rarely explore changes during the middle period of the lifespan. As a consequence, few theories of cognitive change exist that take in both the acquisition and loss of skills and knowledge, and it is fair to say that understanding how memory changes right across the lifespan and how early development affects later changes in memory, even in old age, is at the forefront of research. Recent studies, for instance, show that you can produce earlier autobiographical memories for words that you encountered early in life (Conway, 2005). For instance, you are more likely to produce a childhood memory if cued by the word *dragon* than by *asparagus*. Other studies show that words and concepts encountered earlier in life are better retained in older age, a phenomenon known as the *age of acquisition effect* (Morrison, Ellis, & Quinlan, 1992). As our understanding of memory proceeds, we are likely to uncover more about this special relationship between how and when you encounter skills and knowledge and what that means right across the lifespan.

Lifespan development and the changes in memory across the lifespan is a huge topic. For an overview of cognitive development, we recommend Taylor (2005). For a complete view of the various types of memory covered elsewhere in this book and how they developed in the early years, see Gathercole (1998, 1999, 2002). You can also find reviews of eyewitness memory in children (e.g., Davies, 1995) and older adults (e.g., Moulin, Thompson, Wright, & Conway, 2006). Rather than give a shallow overview of this huge topic, in this chapter we take a detailed approach and discuss some of our own research from either end of the lifespan. We also take the opportunity to introduce a memory system not covered elsewhere in this book: working memory. The first section focuses on learning in childhood development and its most practical impact, on classroom learning. The second section covers a critical debate in studies of cognitive ageing: Are old adults only impaired in the psychologist's laboratory, or do these difficulties extend to everyday life? In addition, we take a quick look at the way in which cognitive ageing theories have been applied to the real world.

WORKING MEMORY

Working memory is a set of cognitive functions that allows a person to hold and manipulate information over short periods of time. It can be thought of as supporting all real-world tasks, from involvement in simple activities such as remembering a telephone number to the support of more complex cognitive processing such as reasoning, problem-solving, and mental arithmetic. Depending on your view— working memory researchers are very fond of telling fellow researchers at conferences that there are as many definitions of working memory as there are working memory researchers—working memory ranges from a useful "desktop" that is necessary to hold and manipulate information, to an essential component for all conscious activity. What is clear is that for most human activity it is very useful to be able to hold some information in mind whilst accessing related information, performing some action upon it, or focusing on another task. Think about how you need to repeat a telephone number over and over in your mind whilst you search for a pen, and you have a basic grasp of what working memory is for, how it works—and how fragile it is. If you are asked a question while looking for the pen and chanting the number, chances are you will lose the number you were once focused on.

The most frequently cited model of working memory (Baddeley & Hitch, 1974) is shown in Figure 11.1. Briefly, working memory is a limited capacity system that

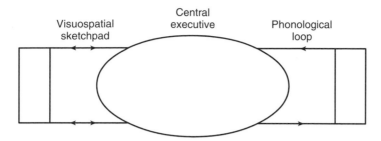

Figure 11.1 The working memory model (after Baddeley & Hitch, 1974).

maintains information over intervals of only a few seconds. Its contents are subject to displacement by new input, and it operates by interacting with other parts of the cognitive system such as stored knowledge or the products of perception. Figure 11.1 shows three components. Information in the auditory and visual modalities is served by separate systems and these are controlled by the third component, a central processor, known as the central executive. The phonological loop is responsible for maintaining and manipulating speech based information whilst the second "slave-system", the visuospatial sketchpad, holds and manipulates visual and spatial information (for recent developments in this model see Baddeley, 2000). The division of working memory into specialised, modality-specific components is supported by findings of selective interference on memory tasks involving visual and verbal information: A secondary visual secondary task interferes with memory for visual but not verbal information, whilst verbal secondary tasks interfere with the retention of verbal but not visual information.

One potential difficulty for the psychology student is the use of the term working memory. Often, people will incorrectly use the terms short-term memory and working memory interchangeably. This is because working memory, like short-term memory, only operates over a period of a few seconds, but this an unhelpful over-generalisation. There is a part–whole relationship between the two: Short-term memory is part of, but not all of, working memory. The area is further confused by the fact that medics, legal professionals, and the general public use the term short-term memory to refer to things that happened in the last few days or weeks, and not technically, as psychologists do, to refer to a brief and temporary store of just a few seconds. To clarify, short-term memory operates as a very brief *store* of memory, whereas working memory has the distinction of being a system that co-ordinates *processing* and *storage*. Working memory can be thought of as acting on the contents of short-term memory.

The utility of the working memory theory is its applicability to real-world situations. It has been applied to many populations and domains. For instance, the phonological loop, a component of working memory that allows the temporary storage of sounds over very brief periods, is thought to play a crucial role in learning new words (Baddeley, Gathercole, & Papagno, 1998; Gathercole, 2006). Tests of phonological loop capacity have advanced understanding of language learning in bilingual individuals (Thorn & Gathercole, 1999) and also in children with developmental impairments of language learning (Archibald & Gathercole, 2006). Working memory also plays an important role in multimedia learning (Gyselinck,

Cornoldi, Dubois, De Beni, & Ehrlich, 2002) and navigation (Garden, Cornoldi, & Logie, 2002).

Garden et al. carried out an experiment where they asked volunteers to find their way around the medieval town of Padova. Of interest was the way in which people use working memory to aid navigation—in particular, they examined the influence of verbal and visuospatial interference on their ability to do so. First, participants were instructed to follow the experimenter on a route through the city, and were told to stop at a particular point. Participants did this whilst either the phonological or the visuospatial component of working memory was occupied. To occupy phonological processes, participants repeated the same word over and over again into a microphone connected to a portable tape recorder on their back. To occupy the visuospatial part of working memory, the participants walked through the streets whilst tapping out a sequence on a keyboard connected to a computer strapped to their back. Having learned the route under these conditions, participants had to complete the same route again, on their own. Route learning and navigation was impaired by both of these concurrent tasks. However, tapping of a repeated sequence was more disruptive for those people who were better at navigation under normal circumstance; for those who were not so spatially proficient, the verbal task was more disruptive.

This study illustrates the value of the individual differences approach in working memory research, and in lifespan studies more generally. Working memory performance is extremely varied between individuals, with some people better at one aspect of working memory, and others better at another. Some people seem to have much larger capacities, whilst others have only a very small temporary memory store. Of relevance developmentally, these differences tend to be greatest at the early and late points of the lifespan. Psychologists have used these individual differences not only to explore the range of abilities in development, but also to explore how different skills and abilities relate to each other. If someone is good at Task A, for instance, and also good at Task B, it suggests that these tasks may be based on similar underlying processes, especially if another person is not good at either Task A or Task B. This focus on individual differences is the predominant scientific approach in the studies described below in children and older adults. It is illustrated by the navigation study: People who spontaneously use spatial strategies are both better at navigation and more susceptible to spatial interference. In contrast, individuals who rely more on verbal strategies are relatively poor at navigation, and are prone to interference from irrelevant verbal material.

Variations in working memory in children

Working memory capacity is usually measured using complex memory span tasks in which participants are required to combine memory for sequences of items with other processing activities. The amount of memory and processing activity is increased over successive trials until memory errors are made. The first complex span task to be used was reading span, in which participants read a series of sentences while attempting to remember the final words of each sentence for recall after the final sentence in the sequence (Daneman & Carpenter, 1980). The number of sentences is increased until the participant starts to make errors, and this point is scored as their reading span. A variety of complex memory span tasks have since been developed that are suitable for use with children. Listening span is similar to reading span, except that sentences are spoken and not read, and participants are required to make a judgement such as deciding whether each sentence is true or false following its presentation. Another complex span task is backward digit recall, in which a sequence of digits is presented and the participant is required to recall them in reverse sequence.

As intimated above, performance on working memory tasks like these is subject to large degrees of individual variation. For example, based on a large sample of 709 children aged between 4 and 11, Alloway, Gathercole, and Pickering (2004) estimate that within an average class of 30 children, differences in working memory capacity corresponding to 5 years of normal development are found between the highest and lowest scoring individuals. That means that even though classes tend to represent a very narrow range in terms of chronological age, the cognitive abilities of the class, especially for working memory, are equivalent to having a class made up of some 5-year-olds and some 10-year-olds, and everything in between. But what does working memory achieve in the real world, and how do these children differ in the classroom and their ability to learn?

Complex memory span measures of working memory are closely associated with children's learning abilities in the key scholastic domains of literacy (Gathercole & Pickering, 2000) and mathematics (Geary, Hoard, Byrd-Craven, & DeSoto, 2004). In fact, these skills are related to scholastic achievement on formal national tests of mathematics and English at the ages of 6/7, 10/11, and 13/14 years. Gathercole, Pickering, Knight, and Stegmann (2003) showed that working memory scores increased with English and mathematics attainment levels: the children with low attainment levels had working memory scores that were considerably below the population mean, the average attainment group had average working memory scores, and the high-attainment group scored considerably above the population mean on the working memory assessments. Indeed, working memory performance measured when children start formal schooling is an effective predictor of later school achievements. Low working memory scores very early on in formal education may therefore be useful in identifying children who are at risk of poor educational progress over the coming years, facilitating prompt intervention.

Many children who are recognised by their school as having learning difficulties in the areas of reading and mathematics have marked impairments of working memory. But is this just because working memory is such a fundamental aspect of cognition, or are working memory deficits characteristic of any specific profile of learning difficulty? Pickering and Gathercole (2004) assessed 734 children aged 4 to 15 years to address this question. Schools were asked to identify whether any children had recognised special educational needs and, if so, to describe the nature of these needs. In all, 98 children had special needs. Significant working memory deficits were found in two groups: in children whose primary problems were related to language, and in children with difficulties in both reading and mathematics. In contrast, children whose problems were restricted to reading alone typically scored in the low average range of working memory scores, and children identified as having behavioural disorders that included emotional and behavioural disturbance and attentional deficits performed entirely normally on the test battery. Learning difficulties that extend across both reading and mathematics, or language, therefore appear to be characteristic of children with poor working memory function. In a follow-up study, it was demonstrated that measures of working memory do not simply act as a proxy for general verbal ability, as specific links with learning attainments are found even when associated differences in general language and verbal IQ are taken into account (Gathercole, Alloway, Willis, & Adams, 2006).

Slow rates of learning therefore characterise children who perform poorly on complex memory measures of working memory. Gathercole and colleagues suggest that the reason for this is that working memory acts as a bottleneck for learning. The acquisition of knowledge and skill in complex domains such as literacy and mathematics requires the gradual accumulation of knowledge over multiple learning episodes, many of which will take place in the structured learning environment of the classroom. Learning is thus an incremental process that builds upon the knowledge structures and understanding that have already been acquired: Any factor that disturbs this acquisition process will have deleterious consequences for the rate of learning, as the necessary foundations for progress will not be in place. It is proposed that working memory capacity is one of the factors that constrains learning success in potential learning episodes. Many classroom activities require the child to keep information in mind whilst engaging in another cognitive activity that might be very demanding for that individual. Mental arithmetic is an example of such a working memory demanding activity for adults. In children, whose working memory capacity is considerably smaller and who do not have the same bedrock of stored knowledge and expertise to support cognitive processing, working memory challenges of a comparable magnitude are present in much simpler activities, such as writing sentences, adding up totals of objects displayed on cards, or detecting rhyming words in a poem read by the teacher. Children with poor working memory capacities will face severe difficulties in meeting the demands of these situations and, as a result of their working memory overload, will fail in part or all of the learning activity. Such situations represent missed learning opportunities and if they occur frequently, will result in a slow rate of learning. The classroom difficulties of children with impairments of working memory are described in more detail in the next section.

The memory-aware classroom

Following on from this exhaustive individual differences approach, Gathercole and colleagues began to investigate the relationship between working memory and learning during the school years in a very different way to previous research in the field. The motivation for the novel approach was straightforward—the existing body of research evidence did not equip working memory researchers to answer two fundamental questions that we were often asked by educational professionals in the real world. The questions were, first: What particular problems do children with poor working memory function encounter in the classroom? And second: How can these children be helped to improve their learning outcomes?

A major limitation of the individual differences approach is that although it has established the close developmental associations between working memory and learning, somewhat paradoxically, it tells us relatively little about the individual child. Studies in this tradition involve the administration of measures of ability completed outside of the context of daily classroom activities, and focus on statistical associations between these measures across relatively large numbers of participants. The individual profiles of children with poor working memory in these studies—in terms of their strengths and weaknesses in the practical context of the classroom—are quite unknown. To address these issues, Gathercole and colleagues returned to observational methods, spending time watching teachers teach and children learn. On the basis of their findings, they recommended an approach to helping children with poor memory skills that was termed the *memory-aware classroom*.

The observations focused in particular on learning situations in which the child frequently failed; in the case of failure, the specific working memory demands of the activities were evaluated. By comparing the observations of these children with those of children with normal working memory function, we aimed to identify the classroom difficulties that are characteristic of poor working memory. The operational definition of working memory demands that guided the observations was the requirement of temporary mental storage, or temporary storage combined with ongoing processing. If the hypothesis that working memory acts as a bottleneck for learning is correct, individuals with low working memory capacity should frequently fail in activities that impose high working memory loads.

Each child was observed for 1 week in school in Year 1 (the second year of full-time education, when children are aged 5 to 6 years) in state primary schools in an urban area of north-east England. David, Phillip, and Joshua were boys selected on the basis of scores at least two standard deviations below the population mean on two complex span measures (backwards digit recall and counting span). Class teachers were asked to comment on the child's behaviour in school, including both their social adjustment and academic profile, but no specific information was supplied to the teacher about why a particular child had been selected to participate in the study. The same procedure was also followed for three children with average memory scores at school entry.

David, Phillip, and Joshua were found to have normal social adjustment, and were relatively popular with their peers. Each child had been placed in the lowest ability group in both literacy and mathematics within the class. Although none of them was timid in general, they were relatively reserved in activities such as "carpet time", in which the teacher works with a large group on a particular activity that typically involves asking questions to the group. The low memory function children rarely volunteered answers to open questions, and frequently failed to provide an appropriate answer when directly questioned by the teacher.

The teachers were aware in each case that the children were struggling in their curriculum activities. The children were described in terms that implied problems with attention and motivation rather than memory, with the teachers using phrases such as "It's in one ear and out of the other" and "He doesn't listen to a word I say". The children, however, demonstrated awareness of their memory failures. Phillip, a child with very poor working memory function, commented to the classroom assistant "I forget everything, me!" On other occasions, failures were noted that were likely to be due to high working memory demands even in children with normal working memory skills for their age. For instance, one child was given a long series of task instructions by her teacher and failed to complete the activity. When asked why, she commented "Mrs. Martin told me a lot and I forgot". In another class-based activity in which children had to clap one more time than the preceding child in a circle, many children failed to clap the correct number of times. Two children spontaneously exclaimed "I forgot the number!" Thus the children appeared to have good metacognitive knowledge of when their working memory fails them, although these failures are less apparent to the teaching staff.

Four areas of frequent failure emerged in all of the low working memory function children, which were associated with significant working memory loads: Following instructions, keeping place in a complex task, coping with simultaneous storage and processing demands, and longer term remembering. Problems of these kinds were rarely observed in either the children with normal memory function, or the children with low phonological loop scores. We discuss *following instructions* as an example of the approach, and what it suggests for practice.

Working memory and following instructions

One commonly observed memory-related failure was an inability to follow instructions from the teacher. The failure appeared to reflect forgetting of the content of the instruction, particularly when it was fairly lengthy and did not represent a routine classroom activity. Here are three examples of this kind of failure:

On one occasion, the teacher gave the following instruction to David: "Put your sheets on the green table, put your arrow cards in the packet, put your pencil away and come and sit on the carpet." David failed to put his sheet on the green table. Teacher asked David if he could remember where he was supposed to put it; he couldn't, and needed reminding.

Joshua's teacher handed him his computer login cards and told him to go and work on computer number 13. He failed to do this, because he had forgotten what computer he had been told to use.

Phillip was asked to go back and put an "n" in the word bean. He went back and asked the classroom assistant what he had been asked to do.

Considered individually, these failures to remember instructions may seem to have relatively trivial consequences. However, the children's frequent forgetting of general instructions and specific task guidance was noted to impair both their individual successes in completing learning activities and the smooth running of the classroom.

Gathercole and colleagues then carried out a systematic investigation of the role of working memory in the comprehension of instructions. Five- and 6-year old children completed two sentence-processing tasks involving spoken instructions that related to the manipulation of a set of objects placed in their full view. The instructions all employed simple structures and high frequency verbs, but varied in length from short ("touch the white bag") to long ("touch the blue folder then pick up the red ball and put it in the green folder"). In one version of the task, the child was asked to repeat the sentence immediately. In the other version, the child was required to carry out the instruction and in both cases, the accuracy of the response was scored.

Each child was also tested on measures of verbal short-term memory, working memory, and nonverbal reasoning ability. The results were striking. Scores on a measure of working memory—backwards digit span—were strongly associated with the child's accuracy of performing the instructions, but not of repeating the instructions. Thus, it seems that there is a highly specific link between working memory and the use of spoken instructions to guide action. Performing a sequence of actions imposes very different demands on memory to the immediate repetition of an instruction, as the instruction has to be retained for a sufficient period to guide action through to the final step of the action sequence, rather than being immediately recalled.

The researchers then turned their attention to how to compensate for working memory difficulties in the classroom. The obvious way of improving the learning outcomes of children with poor working memory capacities would be to improve working memory by training. Unfortunately, however, no training programme has as yet been identified that leads to substantial and generalisable gains in either memory performance or academic attainments. Generally, it seems likely that working memory capacity is genetically determined and is relatively resistant to modification by environmental experience: Working memory scores are not significantly related to measures of the quality of the preschool environment or socio-economic factors, for instance.

Gathercole and colleagues recommend an alternative approach for children with poor working memory function: Controlling the learning environment in a way that prevents working memory overload and consequent task failures. The main focus of this approach is on promoting understanding of working memory and its practical consequences for classroom learning in education professionals (Gathercole & Alloway, 2005).

Consider Joshua, who erroneously copied *Monday 11th November* and underneath, the title *The Market*, as *moNemarket*. Place-keeping errors such as repeating and/or skipping letters and words during sentence writing, or missing out large chunks of a task, are common features of working memory overload. The first step for the teacher is to recognise this error as a working memory failure. The next step is to evaluate the working demands of learning activities. In particular, activities such as keeping track of the place reached in the course of multilevel tasks (e.g., writing a sentence either from memory or from the whiteboard) impose heavy storage demands on working memory. An effective strategy for the teacher to use in order to avoid working memory-related failures is to reduce working memory loads in structured activities. This can be achieved in a number of ways, including breaking down tasks and instructions into smaller components. It would be useful to write the instructions in different coloured ink in order to create a visual cue for the child to keep track of their place. This way, the child can see that the red ink represents the day of the week and the blue ink represents the activity title. By using visual cues to support working memory, the child has external supports to help him/her achieve success in these individual learning activities.

It is also possible to compensate for the difficulties children with low working memory capacities often have in following lengthy instructions. Typically, the children carry out the first or possibly the second action in such an instruction, but rarely complete such a multistep sequence successfully. Teacher repetition of instructions will be useful, but probably will not ensure successful remembering if the amount of information to be remembered is simply too great for the child. In such cases, instructions should be modified to be brief and linguistically simple, and should be broken down into shorter instructions presented separately if possible. When activities take place over an extended period of time, giving the child a reminder that is relevant for that particular phase of the task rather than repetition of the entire instruction is likely to be most helpful. Finally, one of the best ways to ensure that the child has not forgotten crucial information is to ask them to repeat it.

Working memory in children: Summary

We have seen that working memory is a fundamental cognitive ability that varies greatly from individual to individual. This variation is of critical importance, as it has consequences for achievement and attainment amongst children. And yet, once one has understood the basic idea of working memory as a system that—with varying degrees of success—coordinates the storage and processing of information, it becomes relatively easy to identify and remediate errors due to working memory failure. While memory is developing to adult levels of performance, there are knock-on effects on important features of everyday life, such as the ability to follow instructions, and academic progress. The individual differences approach to working memory is also a key element of the research literature on memory function in older adults. In the next section, we consider the parallel literature on changes in memory function as adults become older, and consider the practical implications of this research, too.

MEMORY CHANGES IN OLDER ADULTS

In older adults, the general view is that as you get older your memory gets worse. But is there evidence that memory does actually get worse—or is it just a cliché? There are in fact a great number of social changes that happen across the lifespan, and it seems that the mere fact that everyone expects to have poorer memory as they get older does, to some extent, actually give them poorer memory. For instance, there is evidence to suggest that Chinese cultures, without the negative view of ageing, do not suffer the same memory difficulties as their Western controls (Levy & Langer, 1994). Also, some researchers point to the massive changes in social and cognitive activity in older adults, and suggest these may contribute to memory loss (The "Use it or lose it" theory, e.g., Hultsch, Hertzog, Small, & Dixon, 1999). However, by studying memory in relation to brain function, it is clear that memory is actually impaired in older adults. Particular areas of the brain suffer disproportionate cell loss as you age, and these give the memory deficit a certain flavour.

In particular, older adults' memory function is characterised by a series of deficits common to damage to the frontal lobe area of the brain. Such a model of cognitive decline based on age-related changes in the brain is a useful context in which to discuss memory dysfunction, since armed with the knowledge of which brain locations are most affected by age, it is possible to make predictions of which particular aspects of memory function are most affected by the ageing process. It is, however, very important to note that, while brain cells are being lost, this is an inevitable part of "healthy ageing". Memory loss in older adults occurs ubiquitously, and is not the same thing as Alzheimer's disease or dementia (see Chapter 13), which is a patho-logical condition associated with age.

The most-often cited model of memory change with healthy age is that of memory ageing as frontal lobe dysfunction (for critical reviews of this idea, see Greenwood, 2000; Perfect, 1997). This model of memory dysfunction rests on the observations that the most marked atrophy of cells in the ageing brain is the frontal cortex (e.g., Ivy, MacLeod, Petit, & Markus, 1992), that older adults show deficits on tasks related to frontal function in batteries of cognitive tasks and that these correlate with memory performance (e.g., Parkin & Java, 1999) and that there is a general simi-larity between frontal patients and older adults on the patterns of performance across experimental tasks (e.g., Perfect, 1997). Recent advances in neuroimaging have offered more support for the frontal model. Friedman (2000) has shown that memory tasks allied to electrical activity in the surface of the frontal lobes of the brain are the areas where there are large age-related differences—with a lack of brain activity in the old and a corresponding difficulty with memory. Other work indicates that older adults need to activate more of their frontal lobes than younger people in order to achieve the same memory task, a common finding being that whereas young people use a small, unilateral region of the frontal lobes, older adults show more extensive activation across both sides of the frontal lobes (e.g., Langenecker & Nielson, 2003).

Most of the research focus on the frontal lobes has arisen due to striking simi-larities between the types of memory tasks that frontal patients have difficulty with, and the types of task that yield largest differences between groups of young and old participants. Below, we outline four themes in the ageing and memory literature: Recall compared to recognition, source memory, working memory and metamem-ory. For each, the memory ability and process is thought to be largely reliant on the frontal lobes, and older adults show a particular deficit on that particular function.

Older adults' recall is more impaired than recognition

Numerous empirical studies have indicated that whereas older adults' recall of information may be impaired, recognition performance, even for the same materials, tends to be preserved (e.g., Craik & Jennings, 1992). With recognition being an easier task than recall, this pattern could just be because older adults suffer with difficult tasks. Theoretical research in this area has focused on this difficulty issue. Craik and McDowd (1987) demonstrated that by making recognition extremely difficult by dividing attention during test (asking participants to perform a visual recognition test whilst being administered a recognition test on headphones), young and old still showed no differences in recognition performance. Differences in recall were retained, even though the recall test was much easier (and yielded higher levels of performance) than recognition.

Thus, on quantity of information retrieved, older adults and younger controls seem equal on recognition tasks. However, there is substantial evidence to suggest that the quality of recognition performance in older adults is impaired. Tulving (1983) pioneered a memory test procedure where participants are required to report their subjective experience of remembering (see Chapter 12). In this task, when responding yes or no to whether they have encountered an item before, participants are also asked to give an evaluation of this answer. Participants are required to evaluate whether they "remember" an event or find it "familiar" (sometimes referred to as "just knowing"). Remembering an event includes a sense of "pastness" and an ability to retrieve contextual information about encountering the stimulus before, such as remembering what you were thinking and feeling when you bumped into a man in the chemist's shop a few days ago. Finding an item familiar is a judgement based on a lack of this rich evocative information, such as the type of memory we have for facts.

Parkin and Walter (1992) carried out this procedure on older adults with standard word task experiments. They demonstrated that older adults report significantly fewer remember responses, indicating that their memory performance is characterised by a lack of contextual information and an over-reliance on the mere familiarity of a previously encountered stimulus. This finding was replicated by Perfect and Dasgupta (1997), who also wanted to examine the justifications of recollective experience in older adults. They asked participants to "think aloud" whilst they were learning the words, and they examined what introspections and observations participants made. When they were tested, participants made the usual recollective judgements, as above, and also were asked to justify their response. The younger adults showed clear consistency in their justifications of their remember responses and their reports of thoughts during study, reflecting an ability to consider the contextual information and subjective state of an earlier study episode. In comparison, where older adults made remember judgements, Perfect and Dasgupta found that there was an inconsistency between the justification given at retrieval and what they reported at study. They suggested that this indicated a tendency to produce post hoc rationalisations of their memory experience in the absence of a rich memory of the study episode. This suggests that older adults' memory may be unreliable in this regard: they may reconstruct possibly incorrect contextual information to justify the sensation of remembering.

Source memory in older adults

Older adults, like frontal head injury patients, have also shown deficits in source memory. Source memory can be thought of as the ability to retrieve the context or provider of a certain piece of information; usually this is assessed only for information that a person has correctly retrieved. For example, given that you remember that all lectures have been cancelled for week six, can you remember who told you this information? The evidence that older adults demonstrate difficulties with this kind of memory mostly comes from tests of general knowledge. For instance, in a study by Schacter, Kaszniak, Kihlstrom, and Valdiserri (1991), young and old participants were presented with novel and trivial information by either of two people. At test, participants were asked who had told them the fact. Even though there were no group differences in memory for the facts, older adults were significantly worse at judging who had presented them the information. Such a problem of "source amnesia" is thought to be behind the false fame effect found in older adults (e.g., Dywan & Jacoby, 1990)—this is where older adults show a tendency to attribute fame to a non-famous but highly familiar stimulus due to presentation in an experimental setting. That is, if you present older adults with a non-famous face, and test their memory for it some time later, they are likely to think that the reason the person feels familiar is because they are famous.

Working memory in older adults

Older adults have difficulties with manipulating and storing information in the way described above for children. In particular, they show extreme difficulty with manipulation of information; if you read the average older adult a series of digits to repeat immediately, they will do this as proficiently as the average younger adult. However, ask the older adult to manipulate the information, such as repeating it backwards, or in alphabetical order, they will typically perform at lower levels than their young counterparts.

For example, complex span tasks show clear age differences in older populations. Older adults have difficulty reading a sentence, making a decision about it, moving on to several other sentences, and finally recalling the final word from each. However, it is possible to ameliorate these difficulties, just by providing breaks between each set of sentences (May, Hasher, & Kane, 1999), even though performance never becomes quite as good as that of younger adults. Older adults are also very bad at doing two things at once. This is as a result of a lack of working memory resources being available to coordinate competing tasks.

The extent of these difficulties is neatly demonstrated in Lindenberger, Marsiske, and Baltes (2000) paper, *Memorizing while walking*. Lindenberger and colleagues asked his older adult participants to walk a circular track in the basement of the psychology department, whilst a portable tape-recorder played them words to learn. Older adults had a handrail to help them negotiate the course, which featured a few different low obstacles, but they were told to use this as little as possible, and an electro-conductive glove recorded its use. In a similar fashion, they could press a panic button that briefly paused the words being presented to them. The researchers found that older adults had much greater "dual task costs". Compared to young adults, older adults' memory was more disrupted by negotiating the course than the younger adults' memory was. In addition, the older adults had an interesting pattern of use of aids: Whereas the young adults prioritised memory and rarely used the handrail, the older adults used the handrail and ignored the panic button. So when things got difficult, the young adults paused the tape, but the older adults held the rail.

The literature on working memory in ageing is fast developing, in part at least because it is considered as a key general cognitive resource likely to have impact on a multitude of aspects of everyday mental functioning. Working memory impinges on so much of mental life: How the perceptual systems interact with cognition, for example, so it is a powerful way of describing a range of difficulties from one theoretical viewpoint. We return to this view below.

Metamemory in older adults

Metamemory considers people's beliefs about their memory function, and their ability to control and monitor their memory processes (see Chapter 12). There is considerable evidence that older adults have a deficit in metamemory, but this is largely due to how it is measured and what aspect of function is the focus of study (Dunlosky & Connor, 1997). In general, the ageing process appears to produce predictions of performance that are over confident, suggesting that older adults are not aware of their failing memory. But, despite being over confident in general, the predictions are not actually totally inaccurate: They follow the correct relative pattern. If older adults are given a set of words to remember, they will remember more of the words they judged as being more likely to be recalled, and fewer words to which they assigned a lower probability of recall. The magnitude of these predictions may be exaggerated and inaccurate, but the pattern of which words are remembered and forgotten is—just as with young people—entirely appropriate.

However, It is clear that older adults do have some specific difficulties with metamemory, such as a lack of a relationship between predictions of future performance and time spent studying materials (Dunlosky & Connor, 1997). An older adult may believe an item to be very difficult to memorise, but this will not be reflected in how long they study that item for. When one examines metamemory in detail, a problem occurs when comparing laboratory studies and the real world. For instance, metacognitive evaluations in courtroom situations are largely unreliable (e.g., Perfect & Hollins, 1999) in comparison to the same people's evaluations of general knowledge performance.

Older adults in the laboratory and in the real world

This closer inspection of metamemory reveals an interesting pattern seen elsewhere in the ageing literature: There is a lack of generalisability from laboratory tasks to real-world situations. In the case of metamemory in eyewitness testimony, for example, one difficulty is that whereas most laboratory memory studies indicate *overconfidence* in older adults, in the context of eyewitness testimony, it has been shown that older adults possess lower confidence in their abilities to recall information accurately. This lower confidence may directly relate to the negative perception held about the older adult eyewitness. For example, Brimacombe, Quinton, Nance, and Garrioch (1997) reported that older adults tend to use more unconfident language in their recall of events, e.g., "I think" or "I am not sure".

As another example of the real world—laboratory discrepancy—Salthouse and Saults (1987) tested younger and older expert typists. Even though the older typists showed clear deficits on working memory tasks relative to the young controls, their typing speed was not affected. One would expect copy-typing to be a task very heavily reliant on working memory—sentences have to be held in memory whilst the physical act of typing is carried out, and the place in the text you are copying has to be stored and updated. On closer examination, Salthouse and Saults found that their old typists were completing the task in a different way. Although they were slower than young controls, and working memory was worse, they were able to keep up their typing speed by looking further ahead on the text being copied, and use their greater experience to plan the task better.

This discrepancy between real-world memory performance and laboratory memory performance is a particular problem in the field of ageing, and especially because researchers rarely take the analytic, observational approach seen in the application of working memory to the real world in the educational setting described above. A particular difficulty is that cognitive ageing research, which aims to identify and remediate the memory difficulties in older adults, is off to a very poor start if the very abilities that seem of importance when one considers performance in the laboratory just do not translate to what happens in everyday life. The overwhelming evidence from neuroimaging studies, formal tests of memory, and even anecdotal reports from academics holidaying with their parents, suggests that memory is impaired as you get older. And yet, in a famous study by Sunderland, Harris, and Baddeley (1983), older adults actually reported significantly fewer memory lapses in everyday life than controls. One explanation for this is merely that the older adults forget just how forgetful they are. However, similar findings have been found in several different prospective memory tasks, where older adults are reliably able to carry out a prospective task in the real world while many younger participants fail. Such a positive finding cannot, in this case, be due to forgetfulness or bias in reporting errors: the older adults simply carry out a task (for example, phoning the experimenter) on which the younger adults fare less well. Of course, countless laboratory studies suggest that prospective memory is a particular difficulty for older adults. Thus, real-world studies and laboratory studies often give diverging views of the same issues. The response by cognitive ageing researchers is usually a rather weak compromise—to make laboratory tasks more ecologically valid by changing the materials; for example, studying a list of names rather than a list of unrelated words. However, the motivations to take part, and strategies used to complete tasks in the laboratory, are likely to differ greatly from the real world. For those interested in older adults functioning in a variety of topics covered elsewhere in this book, there are many studies on flashbulb memory (e.g., Cohen, Conway, & Maylor, 1994), memory for names (e.g., Cohen & Faulkner, 1986), prospective memory (e.g., Maylor, 1998), and face recognition (Naveh-Benjamin, Guez, Kilb, & Reedy, 2004).

Finally, some of the differences between the young and the old might not be due to cognitive differences so much as an interaction between the material and the participant. Studies from the eyewitness literature suggest that older adults are influenced by the type of material that they are required to memorise. It has long been known that there are clear effects of race in face recognition, with people being better at recognising faces from their own race. More recently, it has been established that the same effects occur with age. Wright and Stroud (2002) demonstrated that in identification lineups, participants perform significantly better at identifying the culprit when the targets and foils are from their own age group. Similarly, Perfect and Harris (2003) examined the innocent bystander effect in ageing, using either young or old faces as stimuli. Groups of old and young participants saw photographs of target faces (perpetrators), then a series of photographs of nontarget innocent bystanders. A week later, participants were given lineups composed of bystanders and were asked if any of the target faces were present. When younger faces were used, older adults showed higher levels of errors (identifying an innocent person as the criminal), whereas when old faces were used as stimuli, there were no group differences in misidentification. At the very least, these studies suggest that to some extent age differences in eyewitness testimony may be due to social bias, rather than cognitive dysfunction alone.

Bogus callers and older adults

We now turn our attention to the practical applications of theory and data relating to memory changes in older adults, as we did earlier in the context of the memory-aware classroom for children. Where people have special memory needs or difficulties, it is clear that other areas could benefit from this approach—supermarkets, websites, road signs, and household appliances. Another case where working memory principles have been applied to the real world is in work with ID cards for use with older adults. In Leeds, UK, one of the applied memory projects we have been involved in is with the Trading Standards Group, who were worried about bogus callers and distraction burglaries caused by "cold calling"; people making unsolicited calls selling (or pretending to sell) something and taking the opportunity to steal something. This "doorstep crime" was once so prevalent in Leeds that it was once called the "Leeds crime". What troubled trading standards organisations was that this crime was targeted disproportionately towards older adults, with the UK charity *Help the Aged* reporting that between 300,000 and 400,000 older adults were approached by cold callers, bogus or otherwise, each year. Typically, older adults are targeted because they are perceived as more trusting and gullible than younger households, especially where the bogus caller uses a technological excuse to enter the house. As an example, a criminal may enter the house on the pretext that they must check that the new digital phone line is functioning; otherwise the house may well be cut off soon. Whilst the victim is distracted, an accomplice may be looking through the house for valuables.

To work towards preventing these crimes, Trading Standards advocated an ID card approach, and provided collaborating tradespeople and professionals with standard identification cards that older adults could trust. At the same time, they wisely considered older adults as a special population who may need a slightly different design from the general population. Would the older adult get all the information from the card that they need to? Would this information be conveyed so well that it would require little effort to understand and comply? Anecdotal reports suggested that older adults, despite being the most vulnerable group, were the least likely to understand and follow good practice on their doorsteps.

When considering such questions of comprehension, one would tend to turn to the literature on language function in older adults. However, it is generally considered that older adults' language abilities are, on the whole, intact. Older adults do not suffer from a lack of understanding terms and words in isolation. In fact, if anything, vocabulary increases over the lifespan. However, comprehension can be impaired in older adults as it may be secondary to other more fundamental problems. In the real world, older adults may simply not be able to see or hear information properly. Lindenberger and Baltes (1994) suggest that difficulties with visual and auditory acuity accounts for 93% of the decline in intelligence in people aged between 70 and 103. Older adults suffer from specific problems in reading textual material (e.g., Rousseau, Lamson, & Rogers, 1998), and it is possible to design materials that are more older-adult-friendly in the following ways:

1   *Colour vision.* Older adults have difficulties in discriminating colours that are close in hue, especially in the shorter wavelengths. In particular, blues, greens, and violet should be avoided in combination. Perception of yellows and reds are affected least by the ageing process.
2   *Contrast.* Making distinctions between light and dark becomes more difficult with age, especially when alternating patterns of light and dark are small and narrow. Barlow and Wogalter (1991) found that increasing the conspicuity of a warning by increasing the size and the boldness of the type improved young and older adults' memory for the information.
3   *Glare sensitivity.* The susceptibility to glare also increases with age. To minimise glare, information should presumably not be produced on very shiny services,

but the effect of glare on information comprehension in older adults has not been formally tested in research.

4 *Visual acuity*. The ability to resolve details also declines with age. It is estimated that around three quarters of adults have visual acuity worse than 20/20, and one third of older adults report difficulty reading labels on products designed for 20/20 vision. Text should be presented in 12–14 point type and narrow fonts should be avoided. San serif fonts are also more easily resolved, and using exclusively capitals should also be avoided (Morrell & Echt, 1997).

5 *Visual search*. When searching a complex array of information (like an ID card, medicine bottle, etc.) older adults have difficulty selecting the right information and filtering out unnecessary information. This is worse when there is more information to sift through, so information should be displayed in such a way that attention is focused. As such, the object of focus should be presented in the primary fixation point (in the centre of the frame) and in high contrast. Other information can be de-emphasised (Kline & Scialfa, 1997) to help the older adult fixate on what is most important.

It seemed likely that the main problem of understanding these materials was not limited to these lower level characteristics, but that it also extended to working memory difficulties. Older adults have particular difficulties in making inferences in complex sentences such as "The man who sold the car to the woman had red hair". This is because we must hold one clause in memory ("who sold the car to the woman") to get the meaning from the other ("the man had red hair"). Older adults find such sentences particularly difficult to understand as they have to hold one thing in mind and assess another, and they will often report, for instance, that the woman had red hair. A simpler way of conveying the information would be: "The man sold the car to the woman. The man had red hair." Thus complex multiple-clause sentences are best avoided. Working memory is also used to hold meaning in memory whilst we read through longer passages. With impoverished working memory, we may not remember the reason why we started reading a passage. This necessitates the use of reminders, termed *environmental support* by Craik and Jennings (1992). Environmental support can be thought of as anything that exists in the outside world, the environment, that helps our memory. There are obvious real-world examples, like cues such as notes one writes to oneself, or an alarm set on your mobile phone. There are also less obvious examples, which relate to the nature of different memory tasks. Consider *free recall*, where you have to produce—from nothing—the contents of a list that has just been read to you. There is little or no environmental support at all. This gives you less environmental support than *cued recall*. If you are given a list of word pairs such as *water–pond*, on the other hand, then when you are tested with the cue *water*, that cue supports your memory, and it will be easier to recall *pond*. A recognition test provides even more environmental support: *Did you see* water–pond *or* water–ocean? Older adults have poorer memory performance when there is less environmental support, and they show a more exaggerated pattern across these different types of memory task—they are markedly impaired on free recall. So, in drafting material for older adults, one may want to consider environmental support—reminders, and a style that means that working memory is not labouring, and needlessly holding information.

The fact that working memory failures result in a poor coordination of processing and storage may also be behind older adults' failure to make inferences form basic information. Hasher, Zacks, Doren, Hamm, and Attig (1987) suggest that older adults find it more difficult to make inferences whilst reading text information. For example, they suggest that a simple sentence like "Use in a well-ventilated room" causes problems for older adults because they have to make inferences about what well-ventilated means. Rousseau et al. (1998) suggested the use of explicit messages with older adults' such as "*Use in a room that has at least one window open*". Presumably the older adults lack the mental resources necessary to generate sensible images and interpretations of information, whilst at the same time processing it.

In practice, this work with Trading Standards merely led to very straightforward recommendations such as changing the wording from "*Close and lock the door whilst you do this, the officer will not be offended*" to "*Close and lock the door. The officer will not be offended.*"

These simple changes seem like common sense, but their importance becomes clear only once one has understood the nature of memory difficulties in older adults. Some of the other advice seems not to pertain to memory function at all—advice based on clear fonts and appropriate colours does not seem to belong in a textbook about memory. However, consider the Barlow and Wogalter (1991) research. They found that later *memory* for material in older adults improved if it was more conspicuous at the time at which they studied it. This is, in fact, a very familiar pattern in ageing research: Where perception is difficult, information is unclear, and where there is unnecessary distracting information, the differences in memory performance for young and old is accentuated. To explain this, one needs to draw on working memory theory. Concentrating hard on basic perceptual tasks like reading and listening require mental effort and some of the resources otherwise available for working memory function. Thus, for the older adult straining to hear, they will be devoting too much processing power to listening, and not enough to meaningfully interacting with the material.

In the case of irrelevant distracting information, older adults are thought to suffer an inhibitory deficit (Hasher & Zacks, 1988): Working memory becomes overloaded with irrelevant information, and general processing power is diminished as a result. In fact, this is an extremely popular model of cognitive decline in older adults: The whole pattern of memory problems, cognitive slowness, uncertainty, and changes in working memory could be largely due to a failure to prevent unnecessary information from entering working memory.

Several programmes of research are indicative of inhibitory dysfunction in older adults and these often show a striking ironic error: Older adults remember something that they are told to forget. That suggests that older adults not only forget when they would rather remember, but they may also remember when they would be better off forgetting. One oft-cited example used by researchers to explain the applicability of an inhibitory deficit in older adults is relevant to real-world memory: "It is possible that older adults' difficulty in inhibiting the continued processing of information designated as irrelevant or wrong could have an impact on their ability as jurors to comply with a judge's instructions to ignore testimony that has been stricken from the record" (Zacks, Radvansky, & Hasher, 1996, p. 155).

Most of the evidence for inhibitory difficulties comes from tasks that ask participants to complete the last word of high-cloze sentences (e.g., Hasher, Quig, & May, 1997), such as "*Before you go to bed, turn off the _____*". The experimenter then provides a solution that has to be remembered, which either confirms (*lights*) or disconfirms the participant's response (*radio*). The critical condition is the one in which the experimenter's answer disconfirms the high-cloze solution that the participant has given. On disconfirm trials, the task is to remember the experimenter's solution and inhibit or "forget" the first answer. At test, participants are given a different set of sentences to complete. Proficient inhibition is shown by completing sentences with words other than those seen in the previous stage. Deficient inhibition is shown by participants producing responses that were originally disconfirmed. The standard finding is that older adults do not remember the disconfirm items. In fact, older adults are actually better than young adults at remembering these items—which would be good news, were it not the case that they had been instructed *not* to remember those items.

Such inhibitory errors may have considerable impact for everyday functioning in more practical contexts. In eyewitness situations, the failure to inhibit irrelevant information in a lineup of suspects may lead to the wrong person being convicted. Searcy, Bartlett, Memon, and Swanson (2001) report that older adults make more false identifications (of innocent individuals) than young adults when the perpetrator is absent from the lineup. Such inhibitory errors could be behind the observation that older adults are more susceptible to misleading information than younger adults (Bornstein, 1995). It is not that older adults are more gullible than their young counterparts, but that they cannot help but act on their memory and previous experience. When a bogus caller knocks on their door, for instance, the older adult may have difficulty in suppressing very standard, well-learned routines. Informal reports also say that bogus callers talk very quickly and give lots of information— older adults may be overwhelmed by this information and, unlike younger adults, unable to filter out the unnecessary facts in order to turn the criminal away.

CONCLUSIONS

In this chapter, we have examined some important features of memory and the way it changes at both ends of the lifespan. Older adults and children both have difficulties with working memory that are likely to have substantial consequences for their everyday functioning. Theoretical understanding of working memory research is now being applied to the new contexts of the classroom and the ageing process, and is also proving invaluable in understanding emotions and anxiety (Eysenck, Payne, & Derakshan, 2005), and experiential features of mental life such as mind-wandering (Kane et al., 2007). Working memory can therefore be thought of as a fundamental human cognitive process. Studying this form of memory over the lifespan helps build models of how information can be lost and acquired, and what different abilities relate to what others. Such insights into human functioning would not be possible without studies addressing the beginning and end of the lifespan.

REFERENCES

Alloway, T.P., Gathercole, S.E., & Pickering, S. (2004). *Automated Working Memory Assessment*. Test battery available from authors.

Archibald, L.M.D., & Gathercole, S.E. (2006). Nonword repetition: A comparison of tests. *Journal of Speech, Language, and Hearing Research, 49*, 970–983

Baddeley, A.D. (2000). The episodic buffer: A new component of working memory? *Trends in Cognitive Sciences, 4*, 417–423.

Baddeley, A.D., Gathercole, S.E., & Papagno, C. (1998). The phonological loop as a language learning device. *Psychological Review, 105*, 158–173.

Baddeley, A.D., & Hitch, G. (1974). Working memory. In G.A. Bower (Ed.), *Recent advances in learning and motivation, Vol. 8* (pp. 47–90). New York: Academic Press.

Barlow, T., & Wogalter, M.S. (1991). Alcohol beverage warnings in print advertisements. In *Proceedings of the Human Factors Society 35th Annual Meeting*. Santa Monica, CA: Human Factors Society.

Bornstein, B.H. (1995). Memory processes in elderly eyewitnesses—what we know and what we don't know. *Behavioral Sciences & The Law, 13*, 337–348.

Brimacombe, C.A., Quinton, N., Nance, N., & Garrioch, L. (1997). Is age irrelevant? Perceptions of young and old adult eyewitnesses. *Law and Human Behavior, 21*, 619–634.

Cohen, G., Conway, M.A., & Maylor, E.A (1994). Flashbulb memories and older adults. *Psychology and Aging, 9*, 454–463.

Cohen, G., & Faulkner, D. (1986). Memory for proper names—age differences in retrieval. *British Journal of Developmental Psychology, 4*, 187–197.

Conway, M.A. (2005). Memory and self. *Journal of Memory and Language, 53*, 594–628.

Craik, F.I.M., & Jennings, J.M. (1992). Human memory. In F.I.M. Craik & T.A. Salthouse (Eds.), *Handbook of aging and cognition* (pp. 51–83). Hillsdale, NJ: Lawrence Erlbaum Associates, Inc.

Craik, F.I.M., & McDowd, J.M. (1987). Age-differences in recall and recognition. *Journal of Experimental Psychology: Learning, Memory and Cognition, 13*, 474–479.

Daneman, M., & Carpenter, P.A. (1980). Individual differences in working memory and reading. *Journal of Verbal Learning and Verbal Behaviour, 19*, 450–466.

Davies, G.M. (1995). Children's identification evidence. In S.L. Sporer, R.S. Malpass, & G. Kohnken (Eds.), *Psychological issues in eyewitness identification* (pp. 233–258). Hillsdale, NJ: Lawrence Erlbaum Associates, Inc.

Dunlosky, J., & Connor, L.T. (1997). Age differences in the allocation of study time account for age differences in memory performance. *Memory and Cognition, 25*, 691–700.

Dywan, J., & Jacoby, L. (1990). Effects of aging on source monitoring—differences in susceptibility to false fame. *Psychology & Aging, 5*, 379–387.

Eysenck, M.W., Payne, S., & Derakshan, N. (2005). Trait anxiety, visuospatial processing, and working memory. *Cognition and Emotion, 19*, 1214–1228.

Friedman, D. (2000). Event-related brain potential investigations of memory and aging. *Biological Psychology, 54*, 175–206.

Garden, S., Cornoldi, C., & Logie, R.H. (2002). Visuo-spatial working memory in navigation. *Applied Cognitive Psychology, 16*, 35–50.

Gathercole, S.E. (1998). The development of memory. *Journal of Child Psychology and Psychiatry, 39*, 3–27.

Gathercole, S.E. (1999). Cognitive approaches to the development of short-term memory. *Trends in Cognitive Science, 3*, 410–418.

Gathercole, S.E. (2002). Memory development during the childhood years. In A.D. Baddeley, M.D. Kopelman, & B.A. Wilson (Eds.), *Handbook of memory disorders* (2nd ed., pp. 475–500). Chichester, UK: Wiley.

Gathercole, S.E. (2006). Nonword repetition and word learning: The nature of the relationship. *Applied Psycholinguistics, 27*, 513–543.

Gathercole, S.E., & Alloway, T.P. (2005). *Understanding working memory: A classroom guide*. Available from the authors on request.

Gathercole, S.E., Alloway, T.P., Willis, C.S., & Adams, A.M. (2006). Working memory in children with reading disabilities. *Journal of Experimental Child Psychology*, 93, 265–281.

Gathercole, S.E., & Pickering, S.J. (2000). Working memory deficits in children with low achievements in the national curriculum at seven years of age. *British Journal of Educational Psychology*, 70, 177–194.

Gathercole, S.E., Pickering, S.J., Knight, C., & Stegmann, Z. (2003). Working memory skills and educational attainment: Evidence from National Curriculum assessments at 7 and 14 years of age. *Applied Cognitive Psychology*, 17, 1–16.

Geary, D.C., Hoard, M.K., Byrd-Craven, J., & DeSoto, M.C. (2004). Strategy choices in simple and complex addition: Contributions of working memory and counting knowledge for children with mathematical disability. *Journal of Experimental Child Psychology*, 88, 121–151.

Greenwood, P.M. (2000). The frontal aging hypothesis evaluated. *Journal of the International Neuropsychological Society*, 6, 705–726.

Gyselinck, V., Cornoldi, C., Dubois, V., De Beni, R., & Ehrlich, M.F. (2002). Visuospatial memory and phonological loop in learning from multimedia. *Applied Cognitive Psychology*, 16, 665–685.

Hasher, L., Quig, M.B., & May, C.P. (1997). Inhibitory control over no-longer-relevant information: Adult age differences. *Memory & Cognition*, 25, 286–295.

Hasher, L., & Zacks, R.T. (1988). Working memory, comprehension, and aging: A review and a new view. In G.H. Bower (Ed.), *The psychology of learning and motivation, Vol. 22* (pp. 193–225). San Diego, CA: Academic Press.

Hasher, R.T. Zacks, L., Doren, B., Hamm, V., & Attig, M.S. (1987). Encoding and memory of explicit and implicit information. *Journal of Geronotlogy*, 42, 418–422.

Hultsch, D.F., Hertzog, C., Small, B.J., & Dixon, R.A. (1999). Use it or lose it: Engaged lifestyle as a buffer of cognitive decline in aging? *Psychology and Aging*, 14, 245–263.

Ivy, G.O., MacLeod, C.M., Petit, T.L., & Markus, E.J. (1992). A physiological framework for perceptual and cognitive changes in aging. In F.I.M. Craik & T.A. Salthouse (Eds.), *Handbook of aging and cognition*. Hillsdale, NJ: Lawrence Erlbaum Associates, Inc.

Kane, M.J., Brown, L.H., Little, J.C., Silvia, P.J., Myin-Germeys, I., & Kwapil, T.R. (2007) For whom the mind wanders, and when: An experience-sampling study of working memory and executive control in daily life. *Psychological Science*, 18, 614–621.

Kline, D.W., & Scialfa, C.T. (1997). Sensory and perceptual functioning: Basic research and human factors implications. In A.D. Fisk & W.A Rogers (Eds.), *Handbook of human factors and the older adult*. San Diego, CA: Academic Press.

Langenecker, S.A., & Nielson, K.A. (2003). Frontal recruitment during response inhibition in older adults replicated with fMRI. *Neuroimage*, 20, 1384–1392.

Levy, B., & Langer, E. (1994). Aging free from negative stereotypes: Successful memory in China and among the American deaf. *Journal of Personality and Social Psychology*, 66, 989–997.

Lindenberger, U., & Baltes, P. (1994). Sensory functioning and intelligence in old age: A strong connection. *Psychology & Aging*, 9, 339–355.

Lindenberger, U., Marsiske, M., & Baltes, P.B. (2000). Memorizing while walking: Increase in dual-task costs from young adulthood to old age. *Psychology & Aging*, 15, 417–436.

May, C.P., Hasher, L., & Kane, M.J. (1999). The role of interference in memory span. *Memory and Cognition*, 27, 759–767.

Maylor, E.A. (1998). Changes in event-based prospective memory across adulthood. *Aging, Neuropsychology & Cognition*, 5, 107–128.

Morrell, R.W., & Echt, K.V. (1997). Designing written instructions for older adults: Learning to use computers. In A.D. Fisk & W.A. Rogers (Eds.), *Handbook of human factors and the older adult*. San Diego, CA: Academic Press.

Morrison, C.M., Ellis, A.W., & Quinlan, P.T. (1992). Age of acquisition, not word-frequency, affects object naming, not object recognition. *Memory & Cognition, 20*, 705–714.

Moulin, C.J.A., Thompson, R.G., Wright, D.B., & Conway, M.A. (2006). Eyewitness memory in older adults. In M.P. Toglia, J.D. Read, D.F. Ross, & R.C.L. Lindsay (Eds.), *The handbook of eyewitness psychology: Volume I—Memory for events.* Mahwah, NJ: Lawrence Erlbaum Associates, Inc.

Naveh-Benjamin, M., Guez, J., Kilb, A., & Reedy, S. (2004). The associative memory deficit of older adults: Further support using face-name associations. *Psychology & Aging, 19*, 541–546.

Parkin, A.J., & Java, R.I. (1999). Determinants of age-related memory loss. In T.J. Perfect & E. Maylor (2000). *Models of cognitive aging.* Oxford, UK: Oxford University Press.

Parkin, A.J., & Walter, B.M. (1992). Recollective experience, normal aging, and frontal dysfunction. *Psychology & Aging, 7*, 290–298.

Perfect, T.J. (1997). Memory aging as frontal lobe dysfunction. In M.A. Conway (Ed.), *Cognitive models of memory.* Hove, UK: Psychology Press.

Perfect, T.J., & Dasgupta, Z.R.R. (1997). What underlies the deficit in reported recollective experience in old age? *Memory & Cognition, 25*, 849–858.

Perfect, T.J., & Harris, L.J. (2003). Adult age differences in unconscious transference: Source confusion or identity blending? *Memory & Cognition, 3*, 570–580.

Perfect, T.J., & Hollins, T.S. (1999). Feeling of knowing judgements do not predict subsequent recognition performance for eyewitness memory. *Journal of Experimental Psychology: Applied, 5*, 250–264.

Pickering, S.J., & Gathercole, S.E. (2004). Distinctive working memory profiles in children with special educational needs. *Educational Psychology, 24*, 393–408.

Rousseau, G.K., Lamson, N., & Rogers, W.A. (1998). Designing warning labels to compensate for age-related changes in perceptual and cognitive abilities. *Psychology & Marketing, 15*, 643–662.

Rubin, D.C., Wetzler, S.E., & Nebes, R.D. (1986). Autobiographical memory across the adult lifespan. In D.C. Rubin (Ed.), *Autobiographical memory* (pp. 202–221). Cambridge, UK: Cambridge University Press.

Salthouse, T.A., & Saults, J.S. (1987). Multiple spans in transcription typing. *Journal of Applied Psychology, 72*, 187–196.

Schacter, D.L., Kaszniak, A.W., Kihlstrom, J.F., & Valdiserri, M. (1991). The relation between source memory and aging. *Psychology & Aging, 6*, 559–568.

Searcy, J.H., Bartlett, J.C., Memon, A., & Swanson, K. (2001). Aging and lineup performance at long retention intervals: Effect of metamemory and context reinstatement. *Journal of Applied Psychology, 86*, 207–214.

Sunderland, A., Harris, J.E., & Baddeley, A.D. (1983). Do laboratory tests predict everyday memory? A neuropsychological study. *Journal of Verbal Learning and Verbal Behaviour, 22*, 341–357.

Taylor, L.M. (2005). *Introducing cognitive development.* Hove, UK: Psychology Press.

Thorn, A.S.C., & Gathercole, S.E. (1999). Language-specific knowledge and short-term memory in bilingual and non-bilingual children. *Quarterly Journal of Experimental Psychology, 52A*, 303–324.

Tulving, E. (1983). *Elements of episodic memory.* New York: Oxford University Press.

Wright, D.B., & Stroud, J.N. (2002). Age differences in lineup identification accuracy: People are better at their own age. *Law and Human Behavior, 26*, 641–654.

Zacks, R.T., Radvansky, G., & Hasher, L. (1996). Studies of directed forgetting in older adults. *Journal of Experimental Psychology: Learning, Memory and Cognition, 22*, 143–156.

12 Memory and consciousness

*Akira R. O'Connor, Chris J.A. Moulin,
and Gillian Cohen*

INTRODUCTION

The relevance of consciousness

This chapter is concerned with a topic of growing importance in psychology: subjective feelings, sensations, and conscious control of memory processes. The topic is of relevance to every other chapter in this book: When you see someone walking down the street and you recognise their face (Chapter 4), but you do not know where from, how does that feel? When you have a tip-of-the-tongue experience and you cannot think of a word that you want to use—how frustrating is that? When, sat in an exam, you have rich evocative recollections connected to your knowledge—like remembering exactly where and when you were taught about flashbulb memory— how helpful is that conscious awareness to the task in hand? What do these feelings tell us about our memory processes and—in the real world—how do these feelings influence our subsequent behaviours as we search for the answers? This topic is often described as metacognition: your thoughts about your thoughts. The main aim of this chapter is to present the ways in which the study of memory from the subjective viewpoint considering consciousness and states of awareness illuminates our understanding of real-world memory behaviours; in doing so it gives an overview of the topic of metacognition.

Case study—AKP

Patient AKP (Moulin, Conway, Thompson, James, & Jones, 2005) was a man with a very specific and rare memory problem. As a result of cell death in his brain as part of a dementing process, he had an almost persistent sensation, or belief, that he had encountered things in his life before; something that could be described as persistent déjà vu. As a result of this memory difficulty, AKP withdrew from all his hobbies and interests. On refusing to watch the television because he said he'd seen the programme before (he could not have—it was a new programme), his wife once asked him "If you think you have seen the programme before, what happens next?" AKP gave the very self-aware response: "How should I know? I've got a memory problem!"

Clearly, AKP had a problem with his memory. He was not particularly forgetful, but he had a peculiar sensation that he had encountered things before, when in fact he had not. This is not like déjà vu as you or I might experience it (see déjà vécu below), as AKP could not help but act on his feelings. Because he felt as if he had done things before he did not enjoy doing them, and he withdrew from activities: his real-world behaviour was changed by beliefs he had about his memory. We might say his problem was his conscious experience of memory: How it felt when he encountered information. It was his subjective viewpoint that led to his problems.

The importance of consciousness

Traditionally, memory has mostly been studied from an objective point of view—focusing on the observation and measurement of behaviour. It has been relatively easy to explore individuals' abilities and difficulties in this manner. For instance, our understanding of processes such as breaking memory into chunks has been illuminated by studying performance on tasks using lists of words or sequences of digits. These have readily been applied to novel topics and real-world problems, like the memorability of postcodes or classroom practices. In these kinds of study and application, we are interested in the content of memory. Quite simply, we are interested in whether an item is remembered or forgotten. This emphasis is best illustrated by what Koriat and Goldsmith (1996) refer to as the storehouse metaphor, a representation of the way in which traditional psychological research has conceptualised memory, with a priority on the quantity of information that can be stored accurately. Even in more esoteric topics like flashbulb memory, we tend to focus on memory content: Whether we can or cannot remember the facts associated with learning a new event; whether we can remember how we felt, for instance.

Such a bias on the content of memory is pragmatic: These things are easy to test and measure—it is an inheritance from very early studies of memory based on measuring the behaviour of animals. When testing animals, it is impossible to ask them to reflect on their experience—so instead we have to measure what we can observe. Animals have remembered something if they change subsequent performance on the basis of having stored something they encountered earlier. In a similar fashion, psychologists tended not to ask about feelings, sensations, and reflections of their human participants, but concentrated on easily measurable aspects of memory, such as, "if I give a person a list of words, which ones will they be able to remember?" But with AKP above, his behaviour is changed as a result of his own internal feelings and his conscious evaluation of his memory system, not because of forgetfulness. How can we explain this without considering his own first-person experience and how it feels for him? What do cases like his say about how memory and consciousness interact? Just as Koriat and Goldsmith (1996) proposed a shift from the storehouse metaphor to a more subjectively meaningful and naturalistic correspondence metaphor, in this chapter we propose that the study of memory must include conscious sensations and beliefs by recognising self-awareness in order to make a full account of real-world behaviour.

Philosophers (e.g., Gennaro, Herrmann, & Sarapata, 2006) interested in this issue discuss this problem along these lines, in reference to using behaviour to make inferences about mental states:

> If a person leaves her house with an umbrella, we might explain that behaviour by attributing to her a belief that it will rain. However, the behaviour in question cannot be adequately explained merely in terms of that single belief

causing the behaviour. She must also want to keep dry. Thus we must at least attribute a desire in addition to the belief to explain her behaviour.

Gennaro, Herrmann, & Sarapata, 2006, p. 374

That is, we *can* infer that processes are operating in the mind of someone who takes their umbrella with them when they leave the house, but to fully understand their mental state, we might need to know if they hate getting wet, whether they are quite sure it will rain, whether they like the umbrella, and so on. The whole problem gets more complicated it the person forgets the umbrella. How then would we explain the lack of an intended behaviour, if all we can do is measure the behaviour itself? The idea is that it is a complex mental state—consciousness—that drives behaviour. And, as this chapter will demonstrate, failures of some aspects of conscious experience can lead to particular failures of memory. But how do we define consciousness?

CONSCIOUSNESS

Defining consciousness

Consciousness, as in "to regain consciousness", is the state of awareness of which we all have an understanding. You are, at this very moment, conscious whilst you read these words on the page in front of you. You are using your conscious mental monologue to translate and communicate the written words into a stream of language that makes sense to you. As automatic as reading seems, and despite the engrossing nature of this paragraph, your conscious processes are easily distracted. For example, should something more pressing come to mind, like an itch on your ankle, these sensations will temporarily invade your consciousness until you have dealt with the cause of the disturbance, following which you will be able to resume the task of reading again. Of course, you are not consciously aware of every single aspect of reading. You can make yourself aware of some things by diverting your attention to them, such as the way you can mentally vocalise what you are reading, or the movement of your eyes from one line to the next. Other things are much more difficult to notice and almost impossible to control, such as the saccadic movement of your eyes from one group of words to the next. The act of reading the passage illustrates some important aspects of consciousness; that it can be seen as an attentional process, that it can signal to us what we do or do not understand, and that some processes need to go through consciousness to influence our thoughts and behaviour, whereas other processes do not. Much of what makes up our experience of the world comes from this interplay between conscious and unconscious prcesses, which could be seen as a priority system, with conscious processes needing more attention than unconscious processes, which mostly proceed automatically. Tellingly, when something noteworthy enters our consciousness, it is difficult *not* to get distracted by it—this is proof enough that, however hard it may be to measure, consciousness itself impacts greatly on our experience of the surroundings. Just as the overwhelming sensation of itchiness compels us to scratch the offending ankle, so too can an overwhelming sensation of familiarity entering consciousness convince us that a particular face that we encounter must be someone that we have met before.

In this way, whether it is to resolve the sensation of an itch or the sensation of a memory, conscious states capture attention, and guide behaviour.

Although it is fairly easy to produce descriptions of consciousness and the way in which it is engaged in everyday activities, sometimes it seems wise to leave the definition of the term to philosophers. This is mainly because of the difficulty that psychologists have had when settling on a definition that pleases everyone. Some cognitive psychologists will describe only very specific mechanisms as being like consciousness, such as working memory, or the control mechanism that guides attention. Others may like to think of consciousness as metacognition (as outlined later, metacognition is the process of thinking about what we know), or the subjective experience of "knowing about knowing". It is because of well-defined constructs like these that many memory researchers will avoid talking about consciousness wherever possible, and refer instead to these more specific, "safe" entities. In fact, some prominent philosophers suggest that we will never understand the subjective nature of consciousness (e.g., Searle, 1992), since its very subjective nature means it is not likely to be accommodated into objective scientific methods. One of the problems is that the idea of subjective awareness central to consciousness is poorly understood (although measures such as recollective experience—see later— are gradually helping us to get a better grasp of conscious involvement in memory). For instance, if awareness is about monitoring a system and then acting on this information, we might describe a thermostat as being aware, since it can monitor the temperature of a tank of water and control a heating element accordingly. But we would not describe a thermostat as possessing consciousness in any way that we can relate to our own subjective experience.

A further difficulty is historical. Consciousness was often proposed by philosophers as one of the differences between humans and all other species (in the way that theologians still propose the existence of a uniquely human "soul"). It is just this issue that led behaviourism to reject the need to measure or consider consciousness at all, and instead focus on stimulus–response links—observing objective behaviours, not introspective, subjective experiences. This behaviourist approach is often cited as being influential in the development of memory research, and presumably that is why there is still a very large focus on objective tests of memory, things that are remembered and forgotten—as above. Thankfully, there are a growing group of credible researchers beginning to define and explore consciousness from a cognitive viewpoint. Pinker (1997), for instance, suggests that consciousness comprises three distinct parts: *sentience, access to information,* and *self-knowledge.* Sentience describes subjective experience, phenomenal awareness, feelings of what something seems like to you. Access to information considers the ability to report your ongoing mental experience or operations. Self-knowledge considers whether an organism can know itself and its impact on the world. To paraphrase Steven Pinker: We cannot only say we feel happy (sentience) and we can see red (access to information), we can also say, "Hey, here we are, Akira and Chris, feeling happy and seeing red." It is these kinds of debate that dominate discussions of whether memory is comparable in rats and humans, for instance. If rats have memory, can they really reflect on their existence at all? They may remember one maze or another, but are they able to consider how good it was to be in the maze in Colin's laboratory, before they started on this new task in John's laboratory? It seems that animals may lack this kind of self-knowledge, but that this may be a very central part of human memory. These three facets of consciousness are beginning to be taken forward in research illuminated by such things as amnesia, blindsight, and split-brain patients, and in the following review we are careful to consider these three aspects. First, however, we consider an aspect of consciousness that Pinker may have overlooked, but which finds a lot of favour with memory researchers: How consciousness may act to bind our experiences together.

The unity of consciousness

As we have discussed previously, to delve too deeply into the philosophical ruminations on consciousness would not be within the realms of this chapter, nor the academic experience of these writers. However, there is an important notion concerning consciousness that makes it particularly relevant to the exploration of the psychology of everyday life: the notion of the unity of consciousness. Take the example of when you arrive home needing to relax after a hard day. You may put some background music on to help you to get out of the work mindset. It is also nice to sit down in a comfortable chair and take the weight off your feet. As you look out of the window at the hustle and bustle of the world outside, your overall conscious experience may be one of blissful comfort. That you undergo one phenomenological experience and you do not have individual and separable streams of consciousness for your throbbing feet, aching head, comfortable chair, relaxing music, and tired eyes, is down to what is called the *unity of consciousness.*

Since the times of Immanuel Kant (1781/1998), the unity of conscious experience has been considered as an integral characteristic of consciousness itself. Although falling out of favour when the emphasis shifted to behavioural research (as most work on consciousness did), the psychological exploration of consciousness has benefited in more recent times from neuropsychological investigation. Counter-intuitively, as is often the most elegant way to learn from neuropsychological methods, the individuals from whom we have learned most about consciousness are individuals who demonstrate a disruption in the unity of their own conscious experiences. Absence seizures in epileptic individuals may cause minor disruptions of conscious flow for a number of seconds (Revonsuo, 2003). Drug-related experiences can also have similar effects over a much more prolonged period of time, but perhaps the most conclusive division of the normal unity of consciousness has been reported in split-brain patients.

Split-brain patients, as demonstrated famously by Sperry (1984), are a unique group of individuals for whom the unity of consciousness does not hold. Having conducted commissurotomies (the surgical cutting of the corpus callosum; the only part of the brain through which left and right hemispheres can communicate) on a number of epileptic patients, Sperry made a number of interesting observations on the accessibility of the contents of consciousness relevant to the functional specificity of the two hemispheres. The crux of these observations was that aspects of consciousness located within the left hemisphere (for example, speech) were largely unable to utilise the contents of consciousness relevant to the right hemisphere (for example, the tactile sensory input of the left hand) and vice versa. These observations were important for the scientific study of consciousness, placing what is often thought of as a "spiritual" or "otherworldly" construct well within the realms of empirical investigation. Furthermore, these sorts of investigation have resulted in further breakdown of classical Cartesian dualistic ideas (the philosophical viewpoint that mind and body are two separate entities with little to no influence on each other; Descartes, 1641/1970), with the conscious mind demonstrably resulting from neuronal connection and activity. As is the trend, many recent neuroimaging studies have attempted to establish and demonstrate neural correlates of consciousness. However, we do not need to examine such technological means so far to see how a basic knowledge of consciousness can help with our understanding of everyday memory. We often make memory errors if we are distracted, or if our current goals and processes clash with something in memory. For instance, we may run upstairs and forget why we have done so, or be halfway through answering a question only to lose track of what the question was in the first place.

We have established that for most of us, for the vast majority of the time that we are awake, consciousness is unitary and uninterrupted. It acts as a bridge between ourselves and the world with which we interact, making us aware of internal and external states, thereby facilitating decision-making as we know it. But is consciousness needed in order to make accurate judgements? The answer to that question is, of course, no. A thermostat can make far more accurate judgements than you or I could about temperature, yet as we discussed previously, the existence of a thermostat having consciousness similar to our own is out of the question. But it is easy to list thousands of man-made, non-conscious objects designed for a particular function, like temperature control, and observe that they can perform these functions far more consistently and for longer than you or I ever could; that's no surprise at all. After all, their physical constraints do not let them do anything else. What is far more exciting is to find a person who would expect to utilise their conscious processes normally, a person for whom consciousness is an unavoidable part everyday of life, except in certain, very specific situations when conscious awareness leaves them, and they have to rely, quite unnervingly for them, on their unconscious awareness. In *blindsight* patients, that is exactly what we have.

DB, a neuropsychological case study of blindsight reported by Weiskrantz (1986), believed himself to be blind in certain areas of his visual field. When presented with stimuli that he was asked to identify, DB was unable even to notice that he was being presented with anything. However, when asked to guess as to whether what he was currently being presented with was an X or an O, he would invariably guess correctly. His confidence in the accuracy of his judgements was the same as yours would be, were you to stare at a blank piece of paper and say whether what you were seeing was an X or an O. However, DB's accuracy demonstrates that his conscious experience, or lack of it, was not representative of his accurate unconscious experience. Input from his eyes was being processed accurately on an unconscious, implicit level, but was not being made available for conscious, explicit consideration. Of course, for DB's own subjective experience it was probably verging on the irrelevant that he was able to unconsciously perceive things accurately, such is the importance of conscious experience and the way it drives our experience of the world. What use was it to him if he could guess correctly what he was seeing if he did not think that he might be seeing anything at all in the first place? It is this dissociation between two normally congruent aspects of experience, the separation of the *unconscious* and the *conscious*, which has driven much early work on consciousness. The separation of two processes that normally occur as one can tell us about what each component process brings to the experience as a whole. It is not normal for these processes to work out of union, but when they do, it is striking: Think about your own experiences of déjà vu—or of having a word "on the tip of your tongue". We may be able to understand better some of the more nebulous but nonetheless valuable experiences that form part of everyday experience by tackling these topics head-on.

SUBJECTIVE EXPERIENCE AND COGNITIVE FEELINGS

Defining cognitive feelings

When we discuss memory and consciousness, the main thrust of the argument is that as individuals we have "privileged access" to our memory functions. But what sensations does memory give us, and with what apparatus do we judge the qualities of our memory? These sensations and qualities are "cognitive feelings"—they are subjective experiences about processing that guide our behaviours and have consequences for us. One such commonly experienced cognitive feeling is the tip of the tongue state; where we know we know a word, but momentarily we cannot access it. Such a feeling is evidence for a separate conscious contribution to memory. We have the feeling that we know the word and yet the word is not accessible to us to share with another person. The consequent tip of the tongue sensation is a cognitive feeling that drives us to consider using another word, to search harder for the word that we want, or to ask a person to help resolve the feeling. Table 12.1 gives some examples of cognitive feelings. The top four are well established, and discussed here, but in our view this list could be expanded on—the bottom three are examples of feelings that may, like the top four, result in some frustrating feelings and an all-pervading sense of self, and that may signal some important issues for cognitive processing.

The central theoretical questions here are: To what extent are we aware of our memory limitations and functions? How do we act on the states of awareness generated by memory processes? In turn we turn our attention to metacognition, then recollective experience. These two large areas of investigation might be thought of as memory's intersections with consciousness. We might refer to these as quantitative and qualitative cognitive feelings. In metacognition, we use numbers, as you would in a quiz show format, to report subjective experience. Participants make statements like "*I am 90% sure I will be able to remember that word*"—it has a

Table 12.1 Some examples of cognitive feelings

Cognitive feeling	What it signifies
Tip of the tongue	I know that I know this word!
Familiarity	I have encountered this before!
Recollection	I remember this!
Feeling of knowing	I know this!
Aha! (Eureka moment)	I solved it! (Insight)
Uncertainty	I am unsure!
Ease of processing	I can do this!

quantitative focus. In recollective experience, we ask for subjective reports of a state that the person is in, based on how they feel. Participants report feelings, images, and thoughts, as well as the quality of their memory.

Measuring subjective experience

We have already argued that cognitive psychology and, in particular, memory research grew from scientific approaches that sought to remove subjective feelings, and avoid the "bias" of subjective report. The reasoning of early psychologists was that, by using subjective report, the reliability of theories would be weakened—they believed that if psychologists base theories on idiosyncratic reports from certain individuals, then it may not be possible to generalise those theories to others. Moreover, as the discipline developed, we began to understand that factors like social desirability and the Hawthorne effect (that fact that when you are observed by someone your behaviour has a tendency to change) were probably influencing our results if we directly asked people to report their feelings or subjective views. To confound the area further, psychology began to uncover "subconscious" processes critical for healthy cognitive function, that were not available for conscious report anyway. Some researchers who were trained in this period could be forgiven for thinking that their participants would lie to them at every opportunity.

How then, should we measure subjective experience, and be confident that we are reflecting true internal processes and not the idiosyncrasies of a few select participants? There are four general principles that underpin much research on subjective experience:

1   *Subjective evaluations should relate to actual performance.* If someone feels that something has been very well learned, then their performance for that item should be better than their performance for something they feel they have not learned well. This is a general principle that is upheld in the metacognition literature. The fact that people can predict how well they will perform or how well they have performed suggests that their subjective reports are indicative of some access to mental operations. As an example, Lovelace (1984) showed that an individual's prediction of performance for an item was more accurate than an average of everyone's predictions for that item: The individual has a privileged access to their memory function not captured in a group aggregate of predictions.

2   *Subjective evaluations should relate to objective characteristics of stimuli.* Psychologists know that different types of materials produce different levels of performance, and that these appear to be processed in different ways. One such difference is between high-frequency words (such as *house*) and low-frequency words (such as *okapi*). It has long been known that these produce different levels of memory performance but, reassuringly, they generate markedly different reports of subjective experience too. Because the low-frequency words are vivid, and usually bizarre, they tend to generate rich, evocative memories, whereas words like *house* are difficult to differentiate, and tend to generate vague feelings: "Was it the experimenter who showed me the word 'house', or was I thinking about it on the way to work?" This type of difference has been explored with subjective reports of remembering and knowing by Gardiner and Java (1990; also see section on recollective experience later). The two types of

stimulus yield very different types of subjective experience and, unless the participants have studied memory in detail (otherwise how would they know how to produce this pattern) and are very bloody-minded, they would not be able to "fake" this pattern.

3   *Participants should be able to justify their responses.* This is possibly the simplest approach, and one often used by Gardiner, one of the leaders in the field of memory and consciousness (e.g., Gardiner, 2001). Put simply, people's justification of responses should relate to their experience, and the way that they have responded to the test. We regularly collect such justifications from our participants, and they can effortlessly discriminate between feelings such as, *"It's vague—I think I saw it before"* and *"I made an association with Polka dot. It's a Polish word it means woman."* It is particularly persuasive if people spontaneously justify their experience, or draw parallels between what you have produced in the laboratory and what they feel in daily life.

4   *There should be converging evidence from neuropsychology or neuroimaging.* Brain damage and neuroimaging are powerful tools, often regarded as "converging evidence" by cognitive psychologists. If we are measuring a verifiable subjective process, we would hope that we could see it in studies of neuroimaging, or that it might break down in a systematic manner in brain damage. Consider Figure 12.1, the Necker Cube. This image is a classic "ambiguous figure" and can be perceived in one of two ways. You can view it as having point A in the foreground and point B in the background, which will make the cube point upwards (and to the right), and you'll be able to see underneath it, or you can view it as point B in the foreground, which means that the cube is facing downwards (and to the left), and you can see on top of it. We have no way of knowing which way another person is looking at the cube unless we ask them, but then no idea, either, of whether what they have told us is true. The same can be said of the conscious experience of Figure 12.2, either seen as two faces or as a vase. Because we know what area of the brain is responsible for face perception, we can examine what happens when people report that their experience is shifting from face to vase and vice versa. Andrews, Schluppeck, Homfray, Matthews, and Blakemore (2002) showed that significantly different areas of the brain were activated when seeing this as a face or a vase: People's subjective reports mapped onto activation within their brain. The same has been demonstrated for memory: The responses of different brain regions dissociate according to the phenomenology (Henson, Rugg, Shallice, Josephs, & Dolan, 1999). This

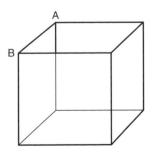

Figure 12.1 The Necker Cube. Which way is the cube facing?

Figure 12.2 The Rubin Vase–Face Illusion. Is it a vase (in white) or two people looking eye-to-eye?

exciting area, how subjective experience is manifest in the brain, is one of the frontiers of neuroscience and it is hopeful that such studies will enable us to map out the functions and operations of consciousness in the future. Of course, another approach is to consider how memory fails in people like AKP, which has yielded similar valuable insights.

Metacognition

Metacognition is "knowing about knowing", and as a topic for scientific study, it considers subjective reports about memory processes, developed from the rationale above. When we try to retrieve something from long-term memory, we can introspect on how difficult it was to reproduce, what else came to mind, how confident we are that what we have retrieved is correct, and sometimes we can even remember where and when we encountered the information. These are "higher order processes", and clearly have a lot in common with Pinker's view of consciousness: We have access to information and self-knowledge. These concepts explain the "meta" part of metacognition. Not only do we produce some content when searching memory, we can report some knowledge about the search for that content, or metaknowledge. The general term "metamemory" has also been used, but Cavanaugh (1988) has pointed out that three kinds of knowing about memory can be distinguished:

1   *Systemic awareness* consists of knowing how memory works, what kinds of thing are easy or difficult to remember, or what kinds of encoding and retrieval strategy produce the best results.
2   *Epistemic awareness* consists of knowing what we know, knowing what knowledge is in store, and being able to make judgments about its accuracy. This is metaknowledge.
3   *Online awareness* consists of knowing about ongoing memory processes and being able to monitor the current functioning of memory, as in prospective memory tasks (see Chapter 5). Cases of absentmindedness occur as a result of failures of online awareness.

As Cavanaugh has noted, the three kinds of metamemory may be interrelated. In trying to recall a particular fact, epistemic awareness may be involved in knowing that the relevant information is in store; systemic awareness may guide the selection of search strategies and direct the search process; and online awareness might be involved in keeping track of the progress of the search.

Evaluating memory failures

One function of systemic awareness is that it provides us with standards against which to evaluate memory failures. People have quite clear expectations about what things they ought to be able to remember and what it is quite acceptable to forget. However, it appears that these expectations are tailored to the age of the person who is doing the forgetting, and they also vary with the age of whoever is making the judgement. Erber, Szuchman, and Rothberg (1990) asked young and elderly participants to evaluate other people's memory failures. The participants were provided with written vignettes describing memory failures of different kinds. Examples are:

> "Mrs X went upstairs to get a stamp and forgot why she had gone up."
> "Mrs X was introduced to someone and shortly afterwards forgot the person's name."
> "Mrs X forgot to buy one item of the three she intended to buy at the grocery store."
> "Mrs X hid money in her house and next day could not remember where it was."

In some examples Mrs X was described as young (23–32 years) and in others as elderly (63–74 years). Participants were asked to rate possible reasons for the memory failures, whether they were signs of mental difficulty, and whether they indicated a need for memory therapy or for medical evaluation. It was strikingly evident that the same memory failure that, when the protagonist was described as young, was dismissed as due to lack of attention and of no consequence, was seen as a sign of mental difficulty and need for memory training when the protagonist was described as elderly. Young participants were also more severe in their judgements than the older participants. These findings show that people have double standards about what level of memory efficiency is "normal" and their judgements are biased by negative stereotypes of ageing.

Knowing what we know

In the recall of general knowledge it is the epistemic kind of metamemory, or metaknowledge, that has received most attention. Our ability to know what we know and, even more importantly, to know what we do not know, is such a commonplace feature of everyone's mental processes that we tend to take it for granted, and fail to realise quite how surprising and how puzzling an achievement it is. Given the enormous range and quantity of information that an adult accumulates and stores over a lifetime, it is surprising that when we are asked a question we can usually say at once and with reasonable confidence whether the answer is in memory or not. Paradoxically, we know whether the search for an answer will be successful or not before it has begun. An example of this ability comes from lexical decision tasks. People are able to decide that a letter string (such as *brone*) does not constitute a real word, and they make this decision so fast that it is hard to believe that they can be searching through the entire mental lexicon to find out whether *brone* is represented. The same ability to know what we know and what we do not know extends to facts as well as lexical items.

Knowledge on the tip of the tongue: The TOT state

Brown and McNeill's (1966) research into the tip-of-the-tongue phenomenon is a classic study of epistemic metamemory. When recall of knowledge is rapid and successful, there is little or no conscious awareness of how that knowledge was retrieved. Direct access to information in the memory system is a fast and automatic process and is not accessible to introspection. Occasions when recall departs from our normal experiences of it, when it is slow, effortful, and indirect, are much more illuminating to the researcher because people are able to report something about *how* they are searching and what fragments or items the search process turns up along the way.

Brown and McNeill focused on cases when a target is known but cannot be recalled. In these cases there is a temporary failure of the retrieval process, but recall is felt to be imminent. This phenomenon was called the TOT state because the target item is felt to be on the tip of the tongue, and Brown and McNeill described this feeling as like being on the brink of a sneeze. The material used in their study consisted of rare words, and their findings are therefore relevant to the storage and retrieval of lexical knowledge rather than factual knowledge, but the basic method they developed has been adapted and used in other studies examining retrieval of general world knowledge. They assembled a large group of participants and read out questions such as "What is the word designating a small boat used in the river and harbour traffic of China and Japan?" and succeeded in inducing 233 TOT states. Of these, 65% were classed as positive because, when the target word was supplied by the experimenter, it was recognised as the one that had been sought, indicating that the feeling of having the word on the tip of the tongue was a valid reflection of what was in the memory store. As in the studies of name blocks, described in Chapter 4, people in the TOT state could often supply partial information about the target word, recalling the first letter, number of syllables, and location of primary stress. They also recalled candidate words that were not the target, but were similar in sound or meaning, and they were able to judge the relative proximity of these candidates to the target.

Brown and McNeill (1966) concluded that words are generically organised in memory into sets with similar meanings or with similar sounds. Recall of partial information, and of nontarget candidates that resemble the target word, reflects this generic organisation. James and Burke (2000) have reported results that reflect links between phonologically related words. Pronouncing prime words that shared phonemes with the blocked target words helped to resolve the TOT because activating these related words strengthened activation of the target. These findings suggest that top-down search processes first access a class of semantically or phonologically related words, and may sometimes stop short at this point without locating the specific target. It is worth emphasising, however, that these findings apply to indirect retrieval processes. They do not apply to rapid automatic direct access to a designated target, which does not necessarily follow the same route as TOT searches.

The feeling of knowing: FOKs and the knowledge gradient

The feeling of knowing (FOK) is distinguished from the TOT state because it relates to a whole range of knowledge states from being sure you do not know something, to being confident that you could recall it if you were given enough time, or, given suitable hints, to being quite sure that you do know the right answer. Retrieval attempts, whether successful or not, are accompanied by a subjective feeling of knowing that falls somewhere along this scale. There are two main questions to be asked about FOK judgements. The first question is concerned with their accuracy: How well does the subjective FOK correlate with objective measures of correct recall? Does the FOK predict actual performance? The second question, which is more controversial, concerns the underlying mechanisms on which the FOK is based.

The accuracy of FOKs

Lachman, Lachman, and Thronesberry (1979) developed Brown and McNeill's (1966) insights using a more experimental technique for investigating epistemic awareness and the retrieval of general world knowledge. Their experiment used a method known as the RJR (Recall: Judgement: Recognition) paradigm in which testing is divided into three phases. In Phase One of Lachman et al.'s experiment, participants had to answer general knowledge questions covering current events, history, sport, literature, etc. such as "What was the former name of Mohammed Ali?" or "What is the capital of Cambodia?". They were told not to guess, but to give the correct answer or respond "Don't know" as quickly as possible.

In Phase Two, participants were re-presented with all the questions to which they had responded "don't know" and asked to make a "feeling of knowing" (FOK) judgement on a four-point scale: 1 = *definitely do not know*; 2 = *maybe do not know*; 3 = *could recognise the answer if told*; 4 = *could recall the answer if given hints and more time*. In Phase Three, after a short delay, the participants were given four multiple-choice alternatives for each of the questions to which they had initially responded "don't know", and had to select one of these alternatives and give a rating of confidence in the correctness of their choice. So, for example, the choices for the question about the capital of Cambodia were Angkor Wat, Phnom Penh, Vientiane and Lo Minh. The confidence-rating scale ranged from 1 = *a wild guess*; 2 = *an educated guess*; 3 = *probably right*; to 4 = *definitely right*.

The results showed that high FOK ratings were positively related to the probability of picking the correct alternative and to the level of confidence. The response times in Phase One were also systematically related to the FOK ratings. Participants took longer to say "don't know" when they thought they might possibly know the answer, so high FOK ratings of 3 or 4 were associated with long response times. When FOK was low, "don't know" response times were fast. Confidence ratings in Phase Three also reflected the correctness of the choice. Participants were more confident when they chose the correct alternative and less confident when their choice was wrong. This experiment takes subjective self-ratings of FOK and of confidence, and validates them against objective measures of accuracy and response time. The results confirmed that there is not a simple two-state dichotomy such that people either know something or they do not know it. Instead, there is a gradient of knowing that is reflected subjectively in the FOK and confidence ratings, and objectively in the speed and accuracy with which a target piece of information can be retrieved.

Nelson, Leonesio, Landwehr, and Narens (1986) reached a similar conclusion using the RJR paradigm like Lachman et al. (1979). They compared three different predictors of memory performance. The FOK supplied by an individual was a better predictor than the average FOK of all the participants, but the best predictor was the objective probability of recall. These findings draw attention to the fact that, although it is generally fairly accurate, the FOK may sometimes be misleading. Krinsky and Krinsky (1988) found that when participants failed to remember a state capital, their FOK for the unrecalled capital city was distorted by a tendency to recognise falsely other large cities as the capital. For example, your estimate of your ability to recall the capital of Kenya will be inaccurate if you think Dar-es-Salaam is the capital. People cannot always judge what they will or will not be able to retrieve from memory. For this reason, metacognition researchers are very fond of testing people on the capital of Australia: Whilst Canberra is the answer, it is Sydney that most readily springs to mind. But the general feeling by the participants is that one really should know what the capital of Australia is.

Metacognition in the real world

The beauty of the metacognitive approach is that it has many real-world applications, and its utility is broadening every day. For an example of some of these applications, see Chapter 13 on memory dysfunction. One aspect of the metacognition approach is that it enables the study of memory difficulties that are not easily captured on everyday tests, or tasks where the focus is on forgetfulness. For example, people who repeatedly check whether the front door is locked or not to a pathological degree do not have a memory deficit, but we could describe them as having a metacognitive deficit: It is their interpretation and evaluation of their memory for locking the door that is dysfunctional. Arguably, it is not these people's memory that is impaired, but their relationship with it. Such a perspective requires a consciousness viewpoint.

One area where there has been a great deal of metacognition research is in memory impairment, particularly in healthy ageing, where there is known to be an impairment in certain types of memory (see Chapter 11). Here, the chief advantage of the metacognition approach is that any deficit that is essentially metacognitive can be remedied by strategy and training. Put another way, if you do not know that you have a memory impairment, how can you implement procedures to compensate for your memory difficulties? Thus, a research priority has been to investigate whether older adults have impaired metacognition. If older adults are not aware of the subtle changes in their memory abilities, their day-to-day functioning will be much worse, since they will not compensate for memory difficulties in their behaviours.

Unfortunately, this persuasive and simple question has not been met with clear-cut data. In fact, the richness and complexity of the data produced by older adults has been driving a lot of the theoretical changes to the way we think about metacognitive processes. For instance, although older adults tend to overestimate their memory performance when compared to younger adults, they are still as able as younger adults to select accurately which items from a memory test they are most likely to remember (Dunlosky & Connor, 1997). That is, they have a general belief that their memory is still as good as when they were young, which suggests that they have a metacognitive deficit, but nonetheless they can still accurately monitor which items in memory they will remember later. This suggests the need for a model that has both general awareness about memory, and more specific online monitoring of information, as outlined by Cavanaugh (1988) above. In turn, even if older adults are able to know which items will be better remembered, and which might need more effort to remember, they are unlikely to act on it during memory processing (Connor, Dunlosky, & Hertzog, 1997). In a series of experiments, Connor and Dunlosky showed that whereas young people's predictions correlated with the amount of time they chose to study items they had to learn, older adults' predictions had little or no bearing on how long they elected to study the items. This of course could be an explanation, or at least an exacerbating factor in memory difficulties: Older adults do not take steps to remediate their memory difficulties—studying items that they judge as more difficult to remember for a longer period of time, for example. Finally, consider the FOK task, which has been studied extensively in older adults. Whereas it appears that FOK is intact and accurate for semantic materials, i.e., general knowledge tests, it is impaired for episodic materials, i.e., newly learned word pairs (Souchay, Isingrini, & Espagnet, 2000). This again raises theoretical issues, as it suggests that the way in which we are aware of general knowledge differs from our awareness of recently learned material.

Theoretical explanations of the FOK

We need to examine models and theories that can explain these otherwise peculiar patterns of results seen in older adults. Koriat (1995) distinguished two very different views about the processes underlying FOKs. According to the *internal monitor view*, sometimes called the trace-based view, there are two stages involved. The first stage is like looking up a directory listing of computer files, and this precedes the second stage of retrieving the desired item. The FOK is based on whether or not the monitor detects the target item in the listing. As Koriat has pointed out, there are some problems with this account. It is consistent with an all-or-none FOK, rather than the graded judgements that are reported, and is also difficult to reconcile with inaccurate FOKs. By contrast, *inference-based models* claim that the FOK is based on inferences. For example, you may believe that you know something because the topic is familiar or because you can remember the context in which you acquired the information originally. Reder and Ritter (1992) elicited FOK judgements for arithmetical problems and varied the amount of exposure to whole problems and to individual terms in the problems. Their results showed that the FOK increased with increased exposure to the terms of the problem. That is, the FOK was based on familiarity with the question, not familiarity with the answer. This result appears to support an inference-based account of FOK.

Koriat's *accessibility model* (1993, 1995) is also an inference-based model. However, according to Koriat, the FOK does not precede retrieval, but is based on the products of retrieval. The products of retrieval may consist of the target item or of partial information about the target provided by the initial retrieval attempt. The FOK is determined by both the quantity and the quality of this information; that is, the amount of information, its intensity, and the ease of accessing it. The main difficulty in testing this model is that partial information may not be consciously available. Given a question like "What is the capital of Uganda?", fragments of the target may be retrieved but remain below the level of conscious awareness. Koriat carried out experiments examining FOKs for the recall of both four-letter nonsense strings (1993) and general knowledge facts (1995). The letter strings allowed Koriat to measure the amount of partial information available when recall of the whole string failed (i.e., the number of letters that were recalled), but in the experiments with general knowledge, the amount of partial information recalled for a given question had to be estimated from normative data based on how many participants could answer the question, that is, if more people could answer the question it was simply assumed that more partial information would be elicited. This method is therefore less satisfactory, although recall of general knowledge has greater ecological validity than recall of letter strings.

The model predicts that:

1   FOK will be higher if a response is given even if it is not correct than when no response is given (because the amount of information available is greater).
2   FOK will be higher if the response is correct than if it is wrong (because the quality of the information is more intense and it is accessed faster).
3   FOK will be higher if there is more partial information than if there is little or no partial information.
4   FOK will be higher for questions that many participants can answer (on the assumption that more partial information is, normatively, available for these questions).

These predictions were supported by the results. The model is also consistent with the graded character of FOKs and the fact that they are not always accurate. In line with his view that the accuracy of the FOK depends on the accuracy of the information retrieved, Koriat showed that, for questions that tended to elicit many wrong answers, FOKs were overestimated. The quantity and ease of access of the information misled participants into feeling overconfident that they knew the correct answer. Thus, for the perplexing finding that episodic but not semantic FOK is impaired in older adults, one merely has to consider that for the two tasks, the cues are different, and therefore that older adults struggle with episodic and not semantic cues. To consider what the difference between these two is, we need a theory of what the difference between semantic and episodic memory is from a consciousness viewpoint—see recollective experience below.

Finally, one very important idea arises from Koriat's model. He concluded that FOK formation occurs neither before nor after retrieval, but as part of an interactive online process contemporaneous with retrieval. This view blurs the distinction between retrieval and FOK, between knowledge and metaknowledge, which are both seen as part of the same process. One might argue that metacognition is not a bolt-on process that occurs alongside memory processes: It is an intrinsic part of memory itself. The contents of memory and the contextual detail retrieved when bringing to mind a memory is the material that generates the feeling of knowing. To understand this interactive online process, one has to turn to the literature on what is most often described as states of awareness.

RECOLLECTIVE EXPERIENCE

The historical context of recollective experience

Up until the late 1980s, psychological research had generally been constrained by what Endel Tulving (1989) called the "doctrine of concordance" of behaviour, cognition, and experience. Gardiner and Java (1990) explain that according to this doctrine, "performance, knowledge and experience are closely correlated" (p. 23), with the assumption that if you measure one, you are going to get an adequate enough picture of the others. This was, of course, convenient for researchers: It is much more reassuring to give someone a memory test and objectively score it out of 30, than it is to question them about their experience of remembering, and interpret the transcript of that interview, introducing subjectivity from both the participant *and* the experimenter. The latter seems especially unnecessary if you are of the opinion that conscious processes contribute little that the final response cannot summarise.

However, in 1985, Tulving argued that it was possible to classify different memory systems on the basis of subjective experience, rather than content or time period. He argued that memory retrieval could either be self-knowing or not. He characterised episodic memory as "autonoetic" (self-knowing). Semantic memory, on the other hand, often described as memory for facts, was "noetic" (just knowing: There is also anoetic memory—memory without awareness, such as implicit memory, or procedural memory). According to Tulving, then, episodic memories are self-knowing—that is, some aspect of the memory includes its source, an awareness of its origin, a feeling of pastness, a conscious evaluation of itself. On the other hand, semantic memories are not. These distinctions, which are still used in the psychological literature, are operationalised to reflect the presence or absence of recollective experience (as detailed in the next section).

Tulving's classifications revitalised the exploration of conscious processes in psychology and, better still, made it a formalised and relatively straightforward task to study the subjective experience of memory. Abandoning the behaviouristic doctrine of concordance, the shift in attention from *the result* of a decision-making process to *the process itself* (including the end-result), recognised the importance of consciousness in decision-making. What's more, the theoretical underpinnings of these memory systems have afforded the development of objectivised measures of subjective experience, called recollective experience, which can be taken alongside standard objective memory tests. Recollective experience measures allow psychologists to trust that participants have an insight into *why* they make memory judgements. So what exactly is recollective experience?

Defining recollective experience

Recollective experience is the subjective report of the sensations attached to the retrieval of an item from memory. Basically, it allows us to distinguish between sensations of "remembering" and "knowing". *Remembering* is the act of bringing something to mind with recollective experience: It includes a subjective state of pastness, and knowledge about the memory's context and source. For example, I may like to think about a recent holiday to New Zealand. On this holiday, I went for a walk in the Abel Tasman national park. I can remember who I went there with, and the sights and the smells of the path, and how I felt at the time. As I dwell on the memory, I begin to recall more detail about it, and I may enjoy the sensation of reminiscence. On the other hand, *knowing* about information, and recalling it from semantic memory, only involves the retrieval of information without recollective experience. There is no rich contextual information, or sense of pastness, I *just know* the information that I have retrieved. Two examples of "knowing" are as follows. If you ask me to name the capital of New Zealand, I can tell you that it is Wellington. I cannot remember how I learned this information and it does not necessarily evoke any feeling in me: It is just a well-established fact. Alternatively, if you ask me whether I have seen the film *Whale Rider*, I can say that I have without bringing to mind any specific memories of watching the film, without any recollective experience for it. Thus, although these two experiences of "knowing" could be considered quite different, the absence of recollective experience means that they are both "know" experiences. "Remembering" and "knowing" can be considered as reflecting either episodic and semantic memory, or autonoetic and noetic storage (Tulving, 1985).

Recollective experience research integrates classical, objective, right or wrong, recognition memory tests with measures of recollective experience. Based on the premise that we make recognition judgements for stimuli after examining our internal responses to them, this paradigm allows the memory researcher to score subjective measures of conscious experience in an objectified way, alongside standard objective measures of memory. A generic, if very short, recollective experience task would proceed as follows:

1   Participants read a list of four words: *heart, postcard, lily*, and *typewriter*.
2   They complete a distractor task, e.g., go through the alphabet backwards.
3   They are presented with the following definitions of judgements they will be asked to make:

- *Remember:* I recognise this word. I can remember aspects of my previous experience of reading it before (e.g., what it made me think).
- *Know:* I recognise this word. I don't remember any aspects of previously encountering the word but I just know it was in the previous list.
- *No recollection:* I do not recognise this word. This is a word I didn't read before.

4   Participants are presented with the test list of words that they are asked to categorise according the above definitions: *tree, postcard, knife, hangar, lily, heart, mug,* and *typewriter.*

In this way, "remember" and "know" judgements allow the researcher to understand what sort of conscious recognition experience the participant is having, as well as acting as positive recognition judgements in their own right. As you have been reading this example, you've probably been making recollective experience judgements of the example words, finding that you "remembered" all four of the words. However, imagine if you had looked at a list of 30 words for 5 seconds each, followed by a real distractor task lasting 15 minutes, and were then presented with a test list of 60 words. You can see how some words would be distinctive enough to be "remembered", others would just be "known", and some would slip through the net altogether. All in all, this sort of memory experiment can help us to examine further the phenomenology involved in the experience of remembering.

Recollective experience research—levels of processing

As we have discussed, one of the groundbreaking aspects of recollective experience research is the help it gives in quantifying the degree to which conscious recollection is involved in our everyday memory. And, due to the nature of the categorical judgements participants make regarding their recollections, we can separate the judgements where conscious recollection helps bring the memories to mind from the judgements not utilising these processes. It would therefore follow that, if we were to engage our conscious processes more when processing something for the first time, we might stand a better chance of recollecting the very same conscious processes and "remembering" the item at test. This is what was tested when the effect of manipulating *levels of processing* on subsequent recollective experience was measured.

When we refer to the level of processing of a stimulus, we consider whether it is encoded mainly using sensory processes (shallow processing) or semantic processes (deep processing). Were I to present you with the word "umbrella" and ask you to count the number of vowels in the word, I am sure you would respond "three". Vowel counting is a *shallow* level of processing; you do not need to do anything more sophisticated than know that *u*, *e*, and *a* are vowels, and count the number of times that they occur in the word. Were I to ask you to think about a memorable encounter with an umbrella, you would give me a totally different response. I could think back to the time I put my umbrella up in Leeds city centre, only to see it get turned inside-out—an embarrassing moment. This would be a *deep* level of processing that requires knowledge of the meaning of the word umbrella, combined with previous experience of using one, and the multitude of associations contextualising the account just described. You are engaging conscious processes and associations much more actively when processing stimuli on a deep level, compared to a shallow level of processing. It has been established that a deep level of processing leads to better performance in standard memory tasks (Craik & Lockhart, 1972) but, crucially, the manipulation has been shown to have an impact on recollective experience, and therefore on our conscious experience of remembering. Java, Gregg, and Gardiner (1997) found that deep processing resulted in higher levels of subsequent recollective experience. It is intuitively plausible that the formation of semantic associations at encoding will increase the network of associations through which conscious awareness of recollection can later be signalled, and it appears that this is what happens. For anyone with an interest in consciousness, this is reassuring.

Consciousness appears to serve a real purpose in signalling to us the degree to which it has been affected by the quality of our memories.

Relying on recollective experience

Interestingly, although subjective experience is an important and often under-investigated aspect of our everyday memory experience, it is not always objectively "accurate" either. As mentioned in Chapter 13, the Deese-Roediger-McDermott (DRM) paradigm can be used to induce false memories at test, in participants previously presented with a list of words associated with an unpresented semantic associate. Based on what we know about levels of processing, it is perhaps understandable that a DRM procedure can have such an effect on standard recognition memory, especially when you consider that the semantics of the presented words and their associates are so similar. However, the fact that participants tend to make these judgements based on recollective experience associated with the semantic associate is much more intriguing. Roediger and McDermott (1995) found that more than half the participants incorrectly identified the associate word as having been previously presented to them and, crucially, they often "remembered" encountering the word previously, including such details as how they felt at the time they encountered it. Now, what the participants report cannot be true, but equally they are not lying; they genuinely believe that they encountered the associate word previously, justifying that belief with a constructed memory of what they thought at the time.

Of course there is the argument that, due to the uneven comparison between the recollection of individual words and the recollection of entire events, procedures such as the DRM are not good analogues of how we form actual false memories (Freyd & Gleaves, 1996). But in this chapter we are not too concerned with the formation of false memories themselves, but rather the conscious processes that go into convincing us that these false memories are part of our previous experience and not a figment of our imaginations. In this respect, the effects of the DRM give us an idea of the predicament faced by individuals such as AKP (see the case study). If we, as individuals without neurological impairment, can have erroneous recollection so convincing that we will confabulate what we "thought" when we "encountered" previously unencountered stimuli, it becomes easier to understand AKP's responses to situations that he also recollects, however erroneously. AKP is not behaving in an abnormal way, he is simply responding as you or I would to the convincing impulses resulting from his conscious experience.

Due to the unity of consciousness, when aspects of our conscious experience such as recollective experience go wrong, we seemingly do not have any superordinate executive processes to convincingly over-ride them. Thus, if you do not have any reason to believe that you have not previously read this paragraph before, and if you can remember what you thought when you read it previously, you would be mad *not* to trust that you had read it before. (We will explore erroneous sensations of memory further in the section on déjà vu). As far as the psychology of everyday memory is concerned, recollective experience appears to be crucial to understanding how we deal with what we encounter. The growing emphasis memory researchers are placing on conscious experience is providing us with a greater understanding of the processes by which we evaluate our own memory experiences. Far from com-plicating the previously objective field of memory research with impenetrable subjective experience, recollective experience is helping to explain the way in which we utilise our memories as a rational and effective, though occasionally error-prone, storage system.

EDUCATION

Understanding the way we learn

The process you are hopefully engaging in now, learning, is another more applied aspect of memory research that has benefited from the use of recollective experience in its investigation. There appears to be a systematic progression we go through in order to acquire and then best use the information we have acquired. Traditionally, psychologists have thought of this as a schematisation process, where learned information (such as your knowledge of standardised experimental processes), through consistent and frequent use, becomes generalised to be universally applicable to all appropriate situations (Conway, Cohen, & Stanhope, 1991). This transfer of knowledge is thought of as a transfer from episodic memory to semantic memory. At first, facts are retained and contextualised, with memory emphasising the contextualising aspects of the fact, such as how, where, and when it was learned. Then, as we encounter the same fact in differing situations, we semanticise the memory, stripping it of the contextualising factors and representing it more as an abstract concept independent of how or when it was first learned. In the case of learning, it appears to be the removal of conscious access to the episodic companion information to a fact that signals our increased understanding of the fact.

For a moment, think about working memory. As a psychology student, you will undoubtedly be familiar with the concept, and you will probably bring to mind automatically, the diagram of the central executive, phonological loop and visuo-spatial sketchpad (and maybe even the episodic buffer) when I ask you to think about it. However, unless learning about it was a particularly momentous occasion, or took place particularly recently, you may find it very hard to think back to the moment you first encountered working memory academically. Who told you about it? Where were you? What did you think of it at the time? You are probably struggling to find answers to these questions because you have semanticised your knowledge of the working memory system. You have studied it, discussed it, and written about it in so many different contexts (in the library, in tutorials, at home) that it makes most sense for your mental representation of it just to abstract it from the multitude of episodic baggage that you could have associated with it. On the other hand, if you think of your knowledge of recollective experience and your first encounter with it was whilst reading this chapter, you will probably, at the moment, have a memory of it that is highly contextualised by the episodic memory associated with how you encountered the information. However rich this memory seems, in order for you to have learned and understood recollective experience to a degree that would satisfy psychologists who study memory, you are probably going to have to sacrifice your memory of reading about it in this book so that, eventually, you *only* have an abstract knowledge of the system and the way in which you believe it works.

We do not yet fully understand the way in which knowledge is transferred from episodic to semantic memory. However, it has been possible to test the assumptions about schematisation using what we already know about recollective experience. In a study examining over 200 students doing psychology modules at university, Conway, Gardiner, Perfect, Anderson, and Cohen (1997) measured participants' recollective experience immediately after lectures, and then following final exam assessment, in order to determine the degree to which memory was semanticised, and how that was associated with final exam performance. They found that, immediately following lectures, high-performing students reported higher levels of "remember" than "know" responses. However, when exam-assessed, these students reported higher levels of "know" responses. Termed the *R-to-K shift*, this effect was found to be stronger in higher performing students, than low performing students. The implication is that students who performed well were able to encode the episodic content of the lectures effectively, and then consolidate it through semanticising it prior to the exam, and this is consistent with our discussions of how learning to takes place most effectively.

Yet again, it seems that conscious experience is tied to more traditional objective measures of memory, in this case memory performance, but not in the way in which we might expect it to be. That we lose recollective experience in order to consolidate and schematise knowledge is intuitively plausible. In order to be able to operationalize our knowledge best, it makes sense to lose the automatic activation of specifics associated with individual and not necessarily generalisable experiences of the knowledge. However, the previously discussed "knowing" was indicative of less elaborative levels of processing and lower memory performance (see recollective experience research—levels of processing), but in this case "knowing" is associated with more rehearsal and, ultimately, better performance. The distinction between the two "know" states is discussed in depth in the Conway et al. (1997) paper but, as with much of the incorporation of consciousness to psychological research, it remains to be fully established.

A similar line of reasoning explains the involvement of consciousness with fluidity and expertise. In order to understand the role of consciousness in fluidity, however, we must first understand fluidity. When we carry out something we are fluid at, we need to devote fewer attentional resources to doing it, and consequently have more resources available for other tasks. In essence, it becomes easy. For example, when I was learning to drive I found that I had to concentrate so much on remembering and implementing how to keep the car going and avoid collisions, that I could not even contemplate talking to a passenger. Now, I can talk readily when driving on the open road, but still find conversation difficult when driving in an unfamiliar city. I have developed fluidity, as measured by my ability to transfer more of it to unconscious processes, for driving on the open road but not for city driving. This development can be measured by this transfer of conscious processes to unconscious control without any detriment in performance (e.g., Fitts, 1964), the act of *attaining fluidity*, of comparing oneself with other more proficient models, of goal setting and error monitoring, also requires consciousness (Rossano, 2003). In this way, and somewhat conversely, consciousness mediates the process of transferring unconscious control of previously cognitively intensive tasks in two ways. First, in order to become this practised, knowledge must pass through consciousness so many times that it becomes so fluid it can be carried out unconsciously. Second, error monitoring, goal setting and self–other comparison all require consciousness to be implemented successfully. So it is perhaps not surprising that the better-performing students in Conway et al.'s (1997) study had started off by "remembering" more of the lectures than they "knew". They had engaged conscious awareness of what they were learning, presumably making it easier to begin the process of attaining fluidity.

HYPNOSIS

Defining hypnosis

Thus far, we have considered how conscious states arise from mental acts such as remembering. There is also considerable interest in how changes in conscious states, in turn, affect memory processes. One such circumstance occurs when individuals' memories are influenced by suggestions given during hypnosis. Hypnosis is an *altered state of consciousness* that can be entered into, in varying degrees, by 90% of the population. Whilst in a state of hypnosis, individuals are able to interact with the world in much the same way as they do normally—they can open their eyes, learn new information, and respond to questions. When this is considered alongside the fact that there are a small number of established, memory-related manipulations associated with hypnosis, it would appear to be a very useful tool for the further experimental investigation of the role played by consciousness in memory.

Posthypnotic amnesia

The most established hypnotic memory manipulation is posthypnotic amnesia. An amnesia suggestion given to the participant prior to deinduction (the process of going from hypnosis into normal, "wakeful" consciousness) can cause some participants to experience a compelling failure to recall material learned during hypnosis (Barnier, Bryant, & Briscoe, 2001). However, this failure of recall is generally thought to apply only to explicit memory (memory that manifests itself through conscious expression) rather than implicit memory (which manifests itself unconsciously), and is reversible following a pre-determined cue. For example, I could present a hypnotised, highly suggestible participant with 20 words, and then suggest posthypnotic amnesia for those words. Following deinduction, even if I were to offer them a per-word financial reward, the participant would not be able to recall the words that they were shown during hypnosis. However, if I were to show them pairs of words, one previously presented and one distractor, and ask them to choose which they preferred, the participant would unknowingly be more likely to choose the one they were implicitly familiar with (the previously presented word), than the distractor. Intriguingly, if I were to shake my keys in front of the participant and whistle, if that was what I had suggested would cancel the amnesia during hypnosis, then this explicit memory failure would be reversed and the participant would be able to remember everything. In fact, this process seems very similar to what can occur with people who have psychogenic amnesia. Psychogenic amnesia is a rare, but scientifically documented, disorder whereby, without any brain damage or organic cause, a person has complete memory loss—usually as a result of trauma. For example, Sharon, a case reported by Eisen (1989), was found naked, unconscious and near starvation in a park. She could not identify herself, and had no idea of how she came to be in the park. For 7 months in hospital she had no idea of who she was, until a media campaign reunited her with her family. Her amnesia was nearly total and affected a large chunk of her life. And yet in hypnotherapy she recovered some memories of the events surrounding her disappearance and was able to shed light on how she came to be in the park. In this case, hypnotic procedures reversed the amnesia, suggesting that conscious processes disrupted memory function.

Posthypnotic amnesia appears only to affect conscious processes. So are participants consciously manipulating their responses to match the suggestions? After all, you cannot control a response you are not conscious of making. The answer to this question delves deep into the heart of hypnosis research, and is one of the reasons why it is often viewed quite critically by scientific empiricists. Consistent with the psychological research detailed so far, the best way to find out about someone's conscious processes seems to involve asking them. In post-experimental interviews with participants experiencing unbreachable amnesia (the amnesia experienced by most participants eventually breaks down if they are questioned and challenged resolutely enough—the 10% for whom it does not are generally extremely hypnotisable and often referred to by hypnotists as *hypnotic virtuosos*), two sorts of *cognitive style* predominate. McConkey, Glisky, and Kihlstrom (1989) examined two participants displaying these two differing styles. The first is a passive style that appears very naturalistic to participants: "when you asked me questions it was like nothing, like dumbfounded. It was totally erased from anything you had done" (p. 136). Participants are unable to remember because it feels as though there is nothing there to remember. The second is an active style, which is more constructive: "It was like there was a wall there" (p. 137). Participants do not remember because they have utilised a number of cognitive strategies to help with the success of the amnesia. The passive style appears not to have any consciously detectable signs of self-control, whereas the participant engaging the active style appears to be aware of why they cannot remember.

The two cognitive styles discussed tell us that there is no clear-cut argument that resolves whether posthypnotic amnesia results from processes that participants are aware of or not—in some participants it does, in some it does not. Nevertheless, because a participant is aware of why they are experiencing amnesia, it does not mean that they are consciously controlling the amnesia. To complicate matters further, suggestions either side of this middle ground have been made. Spanos, Radtke, and Bertrand (1985) argued that conscious control over memory processes is maintained during posthypnotic amnesia, and that memory is manipulated to be consistent with a "deeply hypnotised" self-presentation. On the other hand, Raz, Shapiro, Fan, and Posner (2002) used posthypnotic suggestion (this time that highly suggestible participants would be unable to read) to eliminate an extremely robust measure of automatic processing known as the Stroop effect, which indicates that the explicit–implicit distinction resulting from posthypnotic amnesia can be eliminated in favour of a total and complete amnesia with additional posthypnotic suggestion. We clearly have a great deal to learn about the way in which posthypnotic amnesia is formed and experienced. The important issue, however, is that the subjective experience can be explored to elucidate the intricacies of the various processes that are responsible for producing objectively indistinguishable effects, and just as memory produces conscious states, so it seems that altering conscious states interferes with normal memory processes.

DÉJÀ VU

Defining déjà vu

What happens when the normal relationship between memory and consciousness is disrupted in daily life? To explore this we turn full circle and revisit déjà vu, the strange conflict of sensations that results from feeling that we have experienced the same situation previously whilst knowing that we do not actually have any memory for it. Although patients such as AKP (see the case study) can experience this sensation many times a day, its occurrence in the neurologically unimpaired population is much less frequent, but still extremely common; it is experienced by the vast majority of the population at least once in their lives (A.S. Brown, 2003). Many theories have been proposed to explain the occurrence of the phenomenon. There are those who see it as evidence of reincarnation; it was also thought that it occurred as a result of slight delays in processing the input from one eye and not the other (this seems unlikely, as blind people experience déjà vu in much the same way as sighted individuals do; O'Connor & Moulin, 2006); and Freud believed that it results from the memory of an unconscious fantasy (Freud, 1901/1914). However, current psychological explanations have gravitated towards memory-based explanations that incorporate the role of subjective, conscious experience. We can look at déjà vu as resulting from the conflict between the absence of a memory and the conscious awareness of the sensation of familiarity. Once again, this is of particular interest to us, because it is possible to use traditional memory test methodologies to manipulate the contents of memory, and measures of recollective experience to try and understand exactly how we experience the conscious aspects of the sensation.

The recollective experience of déjà vu

If we were to test experimentally the conscious state associated with déjà vu, we would need some theoretical background on which to base our hypothesis. Vernon Neppe (1983, p. 3) provided this background when he defined déjà vu as "any subjectively inappropriate impression of familiarity of a present experience with an undefined past". If we examine this definition, the notion of recognition related to an undefined past should strike you as being very similar to something we have already examined in detail: The "know" response according to the recollective experience paradigm. According to Neppe's definition, individuals experiencing déjà vu should be recognising the trigger without experiencing any recollective experience for it. So we have a definition-based hypothesis with a strong body of recollective experience literature to draw on. The only problem remaining for us would-be déjà vu researchers is to develop a way by which to administer a test of recollective experience during or immediately after a déjà vu experience; a seemingly thankless task unless you wanted to follow participants around for months on end.

Conveniently for us, an old procedure involving posthypnotic amnesia is often mentioned in reviews of the scientific literature on déjà vu. Banister and Zangwill (1941) showed 10 participants pictures for which they then suggested posthypnotic amnesia. Following the hypnosis, the experimenters presented the to-be-forgotten pictures to participants again, whilst they were still amnesic for them, and asked that they talk about them. Over the course of the experimental procedure, three of the participants experienced *restricted paramnesia*, a sensation the authors compared to déjà vu. We revived this methodology, presenting participants with words, some of which they were amnesic for, and asking participants to make recollective experience judgements of them. We found that 6 (of 10) participants reported a sensation like déjà vu on encountering to-be-forgotten words and that these participants reported higher levels of "know" responses than "remember" responses, whereas those who did not experience déjà vu reported the opposite pattern of responding.

So this goes part of the way to ascertaining the sort of conscious state that gives rise to experimentally induced déjà vu. But there are still a number of questions to answer. How comparable is this "experimental" déjà vu to normal déjà vu? Is it really a surprise that we do not feel recollective experience for something we do not have a memory for (whether that is as a result of never having experienced it before, or of having amnesia for it)? It is hard to answer these questions conclusively without further investigation, but one of the reassuring aspects of this research is that, thanks to the growing emphasis on conscious experience in the field, it can be done, and it is being done.

Déjà vécu

The finding that déjà vu is associated with recognition without recollective experience is, however, surprising when comparing participants under hypnosis to patients such as AKP (see the case study). When Moulin et al. (2005) administered recollective experience tests to AKP and another patient with the same condition, they found that they gave an increased number of "remember" responses compared to control participants, in direct contrast to the pattern shown by people in hypnosis, suggesting that the phenomenon experienced by AKP may not actually be déjà vu as we have conceptualised it, but a more compelling, clinical form of the experience, déjà vécu (already lived). Yet again this distinction is down to a difference in conscious experience.

One of the most apparent differences between what we experience and what AKP experiences lies in how we respond to our respective déjà experiences. When you or I experience déjà vu, we may tell those who are around us about the strange sensation we feel, but we certainly do not act on our feelings in the same way that AKP does. I don't change channels when I experience déjà vu whilst watching television, because I do not actually remember having watched the television programme before: AKP does. That is because AKP's feelings are more overwhelmingly conscious; he cannot ignore them. Not only does he modify his behaviour based on the erroneous memory he experiences, but he also confabulates explanations of how he could possibly have such improbable memories. These confabulations are not lies, because AKP is basing what he says on the truth that he perceived. Herein lies the difference between a sensation that may or may not be wrong, déjà vu (already seen), and a conscious experience that is so overwhelming and overpowering that every time you interrogate it you get the same answer, "You *remember* doing this before"; déjà vécu.

We do not yet fully understand what causes patients like AKP to experience déjà vécu. They have certainly not been presented with a number of semantically related distracters, as would need to have been the case if we were to explain their sensations as resulting from a DRM-like effect. In fact, you might say the opposite is true; patients with déjà vécu tend to find more novel situations familiar (Moulin et al., 2006). For instance, AKP will notice and comment on the day-after-day monotony of the bird singing on the telephone wires as if he has never encountered the situation before. The causes of déjà vécu are to do with the underlying neuropathology, as these patients are usually in the process of cognitive decline related to dementia. However, we can begin to understand sensations similar to déjà vécu if we approximate experiences such as déjà vu with the overpowering sensation of infallibility associated with the certainty of conscious experience. As we have discovered over the course of this chapter, we often learn most about how conscious processes influence our experience of memory and awareness when these systems go wrong. Unlike thermostats, we do not cease to function when one aspect of our everyday functioning departs from its normal behaviour. Consciousness provides us with a grasp of our internal states and some degree of awareness for these entirely subjective, but wholly human states of functioning: It is this conscious understanding that will ultimately help us unravel the impact of consciousness on everyday memory.

CONCLUSIONS

This chapter has reviewed two large research enterprises that are currently enjoying a lot of attention amongst memory researchers: Metacognition and recollective experience. We have seen that both draw on contemporary views of consciousness, incorporating subjective feelings and knowledge about internal processes, and have at their core some aspect of privileged first-person-only access to ongoing memory processes. Moreover, these two approaches are illuminating our understanding of the real world. Despite the belief that consciousness should be ignored or treated as a by-product of processing by early psychologists, it is clearly driving some novel research themes central to daily life. For instance, the déjà vu phenomenon, which has long been ignored by psychologists, has been reinvigorated by a consciousness and cognition viewpoint—and it would appear we have the tools to research this intriguing sensation further. Reports of subjective experience are also helping us understand more mundane activities like student learning.

As a final note, the subjective focus in studies of consciousness and memory has opened the field up to academics wishing to share their cognitive failures with the academic world—but their errors are much more idiosyncratic than the memory failures outlined by Erber et al. (1990) above.

REFERENCES

Andrews, T.J., Schluppeck, D., Homfray, D., Matthews, P., & Blakemore, C. (2002). Activity in the fusiform gyrus predicts conscious perception of Rubin's vase–face illusion. *Neuroimage, 17*, 890–901.

Banister, H., & Zangwill, O. (1941). Experimentally induced visual paramnesias. *British Journal of Psychology, 32*, 30–51.

Barnier, A.J., Bryant, R.A., & Briscoe, S. (2001). Posthypnotic amnesia for material learned before or during hypnosis: Explicit and implicit memory effects. *International Journal of Clinical and Experimental Hypnosis, 49*, 286–304.

Brown, A.S. (2003). A review of the déjà vu experience. *Psychological Bulletin, 129,* 394–413.

Brown, R., & McNeill, D. (1966). The "tip of the tongue" phenomenon. *Journal of Verbal Learning and Verbal Behavior, 5,* 325–337.

Cavanaugh, J.C. (1998). The place of awareness in memory development across adulthood. In L.W. Poon, D.C. Rubin, & B.A. Wilson (Eds.), *Everyday cognition in adulthood and later life.* Cambridge, UK: Cambridge University Press.

Connor, L., Dunlosky, J., & Hertzog, C. (1997). Age-related differences in absolute but not relative metamemory accuracy. *Psychology and Aging, 36,* 34–49.

Conway, M.A., Cohen, G., & Stanhope, N. (1991). On the very long-term retention of knowledge acquired through formal education: Twelve years of cognitive psychology. *Journal of Experimental Psychology: General, 120,* 1–22.

Conway, M.A., Gardiner, J.M., Perfect, T.J., Anderson, S.J., & Cohen, G.M. (1997). Changes in memory awareness during learning: The acquisition of knowledge by psychology undergraduates. *Journal of Experimental Psychology: General, 126,* 393–413.

Craik, F.I.M., & Lockhart, R.S. (1972). Levels of processing: A framework for memory research. *Journal of Verbal Learning and Verbal Behavior, 11,* 671–684.

Descartes, R. (1970). *Meditations on first philosophy.* In E.S. Haldane & G.R.T. Ross (Trans.), *The philosophical works of Descartes, Vol. 1.* Cambridge, UK: Cambridge University Press. [Originally published 1641]

Dunlosky, J., & Connor, L. (1997). Age-related differences in the allocation of study time account for age-related differences in memory performance. *Memory & Cognition, 25,* 691–700.

Eisen, M.R. (1989). Return of the repressed: Hypnoanalysis of a case of total amnesia. *International Journal of Clinical and Experimental Hypnosis, 37,* 107–119.

Erber, J.T., Szuchman, L.T., & Rothberg, S.T. (1990). Everyday memory failure: Age differences in appraisal and attribution. *Psychology and Aging, 5,* 236–241.

Fitts, P.M. (1964). Perceptual-motor skill learning. In A.W. Melton (Ed.), *Categories of human learning* (pp. 253–285). London: Academic Press.

Freud, S. (1914). *Zur Psychopathologie des Alltaglebens/The psychopathology of everyday life.* Translated by A.A. Brill. London: T. Fisher Unwin. [Original German work published 1901]

Freyd, J., & Gleaves, D. (1996). "Remembering" words not presented in lists: Relevance to the current recovered/false memory controversy. *Journal of Experimental Psychology, 22,* 811–813.

Gardiner, J.M. (2001). Episodic memory and autonoetic consciousness: A first-person approach. *Philosophical Transactions of the Royal Society of London, B: Biological Sciences, 356,* 1351–1361.

Gardiner, J.M., & Java, R.I. (1990). Recollective experience in word and nonword recognition. *Memory and Cognition, 18,* 23–30.

Gennaro, R.J., Herrmann, D.J., & Sarapata, M. (2006). Aspects of the unity of consciousness and everyday memory failures. *Consciousness and Cognition, 15,* 372–385.

Henson, R.N., Rugg, M.D., Shallice, T., Josephs, O., & Dolan, R.J. (1999). Recollection and familiarity in recognition memory: An event-related functional magnetic resonance imaging study. *Journal of Neuroscience, 19,* 3962–3972.

James, L.E., & Burke, D.M. (2000). Phonological priming effects on word retrieval and tip-of-the-tongue experiences. *Journal of Experimental Psychology: Learning, Memory, and Cognition, 26,* 1378–1391.

Java, R.I., Gregg, V.H., & Gardiner, J.M. (1997). What do people actually remember (and know) in "remember/know" experiments? *European Journal of Cognitive Psychology, 9,* 187–197.

Kant, I. (1998). *Critique of pure reason.* Translated by P. Guyer & A. Wood. Cambridge, UK: Cambridge University Press. [Originally published 1781]

Koriat, A. (1993). How do we know that we know? The accessibility model of the feeling of knowing. *Psychological Review*, *100*, 609–639.

Koriat, A. (1995). Dissociation knowing and the feeling of knowing: Further evidence for the accessibility model. *Journal of Experimental Psychology, General*, *124*, 311–333.

Koriat, A., & Goldsmith, M. (1996). Memory metaphors and the real-life/laboratory controversy: Correspondence versus storehouse conceptions of memory. *Behavioural and Brain Sciences*, *19*, 167–228.

Krinsky, R., & Krinsky, S.J. (1988). City size bias and the feeling of knowing. In M.M. Gruneberg, P.E. Moms, & R.M. Sykes (Eds.), *Practical aspects of memory: Current research and issues, Vol. 1*. Chichester, UK: Wiley.

Lachman, J.L., Lachman, R., & Thronesberry, C. (1979). Metamemory through the adult life span. *Developmental Psychology*, *15*, 543–551.

Lovelace, E.A. (1984). Metamemory: Monitoring future recall ability during study. *Journal of Experimental Psychology: Learning, Memory, and Cognition*, *10*, 756–766.

McConkey, K.M., Glisky, M.L., & Kihlstrom, J.F. (1989). Individual differences among hypnotic virtuosos: A case comparison. *Australian Journal of Clinical and Experimental Hypnosis*, *17*, 131–140.

Moulin, C.J.A., Conway, M.A., Thompson, R.G., James, N., & Jones, R.W. (2005). Disordered memory awareness: Recollective confabulation in two cases of persistent déjà vécu. *Neuropsychologia*, *43*, 1362–1378.

Moulin, C.J.A., Turunen, M., Salter, A.J.A., O'Connor, A.R., Conway, M.A., & Jones, R.W. (2006). Recollective confabulation: Persistent déjà vécu in dementia. *Helix Review Series*, *2*, 10–15.

Nelson, T.O., Leonesio, R.J., Landwehr, R.S., & Narens, L. (1986). A comparison of three predictors of an individual's memory performance: The individual's feeling of knowing versus the normative feeling of knowing versus base-rate item difficulty. *Journal of Experimental Psychology: Learning, Memory, and Cognition*, *12*, 279–287.

Neppe, V.M. (1983). *The psychology of déjà vu: Have I been here before?* Johannesburg, South Africa: Witwatersrand University Press.

O'Connor, A.R., & Moulin, C.J.A. (2006). Normal patterns of déjà experience in a healthy, blind male: Challenging optical pathway delay theory. *Brain and Cognition*, *62*, 246–249.

Pinker, S. (1997). *How the mind works*. New York: W.W. Norton.

Raz, A., Shapiro, T., Fan, J., & Posner, M.I. (2002). Hypnotic suggestion and the modulation of Stroop interference. *Archives of General Psychiatry*, *59*, 1155–1161.

Reder, L.M., & Ritter, F. (1992). What determines initial feeling of knowing? Familiarity with question terms, not with the answer. *Journal of Experimental Psychology: Learning, Memory, & Cognition*, *18*, 435–451.

Revonsuo, A. (2003). The contents of phenomenal consciousness: One relation to rule them all and in the unity bind them. *Psyche* 9(08).

Roediger, H.L. III, & McDermott, K.B. (1995). Creating false memories: Remembering words not presented on lists. *Journal of Experimental Psychology: Learning, Memory, and Cognition*, *21*, 803–814.

Rossano, M.J. (2003). Expertise and the evolution of consciousness. *Cognition*, *89*, 207–236.

Searle, J. (1992). *The rediscovery of the mind*. Cambridge, MA: MIT Press.

Souchay, C., Isingrini, M., & Espagnet, L. (2000). Aging, episodic memory feeling-of-knowing, and frontal functioning. *Neuropsychology*, *14*, 299–309.

Spanos, N.P., Radtke, H.L., & Bertrand, L. (1985). Hypnotic amnesia as a strategic enactment: Breaching amnesia in highly susceptible subjects. *Journal of Personality and Social Psychology*, *47*, 1155–1169.

Sperry, R. (1984). Consciousness, personal identity, and the divided brain. *Neuropsychologia*, *22*, 661–673.

Tulving, E. (1985). Memory and consciousness. *Canadian Psychology*, *26*, 1–12.

Tulving, E. (1989). Memory: Performance, knowledge, and experience. *European Journal of Cognitive Psychology, 1,* 3–26.

Weiskrantz, L. (1986). *Blindsight: A case study and implications.* New York: Oxford University Press.

13 Memory dysfunction

Céline Souchay and Chris J.A. Moulin

COGNITIVE NEUROPSYCHOLOGY AND COGNITIVE NEUROPSYCHIATRY

Memory dysfunction is a vast topic, and not easily covered in one chapter. Here, several key studies are described in order to give a feel for the variety of approaches used and insights gained from working with people with neurological illness or psychiatric conditions. The overall theme is the application of memory theory and our understanding of memory in the real world to these special populations. For some disorders, such as Alzheimer's disease, memory impairment is central to the disorder, and there is a great deal of information and research available on the disease. Other diseases, such as schizophrenia, are not usually thought of as memory disorders but, nonetheless, a great deal of work has been carried out on the memory difficulties of people with that condition. These two different types of pathology are the focus of this chapter. There are far too many disorders for them all to be included here, so for a complete guide, we recommend a whole book devoted to the topic, *The handbook of memory disorders*, by Baddeley, Kopelman, and Wilson (2002).

Here, we take a cognitive viewpoint. In cognitive *neuropsychology*, the study of the relationship between memory and the brain has led to improvements in diagnosis, rehabilitation, and the understanding of memory impairment and brain damage. The main distinction in this chapter is between the cognitive *neuropsychology* of memory and the cognitive *neuropsychiatry* of memory. The neuropsychological approach—that of understanding brain damage and dysfunction due to physical cause, stroke, cell death, and head injury, is well established and has yielded many helpful insights into a variety of conditions and their treatment. Here we predominantly tackle Alzheimer's disease, a common disorder of memory. The neuropsychiatry approach is less well established, but uses identical tools to understand psychiatric disorders not caused by obvious brain damage; conditions such as schizophrenia, depression, post-traumatic stress disorder and obsessive-compulsive disorder. It would be impossible to give full overviews of these ever-growing areas, but the intersection between common psychopathologies and everyday life is mapped out below to give a flavour of these disciplines.

NEUROPSYCHOLOGICAL DISORDERS OF MEMORY

Disorders of everyday memory tend to be obvious when they occur, and they affect all sorts of memory domains, such as memory for intentions, plans and actions, memory for places, memory for people, autobiographical memory, or memory for knowledge. In fact, for all the topics covered in this book, brain damage can lead to clear problems in everyday life for those domains. In some cases, this damage can be very specific, such as in prosopagnosia, which can lead to very specific deficits in face recognition but not other abilities. In other cases, the damage to the brain is more diffuse, and affects cognitive function and memory for a wider set of abilities.

In the case of neuropsychology, cognitive deficits often result from sudden stroke or a traumatic brain injury (TBI) as a result of a blow to the head. In this chapter, however, the focus is on neurodegenerative disorders, where there is significant and ongoing cell death, such as in Alzheimer's disease. Cognitive neuropsychology is often encountered by the psychology student as a way of understanding how human memory works. For instance, much of what we understand in contemporary theories can be applied to the patient HM (Hilts, 1995), and many theories of cognitive function have been generated by the study of such cases (e.g., Baddeley & Warrington, 1970). HM's brain was damaged in such a precise way, and researched so thoroughly by experimental psychologists, that it gives us insights into the differences between implicit and explicit memory, the role of short- and long-term memory, and so on. However, in the last few years the study of the neuropsychology of memory has begun to have more practical utility, as applied to the real world. Much of this focus stems from the fact that the extent to which memory is impaired is related to the quality of life reported by patients. As one might expect, the worse someone's memory is, the more difficulty they have coping with and enjoying everyday life. For example, memory disorders following stroke have been associated to negative outcomes and poor quality of life in these patients (Clark, Dunbar, Aycock, Courtney, & Wolf, 2006).

With this focus on care and management of patients, some studies have explored the possibility of improving memory by training patients to use efficient memory strategies, whereas others have tried to introduce external help by training patients with memory problems to use portable computers or pagers (Kim, Burke, Dowds, Boone, & Park, 2000; Wilson, Emslie, Quirk, Evans, & Watson, 2005). In addition, a better understanding of memory dysfunction has also led to more effective rehabilitation. For instance, it has been shown that knowing more about one's own memory abilities or failures is a critical factor in the success of memory rehabilitation. Clearly, a better understanding of memory impairment facilitates improvements in remedying and rehabilitating memory disorders.

Most of our knowledge of everyday memory in neuropsychological populations comes from studies of brain damage. Often brain damage occurs due to a blow to the head, a car accident, a fall, blood flow irregularities such as stroke or haemorrhage, or a brain tumour. These different causes of brain injury or damage all vary in how specific the damaged area is, and will often lead to a variety of cognitive difficulties that may or may not change over time. The complexity of the relationship between brain and behaviour in cognitive neuropsychology has led to the description, "each patient may be as unique as a snowflake" (Buxbaum, 2006, cited in Caramazza & Coltheart, 2006). There can be considerable variability even when the damaged area is small, and the area seems the same between two patients. The media depiction of the car crash patient who comes round from coma with a specific clean-cut amnesia without other cognitive difficulties is extremely rare. In turn, whereas patients with specific areas of damage contribute more to student textbooks and our understanding of theory, clinically, such cases are rare. In the real world, it is more common that brain damage is gradual, diffuse, ever-changing, and disruptive to a wide range of cognitive abilities that impinge on social functioning and personality.

Dementia

Dementia is caused by a progressive loss of neurons, and the term comes from the Latin, *"out of mind"*. Someone with dementia experiences, from the age of about 60, massive cell death in the brain. Death of cells is focused on a few locations in the brain, but is much more widespread than the sort of damage caused by brain injury, stroke, or brain haemorrhage. Dementia is age-related, such that the older you are, the greater your chance of having the disorder. But dementia is *not* an inevitable consequence of the ageing process, nor is it correct to label any changes in memory found in healthy old age "dementia".

A recent report in the *Lancet* (Ferri et al., 2006) revealed that a new case of dementia arises every 7 seconds, with the number of people with dementia set to double every 20 years. This report comes nearly 100 years after the first reported case and description of Alzheimer's disease, and estimates that 24.3 million people currently have dementia worldwide—but by 2040 this number will have reached 81.1 million.

Memory impairment is the most common complaint observed in dementia. In fact, this has to be present in order for a diagnosis to be made. Although we know much about cell death in Alzheimer's disease, it is not yet possible to diagnose it with certainty before death. Thus, clinicians have to rule out other causes of memory problems, look for cell loss on a brain scan, and see a certain pattern of impairments in order to make the diagnosis. Critically, patients must have a memory impairment, and this must be affecting daily life in order for the diagnosis to be made.

Even if the memory impairment might be the initial symptom that alerts the clinician, some behavioural disturbance related to memory impairment might be observed by the relatives at an earlier stage of the disease, and changes in real-world functioning are likely to be what alerts the person or their family to go to the doctor. Despite this real-world focus in the experience and diagnosis of dementia, the research into memory dysfunction in dementia has predominantly been concerned with tightly controlled memory tasks with artificial word materials and laboratory studies. This chapter reviews the studies that have focused on real-world memory abilities in dementia.

Three main types of dementia exist: Alzheimer's disease (AD), semantic dementia (SD), and frontotemporal lobe dementia (FTD). These three diseases are all characterised by memory impairments, but because of the different localisation of the brain damage in these different pathologies their presentations are all slightly different. This chapter will focus on Alzheimer's disease, as it is probably the commonest neurodegenerative disorder and it is the disorder that has achieved the most attention from memory researchers.

Alzheimer's disease and everyday memory

Early AD is characterised by impairment of episodic memory. For example, AD patients have been found to perform poorly on recall and recognition tasks of words,

Anatomy of the brain

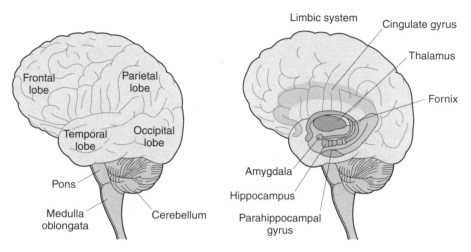

Figure 13.1 A diagrammatic representation of the brain showing the main areas. The hippocampus lies deep within the centre of the brain.

which require deliberate recollection of specific episodes. This episodic memory impairment has been proven to increase the likelihood of identifying AD cases at an early stage—even before they are diagnosed, people will start to have difficulties learning and retrieving lists of words (Buschke, Sliwinski, Kuslansky, & Lipton, 1997). This dysfunction has been connected to pathology in the medial temporal lobe and specifically the hippocampal formation (Braak & Braak, 1997). See Figure 13.1 for a diagram of the different areas of the brain. Alzheimer's disease is also marked by a major impairment of working memory, which has been widely assessed and related to an impairment in frontal lobe functioning (Baddeley, Logie, Bressi, Della Salla, & Spinnler, 1986; Collette et al., 1999). If you consider how critical episodic memory and working memory are in the real world—autobiographical memory and memory for routes is largely episodic and hippocampal (see Chapters 2 and 6), and many of our basic mental operations are facilitated by working memory—you can quickly see how Alzheimer's may affect everyday life. Someone with Alzheimer's disease will lose the thread during conversation, or ask questions repeatedly, due to failures of working memory. They will also not be able to remember routes they take regularly, and will get lost in familiar places due to episodic failure. They may also forget key facts based on their memory for knowledge, such as the number of grandchildren that they have, or who the Prime Minister is.

But the memory impairment in AD is far from total; people with AD have some preserved memory capacities. In particular, they show normal performance on certain implicit memory tests, that is, on tasks that do not require a conscious retrieval of the information (e.g., priming tasks; Fleischman & Gabrieli, 1998). These areas of preservation explain why people with AD may get lost and distracted very easily, but can still use the automatic skills necessary to drive, and why they may have forgotten that they used to work as a music teacher, but they can still, very fluently and expressively, play piano. Next we look at the different memory domains covered in this book in more detail: autobiographical memory, memory for places, memory for people, memory for knowledge, memory for expertise, and prospective memory.

Memory for personal experience in Alzheimer's disease

People with AD find it difficult to learn and remember new information and this impairment has been extremely well researched. In contrast, remote memory—memory for events that happened a long time ago, and information acquired a long time ago, has received relatively little attention. Studies within the domain of remote memory have mainly explored memory for public events and famous faces (Sagar, Cohen, Sullivan, Corkin, & Growdon, 1988; also see Chapter 4). In the last 10 years, cognitive models of autobiographical memory have been developed (e.g., Conway & Pleydell-Pearce, 2000), allowing a better exploration of remote memory in Alzheimer's disease. Autobiographical memory is a complex concept that includes different kinds of knowledge pertaining to oneself. Conway and colleagues (e.g., Conway, Pleydell-Pearce, Whitecross, & Sharpe, 2000) have distinguished between autobiographical memories, which are detailed "episodic" memories of personal experiences situated in time and space (e.g., a memory of an event from your schooldays) and autobiographical knowledge, which refers to more conceptual or "semantic" knowledge of one's past (e.g., the name of your primary school).

The main observation regarding Alzheimer's disease and autobiographical memory is the existence of a very marked pattern of amnesia—memory loss—which obeys Ribot's law (Ribot, 1881): Older memories are better preserved than recent ones (Greene, Hodges, & Baddeley, 1995; Kopelman, 1992; Sagar et al., 1988). Thus, Alzheimer's patients tend to produce fewer memories when compared to older control adults but also tend to recall more memories from the distant past than controls. People with AD have more difficulty recalling recent autobiographical memories than memories for remote events. This is often perplexing for their carer: *Why can my husband remember his school days so vividly, but not remember the holiday we took last week?* In our experience, merely explaining the memory impairment to carers, and the standard pattern of difficulties shared by other carers, can be greatly reassuring. It is normal that memory seems to break down in this ironic manner: Things from longer ago are better remembered.

A few studies have assessed the different components in autobiographical memory to determine whether AD patients have more difficulties in recalling episodic (personal recollections, images, feelings) than semantic information (personal facts). In general, these studies all revealed that AD patients showed impairments in both components (Greene et al., 1995; Hou, Miller, & Kramer, 2005). But Greene et al. found that only autobiographical episodic memories were affected in this pattern according to Ribot's law. Autobiographical personal semantic memories were more uniformly represented over the years. For the neuropsychologist, that suggests that episodic and semantic knowledge in autobiographical memory are probably separate memory systems in the brain. For the real world, these results also suggest that the semantic component of autobiographical memory is slightly more robust than the episodic component, and support the view that preserved remote memories in Alzheimer's disease have a predominantly semantic character (Warrington & McCarthy, 1988). Carers and clinicians could use this information to help them focus on questions and conversations that are easier for the person with AD, and give them some feeling of satisfaction.

Of similar interest is flashbulb memory, which unsurprisingly has also been studied in Alzheimer's disease. In fact, one of our own studies has done this, albeit looking at only a very small number of patients (Thompson et al., 2004). We found that people with Alzheimer's disease were able to remember the terrorist attacks that occurred on September 11 2001, even when tested up to a year later. If they had taken the information in, they were well able to remember it. But interestingly, they were better at recalling the events of the day as recounted by everyone: where it happened in New York, who was the suspect, which building was destroyed, what the global impact was, and so on. In agreement with the above difference between episodic and semantic information, they were much less likely to be able to report their own personal circumstances. We can probably all remember how we heard the information and who we were with—but for the person with AD, this is extremely difficult. Other studies have examined other events in AD within this flashbulb memory framework. They all converge on the usual finding: As found in healthy people, memories of flashbulb events are better than memories of control events. For example, people with AD from the Greater Kobe district of Japan were much more likely to remember the events of the Kobe earthquake than to remember their recent MRI scan (Ikeda et al., 1998). Such findings suggest that the same processes and factors that make flashbulb memory so strong in healthy people, also function in people with AD, so that the disease has less impact on such memories.

But why is autobiographical memory so interesting? In part, it is because in the last few years theories from philosophy, social psychology, and cognitive psychology have related autobiographical memory to the concept of identity (Conway, 2005). Personal identity (or our sense of "self") results from the interpretation of auto-biographical memories into a coherent story about ourselves. Thus, because of this close relationship between autobiographical memories and the constitution of identity, some researchers have suggested that identity would change if autobiographical memories were lost. Indeed, many family members or carers describe personality change as the major difficulty of Alzheimer's disease—something over-looked by professionals, who view it more as a straightforward problem of "forget-fulness". But is there any evidence for this view, or could the notion of personality change be down to other factors, like the carer learning to cope with a loved one with a serious memory complaint?

Recently, this question has been researched empirically. Addis and Tippett (2004) assessed whether the impairment observed in autobiographical memory in Alzheimer's disease was associated with changes in identity. Identity was assessed by using the Twenty Statements test (Khun & McPartland, 1954), requiring participants to give 20 responses to the question "Who am I?" For example, the patient may make a list of 20 items such as: I am a father, I am grey-haired, I am male, I am quick-tempered, I am retired, I am a golfer, I am generous, and so on. Responses are then classified into four categories of identity: attributes ("male"), social identities ("father"), evaluative descriptions ("quick-tempered"), and physical descriptions ("grey-haired"). As expected, the results confirmed a significant impairment on autobiographical memory tests. Patients were found to recall fewer semantic and episodic autobiographical memories compared to controls. Also, AD patients were found to show changes in a number of aspects of identity. Compared to the age-matched control group, AD patients generated fewer responses on the Twenty Statements test and produced a higher percentage of evaluative responses, such as "quick-tempered" or "generous". According to Addis et al., these results suggest that identity becomes weaker in AD and reflect the report of loss of identity made by the family. Most importantly, this study showed that changes in identity were associated with a poorer recall of childhood or early adulthood episodic memories. The worse a person's memory of their own past was, the more difficulty they had on the Twenty Statements test. Thus, there is some evidence that the loss of autobiographical memory in AD leads to changes in identity or the self—again corresponding with many carers' reports.

Finally, the autobiographical memory impairment in AD can tells us about the workings of the brain. Neuropsychology studies and functional neuroimaging studies of autobiographical memory have revealed the involvement of a widespread network of brain cells, including the frontal lobes and temporal lobes (Greenberg & Rubin, 2003). Patients with damage to these areas exhibit a very profound autobiographical amnesia (Vargha-Khadem et al., 1997) and so descriptions of cases with this damage suggest an important role for the temporal lobes and frontal lobes in the recollection of personal experiences. Other researchers then seek to confirm this finding by using converging methods: A different approach to examine the same thing. Happily, functional neuroimaging studies, which look at activation in the brain whilst a person is doing a particular task, have shown increased temporal lobe activations during autobiographical memory retrieval (Maguire et al., 1998).

Neuropsychology often makes great advances like this, looking at the correspondence between areas of damage and deficit in patients, and the areas that are activated when healthy young people are doing the same tasks in the brain scanner. Other researchers then theorise about the function of those areas. In the case of the hippocampus and the temporal lobes, this area seems to play a role in binding together disparate information implicating different brain regions to encode or retrieve information: The more the hippocampus is activated, the more detail is retrieved from autobiographical memory (Gilboa et al., 2005). As for the frontal lobes, their involvement in autobiographical memory has also been supported by neuroimaging. According to Conway, Pleydell-Pearce, and Whitecross (2001), the frontal cortex represents a "working self" in charge of organising all self-related information including personal episodes, personal facts, or future goals.

Returning to Alzheimer's disease, the different sites of cell loss are all relevant to the network of brain regions implicated in autobiographical memory. Thus, the impairment observed in these patients could be related to damage to the temporal lobes, particularly the hippocampus, but could also be related to a frontal lobe dysfunction. In the real world, these cell changes lead to profound changes in identity, and a lack of autobiographical memory.

Memory for places in Alzheimer's disease

As described in Chapter 6, spatial memory is of particular importance for everyday life as it enables us to find our way around and to locate objects in our environment. Topographic disorientation (TD), people's problems in finding their own way, is a common problem among people with AD. TD often forces patients to abandon independent activities and represents a real preoccupation for relatives or carers as patients can become lost even in familiar surroundings. As an example, a change of residence is a major source of TD in AD patients due to the novelty of the environment (Pai & Jacobs, 2004).

Despite the importance of such an impairment in everyday life, only a few studies have tried to demonstrate the underlying cognitive deficits of TD. Cherrier, Mendez, and Perryman (2001) examined AD patients' ability to learn a new route in order to try to understand more about TD in this pathology. AD patients were found to perform significantly worse than controls on a route-learning task and were also found to have a poor learning of environmental details. Some researchers suggest that TD is a consequence of general cognitive deterioration (Passini, Rainville, Marchand, & Joanette, 1995). Caregivers often report that AD patients at an early stage are safe in their familiar environment. As the cell loss worsens, and cognitive abilities deteriorate, spatial abilities get worse. However, even at an early stage, people with AD have been found to be disoriented in a more unfamiliar environment. As a result, people with very early AD tend to stay within familiar territory, and choose not to visit new places or go on holidays.

Like autobiographical memory, TD can be traced to particular brain regions. Data from functional imaging studies of normal navigation (Maguire et al., 1998) suggest that several brain regions may be involved in navigation. These regions include the back of the parietal cortex and, again, the hippocampus (see Figure 13.1). It is widely believed that TD in AD is related to memory failure from the shrinking of the hippocampus that occurs early in the disease (Braak & Braak, 1997). Because the hippocampus is particularly impaired at an early stage of the disease and because AD patients are still able to find their way in a familiar environment but not in a new place at this stage, TD disorientation within new environments is probably related to the hippocampus. The pattern appears to be different, however, according to whether the spatial information was learnt before or after the onset of hippocampus shrinkage. The hippocampus is not involved in the recovery of environments learned long ago (Aguirre & D'Esposito, 1999) and some research shows that the hippocampus is not needed for navigation based on remote memory (see Rosenbaum, Gao, Richards, Black, & Moscovitch, 2005). This would explain why AD patients would be able, at least at an early stage of the disease, to find their way in a familiar environment.

This idea was explored by Rosenbaum et al. (2005). They investigated the role of the hippocampus in the storage and recovery of long-standing topographical knowledge by assessing remote topographical memory in a retired taxi driver diagnosed with Alzheimer's disease. They found that despite the fact that he had a very shrunken hippocampus, he performed as well as control participants on remote tests of spatial location. Thus, memory for locations of well-known places does not appear to depend upon the hippocampus. As the disease affects progressively more and more of the brain, the patient ends up with areas that are critical to knowledge of even familiar locations being damaged, and TD results.

Another way we manage to find our way in environments is to remember the location of objects, such as landmarks, and where they occur. Kessels, Feijen, and Postma (2005) studied this ability in people with AD, finding a deficit in remembering object locations. In their task, conducted on a computer, people had to remember what objects they had seen, and in which room of a house. People with AD could remember what objects they had seen, but not where they had appeared.

This again may explain the disorientation experienced in Alzheimer's disease. People may understand that they passed a church, a fish-and-chip shop, and a primary school on the way to the post office, but not their relation to each other, and their general layout. It may also explain their tendency to lose objects such as their spectacles or keys.

In summary, there is clear evidence that memory for spatial locations and objects in space is impaired in Alzheimer's disease, and we have some understanding of how this is manifest in the brain. But memory for spatial information also seems to have a relationship with severity, and the age at which the information was acquired, just as for autobiographical memory. For well-learned and familiar environments, just as for personal information, it appears that the memory deficit in AD is not so marked. Again, it is memory for new locations and networks that is the most impaired in AD, and information that requires the involvement of the hippocampus—one of the areas affected earlier in the disease process.

Memory for people and faces in Alzheimer's disease

As presented in Chapter 4, memory for people includes different dimensions such as memory for faces, memory for voices, and memory for names. In Alzheimer's disease, patients have difficulty in recognising people, even their own relatives or carers, but only at a very late stage of the disease. In the very early stage of the disease, difficulty in retrieving names of people is a frequent finding among these patients and seems to be present even at a stage when, according to the standard criteria, a diagnosis of AD is not possible. In the laboratory, memory for people has been assessed in AD through the identification of famous faces (Hodges, Salmon, & Butters, 1993) or famous names (Greene & Hodges, 1996). These have all revealed clear difficulties in Alzheimer's patients in the identification of famous faces or names. However, the question of the exact nature of these deficits remains. The main hypothesis is that impaired semantic knowledge regarding the famous person leads to an inability to name the person (Greene & Hodges, 1996) and, again, the age of the material being assessed is critical. People with Alzheimer's disease can name famous faces that they encountered when they were younger, such as Winston Churchill, but they cannot name faces that they may have seen more recently in life, such as Tony Blair. Because memory for people seems to be a problem very early in the course of the disease, some researchers have suggested that name retrieval tasks or face identification tasks might be profitably included in diagnostic tools for the early detection of AD. Thus, memory for real-world materials could then be used for the early diagnosis of AD.

An emergent theme in memory in the real world is that of social cognition—how our cognitive abilities influence our social interactions. As an example, we need to be able to perceive subtle changes in people's faces in order to be able to judge their mood or their intentions correctly; our cognitive abilities impinge on our social abilities. This kind of social cognitive ability was assessed by Lavenu and Pasquier (2005). They assessed memory for faces in Alzheimer's disease in relation to emotions. They showed that recognition of emotion on faces in AD decreases with the progression of dementia in AD. People with Alzheimer's disease are less likely to be able to judge the emotion on the face of a person and, as the disease progresses, this gets worse. This could explain a whole host of social difficulties and lack of confidence in people with Alzheimer's: They cannot correctly interpret social situations, so this leads them to withdraw.

Again, all these difficulties have their basis in deterioration of neurons in the brain. But, unlike autobiographical memory and memory for spatial locations, face recognition is a fundamental social skill related to emotion processing. Brain lesions from stroke or TBI often lead to pure forms of face recognition disorder— prosopagnosia. In this disorder, people are completely unable to recognise faces. If they encounter their wives out of context, and without the clues that they use to recognise and identify them, they completely fail to recognise them. We know, from these cases, which parts of the brain are involved in face recognition—small specific areas of the right temporal lobe (Gainotti, Barbier, & Marra, 2003)—with the names of the faces possibly being stored on the corresponding area on the left-hand side of the brain (Snowden, Thompson, & Neary, 2004).

Alzheimer's disease does not give rise to such a pure deficit but, again, we know that cell loss in AD is encountered predominantly in the temporal and frontal lobes. In a few very rare cases the picture in AD is more bizarre, and quite unlike a pure cognitive failure. People with Alzheimer's disease have been reported to be unable to recognise pictures of themselves (Hehman, German, & Klein, 2005). That is, they correctly identify older pictures of themselves, but fail to recognise more recent photographs. This is again similar to the relationship they have with self-identity and autobiographical knowledge. An even more striking—and extremely rare—disorder is nurturing syndrome, a delusion seen in AD that is, in part, supported by dysfunctional object and face recognition. In this delusion, the AD patient believes a dead person (usually their spouse) to still be alive. Consider this case report (Venneri, Shanks, Staff, & Della Salla, 2000, p. 215):

> [Patient CS] regularly "fed" a photograph of her dead husband to the point that the mouth area of the portrait was worn away. When the family removed the photograph, she formed the same attachment to a record sleeve photograph of Peter Morrison—a well-known Scottish singer. CS mistook this photograph for one of her husband and she formed the same morbid attachment to it. She also tried to feed this record sleeve photograph, and finding difficulty (since it was made of cardboard), on two occasions she went to the dentist asking them to remove the "wires" from the teeth of the photograph. She also took it to bed with her, folding a scarf around the record sleeve, as if it were her husband's neck to protect him from catching a cold.

Also, AD patients have been reported who have had Capgras delusion. This delusion is often described as a "misidentification", where on one level the patient identifies the person, but fails to acknowledge their true identity. Commonly, the patient believes the person to be a copy or double of the person (often their spouse or another relative)—or, in more extreme cases, a robot or other synthetic imposter. The cognitive account of this disorder is that whilst certain aspects of face recognition are preserved, they do not connect properly with the affective "feeling" component, or the area where identity is stored: The subjective experience is that "it looks like the person, but I feel it is not them". Surprisingly, in reviewing this area, and looking at a relatively large sample of 151 people with Alzheimer's disease, Harwood, Barker, Ownby, and Duara (1999) suggested that as many as 10% of all cases of AD have Capgras delusion. These striking delusions are not so easy to pinpoint in the brain, and their relationship to memory in the real world is not as clear. However, as will be developed in the section on cognitive neuropsychiatry, they are less and less thought of as obscure and neglected areas of psychology. Another case of memory disorder in AD that presents as a delusion is given in Chapter 12.

Memory for knowledge in Alzheimer's disease

In the area of memory for knowledge, or semantic memory, deficits are common in Alzheimer's disease. These include problems with knowledge about the world (objects, facts, concepts) as well as words and their meanings. One of the most obvious manifestations of the semantic impairment in Alzheimer's patients' everyday life is in their language production. In general, AD patients are found to have difficulties in finding their words and tend to use inappropriate words by using superordinate responses (for example "animal" for "cat") (Hodges, Salmon, & Butters, 1992). Furthermore, when asked to list items from a specific semantic category, such as tools, AD patients are found to produce fewer words than older control subjects (Hodges & Patterson, 1995). Again, the brain areas that are implicated in this impairment are the temporal lobes. Indeed, a few studies have shown links between impaired performance on semantic memory tasks and a reduced activity in the temporal lobe (e.g., Desgranges et al., 1998).

The question that researchers in this field often ask is: Is this semantic deficit a direct consequence of a loss of information in the semantic store (Hodges et al., 1992) or is the knowledge still there, but difficult to access and manipulate? To answer this question, researchers have used a semantic priming task that does not require any attentional processes (as these are known to be impaired in AD). With these tasks, participants see words appear on a computer screen, and have to make a quick, simple decision, such as: Is this a real word or not? Is this thing living or non-living? Is this item bigger than a football? (The questions that are asked vary from task to task.) Often, experimenters arrange these tasks to look at semantic processes—because if you have just judged *hammer* to be a real word, and then you receive *screw*, you will be much quicker to identify *screw* than if you have seen *three* and then *screw*. The idea is that this is a very basic, automatic, semantic mechanism: Responding to the word *hammer* primes the decision to *screw* because they share a related meaning. According to Shallice (1988), in the case of there being an impaired semantic store, no facilitation resulting from the presentation of the related word should be observed—because the item is missing from the store. If *hammer* has disappeared from the store, it will not be able to facilitate the access to *screw*. If the item *hammer* exists, but semantic deficit is caused by difficulties with conscious, effortful retrieval, people with AD should nonetheless show normal priming because these priming tasks are theoretically low-level automatic tasks, not reliant on these effortful, conscious processes.

The problem is that, at a first look, the data do not answer this question as clearly as one would hope. In different studies AD patients have been found to show impaired semantic priming (Ober & Shenaut, 1988), to have an equivalent priming effect to control participants (Nebes, Martin, & Horn, 1984), or even to show an increased priming effect relative to controls (Balota & Duchek, 1991)! However, with a bit of careful thought, these conflicting results have eventually led to a better understanding of semantic memory deficits in AD. When the results were reappraised in the light of the severity of dementia, a clearer pattern emerged. Results of longitudinal studies, where the same patients were followed as their dementia got worse, showed that the priming effect decreased significantly as the degree of dementia increased (Chertkow & Bub, 1990). Thus, at first, semantic knowledge is normal, and people with AD show normal priming, but as items get lost from the store, priming fails as meanings and concepts disappear. In the case of the superior priming sometimes observed in AD, this could be due to the fact that priming is usually measured as a difference in reaction time for the priming condition (*hammer–screw*) compared to the control condition (*three–screw*). Thus, with people with AD, it is not so much that they are better at responding to primes, but that they are much slower when the words are unrelated. And in general, people with Alzheimer's disease are known to be slow at responding to these kinds of task. Thus, the evidence from priming is in favour of the fact that items are lost from the semantic store.

Metamemory in Alzheimer's disease

Metamemory is a different form of knowledge that concerns people's knowledge about their own memory. Metamemory encompasses a variety of higher order cognitive abilities, including understanding of the functioning and capabilities of one's own memory system, knowledge about memory strategies that can aid memory performance, and prediction of future performance (Flavell, 1979). In everyday life, being able to predict your memory performance, or assess what your performance would be, is of particular importance in being able to choose the most suitable memory strategy to achieve your aims or objectives. The question of how far awareness of memory performance is impaired in clinical populations has been widely studied. Indeed, it has been suggested that an unawareness of deficits represents a difficult obstacle for rehabilitation efforts. If you do not know that your memory is impaired, it is difficult to take steps to improve it.

Many different methods have been used to assess patients' knowledge about their memory capacities, which range from questionnaires to patients' self-rating of their own memory performance on specific tasks. Some studies have assessed AD patients' awareness of their memory deficits by comparing the discrepancy between patients' self-report on questionnaires and their performance on objective memory tests. Despite the variety of methodologies used, results of questionnaire studies are consistent with the hypothesis that AD patients underestimate their memory deficits (Correa, Graves, & Costa, 1996; Green, Goldstein, Sirockman, & Green, 1993; McGlynn & Kaszniak, 1991). The results showed that AD patients reported no more memory decline than did the control subjects. However, the relatively limited predictive validity of self-report questionnaires as suggested by the low correlations between objective memory performance and self-report measures of change has been reported in the literature (Dixon & Hultsch, 1983; Gilewski & Zelinski, 1986), suggesting that the results obtained using this method should be interpreted with caution.

A different way of determining patients' knowledge about their memory capacities is to ask them to predict their memory performance on a specific task. The implicit logic is to assume that the better one's knowledge of one's memory, the more accurate the predictions are likely to be. Different types of prediction have been used: global predictions, in which participants judge how many items from an entire study list they will subsequently recall, and item-by-item predictions, in which they predict the likelihood of subsequent recall separately for each item. Data regarding the accuracy of global predictions have shown that AD patients tend to overestimate their performance (Green et al., 1993; Schacter, McLachlan, Moscovitch, & Tulving, 1986). However, despite this overestimation, several studies also showed that AD patients *were able* to monitor their memory performance by changing their predictions after having experienced the task (Ansell & Bucks, 2005; Moulin, 2002; Moulin, Perfect, & Jones 2000). Furthermore, evidence suggests that AD patients are able to adjust their predictions on different tasks. For example, Moulin (2002) showed that AD patients made reliably higher predictions in a recognition task in comparison to a recall task.

AD studies have also used item-by-item predictions to evaluate AD patients' ability to predict their memory performance. Two types of item-by-item monitoring have been assessed, judgment of learning (JOL), in which predictions are made about the likelihood of subsequent recollection of recently studied items, and feeling-of-knowing (FOK), in which predictions are made about the likelihood of subsequent recognition of non-recalled information (Nelson & Narens, 1990). Studies using item-by-item judgements such as FOK or JOL have found that AD patients do not present a uniform profile of performance across tasks and materials. In semantic memory, studies that explored the FOK did not show any impairment in AD patients (Bäckman & Lipinska, 1993; Lipinska & Bäckman, 1996). However, using an episodic memory task, AD patients were found to be inaccurate at predicting their memory performance with the both the FOK task and the JOL task (Moulin et al., 2000; Souchay, Isingrini, & Gil, 2002). To summarise, a range of studies has found that metamemory is relatively well preserved in Alzheimer's disease. Furthermore, the impairments found were rather specific. What these studies show is a fractionation of metamemory abilities in AD rather than a general degradation of impairment.

Finally, in AD, which part of the brain could be related to the metamemory impairments observed? Several studies have suggested that the frontal lobes are important for memory monitoring. Direct evidence in support of this hypothesis was first provided by brain lesion studies showing that patients with frontal lobe lesions showed metamemory impairments (Janowsky, Shimamura, & Squire, 1989), while patients with damage to the temporal lobes did not show such an impairment (Shimamura & Squire, 1986). Several studies of clinically observed impairment of deficit awareness in AD also suggested a link to frontal functioning deficit (Michon, Deweer, Pillon, Agid, & Dubois, 1994; Reed, Jagust, & Coulter, 1993). As a result, even if the relation has not yet been assessed, it could be suggested that metamemory impairments in AD are related to the frontal lobe dysfunctioning present in this pathology.

Memory for expertise in Alzheimer's disease

As described in Chapter 7, expertise involves skills as well as knowledge. Both knowledge and skills are required to play music or to paint. Interestingly, some studies have documented the maintenance of specific abilities in which patients were considered as experts before the disease. In this regard, Beatty et al. (1994) described AD patients being able to paint or play music without being able to perform more simple actions. In a more recent publication, Fornazzari (2005) described the case of a talented Canadian painter, Mrs Danae Chambers, diagnosed with AD. This case study showed that even at a advanced stage of the disease, this patient was still able to paint portraits despite presenting a variety of severe cognitive difficulties, such as disorientation, agnosia for common household objects, apraxia, and severe memory impairment. This dissociatation between the preservation of a specific expertise and a severe cognitive alteration has been reported several times about artistic painters with AD (Cummings & Zarit, 1987). However, expertise in AD does not always seem to protect against the cognitive decline. To summarise, to some extent it is possible that an intellect of exceptional premorbid quality, and/or a specific expertise, may either protect against cognitive deterioration or enable it to be masked.

Memory for intentions, plans, and actions in Alzheimer's disease

While prospective memory, i.e., timely execution of a previously formed intention, has been widely assessed in patients with specific brain damage (see Burgess & Shallice, 1997), it has not received great interest in patients with Alzheimer's disease. Despite the few studies realised in this area, the results seem to show clear impairment. For example, in a recent study, Kazui et al. (2005) showed prospective memory difficulties in AD patients by using a well-known test of everyday memory: the Rivermead Behavioural Memory test (RBMT; Wilson, Cockburn, & Baddeley, 1991). In a previous study, Maylor, Smith, Della Salla, and Logie (2002) assessed prospective memory in AD by using an interesting laboratory-based task. While viewing a film, participants were asked to say "animal" when an animal appeared on the film, or to stop a clock every 3 minutes. The results clearly showed that AD patients had some difficulties with this kind of task and that it was not due to the forgetting of the task instructions. Interestingly, more studies have been carried out on prospective memory interventions in AD to determine whether it was possible to improve prospective memory in these patients, revealing that prospective memory impairments could be minimised in AD patients. For example, two studies using the spaced-retrieval method (i.e., active attempts to recall information over expanding intervals of time) indicated that individuals with AD could learn a prospective memory task, like selecting a specific coupon and offering it to the experimenter after a week's delay (Kixmiller, 2002; McKitrick, Camp, & Black, 1992). In a more recent study, Oriani et al. (2003) showed that the use of an electronic memory aid significantly improved patients' prospective memory. In summary, even if prospective memory is impaired in Alzheimer's disease, studies suggest that these impairments can be minimised by memory training or external help such as an electronic memory aid. In terms of the brain regions involved, prospective memory has been related to the frontal lobes and has been showed to be impaired in patients with frontal lobe lesions (Burgess & Shallice, 1997). In Alzheimer's disease, the impairment of prospective memory observed could be related to the impaired functioning of the frontal lobes in this pathology. However, this hypothesis needs to be explored further.

THE COGNITIVE NEUROPSYCHIATRY OF MEMORY

With the dominant theoretical viewpoint of *psychology* being cognitive—concerning thought processes and mental abilities—it is unsurprising that the dominant view of *psychopathology*—the dysfunction or disruption of thought, consciousness, the self, or mental life—is also cognitive. This cognitive viewpoint has led to changes in the understanding, care, and treatment of those in psychological distress, and those with psychiatric disorders. For example, the cognitive approach predicates treatment by cognitive behavioural therapy (e.g., Hawton, Salkovkis, Kirk, & Clark, 1989), where the therapist considers people's beliefs and reflections on their thought processes, and seeks to modify or normalise them. For instance, a person who has panic attacks will have complex beliefs and memories of previous attacks, and how they feel. These memories and beliefs about the panic attack, such as the fear of death and the sensation of dizziness, contribute to the panic attack in a vicious circle: The more one panics about hyperventilating, the more one hyperventilates. The therapist needs to challenge beliefs about hyperventilation and the processes in panic attacks and get the sufferer to reconsider and re-evaluate their stored representation. By manipulating their memory—their cognition—the therapist aims to break the vicious circle and treat the psychopathology. There are similar approaches to depression, schizophrenia, and a variety of psychopathologies.

Recently, the impact of psychiatric disorders and, in particular, problems like schizophrenia and people with delusional beliefs on memory performance has started to be examined in more detail—an approach that closely follows the neuropsychology approach above, and is often called cognitive neuropsychiatry. This approach suggests that there is something to be learnt from psychiatric disorders, and that the behaviour and cognitive processes of these people can be understood in the same way as they can be in people following brain damage. From that perspective, care and treatment can be better targeted. The way these difficulties, delusions, and beliefs impact on memory is more complex and more subtle—no one thinks of schizophrenia as a memory disorder—but they can be confusing and debilitating for the carer and patient.

The neuropsychiatry approach borrows heavily from the neuropsychological approach, and its broad aims are similar. But unlike neuropsychology it is not so tightly defined, since it relies not on discernible damage to the brain, but on the cognitive activities and behaviours associated with conditions that are diagnosed by patterns of dysfunctional behaviours. What, then, are psychiatric disorders? A dictionary definition of psychiatry gives it as the branch of medicine concerned with mental disorders. This gives us a good flavour: Psychiatry is interested in a wide range of mental disorders and, as a medical discipline, is largely interested in classifying the disorders into different classes. It aims, through classification, to achieve accurate diagnosis and, largely through pharmacology, to offer treatment. For an example of the unique contribution this approach can make, see Young (2000). For the purposes of this chapter we will concentrate on schizophrenia, one of the more common psychiatric complaints, but the interested student would also find much of interest on memory in depression (where memory tends to be impaired, and autobiographical memories tend to be very general memories of the remote past, see Dalgleish et al., 2007) and post-traumatic stress disorder (where intrusive memories of the traumatic event are frequently experienced as "flashbacks" for the sufferer; see Steel, Fowler, & Holmes, 2005).

Schizophrenia and memory

Schizophrenia is a psychiatric illness that affects, at any one time, approximately 1% of the population. It is a very serious condition that leads to many of its sufferers not being able to work, and that often leads to depression and anxiety. The central features of schizophrenia are hallucinations and delusions, not, as the common belief asserts, split personality or multiple selves. No one would describe schizophrenia as a memory disorder, and yet it has a definite impact on cognitive function; in general, memory is impaired in schizophrenia, including semantic memory and short-term memory (McKenna, Ornstein, & Baddeley, 2002). Other work has shown deficits in episodic memory related to a lack of activation in the frontal cortex (Lepage et al., 2006), although a feeling-of-knowing task demonstrates that metamemory is intact in schizophrenia (Souchay, Bacon, & Danion, 2006). However, these memory deficits are not nearly so severe as those seen in the advanced stages of Alzheimer's disease, and people with schizophrenia would not view these memory symptoms as central to their difficulties; they are much less striking than the disordered thoughts or the beliefs that their thoughts are being controlled by someone or something else.

Perhaps a more alarming cognitive feature of the disorder is remembering events that never happened. The terminology for such memories is varied. Some authors use *false memory*, some *delusional memory*, and others use the term *confabulation*. But the idea is the same: These confabulations are false memories, usually autobiographical; memories for things that did not happen. Critically, confabulations and delusional and false memories are often described as "honest lies" insofar as the patient does not know that the memories are untrue, even though they can be fantastic and implausible. Typically, whereas patients with brain injury or other damage are described as having *confabulations* (and usually the frontal part of the brain is damaged), schizophrenics are usually described as having *delusional memories*. These have no clear organic cause and are usually rather stable; a coherent "memory" based on a long-term false belief or idea. These sorts of false memory are not confined to schizophrenia, but can occur in head injury and Alzheimer's disease.

In some cases the false memories seen in schizophrenia start as delusional beliefs that, over time, become autobiographical memories. Consider the case of patient EN, reported by McKay, McKenna, and Baddeley (1995), who was first admitted to a psychiatric hospital at the age of 22. She was readmitted to hospital a further nine times, until her symptoms were brought under control with the drug clozapine. However, years later, when she had been discharged from hospital, the false memories remained, even though the behavioural difficulties of schizophrenia had all but disappeared. For instance, she described a non-existent identical twin sister, and recalled a series of "memories" of her sister and her involvement with the British Royal Family. Patient WM (Kopelman, Guinan, & Lewis, 1995) was a similar case. She suffered from De Clérambault's Syndrome (sometimes called erotomania), the delusion that someone was in love with her—a delusional state well portrayed in the popular novel *Enduring love* by Ian McEwan (1998). WM claimed that she had met—and fallen in love with—a famous classical music conductor whilst working as a fruit picker in Suffolk. In fact, her whole delusion is supported by these false memories, and she continued to support the non-existent love affair by recalling and repeating these events—all of which, to her, were vivid veridical memories.

A further common perception is that people with schizophrenia are dangerous to society and unpredictable. In general, this view is unhelpful, and denotes a misunderstanding of the disorder. However, of those people in prison who have a serious psychiatric disorder, the most common diagnosis is schizophrenia. To put this into context, people with psychiatric problems make up a minority of the offender population and, in turn, people with a history of criminal acts make up a small proportion of the wider psychiatric population (Blackburn, 1996). Given the profile of people in psychiatric prisons, however, and the fact that these people have a tendency to delusional and false memories, it is perhaps unsurprising that many studies have focused on forensic psychology and schizophrenia, and in particular the tendency to produce false confessions for crimes people could not have committed (e.g., Smith & Gudjonsson, 1995).

There are a number of psychiatric reasons for false confessions, such as the desire for fame, loyalty, or coercion, but false confessions may also be made spontaneously, without prior contact or external pressure from the police. These voluntary false confessions can often be shown to have a basis in psychopathology, and typically occur in the context of mental disorder (e.g., schizophrenia, but also psychotic depression or personality disorder). They are fascinating because, in addition to having a genuine belief in their own guilt, people frequently also develop strong false memories for committing the offence. In such circumstances a person will typically have remarkable certainty regarding their "memory" for the crime.

For example, Gudjonsson (1992) reports the case of Mr M, a man in his 30s who, over the course of 6 years, spontaneously confessed to having committed several well-publicised unsolved murders. Mr M expressed remorse over his "role" in these murders and told police that he was confessing through a desire for these killings to stop. Interestingly, Mr M did not confess to all murders that he saw or read about in the media, but only confessed to those committed in geographical regions that he had visited at some point in his life. In these cases, hearing about the murder appeared to trigger a chain of thoughts cumulating in Mr M becoming convinced that he was the culprit. Gudjonsson also reports the case of Miss S, a middle-aged woman with a diagnosis of paranoid schizophrenia, who confessed to committing a well-publicised local murder. Miss S had been receiving psychiatric treatment at the time of her confession and a doctor involved with her care was able to give an irrefutable alibi proving that Miss S had not been involved in this crime. Miss S's false confession is considered to have resulted from impaired reality monitoring. That is, within the context of being confused by heavy medication and a delusional belief that others were conspiring to harm her, and that she would need to exert violence in order to protect herself from harm, Miss S confused media reports and overheard conversations about the murder as being "memories" from her own life. Such failures of *reality monitoring* (as discussed in Chapter 12) have been considered to be characteristic of psychosis (Gudjonsson, 1992). Reality monitoring (Johnson & Raye, 1981) refers to the ability to differentiate between events that have actually been experienced from those that have been internally generated (e.g., in thoughts, planning or imagination).

Understanding the potential role of false memory in forensic settings is extremely important because it has genuine potential to alter people's lives. A striking example of this is given in the literature through the case of Judith Ward who, after confessing, was convicted of terrorist activities in the 1970s. Nearly two decades later, largely on the basis of psychometric evidence that Ms Ward was vulnerable to false memories, this conviction was overturned (Kennedy, 1992). False confessions are an extreme example of the occurrence and consequences of false memory in offender populations. Smith and Gudjonsson (1995) found that false memory, assessed in laboratory testing, was four times more likely in psychiatric forensic patients than in normal populations.

In fact, there is even a suggestion that within non-psychiatric groups, delusional— or at the least slightly improbable—memories are supported by disrupted or abnormal memory systems. To illustrate this point, Clancy, McNally, Schachter, Lenzenweger, and Pitman (2002) tested the memory of two groups; people who had claimed to have been abducted by aliens, and controls. She also managed to split her sample into people who had "memories" of being abducted, and those who just believed that they had been, but were amnesic for the event. Clancy and colleagues showed systematic differences in memory performance on a very robust and straightforward memory task, the DRM procedure (Roediger & McDermott, 1995). In this procedure, participants are read a list of words that converge on one never-presented item, which they are later tested on. For instance, they might study a list such as: *bed*, *rest*, *tired*, *doze*, *blanket*, *wake*. At test, they are given some words they have and have not seen at study. The critical feature of the task is that participants are presented one never-seen item, such as *sleep*, and may mistakenly identify it as one that had been presented previously. Most people have some susceptibility to this memory error, but Clancy and colleagues showed that people who claimed to have been abducted by aliens were more likely to make this kind of error than people who did not. Moreover, people who "remembered" being abducted were more likely to make this error. Clancy has developed the hypothesis that delusional beliefs, such as alien abduction, are supported by dysfunctioning memory systems. Her work has attracted a lot of attention from the scientific community and the Internet. Naturally, the scientific community generally supports her research, whereas the Internet paranormal community does not appreciate her "debunking" work.

CONCLUSIONS

In 1901 Freud published *The psychopathology of everyday life* (first translated into English in 1914). His aim was to analyse a cornucopia of everyday errors made by healthy people. His reasoning was that by understanding mental errors, slips of the tongue, and forgetfulness, we might better understand the processes at work in everyday mental life. Similarly, in this chapter we have shown that cognitive psychologists have used neurological and psychiatric populations to the same end; we have shown how cognitive neuropsychologists look at the abnormal, pathological states seen in special populations such as schizophrenia, dementia, brain damage, and so on, in order to understand better the brain and its relation to cognition. It has been seen that schizophrenic delusions are somehow sustained by faulty memories and that Alzheimer's disease is characterised by a pattern of memory deficits that one can understand by examining the brain. In all these cases, and throughout this chapter, the study of psychopathology enables psychologists to understand and care better for people with these difficulties. And, quite clearly, proficient memory function is at the centre of a wide range of real-world tasks, and the centre of healthiness and happiness.

ACKNOWLEDGEMENTS

We are grateful to Alan Baddeley for his comments on a draft of this chapter and to Félix Martin Moulin for his help in the latter stages.

REFERENCES

Addis, D.R., & Tippett, T.J. (2004). Memory of myself: Autobiographical memory and identity in Alzheimer's disease. *Memory, 12,* 56–74.

Aguirre, G., & D'Esposito, M. (1999). Topographical disorientation: A synthesis and taxonomy. *Brain, 122,* 1613–1628.

Ansell, E., & Bucks, R. (2005). Mnemonic anosognosia in Alzheimer's disease: A test of Agnew and Morris (1998). *Neuropsychologia, 44,* 1095–1102.

Bäckman, L., & Lipinska, B. (1993). Monitoring of general knowledge: Evidence for preservation in early Alzheimer's disease, *Neuropsychologia, 31,* 335–345.

Baddeley, A.D., Kopelman, M., & Wilson, B.A. (2002). *The handbook of memory disorders.* Chichester, UK: Wiley.

Baddeley, A.D., Logie, R.H., Bressi, S., Della Salla, S., & Spinnler, H. (1986). Dementia and working memory. *Quarterly Journal of Experimental Psychology, 38A,* 603–618.

Baddeley, A.D, & Warrington, E.K. (1970). Amnesia and the distinction between long- and short-term memory. *Journal of Verbal Learning and Verbal Behavior, 9,* 176–189.

Balota, D.A., & Duchek, J.M. (1991). Semantic priming effects, lexical repetition effects, and contextual disambiguation effects in healthy aged individuals and individuals with senile dementia of Alzheimer types. *Brain and Language, 40,* 181–201.

Beatty, W.W.W., Vin, P., Adams, R.L., Allen, E.W., Wilson, D.A., Prince, J.R., Olson, K.A., Dean, K., & Litteford, D. (1994). Preserved cognitive skills in dementia of the Alzheimer type. *Archives of Neurology, 51,* 1040–1046.

Blackburn, R. (1996). Mentally disordered offenders. In C.R. Hollin (Ed.), *Working with offenders: Psychological practice in offender rehabilitation.* Chichester, UK: Wiley.

Braak, H., & Braak, E. (1997). Frequency of stages of Alzheimer-related lesions in different age categories. *Neurobiology of Aging, 18,* 351–357.

Burgess, P., & Shallice, T. (1997). The relationship between prospective memory and retrospective memory: Neuropsychological evidence. In S. Gathercole & M. Conway (Eds.), *Cognitive models of memory.* London: UCL Press.

Buschke, H., Sliwinski, M.J., Kuslansky, G., & Lipton, R.B. (1997). Diagnosis of early dementia by the Double Memory Test: Encoding specificity improves diagnostic sensitivity and specificity. *Neurology, 48,* 989–997.

Buxbaum, L.J. (2006). On the right (and left) track: Twenty years of progress in studying hemispatial neglect. *Cognitive Neuropsychology, 23,* 156–173.

Caramazza, A., & Coltheart, M. (2006). Cognitive neuropsychology twenty years on. *Cognitive Neuropsychology, 23*, 3–12.

Cherrier, M.M., Mendez, M., & Perryman, K. (2001). Route learning performance in Alzheimer disease patients. *Neuropsychiatry, Neuropsychology and Behavioural Neurology, 14*, 159–168.

Chertkow, H., & Bub, D. (1990). Semantic memory loss in dementia of Alzheimer's type: What do various measures measure? *Brain, 113*, 397–417.

Clancy, S.A., McNally, R.J., Schacter, D.L., Lenzenweger, M.L., & Pitman, R.K. (2002). Memory distortion in people reporting abduction by aliens. *Journal of Abnormal Psychology, 111*, 455–461.

Clark, P.C., Dunbar, S.B., Aycok, D.M., Courtney, E., & Wolf, S.L. (2006). Caregiver perspectives of memory and behavior changes in stroke survivors. *Rehabilitation Nurse, 31*, 26–32.

Collette, F., Salmon E., Van der Linden M., Chicherio, C., Belleville, S., Degueldre, C., Delfiore, G., & Franck, G. (1999). Regional brain activity during tasks devoted to the central executive of working memory, *Cognitive Brain Research, 7*, 411–417.

Conway, M.A. (2005). Memory and the self. *Journal of Memory and Language, 53*, 594–628.

Conway, M.A., & Pleydell-Pearce, C.W. (2000). The construction of autobiographical memories in the self memory system. *Psychological Review, 107*, 261–288.

Conway, M.A., Pleydell-Pearce, C.W., & Whitecross, S. (2001). The neuroanatomy of autobiographical memory: A slow cortical study (SCP) of autobiographical memory retrieval. *Journal of Memory and Language, 45*, 493–524.

Conway, M.A., Pleydell-Pearce, C.W., Whitecross, S.E., & Sharpe, H. (2000). Neurophysiological correlates of memory for experienced and imagined events. *Neuropsychologia, 41*, 334–340.

Correa, D., Graves, R., & Costa, L. (1996). Awareness of memory deficit in Alzheimer's disease patients and memory-impaired older adults. *Aging, Neuropsychology, and Cognition, 3*, 215–228.

Cummings, J.L., & Zarit, J.M. (1987). Probable Alzheimer's disease in an artist. *Journal of the American Medical Association, 258*, 2731–2734.

Dalgleish, T., Williams, J.M.G., Golden, A.M.J., Perkins, N., Barrett, L.F., Barnard, P.J., Yeung, C.A., Murphy, V., Elward, R., Tchanturia, K., & Watkins, E. (2007). Reduced specificity of autobiographical memory and depression: The role of executive control. *Journal of Experimental Psychology – General, 136*, 23–42.

Desgranges, B., Baron, J.C., De la Sayette, V., Petit-Taboue, M.C., Benali, K., & Landeau, B. (1998). The neural substrates of memory systems impairment in Alzheimer's disease. A PET study of resting brain glucose utilization. *Brain, 121*, 611–631.

Dixon, A., & Hultsch, D. (1983). Structure and development of metamemory in adulthood. *Journal of Gerontology, 6*, 682–688.

Ferri, C.P., Prince, M., Brayne, C., Brodaty, H., Fratiglioni, L., Ganguli, M., Hall, K., Hasegawa, K., Hendrie, H., Huang, Y., et al. (2006). Global prevalence of dementia: A Delphi consensus study. *The Lancet, 360*, 2112–2117.

Flavell, J. (1979). Metacognition and cognitive monitoring. *American Psychologist, 34*, 906–911.

Fleischman, D.A., & Gabrieli, J.D. (1998). Repetition priming in normal aging and Alzheimer's disease: A review of findings and theories. *Psychology of Aging, 3*, 88–119.

Fornazzari, L.R. (2005). Preserved painting creativity in an artist with Alzheimer's disease. *European Journal of Neurology, 12*, 419–424.

Freud, S. (1914). *The psychopathology of everyday life.* Translated by A.A. Brill. London: T. Fisher Unwin. [Originally published 1901]

Gainotti, G., Barbier, A., & Marra, C. (2003). Slowly progressive defect in recognition of familiar people in a patient with right anterior temporal atrophy, *Brain, 126*, 792–803.

Gilboa, A., Ramirez, J., Köhler, S., Westmacott, R., Black, S.E., & Moscovitch, M. (2005). Retrieval of autobiographical memory in Alzheimer's disease: Relation to volumes of medial temporal lobe and other structures. *Hippocampus, 15,* 535–550.

Gilewski, M., & Zelinski, E. (1986). Questionnaire assessment of memory complaints. In L.W. Poon (Ed.), *Handbook for clinical memory assessment of older adults.* Cambridge, UK: Cambridge University Press.

Green, J., Goldstein, F., Sirockman, B., & Green, R. (1993). Variable awareness of deficits in Alzheimer's disease, *Neuropsychiatry, Neuropsychology, and Behavioral Neurology, 6,* 159–165.

Greenberg, D.L., & Rubin, D.C. (2003). The neuropsychology of autobiographical memory. *Cortex, 39,* 687–728.

Greene, J., & Hodges, J. (1996). Identification of famous faces and famous names in early Alzheimer's disease: Relationship to anterograde episodic and general semantic memory. *Brain, 119,* 111–128.

Greene, J., Hodges, J.R., & Baddeley, A. (1995). Autobiographical memory and executive function in early dementia of Alzheimer's disease. *Neuropsychologia, 33,* 1647–1670.

Gudjonsson, G.H. (1992). *The psychology of interrogations, confessions, and testimony.* Chichester, UK: Wiley.

Harwood, D.G., Barker, W.W., Ownby, R.L., & Duara, R. (1999). Prevalence and correlates of Capgras syndrome in Alzheimer's disease. *International Journal of Geriatric Psychiatry, 14,* 415–420.

Hawton, K., Salkovskis, P.M., Kirk, J., & Clark, D.M. (1989). *Cognitive behavioural therapy for psychiatric problems: A practical guide.* Oxford, UK: Oxford University Press.

Hehman, J.A., German, T.P., & Klein, S.B. (2005). Impaired self-recognition from recent photographs in a case of late-stage Alzheimer's disease. *Social Cognition, 23,* 118–124.

Hilts, P.J. (1995). *Memory's ghost: The strange tale of Mr M and the nature of memory.* New York: Simon & Schuster.

Hodges, J.R., & Patterson, K. (1995). Is semantic memory consistently impaired early in the course of Alzheimer's disease? Neuroanatomical and diagnostic implications. *Neuropsychologia, 33,* 441–459.

Hodges, J.R., Salmon, D.P., & Butters, N. (1992). Semantic memory impairment in Alzheimer's disease: A failure of access or degraded knowledge? *Neuropsychologia, 30,* 301–314.

Hodges, J.R., Salmon, D.P., & Butters, N. (1993). Recognition and naming of famous faces in Alzheimer's disease: A cognitive analysis. *Neuropsychologia, 31,* 775–788.

Hou, C.E., Miller, B.C., & Kramer, J.H. (2005). Patterns of autobiographical memory loss in dementia. *International Journal of Geriatric Psychiatry, 20,* 809–815.

Ikeda, M., Mori, E., Hirono, N., Imamura, T., Shimomura, T., Ikejiri, Y., & Yamashita, H. (1998). Amnestic people with Alzheimer's disease who remembered the Kobe earthquake. *British Journal of Psychiatry, 172,* 425–428.

Janowsky, J.S., Shimamura, A.P., & Squire, L.R. (1989). Memory and metamemory: Comparisons between patients with frontal lobe lesions and amnesic patients. *Psychobiology, 17,* 3–11.

Johnson, M.K., & Raye, C.L. (1981). Reality monitoring. *Psychological Review, 88,* 67–85.

Kazui, H., Matsuda, A., Hirono, N., Mori, E., Miyoshi, N., Ogino, A., Tokunaga, H., Ikejiri, Y., & Takeda, M. (2005). Everyday memory impairment of patients with mild cognitive impairments. *Dementia and Geriatric Disorders, 19,* 331–337.

Kennnedy, H. (1992). *Eve was framed.* London: Chatto & Windus.

Kessels, R.P.C., Feijen, J., & Postma, A. (2005). Implicit and explicit memory for spatial information in Alzheimer's disease. *Dementia and Geriatric Cognitive Disorders, 20,* 184–191.

Khun, M.H., & McPartland, T.S. (1954). An empirical investigation of self-attitudes. *American Sociological Review, 19*, 68–76.

Kim, H.J., Burke, D.T., Dowds, M.M., Boone K.A., & Park, G.J. (2000). Electronic memory aids for outpatients brain injury: Follow-up findings. *Brain Injury, 14*, 187–196.

Kixmiller, J.S. (2002). Evaluation of prospective memory training for individuals with mild Alzheimer's disease. *Brain and Cognition, 49*, 237–241.

Kopelman, M.D. (1992). The "new" and the "old": Components of the anterograde and the retrograde memory loss in Korsakoff's and Alzheimer patients. In L.R. Squire & N. Butters (Eds.), *Neuropsychology of memory* (pp. 130–146). New York: Guilford Press.

Kopelman, M.D., Guinan, E.M., & Lewis, P.D.R. (1995). Delusional memory, confabulation and frontal lobe dysfunction. In R. Campbell & M. Conway (Eds.), *Broken memories: Case studies of memory impairment*. Oxford, UK: Blackwell.

Lavenu, I., & Pasquier, F. (2005). Perception of emotion on faces in frontotemporal dementia and Alzheimer's disease: A longitudinal study. *Dementia and Geriatric Disorders, 19*, 37–41.

Lepage, M., Montoya, A., Pelletier, M., Achim, A.M., Menear, M., & Lal, S. (2006). Associative memory encoding and recognition in schizophrenia: An event-related fMRI study. *Biological Psychiatry, 60*, 1215–1223.

Lipinska, B., & Bäckman, L. (1996). Feeling-of-knowing in fact retrieval: Further evidence for preservation in early Alzheimer's disease. *Journal of the International Neuropsychological Society, 2*, 350–358.

Maguire, E.A., Burgess, N., Donnett, J.G., Frackowiak, R.S., Frith, C.D., & O'Keefe, J. (1998). Knowing where and getting there: A human navigation network, *Science, 280*, 921–924.

Maylor, E., Smith, G., Della Salla, S., & Logie, R.H. (2002). Prospective and retrospective memory in normal aging and dementia: An experimental study. *Memory and Cognition, 30*, 871–884.

McEwan, I. (1998). *Enduring love*. London: Vintage.

McGlynn, S., & Kazniak, A. (1991). Where metacognition fails: Impaired awareness of deficit in Alzheimer's disease. *Journal of Cognitive Neuroscience, 3*, 183–189.

McKay, A.P., McKenna, P., & Baddeley, A.D. (1995). Memory pathology in schizophrenia. In R. Campbell & M. Conway (Eds.), *Broken memories: Case studies of memory impairment*. Oxford, UK: Blackwell.

McKenna, P., Ornstein, T., & Baddeley, A.D. (2002). Schizophrenia. In A.D. Baddeley, M.D. Kopelman, & B.A. Wilson (Eds.), *The handbook of memory disorders*. Chichester, UK: Wiley.

McKitrick, L.A., Camp, C.J., & Black, F.W. (1992). Prospective memory intervention in Alzheimer's disease. *Journal of Gerontology, 47*, 337–343.

Michon, A., Deweer, B., Pillon, B., Agid, Y., & Dubois, B. (1994). Relation of anosognosia to frontal lobe dysfunction in Alzheimer's disease. *Journal of Neurology, Neurosurgery and Psychiatry, 57*, 805–809.

Moulin, C.J.A. (2002). Sense and sensitivity: Metacognition in Alzheimer's disease. In T.J. Perfect & B.L. Schwartz (Eds.), *Applied metacognition*. Cambridge, UK: Cambridge University Press.

Moulin, C.J.A., Perfect, T., & Jones, R. (2000). Global predictions of memory in Alzheimer's disease: Evidence for preserved metamemory monitoring. *Aging, Neuropsychology and Cognition, 7*, 230–244.

Nebes, R.D., Martin, D.C., & Horn, L.C. (1984). Sparing of semantic memory in Alzheimer's disease. *Journal of Abnormal Psychology, 93*, 321–330.

Nelson, T., & Narens, L. (1990). Metamemory: A theoretical framework and new findings. *Psychology of Learning and Motivation, 26*, 125–141.

Ober, B.A., & Shenaut, G.K. (1988). Lexical decision and priming in Alzheimer's disease. *Neuropsychologia, 8,* 273–286.

Oriani, M., Moniz-Cook, E., Binetti, G., Zanieri, G., Frisoni, G.B., Geroldi, C., DeVresse, L.P., & Zanetti, O. (2003). An electronic memory aid to support prospective memory in patients in the early stages of Alzheimer's disease: A pilot study. *Aging Mental Health, 7,* 22–27.

Pai, M.C., & Jacobs, J. (2004). Topographical disorientation in community-residing patients with Alzheimer's disease. *International Journal of Geriatric Psychiatry, 19,* 250–255.

Passini, R., Rainville, C., Marchand, N., & Joanette, Y. (1995). Wayfinding in dementia of the Alzheimer type: Planning abilities. *Journal of Clinical and Experimental Neuropsychology, 17,* 820–832.

Reed, B.R., Jagust, W.J., & Coulter, L. (1993). Anosognosia in Alzheimer's disease: Relationship to depression, cognitive function, and cerebral perfusion. *The Journal of Clinical and Experimental Neuropsychology, 15,* 231–244.

Ribot, T. (1881). *Les maladies de la mémoire.* Paris: Germer-Balliére.

Roediger, H.L., & McDermott, K.B. (1995). Creating false memories: Remembering words not presented in lists. *Journal of Experimental Psychology: Learning, Memory, and Cognition, 21,* 803–814.

Rosenbaum, R., Gao, F., Richards, B., Black, S., & Moscovitch, M. (2005). "Where to?" Remote memory for spatial relations and landmark identity in former taxi drivers with Alzheimer's disease and encephalitis. *Journal of Cognitive Neuroscience, 17,* 446–462.

Sagar, H.J., Cohen, N.J., Sullivan, E.V., Corkin, S., & Growdon, J.H. (1988). Remote memory function in Alzheimer's disease and Parkinson's disease. *Brain, 111,* 185–206.

Schacter, D.L., McLachlan, D.R., Moscovitch, M., & Tulving, E. (1986). Monitoring of recall performance by memory-disordered patients [Abstract]. *Journal of Clinical and Experimental Neuropsychology, 8,* 130.

Shallice, T. (1988). *From neuropsychology to mental structure.* Cambridge, UK: Cambridge University Press.

Shimamura, A., & Squire, L. (1986). Memory and metamemory: A study of the feeling of knowing phenomenon in amnesic patients. *Journal of Experimental Psychology: Learning, Memory and Cognition, 12,* 452–460.

Smith, P., & Gudjonsson, G.H. (1995). Confabulation among forensic inpatients and its relationship with memory, suggestibility, compliance, anxiety and self-esteem. *Personality and Individual Differences, 19,* 517–523.

Snowden, J.S., Thompson, J.C., & Neary, D. (2004). Knowledge of famous faces and names in semantic dementia. *Brain, 127,* 860–872.

Souchay, C., Bacon, E., & Danion, J.M. (2006). Metamemory in schizophrenia: An exploration of the feeling-of-knowing state. *Journal of Clinical and Experimental Neuropsychology, 28,* 828–840.

Souchay, C., Isingrini, M., & Gil, R. (2002). Alzheimer's disease and feeling-of-knowing in episodic memory. *Neuropsychologia, 40,* 2386–2396.

Steel, C., Fowler, D., & Holmes, E.A. (2005). Trauma-related intrusions and psychosis: An information processing account. *Behavioural and Cognitive Psychotherapy, 33,* 139–152.

Thompson, R.G., Moulin, C.J.A., Ridel, G.L., Hayre, S., Conway, M.A., & Jones, R.W. (2004). Recall of 9/11 in Alzheimer's disease: Further evidence for intact flashbulb memory. *International Journal of Geriatric Psychiatry, 19,* 495–496.

Vargha-Khadem, F., Gadian, D.G., Watkins, K.E., Conelly, A., Van Paesschen, W., & Mishkin, M. (1997). Differential effects of early hippocampal pathology on episodic and semantic memory. *Science, 277,* 376–380.

Venneri, A., Shanks, M.F., Staff, R.T., & Della Salla, S. (2000). Nurturing syndrome: A form of pathological bereavement with delusions in Alzheimer's disease. *Neuropsychologia, 38,* 213–224.

Warrington, E.K., & McCarthy, R.A. (1988). The fractionation of retrograde amnesia. *Brain and Cognition, 7,* 184–200.

Wilson, B., Cockburn, J., & Baddeley, A.D. (1991). *The Rivermead Behavioural Memory Test.* Bury St. Edmunds, UK: Thames Valley Test Company.

Wilson, B.A., Emslie, H., Quirk, K., Evans, J., & Watson, P. (2005). A randomized control trial to evaluate a paging system for people with traumatic brain injury. *Brain Injury, 19,* 891–894.

Young, A.W. (2000). Wondrous strange: The neuropsychology of abnormal beliefs. In M. Coltheart & M. Davies (Eds.), *Pathologies of belief.* Oxford, UK: Blackwell.

14 Overview: Conclusions and speculations

Gillian Cohen

MODELS OF EVERYDAY MEMORY

In reviewing research on memory in the real world, this book has included a wide range of different memory functions and has tended to treat them as separate subsystems. Nevertheless human memory is, at some level, a joined-up system and this chapter is an attempt to do some joining up and try to see the big picture. It is a difficult task, though, from such a diverse collection of findings and observations, to formulate any general conclusions or to incorporate them into a general model of memory. Some researchers, such as Tulving, have concluded that there is no single entity corresponding to "memory", but rather that memory consists of:

> a number of different brain behaviour/cognition systems and processes that, through co-operation and interaction with one another, make it possible for their possessor to benefit from past experience and thereby promote survival.
>
> Tulving, 1991, p. 25

Tulving proposed a number of criteria whereby separate systems could be distinguished:

1 Different memory systems have different functions and handle different types of information.
2 Different systems may employ different processes but need not necessarily do so.
3 Different systems are mediated in different brain structures or mechanisms.
4 Different systems have developed at different evolutionary stages.
5 Different systems may have different forms of representation.

Applying these criteria, Tulving identified five separate but interacting memory systems:

1 Procedural memory, which is involved in skills, actions, and simple conditioning.
2 The Perceptual Representation System, which is involved in perceptual priming of the identification of objects.
3 Short-term memory, which includes working memory.
4 Semantic memory, for general knowledge of the world.
5 Episodic memory, for conscious recollection of personal experience.

Each of these five major systems includes multiple subsystems, as yet not fully identified. However, although there is general agreement that memory includes different systems and subsystems, there is no consensus about what these are and how they are related to and interact with each other. Some researchers fear that a proliferation of different systems is conceptually untidy and empirically not confirmable. Johnson (1983, 1992) argued that there is a general system, but that multiple memory functions are served by a number of interacting subsystems. She formulated the multiple-entry modular memory system (MEM), which was specifically designed to accommodate the diversity of memory functions displayed in everyday life. For Johnson:

> the most impressive thing about memory is the range of functions it supports. The same memory system that recalls your vacation learns to play racketball. The same system that memorises a part in a play is startled by faces that resemble the mugger who got your wallet. The same system that can instantly classify a strange animal as a bird struggles to identify the pharmacist when you run into him in the grocery store.
>
> Johnson, 1983, p. 81

In the MEM model, the general system comprises three major subsystems:

1   The sensory system, a low-level system for the detection of stimuli and the development of sensorimotor skills.
2   The perceptual system, for recognising what is familiar, perceiving the relationships between objects, storage of complex patterns.
3   The reflective system, for voluntary explicit free recall of events and for relating new information to stored information.

Any event creates multiple entries in all three subsystems, which can operate in parallel. The first two subsystems handle externally derived information, but the reflective system handles internally derived information allowing us to plan, reminisce, and anticipate. The differential activation of the subsystems is controlled by attention.

   The MEM model is both realist and constructivist and can therefore account for the fact that people have both accurate memories that are precise, specific, and detailed, and also inaccurate memories that are embellished, distorted, or edited. The sensory and perceptual subsystems store surface features and verbatim language, that is, copies of reality. The reflective system is constructivist and stores representations that are integrated, abstracted, and interpreted. According to this model, childhood amnesia can be explained by the later development of the reflective system, and Johnson also advances an evolutionary argument for the separate development of the reflective system. Emotion is primarily associated with the activation of the sensory and perceptual systems, and is weaker in the reflective system. In Johnson's example, this conveys an evolutionary advantage in that we can reflect about tigers, anticipate their movements, and plan how to avoid them without being over-aroused by a full emotional response to tigers.

   One problem with models like Tulving's and Johnson's is that it is difficult to map all the different functions of memory in everyday life onto the proposed subsystems.

Is there a case for adding more specialised subsystems for face memory, spatial memory, or memory for music? Once you start fractionating memory into separate subsystems it is difficult to know where to stop. The assumption that there are specialised subsystems inevitably raises the issue of modularity. Specialisation is consistent with the modular organisation of the brain proposed by Fodor (1983). According to Fodor, a modular brain has domain-specific modules, each of which is specialised to process a particular kind of stimulus input. In addition, modules are said to be "informationally encapsulated" so that there is no interactive processing between different modules at the input processing stage. There is some support for modularity from the kind of highly specific deficits that have been observed following localised brain damage. The neuropsychological evidence from deficits of this type supports the view that there are specialised subsystems for functions such as face recognition or autobiographical memory; and even that there are two distinct subsystems for knowledge about living and non-living things within semantic memory (Farah & McClelland, 1991). However, as the number of distinctions increases it becomes more difficult to incorporate them all into a general model. Moreover, Fodor's "strong" view of modularity has not gone unchallenged, and currently a "weaker" version with some degree of interactivity between specialised subsystems is widely accepted (Farah, 1994).

So far, the diversity of memory in everyday life defies attempts to construct a fully comprehensive model. However, having surveyed most of the functions that an everyday memory system needs to perform, we are in a better position to identify the general characteristics that such a system needs to have. If we cannot yet construct a satisfactory architecture of everyday memory, at least we can identify some of the concepts and theories that prove most useful in the interpretation of memory in the real world.

GENERAL CHARACTERISTICS OF EVERYDAY MEMORY

A Stone Age mind in a modern skull?

Evolutionary psychologists (e.g., Barkow, Cosmides, & Tooby, 1992) believe that human memory evolved to meet the demands of life for the hunter–gatherers of the Pleistocene era. Because the period elapsed since then is too short in evolutionary terms for significant changes to occur, a Stone Age memory system persists in modern times. According to this view, competencies such as memory for routes and places and the ability to recognise individuals and remember personal experiences would have evolved by natural selection and would have been adaptive for the hunter–gatherer society. The approach of evolutionary psychology is speculative and not easily testable. It seems plausible that a Stone Age memory system would clearly be poorly adapted to the problems of modern living, in which demands on memory have vastly increased. However, there have been two important developments in the intervening centuries that have allowed memory to be fit for purpose in the 21st century. First, the use of language and development of communication has clearly transformed the capacity and complexity of human memory. Although we retain the procedural and implicit memory systems of the Stone Age, we rely much more on verbal declarative memory. Second, the use of technology provides an extension to memory of potentially unlimited scope.

Memory in the 21st century

In the kind of simple rural communities that were the norm a few centuries ago, and which still persist in remoter parts of the world, the demands on memory were relatively slight. People rarely encountered an unfamiliar face; they carried out the same activities in daily and seasonal routines all their lives; they rarely travelled beyond the immediate well-known terrain; the same songs and stories were regularly repeated. This sort of life made minimal demands on the memory system compared with a 21st-century urban lifestyle. We are continuously confronted with strange faces; we continually meet new people; we travel to new places and have to navigate in unfamiliar terrain. We have to learn new skills and perform new activities; we are bombarded with written and spoken verbal information almost every waking moment. The result is that in modern urban society the memory system is in danger of being grossly overloaded.

We can, and do, support the overloaded memory system by the use of external aids. In the 21st century, as life gets busier and more complicated, we rely less and less on memory and more and more on information technology. Why bother to try to remember routes when you can use satellite navigation? Why struggle to remember the information for a presentation when you can put it all on PowerPoint? Why keep the day's appointments in your head when you can stick it all on your Palm Pilot, your laptop, or a memory stick? Despite the use of technological back-up, memory is still potentially overloaded. To cope with the information overload the system must be selective. Selective attention and selective perception act to limit the inflow of information but, even so, we still perceive far more than we could hope, or wish, to remember. In many laboratory experiments selectivity emerges as errors, but in the real world selectivity is both a virtue and a necessity. In everyday life, an ideally efficient memory system would make maximum use of external aids and selectively devote its resources to high-priority items, filtering out irrelevant or less important information. Memory does not necessarily need to be complete.

Characteristics of encoding

Memory is elaborative

Although encoding is selective and selectivity may be seen as a strategy to achieve economy, the information that is selected for encoding is elaborated. We encode the context and the source of the information, we generate associations, we link it to pre-existing stored knowledge, scripts, and schemas, and we set up cues and reminders. All these forms of elaboration are designed to enhance the retrievability of the information by providing indices that will locate and identify it. Elaborative encoding is also part of the process of comprehension. New information cannot be understood unless it is related in this way to its context and to the knowledge base already stored in memory.

Memory is dynamic

Besides being enormously complex and rich in information, today's environment is also constantly changing. We move houses, change jobs, and travel around. The skills we learn need frequent updating. The media inform us daily of new events and offer new interpretations of old events. We need a dynamic memory system to cope with changing circumstances and a changing physical environment. We need to be able to update the knowledge we have stored and to transform the models of the world we construct in our heads. We have to revise the concepts we have acquired, or throw them out and acquire new ones. Fixed memory structures are liable to become obsolete or to be inappropriate for the current situation. We noted in Chapter 5 that the kind of mental models needed for planning or problem solving are dynamic models, which are assembled as required. Situation models (see Chapter 8) are part of a dynamic system that can draw on high level general components and low level specific components to construct appropriate memory representations on demand. Fixed memory structures are uneconomical to store because the same high level elements need to be reduplicated in many different representations. Dynamic memories are readily revised, updated, and modified, whereas fixed memories would rapidly become redundant in a changing world.

Characteristics of representation

Memory is integrative and individual

The most important function of memory in the real world is to link past, present, and future. Memory stores retrospective information, monitors current input and output, and constructs and stores future plans. This integration of past, present, and future in a unified personal history is achieved by interactive processes. New memories are stored within pre-existing knowledge structures; old memories are modified by new ones; prospective plans are built out of elements abstracted from past experience. This intricate interaction of past, present, and future allows us to maintain a coherent identity and to develop flexibly and adaptively in knowledge and experience. It is essential to the development of a self-concept and to the maintenance of identity throughout the lifespan and thus is integral to autobiographical memory. Memory is individual to each person, forming a unique record of each individual's personal experiences that is modulated by context and by his or her personality and ability. It is common knowledge that two people who experience the same event will almost certainly report significantly different memories of it.

Memory is able to construct hypothetical representations

A distinguishing feature of the human mind is its capacity for "displacement" in thought. It is because we are able to think about things that are displaced in time and in space, and things that are not the case, that we are able to plan, to predict the outcome of actions and events, to prepare for eventualities. Our ability to construct detailed and accurate hypothetical representations of possible states of affairs is crucial for survival. To meet this requirement we must have a constructive memory system. In the real world, a memory system that could only copy the information it received would be hopelessly maladaptive. It would also be incapable of invention, imagination, and creative art. Johnson's MEM model recognises and accommodates the need to incorporate both a real world and a constructed world.

Memory can store both general and specific information

Many models of cognition, including models of the representation of memories, have a hierarchical structure with more general information represented at a higher superordinate level and specific details at a lower subordinate level (Cohen, 2000). Examples include the action schemas described in Chapter 5 and the autobiographical memories in Chapter 2. From a functional point of view it is easy to see the value of a memory system that abstracts and stores generalisations from experiences. Generalisation allows us to apply the knowledge acquired from one experience to a new experience that is similar but not exactly the same. It is the ability to store general memories that allows us to know what to do in a new restaurant or a different shop, to drive an unfamiliar car, or switch to a different job. Storing knowledge in a generalised form is also economical and reduces the need to store separate representations of repeated or similar events since general representations can provide a basis for reconstruction of lower level specific representations. When we don't know or cannot remember we can fill the gaps with inferences based on general knowledge.

Another advantage of high level general representations is that they are more resistant to error, trauma, and ageing. Koriat and Goldsmith (1996) showed that more general "coarse-grained" memories are less likely to be inaccurate than detailed specific ones. Patients with head injuries or depression tend to retain generalised memories but lose specific ones (Baddeley & Wilson, 1986; Williams, 1996), and a similar pattern is found in old age (Cohen, Conway, & Stanhope, 1992; Holland & Rabbitt, 1990). Studies of long-term retention of knowledge (Chapter 7) also demonstrate better retention of more general information. A general level of representation therefore seems to be relatively robust and long-lasting. Generalised memories are also useful in that they allow us to recognise when a new experience is analogous to a previous one. The ability to solve problems, to avoid a danger, or to respond appropriately to a social situation depends on our recognising that the present situation is analogous to something that worked in the past. Because situations rarely match exactly in every detail, the analogy is only apparent at a higher, more general level.

However, everyday memory also needs to store some information specifically, because in some situations general information is too vague and imprecise to be of much use. We need to remember specific names and specific faces. We need to remember precise information about routes and places and about where objects are located. Similarly, plans and actions represented at a general level, such as "go to London" need to be unpacked at a more specific level in terms of times and dates and mode of travel. It is probably true to say that specific information of this kind does not need to be stored for such a long duration as general information. It is not so important to remember names and faces from the remote past as those you have encountered more recently, and although general information about restaurants is always useful, there is not much point in remembering the menu and prices at a specific restaurant you dined in 10 years ago. Studies of autobiographical memory in Chapter 2 showed that repeated experiences tend to be collapsed into a generalised representation, and specific events are only stored if they are especially salient or unusual. Memory for verbal information exhibits a similar mechanism, retaining a general representation of the gist of what has been read or heard, together with a relatively short-lived specific representation of the verbatim form. The usefulness of general information extends over an indefinite period, but a great deal of specific information can be discarded as life moves on.

Characteristics of retrieval processes

Explicit memories are retrievable

It is a characteristic of explicit memory that it can be recalled by a process of conscious effortful retrieval. As memories proliferate, retrieval must necessarily become more difficult. Retrieval is commonly driven by specific goals and may need to be translated into action, so the memory system must be linked to a response generating system as it is in production system models. Studies of retrieval in everyday life have revealed some of the main strategies used. The retrieval mechanism makes use of the way memory representations are organised in terms of categories, time periods, and levels of generality/specificity. When people search for remote memories, they use complicated search strategies such as partitioning the search context and searching relevant categories or relevant time periods, searching downwards from the higher levels of general schemas, or upwards from idiosyncratic markers placed on specific items at the lower levels. The striking difference that generally emerges between performance on tasks requiring recognition and tasks requiring recall suggests that retrieval is the most vulnerable aspect of everyday memory. One aspect of the memory system that results in economical storage is the way that large amounts of information are only stored indirectly or inferentially, as described in Chapter 7. Explicit pre-stored knowledge is only the tip of the knowledge iceberg, much of which is submerged and consists of inferable information. If we know that all men are mortal and that John Doe is a man, then the fact that John Doe is mortal is inferable and does not need to be represented explicitly. The two forms of information storage are associated with different forms of retrieval: direct access and indirect search. Pre-stored, explicitly represented information can be retrieved directly, but inferable information can only be accessed indirectly by inferential reasoning.

Recall may be involuntary

In everyday life involuntary recall may occur spontaneously, bypassing the effortful processes of retrieval. Memories often come to mind without any deliberate attempt at recall and affect our behaviour and influence our thoughts, moods, and feelings. Sometimes these unbidden memories are distressing ones that we would prefer not to recall, as happens in post-traumatic stress disorder. However, these involuntary memories are sometimes useful ones. For example, memories for targets (like people's names) that had resisted earlier attempts at retrieval may later pop up into consciousness with apparent spontaneity. On other occasions, involuntary memories are triggered by external perceptual or verbal cues or internal cues from current thoughts. A memory system that retrieves information involuntarily, as well as in response to deliberate recall attempts, is suited to the demands of the real world. In many situations we cannot deliberately seek target information because we do not know what the target is. Involuntary memories, triggered by cues in the current situation, can be of analogous past experiences that contain useful hints, warnings, or reminders. Everyday life is full of reminders. For example, when planning a holiday, I involuntarily recalled a previous disastrous experience that reminded me to check the small print of the travel insurance document. Similarly, the sight of a petrol station reminds us to fill up the car, the autumn rainstorms remind us to get the roof fixed, and so on. A retrieval system that only provides information when you already know what it is you want to know is much less versatile.

Memory may be implicit

Implicit memories are not consciously recalled but nevertheless influence behavioural responses. We can recognise faces, places, and objects as being familiar without having any conscious recollection of previous encounters. Implicit memory primes and facilitates identification of current stimuli that have been experienced before. Implicit memory includes procedural memory for the skills and sensorimotor learning that we cannot describe or explain. It is also related to dispositional memory (Damasio, 2000) in which records are dormant and implicit. These dispositions include sensory information about objects that have been perceived as well as associated motor processes and emotions. Implicit memory makes minimal demands on cognitive processing capacity. It is also thought to be earlier in both evolutionary and ontogenetic terms, and represents a sort of reservoir of memory that is better able to survive trauma and to resist the effects of ageing.

CHARACTERISTICS OF MEMORY PROCESSES

Types of memory process

Recent work has concentrated more on the nature of memory representations, so that the importance of memory processes has been underplayed. Most of the characteristics of the memory system that have been outlined so far are ones that have the effect of easing the burden on storage and placing greater demands on retrieval processes. Many other types of process are involved: memories that are dynamic need to be assembled; processes of transformation may be needed to rotate, align, expand, or contract the internal analogues we construct of the real world; processes of selection, abstraction, and generalisation are needed to protect the system from overload. Hypothetical representations have to be constructed, and indirectly represented information has to be recovered by inferential processes. Complex matching processes are required to integrate new information with representations of past experience, and in order to perceive analogies between current problems and previously encountered ones. Elaborative encoding relies on processes of association and matching. All these processes need a temporary storage system like working memory, which can maintain information in consciousness while these operations are taking place.

Metalevels of memory

Metalevels of memory are needed to instigate, monitor, and control memory processes. The operations of working memory need to be driven by some form of central executive or supervisory attentional system linking memory to goals and actions. Retrieval from long-term memory is facilitated by metamemory awareness of what knowledge is in store and what kind of search strategies are most likely to be effective. Memories are more useful if people can make judgements about their accuracy. Metamemory processes also allow people to make judgements about what they *should* be able to remember and what other people should be able to remember. It is these different forms of metamemory that allow memory to be deployed purposefully in real-life situations.

Memory efficiency

Research has tended to emphasise the errors that occur in everyday memory functions. The picture that emerges is of an error-prone system in which memories are liable to be inaccurate, distorted, or fabricated. This emphasis is partly an artefact of research methodology. In experiments it is usually more informative to set task difficulty at a level where people make errors so that the nature of the errors and the conditions that provoke them can be identified. Diary studies such as those recording TOTS and slips of action have also concentrated on failures rather than on successes. People do make many naturally occurring errors in ordinary life situations but, arguably, the methodology has produced a somewhat distorted view of memory efficiency. In daily life, memory successes are the norm and memory failures are the exception. People also exhibit remarkable feats of remembering faces and voices from the remote past, foreign-language vocabulary, and childhood experiences over a lifetime. As well as such examples of retention over very long periods, people can retain very large amounts of information over shorter periods, as when they prepare for examinations, and sometimes, as in the case of expert knowledge, they acquire a large amount of information and retain it for a considerably long time. The conditions of laboratory testing provoke errors and magnify their importance. In everyday life people are not pressed to make forced-choice responses and can always admit ignorance or doubt, so that although omission errors may be more frequent, there are probably fewer commission errors. In any case, errors are the price of having a constructive memory that can fill gaps with best guesses. Considering how grossly it is overloaded, memory in the real world proves remarkably efficient and resilient.

REFERENCES

Baddeley, A.D., & Wilson, B. (1986). Amnesia, autobiographical memory and confabulation. In D.C. Rubin (Ed.), *Autobiographical memory* (pp. 225–252). Cambridge, UK: Cambridge University Press.

Barkow, J., Cosmides, L., & Tooby, J. (1992). *The adapted mind: Evolutionary psychology and the generation of culture.* New York: Oxford University Press.

Cohen, G. (2000). Hierarchical models in cognition: Do they have psychological reality? *European Journal of Cognitive Psychology, 12,* 1–26.

Cohen, G., Conway, M.A., & Stanhope, N. (1992). Age differences in the retention of knowledge by young and elderly students. *British Journal of Developmental Psychology, 10,* 153–164.

Damasio, A. (2000). *The feeling of what happens: Body, emotion and the making of consciousness.* London: Vintage.

Farah, M.J. (1994). Neuropsychological inference with an interactive brain: A critique of the "locality" assumption. *Behavioral and Brain Sciences*, *17*, 43–104.

Farah, M.J., & McClelland, J.L. (1991). A computational model of semantic memory impairment: Modality specificity and emergent category specificity. *Psychological Review*, *120*, 330–357.

Fodor, J.A. (1983). *The modularity of mind*. Cambridge, MA: MIT Press.

Holland, C.A., & Rabbitt, P.M.A. (1990). Autobiographical memory and text recall in the elderly: An investigation of a processing resource deficit. *Quarterly Journal of Experimental Psychology*, *42A*, 441–470.

Johnson, M.K. (1983). A multiple entry modular memory system. In G. Bower (Ed.), *The psychology of learning and motivation*, Vol. 17. New York: Academic Press.

Johnson, M.K. (1992). MEM: Mechanisms of recollection. *Journal of Cognitive Neuroscience*, *4*, 268–279.

Koriat, A., & Goldsmith, M. (1996). Memory metaphors and the real life/laboratory controversy: Correspondence versus storehouse conceptions of memory. *Behavioral and Brain Sciences*, *19*, 167–228.

Tulving, E. (1991). Concepts of memory. In L.R. Squire, N.M. Weinberger, G. Lynch, & J.L. McGaugh (Eds.), *Memory: Organization and locus of change*. New York: Oxford University Press.

Williams, J.M.G. (1996). Depression and the specificity of autobiographical memory. In D.C. Rubin (Ed.), *Remembering our past: Studies in autobiographical memory* (pp. 244–267). Cambridge, UK: Cambridge University Press.

Author index

Subject index